THE SYRIAN UPRISING

Most observers did not expect the Arab spring to spread to Syria, for a number of seemingly good reasons. Yet, with amazing rapidity, massive and unprecedented anti-regime mobilization took place, which put the regime very much on the defensive; what began as the Syrian Uprising in March 2011 has evolved into one of the world's most damaging and protracted conflicts. Despite over seven years having passed since the inception of the Syrian Uprising, this phenomenon remains difficult to fully grasp, both in terms of underlying forces and long-term implications.

This book presents a snapshot of how the Uprising developed in roughly the first two to three years (2011–2013) and addresses key questions regarding the domestic origins of the Uprising and its early trajectory. Firstly, what were the causes of the conflict, both in terms of structure (contradictions and crisis within the pre-Uprising order) and agency (choices of the actors)? Why did the Uprising not lead to democratization and instead descend into violent civil war with a sectarian dimension? With all 19 chapters addressing an aspect of the Uprising, the book focuses on internal dynamics, whilst a subsequent volume will look at the international dimension of the Uprising.

Taking an innovative and interdisciplinary approach that seeks to capture the full complexity of the phenomenon, this book contributes significantly to our understanding of the Syrian conflict, and will therefore be a valuable resource for anyone studying Middle Eastern Politics.

Raymond Hinnebusch is Professor of International Relations and Middle East Politics at the University of St Andrews and founder and director of the Centre for Syrian Studies. He is the author of numerous articles and books on Syria.

Omar Imady is Director for Outreach and Information Dissemination, Centre for Syrian Studies, University of St Andrews. His professional experience combines practical fieldwork as a UN Officer in Syria and as an Academic Dean. He is the author of several UN reports, historical works, and analytic studies on Syria and the Middle East.

ROUTLEDGE/ ST. ANDREWS SYRIAN STUDIES SERIES

Edited by Professor Raymond Hinnebusch, Centre for Syrian Studies, University of St Andrews

Editorial Board:
David Lesch, Trinity University, Texas, **Yezid Sayigh,** Carnegie Research Centre, Beirut, **Christopher Phillips,** Queen Mary University, London, **Eberhard Kienle,** Institut Francaise Proche Oriente (IFPO)

This series aims to be the major venue for the dissemination of research on modern Syria. Although it will not neglect Syria's past, the focus is on the current conflict. It showcases work that locates cutting edge empirical research within innovative theoretical frameworks from all disciplines on, for example, social movements, civil wars, intervention, identity conflicts, failed states, post-war reconstruction, authoritarian resilience, and non-state governance.

The Muslim Brotherhood in Syria
The Democratic Option of Islamism
Naomí Ramírez Díaz

The Syrian Uprising
Domestic Origins and Early Trajectory
Edited by Raymond Hinnebusch and Omar Imady

THE SYRIAN UPRISING

Domestic Origins and Early Trajectory

Edited by Raymond Hinnebusch and Omar Imady

LONDON AND NEW YORK

First published 2018
by Routledge
2 Park Square, Milton Park, Abingdon, Oxon OX14 4RN

and by Routledge
711 Third Avenue, New York, NY 10017

Routledge is an imprint of the Taylor & Francis Group, an informa business

© 2018 selection and editorial matter, Raymond Hinnebusch and Omar Imady; individual chapters, the contributors

The right of Raymond Hinnebusch and Omar Imady to be identified as the authors of the editorial material, and of the authors for their individual chapters, has been asserted in accordance with sections 77 and 78 of the Copyright, Designs and Patents Act 1988.

All rights reserved. No part of this book may be reprinted or reproduced or utilized in any form or by any electronic, mechanical, or other means, now known or hereafter invented, including photocopying and recording, or in any information storage or retrieval system, without permission in writing from the publishers.

Trademark notice: Product or corporate names may be trademarks or registered trademarks, and are used only for identification and explanation without intent to infringe.

British Library Cataloguing-in-Publication Data
A catalogue record for this book is available from the British Library

Library of Congress Cataloging-in-Publication Data
Names: Hinnebusch, Raymond A., editor. | Imady, Omar, 1966- editor.
Title: The origins of the Syrian conflict : domestic factors and early trajectory / edited by Raymond Hinnebusch and Omar Imady.
Description: Milton Park, Abingdon, Oxon ; New York, NY : Routledge, 2018. | Series: Routledge/St. Andrews Syrian studies series | Includes bibliographical references and index.
Identifiers: LCCN 2017037333 | ISBN 9781138310544 (hbk) | ISBN 9781138500501 (pbk) | ISBN 9781315143798 (ebk)
Subjects: LCSH: Syria--History--Civil War, 2011- | Islam--Syria.
Classification: LCC DS98.6 .O75 2018 | DDC 956.9104/231--dc23
LC record available at https://lccn.loc.gov/2017037333

ISBN: 978-1-138-31054-4 (hbk)
ISBN: 978-1-138-50050-1 (pbk)
ISBN: 978-1-315-14379-8 (ebk)

Typeset in Bembo
by Taylor & Francis Books

 Printed in the United Kingdom by Henry Ling Limited

CONTENTS

List of tables	*viii*
Notes on contributors	*ix*
Foreword	*xiii*

1. Introduction: Origins of the Syrian Uprising: From structure to agency 1
   Raymond Hinnebusch and Omar Imady

2. The tragedy of Ba'thist state-building 12
   Adham Saouli

3. The power of 'sultanism': Why Syria's non-violent protests did not lead to a democratic transition 30
   Søren Schmidt

4. The dynamics of power in Syria: Generalized corruption and sectarianism 44
   Stéphane Valter

5. The Uprising and the economic interests of the Syrian military–mercantile complex 56
   Salam Said

6. Revisiting the political economy of the Syrian Uprising 77
   Fred H. Lawson

7 Tutelary authoritarianism and the shifts between secularism and Islam in Syria 92
Line Khatib

8 Organizationally secular: Damascene Islamist movements and the Syrian Uprising 106
Omar Imady

9 Bashar's fateful decision 128
David W. Lesch

10 Syria's Alawis: Structure, perception and agency in the Syrian security dilemma 141
Leon Goldsmith

11 Emergence of the political voice of Syria's civil society: The non-violent movements of the Syrian Uprising 159
Tamara Al-Om

12 Demands for dignity and the Syrian Uprising 173
Juliette Harkin

13 Mediating the Syrian revolt: How new media technologies change the development of social movements and conflicts 188
Billie Jeanne Brownlee

14 Unblurring ambiguities: Assessing the impact of the Syrian Muslim Brotherhood in the Syrian revolution 207
Naomí Ramírez Díaz

15 Sectarianism and the battle of narratives in the context of the Syrian Uprising 223
Enrico Bartolomei

16 Sunni/Alawi identity clashes during the Syrian Uprising: A continuous reproduction? 242
Ola Rifai

17 The rise of Syrian Salafism: From denial to recognition 260
Issam Eido

18 From a window in Jaramana: Imperial sectarianism and the impact of war on a Druze neighbourhood in Syria 271
Maria Kastrinou

19 The Left in the Syrian Uprising 290
Ferdinand Arslanian

20 Political incongruity between the Kurds and the 'opposition' in
   the Syrian Uprising   309
   Deniz Çifçi

21 Conclusion: The early trajectory of the Syrian Uprising: From
   agency to structure   329
   Omar Imady and Raymond Hinnebusch

Index   *336*

TABLES

13.1 Opposition Radio Stations in Syria   196
19.1 The Political Composition of the NCB   294

NOTES ON CONTRIBUTORS

Ferdinand Arslanian is a PhD candidate in International Relations at the University of St Andrews, Centre for Syrian Studies. His thesis is related to explaining Syria's coping with economic sanctions. He holds an MSc in Economics from the University of Kent at Canterbury and has previous professional experience in Syria as a public policy advisor with the German International Cooperation (GIZ). He authored 'Growth in Transition and Syria's Economic Performance' (*Syria Studies*, 2009).

Enrico Bartolomei holds a PhD in History, Politics, and Institutions of the Euro-Mediterranean Area from the University of Macerata. His research interests focus on Palestinian and Arab contemporary political thought. He has recently co-authored 'Gaza and the Israeli Industry of Violence' (2015, in Italian). His articles have been published in miscellaneous and journals, including *Oriente Moderno* and *Afriche e Orienti*.

Billie Jeanne Brownlee (PhD Exeter) was an ESRC Postdoctoral Fellow at the Institute for Arabic and Islamic Studies at the University of Exeter and is currently an Assistant Professor there. Her PhD research studied the development of the new media and civil society in the Middle East, with a particular attention to Syria. She has published several peer-reviewed articles and book chapters on the Arab uprisings and the politics of new media.

Dr Deniz Çifçi (PhD) is a Middle East Analyst and Researcher specialising in ethnic and religious movements in Turkey and among the Kurds in particular. He is a Research Fellow at the University of St Andrews, UK. He is currently working on two books for I.B.Tauris titled *The Kurds and the Politics of Turkey: Agency, Territory* and *Religion*, and *ISIS and the Kurds: The Roots of Conflict in Syria and Iraq*.

Naomí Ramírez Díaz holds a PhD in Arab and Islamic Studies from the Autónoma University of Madrid. Her work focuses on the Muslim Brotherhood in Syria and political Islam in general. She has published various articles and comments on the situation in Syria in English, Arabic and Spanish, including Samira Khalil's *Diary of the Siege of Duma*, 2013.

Issam Eido was a Senior Lecturer at the Department of Religious Studies, Vanderbilt University from 2013 to 2015. In 2012 he was a Fellow of the 'Europe in the Middle East/Middle East in Europe' (EUME) Research programme at the Forum Transregionale Studien in Berlin. Eido's research focuses on the Qur'an in late antiquity, Hadith Studies, and Sufi and Salafi discourses and groups. Eido holds a PhD (2010) in Islamic Studies from Damascus University.

Leon Goldsmith is a political scientist specialising in Middle Eastern and Levant identity politics. He has held a PhD in Politics from the University of Otago since 2012. He was Assistant Professor at Sultan Qaboos University in Oman 2013–16 and currently teaches political science at Massey and Otago universities in New Zealand and continues to work on Syria and the Gulf in his research.

Juliette Harkin is a doctoral researcher in politics at the University of East Anglia. She has a background in international media development with a focus on the Arab world. She has published research about Syria's alternative revolutionary media and user-generated content produced by Syrians. She is a member of the Council for British Research in the Levant, and of St Antony's College, Oxford.

Raymond Hinnebusch is Professor of International Relations and Middle East Politics at the University of St Andrews and founder and director of the Centre for Syrian Studies. He is the author of numerous articles and books on Syria, including *Authoritarian Power and State Formation in Ba'thist Syria* (Westview, 1990); *Syria: Revolution from Above* (Routledge, 2001); and co-edited with Tina Zintl, *Syria: From Reform to Revolt* (Syracuse, 2014).

Omar Imady received his doctorate in Middle Eastern Studies from the University of Pennsylvania in 1993. His dissertation focused on the institutional evolution of the Islamic reform movement in the period 1871–1949. Imady's professional experience combines practical fieldwork as a UN Officer and as an Academic Dean. Imady is the author of several UN reports, historical works, and analytic studies on Syria and the Middle East. He is the Deputy Director for Outreach and Information Dissemination of the Centre for Syria Studies, University of St Andrews.

Maria Kastrinou is a Lecturer in Social Anthropology at Brunel University London. Her research combines anthropology, politics and history to critically interrogate sectarianism and the state; statelessness and refugees; and energy and conflict. She has conducted extensive ethnographic fieldwork in Syria, Greece, Lebanon, and the Israeli-occupied Syrian Golan Heights.

Line Khatib is Assistant Professor of Political Science at the American University of Sharjah. She earned a PhD in Islamic Studies from McGill University and is the author of *Islamic Revivalism in Syria: The Rise and Fall of Baathist Secularism*. Her research and teaching interests lie within the fields of comparative politics, religion and politics, secularism, and authoritarianism and democratization in the Arab World.

Fred H. Lawson is author of *Why Syria Goes to War* (Cornell University Press, 1996) and *Global Security Watch – Syria* (Praeger, 2013), editor of *Demystifying Syria* (Saqi Books, 2009); is past president of the Syrian Studies Association, and in 1992–93 was Fulbright Lecturer in International Relations at the University of Aleppo.

David W. Lesch is the Ewing Halsell Distinguished Professor of History in the Department of History at Trinity University in San Antonio, Texas. He received his PhD in Middle East History from Harvard University. He is the author or editor of 14 books, among which are the following: *Syria: The Fall of the House of Assad* (Yale University Press, 2013); *The New Lion of Damascus: Bashar al-Asad and Modern Syria* (Yale University Press, 2005); and *The Arab-Israeli Conflict: A History* (Oxford University Press, 2009).

Tamara Al-Om is undertaking doctoral research on the Intelligentsia and Civil Society in Syria at the Centre for Syrian Studies, School of International Relations at the University of St Andrews. Her research interests lie in the areas of non-violent movements, civil society, women, liberation, resistance and rebellion. Publications include 'Syria's Women and the Fight to Live in Truth' in *The Routledge Handbook of the Arab Spring*.

Ola Rifai is a Research Fellow at the Centre for Syrian Studies at St Andrews University. Her research interests include the international politics of the Middle East and identity, nationalism and ethnic conflict in the region. Ola received her MPhil in International Relations in 2014 from St Andrews University, Scotland, and a Master of Arts in International Politics in 2011 from City University, London. She is currently working as a freelance political consultant for various research centres and NGOs.

Salam Said is a Syrian economist who graduated from the University of Damascus in 1999 and received her PhD from Bremen University, Germany in 2003. Currently, she is working as a scientific coordinator of the project 'For Socially Just Development in MENA' funded by Friedrich Ebert Stiftung.

Adham Saouli is Lecturer in International Relations and Middle East Politics at the University of St Andrews. Saouli's research interests include historical sociology, state formation, and social movements; politics and international relations of the Middle East; politics and foreign policy of divided states (Lebanon, Syria, and Iraq) and non-state actors (especially Hizbullah); and political violence. He is the author of *The Arab State: Dilemmas of Late Formation* (Routledge, 2012).

Søren Schmidt is Associate Professor at Aalborg University, Denmark. He has a PhD. He worked for the European Commission in Jerusalem and Damascus 1995–2000. His research interests include theories on civil war, regional relations and political economy in the Middle East, and the ongoing civil wars in Syria and Iraq.

Stéphane Valter is an Assistant Professor in Arabic Language and Civilization at Le Havre University (France). Stéphane's publications include *Islamité et identité: la réplique de 'Alî Sulaymân al-Ahmad aux investigations d'un journaliste syrien sur l'histoire de la communauté alaouite* (Institut Français du Proche-Orient, Beirut).

FOREWORD

As series editor, I am pleased to announce the launch of the St-Andrews-Routledge book series on modern Syria sponsored by the Centre for Syrian Studies at the University of St Andrews. This volume, one of the first in the series, is also the first in a projected three-volume set on the Syrian Uprising. Volume two examines the international dimension of the Uprising and volume three looks at its later trajectory. The chapters grew out of several conferences on Syria held at St Andrews. The editors wish to acknowledge their debt to the Asfari Foundation, whose generous funding allowed the foundation of the Centre and the holding of conferences in 2011, 2013 and 2015. In addition to these volumes other studies on Syria will also be published in the series, which aims to become the site of cutting edge work on modern Syria.

Raymond Hinnebusch, Series Editor and Director of the Centre for Syrian Studies,
St Andrews 2017

1

INTRODUCTION

Origins of the Syrian Uprising: From structure to agency

Raymond Hinnebusch and Omar Imady

What began as the Syrian Uprising in March 2011 has evolved into one of the world's most damaging and protracted conflicts. This volume addresses key questions regarding the domestic origins of the Uprising and its early trajectory: 1) what were the causes of the conflict, both in terms of structure (contradictions and crisis within the pre-Uprising order) and agency (choices of the actors); 2) trajectory: a) why did the Uprising not lead to democratization and instead descend into violent civil war with a sectarian dimension? This volume focuses on internal dynamics and leaves to a subsequent second volume treatment of the international dimension of the Uprising. The volume presents a "snapshot" of how the Uprising had developed in roughly the first two to three years (2011–2013). The later development of the conflict will be treated in at least one more subsequent volume. In important respects this volume carries on from an earlier edited volume which examined the first ten years of Bashar al-Asad's presidency, treating this period in its own right, but also looking for the "seeds" of the Uprising (Hinnebusch and Zintl 2015).

Understanding of the Syrian Uprising is aided by contextualizing it within many important broader debates in international and Middle East politics on which it has bearing: the authoritarian upgrading and resilience literature; that on democratic transition; on social movement theory; on civil resistance, on "new wars" and civil wars; and the debates over political Islam. There is also a literature on the Uprising itself, including Wieland (2012), Lesch (2012), Abboud (2015), Hokayem (2013), Kerr and Larkin (2015), Ajami (2012), Starr (2012), McHugo (2015), Pierret (2013), Glass (2015), and Matar (2016). This volume builds on the Syria-specific literatures and zooms in, so to speak, on aspects of structure, such as "Sultanism" (Schmidt in this volume) and agency (e.g. Lesch in this volume on Bashar's choices) in order to address some of the issues raised in the broader literatures – e.g authoritarian resilience. The book includes contributions by veteran scholars of Syria, but also new cutting edge research by junior scholars, most of them originally presented at the periodic conferences on Syria hosted by the Centre for Syrian Studies at St Andrews University, Scotland.

The book consists of 19 chapters, each addressing an aspect of the Uprising. These are framed by this introduction and a conclusion, which together put the chapter cases within a framework that poses a series of key questions or issues raised in the scholarship and debates on the Syrian Uprising and which also summarizes the evidence presented in the chapters.

The introduction will raise the important questions with regard to the origins (causes, grievances, and opportunity structure) of the Uprising and also queries as to how mass protests became possible and why they did not initiate a democratic transition. It takes the view that the structure of the regime goes far to explain the behaviour of the actors – their agency – in the Uprising. The conclusion to the volume summarizes the evidence with regard to the subsequent trajectory of the Uprising that came out of the failure of democratic transition, specifically, why the protests were militarized and sectarianism instrumentalized, resulting in civil war; and how the regime survived despite widespread expectations in 2012 among the Syrian opposition, regional Sunni powers and international powers that it was on its last legs. Specifically, why was it able to keep support of key constituencies, including the military, business, and minorities, in spite of unleashing so much violence against its own citizens? Finally, the impact of civil war on emergent governance in the resulting failed state is summarized, i.e. how the regime adapted itself to civil war and what counter-regime formation took place in opposition-controlled territories. The conclusion elaborates the view that the structures emergent from the Uprising are explained by the agency of the many actors – individuals, groups – discussed in the book chapters.

Why the Asad regime was so vulnerable to the Uprising

When Bashar al-Asad came to power there were widespread hopes for political and economic reform in Syria; yet, not only did reforms not materialize but also in his effort to initiate them, Bashar inadvertently weakened the regime and paved the way for the Uprising. The "reforms" he sought have to be understood as an instance of a region-wide movement from populist (PA) to post-populist (PPA) forms of authoritarianism (or "New Authoritarianism" in King's (2009) words), widely discussed in MENA literature on the 1990–2000 period. A result of the vulnerabilities of populism, chiefly the exhaustion of statist development, PPA aimed to activate private and foreign investment as alternative engines of growth, a strategy pursued, however, at the cost of regimes' sacrificing the original popular support on which they had consolidated themselves. This move was accompanied by what was called "authoritarian upgrading" (Heydemann 2007), on which there is also extensive literature, by which regimes supposedly adapted to the global hegemony of neo-liberal capitalism and tried to compensate for the loss of their populist constituencies by co-opting new more privileged constituencies; yet for every vulnerability of the populist period supposedly fixed by this, such "upgrading" had negative side effects and produced new vulnerabilities. It is therefore the political economy literature on post-populism and that on authoritarian upgrading of regimes that provides the essential context for understanding the Syrian Uprising.

The political economy of Ba'thist Syria

As Adham Saouli's chapter on Ba'thist state-building indicates, Ba'thist populism's special vulnerability was dominance of the regime by Alawi officers in a Sunni-majority society; this was initially overcome by nationalization and land reform, which broke the dominance of the Sunni oligarchy and gave the regime the means to win over popular constituencies, notably Sunni peasants. Stability, however, was only achieved when Hafiz al-Asad concentrated power in a presidential monarchy, backed by Alawi clients commanding key military and intelligence machinery, which nevertheless shared power with a cross-sectarian elite, and rested on party and bureaucratic institutions which incorporated a cross-sectarian rural-centric constituency. The regime achieved a measure of legitimacy on nationalist grounds, notably from the 1973 war and the on-going struggle with Israel, and also from a "social contract" in which political loyalty was contingent on regime delivery of material benefits to its constituencies. In parallel, though, the regime could never relax its repressive control, particularly over the half of society, initially mostly remnants of the old oligarchy and Islamists, un-reconciled to Alawi-Ba'th rule.

This neo-patrimonial state, mixing traditional practices, notably clientalism, and modern bureaucratic instruments, required significant revenues to sustain itself; but the state, overdeveloped relative to its economic base, generated a permanent fiscal deficit that could only be sustained by external "rent". Hafiz al-Asad deftly used his nationalist foreign policy, making Syria a front-line state with Israel, to access aid from the Arab Gulf states and Iran and cheap arms from the Soviet Union; however, in the 1990s economic aid declined and while the gap was filled by Syria's own modest oil revenues these were set to decline in the 2000s. The cumulative economic vulnerabilities of the system were already exposed by the economic slump of the late 1980s which was met by an austerity policy that starved the public sector, froze social benefits and slashed the earning power of the state-employed middle class. In the early 1990s, a new investment law was promulgated to entice private and foreign investment to supplement the declining public sector. Together, these measures revived the private sector, thus appeasing the bourgeoisie, parts of which were incorporated into the regime support base; the regime was thus starting on a post-populist tangent but it did not wholly renege on the social contract and continued, for example, to provide subsidized bread and agricultural inputs. However, in parallel with the fall of Syria's Soviet patron, external aid declined and the Ba'th's anti-imperialist nationalist tangent now collided with the imperative to access inward investment from the capitalist world as a substitute for aid; as a possible solution in the 1990s Syria pursued, under US auspices, a peace settlement with Israel that was expected to open the door to foreign aid and investment yet which, in also allowing recovery of Syria's lost Golan territory, would also sustain nationalist legitimacy.

Bashar al-Asad's presidency: "authoritarian upgrading" in Syria

According to Volker Perthes (2004), Bashar al-Asad's project was to "modernize authoritarianism". Regime survival required preserving the fiscal base of the state, hence reforming the economy by a move toward the market, and integration into the global world of the Internet, cell phones, etc.; but such economic reform required consolidating the power of reformers within the regime and adapting Syria's nationalist foreign policy and its populist social contract to the requisites of capitalism without de-stabilizing the regime. Bashar al-Asad initially appeared to deftly manage this balancing act, but in the end it proved beyond him.

The contradiction between revenue needs and nationalist legitimacy had sharpened owing to the failure of the 1990s peace process with Israel that led Syria to shift toward a foreign policy of "resistance" (opposing the invasion of Iraq, alignment with Iran), which closed off the initially attempted avenue of reform via integration into the Western market, as symbolized by the nearly signed association agreement with Europe. US-imposed sanctions, aiming to economically isolate Syria, discouraged Western investment and caused difficulties for the financial services and telecommunications industries by which the regime sought to propel the globalization of the Syrian economy. Pre-Iraq war oil deals with Saddam Hussein, which antagonized Washington, were cut off after the US invasion. To counter isolation from the West, trade was switched toward Turkey through which Bashar sought back door access to Western economies; creation of a stock market and private banks were designed to attract expatriate capital and surplus liquidity from the Gulf. In fact, investment inflows drove a boom in trade, housing, banking, construction, and tourism, steadily increasing the proportion of GDP generated in the private sector and solidifying the support of the emerging new capitalist classes. As Lawson (this volume) shows, the Syrian economy preformed relatively well in the 2000s, and even unemployment was below the Arab average. However, the drive to evade isolation and access resources meant that the "social contract" with the regime's traditional constituency was sacrificed as the priority shifted to capital accumulation and growth to the neglect of equality and distribution. Economic liberalization removed former limits on corruption and the managers of the new banks and businesses earned high salaries, while cuts were made in the subsidies that kept low income citizens from falling into extreme poverty. Public education and services were run down and parallel private ones for the rich sprang up. Agriculture was neglected and despoiled by drought, which propelled urban migration that, together with the influx of Iraqi refugees, exacerbated a housing crisis originating in Syria's population boom and propelled as well by the increase in real estates prices from the influx of Gulf money. The conspicuous consumption by the new crony capitalists and their foreign partners alienated the regime's original rural constituency. Studies by Ahmad (2012) and Sudermann (2011) showed how, even as the decline in public spending on education left the poor in informal settlements around Aleppo with reduced opportunities, in Damascus gentrification of the traditional city sparked an explosion in consumerism for the rich; the middle class was pushed out and investors co-opted. The end to tariff protection devastated small manufacturers in the suburbs. Upward social mobility for lower class elements became blocked, causing resentment of the Alawis and crony capitalists who were perceived to corner the new opportunities.

Parallel to this move to post-populism, Bashar al-Asad sought to concentrate power in the presidency in an extended struggle with his rivals among his father's old guard, using his powers of office to retire the elder generation; inserting his loyalists in the army and security forces; and, in a tug-of-war with the party leadership, appointing reforming technocrats to the council of ministers. In uprooting mostly Sunni regime barons, Asad reduced obstacles to his power and reforms but also weakened powerful interests with clientele networks that incorporated key Sunni segments of society into the regime, making him over-dependent on the presidential family, Alawi security barons and technocrats lacking bases of support. An over-concentration of patronage opportunities in the presidential family came at the expense of other regime clients. At the same time, Asad debilitated the party apparatus and the worker and peasant unions which he saw as obstacles to economic reform, withering the regime's organized connection to its constituency and its penetration of neighbourhoods and villages. The narrowing of the regime core from the ruling party to the presidential family is a dangerous move for authoritarian regimes but one that was common across the region and a key grievance driving the Arab uprisings.

A main technique of authoritarian upgrading everywhere was the fostering of alternative constituencies that could be balanced against each other. The Syrian regime co-opted a new alliance of reforming technocrats and the business class, a powerful social force that was dependent on the state for opportunities (contracts, licences). The new rich and the urban middle class were encouraged to develop their own civil society organizations, such as junior chambers of commerce. Bashar al-Asad intensified his father's strategy of fostering moderate (Sufi) Islam as a counter to both radical Islamists and the secular opposition, resulting in the further spread of Islamic schools and charities, conservative attire, and mosque attendance (see Khatib and Imady, both this volume). Efforts were made to off-load welfare responsibilities from the state to private charities (Ruiz de Elivra 2012). The political dimension of authoritarian upgrading chiefly took the form of co-optation, divide and rule and selective political decompression; little movement forward took place in incorporating co-opted social forces through a pluralized party system, which might have compensated for the shrinking of the regime's traditional populist political base. In summary, authoritarian upgrading's lag behind post-populist change meant the regime had not sufficiently cultivated new constituencies to compensate for its former support base (Hinnebusch and Zintl 2015). The chapters in this volume by Saouli, Valter and Schmidt document the vulnerabilities of the regime.

Explaining anti-regime mobilization

Most observers did not expect the Arab spring to spread to Syria, for a number of seemingly good reasons (Haddad 2011). Yet, with amazing rapidity, massive and unprecedented anti-regime mobilization took place, which put the regime very much on the defensive. Indeed, mass protests spread to most of Syria's cities (if much less so in Damascus and Aleppo), with hundreds of thousands mobilizing on successive Fridays. Whole quarters, suburbs and towns fell out of regime control. Social movement theory specializes in understanding such phenomenon and particularly how the collective action problem (by which rational agents would tend to free-ride) is overcome and typically looks at movements' ability to frame grievances, the opportunity structure for mobilization, including the existence of networks enabling collective action, and the material means to mobilize.

Grievances were significant in Syria but in some respects they may have been lower than in other Uprising states: Syria had, as opposed to Egypt, a young president with a nationalist image (countering this, Bashar had, of course, inherited his post, which, in a republic, must have dubious legitimacy); authoritarian upgrading had co-opted new support to make up for those being excluded, with the inclusion of business actors, returning expatriates, and Sufi clergy; there was an image of modernization and for the upper middle classes a new life of consumption in the big cities; Syria's economy had done comparatively well in the 2000s and, as Lawson indicates (this volume), although the world financial crisis started to bring Syria's boom to an end there was no sharp downturn prior to the Uprising resembling the typical revolutionary scenario of boom followed by bust; moreover, neo-liberal exclusion of the lower strata was recent and less advanced than, e.g. in Egypt. The negative demonstration effect of civil war in Iraq and Lebanon, showcases of American democracy export, should have made Syrians cautious about rocking the boat. Importantly, it was understood, notably from the memory of the brutal repression of the Hama Uprising (1982), that the security forces were more cohesive and more loyal to the inner core of the regime than elsewhere and would not hesitate to use unrestrained violence. All these factors would dilute the breadth of anti-regime mobilization compared to cases such as Tunisia and Egypt where the vast majority bandwagoned with the opposition against the ruling elite.

Working in favour of mobilization were grievances from the sectarian cleavage between the regime inner core and the Sunni majority and a perception of sectarian discrimination against the latter. Moreover, as Tamara al-Om (this volume) suggests, the lack of political voice in civil society meant grievances accumulated rather than being addressed. Indeed, as the party and corporatist infrastructure of the regime contracted, the intrusive and arbitrary behaviour of the corrupt security forces that filled the vacuum became more intolerable, hence the ubiquitous demand for "dignity" during the protests (Harken, this volume) and the slogan widely raised at the outset of the protests: "The Syrians won't be humiliated." And, decisively, the decision of the regime to use violence against peaceful protestors had the effect of inflaming, not dampening the protests.

Given this relative balance between grievances and stakes in the status quo, what, arguably, ought to have made the difference for outcomes was the "opportunity structure" and this appeared to be sufficiently unfriendly to anti-regime mobilization to tilt the balance against it. Indeed, theories of collective action have a hard time explaining the Uprising. Even compared to other authoritarian Arab states, the opportunity structure was low. Civil society was much more controlled and atomized than in the other Uprising states and Syria less penetrated by Western NGOs; it had low and recent IT penetration compared to Egypt and Tunisia. There were no recognized charismatic leaders to mobilize protestors and no pre-existing organization; insofar as these emerged, they were the product of mobilization, not the cause of it. Thus, decisions to join protests were individual ones, but rational choice theory can't explain such choices: the collective action problem was likely to be especially dire given the high costs for protestors and also the fact that, in an authoritarian state intolerant of public dissent, oppositionists can't know how many are with them and hence rational actors would be risk adverse and free ride. Calculations of the likely success of protest are important and, as such, crucial to overcoming the collective action problem was the demonstration effect of the uprisings in other Arab states where in fact the military did turn against presidents, encouraging wishful thinking that Syria was not that different from them (thus inaccurate analogies). There was also a loss of fear among the younger generation that had not lived through the repressions of Islamist insurgencies in the early 1980s and who spearheaded the Uprising. The initial protestors also refrained from mass demonstrations in public squares and adopted guerrilla tactics, demonstrators dispersing when the security forces approached. Nevertheless, individual self-interest cannot explain the scale of mobilization; moral outrage at government killings (rather than calculations of interest) seem to have motivated many and explain the rapid spread of protests; Brownlee (this volume) argues that mobile phone images of the brutality of the regime uploaded to YouTube spread rather than deterred protests, especially when this was connected to satellite TV which amplified its message. This broke the barrier of apathy and people recognized their neighbours were no longer afraid. The demand for citizens to be treated with dignity resonated widely among people who shared an experience of the security forces' arbitrariness and corruption (Harkin). That Sunnis appeared to be the target of Alawi-dominated security forces and pro-regime militias (*shabiha*) would have activated a sense of sectarian solidarity – what Bayat (2005) called "imagined solidarities" – and mosques became focal points for protests (Rifai, this volume). Other factors helped overcome the collective action problem by enabling the sharing of views and experience: as Brownlee, al-Om and Harkin document, satellite TV and the Internet helped overcome atomization among educated Internet-connected youth and fostered the impression that individuals were part of a national movement that collectively disdained the regime's narratives. Media penetration – mobile phones and Internet had, in fact, increased exponentially just prior to the Uprising. The use of the media to mobilize protest began with the Facebook page of the Syrian revolution, used as a manifesto and to coordinate and theme protests. Expatriates played a key role in using the new media to encourage protests (Almqvist 2013). The role of tribal ties in overcoming atomization in the rural suburbs, e.g. in Daraa where resistance to the regime first flared up before spreading elsewhere, was important: when fellow tribesmen were killed by the security forces, honour required exacting revenge (Dukhan 2014).

Why peaceful protests did not lead to democratic transition

There was enough mobilization to lead to democratic transition under the right circumstances. Indeed, as several of our chapters document, the weakening of the repressive apparatus unleashed a wave of expression and associational activity among Syrians that had been stifled for decades (Al-Om; Harkin) and could have provided the basis for democratization.

Two theories that suggest how such activism could be harnessed to a transition also allow us to understand why it did not happen. In the thinking of the non-violent resistance paradigm, mobilization levels in Syria were easily enough to force democratization on the regime and its use of violence was expected to inflame opposition and spur large defections from the security forces or lead to foreign intervention (Stephan and Chenoweth 2008). Indeed, this was the calculation of the protestors. However, the first happened but not the last two. There was no abandonment of the president by the military, as in Egypt and Tunisia, where its interests were distinct from the presidential families and where it enjoyed sufficient institutional autonomy to turn against Mubarak and Ben Ali. This can be understood as a symptom of Syria's "Sultanism", as Schmidt (this volume) argues, in which no institutions had much autonomy from the ruler. Indeed Said (this volume) documents how the Syrian military did not enjoy institutional cohesion vis-à-vis the ruler; rather there were interlocking interests between the political and military elites. They were intimately intertwined by sectarian ties, with the Alawi community that staffed the most powerful military units particularly invested in regime survival (Goldsmith this volume); but also by political and economic ties, as can be seen by Said's analysis of the military industrial complex, exposing how elements of the military elite had become crony capitalists benefiting from the regime's turn to neo-liberalism while others, many Sunni, had enjoyed upward professional mobility from modest backgrounds and identified with the military institution. The security forces were thus willing to use coercion against protestors and while there were defections from the wider army, this was not enough to endanger the regime's control of the core of the coercive apparatus. As for external intervention, although protestors were encouraged by Western rhetoric to think that the regime would be forced to restrain its repression of protestors or face such intervention, especially after the Libyan intervention and support demonstrated by Western ambassadors for the protests, this again proved wishful thinking.

A "pacted transition" was an alternative transitional pathway. In this scenario, soft-liners (moderates) marginalize the hardliners on both sides and come to an agreement for a transition in which the interests of incumbents are respected in return for a pluralistic opening in which the opposition is allowed to compete for power in elections. Non-violent resistance encourages moderates within the regime to push for reform and withdraw their support from hard-line authoritarians; but this requires that the opposition refrain from maximalist demands such as regime change. In Syria, the soft-liners on both sides were pushed aside by hardliners. The Sultanistic explanation argues that soft-liners in the regime had insufficient autonomy to reach out to the opposition; indeed, soft-liners such as Vice President Farouk al-Shara and General Manaf Tlas, appear to have been easily side-lined by hardliners. The debilitation of any political alternative, including the worker and peasant unions and civil society meant, as Schmidt points out, that there were no interlocutors between regime and protestors that could have channelled protest into a bargain for a pacted transition, as in Tunisia.

But what if Bashar al-Asad has led the soft-liners instead of the hardliners? His choices, as Lesch (this volume) shows, were decisive and had he led the reform process he might have won a free election (see also Wieland 2012: 34–45). Why did he not? Whether Bashar intended the over-reaction of the security forces is debatable, observes Valter (this volume), but the regime modus operandi had always been to respond to challenges with harshness out of a feeling that to do otherwise would be taken as weakness and hence encourage rebellion. The domination of the regime core by the Alawi military elite meant those most invested in the status quo would have the upper hand in any debates with soft-liners, who were often Sunnis, inside the regime. The perception among the security services was that making concessions had led to the fall of other presidents; yet why did they not learn from Qaddafi's demise that the use of violence was counter-productive because it inflamed opposition and invited intervention? For Vatter, the Asad family saw its right to rule as a personal legacy to be defended at any cost. Bashar likely perceived that the opposition was dominated by hardliners that would not be content with anything less than regime change; this was not the initial demand of the protestors, but determined activists, many of them exiles, had systematically set out to spread the Arab Uprising to Syria, using the Internet and promoting a discourse of democratization meant to de-legitimize the regime (Almqvist 2012); Ramirez (this volume) notes the early involvement of the regime's traditional enemy, the Muslim Brotherhood, in these activities. No doubt, in some instances, the regime was deliberately provoked by attacks on government and party buildings and statues of Hafiz (Worth 2013). On the other hand, as Qureishi (2012) showed, the Syrian ulama's first response to the Uprising was to caution against *fitna* (discord) and it was only with increased regime repression that this discourse evolved to defence of the right to protest, an ambivalence that probably reflected the views of a large part of society. Indeed, it was with the increased violence of the regime against protestors that popular demands became maximalist – fall of the regime; up to that point there remained a way back for both sides. Arguably, however, the regime could not afford to make sufficient concessions to appease the protestors for, although Bashar ostensibly had sought both political and economic liberalization, the toxic combination of sect and crony capitalism on which his regime came to be overly based was incompatible with thorough liberalization. Since the system had politicized sectarian identities, while his "reforms" had debilitated the Ba'th party's capacity to deliver cross-sectarian voting support in post-transition competitive elections, majoritarian democratization risked disempowering the Alawi core (and base) of the regime in favour of Sunni politicians; moreover democratization would also empower the masses deprived by the turn to neo-liberalism, and possibly enable them to attack the policies that constituted crony capitalism.

Once the transition to democracy failed, Syria was set on a trajectory that could lead *either* to regime collapse in a revolution from below or else civil war and stalemate. Many of the following chapters will detail this evolution of Syria's trajectory and the conclusion will summarize the evidence they present, particularly as to why it evolved into civil war rather than revolution from below and the consequences of this for governance.

Plan of the book

Several initial chapters focus on the pre-existing structure to explain the origins of the Uprising, including Saouli's on the flaws of Ba'thist state-building, Schmidt on the consequences of its "Sultanist" character, Valter on its use of sectarianism and corruption, Said on the military-mercantile complex at its heart, Lawson on the differential impact of economic change on Syria's social forces and Khatib and Imady on the regime's relations with the ulama and Islamic activists. Bridging structure and agency are Lesch's focus on President Asad's decisions and Leon Goldsmith's examination of the Alawi community. Turning to agency in the Uprising, Tamara Al-Om looks at the non-violent protest movement and Juliette Harkin at the role of the dignity in them; Billie Jean Brownlee analyses the role of the media in anti-regime mobilization and Naomi Ramirez the role of the Muslim Brotherhood. Enrico Bartolomei and Ola Rifai dissect the dynamic of militarization and sectarianization of the conflict and Isam Eido examines the Salafist Jihadi groups that became, as a result of this, the most potent opposition. There follows analyses of "in-between" groups, the Druse (by Kastrinou); the Left (by Arslanian) and the Kurds (by Cifci).

Bibliography

Abboud, Samer (2015), *Syria*. London: Polity Press.
Ahmad, Balsam (2012), "Neighbourhood and Health Inequalities in formal and informal neighbourhoods of Aleppo", *Syria Studies*, 3:2, 30–70.
Ajami, Fouad (2012), *The Syrian Rebellion*. Stanford, CA: Hoover Institution Press.
Almqvist, Adam (2013), "The Syrian Uprising and the Transnational Public Sphere: transforming the conflict in Syria", *Syria Studies*, 5:1, 49–80.
Bayat, Asef (2005), "Islamism and Social Movement Theory", *Third World Quarterly*, 26: 1, doi:10.1080/01436590500089240.
Dukhan, Haian (2014), "Tribes and Tribalism in the Syrian Uprising", *Syria Studies*, 6: 2, https://ojs.st-andrews.ac.uk/index.php/syria/issue/view/97/showToc.

Glass, Charles (2015), *Syria Burning*. New York: OR Books.
Haddad, Bassam (2011), "Why Syria Is Not Next – So Far". 9 Mar. http://www.jadaliyya.com/pages/index/844/why-syria-is-not-next-.-.-.-so-far_with-arabic-translation-.
Heydemann, Steven (2007), *Upgrading Authoritarianism in the Arab World*. Washington, D.C.: Saban Center, Brookings Institution, November.
Heydemann, Steven and Reinoud Leenders (2013), *Middle East Authoritarianisms: Governance, Contestation, and Regime Resilience in Syria and Iran*. Stanford, CA: Stanford University Press.
Hinnebusch, Raymond and Tina Zintl (2015), *Syria: From Reform to Revolt*, vol. 1, Syracuse: Syracuse University Press.
Hokayem, Emile (2013), *Syria's Uprising and the Fracturing of the Levant*. London: International Institute of Strategic Studies, Adelphi Series.
Kerr, Michael and Craig Larkin (2015), *The Alawis of Syria*. London: Hurst.
King, Stephen K. (2009), *The New Authoritarianism in the Middle East*. Bloomington, IN: Indiana University Press.
Lesch, David (2012), *The Fall of the House of Assad*. New Haven: Yale University Press.
McHugo, John (2015), *Syria: A Recent History*. London: Saqi Books.
Matar, Linda (2016), *The Political Economy of Investment in Syria*. London and New York: Palgrave Macmillan.
Perthes, Volker (2004), *Syria under Bashar al-Asad: Modernization and the Limits of Change*. London: Oxford University Press.
Pierret, Thomas (2013), *Religion and State in Syria: The Sunni Ulama from Coup to Revolution*. Cambridge: Cambridge University Press.
Qureishi, Jawad (2012), "The Discourses of the Damascene Sunni Ulama during the 2011 Revolution", *Syria Studies*, 4:1, 59–98.
Ruiz de Elivra, Laura (2012), "State-Charity Relations in Syria: Between Reinforcement, Control and Coercion", *Syria Studies*, 4:2, 7–32, https://ojs.st-andrews.ac.uk/index.php/syria/issue/view/82/showToc.
Starr, Stephen (2012), *Revolt in Syria: Eye-Witness to the Uprising*. London: Hurst.
Stephan, Maria J. and Erica Chenoweth (2008), "Why Civil Resistance Works: The Strategic Logic of Nonviolent Conflict", *International Security*, 33:1 (Summer), 7–44.
Sudermann, Yannick (2011), "Contested Heritage: Gentrification and Authoritarian Resilience in Damascus", *Syria Studies*, 3:2, 31–56.
Wieland, Carsten (2012), *Syria: A Decade of Lost Chances: Repression and Revolution from Damascus Spring to Arab Spring*. Seattle, WA: Cune Press.
Wieland, Carsten (2013), "Asad's Decade of Lost Chances", *Syria Studies*, 5:1, 7–45.
Worth, Robert (2013), "The Price of Loyalty in Syria", *New York Times*, June 19. Available at: http://www.nytimes.com/2013/06/23/magazine/the-price-of-loyalty-in-syria.html?partner=rss&emc=rss&_r=2&pagewanted=all&.

2

THE TRAGEDY OF BA'THIST STATE-BUILDING

Adham Saouli

'The secret of Syria's strength and immunity', announced a nervous President Bashar al-Al-Asad at the start of the Syrian Uprising in March 2011, 'lies in the many crises it has faced in its history, especially since independence'. Crises can be positive, he asserted, but only if 'we were able control them, and emerge triumphant' ('Bashar Al-Asad' 2011). Strength, immunity, and control, have certainly motivated the Ba'thists since their rise to power in March 1963. But, ironically and tragically, Ba'thist state-building has generated, not immunity but vulnerability; not strength, but weakness; and not control but chaos. Why has the Ba'thist regime, which carried to power progressive ideals of national independence, socio-economic development, and Arab unity, succumbed to authoritarianism, sectarianism, corruption, and external dependence?

I argue that Ba'thist state-building has generated the seeds of regime erosion and state disintegration due to three interdependent processes. First, intra-regime and regime-society struggles for domination have led to the monopolization of power by a narrow elite, leading to mass political exclusion. Second, to consolidate and reproduce its power, the ruling Ba'thist military elite resorted, like its predecessors, to kinship (sectarian, tribal, familial) and regional ties, effectively activating identity and regional cleavages which Ba'thist ideology had hoped to transcend. Third, domestic political exclusion and identity divides have exposed Syria and its regime to external threats and intervention, which have in several episodes reinforced the regime's authoritarian drive and deepened domestic sectarian and political cleavages. When the Uprising took place in 2011, Syria was ripe for popular mobilization and external penetration.

State-building in Syria

The context of state formation

State-building in modern Syria came against a backdrop of major socio-political changes in the Middle East region, specifically in its Arab core. The disintegration of the Ottoman Empire (circa 1299–1922) and slow but steady expansion of European colonial powers to the region constituted a political shock raising questions about boundaries and identity: How is the region going to be organized politically? Which identity and/or ideology will form the basis for the new political order? Arab and Muslim intellectuals provided three visions. Arab Nationalism, calling for establishing of a state that would unite all Arabs; Islamism, in its various colours, calling for the re-establishment of the Caliphate; and national-state projects – such as pan-Syrian nationalism of the Syrian Social Nationalist Party, Lebanese nationalism, and Egyptian nationalism.

However, to the chagrin of many regional intellectuals and political movements, what determined the political boundaries and order in the region was colonial (French, British, and Russian) rivalries, compromises, and conspiracies. The Sykes–Picot agreement of 1916, led to the division of the region into British and French spheres of influence, ingraining the seeds of the current regional state-system. What historically was known as *Bilad al-Sham* (Greater Syria: the current states of Syria, Lebanon, Jordan, and Palestine/Israel) was divided between France (controlling Syria and Lebanon) and Britain (controlling Palestine, Jordan (initially 'Transjordan'), and Iraq). These divisions and the Mandate System – the League of Nation's distribution of former Ottoman territories to victorious Allied powers – created another frustrating grievance for Arab political movements and demands for independence from colonial control.

Unlike Egypt, Turkey, or Morocco, Syria lacked a history of statehood. Its newly imposed political boundaries left the nascent state caught between three sources of identities with important implications for state-building: *sub-state identities*: religious (Muslim and Christian), sectarian (Sunni, Alawi, Druze), and ethnic (Arab, Kurdish, and Turkman);[1] *supra-state identities*: primarily pan-Arab and pan-Islamic; and *National Syrian identity*, which relates to Syria's historical boundaries or else, with time, naturalized the political boundaries of post-colonial Syria.

Combining mercantile cities (Damascus, Aleppo or Homs), largely self-contained and dispersed communities, and a desert covering half of the country, Syria was also divided between the city, the village, and the tribe. Ottoman rulers exercised power indirectly through urban notables, mostly Sunni families, *Ayan*. The Ottoman Land Code of 1858 – a component of the 19th century Ottoman reforms (Tanzimat) that permitted private ownership of land – gradually transformed the *Ayan* into a large land-owning class. Land ownership, patron–client relations with dependent peasants, and strong ties to urban politicians provided the landed class with political power. Before the Ba'thist land reforms of 1963, landowners of more than 100 hectares formed 1 per cent of the agrarian population and owned 50 per cent of land. Landless peasants constituted 60 per cent of the population (Waldner 1999, 84–85; Hinnebusch 2001, 16–18).

Syria's incorporation into the Western-dominated international economic system in the 19th century had a dual effect. First, through unfavourable trade treaties, Syria became a recipient of manufactured products, which debilitated the country's infantile and unprotected (especially the textile) industries. Second, Western need for primary products transformed Syria into an exporter of cash crops, turning the country into a dependent economy (Hinnebusch 2001, 16–17). French colonial rule also constrained Syrian industrialization and continued the Ottoman policy of indirect rule, constructing a 'mediated oligarchic state' (Waldner 1999, 76), effectively reproducing Syria's late Ottoman socio-political structure.

Syria's 'ecological-cultural division' (Batatu 1981, 336) and its geopolitical location form the historical-sociological contexts (structures of constraints and opportunities) that explain post-colonial state-building. No one factor – whether class, identity, coercion, ideology or geopolitics – can on its own account for Syria's state-building. Rather, these factors formed the *social resources* that political actors capitalized on – such as the *political* mobilization of peasants or sectarian networks or ideological articulation – to advance their projects of domination and institution building (Saouli 2012, 15–28). Thus, an analysis of Syria's state-building process and the causes of its vulnerability requires consideration of how a *configuration* of factors determined the country's state-formation and de-formation trajectories.

Understanding state formation

But it is important to conceptually distinguish the state-formation process, which is not unique to Syria, from the context in which it takes place. State formation is a socio-political process that culminates in the emergence of a legitimate centralized political authority that monopolizes the use of violence within a territory, supplies order and social services, and adjudicates social conflicts (Tilly 1992; Fukuyama 2012; North 2013). Syria shared two characteristics with many emerging states in the developing world: first it was in the stage of *early* state-making and, second, it arrived *late* to an existing (Western-dominated) international system (Saouli 2012, 49–67).

Building new states involves the monopolization of three areas of social life: coercive, ideological, and economic. The monopolization of coercive force – police, security agencies, and army – is a prerequisite to establish political order (law, economic exchange, adjudication) in a demarcated territory. The ideational sphere provides meaning to a society: a narrative of a country's sense of identity, history, and symbols; state-building, thus, also involves nation-making. Relative control over the economic sphere provides regimes with a fiscal base but also the leverage to structure the economy (e.g. through land reform, marketization, economic exploitation, or industrialization) in ways that affect the balance of class forces and, consequently, suit the interests and ideology of the ruling coalition and their social allies (Saouli 2012, 8–21).

In early state formation, these spheres form spaces of contention among and between various socio-political actors (classes, communal groups, and/or political parties). When a socio-political group manages to control these three spheres, it institutes a 'regime': a coalition of socio-political forces that dominates over a society, capturing and designing state institutions, and preventing alternative social forces from challenging its rule. Domination, however, always generates *resistance* from dissatisfied groups who contend with the dominant coalition in and over the three identified social spheres (Saouli 2015a). State-building in post-colonial Syria involved a series of attempts to establish political order in a country that inherited 'a patrimonial culture, a fragmented society and a dependent economy' (Hinnebusch 2001, 18).

Domination and resistance as state-building: the rise of the Ba'th

Under French colonial rule, Syria accumulated a combination of socio-political grievances (the 'division' of Syria, colonial rule, emergence of Israel) that would later translate into competing political visions and consequently bloody rivalries. These grievances and attempts to overcome the normative standards for legitimate political discourse and action. Arab unity, socio-economic reform, political independence, and liberation of Palestine were the goals that many political movements aspired to achieve. Whilst these goals set the standards of accepted political aspirations, the organizational and ideological vehicles for their achievement varied. By the early 1950s, competing political movements in Syria included Arab Nationalists, the Syrian Socialist Nationalist Party (SSNP), the Muslim Brotherhood, and the Communist Party, revisionist movements with opposed state-building visions. They competed for power and legitimacy with the old oligarchy, some of which had begun to resist French power in Syria and, capitalizing on British–French rivalries, contributed to Syria's independence in 1946.

Social change in the 1940s and 1950s – education, mechanized farming, and industrialization – and increasing socio-political consciousness and mobilization sharpened class and regional divides and weakened the power of the old elite. Post-colonial governments' neglect of the countryside, the Arab defeat in the Palestine war of 1948, and absence of economic reform fuelled existing political grievances. The overthrow of the old oligarchy, however, was not channelled through political contestation within existing political institutions, but by the increasing role of the military in Syrian affairs. Despite the presence of a parliament and the occasional elections, socio-political grievances and ideological rivalries exceeded existing institutional capacity to absorb and channel political demands: 'secure in their local power bases, the traditional politicians had no incentive to draw the masses into participation' (Hinnebusch 2001, 23). On the other hand, the presence of radical ideologies with hegemonic state-building visions meant that democracy did not capture the imagination of political parties or society at large (contrast this with the 2011 Uprising).

Slowly but steadily, the army became an arena of political contention and a vehicle for political control and change. However, like other institutions of the nascent Syrian state, the military was a malleable institution that was open for socio-political construction. Ottoman and later French control did not permit nor facilitate the rise of an independent local military institution (compare to Muhammad Ali who in quest for independence from Ottoman authorities in the early 19th century established a strong standing army in Egypt). French policy encouraged the recruitment of members (especially influential families) of minority and tribal groups (Alawis, Christians, Druzes, Ismailis, and Kurds) remote from the centre to the *Troupes Speciales du Levant* (which would later become the Lebanese and Syrian armies) to weaken Sunni notables, especially ones demanding independence from France (Van Dam 2011, 26; see also Neep 2010). For example, Batatu (1981, 341) observes that of the eight infantry battalions in the *Troupe Speciale*, three were entirely formed from the Alawite community. Sunni notables' resistance to French colonial rule and their disdain for the military profession 'reinforced the trend towards strong representation of minorities in the Syrian army' (Van Dam 2011, 27).

However, despite French colonial policy, the majority of officers continued to be Sunni, urban, and from middle-class backgrounds. This was reflected in the first three military coups in 1949, which were led by middle-class Sunni officers: two came from Aleppo and had served in the army under Ottoman and French rule (Husni al-Zaim, 1897–1949; Sami al-Hinnawi, 1898–1950) and a third came from Hama and had served under the French (Adib al-Shishakli, 1909–1964). It was only in the post-colonial period, especially with the rise of the Ba'th in 1963, that a salient number of officers of minoritarian and rural background began to emerge. Access to primary and secondary education in rural areas and the lure of a military career, especially after the introduction of scholarships in 1950, attracted many members of rural areas and minority groups to join the army (Hinnebusch 2015b, 110; Batatu 1981, 334).

Military recruits, minoritarian or otherwise, carried with them their socio-political grievances, ideologies, and ambitions. Establishing influence in the army became, especially after the first three coups, a strategic goal for various political factions. The political logic for this is straightforward, and is a symptom of early statebuilding: monopolizing coercive force is a *prerequisite* for the realization of other political goals such as economic reform or nation building. Attempts to monopolize coercive power involved a set of interdependent factors that have shaped Syria's state formation/de-formation; these factors predated and continued, albeit with a greater intensity, as I will elaborate, after the rise of the Ba'th to power in 1963.

First, the early military coups underlined the role of violence and the threat of its use (Tilly 2003, 36) as a major resource among other ingredients of political contention in Syria. Al-Zaim's military coup and his later ousting and execution through another military coup a few months later revealed that those who possessed the tools of violence had the power to shape and direct politics according to their visions and interest, despite the presence of influential civilian leaders such as Presidents Hashem Al-Atasi (1936–1939; 1949–1951; 1954–1955) or Shukri al-Kuwatly (1943–1949; 1955–1958).

Second, military coups facilitated the imposition of specific political visions and identities and the repression of alternative political models. Shaped by his ethnic Kurdish ancestry, al-Zaim tried to impose a secular model on Syria. Adib al-Shishakli, on the other hand, promoted an 'Arab-Muslim state' (Van Dam 2011, 29) and attempted to centralize power, targeting separatism in the Alawite and Druze mountains (Hinnebusch 2001, 28). These attempts were not mere functions of political survival; rather, they reflected underlying identity and political cleavages, which characterize divided societies' attempts (comparable to those in Iraq and Lebanon) to construct their national identity, political system, and foreign policy. Al-Shishakli's opposition to Sami al-Hinnawi and President Atasi stemmed from his (and the SSNP's) opposition to Syria's union with Hashemite Jordan and Iraq. After he consolidated his power, al-Shishakli arrested members of the opposition and banned most political parties, including the Ba'th Party, the Communist Party, and the Muslim Brotherhood.

Third, in order to consolidate their power in a context of political uncertainty and military intrigues, rulers began to promote trusted members of their own political party, region, ethnic, or sectarian group to strategic positions in the army and other state institutions. For example, al-Zaim promoted Kurdish and Circassian officers, whilst Shishakli entrusted Hamwi and generally Sunni officers with positions of power (Van Dam 2011, 28–29; Hinnebusch 2001, 28). One early effect of this process was the activation of latent identities as a social resource in political rivalries. However, unlike Lebanon were the activation of sectarian identities was visible, vocal, and institutionalized as part of the country's consociational democracy, in Syria (similar to Iraq) the expression of sub-national identities was socially *tempered* because of the dominant nationalist and secular norms of the day. Dominant norms disparaged regionalism, tribalism, and sectarianism as parochial and reactionary ideologies that spoke to the past. Many politicians and groups had to appear to conform to these norms; these actors engaged in what social psychologists (Klein, Spears, and Reicher 2007, 29) have described as 'identity performance': the 'purposeful expression (or suppression) of behaviours relevant to those norms conventionally associated with a salient social identity'. Whether political actors actually uphold these norms is a different matter: what is crucial is that this is the 'meaning that they, as social actors, consciously or unconsciously, wish to have others believe' (Alexander 2006, 72). Thus, what emerged in Syria's state-building is a bi-polar political order (or disorder!): on the one hand, most leaders relied on identity networks to safeguard their power; but on the other hand, they shamed sectarianism as divisive and as a tool of external subvention, going as far as condemning their rivals as 'sectarian' – as we shall see, this was a tactic that opposition forces have also used to delegitimize regimes.

Finally, is the role of external forces in shaping Syria's state-formation trajectory. The interregnum (1943–1956) between the fall of France and Britain and the rise of Cold War powers (the US and the Soviet Union) provided ample opportunities for revisionist forces in the region to bid for power – the military coups starting as early as 1939 in Iraq, followed by major coups in Syria (1949) and Egypt (1952) and later in Iraq (1958) with the toppling of the British-installed monarchy reflected a change in the balance of power *within* and, thus, *among* the nascent states of the region. Syria's geopolitical location made it vulnerable to regional and international political influence. Power struggles within Syria shaped and were shaped by the regional balance of power (compare with the Syria war since 2012). The first three military coups in 1949 were not entirely immune from regional and international rivalries: al-Zaim's military coup was inspired by the CIA, largely due to his friendly overtures to Israel and Turkey, his promise to ratify the Trans-Arabian pipeline, and willingness to host Palestinian refugees; al-Zaim's overthrow by al-Hinnawi was due to the latter's affinities to Hashemite visions of Arab union; al-Shishakli, close to the SSNP, overthrew Hinnawi to prevent an Iraqi–Syrian federation or union that, it was feared, would subordinate Syria to Britain's influence over Iraq. In 1954, a Ba'thist colonel, Adnan al-Malki, overthrew al-Shishakli to curb Syria's orientation to the US. By 1954, Syria had become an arena of rivalry between the US and the USSR. To protect its allies and interest in the region and to block Soviet penetration, the US had, by 1957, engaged in 'nearly a decade of covert American meddling in Syria' (Little 1990, 51).

The configuration of the above factors formed the framework and direction of Syria's state-building process, which predate the rise of Hafiz al-Asad. Two phases need to be demarcated. First, is the pre-1963 phase when various ideological groups (rightists, Arab Nationalists, SSNP, Communists) were competing for power. Second, is the post-1963 phase when intra-Ba'thist rivalries led to the rise of Hafiz al-Asad who managed to establish a comparatively stable regime, extending from 1970 to 2011. Like the case of Iraq in the late 1950s and 1960s, the contentious politics in Syria involved intra-regime and regime-opposition struggles for power, reflecting Syria's fragmented social order, which by 1958 had reached the verge of civil war.

In 1958 Syria entered into an ill-conceived political union with Egypt, which was imposed on a reluctant Jamal Abd al-Nasser. The popular union resulted in the dissolution of all political parties and, to the frustration of the Syrian military and political elites, extended Nasserite control over Syria. However, in 1961 a military coup led by Abd al-Karim al-Nihlawi brought the union to an end. Condemned, however, as a 'separatist regime', Al-Nihlawi's Damascene coalition was toppled in 1962, giving way to a predominantly non-Damascene military command, but still reflective of the regional (Damascus–non-Damascus) cleavage and ideological divides (right-left) within the Sunni military officer corps of the time (Van Dam 2011, 29–30).

Until 1962 intra-elite divisions centred on the old elite, albeit often challenged by the military backers of radical parties. However, the military coup of 1963, which was orchestrated by a coalition of Arab nationalist forces, would alter Syria's ruling regime and its socio-economic basis. The 1963 coup diminished the power of conservative forces in Syria, particularly urban Sunni forces in the military, whose rivalries and purges within the army had weakened their representation; conversely, it increased the representation of religious minorities in the Syrian army command: nine out of the 15 members of the Syrian command came from religious minorities (Van Dam 2011, 30–38).

Nevertheless, soon after the military coup, Arab Nationalists (who wanted to revive the union with Egypt) and Ba'thists (who preferred a loose federation with Egypt and autonomous power in Syria) clashed. In July of 1963, however, the more organized Ba'thists managed to purge their Nasserite opponents and to abort their coup attempt, paving the way to Ba'th rule.

Founded by two Damascene school teachers, Michel Aflaq (Christian Orthodox) and Salah al-Din Bitar (Sunni Muslim), Ba'thism – like other contemporary political visions (SSNP, Muslim Brotherhood, Communism) – was more than an ideology: it was a state project that addressed problems of identity, political boundaries, and socio-economic reform in the post-Ottoman Arab territories. The Arabs, it proposed, form a 'cultural unity' that ought to be united in one secular state; religious, sectarian, and tribal cleavages were deemed trivial and would fade away. State-led socialist development would achieve domestic economic equality and political independence. The party would be the vanguard and vehicle that would lead state and society to Arab unity and socialism. These ideals appealed to various segments of Syrian society. Its moderate version of socialism attracted peasants, workers, students, and white-collar employees. Despite Ba'thism's weak base in Syria's main urban centres (Damascus, Aleppo, Hama, Homs), its Arab nationalist goals reflected the aspirations of the vast majority of Arab Syrians. Its secularism promised to put members of religious minorities on a par with the Sunni majority (Van Dam 2011, 15–18; Batatu 1981, 339).

The social-sectarian background of Ba'thist officers reflected the underlying social change in Syria, and the Ba'th's hope to lead it: most Sunni members came from a rural background, including President Amin al-Hafiz (1963–1966) and the majority (9 out of the 15) came from a rural/minoritarian background. Of these, three were Alawis: Salah Jadid (Chief of Staff), Hafiz al-Asad (commander of the Syrian Air Force), and Muhammad Umran (head of the 70th Armoured Brigade that protected the capital).

However, the coming of the Ba'th to power would not end intra-elite divisions. Shortly after the purging of the Nasserites, an intra-Ba'thist elimination contest ensued. First, Jadid and al-Hafiz purged Umran; later Jadid, in 1966, purged al-Hafiz and Salim Hatoum – both of whom had attempted to topple him. In 1970, al-Asad toppled Jadid and monopolized both political and military power in Syrian, ending one of Syria's most intense period of political struggle (1963–1970). This phase evokes crucial questions regarding the role of identity, particularly sectarianism, ideology, and violence in Syrian state-building.

On the face of it, the purges correlate with rivalries between sectarian blocs in the army. The purging of the Nasserites and then of Amin al-Hafiz by a cabal of officers who predominantly came from religious minorities (Alawis, Druze, and Ismailis) weakened Sunni influence in key positions in the army. The purging of Selim Hatoum, the Druze head of the special forces, weakened Druze influence and paved the way for Alawi dominance in the army, before Jadid and al-Asad turned against one another in an intra-Alawi elimination contest.

Sectarianism certainly played a key role in these battles. To consolidate their power, extend their influence, promote their ideological preferences and to curb the power of their opponents, Ba'thists installed trusted allies from their tribe, region, or sect in key positions within the army and transferred threatening rivals to marginal posts. They capitalized on sectarianism as a social resource in their political battles and in doing so activated sectarian boundaries. In Ba'thist Syria, behaviour that appeared to be motivated by sectarian calculation generated two contradictory effects. First, the use of sectarianism by one group led its opponents to mobilize sectarian feelings and forces. Increase in minoritarian influence in the armed forces and the emergence of sectarian networks after the Ba'thist coup, observes Van Dam (2011, 42), led Sunni supporters of Amin al-Hafiz to 'create a cohesive Sunni bloc, opposing Alawi and Druze officers in particular'. These sectarian cleavages eroded the role of ideology as a unifying factor in Ba'thist Syria.

However, overt sectarianism generated a second reaction: it exposes individuals to attacks by their opponents. In Ba'thist ideology, sectarianism is a sin. The ousting of Mohammad Umran, who allegedly used sectarian discourse and who sought to establish a sectarian block against his opponents, Jadid and al-Hafiz, was justified on this basis (Van Dam 2011, 39–40). This second reaction links directly to ideology. Ba'thism as the salient ideology since 1963 *constrained* the expression of sub-state identity (sectarianism, tribalism, or regionalism) first among Ba'thists but later in society as a whole. Ideology, thus, mattered because it constrained the overt expression of sectarianism and its use for popular mobilization (compare to the difference in Lebanon).

But ideology mattered in other ways. It constituted the ideological *context* for intra-Ba'thist battles defining what could or could not be done. Like any ideological party, the Ba'th faced questions about the pace and priorities of socio-political change. Against the more moderate orientation of the party founders and his opponents in the military, Jadid represented the radical branch. His 1966 military coup deepened a process of 'socialist transformation': the nationalization of industry and major businesses; state control of trade and agriculture, and promotion of workers', peasants', and women's syndicates. Jadid repressed all forms of political activity except those under Ba'thist control (Hinnebusch 2001, 52–54; Waldner 1999, 84–88). His opponents, now led in the army by his Alawi opponent, Hafiz al-Asad, wanted gradual change and, after the humiliating defeat against Israel in 1967, prioritized the recovery of the occupied territory over ideological goals. The period 1966–1970 marked a major development in regime formation in Syria. For the first time, a regime came very close to monopolizing all spheres of power. But this period also marked a salient division between ideology, as represented by the party's formal institutions, now in the hands of Jadid and President Nur al-Din Atassi, and coercive power that, ultimately, lay in the hands of the army, namely with Hafiz al-Asad (Van Dam 2011, 64).

Thus, just as sectarianism was constrained by ideology and vice-versa, coercive power limited the role of ideology. The last batch of intra-Ba'thist military purges, not only left Alawi officers in a dominant position in the army, but also left the youngest of the three Ba'thist Alawi officers, Asad, in a strong position to buttress his own power in the army and to extend it into the party, state, and society. Jadid, who retired to the leadership of the party, tried to weaken Asad's power, in some cases by mobilizing armed organizations (such as the Ba'th-led Palestinian *Saiqa*) as a counter-balance to the Syrian army. In a last attempt to topple Asad, in 1970 Jadid and the Ba'th Party relieved Asad and his close ally Mustafa Tlas from their military responsibilities; this came after the party had pursued policies (such as the failed military intervention in Jordan), which Asad opposed. In November 1970, Asad-loyal army units occupied the Ba'th Party's offices and arrested several comrades, including Jadid and al-Atasi (Van Dam 2011, 66–67). The latter two would remain in detention until their deaths in the early 1990s.

The ironies of regime consolidation and erosion

Asad's military coup of 1970, as ever, highlighted the role of violence as the factor that determines political power in Syria. The coup, framed as the 'Corrective Revolution' in Asad's Syria, ended the duality of authority and power (between civilian institutions and the army) in Syria since 1949. In 1971, Asad became the first non-Sunni president in Syria's modern history. Monopoly over coercion enabled control over the interpretation of (Ba'thist) ideology and the determination of socio-economic, defence, and foreign policies. Al-Asad's coup ended the long phase of instability (1949–1970) in Syrian politics and inaugurated a relatively stable political regime.

In some ways, Asad's coup signalled the beginning of the end of Ba'thism. Despite its continuing role as a state religion, Ba'thism would give way to pragmatist and realist policies, reflecting Asad's regime's urge to survive in a fragmented society and within a hostile geopolitical context. Asad's pragmatism, one could argue, originated in his personality as a cautious and ambitious member of a minority sect and his rural background; however, it was also born from the punishing lessons of Syria's political context since independence, and the Ba'th's attempts to consolidate power. Jadid's regime had alienated several segments of Syrian society: repression excluded political opponents and potential allies; his socio-economic policies alienated conservative (Sunni) capitalists of major cities; his strict secularism alienated moderate and Islamist forces in Syria; and last, but not least, his foreign and defence policy threatened to isolate Syria in the Arab world and in regional politics and brought on the 1967 defeat by Israel (Van Dam 2011, 47–55; Hinnebusch 2001, 51–54).

On the other hand, Asad, shrewd, Machiavellian, and, crucially, conscious of Syria's fragmented social order, reversed the radicals' policies and established an authoritarian corporatist regime that included influential segments of Syrian society (Seale 1992). First, he launched partial economic liberalization that contributed to the acquiescence of urban merchants, most of whom were Sunnis, and to the emergence of a state-dependent bourgeoisie that was hungry for political stability. Additionally, he co-opted many urban Sunni members to high-level positions in the party and state. Asad's agricultural policy encouraged former landlords to invest in the development of the countryside, particularly in areas where corporatization had failed or where the state lacked the resources to invest (Hinnebusch 2001, 115); but this did not alienate the peasants who had been co-opted by land reforms and through trade unions and party organizations. Politically, Asad established the People's Assembly and the National Progressive Front (a coalition of small leftist and Arab nationalist political parties that were willing to work with and under Ba'th rule); whilst both were far from being democratic fora, they formed channels through which non-Ba'thists could voice their views always within the parameters set by Asad. The Ba'th Party and its statist political development contributed to the co-option of lower and middle classes who through the state, party, and army found channels for social mobility.

But Asad's regime was ultimately based on his ability to monopolize coercive force. Co-optation of socio-political forces was only possible after Asad had eliminated all threats from the military; consolidation of the regime rested ultimately on his ability to establish a coup-proof military, to divide and control the security agencies, and to rely on multiple and competing intelligence agencies. That also required an increasing reliance on trusted networks of Alawi groups and increasingly his own family, who dominated major army and security posts. Van Dam (2011, 3) observes that many Alawi officers who continued to hold senior positions until the 1990s replaced Sunnis purged in the 1960s. By the 1980s, Rifaat and Jamil, Hafiz al-Asad's brothers, and his brother-in law, Adnan Makhluf, commanded the 'Defence Units', which were tasked to protect the regime and the Alawite community. Other Alawi officers commanded major units: Muhammed al-Khawli was the chief of intelligence and chairman of the Presidential Intelligence; Ali Dubah was Head of Military Intelligence; Ali Aslan was Deputy Chief of Staff. Most of these are not only Alawis, but also belonged to Asad's tribe, al-Matawirah (Batatu 1981, 331–333; Hinnebusch 2015b, 114–115).

Whilst the Alawi-dominant army and security agencies formed the backbone of Asad's rule, his regime stood on other important foundations. The Ba'th Party continued to play a crucial role in the articulation of a dominant narrative – the set of norms and standards of behaviour that constrained social and political action – and in suppressing alternative ideologies. The party, with its various organizations, played an important role in the mobilization and socialization of social forces, in the recruiting of the elite, and in forming an institutional bridge between regime and society. Politically, the party formed a counter-balance to the army, diluting the sectarian dominance of the Alawis and forming a context within which other social forces could be co-opted (Hinnebusch 2001, 81). Its Arab nationalist ideology continued as a durable ideal for most Arab Syrians. Finally, the bureaucracy, which continued to grow since 1965, offering employment and services for millions of Syrians, buttressed the regime's power; it played a key role, parallel and sometimes in contradistinction to the party, in executing regime policy.

Over all the above stood Asad, autonomous from any specific social forces, yet dependent on all of them for survival. His authoritarian rule disciplined both his allies and enemies, giving him the power to be the final arbitrator in the resolution of conflict within his relatively broad-based diverse ruling coalition. Asad's domestic monopolization of power enabled him to project power across the border. His foreign policy centred on the liberation of the occupied territories, specifically the Syrian Golan Heights controlled by Israel. Toward this end, he strengthened his relations with the Gulf states (needed to finance the build-up of the army), buttressed his alliance with Egypt (needed to confront Israel), and deepened the alliance with the Soviet Union (which provided arms and protection), policies which have given his regime autonomy at a regional level and the ability to project power in neighbouring countries of Lebanon, Jordan, Iraq, and the Palestinian territories.

In consolidating power, Al-Asad's regime had deepened trajectories of state-building that had long preceded his rise to power as mentioned above. Paradoxically, however, Al-Asad's consolidation of power sowed the seeds for regime erosion and paved the way for state de-formation and collapse in Syria after 2011. Regime erosion and state de-formation can be explained by three interdependent factors: political exclusion, political mobilization of sectarian and identity divides, and, consequently, Syria's vulnerability to geopolitical threats and external intervention (Saouli 2015a).

Whilst Asad incorporated various social forces, this was far from democratic political inclusion. Asad and a narrow circle of military and political advisors made all major political decisions. The 'political' – the public sphere where political forces contend over visions, policies, and power – was monopolized by Asad and the Ba'th Party, leaving little, if any, margin of freedom for the public to express independent political choices. All forms of political expression were controlled or if deemed threatening, repressed, which had negative effects on the production of knowledge, the media, and education. Stories of violent treatment of prisoners in the notorious prisons of Palmyra and Mezze terrorized and deterred political actors. The Ba'thist political order – a set of social expectations built on the use and threat of violence – were eventually internalized by the Syrian public: religious, sectarian, political, and ideological feelings and expressions were repressed. The regime had 'disciplinary effects' on the Syrian public who had to 'act *as if* they do' believe in Ba'thist ideology and increasingly Asad's cult of personality (Wedeen 1998, 505).

Political repression also meant the absence of accountability: by excluding all organized political opposition, Asad's regime had also eliminated the social constraints that would have otherwise restrained and disciplined its own power. Trusted members in the military, security agencies, and party established their own networks of social (tribal, sectarian, religious) clients. These networks did not only compete with the party as a bridge between regime and society, but also weakened Ba'thist ideology which ceased to be an ideational glue that tied various members of the regime together. Whilst these networks contributed to the informal co-optation of social forces, they gave rise to regime barons, each leading its own patronage network. Unrestrained, these networks formed a breeding ground for corruption, which debilitated both the Ba'th's socio-economic strategy and the institutional capacity of state organs. The inter-dependence that Asad established with these barons (including, for example, in the 1970s and early 1980s his brother Rifaat al-Asad) presented him with a dilemma: challenging these networks would contribute to limiting corruption and to boosting accountability and trust in the regime; but this would also threaten the integrity of a regime that relied on these networks for its survival. For example in 1977, Asad formed a committee to examine illegal profits, but as Van Dam (2011, 73) observes:

The campaign was doomed to failure from the very beginning, since some high-placed military officers in the direct entourage of President Hafiz al-Asad, who constituted an indispensable part of the hard core of his (mainly Alawi) officers' faction, were also found to have been guilty of involvement in corrupt practices.

Political repression, corruption, and the absence of effective channels for accountability made Asad's regime vulnerable to opposition by his domestic and external political foes.

Another aspect that has equally contributed to regime erosion was the apparent dominance of Asad's family and his sectarian community. Despite his best efforts to present his regime as a cross-class-and-sectarian coalition, which to an extent it was, Asad had no control over how his enemies (Ba'thists, secularists, or Islamists) would politically portray and frame his regime. As early as the 1960s, Ba'thist opponents of Jadid and Asad had attempted to delegitimize their rule by portraying them as sectarian leaders who hid behind a Ba'thist mask to advance the interests of their communities. The Asad regime's exclusion of independent social forces and visible reliance on the Alawi community formed the basis for *popular mobilization* of sectarian and religious identity in Syria (McAdam, Tarrow, and Tilly 2001). Identity boundaries had already been demarcated, but were also tempered by Ba'thist ideology as mentioned above. As Tilly argues, 'identities become *political* when governments become parties to them' (Tilly 2006, 210–216, emphasis original) and when 'political entrepreneurs draw together credible stories from available cultural materials, similarly create we–they boundaries, activate both stories and boundaries as a function of current political circumstances, and manoeuvre to suppress competing models'. Framing, which 'provides the sorts of shared meanings necessary to facilitate social mobilization' (Schwedler 2005, 162), is key in this process.

In 1973, the historical animosity between the Muslim Brotherhood (MB) and the Ba'th began to assume a new dimension. The MB, which began to radicalize in that period, triggered, through discursive and violent challenges to the regime, a wave of resistance to the Asad/Ba'thist regime. In essence, the MB insurgency aimed to de-monopolize the regime's control over violence and the national narrative. In their challenge to the regime, the *Mujahedeen*, a group with blurred connections to the MB, attempted to activate Sunni identity for political mobilization: it claimed to be fighting against regime 'oppression and terror', which specifically targeted Syria's Muslims; it proclaimed that a '[Alawi] sectarian party militia [had] replaced the armed forces' and that the regime was composed of the 'Nusairi [Alawi] enemy [of Muslims]' (Van Dam 2011, 90–91; Lefevre 2012, 6).

The Islamists initiated a violent campaign against the regime. In 1979, a Sunni officer in the Aleppo artillery school killed 32 students, many of which were Alawi, leading the regime to respond with further violence and repression. In 1981, an assassination attempt against Asad by a member of his presidential guard led to unprecedented regime violence against its opponents, starting with Rifaat al-Asad's 'Defence Companies' murder of political prisoners (most of which were MB) in

Palmyra prison and culminating in the Hama massacre, where thousands were killed after a failed insurgency. The traumatizing Hama massacre brought Syria's civil war (1978–1982) to an end and re-established Asad's dominance in Syria.

The Islamists' challenge to the regime, their activation of identity boundaries, the use of violence by both parties, and international intervention, as I will elaborate below, all formed a precursor to Syria's war since 2011. The confrontation heightened and deepened identity divides, grievances, and fears. The Islamists' discourse and violent campaign challenged the regime's monopoly over coercion and the ideational sphere, questioning its legitimacy as an Arab nationalist and secular regime. The Islamists' discourse, however, also hardened the communal solidarity of the Alawis and other minority groups, who, whether intentionally or unintentionally, became embroiled with and had a stake in regime survival (Hinnebusch 2015b, 117–119).

Why did not Syria witness at this time an Uprising by the (Sunni) majority? Though one cannot provide a conclusive answer to this question, there are influential factors that might have stood in the way of a national Uprising against the regime. As with previous episodes, Syrian Sunnis did not form a monolithic group; they were divided on class, regional, and political-ideological levels. The regime's co-optation of members of the Sunni urban classes and of Sunni peasants from the peripheries weakened the Islamists' ability to mobilize them. Ba'thist discourse, on the other hand, which continued until the 1980s to address Syrian aspirations (pan-Arabism; liberation of occupied territories and Palestine; national independence), effectively competed with the more conservative ideology of the MB, whose Islamist manifesto did not resonate with many secular and/or Arab nationalist Sunnis. Finally, regime violence was a deterrent to and constraint on collective political action.

However, Asad's domestic authoritarianism made it vulnerable to external subversion. Among other things, Asad's grip on power aimed to minimize external intervention in Syria. Ironically, however, as with other Arab regimes, Syria faced one of the dilemmas of late state formation: whilst political incorporation of domestic opposition would narrow the avenues for external subversion, it diminishes the monopolization of power by authoritarian regimes; on the other hand, lack of political incorporation consolidates the ruling regime, but exposes a state to external intervention (Saouli 2012, 49–67). External intervention takes place when regional and international enemies of a regime support its domestic opposition to weaken its grip on power and to curb or re-orientate its foreign and defence policies – a mechanism that has shaped Middle East regional dynamics from the fall of the Ottoman empire to the ongoing wars in Syria, Iraq, Yemen and Libya.

Asad's repression of the Ba'thist comrades, of the MB, and other oppositional groups created opportunities for his regional enemies to intervene in Syrian politics. Depending on the period, Asad's enemies ranged from his Ba'thist counterpart in Iraq, Sadat's Egypt, Lebanese Christians, the PLO, Jordan, Israel and the US. When external pressure increased on Asad, his domestic foes perceived this as an opportunity to weaken or topple his regime. The civil war in 1978–1982 in Syria correlated with Asad's regional isolation. Egyptian–Syrian relations had deteriorated after the 1973 war and Egypt's strategic shift, which culminated in the signing of a treaty with Israel. To weaken his Syrian counterpart and to counter the Ba'thist campaign against him, Egypt's president, Anwar Sadat, tried to delegitimize Asad's regime as an 'Alawi-sectarian regime'. The MB on the other hand found refuge in and support from Iraq and Jordan, each of which aimed to weaken Asad for various reasons (Lefevre 2012, 12). Asad's Lebanon intervention against the PLO and Lebanese Muslim/Leftist coalition in 1976 and his support for Iran's Islamic Republic in its war with Iraq in 1980, both dictated by geopolitical threats (in Lebanon from Israel) and opportunities (an alliance with Islamist Iran), threatened his Arab nationalist credentials, exposing his regime further.

The higher the external pressure on Asad, the more he sought to monopolize power domestically (the Hama massacre should be contextualized within these regional developments) by relying on a narrow circle of power, and the more he sowed the seeds of domestic fragmentation and external vulnerability.

The tragic conclusion to Ba'thist state-building

In 2000, Hafiz al-Asad died. His son, Bashar al-Asad, assumed power. The speedy elevation of the 34-year-old doctor to the presidency in Syria deepened the process of Syria's gradual transformation from the rule of a progressive coalition of Arab nationalist forces to the predominate rule of a family headed by a 'Presidential Monarchy' (Hinnebusch 2001, 67; Hinnebusch 2015a). The visible signs of the shift to presidential monarchy, however, took place by the early 1980s, when Hafiz al-Asad fell sick his brother Rifaat made a bid for power, before he was curbed and sent into exile.

Like a private estate (states initially were nothing but the private property of patrimonial leaders), Hafiz al-Asad bequeathed his political regime, with all its inherent paradoxes, and Syria's fate to his son, Bashar. The regime, however, was designed, whether intentionally or by virtue of the challenges and constraints it aimed to overcome, to operate in a world that does not change. Like all heirs of authoritarian regimes in the Arab world, Bashar al-Asad promised some reforms, freed some political detainees, and enabled limited political expression: regime survival techniques which have fashionably come to be called 'Authoritarian Upgrading'. But it did not take long before he realized the 'dangers' of political opening and economic liberalization. Regime vulnerabilities – political repression, corruption, repressed sectarianism – and dilemmas – political opening versus regime dissolution – left Bashar, like his father, with restricted options.

Faced with the prospect of a widening political sphere, emerging from the so-called 'Damascus Spring' of 2000–2004, which began to question the Ba'th's political legitimacy, Bashar began to gradually reverse his initial liberal discourse and to tighten his grip over the political opposition. Asad's reversal, once again, correlated with external pressures. His opposition to the US-led Iraq invasion, the US challenge to his control of Lebanon, and to his enduring alliance with Iran, Hizbullah and

Hamas all exposed the regime to further external pressure (Wieland 2013). The Syrian army's humiliating withdrawal from Lebanon in 2005, following the assassination of PM Rafic Hariri, which Asad was accused of perpetrating, presented a strategic loss, deepening the regime's reliance on Iran and Hizbullah; the latter accentuated the sectarian image of the regime as a member of a 'Shi'a alliance'. As in the 1950s, Syria once again was developing into an arena for external rivalries, this time an Iranian–US competition.

Bashar al-Asad's attempts to reform the economy, to limit corruption, and boost his legitimacy, demanded autonomy from the 'old guard' of the Ba'th Party. This initially strengthened his presidency, but it also threatened his regime's integrity. As with other authoritarian systems, and in the absence of transparent and fair procedures to transform public property to private hands, Asad's economic reforms produced crony capitalism that benefited regime barons (mostly Alawi and urban Sunni regime strongmen). By curbing and ultimately diluting the Ba'th Party, Asad not only lost the party as a main pillar of his regime, but also isolated many of the informal networks of patronage Ba'th strongmen had knitted with the countryside:

> The fall of the old guard was paralleled by a concentration of power in, not just the presidency, but also the presidential family. The tendency of Asad to rely on his kin in place of the purged old guard seemed to simply transfer opportunities of rent-seeking from the latter to the former. (Hinnebusch 2015a, 39)

The gradual erosion of Ba'thism raised crucial questions about an alternative ideological framework. Bashar al-Asad's regime toyed with various ideological alternatives: a 'market socialism' or a 'Ba'thist Islam' or a national Syrian narrative that maintains pan-Arab features. To counter the Islamist threat and to divide and control the Islamist social sphere in Syria, Hafiz al-Asad and later Bashar al-Asad promoted moderate Islamist figures and schools of thought. But this enabled the emergence of religious networks and institutions, many of which were funded by external bodies, who, despite their operation within the bounds set by the regime, nevertheless provided alternative ideational bases that were ripe for mobilization if and when the opportunity arose (Khatib 2012).

When boys from Deraa and a new generation of rebels from Baniyas, Latakia, Idlib, Tartus, and Hama challenged the regime (the uprisings started in the peripheral areas where socio-economic grievances overlapped with sectarian, specifically Sunni, belonging), Syria was already a fragmented society. The Uprising and the consequent civil war in Syria brought all of its contradictions to the fore: on the one hand it was a break from the past (a new context of opportunities and threats); but on the other hand it was a continuation of a process that started in the 1950s, as this chapter has shown. The war signalled total state de-formation; the Asad regime had now visibly become one actor amongst many struggling for control of the Syrian space. But it did not disappear: it intensified its use of violence; it continued to manipulate ideology to maintain a cross-sectarian alliance; it mobilized its sectarian base, moving it beyond the circle of Asadist loyalists; it continued to act like a 'state'; and it increased its dependence on its external alliances. Its domestic and external enemies, as ever, found in the 2011 Uprising a golden opportunity to 'de-monopolize' the regime's control over violence and the ideational sphere. By 2012 Syria's state de-formation had been completed. International rivalries over and in Syria reached unprecedented levels (Saouli 2015a). By 2015 al-Asad's regime and other Syrians seemed to have lost control over their political fate.

Note

1 Roughly, Sunni Arabs in Syria constitute around 60 per cent of the population; 40 per cent is made up of minorities: Alawites (12%); Druze (3%); Ismailis (1.5%); Christians (14.5); Kurdish (8%); Armenian, Jews, and Turkomens (2–3%) (Van Dam 2011, 1; Hinnebusch 2001, 20).

Bibliography

Alexander, Jeffrey C. (2006), 'Cultural Pragmatics: Social Performance between Ritual and Strategy'. In *Social Performance: Symbolic Action, Cultural Pragmatics and Ritual*, edited by Jeffrey C. Alexander, B. Giesen, and J.L. Mast, 29–90. Cambridge: Cambridge University Press.
'Bashar al_Al-Asad' (2011), March 30. www.presidentAl-Asad.net/index.php?option=com_content&view=article&id=1093:30&atid=303&Itemid=469.
Batatu, Hanna (1981), 'Some Observations on the Social Roots of Syria's Ruling, Military Group and the Causes for Its Dominance'. *Middle East Journal* 35: 3, 331–344.
Fukuyama, Francis (2012), *The Origins of Political Order: From Prehuman Times to the French Revolution*. London: Profile Books.
Hinnebusch, Raymond (2001), *Syria: Revolution from Above*. London: Routledge.
Hinnebusch, Raymond (2015a), 'President and Party in Post-Ba'thist Syria: From the Struggle for 'Reform' to Regime Deconstruction'. In *Syria from Reform to Revolt: Political Economy and International Relations*, edited by Raymond Hinnebusch and Tina Zintl, 1: 21–44. New York: Syracuse University Press.
Hinnebusch, Raymond (2015b), 'Syria's Alawis and the Ba'th Party'. In *The Alawis of Syria: War, Faith, and Politics in the Levant*, edited by Michael Kerr and Craig Larkin, 107–124. London: Hurst & Company.
Khatib, Line (2012), 'Islamic Revival and the Promotion of Moderate Islam'. In *State and Islam in Ba'thist Syria, Confrontation or Cooptation*, 29–58. St Andrews, Scotland: The University of St Andrews.
Klein, Olivier, Russell Spears, and Stephen Reicher (2007), 'Social Identity Performance: Extending the Strategic Side of SIDE'. *Personality and Social Psychology Review: An Official Journal of the Society for Personality and Social Psychology, Inc* 11: 1, 28–45, doi:10.1177/1088868306294588.
Lefevre, Raphael (2012), 'Hama and Beyond: Regime-Muslim Brotherhood Relations since 1982'. In *State and Islam in Ba'thist Syria, Confrontation or Cooptation*, 3–28. St Andrews, Scotland: The University of St Andrews, Centre for Syrian Studies.
Little, Douglas (1990), 'Cold War and Covert Action: The United States and Syria, 1945–1958'. *Middle East Journal* 44: 1, 51–75.
McAdam, Doug, Sidney Tarrow, and Charles Tilly (2001), *Dynamics of Contention*. Cambridge and New York: Cambridge University Press.

Neep, Dan (2010), 'Policing the Desert: Coercion, Consent and the Colonial Order in Syria'. In *Policing and Prisons in the Middle East: Formation of Coercion*, edited by Laleh Khalili and Jillian Schwedler, 41–56. London: Hurst & Company.

Niebuhr, Reinhold (1932), *The Irony of American History*. Chicago: University of Chicago Press.

North, Douglass C. (2013), *Violence and Social Orders: A Conceptual Framework for Interpreting Recorded Human History*. Reprint edition. Cambridge: Cambridge University Press.

Saouli, Adham (2012), *The Arab State: Dilemmas of Late Formation*. Abingdon: Routledge.

Saouli, Adham (2015a), 'Back to the Future: The Arab Uprisings and State (re) Formation in the Arab World'. *Democratization* 22: 2, 315–334.

Saouli, Adham (2015b) 'Performing the Egyptian Revolution: Origins of Collective Restraint Action in the Midan'. *Political Studies* 63: 4, 730–746.

Schwedler, Jillian (2005), 'Cop Rock: Protest, Identity, and Dancing Riot Police in Jordan'. *Social Movement Studies* 4: 2, 155–175. doi:10.1080/14742830500191410.

Seale, Patrick (1992), *Asad: The Struggle for the Middle East*. Berkeley: University of California Press.

Tilly, Charles (1992), *Coercion, Capital, and European States, AD 990–1992*. Oxford: Blackwell.

Tilly, Charles (2003), *The Politics of Collective Violence*. Cambridge: Cambridge University Press.

Tilly, Charles (2006), *Identities, Boundaries and Social Ties*. Abingdon: Routledge.

Van Dam, Nikolaos (2011), *The Struggle for Power in Syria: Politics and Society under Al-Asad and the Ba'th Party*. 4th edition. London and New York: I.B.Tauris.

Waldner, David (1999), *State Building and Late Development*. Ithaca, NY: Cornell University Press.

Wedeen, Lisa (1998), 'Acting 'As If': Symbolic Politics and Social Control in Syria'. *Comparative Studies in Society and History* 40: 3, 503–523.

Wieland, Carsten (2013), 'Al-Asad's Decade of Lost Chances'. In *The Syrian Uprising*, 5–46. St Andrews, Scotland: The University of St Andrews, Centre for Syrian Studies.

3

THE POWER OF 'SULTANISM'

Why Syria's non-violent protests did not lead to a democratic transition

Søren Schmidt

The popular mobilization during the Arab Spring against the authoritarian political systems in the Middle East had very different results in different countries. While Tunisia today has democracy, the Muslim Brotherhood in Egypt gained power by means of democratic elections and had that power for over a year until the old regime retook it. In Syria, however, civil war has been raging for over six years and has killed more than 300,000 people and made millions into refugees.

What started as a secular and democratic protest against an authoritarian regime has ended in sectarian civil war. Why did these non-violent protests in the beginning of the Syrian Uprising not create a dynamic leading to a democratic transition as they did in Tunisia and partly in Egypt? This is the question to which this chapter will contribute an answer.

Theory

Authoritarian systems exist in many variations and the further these systems are from what we understand to be a democracy, the more difficult it is to make the transition. Although democracy is characterized by free and equal elections of a country's political authorities, democratic elections do not necessarily lead to democracy. Democracy requires, also, that a number of non-electoral conditions are met: that civil society may organize itself freely, that the execution of power is based on the rule of law and that there is a separate legal regulation of economic life; i.e. an economic realm that is relatively autonomous from the political realm. The more authoritarian systems fulfil such non-electoral conditions, the greater the probability that they may successfully also introduce the last element necessary for democracy: elections (Linz and Stepan 1996); the farther they are from these conditions the less likely is such a transition. The least democracy-friendly version of authoritarianism is what has been called sultanism. Sultanism is a concept from

Max Weber (1964:347; 1978:1020; Nadiri 1990) and describes a highly centralized version of a patrimonial political system without institutions, but based on clientalistic relations of the citizens to the ruler and his family qua patrons; an atomized civil society that doesn't allow independent political actors to emerge; and a state-dependent market economy, which therefore doesn't support pluralism. H.E. Chehabi and Juan J. Linz (1998:10–25) elaborated Weber's characterization of sultanism into five specific empirical characteristics: blurring of difference between regime and state, personalism, constitutional hypocrisy, weak social roots of the regime and distortion of the capitalist economy.

The usual way for a peaceful democratization to take place is that reform-friendly forces within the regime and moderate forces in the opposition prefer an alliance with each other instead of supporting extremist forces on either side; i.e. respectively regime-hardliners and radical oppositionists (O'Donnell and Schmitter 1986). Whether such actors exist at all, and whether they are able to articulate a democratic political strategy, is related to the extent to which the non-electoral conditions are met in that particular society. For example, the more sultanist, hence less pluralistic the political system is, the less probable it also is that there is sufficient differentiation of actors (between moderates and hardliners) on both sides of the conflict; and the harder it will be for them to initiate a dialogue, if such a differentiation exists at all.

In cases where there's a potential for a coalition between reformists in the regime and moderates in the opposition, the military is crucial for allowing that potential to be realized. The reason is that the military is the only national actor which may give the reformists a guarantee that they would not lose all if they were to separate from the old regime. In principle, both parties could renege on any deal that had been made before the transition. If the quid-pro-quo deal made between the moderates and the reformists does not hold, the military would always by means of a coup be able to bring back the situation to its ex-ante situation.[1] The military is therefore the only actor that may give both parties (and in particular the regime-reformists) a credible guarantee that a prospective bargain will be enforced.[2] Because the military is the only actor that may facilitate (or obstruct) a negotiated transition, it is also important to analyse whether it is organized in such a way that would allow it to play that role (Przeworski 1991).

Background

Tunisia is a country where a number of the non-electoral conditions for democracy were met and where the distance between its authoritarian system and democracy was not great.[3] Egypt is in the middle of the scale, while Syria is at the other democratic-unfriendly end. In the immediate post-colonial period Syria was an unstable state with a moderate degree of institutionalization of political life, some degree of rule of law, a relatively independent civil society and with a reasonably capable state. However, since 1963, when the Ba'th party with the help of the military came to power, Syria developed towards what may be called a 'semi-sultanistic' system.[4] The pre-fix 'semi' is used to indicate that the Syrian political system also incorporates ordinary authoritarian traits, such as some degree of power pluralism and some normative and legal restraints on the exercise of power (Stacher 2012).

While the Syrian opposition was heavily suppressed during 1970–2000, during the period from the summer of 2000 to the spring of 2001 a degree of political liberalization took place, the so-called Damascus Spring (George 2003). An opposition emerged during this period that demanded political and economic reforms, but without challenging the overall power of the president. However, the popular support for this moderate political opposition did not exceed intellectual and cultural circles in Damascus. After the failed Damascus Spring, the regime moved towards concentrating power around the Asad family while reforms of political and legal institutions were put on hold.

When the present Uprising started in the spring of 2011, the opposition tried again to propose that the regime enact cautious political reforms. The two actors – the regime and the moderate opposition – attempted during a few months to see if a deal could be made about political reforms. But at the same time, the security forces of the regime came down hard on the demonstrators and undercut in this way the moderate opposition's ability to stand as a representative of these same demonstrators, who then quickly replaced their demand for reforms with the demand for the head of the ruler. It was in this way that the moderate opposition lost its opportunity to mediate and therefore allowed the struggle against the Syrian dictatorship to become militarized and to take on a more Sunni Islamist identity, which further cooled the inclination of the minorities – the Kurds, the Alawites, the Druzes and the Christians – as well as the secular urban middle classes to support the Uprising (International Crisis Group 2014).

The character of the political system does not only have a bearing on understanding the causes of Syria's failed attempt to democratize but as well on what to expect, if and when Asad one day should leave the scene. Will a more human and democratic Syria then emerge, or will the state instead implode and leave a fully failed state where Islamist militias will fight each other and terrorize people? If the Syrian political system may be characterized as semi-sultanistic, as is my claim, there is a great risk that the result of the downfall of the Asad regime would be a failed state rather than a democratic Syria. Even a new military dictatorship presupposes that the military is able to act as a unitary actor and is not split into smaller units, each having its own lines of command to the sultan. If the latter is the case, then the military will also fragment when the sultan disappears.

More specifically, I intend in this chapter to assess the degree to which the Syrian regime may be characterized as sultanistic, using Chehabi and Linz's criteria, and how this contributes to blocking a transition to democracy. The focus is on the structural reasons why the non-violent protests in the beginning of the Uprising did not create a dynamic leading to a democratic transition. This is not to say that the choices actors made between alternative options during the Uprising did not matter. The fateful decision by Asad and the hardliners in the security forces to come down hard on the demonstrators in 2011 instead of reaching out to them and meeting some of their demands, illustrates that agency is also important in explaining why transition failed.[5] I will recapitulate the character of the Syrian regime in the conclusion and what it has meant for the possibility of transition to democracy.[6]

Regime characteristics deterring a democratic transition in Syria

Blurring of the difference between regime and state

Institutionalization of political life entails differentiation of the rule-setting organizations (the regime or government) and the executing organization (the state) and the latter given a degree of autonomy making it possible to solve societal issues by delivering public goods. The relative autonomy of state organizations in relation to the regime presupposes norms, which secures such a differentiation and gives the state organizations the possibility to organize their tasks with a degree of inner coherence and professionalism. The opposite of such institutional differentiation is neo-patrimonialism, where state organizations tend to be penetrated by and act as the extension of the regime and chiefly cater to its short-term self-interests. Sultanism implies even less autonomy of the state institutions. To what degree may the Syrian regime be characterized by institutionalization of the difference between regime and state?

Although Syrian state institutions give the impression of being independent and with internal cohesion, the reality is different. For instance, none of the ministers, not even the prime minister, has the slightest autonomy vis-à-vis President Asad. The ministers serve only at the pleasure of the president and have no independent, actual or institutional powerbase; and may therefore be replaced at any time. Ministers are, to a large degree, technocrats or window dressing and kept under a close eye of a personal representative of the president (typically with the rank of deputy minister), who, in line with Leninist power management, previously represented the party and its ideological programme, but today represents the president as a person on basis of a self-interested patron–client relationship. The president may at any time interfere at any level of the bureaucratic machinery in order to change and dictate specific decisions. Promotions and appointments above a certain level depend on whether the candidate enjoys the goodwill of the president. The effect is that it becomes very hard for the prime minister to make the administrative apparatus work professionally in order to serve the common good. The distinction between the administrative apparatus of the state and the political regime exists therefore only on the lower levels, while it has almost completely disappeared on the central and decisive levels.

The most important relationship between regime and state is the relationship to the military. In any state, it is the military that is the guarantee of regime survival. When this relationship is institutionalized, the military will organize itself as an autonomous hierarchical unitary organization that obeys the political rulers based on fixed rules and regulations. In a sultanistic regime, the ruler weakens the autonomy of the military by interfering in how it organizes itself as well as in appointments and promotions at all levels.

In Syria, the military is divided into two main groups. One part consists of elite forces, which are manned by soldiers and officers from the Alawite minority and is under direct command of members of the Asad family. The second part is the national military, which is manned through national conscription and has a certain leeway to organize itself based on meritocratic criteria with a view to retain a certain effectiveness and deterrence in relation to external enemies (Lutterbeck 2011). However, all major military units report directly to the president and not to a common Joint Command, and they are all subject to the scrutiny of mutually competing security services. The incentive that makes the officers act loyally in relation to the ruler is that loyalty gives them the opportunity to get a cut of the patrimonial cake by allowing them to make use of their power and authority for predatory material exploitation of the rest of society.[7] The reason for the splitting up of the military and the security services is to coup-proof the elite services charged with regime protection and to keep the rest of the military under surveillance (Huntington 1957; Quinlian 1999).

It is particularly at the time of political crises that it becomes clear if the ruler does indeed control the military and can make use of it for his own or his regime's interests (Brownlee et al. 2013). The three most important crises, which the Asad-dynasty has experienced, are the Islamist insurgency and civil war during the 1980s, the conflict about who was to succeed Asad père in 2000, and finally the current Uprising. In all three situations the control of the ruler over the military has been complete. The military did repress the Islamist insurgency in the 1980s, although it had its roots in the Sunni Muslim majority population. Asad père managed also to transfer power to his son, Bashar al-Asad (fils) in year 2000 without major opposition;[8] and finally Bashar al-Asad by and large succeeded in keeping the military intact during the current Uprising. Some defections took place in the beginning, but of limited scale and only as individual persons and not as whole units. The system may be said to have worked.

It is still important, however, to acknowledge the constraints within which the ruler exercises power in Syria. First of all, the ideological underpinning on which the regime came to power was nationalist populism. This was the ideology on which the Ba'th was founded. And the Ba'th was an important constraint on the exercise of power for many years and represented an independent voice in how Syria was ruled. Clearly, however, during the rule of Hafiz al-Asad the power of the Ba'th steadily declined. Between 1985 and 2000 Asad did not even bother to convene the ruling body of the Ba'th – the Regional Congress. Aside from year 2000 when the Regional Congress was convened shortly to rubberstamp the succession from Asad père to Asad fils, it has only been convened once under Bashar al-Asad; namely in 2005, where it also basically rubber-stamped the propositions which the president put to it. However, the legitimacy of the ruler still made it necessary for him to relate to the ideology of the Ba'th: populism and nationalism.

Rather than the Ba'th being considered an independent organizational actor during the presidency of the Bashar al-Asad, it would be more appropriate to consider Ba'th ideology as a normative constraint on how he exercised power. Bashar al-Asad could e.g. not make peace with Israel on Israel's terms even if he had wanted to do so. Neither could he completely do away with the pretence of any social considerations in formulating economic policies. These norms undergirded his legitimacy and would therefore be politically costly to ignore. In that way, even the sultan was constrained in how he exercised power.

Likewise, the security establishment may also be considered as a power base with which the sultan had to contend. Several authors point out that during the beginning of his presidency, Bashar al-Asad was constrained by the security barons (leaders of the different intelligence services), who were instrumental in securing his passage to power.[9] However, power is based on the control of power assets: the ability to mobilize people or arms. All security barons were, however, as individuals disposable at any time and did not have any organizational means with which they could collectively gang up against the president. As long as the president refrained from simultaneously antagonizing the majority of these barons on which his rule is based and satisfied their expectations of getting a cut of the patrimonial proceeds, his challenge seems to have been managerial, rather than political.

For that reason one should not expect that reformists, neither within the security organizations nor within the military would or could ally themselves with moderate oppositionists or that the military would support reformists within the regime. Also, nothing indicates that the military as such would turn against the ruler and replace him by means of a military coup.

There were restraints on the sultan in Syria; normatively and from his henchmen, which is the reason why I characterize the political system as semi-sultanistic. But they were manageable and events have indeed supported this. At no point is it possible to document that the president took a particular major decision or initiated an important action that could be explained by giving in to either the Ba'th or to the political concerns of the security barons.

Personalism

Personal cult and dynasticism are typical traits of sultanism. The leader tries to compensate for his weak social and ideological roots by fostering a cult around himself, which puts him above all other people. This personal cult was indeed very strong under Hafiz al-Asad, as it was said, that wherever you went in the Syrian cities, you could always find at least three portraits of him. There was also no limit to how wise Hafiz al-Asad was and the fantastic deeds that were attributed to him. In the national newspapers he was often described as 'the father', 'the fighter', 'Lebanon's saviour', 'the eternal leader', 'the gallant knight' or as the 'nation's teacher', 'lawyer' or 'doctor'; in company with other statesmen, he showed 'complete understanding of all subjects' (Wedeen 1998:504). When during the 1970s a huge artificial lake was created by the new dam on the Euphrates in northern Syria, it was named 'Lake Asad'. In the beginning of his presidency Asad fils had the personal cult reduced, but immediately after the failed Damascus Spring, the Asad cult was restarted and the portraits came up again.[10]

Such a state-directed personal cult is usually associated with the absence of natural charisma of the leader, and often also with his social insecurity stemming from low social status and/or coming from a communal group looked down upon by the majority group. For the Asad-dynasty both aspects apply: everyone who has been acquainted with either Asad père or fils reports an impression of pleasant and cultured people, but not in any way of particularly charismatic persons (Lesch 2016). The Asads also belong to a culturally and economically low-status minority group, the Alawites, which the Sunni Muslim urban elite traditionally frown upon.

The dynastic element is also a characteristic of sultanistic regimes. There are in such uninstitutionalized regimes no rules, except possibly dynastic inheritance, for how the successor of the ruler is chosen, and the whole political system is based upon patron–client relationships to the ruler as a person. The congruence between the ruler's personal interests in pursuing the interests of his own family and his political interest in securing the political system by continuing the clientalistic network ensures that sultanistic regimes almost always become dynastic. The desire of the ruler to pass on power to someone within the family is usually compatible with the clientalistic network's self-interests. This network will therefore usually support a dynastic succession, unless the greed of the sultan is so great that it leaves very little for the clientalistic network itself.[11] Likewise, there is a congruence between the personal and the political interest in appointing close family members to important positions, not least in the military. Today, Bashar al-Asad's brother, Maher, is the actual chief of the Syrian military, while other parts of the family (including the Makhlouf and Shalish branches of the family) have important positions within the security services. As I will show later, the influence of the family is not restricted to the state apparatus, but prevails also in the economy. Personal cult and dynasticism contribute to confound private and public power and does not allow space for dissidence that could incubate an independent moderate wing of the regime.[12] In the sultanistic regime, persons are not important because of their formal positions, but only because they are personal assistants to the sultan.

Constitutional hypocrisy

Sultans lack institutional legitimacy and therefore often hide behind ideologies that previously had popular appeal. One of the strongest modern ideologies is the idea of public participation in political decision-making. This is why all the façades of democracy are maintained in Syria: elections, parliament, party pluralism and constitution.[13] But it is only a façade. The president is elected in a referendum, wherein there is only one candidate on the ballot list. Candidates need the permission of the regime to run for parliament and the 'parties' and independent candidates who are allowed to run are meticulously selected on condition that they don't cross pre-set limits for how much the regime's policies may be criticized.

None of the parties have any form of independent social basis and ought rather to be understood as groups of persons organizing themselves in order to gain advantages through privileged access to the state apparatus than as genuine representatives of constituencies in society (Gandhi and Lust-Okar 2009). The Ba'th party is already guaranteed an overwhelming majority in parliament, which through the years has functioned as an obedient tool in the hand of Asad (Hinnebusch 2001).[14]

The stipulations about liberal rights in the constitution are likewise without content as long as a de facto state of emergency is maintained which allows the regime to incarcerate anyone at any time for whatever reason. The law on a state of emergency from 1963 was indeed repealed in 2011; but this has not changed anything, as there is not any independent and objective law enforcement mechanism. In Syria, judges are corrupt and take orders from the rulers. Since the start of the civil war both the military and the security services make no pretence of being in line with the law or following legal procedures.

To make sure that a constitution functions as a sort of supra-law it would ordinarily require particular stringent procedures and more than an ordinary majority to change it – but not in Syria. When Bashar al-Asad was to be elected as new president and succeed his father in year 2000, he did not fulfil the requirement of minimum age of the constitution. However, what was important was that Bashar was to become president – and the constitution had therefore in all haste to be changed over a weekend! Therefore, there is no respect for the constitution in Syria, neither by the power holders, within the legal system nor from ordinary people. Respect for the constitution, i.e. constitutionalism, would therefore have to be established from a very low level were democracy at some time to be introduced in Syria.

Weak social roots

Modern sultans have usually come to power by heading a popular movement against traditional oligarchs. In the immediate period after taking over power, the popular legitimacy of the new rule was often based on programmatic demands for inclusion, redistribution and nationalism. However, the first act after gaining power for such leaders of populist movements has also been to use power to eliminate or coopt independent political power centres which might pose resistance to the new rulers' direct control over the country and its citizens (Migdal 1988). Where the elimination or the cooption of elites was comprehensive, the political space for any opposition was likewise very limited.

In Syria, this process took place by expropriating the old oligarchy's property by the state, through the organization of peasants into pseudo-cooperatives, whose survival depended on state subsidies and who had to follow state production directives; and finally by implementing a centralistic Leninist party-system, which monopolized the access of the general population to political influence and access to state privileges, while at the same time secured the state's and the party's control with the population. Free and independent expression of opinion as well as other liberal rights were abolished (Yapp 1996). The centralization of power and elimination of pluralism were the first steps towards sultanism.

As the state and the ruler acquired unlimited power, the party organization withered and became an empty shell, which in turn cut the link between the ruler and his social roots.[15] The ruler did not any longer represent anyone, but due to the centralization of power he was at the same time able to prevent others from organizing structures of social representation. Society became depoliticized and the role of citizens was reduced to celebrating the achievements and abilities of the ruler.

When the socialist planning economy broke down in Syria – as it did in other populist Arab states during the 1980s – the regime began to transform its socialist economy into an economy based on the private market. The neo-liberal economic reforms of the mid-1980s dramatically increased the ability of the ruler and his cronies to extract rent. The reforms eradicated many of the elements of the social security system for ordinary people and exhibited the claimed social responsibility of the regime as hypocrisy (Perthes 2004 and Hinnebusch 2006). Raw neo-liberal capitalism ruled Syria and any pretence that the regime had a social project for ruling the country was gone. The ruler and his cronies lived in hedonistic luxury and it was clear for ordinary people that they were left, so to speak, 'on their own'. When the rural areas of the north-east of the country were hit by drought during 2006–9, it was typical that the sultan did not give any priority to help the huge number of people who because of this natural disaster lost their livelihood and were forced to settle in the already crowded slums of the big cities in the north; in particular in Idlib and Aleppo. Quite characteristically, it was also especially from those segments and places, that the opposition militias recruited its greatest number and most dedicated activists.[16]

When the regime started to lose links with its original constituencies from the mid-1980s, it began instead as a countermeasure to establish ties with traditional leaders from the religious communities and tribes. In addition to the traditional material reward systems, such co-optation was facilitated by the aversion towards radical Sunni Islamism felt among the religious minorities, mainstream Sunni Muslim authorities and secularists. This opportunistic alliance seems to have succeeded as during the present Uprising hardly any prominent representatives with independent social constituencies within the social (prominent families from the minorities), the religious (prominent imams) or the economic life (prominent businessmen) have defected to the rebels, although the tribes are split between pro and anti-regime ones.

As the contract between the unprivileged in society and the regime became a hollow shell, and as the Ba'th no longer played this role, the grip of the regime on these lower strata weakened. This led the unprivileged to become attracted to the new networks of ideologically maximalist Islamist oppositionists (Sayigh 2014). The attraction to such networks was further strengthened by the weakly organized and weakly articulated moderate and democratic opposition due to the many years of atomization of political life.

Distortion of the capitalist economy

In the same way as there are several versions of authoritarian systems, there are also several versions of capitalism. One of the decisive variables which influences whether capitalist economic activity is focused on the here-and-now or has a longer-term view, is the degree of certainty of political conditions and degree of rule of law under which business is conducted. If there is much uncertainty about future political conditions, businessmen will optimize on the short-run; and vice versa. Short-term capitalism is characterized by commercial dealings and is more akin to a zero-sum type of game; while long-term capitalism is characterized by longer-term investments generating higher productivity and economic growth. This latter gives at least the possibility of the state redistributing income from the wealthy to the ordinary man.

Because sultanistic systems are not grounded in institutions, they are characterized by uncertainty as regards political conditions for business, including risk of expropriation and absence of independent and objective law enforcement. Therefore, sultanistic systems do not promote long-term sustainable economic growth. Instead they promote mafia-capitalism, which works by allowing the ruler and his cronies from time to time to expropriate property from other elite members who don't toe the line and to monopolize markets. Mafia-capitalists in turn support sultanism, as they themselves don't value institutions.

The stories about how property has been confiscated in Syria; either because businessmen fell from political grace, or because the cronies of the ruler could not resist the temptation to secure for themselves yet another economic benefit, are many (Schmidt 2009). Also, in Syria it is a condition for doing business that one obtains a licence for that particular business. The criteria for giving these licenses are not fixed beforehand and/or objectively enforced and therefore lends itself to corruption and monopolies. The crudest example of how state power has been used to further the private interests of the cronies of the ruler is the licence given to the cousin of the president, Rami Makhlouf, to operate so-called tax-free shops at the borders and at the international airport.[17] By contrast to commercial transaction inside Syria, upon which is levied high levels of tax and duties, all goods in these shops are sold 'tax-free'. This means that anyone who crosses the border may buy these cheaper goods, of which many may not even be bought inside Syria. This is an example of the state privileging an individual, who need not be a good businessman, since he can easily prosper from such a monopolistic arrangement. However, while such an individual may profit, other businessmen, who are obliged to follow the rules, are hurt and this sends a signal to all businessmen that competition does not take place on equal terms (i.e. on the basis of who is most efficient, price-quality wise, to produce) but is based on who has the best connections. Syrians in general suffer from this type of capitalism because its overall effect is to diminish investments (and particularly long-term investments) in the economy. This form of capitalism explains the absence of reform-minded businessmen, who could contemplate allying with moderate oppositionists.

In Syria, a so-called 'economic society' was never developed. The term 'economic society' is developed by Linz and Stepan (1996:13) and describes a relationship between state and market, which is based on norms, institutions and rules and makes up the framework for conducting business. The relationship between state and market provides a stable framework for independent business activities. When economic society does not exist, business is regulated at the pleasure of the ruler. If the ruler fails, they also fail and this is the reason why such state-dependent actors are not able to constitute an independent middle-force between ruler and masses that might push for democratization and constitute part of the opposition soft-liners supportive of a transition pact.

Conclusion

Contrary to mature authoritarian regimes, sultanistic Syria has neither a robust civil society, a legal culture which supports constitutionalism, rule of law, a state bureaucracy based on professional norms nor reasonably institutionalized norms for the relationship between market and state. All of these crucial aspects for building democracy are sorely lacking in Syria and the road to democracy is therefore very long.

A negotiated transition to democracy would usually take place by negotiation between moderates within respectively the regime and the opposition, who each has an interest to counter the hardliners in their respective camps.[18] However, such a game of four players requires that moderate players in each camp possess sufficient autonomy to conduct strategic and tactical negotiations with each other. This has not been possible in Syria because any potentially moderate actors lack the autonomy or capacity to act as a result of the way Syria is politically organized. The option that the military could distance itself from the regime and act as midwife for democracy, as in Tunisia, was also not present because of lack of internal cohesion and lack of dedication to national rather than regime interests by the military.

There is of course a final solution to sultanism; namely that the sultan is removed. However, as the sultan and the state (as a spider and its web) hardly are distinguishable in Syria, this would most probably lead, not to a transition to democracy, but rather to the implosion of the state, which clearly is part of the reason why the US and other Western powers have been so reluctant to intervene militarily in Syria in order to bring about regime change. The negative lessons from Iraq and Libya, where the removal of the sultan led to implosion of the state and all-out civil war instead of to democracy, is obviously looming in the background.

Authoritarian political systems come in many variations and the semi-sultanistic version that exists in Syria is clearly the variant that provides the worst conditions for transition to democracy. Therefore, sultanism, in combination with the regime's fateful choice to come down hard on demonstrators in 2011, is an important element in explaining why the non-violent protests in the beginning of the Uprising did not create the dynamic leading to a democratic transition.

Notes

1 To some degree this was what happened in Egypt, where the military believed that the Muslim Brotherhood was not sticking to their part of the bargain.
2 This is the role that the Tunisian military played in that transition.
3 See Schmidt (2013) for a comparative analysis of Tunisia's, Egypt's and Syria's conditions for transition to democracy.
4 When I use the term 'sultanism', I mean 'neo-sultanism', i.e. where power is exercised through bureaucracies and a national military and where power is based on repressive means as well as legitimacy.
5 David Lesch (2016) describes that until the very last moment before Bashar al-Asad's speech on 30 March 2011 before the Parliament, two versions of the speech existed. One, where he reached out to the demonstrators and one, which characterized the demonstrators as terrorists cooperating with external forces. Unfortunately, Asad chose the last version.
6 See Linz and Stepan (2013) for general reflections on the relevance of the concept of sultanism for understanding The Arab Spring. See also Goldstone (2011).
7 E.g. by officers having their soldiers work as labourers building their houses, by 'taxing' civilians crossing check-points and by participation in the lucrative drug-trafficking in the parts of Lebanon which were controlled by the Syrian army until 2005.
8 Although it seems that he partly had to share that power with members of the old guard during the first years of his presidency.
9 In particular Stacher (2012) makes the argument that these security chiefs had real independent power, although he hardly gets beyond claiming it and does not prove it.
10 The Syria expert professor David Lesch met Bashar al-Asad several times and explains: 'In the beginning he told me, that he wanted to do away with the personal cult, of his predecessor, his father. But from 2007 gigantic posters with adoring pictures were up again, now with pictures of Bashar, the son. And it hit me, that he had lost his sense of reality, when he told me that "it was an expression of the will of the people". Suddenly, he believed it himself.' *Politiken* 26.3.14.
11 The importance of the person in weakly institutionalized organizations is also evident within the Mafia, which is organized in families, where sons or nephews succeed the leader when he dies (of natural or other causes) and may in a similar way be explained by the congruence between the interest of the leader in promoting his own family and the lieutenants' interest in securing their own interests, which are based on a continuation of the existing patron–client network. The alternative to the dynastic principle is a war where everyone fights everyone, where in costs would be much greater for the lieutenants than the cost for them to continue the old patron–client hierarchy under the leadership of the family (Forte 2004).
12 Some people hoped the former vice president Farouk al-Shara' would lead such a moderate wing.
13 What goes on here may be described by the bon mot: Hypocrisy is the tribute vice pays to virtue.
14 Therefore, it is also not correct to characterize Syria as a state governed by the Ba'th party. The Ba'th played a role in Syrian history, but hardly plays a role any longer.
15 Membership numbers of the party were e.g. hugely inflated during the 90s, when people were made members without knowing it themselves (author's conversations with such 'ghost' members in 1999).
16 Francesca De Châtel (2014:35) says about the incompetence of the regime in relation to the drought: 'The lack of transparency, corruption and absence of reliable data leads to a lack of accountability. Ambitious policies are drafted on paper, but never implemented; special committees are formed to "study" various aspects of sector modernization, but final reports are never produced, studies are carried out, but never followed up on; laws are issued; but inconsistently enforced. This has enabled years of unsustainable management.'

17 Makhlouf was said to be worth $5 billion before 2011, and to have dominated 60% of Syria's economy (Cole 2016).
18 The transition to democracy in Poland is a good example of such negotiated transition. See Przeworksi (1991).

Bibliography

al-Jazeera (2011), Thousands Rally in Support of Syria's Asad (12.10.2011).
Brownlee, Jason, Tarak Masoud & Andrew Reynolds (2013), 'Tracking the "Arab Spring". Why The Modest Harvest?' *Journal of Democracy*, 24:4, 29–44.
Chehabi, Houchang E. & Juan J. Linz (1998), 'A Theory of Sultanism.' In *Sultanistic Regimes*, edited by Chehabi and Linz, 3–48, Baltimore, MD: Johns Hopkins University Press.
Cole, Juan (2016), In *Informed Comment*, April 6.
De Châtel, Francesca (2014), 'The Role of Drought and Climate Change in the Syrian Uprising: Untangling the Triggers of the Revolution.' *Middle Eastern Studies*, 50:4, 1–15.
Forte, Guido Lo (2004), 'The Sicilian Mafia: A Profile Based on Judicially Confirmed Evidence.' *Modern Italy*, 9:1, 69–94.
Gandhi, Jennifer & Ellen Lust-Okar (2009), 'Elections under Authoritarianism.' *Annual Review of Political Science*, 12, 403–422.
George, Alan (2003), *Neither Bread nor Freedom*. London: Zed Books.
Goldstone, Jack A. (2011), 'Understanding the Revolutions of 2011.' *Foreign Affairs*, 90:3, 8–16.
Hinnebusch, Raymond (2001), *Revolution from Above*. London: Routledge.
Hinnebusch, Raymond (2006), 'Authoritarian Persistence, Democratization Theory and the Middle East: An Overview and Critique,' *Democratization*, 13:3, 373–395.
Hinnebusch, Raymond (2009), 'The Political Economy of Populist Authoritarianism.' In *The State and the Political Economy of Reform in Syria*, edited by Raymond Hinnebusch, St. Andrews Papers on Contemporary Syria, St Andrews: University of St Andrews.
Huntington, Samuel (1957), *The Soldier and the State: The Theory and Politics of Civil-Military Relations*. Cambridge, MA: Harvard University Press.
ICG (International Crisis Group) (2014), 'Flight of Icarus? The PYD's Precarious Rise in Syria,' *Middle East Report*, 151. Bruxelles: ICG.
Lesch, David W. (2005), *The New Lion of Damascus: A Social Transformation. Bashar Al Asad and Modern Syria*. New Haven, NJ: Yale University Press.
Lesch, David W. (2016), 'Assad's Fateful Choice.' *Syria Comment*, April 6.
Linz, Juan J. & Alfred Stepan (1996), *Problems of Democratic Transition and Consolidation*. Baltimore, MD: Johns Hopkins University Press.
Linz, Juan & Alfred Stepan (2013), 'Democratization Theory and the 'Arab Spring'.' *Journal of Democracy*, 24:2, 15–30.
Lutterbeck, Derek (2011), 'Arab Uprisings and Armed Forces: Between Openness and Resistance,' *SSR Paper*, 2. Geneva: Geneva Centre for the Democratic Control of Armed Forces.
Migdal, Joel S. (1988), *Strong Societies and Weak States: State-Society Relations and State Capabilities in the Third World*. Princeton, NJ: Princeton University Press.
Nadiri, Nader (1990), 'Max Weber and the Study of the Middle East: A Critical Analysis.' *Berkeley Journal of Sociology*, 35, 71–88.
O'Donnell, Guillermo & Philippe C. Schmitter (1986), *Transitions from Authoritarian Rule: Tentative Conclusions about Uncertain Democracies*. Baltimore, MD: Johns Hopkins University Press.
Perthes, Volker (2004), *Syria under Bashar al Asad: Modernisation and the Limits of Change*. Oxford: Oxford University Press.

Politiken (2014), 'Asad har tabt, men ingen har vundet – og sådan kan det blive ved længe.' March 23.
Przeworski, Adam (1991), *Democracy and the Market: Political and Economic Reforms in Eastern Europe and Latin America.* Cambridge: Cambridge University Press.
Quinlian, James T. (1999), 'Coup-Proofing: Its Practice and Consequences in the Middle East,' *International Security*, 24:2, 131–155.
Sayigh, Yezid (2014), 'The Syrian Opposition's Bleak Outlook.' Carnegie Middle East Center, Tilgængelig på http://carnegie-mec.org/2014/04/17/syrian-opposition-s-bleak-outlook/h8e.
Schmidt, Søren (2009), 'The Developmental Role of the State: Lessons from Syria.' In *The State and the Political Economy of Reform in Syria*, edited by Raymond Hinnebusch, St. Andrews Papers on Contemporary Syria, St Andrews: University of St Andrews.
Schmidt, Søren (2013), 'Militærets betydning for demokratisering under det arabiske forår – tilfældene Tunesien, Egypten og Syrien,' *Internasjonal Politikk*, 71:4, 479–502.
Stacher, Joshua (2012), *Adaptable Autocrats: Regime Power in Egypt and Syria.* Stanford: Stanford University Press.
UNHCR (United Nations High Commissioner for Refugees) (2015), 'UNHCR Country Operations Profile – Syrian Arab Republic.' www.unhcr.org/cgi-bin/texis/vtx/page?page=49e486a76&submit=GO.
Weber, Max (1964), *The Theory of Social and Economic Organizations.* New York: Free Press.
Weber, Max (1978), *Economy and Society: An Outline of Interpretive Sociology.* Berkeley, CA: University of California Press.
Wedeen, Lisa (1998), 'Acting 'As If': Symbolic Politics and Social Control in Syria.' *Comparative Studies in Society and History*, 40:3, 503–523.
Yapp, Malcolm E. (1996), *The Near East Since the First World War: A History to 1995.* London: Longman.

4
THE DYNAMICS OF POWER IN SYRIA
Generalized corruption and sectarianism

Stéphane Valter

The Syrian regime can rightly be characterized by its monopoly of power. This has been the case since 1970 when general-turned-president Hafiz al-Asad carried out a coup against rival left-wing Ba'thist officers and civilians. The previously erratic and collective leadership thus became progressively more organized and centralized, until it turned into a strong presidential system based on the control of one man.[1] This legacy of power-wielding is necessary to understand the nature of the current system and the level of authority and margin of autonomy enjoyed by Hafiz's son, Bashar, in the decision-taking process.

Neo-patrimonial leadership

Despite the regime's power monopoly, one can still doubt whether power, conceived as a well-organized, coherent, and structured phenomenon able to get things done, really does exist as far as the Syrian presidency is concerned. Some years ago, Patrick Seale, Hafiz al-Asad's privileged biographer who sometimes adopted discreetly laudatory stances vis-à-vis Syria's strong man, already admitted that the presidency was in a certain way weak, in the sense that it was not totally controlling the whole administration and state apparatus, despite its authoritarian nature. During Hafiz's time, it can be argued that the president did not wield total control over the state administration, but rather kept up strong personal relations with people directly nominated by himself (like army and security officers) who commanded various levers of power. Although Bashar did not at first enjoy the same amount of authority and power, because of his youth and deficient military background, individual links between the president and the top brass in charge of loyal army brigades and sensitive security branches can still be described as functioning in a similar way: based on personal allegiance and shared interests.

What may be dubbed the inefficiency of the state in applying directives and orders was mainly due to multiple causes: the personal nature of command, widespread corruption, when personal interests prevail; sociological barriers, when allegiance goes first to the proximity group; ideological fuzziness when the collective aims remain opaque and thus not mobilizing. Hafiz al-Asad himself is thus quoted as having said: 'I can appoint a policeman for each person who needs to be controlled, but I cannot put a conscience into a policeman's head.' Yet, the state's inefficiency was, paradoxically, encouraged by the ruling system itself that was seen by its architects as a convenient and cheap way to satisfy both affiliates and clients, and to allow the sword of Damocles to hang over everyone's head. The kind of disorderliness affecting the whole political system and all the state institutions was mixed with a high degree of arbitrariness and cruelty on the part of the security (or rather insecurity) services, that thrived in an environment of total constitutional impunity (Ziadeh: 2013).[2]

A salient manifestation of political brutality was the role played by Hafiz's brother Rif'at[3] who reportedly ordered the massacre at the Palmyra prison when some 500 (or maybe more) inmates from the Muslim Brotherhood were liquidated (summer 1980). As vice-president and chief of the Defence Brigades (*Saraya al-difa'*), his name is associated with all of the regime's ignominies (although the opposition stemming from the Muslim Brothers was far from being smart and pacific, but rather aggressive, violent, and even terrorist, not to mention their inner anathematizing tendency to view Ba'thists as secular infidels and Alawites as deviant heretics deserving to be fought and ultimately slaughtered).

This heritage has not changed at all under Bashar except that while power was personal and centralized under Hafiz it seems to have been, to a certain degree, more collective under Bashar, or at least it was so at the beginning. Initially, he had to share power with the old guard, who were part of Hafiz's legacy but these were progressively sidelined or neutralized, to the point that Bashar's grip on power looked stronger in the second half of the 2000s than at the time of succession. Since 2011, the civil war experience has turned him into a skilled politician.

Rule by family and sect

When Rif'at revolted against his brother, a decisive rupture within the ruling group happened, and the previous political inner core, which had been based on the large Asad family (or even tribe), became more restricted to Hafiz's sole progeny, for stability's sake. The first heir was Hafiz's eldest son, the paratrooper officer and Republican Guard major Basil, until his fatal car accident in January 1994, and then the ophthalmologist Bashar (assisted by his younger brother Mahir who became the Republican Guard commander and the chief of the 4th Armoured Division after 2000). It is unclear whether this shift of leadership – from the large family to the cellular one – has altered in any manner the dynamics of sectarianism both within the Alawite community and, by extension, on the national level. But one thing appears to be certain: power, already monopolized by the father, has been transmitted to his sons as a personal legacy to be conserved at any cost, which is assuredly an element that can contribute to explaining the rapid deterioration of the Syrian Spring. Thus, when popular legitimate claims were unmet by the not very legitimate leadership, who opted for a very brutal crackdown, leading the protesters to demand regime change, the situation deteriorated quickly. Yet, although sectarianism is prevalent in the whole political system and security apparatus, the argument of this article tries to show that corruption is actually a more convincing paradigm of explanation.

How far does sect motivate the Asads? Hafiz al-Asad certainly had a sectarian side; for example, he used to speak his coastal dialect in all possible circumstances, except when he was delivering an official speech, which occurred in standard Arabic (yet with a touch of western intonation). His main language was thus the old Alawite dialect. In contrast, Bashar is largely able to speak the Damascene dialect even if he knows the coastal one well. But even if he is more cosmopolitan than his father, since he was raised in Damascus and England, and married a woman originating from central Syria, he nevertheless showed a marked preference on some occasions for his coastal homeland idiom. In one circumstance, he received a young female reporter from the national media who was an Alawite born in the capital. As she conversed with him in the Damascene dialect, he gently rebuked her and firmly recommended that she be proud of her sectarian mother tongue and use it more frequently.

Rule through the security services

The first keys to power in the Syrian political system are the security services. Hafiz al-Asad created multiple security services which were all totally dependent on his close scrutiny and moreover entirely independent from each other, so as to avoid any collusion between some of them against his regime. Therefore there was scarcely any collaboration between them. The relationships between these various agencies were even – purposely – bad, sometimes execrable: *divide ut regnes*. These ominous security services were thus competing against one another, to the point that any attempt by one of them to threaten the regime was doomed to failure. In addition to mutual distrust and reciprocated fear, no one possessed the necessary heavy weaponry to constitute a real danger, only towards the people. They could – and still can – be described as deprived of military power but endowed with a high degree of coercion, the manifestations of which were – and remain – violence, criminality, corruption, etc., with the tacit approval of the president.

Under Hafiz, most of the orders to them were given through telephone calls, so that there would be no written instructions, no compromising papers, no traces of any kind. The orders were given in a concise way, sometimes coded, by a distant and almighty voice, just like Stalin or Saddam Hussein did. Muhammad Da'bul (known as Abu Salim), the irremovable presidential cabinet's chief, used to summon army and security officers whenever an order transmitted by phone needed to be clarified and then a secret meeting took place between the president and the concerned person. The names of the main army and security officers, directly nominated by the president alone, were *officially* not divulged to the public, although their identities were more or less known. Thus no photographs of these mysterious people were circulated, and no publicity was given to these secretive men who used to avoid public spaces. The consequence was that a halo of inscrutability prevailed around them in order to scare the people, as if they represented an invisible force ready to suppress any dissent, at the president's slightest behest.

The impunity enjoyed by the security services came at a price to the state and population. There were gang-like wars between secret services over lucrative activities: the levying of illegal taxes on imports, racketeering, smuggling, kidnapping, and the like. Although these unlawful deeds were detrimental to the state's budget and prestige, they were tolerated and even encouraged by the regime, which considered them as an easy way to keep thugs busy and enrich thousands of men (mainly from the Alawite sect) without laying out – directly – a single penny. Today, in Latakia, a regime stronghold, ransoming, abducting, raping, killings are common and carried out by competing Alawite gangs with the complicity of security services. And these crimes plague the whole (mostly Alawite) local population. There has even been recently an overt war, which the regime is unwilling or unable to stop, over land ownership in coastal places where oil is supposed to have been discovered.

The regime's Machiavellian aptitude to terrorize its own people may derive from middle-eastern inclinations towards masculinity and virility, sometimes brutally, in the sense that consensus and concession are often deemed a proof of male weakness. Hafiz's regime also learnt from other dictatorial experiences: for a long period of time, East German secret services (the Stasi) used to operate in Damascus. Thus, there has been a remarkable accumulation of repressive know-how to be used against the Syrian people, and eventually external foes.

The regime's modus operandi did not radically change with the accession to power of Bashar. The new president was certainly unwilling to change the surveillance system. But he tried to put a more modern and civilized stamp on the army and the security apparatus, at least during the first years of his accession to power since he could then fairly be dubbed as a reformist president. The National Institute for Security (*al-Ma'had al-watani al-amni*) is an emblematic endeavour to reform the system, but only superficially. This Institute was located near the city centre, in the Baramkeh district, close to security and military compounds, in a closed and controlled area. Administratively independent from other state agencies, it fell within the realm of the presidency (more precisely of the Bureau for National Security, or *Maktab al-amn al-qawmi*). It was intended to train high-ranking officers, the majority of whom were Alawites, and to inculcate the basics of urbanity in them so as to give the impression to the people as well as to foreign partners that the regime had started its ascent towards modernity, education, and refinement. So, apart from acquiring new spying techniques and the like, officers used to undergo mandatory training sessions, that could usually range from one week to one month, during which they were taught the etiquette's fundamental tenets (*suluk raqi* was the

Arabic accepted expression). The participants were security chiefs as well as high officers about to be sent abroad to Syrian embassies. For instance, the university professor Samir Taqi used to teach the mysteries of international politics. But the initiation to the rules of protocol constituted an important part of the *curriculum*, like how to shake hands in a gentlemanly manner, how to speak nicely on the phone, how to welcome people, to say goodbye, to dress smartly and behave politely during cocktails and receptions, etc. The main idea was therefore to render them – externally – more refined. And indeed, some palpable progress was made in this respect, since a routine convocation to a security branch meant a beating under Hafiz's reign (for those who were lucky enough), whereas under Bashar, tea or coffee could sometimes be served before engaging in serious talking. The great flaw of this training endeavour, which was directly encouraged by the president, was that absolutely nothing was said about human rights and legal constraints. Apart from the essential – but in the end superficial – rules of politeness, virility and masculinity were still highly promoted. If we admit that these two concepts convey a high amount of implicit or exteriorized violence, they certainly mean that the final aim of the training was to impose the will of this security caste on the Syrian people. The trainees were usually married and had children, but the education of their offspring was corrupted, because the fathers constantly lived a life of misconduct and illegality and the rural spouses behaved like arrogant *nouveaux riches*.[4]

Bashar's authority over the coercive apparatus may be less unqualified than was the case under Hafiz, since he has been contested by members of his own family. When he took power, the new president had to make do with his turbulent and ambitious brother-in-law Asif Shawkat as military intelligence chief, until he was killed in a bomb explosion in July 2012. Bashar also had to tolerate the virile initiatives taken by his own younger brother Mahir, who seems, despite rumours of his assassination, to remain in charge of counter-insurrectionary operations. Bashar gives similar orders and relies on the same method for contacting officers and aides as did his father. Yet one difference consists in giving more independence than before to those who are supposed to apply orders, which means that instructions, especially overly concise ones, can be easily overstepped, or even slightly transgressed. Thus, when the first demonstrations started to degenerate into some kind of uncontrollable Uprising (March 2011), the president gave both precise and vague orders so as to contain the upheaval and repress the people, if necessary. But the loose interpretation of the directives led to an immoderate use of violence (like in the southern city of Dar'a), maybe beyond the president's first intention (a point which remains to be clarified). Whatever the causes, the result was that the army and security services acted with a certain amount of autonomy, to the point that the repressed local people felt that the officers were only animated by an inculcated security mentality, vested corporatist interests, and – probably most of all – sectarian animosity (Valter: 2011).[5] In any case, this was a partly uncontrolled situation, barely seen under Hafiz who used to supervise closely all military actions.

At the same time, the regime uses incarceration centres as tools to terrorize the population. Prisoners are frequently detained without any legal basis and exposed to mistreatment, torture and killing. The living conditions in jails are fiendish: overcrowding, lack of hygiene, scarcity of food (if any). One can thus rightly speak of a methodical policy of humiliating, weakening, starving, torturing, to eliminate useless inmates and terrorize the rest of the people.

Controlling the army: Sect and inter-sectarian divisions

How has the regime controlled the army and, in particular, kept it largely loyal, and defections to a minimum, during the Uprising? The regime has relied firstly on sectarian solidarity. One manifestation of this is the rather well-known fact that many Sunni officers have been – and are – under the close scrutiny of subordinate (generally) Alawite officers, as if the latter ones constituted a kind of political police within the armed forces. Thus, whenever there has been a prominent Sunni high-ranking officer, an Alawite aide has generally been controlling his boss from behind the curtains. As always, this rule is assuredly confirmed by many exceptions, particularly during Hafiz's period when fellow officers and Ba'th party members (hailing from all communities), who constituted the 1970 Rectification Movement's old guard, were promoted to high security positions. For instance, the previous defence minister Mustapha Tlas probably stands as a noticeable exception (which needs yet to be confirmed) since he was a faithful old companion of the defunct president. Whatever the truth, testimonies and observations clearly expose the existence of a sectarian system that aimed to control the military hierarchy, from the 1970s onwards, with an apparent increase of (usually) Alawite political mentors and close advisers under Bashar's presidency. The hierarchical inferiority of Sunni officers (and more largely of all the officers whose loyalty towards the regime is not totally sure) manifests itself in the fact that Sunni commanders are (according to well-informed persons) obliged to defer to the powerful Alawite subordinates on certain sensitive issues who are theoretically under their orders, which is a bizarre way to behave within any normal army. Another manifestation of this is the fact that Hafiz Makhluf, one of the president's cousins, when still a rather young (under 40) non-commissioned officer (*naqib*, or lieutenant), supervised the transfer process of almost all officers, a prerogative far superior to his official rank.

After March 2011 when the use of unrestrained violence against protesters raised the prospect that the army might turn against the president, as in Egypt, or defect, the techniques of control became more brutal. 'Ammar Isma'il, an Alawite from Qardaha, the Asad family's birthplace, ran a private radio emitting from Damascus at the start of the upheaval. He used to attack anybody on the waves, with the tacit approval of the president (according to 'Ali Isma'il, 'Ammar's own brother, an engineer, cited by our informants). He thus even ventured to criticize violently high-ranking Alawite officers because of their supposed half-heartedness in implementing what he viewed to be a necessary fierce and blind repression. In this sense, the regime's dynamics have contravened the logic of pure sectarian bonds. His violent diatribes and threats were thrown at whoever was deemed weak and hesitant. He said in substance that he who had the physical or mental capacities to defend the regime but was reluctant to do so in the required brutal and efficient manner could be considered a traitor, and therefore somebody to gun down. The presidential encouragement plus the notoriety of his family appear to have protected him.

After the triggering of the revolt, he launched a media attack against Firas Tlas, a Sunni 'friend' of Bashar and son of the ex-minister of defence. An important industrialist and entrepreneur who had benefited from lucrative import licences, Firas thought that the best way to save the country – and incidentally his own interests – was to implement reforms and call for national reconciliation, which he did on his Facebook account. 'Ammar Isma'il, out of rage, stopped his car on the southern Mezzeh highway and reportedly presented some bullets to him, which meant that his life was in jeopardy and his family endangered. Another son of the previous defence minister, Manaf, who was still closer to the president and moreover a general ('*imad*) from the Republican Guard (the regime's ultimate shield against popular rebellion), went with his brother Firas to complain in front of the president. According to reports from insiders, the president laughed in his 'idiotic' habitual manner instead of showing understanding for the gravity of the situation. A few days later, Firas moved to Dubai with his family whereas Manaf defected and travelled to Paris (July 2012). 'Ammar Isma'il is also mentioned as the head of the regime's electronic army.[6] A famous Syrian actor and an Alawite born in Damascus, Jamal Sulayman, has also been physically threatened by 'A. Isma'il who spares no coreligionist.

As it was unwilling to make any real concession, the regime had to rely on violence, and from the very beginning of the rebellion. To be fair, some acts of gruesome violence were also committed by protesters against (mostly) minority individuals when the unrest erupted. But the security apparatus, packed with Alawites, overreacted because of a history loaded with sectarian blood spilling. Before the disturbances became an overt war, a usual way of scaring the Sunni population was the following: green public transport buses would bring tall, strong, violent, and savage soldiers or paramilitaries – the dregs of Alawite society – into seditious Sunni places. These fanatical thugs just came to take revenge against those they considered to be traitors to the country and foes vis-à-vis the Alawite community, even to the point that the Sunni population was perceived by them as the descendants of the Umayyad dynasty, which was responsible for the hideous slaughter of the imam Husayn, the Prophet's grandson. They used to wear green headbands with the written incantation: 'O! Husayn.' Their mission was to abuse, rape, torture, kill, and rob valuables. The 'regular' army usually arrived shortly later to put the heavy furniture on trucks. According to many reports, some officers have acknowledged that they were not able to master their own soldiers who had not been on furlough for a long time, and if they had attempted to impose martial discipline, they would probably have been killed in mutinous retaliation. One cause of this primitive violence is certainly a very prejudiced religious education, although Alawites do not carry out the Shiite rites of '*Ashura*', or the annual celebration of Husayn's martyrdom. Whatever the case, these ruffians have been writing on the walls of all rebel Sunni districts and villages: '*Bab al-janna, qatl-u al-sunna*', or 'The door to

Paradise consists in killing the Sunnis'. The Alawite community will continue to enjoy certain economic and political prerogatives, at least for those who are loyal and voracious. But if the regime collapses, it will have to pay collectively for the blood bill. Internal dissent has been strong within the Alawite community, and desertion has occurred among Alawite officers, yet on an insufficiently strong scale to decisively alter the power balance and propose a political alternative. If the regime, from Hafiz to Bashar, has relied heavily on sectarian dynamics, it appears that the ultimate beneficiaries are much less numerous than the losers: all those who have become hostages of favouritism, corruption, and violence. As war takes a heavy toll on all sides, the sectarian nature of the regime bears some responsibility: first in having caused blind violence and then in having generated indiscriminate counter-violence.

Economic sleaze and administrative dysfunction

The state administrative apparatus has always functioned on loyalty (reinforced by sectarian affinities) rather than on competence. In this sense, there has never been a recruitment process based on expertise, but rather on co-optation of clients (Gellner and Waterbury: 1977).[7] Bashar at first did want to reform the system (at least partly) and was rather liked by the people, but his irresolution prevented him from taking firm action, even in the administrative sphere. Nibras al-Fadil, the son of the (Alawite) assassinated rector of Aleppo University and a PhD graduate from the famous Institut d'Études Politiques de Paris, was nominated by the president as coordinator of the Syrian team in charge of working with French experts to reform the administrative system. One of the first recommendations of the French experts was for Bashar to move all the Ba'thist civil servants from sensitive positions. The situation deteriorated when some security services accused Nibras of collaborating too intimately with the French. From that time onwards, the rather friendly relations with the French got worse since it was clear that the president had no real intention of profoundly modernizing the administration.

In a system based on favouritism, sectarianism, and repression, corruption cannot but be widespread, especially now that the country is war-ravaged. Rami Makhluf, the president's cousin and notorious tycoon, is one of the most famous examples of corrupt practices and economic voracity, before and during the war. He has been running many big companies and thus controlled (before the Uprising and certainly after as well), directly or not, and together with members of the Asad clan, according to some estimates, half of the national economy, since the mid 1990s.[8] If he can be credited for having attracted investment and created jobs, he has obviously served his clan's interests first and then financed the war effort, particularly the (largely Alawite) pro-regime militia (or *shabbiha*). When the revolt flared up, he was one of the first to declare that the Syrian regime's fall would hurt Israeli interests. Other Alawite personalities are notorious for their illegal involvement in business, corruption, and financial contributions to pro-regime paramilitary activities: Dhu al-Himma Shalish, a cousin of the former president and chief of Bashar's close protection guard; Kamil al-Asad, another relative and president of Latakia's chamber of commerce and industry; Muhammad Makhluf, an elder cousin in charge of oil revenues management;[9] Asif Shawkat, the brother-in-law who controlled the economic activity in the coastal city of Tartus (before his assassination); Nizar al-Asad, an influent entrepreneur in the oil sector; and so on.[10]

Kidnapping and ransoming are common among many rebel armed groups, to the point that in many instances, the lines between financing the war effort and conducting criminal activities are blurred, and one should sometimes rather speak of venal warlords than of dedicated rebellion commanders. But the same is true for regime supporters.[11] As the regime is both unable (because of an inherent disorganization) and disinclined (for security reasons and lack of resources) to monitor closely the secret services and the police, arbitrariness and graft prevail. In order to visit a prison detainee, relatives have to pay a ransom: around 100,000 Syrian pounds, that is about tenfold the average monthly salary (when there is one) and double that, or more, to get him free, if he is innocent. This kind of trade has thrived on mayhem even though the wardens know that many prisoners have no link with the armed opposition.

According to the law, students are allowed a postponement of conscription (which means high risks in the current circumstances). But they frequently have to pay between 20 and 25,000 SP to obtain the official document from the appropriate service, in which Alawite staff is numerous. To be fair, Sunni personnel are usually just as corrupted, but things work under the supervision of Alawite officers, who are more empowered. High officials also facilitate the flight of capital from Syria to Lebanon, although this is forbidden.

Under Hafiz, the illegal trafficking of antiquities was already a prosperous business, carried out by high officers (Rif'at in the first place) with the collaboration of well-established merchants connected to a clientele of foreign diplomats. Since the war, archaeological sites, in theory falling under the UNESCO's protection, have been partially destroyed by the regime, like the Crac des Chevaliers. Many historical mosques have been shelled by the regime's armed forces: the Khalid b. al-Walid mosque in Homs, the 'Umari mosque in Dar'a, the Umayyad mosque in Aleppo, etc. But the rebel factions are far from being innocent in the global destruction (like the Islamic State which destroys whatever pre-Islamic vestiges it cannot sell). In all, some 850 mosques have been destroyed, a third of which belongs to the historical patrimony. And now that nobody keeps an eye on archaeological sites, smuggling of antiquities has taken on unknown proportions. Bashar's wife, Asma, suggested once that archaeological sites and museums be placed under her direct responsibility, and though the suggestion was dropped, it shows how the Asad family's personal interests and the state's prerogatives overlap.

The media, which have often been generously financed by the regime, constitute another example of political interference. Before the war, there were some 5,000 employees at the Syrian television and broadcasting establishment,[12] with high salaries and bonuses. Whenever a Lebanese journalist took part in a programme, the remuneration oscillated between $500 and $5,000, a high sum sometimes paid in advance. For TV news bulletins, directives are given by both the secret services and the Ministry of Information. And in general, the task of controlling television and radio (and especially the news bulletins) is incumbent upon the Political Security Agency, which transmits the instructions to the managing staff.[13] But *in fine*, the presidency's press office is the key organ that checks all the information, in coordination with the secret services. In the event of an error, the person in charge is dismissed (as happened for example to Fawaz al-'Amiri). If there was, at least before the war, a certain margin of autonomy for the coverage of social and economic issues so as to give the illusion that freedom of expression existed, political questions remained under total control.[14]

Private channels have also recently appeared, like Arab News Network, owned by Rif'at and broadcast from London; it was quite popular at the beginning of the Uprising but it has now fallen into semi-oblivion. Orient News, based in Dubai, has tried to be balanced and critical: it admits that atrocities have been committed but tries to distance the president from the carnage carried out by the official armed forces; this channel was founded by 'dissident' MPs with, for instance, the collaboration of Ayman 'Abd al-Nur, a previous economic adviser of the president. Iranian, Russian, and pro-Shiite Lebanese and Iraqi media are for their part always showering praise on the regime. Such is the case of the ANNA news agency, based in the separatist part of Abkhazia (the irredentist claims of which are supported by Russia). Its diffusion of war images via the Internet clearly indicates a bias in favour of the Syrian regime.[15]

Intellectual servility goes hand in hand with the cult of personality. Pictures of the president can be seen everywhere, frequently with the trinity's two other deified hypostasis: the father and the deceased brother. Fanatical Alawites have written on city walls: 'Asad for ever or we burn the country', an ominous warning; photos of Bashar are hung in shops, sometimes out of conviction, sometimes to prevent the application of commercial and fiscal administrative rules.

Rape has become a weapon in the civil war. When IS fighters capture women hailing from minority communities (Alawites, Christians, Yazidis, etc.), if they do not kill them straight away, they enslave them before raping or selling them (Valter: 2014). From the regime's side, rape is also systematic. Wardens were sometimes compelled by their superiors to rape men or women, of all ages, before getting accustomed to it and finally doing it out of sadistic pleasure. The motives pushing regime servicemen to commit rape are numerous: sexual frustration, lack of moral education, etc. Raped women seldom mention their ordeal for fear of being killed by their own family in so-called honour crimes. If rapes are very frequent in prisons, they also occur in houses, in front of relatives, when militaries, secret agents, or militiamen break in.

Conclusion

In summary, the Asad regime was built on dysfunctionalities. The concentration of power in the presidency, and the personal character of rule, translated into inefficient administration. The inheritance of power by Bashar al-Asad was seen as a personal bequest to be defended at all costs. The security of the leader depends on divide and rule, especially among the multiple security services whose officers are key power brokers. While they have always enjoyed impunity, since the Uprising, restraints of their brutality have disappeared. Control of the army depends on a network of loyal Alawi officers. The businesses of crony capitalists close to the Asad family have prospered during the Uprising.

The regime is built on a combination of generalized corruption, violence, and sectarianism.

Notes

1 Some analysts suggest that President Asad was both dominating and prisoner (to a certain point) of the security apparatus (*al-mu'assasa*, which could be translated by 'the Institution' or 'the deep state') he had contributed to creating.
2 R. Ziadeh has relied on the constitution's articles which clearly mention that the security services (which should rather be called the insecurity services) are totally above the law and thus not responsible to anyone except the politico-military leadership.
3 http://www.souriyati.com/2015/09/02/19806.html.
4 For example, testimonies from the prestigious Lycée Français in Damascus, where many siblings of Alawite officers have been educated, confirm this assertion.
5 The overwhelming majority of the security services are made up of Alawites, as are the elite army units (like the 3rd and 4th Divisions, or the Republican Guard), whereas the Dar'a demonstrators were Sunnis.
6 http://www.lemonde.fr/proche-orient/article/2013/08/15/piratage-des-liens-pro-assad-sur-le-site-de-plusieurs-grand-medias_3462224_3218.html and http://www.lemonde.fr/pixels/video/2015/01/20/qui-sont-les-pirates-de-l-armee-electronique-syrienne_4560026_4408996.html.
7 For Gellner, there is a link between patronage and the dysfunctions of a semi-capitalist system. Although Syria pretends to be a socialist state, the following shortcomings can be identified: an inefficient and corrupted bureaucracy, a market not submitted to competition, the prevalence of dominating groups' norms and dynamics, etc.
8 See for example http://syrie.blog.lemonde.fr/2011/06/28/rami-makhlouf-de-laffairisme-a-lillusionnisme/.
9 When he was director of the Bank for Real Estate Investment, he used to carry out private forward transactions with public money.
10 Many high officers, involved in illegal trade, have amassed huge fortunes. See http://syrianobserver.com/EN/Features/29691/Regime_Loyalists_Amass_Fortunes_From_Misery_Syrian_War/.
11 http://syrianobserver.com/EN/News/29708/Assad_Loyalists_Voice_Fear_Gangs_Homs_Tartous_Highway/.
12 Two in Arabic plus a trilingual one (Arabic, English, and French).
13 Similarly, sermons in mosques are supervised by the security services.
14 Technical security units, with Iranian assistance, have tried for a long time to scramble foreign channels, like the Qatari al-Jazira or the Saudi al-'Arabiyya, overtly opposed to the regime from the very start of the revolt.
15 The political written press is mostly made up of the journals edited by (or connected to) the authorized political parties, i.e. those that are members of the National Progressive Front dominated by the Ba'th. And the allowed private papers have always been financed by the state, often through cash money given to some personalities.

Bibliography

Aarts, Paul & Francesco Cavatorta (2012), *Civil Society in Syria and Iran: Activism in Authoritarian Contexts*. Boulder: Lynne Rienner.

Al-Khatib, Muhammad Kamil (n.d.), *One Hundred Years of Suffering* (in Arabic). Beirut: Manshurat 0021.

Atassi, Karim (2014), *Syrie, la Force d'une Idée. Architectures Constitutionnelles des Régimes Politiques*. Paris: L'Harmattan.

Chouet, Alain (1995), 'L'Espace Tribal Alaouite à l'Épreuve du Pouvoir. La Désintégration par le Politique,' *Monde Arabe Maghreb-Machrek* 147: 93–119.

Friedman, Yaron (2010), *The Nusayri-Alawis: An Introduction to the Religion, History, and Identity of the Leading Minority in Syria*. Leiden: Brill.

Gellner, Ernest & John Waterbury (ed.) (1977), *Patrons and Clients in Mediterranean Societies*. London: Duckworth.

Khadduri, Majid (2006), *War and Peace in the Law of Islam*. Clark, NJ: The Lawbook Exchange.

Le Gac, Daniel (1991), *La Syrie du Général Assad*. Brussels: Éditions Complexe.

Paul, James A. (1990), *Human Rights in Syria*. A Middle East Watch Report, September, New York and Washington.

Seurat, Michel (2012), *Syrie, L'État de barbarie*. Paris: Presses Universitaires de France.

Valter, Stéphane (2002), *La Construction Nationale Syrienne: Légitimation de la Nature Communautaire du Pouvoir par le Discours Historique*. Paris: CNRS Ed.

Valter, Stéphane (2003), 'La Réplique à Ibn Baz (1912–1999) de 'Abd al-Rahman al-Khayyir (1904–1986),' *Bulletin d'études orientales* 55: 299–383.

Valter, Stéphane (2011), 'Rivalités et Complémentarités au Sein des Forces Armées: Le Facteur Confessionnel en Syrie,' *Les Champs de Mars* 23: 79–96.

Valter, Stéphane (2014), 'La Justice Chariatique en Syrie "Libérée": Un Modèle Juridique Consensuel?,' *Confluences Méditerranée* 90: 155–173.

Van Dam, Nikolaos (1996), *The Struggle for Power in Syria: Politics and Society under Asad and the Ba'th Party*. London: I.B.Tauris.

Ziadeh, Radwan (2013), *Syria's Role in a Changing Middle East*. Basingstoke: I.B.Tauris.

5

THE UPRISING AND THE ECONOMIC INTERESTS OF THE SYRIAN MILITARY–MERCANTILE COMPLEX[1]

Salam Said

Introduction

During the Arab Spring, the role and behaviour of national armies has been crucial. While the military institutions in Tunisia and Egypt detached themselves from the collapsing regimes, the Syrian military has been involved in suppressing the protest movement from the uprising's outset. Despite many defections of soldiers and low-ranking officers since 2011, the majority of the Syrian army's officer corps still adheres to Asad's regime. Relations between the military and the regime are very complex. The loyalty of high-ranking officers has been widely attributed to sectarian and ideological factors but also needs to be seen in relation to their economic interests.

The army's economic activities go back five decades and happened with the regime's consent and even encouragement. During the 1980s and 1990s, the limited and controlled market opening by Hafiz al-Asad encouraged business partnerships between the private sector and military officers. In the 2000s, Bashar al-Asad accelerated the transition to a neoliberal economy that allowed military officers and their offspring an even larger involvement in the private sector. By contrast with Egypt, where the military institution owned large-scale enterprises as a whole, in Syria ownership was more often located at the individual level. Using their influence to access governmental institutions, army officers either created their own private companies or acted as patrons of business monopolies. In many cases, sons of the generals opened their own firms enjoying a high degree of favouritism.

This chapter examines the economic factors underlying the army's proven loyalty to the regime by looking at its economic activities since the military coup in 1970. The first section of the chapter focuses on socioeconomic developments within the Syrian military prior to the Uprising. The second section investigates the military's economic interests by analysing the different developmental stages of the military economic institution since 1970 on the one hand, and by tracing the relations between officers and private businesses as well as the illicit economic activities of the military on the other hand. The third part of the chapter takes up the question as to whether the proven loyalty of the military to the regime during the Uprising and thereafter can be explained by the tight economic connections between the regime inner core and the officer corps. The chapter concludes by addressing the effects of the militarization of the state by the Syrian military.

Socioeconomic background of the military

Since its formation in 1930 during the French mandate period, the Syrian army has attracted persons with low socioeconomic status, in particular peasants and disadvantaged urban social classes (Batatu: 1981, p. 341; Van Dam: 2011, pp. 26–27). Not only does the army offer economic advancement and advantages, but also social prestige, pride and power. Due to their increasing influence in domestic politics in the post-independence period, the armed forces attracted not only those who aimed to improve their socioeconomic status but also those with political ambitions. Military coups characterized the time between 1949 and 1970 and emphasised the importance of being a military officer to seize political power. In the 1950s and 1960s, military officers were of different religious, economic and geographical backgrounds. Struggles and alliances within the military officers took place according to political ideology, socioeconomic class and ecologic-cultural divisions rather than according to religion and tribe. For instance, the mostly rural-oriented Ba'thist Sunni officers supported the Alawite and Druze ones against the Sunni urban officers. However, the internal struggle among the Ba'thist officers after 1963 led to a concentration of military power in the hands of Alawite officers and later on in the hands of officers loyal to Hafiz al-Asad (Batatu: 1981, pp. 242–243; Seale: 1990, pp. 72–75). From the end of the 1960s onwards, the dominance of the Alawites in the military increased. Hafiz al-Asad, himself an Alawite officer of peasant origin, became president in 1970 following a military coup. He consolidated his power by appointing loyal officers and relatives to key positions and units within the military. In order to prevent any defection of army officers to the opposition, moreover, he developed strong loyal paramilitaries and an intelligence apparatus (Makara: 2013, p. 348). Paramilitaries were well equipped and trained, mainly Alawite and headed by loyal leaders and relatives of Asad (Batatu: 1981, p. 331; Picard: 1990, p. 202; Mora & Wiktorowicz: 2003, p. 23). This strategy seemed to be successful not only in terms of the survival of the Hafiz-led regime, but also for the one led by his son Bashar, who, in his military confrontation with the opposition since 2011, has relied mainly on the Republican Guards, Special Forces and 4th Armoured Division as well as paramilitaries (Holliday: 2013, p. 6).

Prior to the Syrian Uprising in 2011, the majority of enrolled students in the armed force's academies (military, police and intelligence) came mainly from the rural population as well as from the lower and lower-middle classes of the urban population. As the Syrian journalist Youssef said, "If you ask a young man in one of the coast Alawite villages 'what is your dream?' he will answer, 'to become a military officer'."[2] Another journalist from Raqqa stated, "Only the sons of unimportant and poor tribes in the province seek to enrol in the police forces or in the military. Prominent and rich tribes despise this profession, even if they need to pragmatically deal with them or need their help."[3] By contrast, the offspring of the first generation of the Ba'thist officers are not necessarily involved in the armed forces. According to the Syrian journalist Youssef "they don't need to! They take advantage of the network of their fathers, without needing to be involved directly in the patronage system."[4] Thanks to the connections of their fathers, they enjoy high standards of living, receive excellent education, get jobs easily in the public administration, and can easily get loans from public banks. Moreover, the economic wealth and elite education of the offspring of senior army officers make them competitive in both the national and international business worlds.[5]

The military's economic role and interests

The doctrine of the Syrian military under Hafiz al-Asad stated that the Syrian Arab Army has two missions: a regional Pan-Arab "*qaumi*" and state "*qutri*" mission. As a military of the Pan-Arab Nation, the Syrian military's ideological doctrine defines it as the protector of all-Arab interests, including being the defender of the Palestinian land. According to the military slogan "the military for war and reconstruction" the state (Syria-specific) mission of the military is twofold: to protect people against all internal and external threats and to participate in the domestic social and economic development process by providing social services and by building up the socio-economic infrastructure (Al-Haj Ali: 2012). For this purpose, from the 1970s onwards many economic establishments were created and operated by the military, such as the Military Housing Institution, the Institution of Defence Factories, the Institution for the Execution of Military Construction, the Social Military Institution, the Administration of Productive Projects, the Institution for Military Transport and the Institution for Blood Transfer and Medical Industries. In addition, military institutions contributed to social development by providing medical services, high education and training (Al-Haj Ali: 2012). At the beginning, these establishments aimed at meeting the needs of the military and achieving self-sufficiency. Later on, they expanded their economic activities to the civilian sector. In the 1980s some of them dominated more than 75 per cent of the domestic market in a particular field. Despite the fact that military companies are considered state-owned enterprises, they were given more entrepreneurial freedom than other state-owned enterprises. They were free to hire and fire their employees and enjoyed a lot of exemptions from foreign trade and currency regulations. They belong administratively to the Ministry of Defence and were therefore not controllable by or accountable to the government (Perthes: 1995, pp. 147–152).

The nature and extent of the military's institutional economic activities developed according to broader state economic policy and can be analysed through three distinct phases: The creation and development in the 1970s (phase I), the expansion and operation in civil economic sectors in the 1980s (phase II) and the decline of their economic activities from 1991 onwards (phase III). These phases are discussed in the following.

Phase I: Creation and development – from socialism to the first infitah[6]

The constitution of 1973 declared Syria a "socialist state with a planned economy". Its socialist economic policy was characterized by the implementation of radical land reforms and the nationalization of private industrial and commercial enterprises, which resulted in the enlargement of the public sector at the expense of the private one. In addition, a large number of restrictions on imports and financial transfers were imposed. Almost all international economic transactions were conducted by the public sector or highly controlled by the state authorities. In line with the socialist economy, Syria also followed an import-substitution policy that influenced the activities of the state-owned enterprises, including the military ones.[7]

The founding of military economic establishments

In accordance with the socialist economic policy, military economic establishments were created to achieve the aim of self-reliance. The formation of extensive military economic institutions was possible in the 1970s due to the earnings from oil exports and the inflow of state assistance from the Gulf, which was estimated at $850 million between 1973 and 1978 and $1.6 billion from 1979 to 1981 (Perthes: 1995, p. 34). In addition to their military production and services, military economic enterprises also operated in the civil economic sector. Their civil production (e.g. clothes, furniture, food products) and services (medical, sport and leisure facilities and transport) were at the beginning limited to military use and members. For instance, the Institution of Defence Factories (14 factories) fabricated uniforms, shoes, water and electricity meters, spare parts and furniture for the military. The Military Housing Institution (MHI) and the Institution for the Execution of Military Construction (MATA) undertook construction and infrastructure work for the army, including roads, bridges, dams, airports, ports, barracks, dwellings, hospitals, colleges and leisure houses. The Military Social Institution provided medical and social services for the armed forces. The Administration of Productive Projects ran agricultural activities, such as land restoration, breeding farm animals, and providing agricultural and food products for military consumption. The military was also involved in import and trade activities, so it owned supermarkets, where only employees of military institutions had access to imported and domestic goods at subsidized prices. Through this institutional complex, the military not only sustained a kind of self-sufficiency, but also enjoyed privileged access to the best social and medical services as well as to prohibited imports.[8]

The workers and employees of the military economic institutions were mainly from the military: conscripts, soldiers, graduates of military academies and officers.

Civilian workers (permanent and temporary) were estimated – depending on the institution and the season – at only between 9 and 25 per cent. Except for the conscripts, all labourers received salaries according to the labour regulations for state-owned enterprises, attractive bonus payments and access to the privileges of the military. Therefore, military companies were an attractive employer for highly skilled labour, especially for engineers.[9]

The emergence of informal military–businessmen relations under economic liberalization

Apart from the official economic activities of the military institutions, which were part of the official socialist economy, informal business relations were built between the military elite and the newly emerging private capital, indicative of a cautious economic transformation from socialism to more liberalized economy.

After becoming president in 1970, Hafiz Asad diluted the orthodox socialist policies that had been followed by the Ba'th Party in the later 1960s in order to reduce dependence on the socialist bloc and open up the economy to the West, Gulf states as well as to private investors (Perthes: 1995, p. 41). Asad, moreover, liberalized economic regulations, which increased the role of the domestic private sector in the economy and resulted in creating a kind of bourgeoisie-public sector alliance (Perthes: 1994, pp. 48–55). According to Hinnebusch (1994), the bourgeoisie in this alliance is a pro-regime new bourgeoisie, which took advantage of its relations to the state elite to enlarge its economic activities and accumulate capital mainly through corruption and patronage. They are "speculators", contractors and "brokers" rather than industrialists (Bahout: 1994, p. 75). According to Mora & Wiktorowicz (2003, p. 23): "several hundred officers with personal connections to the regime used their relationships to evade regulations, garner favours, and generate vast personal wealth. Much of this wealth has been produced as a result of political privileges rather than productive activities."

Elizabeth Picard and Sadiq al-Azm used the terms "military mercantile complex" to describe these clientelist networks between (mainly Alawite) military officers and new businessmen. Military officers were brokers of the state's big construction contracts, monopolized distribution of contracts to private clients and took considerable commissions (Interview, Sultan). Official military companies were also contracting with favoured private clients who had good connections to influential officers in the administration of the companies. Private clients (usually small enterprises) would have to pay a percentage of the contract/deal to the officer in order to win a tender with the military company.

In addition to evading laws and manipulating government contracts with private businesses, military officers were also involved directly in illicit, sometimes mafia-like activities. They protected businesses for fees or shares of the business and smuggled banned imports, arms and drugs, especially after the Syrian military intervention in Lebanon (Mora & Wiktorowicz: 2003, p. 24). Consequently, powerful generals such as Ghazi Kan'an and Shafiq Fayyad could constitute "islands of wealth and power as a result of Syria's involvement in Lebanon" (Haddad: 2012, p. 225, fn. 256 cited in Mora & Wiktorowicz: 2003, p. 24).

The illegal earnings of the military officers allowed them to accumulate capital, making them and their offspring part of the new economic elite that encouraged further economic liberalization in state policy. By the end of this phase, the first generation of officers, who came from rural background or lower income classes, became gradually a part of the new middle- and high-income classes in Syria.

Phase II: Expansion and development – the 1980s

By the end of the 1970s the first signs of an economic crisis appeared and led to a re-orientation of the economic policy. The enlargement of a bureaucratic public sector at the expense of the private one and the declining of rent – both oil revenues and Arab aid – led to a fiscal crisis. The Syrian government had to follow an austerity programme, including decreasing governmental spending and investment (Hinnebusch: 1994, pp. 100–101, Perthes: 1995, p. 52). Under these circumstances, a second *infitah* was announced in order to revive the stagnated economy. In other words, the economic crisis forced the government to undertake market opening measures facilitating a larger contribution by the private sector in the economy, by easing foreign exchange regulations and relaxing export and import restrictions. Still, strategic economic sectors such as oil, energy, infrastructure and heavy industries were not open to private investments (Hinnebusch: 1994, p. 101, Perthes: 1994, pp. 55–56). The beneficiaries of the second *infitah* were the crony capitalists, whose economic success depended on their connection with the regime elite (Perthes: 1994, p. 57), and of course, the emerging wealthy military officers, governmental elite and members of Asad clan.

Expansion of military economic establishments

Yet, the one part of the public sector, which not only did not contract or stagnate but continued to expand, were the military economic institutions. In non-democratic regimes like the Syrian one, an economic crisis and the reduction of revenues are potentially risky if the crisis damages the interest of the military, the main pillar of the regime's power. In order to ensure the loyalty of the military and political survival, the regime responded by fostering military-controlled businesses and supporting the creation of business opportunities for key officers (Mora & Wiktorowicz: 2003, p. 4). This might explain the expansion of military establishments' civil economic activities in this period, which was described by Syrian journalists and economists as the "peak" of military–business activities.[10]

As state-owned enterprises, the military enterprises were – at least officially – in competition with both public and private sectors. Their monopoly was due to their competitiveness and efficiency, as the Syrian journalist Youssef stated: "no other private company could at that time offer the same performance at competitive prices like the military ones".[11] This statement is not fully accurate if one takes into consideration the fact that the military enjoyed economic advantages compared with their competitors in both public and private sectors. They had access to raw materials, electricity, land and fuel at subsidized prices, but also to unlimited and duty-free imported inputs in a country with a highly restrictive trade system. Also, they did not have to go through an expensive and time-consuming bureaucracy to get import or operational licences. There were no private banks in this period and the military had favoured access to loans and financial resources from public banks compared with similar private enterprises. Military establishments also had low labour expenses, since a considerable number of their workers were conscripts that did not receive any wages for their work.[12] In Syria's state-controlled economy, military enterprises were also favoured in obtaining modern technology and in co-operation with the sole research technological institute (Scientific Studies and Research Center) in the country. All these economic privileges enabled the military to expand its economic activities to the civil sector, to be efficient and to offer goods and services of good quality at competitive prices, while still keeping a low profit margin (c. 5 per cent) in accordance with social goals.[13] As a result, the military succeeded in monopolizing several domains of the domestic market. Only military supermarkets could at the time of a highly restricted trade system offer prohibited import products (e.g. cigarettes and alcohol) at subsidized prices; and only military hospitals and medical centres could provide patients with foreign medicines. Although military supermarkets, leisure and sport facilities, hospitals and medical centres partially opened for non-military customers, military personnel maintained preferential access to these services.

Simultaneously, the Military Housing Institution (MHI) became one of the most important and biggest economic establishments in the country, with more than 100,000 permanent and 50,000 temporary employees in the 1980s. It was the sole contractor for huge construction contracts, such as roads, tunnels, airports, ministries, schools, universities, and dwelling projects. It monopolized more than 85 per cent of the domestic market.[14] In order to meet the need of its expanding business and in accordance with the self-reliance strategy, the MHI expanded the value added chain of its activities by producing cement, stones, sand, cement blocks and other construction raw materials, as well as electricity cables and furniture. This company became very sophisticated and even started to operate internationally. Some construction projects in Algeria and Sudan were undertaken during the 1980s by the MHI.[15] Domestically, it grew to be the most influential actor in the economy. To express its huge economic size, its autonomy and being above the law, Syrian people considered this institution an economic empire. A Syrian journalist quoted Patrick Seale by describing this institution as "a State within the State".[16]

The second military construction enterprise (MATA) also expanded and conducted contracts with the public sector as well as with MHI. MATA executed many construction projects such as irrigation projects, dams, land reclamation, sanitation projects, sewage treatment plants, transport infrastructure, universities, schools, hospitals and housing projects (Aljerdi: 2011, p. 2). However, its activities were not as large as that of the MHI. Other military institutions such as the

Institution of Factories of Defence and the agricultural enterprise Administration of Productive Projects also expanded their activities in this period without private investment and import opportunity. Yet, their market share did not exceed 2 per cent and 3 per cent in the peak period respectively.[17] Military involvement in the economic civil sector has been described by the regime as the contribution of the "[a]rmy of dignity and reconstruction" in the development process and in supporting the economy in Syria (Aljerdi: 2011, p. 1, see Hasan: 2011, p. 1).

Corruption, illegal businesses and the interdependent military–business relations

The new wave of economic liberalization strengthened both the alliance and interdependency between the military officers as a part of the state elite and the private sector that emerged in the 1970s. While businessmen, regardless of the size of their businesses, needed connections with the power structure (state officials, military or security officers) in order to secure their business, officers and officials needed the private sector to access financial sources and networks (Hinnebusch: 1994, p. 101; Perthes: 1995, p. 149, also interview with Youssef). The new economic elite, including state officials, military and security officers who had accumulated wealth over the previous years, was ready for a new wave of economic liberalization that opened up new investment and business opportunities.[18] As a result, sons of high-ranking officers and government officials opened businesses in tourism, gastronomy and media. They could dominate the market and eliminate competitors using the power of their fathers, by threatening and blackmailing potential rivals. "No one ventured to compete with them", said the Syrian journalist Ahmad.[19]

In order to maintain the loyalty of the military officers in a time of economic crisis, the regime not only fostered clientele affairs between the officers and the private sector, but also tolerated corruption and involvement of military officers in illicit economic activities that ranged from smuggling prohibited imported goods like arms and drugs to money laundering and trading antiquities (Haddad: 2012, pp. 99–100). The smuggling activities of the military reached their peak in the 1980s, when foreign trade was heavily restricted and the Syrian army was positioned in Lebanon (Perthes: 1995, pp. 149–150). The so-called "military line" between Damascus and Beirut was out of the control of customs authorities and other security apparatuses. Military officers could transfer and smuggle whatever they wanted from and into Syria according to a quota-system among them.[20] The drugs business in Lebanon was protected and encouraged by high-ranking Syrian officers, such as Rifat Asad, the president's brother, who had collected considerable wealth from his involvement in the drugs trade (Human Rights Watch: 1991, pp. 163–165). Financial resources from Lebanon were not limited to smuggling prohibited imports and drugs only, but also protection money extorted from Lebanese businessmen. A large number of Lebanese enterprises had to pay fees to Syrian officers to be able to run their business without risking having "troubles" with the Syrian army.[21] After the import bans on some commodities (e.g. cigarettes and alcohol) had been removed in Syria and the hashish cultivation in Lebanon declined (Perthes: 1995, p. 153), the "illegal" military earnings in Lebanon started to decrease.

In addition to illegal business, it was quite common in the military to earn additional income from corruption and bribery, which were not restricted to the high-ranking officers (Perthes 1995, p. 150). The conscripts were the main victims. Petty bribes could be paid to obtain some more holidays during military service or to get exemption from certain regulations. Officers used conscripts and rank-and-file soldiers in their private businesses.[22] Officers of low ranks stole materials (food, construction materials) from the military storages to sell it in the market. It was well known that to be a member of the so-called "purchasing committee" in any military department was an attractive opportunity to earn additional income.[23] Corruption of a larger scale occurred in higher positions. High-ranking officers could charge a percentage (commission) of the transaction from the private contracting firm as a reward for helping to get the firm a subcontract from one of the military economic establishments, in particular from MHI and MATA.[24]

Phase III: Decline of military economic activities from 1991 onwards

In the 1990s, economic liberalization measures were extended to include the investment sector. According to Investment Law No. 10 in 1991, the private sector was allowed to invest in additional agricultural, industrial and service sectors. Not only Syrians abroad, but also Arab and foreign investors were welcome to launch joint ventures (Perthes: 1994, p. 60, Pölling: 1994, p. 14). Further – and more important – liberalization steps were undertaken in the mid-2000s under Bashar Asad, who took over the presidency after the death of his father in 2000. In 2005, state monopolies in many sectors, such as banking, insurance, telecommunication and cotton ginning, ended. A large number of import bans were abolished and import duties were unilaterally decreased. In addition, a number of free trade agreements with regional partners (Arab countries and Turkey) were signed allowing wider foreign trade exchange and foreign investments. Syria also revived the negotiation of an Association Agreement with the EU and applied to join the WTO in 2001 and again in 2004 (Said: 2011, pp. 226–232).

These steps provoked debate as to the incentives for such economic reforms in an authoritarian regime like the Syrian one. Syrians traced these reforms back to the Western educated young president with a non-military background. He was considered as a "white hope" for more economic and political freedom, for fighting corruption, for institutional modernization and supporting civil society. Economic liberalization was propagated as a necessity to attract investments and ensure economic growth, to compensate for the decrease in oil revenues,[25] and to enhance international credibility and competitiveness. Politically, the regime promoted the economic transformation to a liberal economy legitimized as a "Social Market Economy", the German economic model that was said to be in accordance with the socialist Ba'th Party's doctrine. In a conversation in January 2013 with Abdullah Dardari, the former prime minister and supporter of liberal economic reforms, he stated that

Syria might follow the "successful" Chinese model that applied liberal economic reform without the need to undertake political one.[26]

Perhaps more important, however, economic liberalization was a demand of the Syrian crony capitalists, who were ready for such an opening after years of privileges and state-protection, in order to expand their domestic business and launch export markets abroad. The competitive and sophisticated young generation of the economic elite welcomed the neoliberal reforms that opened new areas of investments. In contrast, small businesses and some other stakeholders suffered under the reforms. For instance, the market opening with Turkey in 2007 damaged dramatically small textile manufacturers, but not the big well-connected ones. New economic regulations were reputedly tailored to advantage the well-connected business elite and open new channels for corruption and briberies to evade regulations. Hence, the economic liberalization was again unfair, undemocratic, non-transparent, discriminating, corrupt, and deliberately in favour of the elite only.

In addition, the liberalization of the 2000s led to an accumulation of wealth in the hands of Bashar's inner circle. Gambill (2004) observes that economic opportunities under Bashar became increasingly concentrated within Asad's own clan. An example of this was the monopoly of the private part of the telecommunication (mobile phone) sector by Rami Makhlouf, the cousin of the president; liberalization moved state monopolies to "private" monopolies of crony capitalists. Mora & Wiktorowicz (2003) argue that the regime increasingly favoured the businesses of pro-reform officers, the so-called "New Guard". They suggest that the reform challenged the economic interest of many other military officers, the "Old Guard", who relied on their connections to political power and a favourable economic environment to run profitable businesses. However, some other authors believe that there is hardly a difference between the old and the new guards (George: 2003, p. 162; Gambill: 2004, p. 5). The personnel change of some key positions under Bashar was not a matter of anti-reform old guards, being replaced by pro-reform ones; rather, it was needed to consolidate the power of Bashar and to exclude figures threatening to his succession (Gambill: 2001, p. 4).

Economic Liberalization and Military Enterprises

Undoubtedly, the neoliberal economic policy affected the economic activities of military-owned enterprises. The removal of restrictions on private investments and foreign trade on the one hand, and the opening of new investment domains in banking, health, manufacturing and tourism sectors on the other hand, cost the military a lot of its old advantages vis-à-vis private businesses. Moreover, several subsidies were reduced due to the reforms, even for the military institutions (IMF: 2010, p. 4).[27] So, military economic institutions not only had to give up their monopoly position, but had also to compete with modern and efficient private companies, which had likewise access to state-granted privileges due to their tight connections to the political regime. In addition to the increasing competition, there were other factors that impeded an expansion in the military's economic activities in this period, such as heavy bureaucracy, high administrative costs, huge size, out-dated machinery, corruption and low productivity. For instance, the Administration of Productive Projects, which was the single producer of medical herbs in Syria, from the late 1990s onwards had to share the market with other producers. Alcohol and tobacco could be imported by private companies and were thus available in the private supermarkets.[28] The military resorts and hospitals were neglected and needed renovations, while private hospitals and resorts were outfitted with modern and luxury equipment. Wealthy and high-raking military officers were able to pay the high costs of the private services while mainly low-ranking officers and ordinary soldiers used the military medical and tourist services.

The regime did not aim to challenge the military businesses, which were a core constituency. They were not affected by the privatization wave of dozens of industrial state-owned enterprises that took place between 2005 and 2008. While some economic activities declined, military enterprises were allowed to maintain monopolies in some market segments. For example, Factories of Defence were still the main producer of gas cylinders, electricity, water meters and oxygen. The MHI and MATA remained the major and most competitive contractors in the construction sector due to their huge capacity, long experience, skilled workers, engineers and, of course, their access to the cheap building materials.[29] The MATA even benefited from the real estate price inflation following the neoliberal economic reforms. As a state-enterprise, MATA contracted new construction projects for civilian housing in the Damascus suburbs Dahiet al-Asad. Similar to the corrupt contracting pattern in the 1980s, MATA also contracted construction projects for private firms owned by regime members and their partners. Through this construction boom MATA became "flush with cash" (Khaddour: 2015, p. 3). After the liberalization, the MHI succeeded in securing a contract to build hotels in Syria for an American-based hotel chain (Mora & Wiktorowicz: 2003, p. 27). However, compared with the 1980s, the activities of the MHI declined and the institution became less powerful than before. According to Sultan, it lost more than 35 per cent of its market share and 60 per cent of employees. In 2011, there were only 25,000 workers compared with 100,000 in the 1980s. In an interview with the general director of the MHI published in the state-owned daily newspaper *Al-Thawra* on the 66th anniversary of foundation of the Syrian Arab Army, he indirectly stated that many building material factories (e.g. Ceramic) belonging to the MHI needed modernization to be profitable again.[30] This shows the economic situation of the most important economic institution (MHI) of the military prior to the Uprising in the country.

Corruption and the private businesses of military officers

The living standards of many military personnel seem to have been negatively affected by the increasingly neoliberal economic reforms undertaken since 2001. It seems also that the regime was not able to continue financing the sweeping and generous privileges of the military.[31] A project on professionalizing the army by concentrating on special units and the loyal key figures and making others redundant was proposed and triggered resistance within the military institution. Due to high inflation – according to IMF (2010) it reached 19 per cent in 2008 – and the depreciation of real wages, officers of lower ranks needed to take on additional work in the private sector, for instance as taxi drivers.[32] The disparity within the military seemed to have grown. So, there were wealthy, middle-income and low-income officers.

The private businesses of influential officers flourished in the time of market opening. Being above the law and rich, the new generation of the economic elite furthermore enjoyed state-protection and privileges vis-à-vis the unconnected private investors. Even foreign affairs were deployed to protect the economic interests of this elite; for example, clientele connections between the Syrian and Egyptian economic elite made it possible for a well-connected businessman to monopolize the export of cotton yarn to Egypt (Said: 2011, pp. 246–247).

Also, corruption, bribery, and blackmailing remained important financial sources for military personnel. They became even more regular in the last years prior to the Uprising, since the officers' official salaries failed to keep up with inflation and were not lucrative compared with the ones in the private sector. Conscripts and ordinary soldiers, who were in the bottom of the hierarchic military ranks, know "the price list of escaping regulations and gaining privileges from the first day in the military", as a former conscript claimed.[33]

After all, over a period of 40 years the merchant–military relationship generated the "business-officers" who in the 1970s had power and lacked capital. Later, they had both: power and capital. The old generation of military officers and their offspring now aimed at developing their businesses and becoming the richest of the rich.

Economic interest as a loyalty-factor during the Uprising

The Egyptian military's forcing of President Mubarak to step down in early 2011 inspired Syrian protesters and activists who tried to motivate the Syrian military to similarly defect and avoid bloodshed in the country. One of the initiatives to win over the military was to give army personnel flowers and water bottles during the peaceful demonstrations in 2011. This campaign ended up with detention and murder of dozen of activists and the expansion of military involvement in repressing the protests.[34]

The Syrian army has neither defected, as in the case of Egypt, nor collapsed due to the mass defection of its personnel since the Uprising in 2011. The majority of the army remains loyal to the president and is still fighting for his survival. That this majority includes many Sunni officers is indicated by the continued loyalty of senior Sunni officers in sensitive command positions, including Minister of Defence Fahd al Friej and intelligence barons Ali Mamluk and Mohammad Dib Zaitoun; Major General Ramadan Mahmoud Ramadan, commander of the Thirty-Fifth Special Forces Regiment, which is tasked with the protection of western Damascus, and Brigadier General Jihad Mohamed Sultan, the commander of the Sixty-Fifth Brigade that guards Latakia.[35]

While the military – as an institution – in the Egyptian case acted independently from the president of the state to protect its collective economic interests and control the political transition,[36] the Syrian army demonstrated an inability and unwillingness to act independently or to direct a political change.

The *unwillingness* of the military to distance itself from the president despite the brutal escalation against civilians and increasing opposition to this in military ranks lies in the fact that the president and influential military officers have a lot of common economic interests. The army's officer corps would lose a lot of economic privileges if the clientelist and corrupted state system falls. The private businesses of military generals and officers that have grown over the years due to the regime's support would suffer under any change that might allow greater or different political participation and power sharing arrangements. Similar to the Egyptian officers, the Syrian ones have acted mainly according to their economic interest, rather than according to ideological or religious reasons. The difference is that the Egyptian officers have not a lot of economic privileges beyond the military's corporate business and were in competition with a young civilian economic elite that was well connected to the political party of Mubarak and his son (see Abul-Magd: 2012, pp. 5–8). The officers in Syria – on the contrary – are a part of the economic elite and are associated with the policy makers. Hence, the Syrian regime and key military officers are interdependent vis-à-vis each other. Therefore, the decline of the importance of the military institution in the Syrian economy as a result of the neoliberal economic reform up to 2011 and the greater role of the crony capitalists did not drive the military to change sides after 2011. This argument can also explain the loyalty of a wide range of the business community to Asad in spite of existing economic sanctions against Asad's regime imposed by United States, the European Union and the Arab League in 2012. The business community not only remained loyal but also supported Asad's troops financially and logistically (Yazigi: 2014, p. 3).

Not only officers who run large businesses are loyal to Asad, but also middle-ranking officers, who benefit from military housing, a welfare system and from the state corruption network. Khaddour (2015) argues that the military's housing system is an important reason for the coherence of the army's officer corps and its loyalty to the regime. This system created in the suburbs of big cities so-called "officer ghettos" that are usually detached from the society and the culture of the city centres (Khaddour: 2015, pp. 3–5). Resident officers in these housing projects are mainly of rural and low socioeconomic background and cannot afford property elsewhere. High-ranking officers used to live in the centres or in villas in luxury neighbourhoods. The officer ghettos' inhabitants, who are of different religious background, share social values, life style, political ideology as well as loyalty to Asad. They also identify themselves with the military as an institution and are ready to fight for its survival. The housing projects were initially for military personnel only. However, the share of civilian inhabitants increased in line with the growing demand for houses and the increasing prices of real estate in the urban centres (Khaddour: 2015, pp. 3–6). The civilian population of these areas might not be completely integrated in the "society" there. Still, to buy a home from an officer, one needs to be very rich or well connected. In both cases one needs to go through the patronage system of the regime. Dahiet Al-Asad in Damascus' suburbs, an example for this ghetto-like residential area, has been considered an important stronghold of the regime.

Economic interests were not only a factor for loyalty, but also for desertion and defection. Officers who enjoyed some, but not exceptional, economic privileges defected more easily due to ideological factors than officers with high privileges. At the same time, enrichment chances on the opposition side were a pull factor. Businesses in line with the war economy and receiving foreign support (high salaries and modern equipment from the opposition's allies) attracted many officers to change sides (Albrecht, Koehler and Ohl: 2015, p. 8). Defecting or being loyal is a matter of material cost-benefit calculation.

The *inability* of the military to act independently from the president lies in the power consolidation strategy of the regime within the armed forces followed since the 1970s. Hafiz Asad followed a strategy to prevent any military coup based on three elements: a) creating parallel loyal, well-equipped and trained military units (paramilitaries), which are able to defend the regime and replace the regular military units in case of an Uprising (The Carter Center: 2013, p. 7); b) bolstering a strong security apparatus (*Mukhabarat*), which controls the military personnel, mainly officers, to prevent any coup; c) involving officers in the state corruption network by tolerating their personal economic gains in order to increase their loyalty or to extort opponents;[37] and lastly d) instrumentalizing sectarianism manifested in the strategy of giving key positions to relatives and reliable persons of the sect of Asad. Consequently, Alawites have been overrepresented in the officer corps, especially armoured units, the key security and intelligence armed units and paramilitaries (Holiday: 2013, p. 7, Albrecht, Koehler and Ohl: 2015, p. 5).

The sectarianism of Asad's regime does not only mean favouring Alawites or other minorities at the expense of the majority (Sunnis). It aims also at establishing loyal allies within each religious or ethnic (Kurds) community, which are not homogeneous, neither politically nor economically.[38] Hence, there were in the society and in the military pro-regime Sunnis and anti-regime Alawites based on their economic interests and sometimes on ideological belief. While sectarian dominated paramilitaries and security forces have been essential for the survival of Bashar since 2011, the sectarian strategy also succeeded in ensuring the loyalty of the officer corps and in preventing large-scale defections of Alawite low-ranking officers and soldiers. Moreover, it has been progressively instrumentalized to recruit fighters for pro-regime militias.[39] Khaddour (2015) argues that the religious factor became more important relative to the socioeconomic factor or military affiliations since the Uprising in 2011. Albrecht, Koehler and Ohl (2015) note that the regime fostered its desertion-proofing strategy by reinforcing control mechanisms; by stimulating sectarian narratives; and by pay raises and tolerating officers' wider corruption and self-financing through illicit businesses.

The regime's ability to keep on paying salaries to the armed forces and maintaining business interests of military officers for more than five years of war was essential for preventing a military collapse and increasing loyalty and confidence. This would not have been possible without the considerable and steady financial, political and military support of the regime's allies, Iran and Russia, since 2011.

Finally, the army's inability to act collectively to enable a political transition in Syria, as did Egypt's army, is, in part, attributable to its lack of cohesion. The Syrian military is not a homogeneous institution but, rather, consists of different groups with different interests according to place in the hierarchy, family ties to the president and religious background. The army's officer corps does not share the privileges and interests with soldiers and low-ranking officers. Also, members of the elite units with Alawite background or strong family ties to the president have different degrees of loyalty and advantages than the personnel of "normal" or neglected units. Finally, the military patronage system that was based on benefiting army officers as individuals and not the army as an institution led to competition and mistrust among them and discouraged any alliances or collective representation.

The Syrian military after the Uprising

Despite the narratives about the loyal Syrian military's coherence and the lack of mass defection by whole units, and its efficacy in defending the regime over five years of military conflict, facts on the ground display a less optimistic picture. By April 2014, it was estimated that the Syrian military had lost more than 60 per cent of its personnel of 2011 (295,000) and has been forced to withdraw from wide territories in the north, east and northeast of the country (Lister: 2014, p. 11). While the fatalities exceeded 35,000 and the number of wounded personnel was more than 100,000, defections were estimated to reach 50,000 (Lister: 2014, p. 11). Other sources assessed the number of deserted personnel (including defectors who joined the opposition troops, but not the evaders of military service) as up to 100,000 in July 2014 (Albrecht, Koehler and Ohl: 2015, p. 2). Some researchers claim that defections have not massively weakened the military, as they occurred individually, rather than en masse, and mainly among conscripts, rank-and-file soldiers and low-ranking officers (Khaddour: 2015, p. 1; Albrecht, Koehler and Ohl: 2015, p. 3). Still, defections were a turning point in the Syrian conflict, since they contributed to the militarization of the Uprising, internationalization of the conflict and to militarization of the state.

The regime at first relied on the security forces and the so-called "*Shabbiha*" to supress the peaceful protest movement and to persecute activists and political critics during the Uprising. *Shabbiha* has become a term to describe regime loyalists, who were self-organized to intimidate protesters, critical journalists and human right activists in their neighbourhood either by arms, brawls or threats. They were mainly civilians of different religious backgrounds. Shortly afterwards, they were reorganized in coordination with the security apparatus under the name Popular Committees (*Lijan Al-Sha'bia*). Since then, they have taken up arms and started controlling checkpoints (Lund: 2013, p. 2; The Carter Center: 2013, p. 7). In reward for their services, they were allowed to generate economic gains from looting, kidnapping, extorting, and briberies in their territory, an early sign of warlordism and the decentralization of the regime's military power (see Lund: 2015).

As a result of the financial, military and logistical support of its allies (Saudi Arabia, Qatar, USA and Turkey), the armed opposition has succeeded in controlling territories in different parts of the country since 2012. Fighting on many fronts simultaneously and growing defections and desertions challenged the Syrian military, despite the financial and military support by the regime's allies, Iran and Russian. In order to overcome the lack of manpower of the regular military, the regime founded the National Defence Forces (NDF) in 2012 to replace the popular committees and other pro-regime groups as well as to attract civilian volunteers of both sexes. With around 100,000 personnel, they represent the largest pro-regime militia. Some are heavily armed with tanks and rocket launchers and organized under regional commanders (Lund: 2015, p. 2). It was reported that the NDF received training from Hezbollah and Iran's al-Quds forces (Lister: 2014, p. 4). Other NDF-units seem to behave like criminal sectarian gangs and are poorly equipped (Lund: 2015, p. 2). In addition to the NDF, there are a series of smaller pro-regime militias of some thousands of fighters that command local operations. Some of them bear politically symbolic names such as the Ba'th Battalions, the Syrian Resistance, or are pre-existing organizations that support the regime, such as The Popular Front for the Liberation of Palestine-General Command and the Syrian Social Nationalist Party. Others are religious militias that include Shia foreign forces such as Abul-Fadl al Abbas Brigade (see Lund 2013, 2015). Alongside the Syrian army, NDF and pro-regime militias, Hezbollah, Iran's strong ally in Lebanon, supported the regime in its recapture of strategic areas such as al-Qusayr nearby Homs in 2013. Since then, Hezbollah forces even commanded Syrian army forces in certain battles (Lister: 2014, p. 12). These groups have helped the regime to survive, but not the Syrian army. The fragmentation of the pro-regime forces and growing dependency on Iran and its local proxies create rivalry among them for power and economic gains in line with the war economy. For the time being, the Syrian military with a centralized command belongs to the past.

At the end of September 2015, the regime announced the formation of "The 4th Corps" in parallel to the direct Russian military intervention. This corps was established under Russian supervision and support to serve as effective ground troops against the military opposition groups in central and northern Syria. Its aim lies in replacing the NDF and integrating all pro-regime armed forces under one centralized command (OE Watch: 2015, pp. 13–15). The establishment of the new military body reflects not only the rivalry between the main regimes' allies – Russia, that prefers one disciplined centralized military under Asad, and Iran, the sponsor of the NDF – but also the incapability of the existing ones. While corruption has been widespread in the Syrian military, the NDF were increasingly taking part in illicit activities (looting, kidnapping and smuggling), and were allegedly involved in sectarian massacres, and in fighting each other (Al-Quwatlī: 2015, pp. 1–2). Russia's concern was, first, that because of this Asad could lose further control over territory and, second, that locally influential leaders could change the partnership conditions with Russia.

Currently it is too early to know whether the Russian efforts to recentralize the pro-regime armed forces under Asad will be more successful than the earlier attempt with the NDF. Also, it is quite challenging to convince warlords to give up their small "empires" and enrichment sources in an ongoing war.

Conclusion

The main aim of this chapter was to examine whether the economic interests of the Syrian military have underlined its loyalty to Asad's regime since 2011. In fact, the Syrian military shared a lot of economic interests with Asad's regime prior to the Uprising. However, the Syrian military cannot be understood as an independent institution that has collective economic interests like the Egyptian one. The interlocking of interests between military officers, political regime and business community represented an important factor fostering the loyalty of the military elites, whose economic existence and prosperity depends on the patronage system of the regime. The economic interests of the middle and low-ranking officers lie in the military welfare-benefits and housing system, petty corruption as well as small businesses. The military as an economic institution – represented by the military-owned enterprises – does not share a lot of interests with the regime, as the neoliberal economic policy in the 2000s limited its activities. It is indicative that only military construction enterprises (HMI and MATA) have maintained a reasonable market share.

Economic interests are not the sole factor behind the loyal behaviour of the Syrian military. Historically, promoting the loyalty of the Syrian military played a major role in Hafiz Asad's power consolidation strategy since 1970. It was successful in weakening the military as a collective and independent institution by promoting individual power centres that were competing with each other. The fragmented power within the military made a defection en masse or an officers' alliance against Asad improbable. Asad's power consolidation was based on four elements: firstly, formation of reliable paramilitary groups; secondly, bolstering control networks (*mukhabarat*) over the military; thirdly, making officers vulnerable to blackmail by involving them in state corruption; and finally instrumentalizing sectarianism to ensure high loyalty and create mistrust among officers of different religious backgrounds.

Since 2011, the Syrian military has been facing fundamental challenges affecting its performance and influence: the loss of manpower due to defections, desertions, fatalities and wounded personnel; the emergence of powerful but fragmented pro-regime militias under local (warlords) or with foreign (Iran) loyalties; the increasing role of foreign pro-regime military actors such as Hezbollah, Iranian Revolutionary Guards and currently Russian forces at the expense of the Syrian army; and, finally, the ongoing proxy war on various fronts. It is, therefore, questionable whether the Russian efforts to recentralize the pro-regimes militias and defeat the armed opposition will help to overcome these challenges and to re-build the Syrian military as it had been before the Uprising.

Notes

1 This research is part of a regional research project entitled "Economic interests and actors in Arab countries and their role during and after the Arab Spring", hosted by the Bonn International Center for Conversion (BICC) and funded by Volkswagen Stiftung. The interviews used in this research were conducted between 2011 and 2015. All interviewees are anonymized. I would like to thank Maria Kastrinou and Samer Abboud for their valuable comments.
2 Author's interview with Youssef on 17 January 2013 in Beirut. Youssef is a Syrian journalist.
3 Author's interview with the journalist from Raqqa on 18 January 2013 in Beirut.
4 Author's interview with Youssef on 17 January 2013 in Beirut.
5 Author's interview with Youssef on 17 January 2013 in Beirut.
6 *Infitah* refers to the Arabic word for market opening policy or economic liberalization.
7 For more information about socialist policies and their impact on Syrian economy and society, see Perthes: 1995; Batatu: 1999; and Hinnebusch: 1994.
8 Author's interviews with Sultan (25 August 2012/Berlin) and Ahmad (30 August 2012/Berlin). Sultan is a Syrian economic consultant and former employee of MHI, and Ahmad is a Syrian journalist and former consultant in the Palace of the president Bashar al-Asad. See also Aljerdi: 2011 and Aljerdi: 2012 and Mualla: 2011.
9 Author's interview with Sultan on 25 August 2012 in Berlin.
10 Author's interviews with Sultan (25 August 2012/Berlin), Ahmad (30 August 2012/Berlin) and Youssef (17 January 2013/Beirut).
11 Author's interview with Youssef on 17 January 2013, Beirut.
12 Author's interview with Youssef on 17 January 2013, Beirut.
13 Author's interviews with Ahmad (30 August 2012/Berlin) and Sultan (25 August 2012/Berlin).
14 Author's interview with Sultan on 25 August 2012 in Berlin.
15 Author's interviews with Sultan (25 August 2012/Berlin) and Youssef (17 January 2013/Beirut).
16 Author's interview with Youssef on 17 January 2013 in Beirut.
17 Author's interview with Sultan on 25 August 2012 in Berlin.
18 Author's interview with Ahmad on 30 August 2012 in Berlin.
19 Author's interview with Ahmad on 30 August 2012 in Berlin.
20 Author's interviews with Sultan (25 August 2012/Berlin), Ahmad (30 August 2012/Berlin).
21 Author's interview with Ahmad on 30 August 2012 in Berlin.
22 Author's interview with Munzer on 14 February 2015 in Berlin. Munzer was a conscript in the Syrian army between 2008 and 2010.
23 Author's interview with Munzer on 14 February 2015 in Berlin.
24 Author's interviews with Sultan (25 August 2012/Berlin), Ahmad (30 August 2012/Berlin) and Youssef (17 January 2013/Beirut).
25 According to IMF, oil revenues dropped from 7.1 per cent of GDP in 2005 to 4.6 per cent in 2009.
26 Author's interview with Abdullah Dardari, the former prime minister and supporter of liberal economic reforms in Syria, on 16 January 2013 in Beirut.
27 According to the IMF, the Syrian government reduced the energy subsidies by 7 per cent of the GDP. As compensation it increased public wages and issued coupons for diesel at a lower price, which amounted to about 4.5 per cent of GDP, see IMF (2010).
28 Author's interview with Sultan on 25 August 2012 in Berlin.

29 Author's interviews with Sultan (25 August 2012/Berlin) and Youssef (17 January 2013/ Beirut).
30 See Mualla 2011.
31 The budget deficit was estimated at 5.5 per cent of GDP in 2009, see IMF 2010, p. 5.
32 Author's interviews with Ahmad (30 August 2012/Berlin) and Munzer (14 February 2015/Berlin).
33 Author's interview with Munzer on 14 February 2015 in Berlin.
34 In 2011, Ghiath Mattar, an activist and organizer of peaceful demonstrations in Darya/ Damascus, launched the "Flowers and Water" for military and security forces. His attempt to win the army over ended up, like dozens of other activists from his city, with his death under torture in the Air Force intelligence branch. See Ghiath Mattar Foundation (ghiathmatterfoundation.org).
35 Kamal Alam, "Why Asad's Army has not Defected," *The National Interest*, 12 February 2016, http://nationalinterest.org/feature/why-Asads-army-has-not-defected-15190?page=2.
36 The Egyptian military, which controls between 25–40 per cent of the domestic economy, did not move to the opposition purely to ensure a democratic transition or to protect civilians against the brutal repression of security forces. Its changing sides was rather an important step to protect its own economic interests that were increasingly threatened by the neoliberal economic reform by Mubarak, the rise of an influential young business elite supported by Gamal Mubarak as well as the growing "civilisation" in Egyptian politics (Abul-Magd: 2012, pp. 5–8, Makara: 2013, p. 346).
37 Author's interview with a defected former intelligence officer, who worked on a project for digitally archiving military officers' files. He stated that he went through corruption cases of famous and high-ranking officers that were registered in the files. The aims of documenting corruption cases and collecting evidence of officers' financial embezzlement were to put pressure on them by blackmailing them, in case of conflict or suspicion falling on them. Author's interview in Berlin on 25 January 2015.
38 See the chapter of Maria Kastrinou in the book.
39 For more information about the role of sectarianism in the military after the Uprising see Holiday (2013), Makara (2013), Lister (2014) and Albrecht, Kohler and Ohl (2015).

Bibliography

Abul-Magd, Z. (2012), "Understanding SCAF", *The Cairo Review on Global Affairs* 6, 2012. Available from <www.thecairoreview.com/essays/understanding-scaf/> [22 February 2016].

Albrecht, H., Koehler, K. and Ohl, D. (2015), "For Money or Liberty? The Political Economy of Military Desertion and Rebel Recruitment in the Syrian Civil War", Carnegie Endowment for International Peace, Regional Insight, 24 November 2015. Available from <http://carnegieendowment.org/2015/10/24/for-money-or-liberty-political-economy-of-military-desertion-and-rebel-recruitment-in-syrian-civil-war/ilqf> [21 January 2016].

Al-Haj Ali, M. H. (2012), "al-jaysh al-ʿarabī al-sūrī: min al-ḥaraka al-taṣḥīḥīya ḥatta al- ān". Available from: <www.baath-party.org/index.php?option=com_content&view=article&id=5839:2012-05-13-08-26-30&catid=67&Itemid=121&lang=ar> [15 March 2013].

Aljerdi, M. (2011), "Jaysh al-karāma wa al-"iʿmār…mu"assasat tanfīdh al-"insha"āt al-ʿaskarī ya", *Al-Thawra*, 2 August 2011. Available from: <http://thawra.sy/_archive.asp?FileName=30338110220110801214910> [2 October 2014].

Aljerdi, M. (2012), "60 ʿām min al-ʿaṭā…maʿāmil al-difāʿ, *Al-Thawra*, 1 August 2012. Available from: <http://thawra.alwehda.gov.sy/_print_veiw.asp?FileName=87090842220120731172539> [10 December 2012].

Al-Quwatlī, M. (2015), "Mīlīshīa "ādifāʿ al-waṭanī" muhadda bifeʿel al-juhūd al-rūssīya liḥallahā wa al-istiʿāda be "al-fylaq al-rābeʿ"", *Alsouria*, 1 December 2015. Available from <www.

<ميليشيا-الدفاع-الوطني-مهددة-بفعل-الجهود-الروسية-لحلها-والاستعاضة-الفيلق-الرابع/alsouria.net/content> [10 January 2016].
Bahout, Joseph (1994), "The Syrian Business Community, its Politics and Prospects". In *Contemporary Syria: Liberalization between Cold War and Cold Peace*, edited by Eberhard Kienle, 72–80. London: British Academic Press.
Batatu, H. (1981), "Some Observations on the Social Roots of Syria's Ruling, Military Group and the Causes for its Dominance", *Middle East Journal* 35: 3, 331–344.
Batatu, H. (1999), *Syria's Peasantry: The Descendants of its Lesser Rural Notables, and their Politics*. Princeton: Princeton University Press.
Gambill, Gary (2001), "The Political Obstacles to Economic Reform in Syria", *Middle East Intelligence Bulletin* 3: 7. Available from: <www.meforum.org/meib/articles/0107_s1.htm> [19 November 2012].
Gambill, Gary (2004), "The Myth of Syria's Old Guard", *Middle East Intelligence Bulletin* 6: 2–3. Available from: <www.meforum.org/meib/articles/0402_s1.htm> [18 December 2012].
George, Alan (2003), *Syria: Neither Bread nor Freedom*. London: Zed Books.
Haddad, Bassam (2012), *Business Networks in Syria: The Political Economy of Authoritarian Resilience*. Stanford: Stanford University Press.
Hasan, C. (2011), "Jaysh al-karāma wa al-"i'mār…al-idāra al-intajīya li-l-mashārī' al-'askarī ya", *Al-Thawra*, 2 August 2011. Available from: <http://thawra.sy/_print_veiw.asp?FileName=30338110220110801214705> [2 October 2014].
Hinnebusch, Raymond (1994), "Liberalization in Syria: The Struggle of Economic and Political Rationality". In *Contemporary Syria: Liberalization between Cold War and Cold Peace*, edited by Eberhard Kienle, 97–113. London: British Academic Press.
Holiday, J. (2013), *The Syrian Army: Doctrinal Order of Battle*. Institute for the Study of War, February. Available from <www.understandingwar.org/sites/default/files/SyrianArmy-DocOOB.pdf> [21 November 2013].
Human Rights Watch (1991), *Syria Unmasked: The Suppression of Human Rights by the Asad Regime*. New Haven: Yale University Press.
International Monetary Fund (IMF) (2010), Syrian Arab Republic: 2009 Article IV Consultation – Staff Report; and Public Information Notice. Country Report No. 10/86, March.
Khaddour, K. (2015), "Asad's Officer Ghetto: Why the Syrian Army Remains Loyal", Carnegie Endowment for International Peace, Regional Insight, 4 November. Available from <http://carnegie-mec.org/2015/11/04/Asad-s-officer-ghetto-why-syrian-army-remains-loyal/iigr> [2 January 2016].
Lister, Charles (2014), "Dynamic Stalemate: Surveying Syria's military Landscape", Brookings Doha Centre, Policy Briefing, May 2014. Available from <www.brookings.edu/~/media/research/files/papers/2014/05/19-syria-military-landscape-lister/syria-military-landscape-english.pdf> [20 January 2016].
Lund, Aron (2013), "Gangs of Latakia: The Militiafication of the Asad Regime", *Syria Comment*, 23 July. Available from <www.joshualandis.com/blog/the-militiafication-of-the-Asad-regime/> [3 February 2016].
Lund, Aron (2015), "Who Are the Pro-Asad Militias?", *Syria in Crisis* – Carnegie Endowment for International Peace, 2 March. Available from <http://carnegieendowment.org/syriaincrisis/?fa=59215> [18 February 2016].
Makara, M. (2013), "Coup-Proofing, Military Defection, and the Arab Spring", *Democracy and Security* 9: 4, 334–359.
Mora, F. & Wiktorowicz, Q. (2003), "Economic Reform and the Military: China, Cuba and Syria in Comparative Perspective". Proceedings of the 2003 meeting of the Latin

American Studies Association (LASA); Dallas, TX, 27–29 March 2003. Available from: <http://lasa.international.pitt.edu/Lasa2003/MoraFrank.pdf> [26 June 2015].

Mualla, B. (2011), "Jaysh al-karāma wa al-'i'mār...al-iskān al-'askarī", *Al-Thawra*, 2 August 2011. Available from: <http://thawra.sy/_print_veiw.asp?FileName=30338110220 110801214826> [2 October 2014].

OE Watch (2015), Russia in Syria: Perspectives on the Russian Intervention in Syria, Vol. 5, November 2015. *Available from*: <http://fmso.leavenworth.army.mil/OEWatch/201511/201511.pdf> [21 February 2016].

Perthes, Volker (1994), "Stages of Economic and Political Liberalization", in *Contemporary Syria: Liberalization between Cold War and Cold Peace*, edited by Eberhard Kienle, 44–71, London: British Academic Press.

Perthes, Volker (1995), *The Political Economy of Syria under Asad*. London: I.B.Tauris.

Picard, Elizabeth (1990), "Arab Military in Politics: From Revolutionary Plot to Authoritarian State". In *The Arab State*, edited by Giacomo Luciani, 189–219. Berkeley and Los Angeles: University of California Press.

Pölling, Sylvia (1994), "Which future for Private Sector?" In *Contemporary Syria: Liberalization between Cold War and Cold Peace*, edited by Eberhard Kienle, 14–25. London: British Academic Press.

Said, Salem (2011), *Globalisierung und Regionalisierung im arabischen Raum*. Berlin: Klaus Schwarz Verlag.

Seale, Patrick (1990), *Asad: The Struggle for the Middle East*. Berkeley, California: University of California Press.

The Carter Center (2013), Syria Pro-Government Paramilitary Forces, 5 November. Available from <www.cartercenter.org/resources/pdfs/peace/conflict_resolution/syria-conflict/Pro-GovernmentParamilitaryForces.pdf> [30 January 2016].

Van Dam, N. (2011), *The Struggle for Power in Syria: Politics and Society under Asad and the Ba'th Party*, 4th edn. London: I.B.Tauris.

Yazigi, J. (2014), "Syria's War Economy", European Council on Foreign Relations, ECFR/97, April 2014. Available from <www.ecfr.eu/page/-/ECFR97_SYRIA_BRIEF_AW.pdf> [1 January 2016].

6
REVISITING THE POLITICAL ECONOMY OF THE SYRIAN UPRISING

Fred H. Lawson

Existing scholarship on the popular revolts that erupted across the Middle East and North Africa during the winter of 2010–11 pays scant attention to trends in the regional and global economy, and concentrates instead on the institutions of governance and policy-making processes that characterize authoritarian regimes. This perspective is evident in the initial wave of studies of the Syrian Uprising, which focuses almost exclusively on the political and legal demands voiced by the protesters and the tactics used by the authorities to deal with widespread challenges from below. Only a handful of analyses explore the connection between trends in Syria's domestic economy and the outbreak of large-scale popular revolt. For the most part, such explorations highlight the detrimental consequences of the regime's privatization policies, the burgeoning inequality of wealth, the steady decline in oil revenues and the plunge in labor force participation, especially among well-educated young people, that afflicted the country beginning in the mid-1990s (Marzouq 2011; Haddad 2011; Goulden 2011; Nasser, Mehchy and Abu Ismail 2013; Darwisheh 2013; Achcar 2013; Azmeh 2014).

What remains absent from analyses of the Syrian Uprising is the impact of the global financial crisis that occurred in 2008–09 (Habibi 2009; Brach and Loewe 2010; Mashal 2012). This worldwide economic disruption affected different Middle Eastern countries in divergent ways, depending not only on the peculiar form and level of each country's integration into the international market, but also on the social structure of accumulation (SSA) that governs each country's domestic political-economic order (McDonough, Reich and Kotz 2010). It is by tracing the specific ways in which the global crisis exacerbated tensions inherent in Syria's early twenty-first-century SSA that one can best explain why the Uprising broke out when it did, and why the early protests by civil rights activists and impoverished laborers in marginal districts elicited no backing from well-to-do businesspeople and public sector workers (Bassyouni 2011). The absence of support from these two actors prompted opposition forces to resort to violent measures in a desperate bid to overthrow the Ba'th Party-led regime.

Global crises and local outcomes

Studies of the domestic political consequences of global economic crises usually advance broad generalizations that contribute little to our understanding of the peculiar events that occur in any one country at a particular moment in time (Gourevitch 2009; Helleiner 2011). One important exception to the rule is Paul Chaisty and Stephen Whitefield's (2012) meticulous explication of changes in political attitudes that took place in Russia in the aftermath of the 2008–09 financial crisis.

Chaisty and Whitefield find that the global downturn had little immediate impact on Russian politics. Public approval ratings for the country's successive presidents remained comparatively high, as did indicators of popular confidence in the government (Chaisty and Whitefield 2012, 187). By December 2011, however, the level of electoral support for the dominant political party dropped off precipitately. Furthermore, the decline in backing for the ruling party accompanied a notable upsurge in the number and frequency of public protests. Disgruntlement arising from the crisis "made the middle classes less willing to put up with negative factors like corruption and the overconcentration of political power, which were associated with [President Vladimir] Putin's rule" (Habibi 2009; Brach and Loewe 2010; Mashal 2012). Chaisty and Whitefield (2012, 192) go on to show that actors whose livelihoods or other material interests were damaged as a result of the crisis were more likely to move into active opposition against the leadership in Moscow. On the other hand, actors who managed to avoid the ill effects of the downturn remained loyal both to the president and to the dominant political party. These findings hold for private sector workers and government employees alike. Moreover, both workers and members of the salaried middle class who suffered as a result of the crisis became more apt to vote for alternative presidential candidates.

All of these connections between global crises and domestic discontent take place with a substantial time lag. In the Russian case, the delay amounted to more than two years – from mid-2009 to the end of 2011. Chaisty and Whitefield point out that this interval resembles the lag that has been discovered in other empirical studies, in particular the analysis by Minxin Pei and Ariel Adesnik (2000), of the association between external downturns and regime change in two dozen Asian and Latin American countries from 1945 to 1998. Pei and Adesnik (2000, 141) conclude that global crises are most likely to be correlated with the collapse of a country's leadership "with a time lag of about 18 to 30 months." Consolidated liberal democracies cluster at the near end of this spectrum; authoritarian regimes hover around the far end (Pei and Adesnik 2000, 142).

Pei and Adesnik (2000, 142) propose that the effects of international financial troubles can be offset – and in effect postponed – by a wide range of internal "political" factors that obscure or overshadow the impact of external trends and thus focus public attention on other matters besides the damage caused by an external crisis – at least for a while.

More cogently, one might argue that the effects of global crises take time to alter the attitudes and actions of domestic actors, due to the fact that such disruptive episodes set a baseline for subsequent expectations. Whether later trends confirm or contradict these expectations will determine the kind of response that local actors choose, and the process plays out over the course of many months. During that interval, state officials, military officers, businesspeople and workers constantly compare their current situation to the baseline laid down during the crisis. To the extent that circumstances seem to be improving with respect to that fixed reference point, actors are likely to consider themselves to be operating in "the domain of gains;" to the extent that things keep deteriorating, they will find themselves in "the domain of losses." Actors in the domain of gains tend to be comparatively risk-averse, whereas ones situated in the domain of losses exhibit a pronounced tendency to engage in risk-acceptant forms of behavior (Kahneman and Tversky 2000).

Effects of the 2008–09 global financial crisis

Economists for the most part agree that three aspects of the 2008–09 global financial crisis had the greatest impact on the countries of the Middle East and North Africa (MENA). First, and arguably most important, was the abrupt contraction of international capital that soon became apparent in the diminished flow of foreign direct investment (FDI) to the region, both directly from the rich industrial world and indirectly through the oil-producing states of the Gulf (Danmark and Helali 2013, 18; Brach and Loewe 2010, 48 and 53; Pfeifer 2012). Second was the collapse of external markets for locally produced manufactured goods, which in turn boosted unemployment levels in the industrial sectors of economies throughout the region (Habibi 2009, 5 and 7; Behrendt, Haq and Kamel 2009, 4–7). Third was the lack of access to credit, along with the much more stringent requirements that were imposed by lenders in the aftermath of the crisis (Brach and Loewe 2009, 4). Moreover, these three effects of the global downturn coincided with a sharp increase in the level and volatility of world food prices, especially for such staples as wheat (Clapp 2009). Price instability turned into dramatic price rises for cereals all across the MENA by the winter of 2010–11 (Zurayk and Gough 2014).

For the region as a whole, the Great Recession produced a variety of negative consequences. FDI inflows peaked at approximately USD 95 billion in 2008, then plunged 25 percent the following year and a further 12 percent the year after that (Chauvin 2013, 5). Investments undertaken by the oil-producing Arab Gulf states in the other MENA countries trailed off more gradually after 2008, although a handful of Gulf-based private equity firms resumed operations in Egypt, Tunisia, Morocco and Algeria during the course of 2009–10 (Pfeifer 2012, 20–22). Access to credit, in the words of an International Monetary Fund (IMF) study, "decelerated sharply" as a result of the global downturn (Barajas, Chami, Espinoza and Hesse

2011, 153), and a number of major investment banks, including Credit Suisse and Deutsche Bank, quickly scaled back their regional operations (Reuters, September 18, 2011).

MENA countries that exported manufactured goods and agricultural products to Europe experienced a steep decline in the value of such exports from 2008 to 2009 (Habibi 2009, 5). As a result, the International Labor Organization estimates that the rate of unemployment in the Middle East jumped 25 percent between 2007 and 2009, and rose 13 percent in North Africa during that same period (Habibi 2009, 7). Furthermore, world food prices, which had doubled from 2004 to 2008, plunged from 2008 to 2009, but then rebounded by almost 50 percent from 2010 to 2011 (Lagi, Bertrand and Bar-Yam 2011; USAID 2011).

Syria weathers the crisis

Aggregate statistics that chart the impact of the 2008–09 crisis on the Middle East and North Africa as a whole mask crucial differences across the discrete economies that make up this part of the world. More important, they skew the overall picture in the direction of the oil-producing states of the Gulf, since it is this small subset of countries that was most tightly connected to the international financial, commercial and labor markets at the time that the downturn occurred. It is therefore imperative to lay out, as best one can, the specific ways in which the Great Recession affected the Syrian economy (Marshall 2008; Marshall 2009).

Estimates of foreign direct investment in Syria vary widely from one source to another. Data compiled by the United Nations Conference on Trade and Development (UNCTAD) show a steady increase of FDI coming into the local economy during the first decade of the twenty-first century, with a 38.9 percent jump in total inward FDI from 2006 to 2007, a 33.1 percent rise from 2007 to 2008 and a 43.6 percent increase from 2008 to 2009 (unctadstat.unctad.org). Figures drawn up by the International Monetary Fund (IMF), on the other hand, exhibit more pronounced year-to-year fluctuations, with an increase of 88.5 percent in net inflows of FDI from 2006 to 2007, an 18 percent rise from 2007 to 2008 and a 73.3 percent increase from 2008 to 2009 (indexmundi.com). The two databases concur that investment capital entered the country at a remarkably high rate in the years just prior to the 2008–09 crisis (albeit from a comparatively low starting point), and that outside funds continued to arrive in the immediate aftermath of the global downturn.

By 2010, however, foreign investment in Syria started to stagnate. UNCTAD reports that total inward FDI rose from USD 8.47 billion in 2009 to 9.94 billion in 2010 (a 17.3 percent increase), and then to 10.74 billion in 2011 (an 8.1 percent increase). The IMF, by contrast, estimates that net inflows of FDI actually declined from a peak of USD 2.57 billion in 2009 to just under 1.47 billion in 2010. Either way, the available data indicate that it was some two years after the Great Recession that the contraction of global capital started to afflict the Syrian economy.

Trade data paint a somewhat different picture. According to UNCTAD, Syria's total merchandise exports increased 5.7 percent from 2006 to 2007, and rose another 33.5 percent from 2007 to 2008, but plunged by some 30 percent from 2008 to 2009. From 2009 to 2010 exports recovered by 18 percent, but then fell 22 percent from 2010 to 2011 (unctadstat.unctad.org). It therefore appears that foreign markets for Syrian goods shut down much faster in the wake of the 2008–09 crisis than did inflows of investment capital.

Different types of Syrian exports nevertheless display markedly divergent patterns. External sales of manufactured goods, which had shown a marked rise beginning in 2001, reached their peak in 2007. Manufactures exports then trailed off steadily from 2007 to 2010 (indexmundi.com). Food exports, by contrast, increased continuously from 2001 to 2009, only to collapse abruptly in 2010. The impact of the drop in exports in both sectors was offset to some degree by a short-term increase in the production and overseas sales of Syrian hydrocarbons (IMF 2010, 4).

To what extent the 2008–09 crisis affected access to credit is harder to ascertain. Figures collected by the IMF indicate that total external credit available to Syria decreased from USD 594 million in 2007 to 540 million in 2008, and was projected to plunge to 290 million in 2009 (IMF 2010, 20). At the same time, however, the country's outstanding foreign debt fell from a high of USD 73 million in 2004 to only 14.5 million in 2007, and then dropped to 10.5 million in 2008 (IMF 2010, 24). In the domestic arena, the IMF reports that aggregate credit increased from 635 billion Syrian pounds in 2006 to 740 billion in 2007, and then to 917 billion in 2008. Domestic credit was expected to grow to 1.14 trillion pounds in 2009, and then to 1.44 trillion in 2010 (IMF 2010, 19). The same IMF report estimates that the amount of credit that was extended to private sector companies increased 3.8 percent from 2006 to 2007 and 5.7 percent from 2007 to 2008; such credit was projected to rise another 5.9 percent from 2008 to 2009 (IMF 2010, 40). The steady expansion of credit to private enterprises was attributed by IMF officials to the reopening of private banks inside Syria beginning in 2004 (IMF 2010, 6; but see also Matar 2012).

Just how the global crisis affected Syrian food prices is equally hard to gauge. On one hand, overall food prices in the local market surged some 35 percent from 2006 to 2010 (USAID 2011). Steadily rising imports of expensive foreign wheat accompanied a marked rise in the cost of domestically grown cereals during these years. Furthermore, structural features of the Syrian economy led increases in world food prices to get passed along to domestic consumers comparatively rapidly (Ianchovichina, Loening and Wood 2012). On the other hand, the rate of inflation with regard to food spiked in the spring of 2008, then fell off sharply between that time and the end of 2009 (Ianchovichina, Loening and Wood 2012). Food prices rebounded during the course of 2010, but did so at a more moderate pace – peaking during the winter of 2010–11 at about one-third of the rate that had obtained in the spring and summer of 2008. More important, Syria continued to be largely self-sufficient in wheat and sugar in the years surrounding the 2008–09 crisis, and it exported these two staples to neighboring countries in substantial quantities until the late spring of 2011, when the Uprising started to disrupt routine commercial relations with Iraq, Turkey, Lebanon and Jordan (IRIN 2012).

External crises and internal challenges in Syria

How the trends that accompany a global crisis affect a given state's political-economic order depends on the *social structure of accumulation* that governs the domestic economy. Each country's SSA consists of the class conflicts and alliances that shift kaleidoscopically in accordance with the changing dynamics of capital accumulation, plus the institutional arrangements – particularly those related to the state apparatus – that organize markets and regulate investment. For the most part, the SSA operates so as to facilitate the orderly expansion of the local economy, but in times of crisis it can instead compound the difficulties that are inherent in the accumulation of capital, since "the integrated character of the SSA accelerates the decline [of profits and expectations] as failing institutions destabilize each other" (McDonough, Reich and Kotz 2010, 3). Underlying configurations of class antagonism and alignment, together with established modes of state intervention in the domestic economy, play a crucial mediating role between global trends and internal outcomes.

Syria's social structure of accumulation

Syria's SSA at the time of the 2008–09 crisis entailed a high level of state involvement in economic affairs. Extensive government ownership and regulation of industry, trade and agriculture remained enduring legacies of the socialist era of the late 1960s, and reflected as well the dominant role of the central administration in collecting and distributing revenues derived from the production and sale of hydrocarbons (Hinnebusch 2001; Lawson 2013). Liberalization policies adopted during the 1990s ended up transferring a number of public sector enterprises into the hands of businesspeople who enjoyed close ties to senior figures in the regime. Investment capital was almost entirely controlled by the state-run Commercial Bank of Syria (CBS), whose managers disproportionately targeted credit toward companies owned by members of this well-connected, rent-seeking class. Bassam Haddad (2012b) calls this social force the "state bourgeoisie," while Samer Abboud (2013) designates it the "'integrated' elite."

At the turn of the twenty-first century, the state bourgeoisie was joined by an assortment of private entrepreneurs, whose companies took root and flourished in the interstices between the monopolistic conglomerates of the state bourgeoisie and the obsolescent enterprises that made up Syria's public sector. These private companies, whose owners Abboud (2013) calls the "'dependent' business elite," created a substantial number of jobs for previously unemployed and underemployed workers, and by 2010 accounted for more than half of all non-oil economic output (Strategic Research and Communication Centre 2011). The emergence of this dynamic entrepreneurial class prompted government officials to enact a series of laws to facilitate the establishment of private financial institutions that might complement the operations of the CBS. Law No. 28, promulgated in April 2001, for instance, laid down the procedures whereby private banks and joint ventures between private and public banks could be set up. Nevertheless, private banking remained a minor component of local finance. Data for 2006 show that the private sector accounted for no more than 18 percent of total bank deposits, and that private institutions extended no more than 7.5 percent of all outstanding credits, which were heavily concentrated in light manufacturing (Seifan 2010, 15).

Meanwhile, state officials encouraged the formation of public–private partnerships, in which the country's struggling state-owned enterprises contracted with private companies to undertake renovation and expansion in exchange for a share of the resulting profits. The Council of Ministers in 2009 prepared a draft statute that spelled out the broad principles and legal framework that would regulate such arrangements. The new law was intended to apply to 10 percent of all future energy and infrastructure projects, along with major initiatives in housing, sanitation and water supply (Abboud and Lawson 2013). Public–private partnerships gained traction in various sectors of the domestic economy during 2008–09. At the same time, the Ministry of Industry stepped up its campaign to attract investment funds from the oil-producing countries of the Gulf: More than a dozen public industrial enterprises were opened up to investors from Saudi Arabia during the spring of 2010, and a law was promulgated in February 2011 that permitted public sector enterprises to reconfigure themselves into joint-stock companies as a way to attract new capital (*Syria Report*, February 21, 2011).

Well-to-do property owners who were not part of the state bourgeoisie therefore found themselves accorded avenues for capital accumulation and leverage in industrial and commercial affairs that had been tightly restricted if not completely blocked in previous decades. The central administration's concurrent scaling back of state-sponsored social welfare programs opened up additional room for the exercise of private authority (Pierret and Selvik 2010; Donati 2013; Ruiz de Elvira and Zintl 2014). Under these circumstances, a somewhat less advantaged class of "middle merchants," many of whose members had deep roots in the pre-1963 commercial and industrial elites of Aleppo and Damascus, assumed positions in the domestic political economy that gave them the capacity to act more or less autonomously of the state bourgeoisie and government agencies alike (Ismail 2009; Abboud 2011).

Organized labor, which had exercised considerable influence in policy-making circles during the 1960s and 1970s, played little if any active role in Syrian politics by the early 2000s. The great majority of the country's manufacturing and transportation workers continued to cluster in the component organizations of the Ba'th Party-affiliated trade union federation, the General Federation of Worker's Unions (GFWU). But what little of the GFWU's political clout survived the liberalization policies of the 1990s ended up getting siphoned off during the early months of Bashar al-Asad's presidency (Hinnebusch 2011, 124; Hinnebusch 2012, 99). Independent labor associations like the ones that emerged so prominently in Egypt during the first decade of the twenty-first century were non-existent in Syria.

Senior military and internal security commanders constituted the power-brokers of last resort, setting the broad parameters of political and economic life and occasionally stepping in to deal with regulatory problems that state officials could not manage by themselves. President Bashar al-Asad embarked on an ambitious campaign to scale back the influence of the officers' corps and consolidate policy-making authority in the office of the presidency, but found himself stymied in the attempt to displace the generals (Hinnebusch 2012, 98–99). More important, the new president's efforts to curtail the purview and prerogatives of the regular armed forces accompanied a deeper entrenchment of the internal security services, whose commanders had tightened their grip on the country during the struggle against Islamist militants that occurred in the 1980s (Haddad 2005).

From global crisis to popular Uprising

Members of Syria's industrial and commercial elite who were not part of the state bourgeoisie, and who had started to experience difficulties due to the bilateral free trade agreement with Turkey that had come into force in January 2007, found themselves in serious trouble when the global financial crisis took shape during the winter of 2008–09. Turkish manufactured goods were already flooding the domestic market, and less expensive products from the People's Republic of China had begun to penetrate the local marketplace as well. Faced with intense competition from these imports, 41 textile and clothing factories in Aleppo shut down during the last quarter of 2008, and as many more followed suit in the winter of 2009–10 (Marshall 2008; Lawson 2013, 50).

Meanwhile, private manufacturers outside the state bourgeoisie found it increasingly difficult to obtain investment and operating capital. State-run financial institutions took steps to prop up foundering public sector textile factories and other state-owned enterprises in the wake of the 2008–09 crisis, but turned a deaf ear to appeals for assistance that emanated from nouveaux riches entrepreneurs and smaller private companies. The proportion of total investment to gross domestic product, which had been projected to reach 25 percent by 2010, barely reached 10 percent (*Syria Today*, April 2010). Deputy Prime Minister of Economic Affairs 'Abdullah al-Dardari explicitly addressed the problem in February 2010, and promised to augment government support for small and medium-sized enterprises (SMEs) (*The Syria Report*, February 22, 2010). Despite this pledge, the eleventh five-year plan (2011–15), which was drawn up in the fall of 2010, earmarked additional state funding for ailing public sector enterprises, but allocated no new monies to assist private industry (Haddad 2011, 43; Oxford Business Group 2011).

Nevertheless, prospects for privately owned companies were not entirely bleak. The eleventh five-year plan opened up new sectors of the Syrian economy for public–private partnerships. Selected for special attention were the struggling state-run tire company, the network of state-owned cement factories and the rapidly collapsing web of government-run sugar beet refineries (Monajed 2011). More important, the Ministry of Industry announced that the public sector would no longer engage in the manufacture of pasta, cookies, fruit jellies, shoes, laundry detergent and paper towels. The state-owned enterprises that had previously produced these items were slated to be closed down, so that private companies could take over production (Monajed 2011). Consequently, by the last quarter of 2010, private manufacturers could look forward to opportunities for expansion in the domestic economic arena, even as export markets remained scarce in the wake of the global crisis.

Beleaguered private industrialists found additional cause for optimism in the revival of Syria's hydrocarbons production that took place immediately after the Great Recession. The jump in oil revenues contributed to an increase in real gross domestic product of approximately four percent from 2009 to 2010 (IMF 2010, 21; Haddad 2011, 47). State officials took advantage of the windfall to initiate long-delayed improvements in infrastructure, thereby laying the foundation for future industrial and commercial growth (Haddad 2011, 48; Oxford Business Group 2011). Furthermore, the government set up an Export Development and Promotion Agency and charged it to provide advice and financial assistance to any private companies that undertook to manufacture clothing, cotton yarn, canned vegetables and olive oil for sale outside the country (*The Syria Report*, July 5, 2010).

However, Syrian hydrocarbons production fell off during the fall of 2010, forcing state officials to reassess their overall economic strategy. In a bid to convince local consumers to moderate their use of subsidized fuel oil, the retail price of this commodity was raised 13 percent in late September (*The Syria Report*, September 26, 2010). Two months later, the Council of Ministers asked the People's Assembly to boost government income by increasing direct taxes and fees by 15 percent and increasing indirect taxes by 22 percent (*The Syria Report*, November 8, 2010). Meanwhile, salaries for state employees and public sector workers were kept at existing levels. Grumbling on the part of civil servants and armed forces personnel over these initiatives prompted President al-Asad to grant a one-time bonus to all government and public sector employees on the occasion of the festival of 'Id al-Adha (*The Syria Report*, November 15, 2010).

In sharp contrast to the dynamic private sector, employment in stagnant state-run enterprises plummeted. The number of workers in public sector manufacturing had stood at 105,000 in 2005, but dropped to 96,000 four years later. Even with the high priority that was accorded to state-owned industry in the eleventh five-year plan, it was estimated that public sector employment would continue to decrease, perhaps to a total of no more than 80,000 workers by 2015 (Monajed 2011). In an attempt to soften the blow from the expected contraction in the public sector labor force, Minister of Industry Fu'ad 'Isa al-Juni asked the People's Assembly to allocate 55 billion Syrian pounds to restructure state-owned industrial enterprises during the course of the 2010–15 plan.

President al-Asad in January 2011 issued an executive order that created a National Welfare Fund to help state employees and other low-income families cover their basic living expenses. He then promulgated a regulation that effectively doubled the monthly subsidy paid to civil servants to offset the rising cost of heating their homes (*The Syria Report*, January 17, 2011). Partly to enable it to pay for these initiatives, the government at the end of the month announced plans to raise fuel oil prices for manufacturing companies by more than 50 percent as of April 1 (*The Syria Report*, January 31, 2011). The president subsequently ordered a substantial reduction in the consumption tax on sugar and vegetable oil, and imposed a cut in the customs duties levied on imported tea and rice (*The Syria Report*, February 21, 2011).

This package of policies constituted a concerted effort by the authorities to ameliorate the lingering impact of the 2008–09 crisis on public sector workers, while at the same time brightening the prospects for future recovery among private manufacturers. The actual cost of the global downturn as a result shifted to the agricultural sector of the Syrian economy, which was already reeling from the cumulative effects of five successive years of drought (Nasser, Mehchy and Abu Ismail 2013, 20 and 26; De Chatel 2014). Unable to survive any longer in rural areas, tens of thousands of impoverished laborers flooded to the fringes of the country's major cities, where they clustered in shanty towns that were almost entirely devoid of public services. It was in such marginal districts that the popular Uprising broke out in the early spring of 2011 (International Crisis Group 2011, 18).

Yet the political opportunity structure that made it possible for widely held grievances to explode into large-scale collective action was anchored in escalating friction between the central administration and state bourgeoisie on one hand and the dependent business elite and middle merchants on the other. As competition for investment capital intensified in the months following the 2008–09 crisis, private manufacturers outside the state bourgeoisie scaled back their operations (Yazigi 2012). This trend exacerbated pervasive anxiety among unemployed and underemployed workers, recent migrants to the cities and well-educated young people just entering the labor market. So, when the price of food and other necessities ratcheted up during the winter of 2010–11, simmering discontent among social forces that were operating in the domain of losses flared into anti-regime protest in a desperate bid to turn things around.

Influential forces refrain from joining the opposition

By contrast, well-to-do businesspeople who were not part of the state bourgeoisie found themselves operating in the domain of gains. Sadik al-Azm (2014) reports that shortly before the Uprising broke out, industrial and commercial elites in Damascus "were optimistic about the future of the country and its economy. They were investing generously, negotiating all sorts of arrangements with incoming German investors, and closing highly profitable deals with outgoing Dutch business delegations." So, when civil rights activists, impoverished laborers and disgruntled students took to the streets in February and March 2011, private manufacturers and successful entrepreneurs exhibited little if any interest in joining the protests, and signaled instead that they would be willing to tolerate a perpetuation of the existing order.

There was, as one might expect in any heterogeneous collection of autonomous actors, a handful of members of Syria's industrial and commercial elite that expressed sympathy for the protesters. Samer Abboud (2013, 3) notes, for instance, that a trio of influential businesspeople "who had lost out on key contracts to the Makhlouf family [a central component of the state bourgeoisie]" sponsored a gathering of opposition figures in the Turkish city of Antalya at the outset of the revolt. Yet for the most part prominent businesspeople did their best to stay out of the conflict. As Abboud (2013, 4) points out, "Syria's dependent elite may not have political affinities with the regime but cannot take the chance that their political bets lead to exile or isolation down the road." Rather than exercising what Albert Hirschman (1970) calls voice during the inaugural phase of the Uprising, those who could manage to do so left the country. "At best," Abboud (2013, 5) observes, "they have maintained regular communication with both the regime and opposition intermediaries. In many cases, they have provided covert financial support to the political activities of both sides." That is to say, they "hedged their bets in anticipation of a political outcome that would facilitate their continued access to political power in post-revolution Syria."

Abboud explains the ambivalent posture that was adopted by influential private interests outside the state bourgeoisie in two ways. First, potentially pivotal businesspeople lacked sufficient incentive to break completely with the Ba'thi regime. Their unwillingness to join the challengers was compounded by their profound misgivings about the political-economic programs that were articulated by key components of the opposition, as well as a lack of conviction that anti-regime forces would actually be able to overturn the existing order (Abboud 2013, 5). Second, members of the dependent business elite had an overriding interest in keeping a foot in both camps, in light of the fixed capital – "land, factories, buildings and other assets" – that they had implanted in the country. These considerations pushed propertied interests to adhere to a neutral course of action, or at least to present "a public display of neutrality" (Abboud 2013, 5).

It is therefore misleading to assert that Syria's industrial and commercial elite rallied to the defense of the Ba'thi regime when the protests picked up speed as the spring of 2011 went by. The state bourgeoisie, whose members were virtually inseparable from the top ranks of the central administration, armed forces and security apparatus, certainly had no interest in abandoning the president. In Bassam Haddad's (2012a) words, "the moguls [sic] know very well that their fate is bound up with that of the regime by virtue of intertwined investments and also their years of self-enrichment at regime behest." Members of the dependent business elite and middle merchants who remained in the country, on the other hand, made little if any effort to prop up the existing order as the protests gathered momentum. The fact that they also took no steps to defect from the dominant social coalition reflects not so much their inherent loyalty to President al-Asad and the Ba'thi system of rule as it does the underlying tendency to avoid risky behavior that comes into play whenever political actors find themselves in the domain of gains.

Conclusion

In retrospect, it seems clear that the popular Uprising in Syria emerged from a conjunction of economic trends that took shape beginning in the mid-1990s. Youth unemployment grew as a result of the government's declining expenditure on the public sector; declining oil revenues prevented the central administration from maintaining adequate levels of subsidies on staples for the working poor; wealth gravitated inexorably into the hands of a "crony capitalist" stratum at the pinnacle of local society (Azmeh 2014, 13); and impoverished laborers from the countryside swelled the population of peripheral neighborhoods in and around the larger cities, particularly in the north-central provinces.

Yet none of these trends offers a satisfactory explanation for the outbreak and subsequent trajectory of the 2011 revolt. Syria's gross domestic product exhibited "relatively high growth rates" during the opening decade of the twenty-first century (Nasser, Mehchy and Abu Ismail 2013, 18); local production steadily shifted toward manufacturing and away from an inordinate reliance on hydrocarbons (Nasser, Mehchy and Abu Ismail 2013, 21); inflation, public indebtedness and the balance of trade all remained comparatively stable (Nasser, Mehchy and Abu Ismail 2013, 22); even unemployment stood at a level that was "below the average in the Arab region" in the years leading up to the revolt (Nasser, Mehchy and Abu Ismail 2013, 22).

What explains the outbreak of large-scale upheaval in the spring of 2011 is the peculiar way that the 2008–09 global financial crisis intersected with the dynamics of Syria's social structure of accumulation. The impact of the external crisis put some social forces squarely in the domain of losses, but left others operating in the domain of gains. The latter included a pivotal assortment of well-to-do private manufacturers and traders who were not connected to the ruling elite by blood, marriage or long-time comradeship. Friction between these relatively autonomous businesspeople and the state bourgeoisie created the opportunity for revolt to occur, but the generally bright prospects that the dependent business elite and middle merchants enjoyed in the aftermath the Great Recession convinced them not to take the risky step of joining the opposition. The upshot was a tactical stalemate, which provided the context in which the popular protests of February and March 2011 eventually devolved into a sectarianized civil war.

References

Abboud, Samer N. (2011), "Economic Transformation and Diffusion of Authoritarian Power in Syria." In *Unmaking Power: Negotiating the Democratic Void in the Arab Middle East*. Edited by Larbi Sadiki and Heiko Wimmonen, London: Routledge.

Abboud, Samer (2013), "Syria's Business Elite: Between Political Alignment and Hedging Their Bets." SWP Comments 22, Berlin: *German Institute for International and Security Affairs*, August.

Abboud, Samer N. and Fred H. Lawson (2013), "Antinomies of Economic Governance in Contemporary Syria." In *Governance in the Middle East and North Africa: A Handbook*. Edited by Abbas Kadhim. London: Routledge.

Achcar, Gilbert (2013), *The People Want: A Radical Exploration of the Arab Uprising*, Berkeley: University of California Press.

al-Azm, Sadik J. (2014), "Syria in Revolt: Understanding the Unthinkable War." *Boston Review*, August 18.

Azmeh, Shamel (2014), "The Uprising of the Marginalized: A Socio-Economic Perspective of [sic] the Syrian Uprising." *LSE Middle East Centre Paper No. 6*, Middle East Centre, London School of Economics and Political Science, November.

Barajas, Adolfo, Ralph Chami, Raphael Espinoza and Heiko Hesse (2011), "Further Fallout from the Global Financial Crisis: Credit Crunch in the 'Periphery'." *World Economics* 12: 2, 153–176.

Bassyouni, Mustafa (2011), "Labor Movement Absent in Syrian Revolt." *al-Akhbar English*, October 18.

Behrendt, Christina, Tariq Haq and Noura Kamel (2009), "The Impact of the Financial and Economic Crisis on Arab States." Policy Note, April, Beirut: International Labor Organization Regional Office for Arab States.

Brach, Juliane and Markus Loewe (2009), "Getting Off Lightly? The Impact of the International Financial Crisis on the Middle East and North Africa." GIGA Focus No. 1/2009. Hamburg: German Institute of Global and Area Studies.

Brach, Juliane and Markus Loewe (2010), "The Global Financial Crisis and the Arab World: Impact, Reactions and Consequences." *Mediterranean Politics* 15: 1, 45–71.

Cammett, Melani and Ishac Diwan (2014), *The Political Economy of the Arab Uprisings*. Boulder, CO: Westview Press.

Chaisty, Paul and Stephen Whitefield (2012), "The Effects of the Global Financial Crisis on Russian Political Attitudes." *Post-Soviet Affairs*, 28: 2, 187–208.

Chauvin, Nicolas M. Depetris (2013), "FDI Flows in the MENA Region: Features and Impacts." IEMS Emerging Market Brief, January, No. 13–01. Moscow: Institute for Emerging Market Studies. SKOLKOVO School of Management.

Clapp, Jennifer (2009), "Food Price Volatility and Vulnerability in the Global South." *Third World Quarterly* 30: 6, 1183–1196.

Dahi, Omar S. (2011), "Understanding the Political Economy of the Arab Revolts." *Middle East Report* 259 (Summer), 2–6.

Dahi, Omar S. (2012), "The Political Economy of the Egyptian and Arab Revolts." *IDS Bulletin* 43: 1, 47–53.

Danmark, Thouraya B. and Kamel Helali (2013), "The Repercussions of the 2008 Financial Crisis on the Labour Market in Tunisia." *Journal of Business and Finance* 1: 1, 17–26.

Darwisheh, Housam (2013), "From Authoritarianism to Upheaval: The Political Economy of the Syrian Uprising and Regime Persistence." IDE Discussion Paper No. 389, Chiba, Japan: Institute of Developing Economies.

De Chatel, Francesca (2014), "The Role of Drought and Climate Change in the Syrian Uprising." *Middle Eastern Studies*, 50: 4, 521–535.

Donati, Caroline (2013), "The Economics of Authoritarian Upgrading in Syria." In *Middle East Authoritarianisms*. Edited by Steven Heydemann and Reinoud Leenders. Stanford, CA: Stanford University Press.

Freund, Caroline and Carlos A. Primo Braga (2012), "The Economics of Arab Transitions." In *Arab Society in Revolt*. Edited by Cesare Merlini and Olivier Roy, Washington, D.C.: Brookings Institution Press.

Goulden, Robert (2011), "Housing, Inequality and Economic Change in Syria." *British Journal of Middle Eastern Studies* 38: 2, 187–202.

Gourevitch, Peter A. (2009), "The Great Meltdown of '08: Six Variables in Search of an Outcome." *APSA-CP Newsletter* 20: 1, 1–7.

Habibi, Nader (2009), "The Impact of the Global Economic Crisis on Arab Countries: A Year-End Assessment." *Middle East Brief* 40 (December). Waltham, MA: Crown Center for Middle East Studies.
Haddad, Bassam (2005), "Left to its Domestic Devices: How the Syrian Regime Boxed Itself In." *Working Paper* 43, March 10, Madrid: Real Instituto Elcano.
Haddad, Bassam (2011), "The Political Economy of Syria: Realities and Challenges." *Middle East Policy* 18: 2, 46–61.
Haddad, Bassam (2012a), "The Syrian Regime's Business Backbone." *Middle East Report* 262 (Spring).
Haddad, Bassam (2012b), "Syria's State Bourgeoisie: An Organic Backbone for the Regime." *Middle East Critique* 21: 3, 231–257.
Helleiner, Eric (2011), "Understanding the 2007–2008 Global Financial Crisis: Lessons for Scholars of International Political Economy." *Annual Review of Political Science*, 14: 67–87.
Hinnebusch, Raymond (2001), *Syria: Revolution from Above*. London: Routledge.
Hinnebusch, Raymond (2011), "The Ba'th Party in Post-Ba'thist Syria: President, Party and the Struggle for 'Reform,'" *Middle East Critique* 20: 2, 109–125.
Hinnebusch, Raymond (2012), "Syria: From 'Authoritarian Upgrading' to Revolution?" *International Affairs* 88: 1, 95–113.
Hirschman, Albert O. (1970), *Exit, Voice and Loyalty*. Cambridge, MA: Harvard University Press.
Hossain, Naomi, Rizki Fillali, Grace Lubaale, Mwila Mulumbi, Mamunur Rashid and Mariz Tadros (2010), *The Social Impacts of Crisis*. Brighton: University of Sussex, Institute of Development Studies, May.
Ianchovichina, Elena, Josef Loening and Christina Wood (2012), "How Vulnerable are Arab Countries to Global Food Price Shocks?" World Bank Working Paper, February, Washington, D.C.
International Crisis Group (2011), "Popular Protest in North Africa and the Middle East (VI): The Syrian People's Slow Motion Revolution." *Middle East North Africa Report* 108, July 6, Brussels.
International Monetary Fund (2010), "Syrian Arab Republic: 2009 Article IV Consultation Staff Report." *IMF Country Report* 10: 86, March, Washington, D.C.
IRIN (2012), "Analysis: Syria and the Regional Food Chain." www.irinnews.org. October 18.
Ismail, Salwa (2009), "Changing Social Structure, Shifting Alliances and Authoritarianism in Syria." In *Demystifying Syria*. Edited by Fred H. Lawson. London: Saqi Books.
Kadri, Ali (2012), "The Political Economy of the Syrian Crisis." *Working Papers in Technology Governance and Economic Dynamics* 46, December. Tallinn: Tallinn University of Technology.
Kahneman, Daniel and Amo Tversky (2000), *Choices, Values and Frames*. Cambridge: Cambridge University Press.
Lagi, Marco, Karla Z. Bertrand and Yaneer Bar-Yam (2011), The Food Crises and Political Instability in North Africa and the Middle East. Cambridge, MA: New England Complex Systems Institute, September 28.
Lawson, Fred H. (2013), *Global Security Watch Syria*. Santa Barbara, CA: Praeger.
McDonough, Terrence, Michael Reich and David M. Kotz (2010), *Contemporary Capitalism and Its Crises*. Cambridge: Cambridge University Press.
Marshall, Shana (2008), "Syria and the Global Financial Crisis: Insulated or Isolated?" *Syrian Studies Association Newsletter*, 14: 1.
Marshall, Shana (2009), "Syria and the Financial Crisis: Prospects for Reform?" *Middle East Policy* 16: 2, 106–115.

Marzouq, Nabil (2011), "The Economic Origins of Syria's Uprising." *al-Akhbar English.* August 28.
Mashal, Ahmad M. (2012), "The Financial Crisis of 2008–2009 and the Arab States Economies." *International Journal of Business and Management* 7 (February), 96–111.
Matar, Linda (2012), "Syria Reverts to Statist Policies in the Course of its Political Uprising." *Middle East Insights* 73, August 15. Singapore: Middle East Institute, National University of Singapore.
Monajed, A. (2011), "The Future of Syrian Industry under the Eleventh Five-Year Plan. 2011–2015." www.scpss.org. March 2.
Nasser, Rabie, Zaki Mehchy and Khalid Abu Ismail (2013), Socioeconomic Roots and Impact of the Syrian Crisis. Syrian Center for Policy Research. January.
Oxford Business Group (2011), "Syria: Planning Ahead." February 17.
Pei, Minxin and Ariel David Adesnik (2000), "Why Recessions Don't Start Revolutions." *Foreign Policy* 118 (Spring), 138–151.
Pfeifer, Karen (2012), "Gulf Arab Financial Flows and Investment, 2000–2010: Promises, Process and Prospects in the MENA Region." *Review of Middle East Economics and Finance*, 8: 2, 1–36.
Pierret, Thomas and Kjetil Selvik (2010), "Limits of 'Authoritarian Upgrading' in Syria: Private Welfare, Islamic Charities and the Rise of the Zayd Movement." *International Journal of Middle East Studies* 41: 4, 595–614.
Ruiz de Elvira, Laura and Tina Zintl (2014), "The End of the Ba'thist Social Contract in Bashar al-Asad's Syria." *International Journal of Middle East Studies* 46: 2, 329–349.
Seifan, Samir (2010), "Syria on the Path to Economic Reform." St Andrews Papers on Contemporary Syria. Boulder, CO: Lynne Rienner.
Sika, Nadine (2012), "The Political Economy of Arab Uprisings." *IEMed Papers* 10 May, Barcelona: European Institute of the Mediterranean.
Springborg, Robert (2011–12), "The Precarious Economics of Arab Springs." *Survival* 53: 6, 85–104.
Strategic Research and Communication Centre (2011), "The Performance of the Syrian Economy and the Industrial Sector." January.
USAID (2011), "Food Price Trends in the Middle East and North Africa." www.fewsnet. February 16.
USDA (2011), Foreign Agricultural Service. Washington, D.C. April 4.
Yazigi, Jihad (2012), "No End in Sight to Syria's Economic Woes." *Perspectives* 3 (February), 24–27.
Zurayk, Rami and Anne Gough (2014), "Bread and Olive Oil: The Agrarian Roots of the Arab Uprisings." In *The New Middle East: Protest and Revolution in the Arab World*. Edited by Fawaz A. Gerges. Cambridge: Cambridge University Press.

7

TUTELARY AUTHORITARIANISM AND THE SHIFTS BETWEEN SECULARISM AND ISLAM IN SYRIA

Line Khatib

Introduction

Studies on the robustness of authoritarianism and authoritarian upgrading in the Middle East have helped to explain many elements of the region's 'resistance to democratization' (Bellin: 2004). In particular, these studies have shown that a key element in the ability of states in the region to consolidate power and resist democratization is their fiscal rentier power, their effective control of the economy, the weakness and illiberalism of civil society, elements within Islam, as traditionally interpreted, and the complementarity of their repressive and co-optive measures (Heydemann: 2007, 2014; Heydemann and Leenders: 2011; Hinnebusch: 2012, 2001; Perthes: 2004; King: 2009; Guazzone and Pioppi: 2009). Studies on authoritarian upgrading have also looked at questions of legitimation: they have, for instance, shown how autocratic regimes have sometimes had to temper their opposition to Islamic political participation to legitimize and thus consolidate their autocratic rule. Very few studies, however, have attempted to explore how some Middle Eastern regimes have tried to use secularism, used here to denote separation – or distancing – of church and state, as an instrument for legitimation and stabilization. Indeed, secularism has been instrumentalized in Syria to boost the autocratic effectiveness of the regime, to blur state-society distinctions, to divide the people, as well as to marginalize some of the regime's staunchest critics and unfaltering dissidents: Syria's secularists.

In order to explicate this argument, the present chapter looks at the survival and consolidation of the Asads' authoritarian regime in Syria, paying particular attention to secular–religious interactions and dynamics in the country, the regime's manipulations of these, and the results of the manipulations for Syrian state and society. Questions examined include: how do regime discourses and policies intertwine with secularism and Islam in an authoritarian state context such as that in Syria? And, what do the adaptive practices of the Syrian regime tell us about Syria's society and the Islamist threat in the country?

This chapter relies on post-Democracy/authoritarian resilience theoretical approaches in arguing that authoritarian regimes have a robust repertoire of responses and tools, and can adapt and transform their practices in times of crisis. The chapter looks at the state's dynamic relations with secularism and Islamism in Syria to draw out aspects of the regime's transformative capacity, which are sometimes hidden in plain sight, as well as to consider their significance and the resulting outcomes. The argument is that authoritarian persistence takes many forms. In Syria, the political regime has consistently relied upon and alternated between both secularism and Islam to sustain its authoritarian rule, by frequently shifting between secular and Islamic bases of legitimacy. In other words, secularism and Islam have become mere reference points that are invoked in alternation to strengthen the power of the state. Thus the Asads' regime has posited itself as the guardian of secularism in Syria and, in this capacity, as the sole guardian of the country's minorities, as well as the minorities' best option for protection. At the same time, it has halted secular institutionalization, imprisoned and silenced Syria's most prominent secular intellectuals and activists who have dared over the years to challenge the state, and provided organizational and ideological openings for Muslim religious figures, and Islamic militants fighting in neighbouring countries to organize. The silencing of secularism, it has been argued, was due to pressures from the Islamic opposition in Syria and the regime's need to co-opt this powerful opposition. The chapter adds nuance to this argument by showing that the halt to secular institutionalization was also due to the regime's fears of Syria's pro-democracy secular activists, concerns that drove the regime to placate the pious but also to silence Syria's secular political dissidents.

One of the key considerations at the root of the regime's aggressive fight against pro-democracy secularist parties and activists is that these anti-regime secularists promise the same thing as the Asads' regime: equal citizenship, protection of minorities, and a secular state. But the secularist dissidents also go further in promising the rule of law, free and fair elections, as well as transparency and civil freedoms and rights. Moreover they can potentially become very powerful if permitted to organize and spread their messages precisely because Syria is made up of a diverse blend of ideological, religious and ethnic groups, many of whom perceive their interests as being best served by the inclusive secularists rather than by the exclusive, radical Islamists. Important to keep in mind as well is that this diversity is even found within particular communities – thus for example Syria's Sunnis are ideologically diverse and include avowed secularists. At the same time, Islam and the Islamists have been used instrumentally by the regime to divide the opposition, to rule by fear, and to manipulate the regional environment, e.g. through the support and use of Hamas in the Palestinian territories and Hizbullah in Lebanon.

Political contestation during the time of Hafiz al-Asad

The Syrian regime's instrumental usage of secularism as an ambiguous signifier and a mere tool to legitimize power started with the presidency of Hafiz al-Asad.

Indeed, when we examine the nearly 30-year rule of Hafiz al-Asad, there is a clear pattern of the regime opting to prioritize regime survival above any particular ideological goals such as establishing or institutionalizing secularism in the country. This, for example, is evident in the fact that the secularization of the Shari'a-based Family Law initiated by the Ba'thist state in the mid-1960s was halted under Hafiz al-Asad, and plans to secularize the educational system by removing all religious classes from the curriculum were discarded entirely. Instead, secularism was in fact muted by the regime and became a mere sermon used by the political elite to assert the regime's vital position in ensuring order and promoting cohabitation between the different religious groups. The Islamic rebellion in the country, which simmered and boiled throughout the 1970s and was definitively and brutally put down in Hama in 1982, facilitated this instrumental use of secularism as a means for the regime to boost its legitimacy. This is because the rebellion allowed the regime to foster national unity around 'us' (the secular nationalists) versus 'them' (the radical Islamists).

This tactic has allowed the state to characterize itself as a tutelary state and as society's saviour in the face of the threat represented by the Islamists. The creation of the Islamist 'Other' has served to blur the lines between the anti-regime secular intellectuals and activists (who are pro-democracy) and the secular political elite and its cronies (who uphold the autocratic regime in Syria), since the regime claimed to represent and speak in the name of all of Syria's secular nationalists. To effectively act as the only acceptable bearer of secular values, however, the state has had to ensure that the secular intellectuals and political activists are either co-opted and incorporated, or constrained and marginalized since otherwise these actors would represent an alternative pole of power that could threaten regime hegemony.

It is important to underline here that the instrumental use of the Islamists by the Syrian regime does not obviate the fact that radical Islamists may very well pose a threat to the unity of Syria's society. We need only recall the very strong challenge to Hafiz al-Asad's regime by the Islamist Fighting Vanguards in the 1970s and 1980s. Indeed, this Islamist rebellion was one of the strongest instances of Islamic rebellion in the modern Arab world. It lasted for six years, targeted civilians, military officers and government officials, and caused terror. But this threat was manageable and controllable by the state because the movement failed to attract the majority of Syria's population which, as noted above, is diverse ideologically even within the same ethnic and religious community. At the same time, the Islamic rebellion led to instances of 'authoritarian learning' by the regime of Hafiz al-Asad, including the need to concede some space to the pious in Syria as well as to allow some apolitical and semi-independent religious civil society groups to form, organize, and be active.

In parallel to this controlled opening up, independent secularists continued to be ruthlessly silenced, harassed and policed under emergency laws (nominally lifted in April 2011). This is because, as mentioned earlier, Hafiz al-Asad and his regime claimed to speak in the name of the secularists. As the following quote from a June 1979 public address shows, Asad did so by asserting a national culture that transcended and maybe even superseded divisive sectarian identities such as Muslim or Christian, and implicitly that this secular identity was embodied by his regime:

> The concept of 'homeland' loses its meaning if its citizens are not equal. This equality is an integral part of Islam. We are leading the country in the name of the Arab Ba'th Socialist Party and as President of the Republic, not in the name of a religion or of a religious community, despite the fact that Islam is the religion of the majority. (Van Dam 1996: 94–95)

This concern on the part of the regime with solidifying its place as leader of the secularists also points us towards an all too often ignored aspect of the Islamic rebellion of the 1970s and 1980s: that the rebellion did not only involve Islamists. Indeed, it included secularist intellectuals and prominent politicians and unified two groups that opposed the regime, the Islamists and the Democratic National Bloc, the latter of which was made up of the Arab Socialist Union (led by Jamal al-Atasi), the same old Ba'thists; the Arab Socialists under Akram Hawrani and the communist faction of Riyad al-Turk (Seurat: 1980). During the Uprising, human rights activists were detained without trial with some forced to flee the country (Drysdale: 1982), and the Committee for Human Rights that was publishing accounts of human rights abuses was targeted and closed (Seurat: 1989; Seale: 1988). Indeed, the regime was not only fighting sectarian Islamists, but it was also fighting secular democrats and nationalists who aimed to challenge the authoritarian nature of the regime. By ignoring or downplaying this part of the struggle and focusing on the Islamists in its discourse, the regime successfully side-lined the secular pro-democracy movement. This in turn facilitated the regime's claim to be the sole representative of secularism in the country.

By February 1982 and the Hama massacre, the regime had effectively put down the entire rebellious movement in Syria: anti-regime Islamists and secularists were either dead, in prison, or in forced exile. As a result of that ferocious regime response, the remaining Sunni religious leaders and the country's religious class overall acquiesced to the new order, shunned political activism and started focusing on social and moral change at the individual level. This change in attitudes and approach was partly due to the fact that the regime had fought ruthlessly against the opposition, but also because the Muslim religious leaders could still deflect some of the state's control by focusing on *da'wa* (proselytizing) and promoting Islamic piety at the societal level. This reconfiguration of the religious phenomenon away from the politics and towards society satisfied the authoritarian regime. At the same time, it allowed Muslim religious leaders to maintain a certain organizational and ideological space and autonomy, and meant that they could work on their longer-term goals of Islamizing the state by promoting Islamic piety as part of a bottom-up strategy (Khatib: 2011).

Unlike the Muslim religious leaders, the anti-regime secularists were never really permitted similar organizational and intellectual space post-1982. Instead, they were continuously monitored and harassed, many were imprisoned, and they were not allowed to organize or assemble. These actions did not entirely stop diversity and contention, at least not within the 'cultural field' in which artists negotiated and pushed the boundaries of the permissible (Boëx: 2011). But they underline the extent to which anti-regime secularists were perceived as a political threat because they risked challenging the regime's characterization of itself as the sole representative of Syrians with secular sympathies. Moreover, the harassment and persecution included a strong legal dimension. For example, Article 355 of the penal code bans 'attending a meeting that is not of a private nature … where an individual issues calls for rioting or displays signs that perturb the general safety, or undertakes any form of rioting'; article 336 states that 'gathering in a public space is considered a riot if … (b) there are at least seven people gathered to protest a decision or measure taken by the public authorities or (c) if they are more than 20 people and they appear in a way that can threaten the public peace'; and Article 288 bans being a member of a 'political or social organization or an international group without the permission of the government' (US Department of State: 2010). These articles of the penal code are regularly placed within the wider context of repressive governmental measures since they limit free assembly and freedom of expression in general. But it is important to note here that they have mostly affected the secularists because they enabled the government to prevent any gathering of secularist activists from occurring while religious leaders (both critical and co-opted ones) were still permitted to engage the public and propagate their ideas and vision within mosques and other privately owned religious institutions (Pierret: 2013; Khatib: 2011).

Overall what we can see is that, in its management of political contestation, the state suffocated the secularists. Secular intellectuals such as 'Aref Dalila, Haitham al-Maleh, and Riad Turk were harassed and imprisoned, often for many years. Secularists such as Nazih Abu 'Afash and Mamduh 'Adwan were forced to retire or quit their jobs within cultural institutions like the Ministry of Culture and Syria's Writers' Union. Others such as Sa'adallah Wannous, Muhammad al-Maghut, 'Ali Ferzat, and Michel Kilo continued to work in Syria, but at great personal risk and often with impacts upon their ability to work as well as their peace of mind. And many other secularists were directly or indirectly forced into exile, including people such as Burhan Ghalioun, Subhi al-Hadidi, Bashar 'Issa, and Zakaria Tamer just to name a few.

This effort at control and containment of the secularists also involved banning independent secular parties and allowing only those included in the state-sanctioned National Progressive Front and thus under the umbrella of the ruling Ba'th party, as well as banning human rights organizations, and ensuring that no independent secular civil society groups could be formed. Indeed, until 2001, NGOs were not allowed to form unless they fit into one of two organizational categories: welfare organizations soliciting donations to provide services for specific target groups (such as orphans or the disabled), and the regime-sponsored populist corporatist organizations in existence at the time. By allowing the former type of organization, Asad effectively reduced reliance on the government to provide such services. The latter type of organization, which includes such groups as the General Union of Women

(GUW), trade unions and the Revolutionary Youth Union, are in fact quasi-governmental and are overseen by *al-qiyadah* (the Ba'th party command) which exercised great influence over them (Camillia, El-Solh, and Barmada: 2005). While these populist corporatist organizations were effective administrative and service structures that incorporated teachers, workers and peasants, they simultaneously served as tools of authoritarian control to indoctrinate the public and curtail independent thinking and activities.

Continuity and Bashar al-Asad's new era: après moi, le déluge

After the death of Hafiz al-Asad in 2000, the new regime of Bashar al-Asad went through a period of uncertainty before the new president was able to consolidate his control over the governmental apparatus. This fact, coupled with threats that included an economic crisis exacerbated by strong demographic growth, a new geopolitical reality as a result of the war in Iraq, and the inability of the regime to sustain the populist policies, made regime adaptation of paramount importance.

This moment of crisis is arguably the natural outcome of the built-in structural limitations of the Populist Authoritarian regime model created by the Ba'th in 1963 (Hinnebusch: 2001). Indeed, while the regime's survival strategies were successful in postponing the need for larger structural adjustments during the time of Hafez al-Asad's presidency, they became increasingly insufficient to secure the loyalty of strategic sectors. The main predicament was an outgrowth of the selective economic liberalization adopted by the state in the 1990s. While this liberalization addressed the demands of the newly emerging capitalist and *arriviste* elements linked to the regime, it also led to the gradual abandonment of the regime's social welfare programmes that underwrote its populist identity. Thus, the gap between the impoverished classes and the economic elite in the country widened. More particularly, the wealth gap widened by 11 per cent between 1996 and 2004, with 11.4 per cent of Syrians living in extreme poverty and unable to obtain their most basic needs in 2003–2004 (Al-Laithy and Abu Ismail: 2005). In that year, the bottom 20 per cent of the population consumed only 7 per cent of all expenditures in the country, and the richest 20 per cent consumed 45 per cent. Thereafter, the economic situation further deteriorated for the poor (Syrian Central Bureau of Statistics: 2006; UN Development Programme: 2008), while, at the same time, in 2009 sales of such luxury items as Maserati, Porsche and BMW cars were soaring in Syria such that the country was BMW's top-performing Middle Eastern market for the year (*The National*, 5 July, 2010).

The widening gap between rich and poor meant that the state could no longer maintain its balancing act of satisfying its broad base of support rooted in the middle and lower classes as well as its newer supporters among the richer, capitalist class. This narrowing strategic alternatives available to the political command resulted in a greater reliance on the regime's most powerful clients, namely the newly established business class as well as the numerous religious leaders who had taken advantage of the organizational space provided by Hafez al-Asad. Overall, this deepening of the alliance between the state and the economic and religious elite under Bashar al-Asad is a continuation of the strategy pursued by his father, who had himself pragmatically reinforced and empowered from above those individuals – including religious leaders – who agreed to serve, support or become a more or less integral part of the ruling coalition. But this social engineering has had important ramifications in that it has led to a transformation in the form and size of the piety movement in Syria: as religious leaders were increasingly co-opted, they were also becoming increasingly vocal, more structured, and more effective in Islamizing society and in recruiting members (Khatib: 2011). And the decreasingly populist regime was relatively powerless to push back because it in turn depended upon their support.

President Bashar al-Asad's foreign policy also indirectly and unwittingly reinforced this Islamization trend. Regional Islamist militants harboured and trained within Syria were used to influence Syria's larger geopolitical environment. Religious leaders, such as Mahmoud Gul al-Aghassi (also known as Abu al-Qa'qa'), were emboldened and allowed to recruit and train militants transiting into Iraq from Syria. Syria increasingly became a hub for Jihadists wanting to fight against the Americans in the neighbouring country. In 2003, one secular political dissident said that '[t]here is no overt political Islam ... but they are building a base, and the moment they have the chance, they will act to become fanatic, extremist movements' (MacFarquhar: 2003). While this activity was soon halted due to international pressure and domestic concerns, it contributed to the expansion of the Islamic sector at both the organizational and the ideological level. The new Islamic sector came to encompass such different groups as non-political neo-fundamentalists (salafists) and militant Islamists (jihadists), with each increasingly pitted against the other.

The key point for this chapter is that a new Islamic civil society emerged, and was moreover allowed to flourish by the regime outside the purview of the state. In response, the regime attempted to promote a 'moderate' interpretation and practice of Islam in Syria. The move was spearheaded by Syria's Ministry of Awqaf (religious endowments) and by prominent religious leaders such as Ahmad Hassoun and Muhammad Habash (at the time a close friend of the Syrian political elite). Promotion of moderate Islam was the reason for its organization in 2004 of the country's first religious conference in 40 years, entitled *Tajdeed al-Khitab al-Dini* (Renewal of the Religious Message), which attracted many globally known Islamic thinkers and leaders. The state seemed at the time to be determined to contain and appropriate religious social activism, but not to stop it. And from the point of view of religious leaders and their organizations, it was treated as an opportunity to expand their work and increase their visibility. In this sense, 'Islamic groups were not just pawns of the state. Rather, they successfully operated within the space available to them to advance a comprehensive cultural system, and thereby to expand their effective control over society in a way that altered the governing political coalition and challenged the secular heritage of the country' (Khatib: 2011).

This opportunity for the different Islamic groups to organize, recruit and 'renew' their message was not enjoyed by the anti-regime secular activists but this did not stop them from taking advantage of the few opportunities that arose when the regime either appeared to be more tolerant of criticism or vulnerable to it. In a brief 2000–2001 interlude known as the Damascus Spring, seemingly encouraged by the president's call for constructive criticism, the secularists made clear their views regarding the need for democratic change and respect for human rights as being vital for Syrians to remain a united people in a straight-forward, bold and unapologetic statement that was signed by 99 Syrian intellectuals:

> Democracy and human rights today constitute a common humanitarian language, gathering and uniting peoples' hopes in seeking a better future ... As Syria enters the 21st century, it is in need for all of its citizens to join forces to face the challenges posed by peace, modernization and opening up to the outside world ...
>
> From this subjective need, and in order to secure our national unity, believing that the future of our country cannot be dictated, being citizens in a republican system where everybody has the right to express themselves freely, we, the undersigned, call upon the state to implement the following demands: End the state of emergency and martial law being applied in Syria since 1963; Issue a public pardon to all political detainees and those who are pursued for their political ideas and allow the return of all deportees and exiled citizens; Establish a rule of law that will recognize freedom of assembly, freedom of the press and freedom of expression; Free public life from the laws, constraints and various forms of surveillance imposed on it, allowing citizens to express their various interests within a framework of social harmony and peaceful [economic] competition ... (al-Hayat: 2000)

The Statement of 99, launched in September 2000, was signed by long-time anti-regime secular activists who had hitherto been silenced but remained within Syria's cultural milieu, such as Abd al-Razzak 'Eid, Anwar al-Bunni, Mamdouh 'Adwan, Haidar Haidar, and Michel Kilo. The Damascus Spring also led to the launch of the Statement of the 1,000 in January 2001, which established the Committees for the Revival of Civil Society in Syria. The period furthermore saw the launch of the Forum of National Dialogue (*Muntada al-Hiwar al-Watani*) by Riyad Sayf in August 2000, the formation of the Cultural Forum for Human Rights (*al-Muntada al-Thaqafi li-Huquq al-Insan*) by Khalil Ma'tuq in 2001, and the launch of the Suhayr/Jamal al-Atasi forum. These various initiatives were met with some compromises by the regime at first, but compromise quickly turned to repression and persecution since unlike their religious counterparts, the secularists asserted their normative commitment to political liberalization.

Despite the repression and harassment of secular activists, October 2005 saw the emergence of the Damascus Declaration, at a time when the regime seemed vulnerable to intense external pressure. The Declaration was written by Michel Kilo and Abdul Razzaq 'Eid, and was signed by hundreds of dissidents (including members of Syria's exiled Muslim Brothers). It criticized the totalitarian nature of the regime and called for the abolition of martial law and a return to democratic rule.

In May 2006, the Damascus-Beirut Declaration was published. It carried the signatures of hundreds of Syrian and Lebanese activists. That declaration called for the normalization of relations between Lebanon and Syria following the assassination of former Lebanese Prime Minister Hariri – which the Syrian regime is widely believed to have been implicated in – and more generally for an end to the policy of political assassinations. The release of the declaration led to Michel Kilo and ten other secular dissidents being arrested. Eight of them were soon after released, while Michel Kilo and Mahmoud 'Issa were released in 2009 and Anwar al-Bunni and Kamal Labwani were released in 2011. Mahmoud 'Issa was again imprisoned in April 2011 following an interview with al-Jazeera in which he called for a democratic regime (Shaam News: 2011).

The various mechanisms of control and harassment that secular activists have faced underlined the robust repertoire of tools deployed by the authoritarian regime in response to a perceived challenge. They included forced exile, imprisonment, disappearance, degrading treatment and torture, and state-sanctioned murder. Abdularazak 'Eid's story can shed light on the determination of the regime to pursue its opponents and to ensure they could not mount a serious challenge. 'Eid had drafted the Statement of the 1000 and helped found the Committees of Civil Society in Syria. In 2004, he had to appear in front of a military tribunal in Aleppo because he wrote critically about the regime in *An-Nahar*, a Lebanese newspaper (Abdel Hadi: 2004). 'Eid was also detained by agents of the Syrian Mukhabarat in February 2007 because he had written an article that appeared in a Lebanese newspaper (Al-Safir) that was critical of Hizbullah, Syria and Iran (Bureau of Democracy, Human Rights and Labor, 2008). He was freed a few hours later after being threatened with physical harm if he continued to challenge the authorities. His 2009 presentation at the German Goethe Institute in Damascus was cancelled because he was accused of indirectly criticizing the regime through his critique of the Iraqi Ba'th Party. Importantly, 'Eid's experience is not exceptional and is in fact typical of the relentlessness with which the regime pursued its opponents. Despite the fact that the secularists were not bearing arms and were not radical militants who represent a threat to Syria's people, they were nonetheless targeted, persecuted and silenced with the same zeal that was applied to the militant radical Islamists.

In parallel, the regime sponsored regime-affiliated elements of secular civil society. This affiliation is made visible by the fact that the first lady, Asma Akhras, was the official sponsor of Syria's most visible NGOs. These groups focused on youth development (Shabab), women's empowerment (MAWRED, which stands for Modernising and Activating Women's Role in Economic Development), education issues, the environment, and overall development of Syria (FIRDOS, which means Paradise in Arabic). This civil society was secular and helped the regime to portray itself as a secular actor that supported a society founded on the ideal of empowering women and youth, and that it is concerned about 'modern' issues such as the environment, gender equality and technological reform.

The secular threat and the March 2011 Uprising

The Syrian Uprising of March 2011 started as a secular, non-sectarian Uprising (Kahf: 2013). In the earliest demonstrations, protesters asserted that their sectarian affiliations were not the driving force behind their political demands, reflected in their secular and non-sectarian chants. For example, in the Hamidiyya market in Damascus in March 2011, protesters chanted, 'We are Alawites, Sunnis, people of every sect, and we want to topple the regime' (Kahf: 2013). 'The first Banyas crowds of March 18, 2011, memorably sang "Sunnis and Alawites, we all want freedom"' (Kahf: 2013). The early protesters also displayed both crosses and crescents at the protests to demonstrate their non-aligned stance, and Syrians from all ethno-sectarian backgrounds gathered, sometimes in mosques, in solidarity against the regime. Veiled women at the protests also chanted 'silmiyeh (peaceful), Islam and Christians.' One observer noted at the time the, '[s]olidarity across lines of sect, religion, and ethnicity among the grassroots population that began and drove the Syrian Uprising in its first phase ... The majority of the protesters are Sunni because the majority in Syria is Sunni. Despite their smaller numbers, minority members played not only proportionate but historical roles in the Uprising' (Kahf: 2013). The protesters were indeed making an important point that sectarian identifications in Syria did exist and should not be negated or dismissed as often done by the Ba'thi regime, but that these affiliations were not the driving force behind the protests.

The regime's response to the Uprising demonstrates how it used secularism to assert its legitimacy and to mobilize support in much the same way that its response to the earlier Islamic rebellion and to Islamism more generally was used to divide the people and discredit dissidents. The regime's instrumental usage of secularism began only two weeks into the protests, at the end of March 2011, when Bashar al-Asad's first speech portrayed the Uprising as *fitna* (sedition or incitement to rebellion and civil strife): a foreign conspiracy against the coherence of Syria. The purpose of this *fitna*, according to his speech, was to divide Syrians based on their *ta'ifa* (sect) and to destroy the unity of Syrians, thereby turning the country into a patchwork of *tawa'if* (sects) (Bashar al-Asad's Presidential Speech: 2011). The discourse was meant to reinforce the idea that the state was the only secular actor in Syria and the sole protector of the minorities. It was also meant to demonize the demonstrators: first, the arrest and removal of pacifist activists and secular intellectuals from the ranks of the protesters 'aimed in part at depriving the opposition of its more sophisticated members, but also at validating the government's argument that it was fighting only militants and religious extremists' (*New York Times*: 2012). It was under this strategy that 'Ali Farzat, Syria's internationally known cartoonist and secular dissident, was attacked in Damascus and had both his arms broken. Second, the strategic invocation of an Islamist threat (Presidential Speech: 2013) led to the regime immediately pointing the finger at the Islamists even while protesters were peacefully marching in the streets. The manipulation of Islamist threat can be seen in the fact that while secularist activists were imprisoned, Zahran Alloush, the founder of the Salafist group Jaish al-Islam who had been in prison since 2009, was released in June 2011 (Helberg: 2014). The regime also played upon the fears of minorities about a radical Islam sweeping the nation, forcing all to submit to its radical rule, and taking away whatever social freedoms they have enjoyed under the secular regime of the Asad family. The regime's ability to do so was heightened because it had been warning Syrians about the Islamist threat since the Islamic rebellion of the 1970s and early 1980s (Mayer: 1983), and because Syria's middle class appeared to believe in the regime's performance as a secular actor. The regime's ability to do so was also the result of its jealous guarding of the political space which denied the secular opposition the political experience, which contributed significantly to their failure to work together and organize effectively once the Uprising presented them with the opportunity, and to agree on a common platform that included the main Syrian opposition groups and encompassed the wide spectrum of ideological stances.

The result has been the rise of a plethora of opposition groupings that did not see eye to eye on key issues such as foreign intervention, alliance formation, militarization of the Uprising, and the possibility of negotiations with the regime. Indeed, five main secular opposition groups emerged with the Uprising: The National Democratic Gathering, the Damascus Declaration Group, the left-leaning National Co-ordination Committee for Democratic Change (NCC), Local Coordination Committees that form the backbone of the secular resistance, and the Syrian National Council (SNC), which represented those outside Syria. Each of these groupings included several political parties and movements, as well as independent actors. The distinction between the internal opposition and the external opposition also grew as they disagreed on how they should topple the regime. The SNC for instance formed external alliances and depended on external funding and backing; supported economic sanctions against the regime and some sort of foreign intervention, in addition to the militarization of the resistance movement and the creation of humanitarian corridors to help civilians; it did not perceive a difference between the state apparatus and the regime in Syria. The internal opposition by contrast, and particularly the NCC, opted for the continuation of pacifist resistance at the local level. It viewed the regime and the state as two different entities and argued that the latter should be safeguarded for the sake of those living in Syria, to ensure stability and institutional continuity. It focused on questions of economic and political corruption, citizens' marginalization, and on the need to stop the violence and to negotiate a political solution and programme with those in power in Syria as well as their external allies. Being inside Syria, it claimed to be more authentically representative of the people's wishes and needs as compared to others such as the SNC that are populated by exiles and that depend on external funding (Haddad: 2012). According to SNC members, however, it is more realistic to work with external powers than it is to be, like the NCC, at the mercy of the regime and its allies.

During the first two years of the Uprising, the SNC was often riven by discord owing to the conflicting interests of its patrons, Turkey, the Gulf States, the European Union and the United States. On 8 November 2012, the National Coalition for Syrian Revolutionary and Opposition Forces (NC) was created in an attempt to broaden the SNC and unify the entire resistance movement. The NC initially included the Syrian National Council, the Muslim Brotherhood, the Coalition of Secular and Democratic Syrians (Chaired by Randa Kassis), the Damascus Declaration Group, the Democratic People Party (under the leadership of George Sabra), the Communist Labour Party, the National Kurdish Council, the Democratic Turkmen Movement, the Turkmen National Bloc, the Local Coordination Committees (*al-tansiqiyat*), the Free Syrian Army and the Higher Military Council. But the NC failed to include the NCC, the Kurdish Democratic Union Party (PYD) and the left-leaning National Democratic Front. And in 2013, divisions were already emerging within its ranks: the NC's first president, Mo'az al-Khatib, resigned, complaining of external powers' meddling and manipulation. Then in May 2013, the Local Coordination Committees issued a statement that the NC had failed to represent the interests of the Syrian people. In January 2014, the SNC broke with the coalition because the NC agreed to talks with the Asad regime in Geneva.

What emerges then is that Syria is not short of secular democratic activists, but these activists are divided, politically inexperienced, and weak. Perhaps one of the key measures of their lack of success is that as of the end of 2015, the movement seemed to control very little of the Syrian territory and had to rely on alliances with Islamists. Manipulation from above played a key role in isolating and weakening the secularists, while, in parallel, the regime soon found that, not only could it not control the Islamists but that they soon came to constitute a powerful militarized opposition. The marginalization of the secular opposition contributed greatly to the rise of radical Islamists.

Conclusion

This chapter has argued that secularism is an important element to examine when studying autocratic regimes' persistence in the Middle East. In Syria, it has been a key ground of contention between the state and the opposition since 1982, with the opposition manipulated both in fact and in the popular imagination to reinforce the regime's domination of this ground. This was demonstrated through a focus on the Syrian regime's different ways of dealing with and of containing both the Islamists and the secularists, including according some ideological and organizational space for Islamic groups to flourish and expand the so-called Islamic sector, space that was not accorded to the secularists. Meanwhile, the regime, claiming to be the sole secular actor in Syria, consistently pushed the secular dissidents into exile or underground, sowing divisions and undermining attempts to organize such that secularism as an ideology has become muted and moribund.

This chapter has highlighted the often ignored history of the anti-regime secularists in Syria over a period of shifting state policy starting with the Islamic rebellion in the 1970s and early 1980s and continuing until the Syrian Uprising that began in 2011. It has also sought to explain their fragmentation and ineffectiveness, and to add nuance to our understanding of the Syrian Uprising by demonstrating that despite the prominence of and attention being given to the Islamist opposition, the contest with the secularists has been at least as important for the regime as it has grappled to stay in control. These various insights point to the need for empirical and theoretical works on the robustness of authoritarianism in the Middle East to give greater consideration to the use of secularism and not just to religion, as an instrument for consolidation of power by authoritarian regimes.

Bibliography

Abdel Hadi, Majd (2004), 'Syrian Dissident Walks Free', BBC (2 June), http://news.bbc.co.uk/2/hi/middle_east/3769309.stm.

Al-Hayat, 27 September. (2000), Translation by Suha Mawlawi Kayal, available in the Middle East Intelligence Bulletin 2, 9 (5 October 2000).

Al-Laithy, Hiba and Khalid Abu Ismail (2005), 'Poverty in Syria 1996–2004: Diagnosis and Pro-Poor Policy Considerations', UNDP Report (June), http://www.undp.org/content/dam/rbas/report/PovertInSyriaEnglishVersion.pdf.

Al-Monitor (2015), 'Will Syrian Opposition Move Interim Government to Idlib?' (April), http://www.al-monitor.com/pulse/politics/2015/04/syria-opposition-idlib-nusra-government-in-exile.html.

Bellin, Eva (2004), 'The Robustness of Authoritarianism in the Middle East: Exceptionalism in Comparative Perspective', Comparative Politics, 36: 2 (January), 139–158.

Boëx, Cécile (2011), 'The End of the State Monopoly over Culture: Toward the Commodification of Cultural and Artistic Production', Middle East Critique 20: 2, 139–155.

Bureau of Democracy, Human Rights, and Labor (2008), Syria, US Department of State, 11 March, www.state.gov/j/drl/rls/hrrpt/2007/100606.htm.

Camillia, Leif Ole Manger, Fawzi El-Solh and Warka Barmada (2005), Country Evaluation: Assessment of Development Results Syria. UNDP.

Cavatorta, Francesco (2010), 'The Convergence of Governance: Upgrading authoritarianism in the Arab World and downgrading democracy elsewhere?' Middle East Critique, 19: 3, 217–232.

CIA (n.d.), The World Factbook, Syria, www.cia.gov/library/publications/the-world-factbook/geos/sy.html.

Drysdale, Alasdair (1982), 'The Asad Regime and its Troubles', MERIP Reports (Nov.–Dec.).

Guazzone, Laura and Daniela Pioppi (2009), The Arab State and Neo-Liberal Globalization: The Restructuring of the State in the Middle East. Reading, UK: Ithaca Press.

Haddad, Bassam (2012), 'The Current Impasse in Syria: Interview with Haytham Manna', Jadaliyya (30 June), www.jadaliyya.co/pages/index/6245/the-current-impasse-in-syria_interveiw-with-haytham-manna.

Helberg, Kristin (2014), 'al-salafi al-suri zahran alloush wa al-huquqiya al-suriyya razan zaitouna', translated from German by Raed al-Bash, http://ar.qantara.de.

Heydemann, Steven (2007), 'Upgrading Authoritarianism in the Arab World', Analysis Paper 13. Washington DC: Saban Center for Middle East Policy at the Brookings Institution.

Heydemann, Steven (2014), 'Mass politics and the future of authoritarian governance in the Arab world', 16 December, http://pomeps.org/2014/12/16/mass-politics-and-the-future-of-authoritarian-governance-in-the-arab-world/#_ftn4.

Heydemann, Steven, and Reinoud Leenders (2011), 'Authoritarian Learning and Authoritarian Resilience: Regime Responses to the Arab Awakening', *Globalizations*, 8:5 (October), 647–653.
Hinnebusch, Raymond (2001), *Syria: Revolution from Above*. London: Routledge.
Hinnebusch, Raymond (2012), 'Syria: From Authoritarian Upgrading to Revolution?' *International Affairs* 88: 1, 95–114.
Kahf, Mohja (2013), 'Then and Now: The Syrian Revolution to Date', *A Special Report from Friends for a Nonviolent World*, 1. 1 (28 February), 2–9.
Khatib, Line (2011), *Islamic Revivalism in Syria: The Rise and Fall of Bathist Secularism*. London: Routledge.
King, Stephen (2009), *The New Authoritarianism in the Middle East and North-Africa*. Bloomington: Indianan University Press.
MacFarquhar, Neil (2003), 'Syria, Long Ruthlessly Secular, Sees Fervent Islamic Resurgence', *New York Times*, 24 October.
Mayer, Thomas (1983), 'The Islamic Opposition in Syria, 1962–1982', *Orient*, 24.
New York Times (2012), 'Syrian Arrests Are Said to Have Snared Tens of Thousands' (27 June), www.nytimes.com/2012/06/28/world/middleeast/beyond-arms-syria-uses-arrests-against-uprising.html?_r=0.
OMRAN Centre for Strategic Studies (January 2016), http://goo.gl/P02gKa.
Perthes, Volker (2004), 'Syria under Bashar al-Asad: Modernization and the Limits of Change', Adelphi Papers. London: Oxford University Press for International Institute for Strategic Studies.
Pierret, Thomas (2013), *Religion and State in Syria: The Sunni Ulama from Coup to Revolution*. Cambridge: Cambridge University Press.
Presidential speech Bashar al-Asad (2013), al-Dunia TV, 1 January.
Presidential speech Bashar al-Asad (2011), Syrian TV, 20 June.
Presidential speech Bashar al-Asad (2011), Syrian TV, 30 March.
Qurna, Ahmad (1986), *Hafez al-Asad: Sane' Tarikh al-Umma wa Bani Majd al-Watan: 1970– 1985*. Aleppo: Dar al-Sharq al-'Arabi.
Seale, Patrick (1988), *Asad of Syria: the Struggle for the Middle East*. London: I.B.Taurus.
Seurat, Michel (1980), 'La Société syrienne contre son Etat', *le Monde Diplomatique*, April.
Seurat, Michel (1989), *L'Etat de barbarie*. Paris: Collection Esprit/Seuil.
Shaam News (2011), www.facebook.com/notes/snn-shaam-news-network/political-security-branch-arrested-dissident-mahmoud-issa/182117951835988.
Syrian Central Bureau of Statistics (n.d.), Reports available at http://www.cbssyr.org [Arabic].
Telegraph (2012), 'Syria's First Lady Asma al-Assad Breaks her Silence', (7 February), http://www.telegraph.co.uk/news/worldnews/middleeast/syria/9065611/Syrias-First-Lady-Asma-al-Assad-breaks-her-silence.html.
UNICEF and the Syrian Central Bureau of Statistics (2006), 'al-Maseh al-'Unqudi Muta'aded al-Mu'ashira,t', www.cbssyr.org/people%20statistics/Final_Report_Syria_ARB.pdf.
United Nations Development Programme Syria (n.d.), www.undp.org.sy/ (accessed September 2008).
US Department of State (2010), 'Human Rights Report–Syria', www.state.gov/j/drl/rls/hrrpt/2010/nea/154473.htm (accessed 20 June 2015).
Van Dam, Nikolaos (1996), *The Struggle for Power in Syria: Politics and Society under Asad and the Ba'th Party*. London and New York: I.B.Tauris.

8

ORGANIZATIONALLY SECULAR

Damascene Islamist movements and the Syrian Uprising

Omar Imady

Two Islamist movements predominantly active in Damascus, the *Kaftariyya* and the *Qubaysiyyat*, are analysed in this chapter. The analysis focuses on the distinct organizational features of these movements and how these have, over time, shaped the way in which they interacted with the Syrian regime and the Syrian Uprising. To further elucidate the findings, the analysis makes use of interviews with the late Muhammad Bashir al-Bani (1911–2008), Kaftaru's right hand and spiritual successor, that are here shared for the first time. The conceptual framework for this analysis is grounded in various scholarly contributions, including Niklas Luhmann's idea of organizations as constituting systems of communication, the distinction first made by Gordon and Babchuck (1959), between expressive and instrumental organizations; and elements of organizational typologies from various disciplines.

After identifying the theoretical contributions that are employed by this analysis, an analytic narrative is provided of the *Kaftariyya* and the *Qubaisiyyat*. The narrative explicates how these movements evolved organizationally, and focuses on the linkage between their organizational features and how they interacted with state and society. The narrative culminates in how these movements responded to the Syrian Uprising.

The essential idea advanced here is that the *Kaftariyya* and the *Qubaysiyyat* are organizationally secular, irrespective of the religious discourse articulated by their leaders and adhered to by their followers. It is this organizational quality that explains why these movements chose to not confront the Asad regime, despite the heavy costs which they incurred as a result of this position, both with members of the opposition, who often brand them as traitors, as well as with loyalists, who suspected their loyalty.

Conceptual framework

Popular classifications of Islamist movements, e.g. *sufi, salfi, jihadi,* not only fail to capture the significant intellectual nuances within these movements, but, far more importantly, they provide very little, in terms of empirical understanding, of how these movements are organized. An alternative conceptual framework is outlined here that identifies the key organizational features that govern how a movement evolves, and interacts with its external environment.

Niklas Luhmann was a German sociologist and an important organizational theorist (Bechmann and Stehr, 2002). Elements of his understanding of the relationship between communication and organizations have significant implications on how movements, in particular those that may be described as popular, are identified. In essence, Luhmann regarded organizations as social systems, which differentiate themselves within society on the basis of 'decision communications' (Seidl and Becker, 2006; Mykkänen and Tampere, 2014). This initial 'decision communication' mutates as it were and moves on to permeate the organization as a whole. The end result is a group of people who have been differentiated organizationally from others by the fact that they identify with a specific 'decision communication'.

This important contribution allows us to understand how popular informal movements are defined on the basis of 'decision communications'. In the context of a large movement, for example, in which followers are more akin to supporters rather than formal members, how does one determine the size of such a movement and who actually belongs to it? Employing Luhmann's theory helps us understand that followers are determined by the extent to which they communicate the initial 'decision communication'. For example, the decision to protest (rather than not to protest) at a specific place (rather than at a different place) will be recommunicated by supporters of a popular movement and will in turn differentiate this specific movement from another, which initiated a different type of 'decision communication'. In short, communication is not merely about conveying ideas, it also plays a critical role in differentiating an organization from its external environment.

The distinction between expressive and instrumental organizations was first introduced by Gordon and Babchuk (Gordon and Babchuk, 1959; Lu, 2008; Hopkins, 2015). Expressive organizations 'express or satisfy the interests of their members in relation to themselves – i.e. they have no public service function outside the immediate sphere of their members' interest' (Robinson and White, 1997, p. 5). Instrumental organizations, on the other hand, 'seek to achieve a condition or change in a limited segment of society' (Robinson and White, 1997).

This distinction among religious organizations, Islamist in particular, is highly significant. Islamist movements that are primarily based on an instrumental organization have frequently proven to be irreconcilable with the idea of a civil society, hostile to state sovereignty, and at times, associated with indiscriminate violence (Imady, 2005b). Islamist movements, on the other hand, that are embodied in organizations that are primarily expressive have historically proven to be easily reconciled with the idea of a civil society, respectful of state authority, however repressed by the state, and against the use of violence to achieve religious or political objectives (Imady, 2005b).

Analytic narrative: The *Kaftariyya*, and the *Qubaysiyyat*

Beginnings

The story of the *Kaftariyya* and the *Qubaysiyyat* first begins with the Naqshbandi Sufi order, in particular the *Khalidi* branch of this order. This branch was named after Khalid al-Baghdadi (1779–1827), a Kurdish Sufi, who spread a reformist version of the Naqshbandi order in areas under Ottoman control (Weismann, 2003). From al-Baghdadi several sub-branches emerged and in Damascus the *Khalidi Naqshbandiya* was destined to play a highly significant role in Syria's recent religious and political history. Sufi orders are headed at any given point in time by a master who was entrusted with this position, explicitly or implicitly, by the previous master of the order. From the information available to us, Isa al-Kurdi (1831–1912), was the master who played a pivotal role in the modernization of the order in Damascus, in adopting a new organizational form, that of the *jam'iyyah* or the association, an essentially secular organization (Weismann, 2003). When some of his disciples decided to create an association to support the Ottoman war effort in the Balkans, al-Kurdi not only supported this action, but also rewrote the articles of this association in a manner that reflected his own vision, which emphasized that the primary objective of this association was neither leadership nor material gain (Weismann, 2003). After his death, one of his primary disciples, Abu al-Khair al-Midani (1876–1961), was one of the founders of the *Rabitat al-'Ulama* (the League of Religious Scholars), which was in essence a religious association formalized in 1949, that sought to articulate the position of religious scholars regarding important social and political issues (al-Humsi, 1991). In addition to al-Midani, the board of administrators of this association included Ahmad Kaftaru (1912–2004) (Böttcher, 2004).

From 1936 onwards, Ahmad Kaftaru had become one of the prominent masters of the *Khalidi Naqshbandi* order in Damascus succeeding his father Amin Kaftaru, who had designated him as his spiritual heir (al-Humsi, 1991). Gathered around him were a number of figures who were previously disciples of his father, but who would now form his inner circle, including Muhammad Bashir al-Bani (1911–2008); Kaftaru's principal deputy and heir (al-Humsi, 1991). In 1949, Kaftaru established *Ma'had al-Ansar*, a religious institute for secondary education, which in 1952 became part of the larger framework of *Jam'iyat al-Ansar al-Khairyyah* (the benevolent association of al-Ansar) (al-Humsi, 1991).

There was nothing innovative at this point regarding what Kaftaru and his predecessors were organizationally pursuing. Indeed, by the late 1940s, Damascene religious scholars had fully internalized the model of the association and had created a large number of them, which, despite their various orientations and intellectual inclinations, were secular organizations through which the *'ulama* sought to advance their educational and social objectives in a manner that was autonomous from the government. It may seem surprising to describe these organizations as secular since they were established by religious scholars and were meant to advance religious objectives. Their secular nature, however, is not related to their membership or to their objectives. It is rather grounded in the fact that the 'association' was an organizational type that, in contrast to traditional organizations, was created under rules that were rooted in the idea of civil society, rather than in religious traditions (on which see more below). Putting aside whatever restrictions or even manipulations, which the government applied on associations, this organization, even when created for the sole purpose of advancing religious principles, was, nevertheless, an organization operating in a 'secular space' and under 'secular rules' (Berger, 2003; Salvatore, 2005; Sahgal, 2013).

Ironically, it is precisely this secular aspect of the association that attracted religious scholars the most. They had by now fully understood that in the modern nation state not only were their traditional organizations not reliable, since their economic basis (the *awqaf*) was no longer safe from government tampering, but also that the government would systematically seek to assert its authority over everything that was formally religious (Skovgaard-Petersen, 2004; Imady, 2005b; Qahf, 2006). In contrast to the realm of the 'formally religious', which fell under the authority of the Ministry of Awqaf, benevolent associations, irrespective of their orientation, fell under the authority of the Ministry of Social Affairs and Labour, and hence enjoyed far more freedom, albeit in a relative sense.

Long before the Ba'th arrived on the scene, the process of taking over formal religious activity by the government had been initiated. The Awqaf Administration, the administrative prelude to the Ministry of Awqaf, was established in 1947 during the reign of Shukri al-Quwatli (Pierret, 2013). Along with it, laws were decreed that effectively transformed the *a'lim* into a government employee, and placed all local muftis under the authority of a grand mufti, a measure which may be described as the culmination of what the Ottomans initiated centuries earlier with their creation of the position of the grand mufti (Makdisi, 1981). Even mosques were not spared since they all became formally owned by the government irrespective of the source of funds used to build them (Badawi, 2011). All of this, along with the measures that would follow served to heighten the awareness of the *'ulama* that the only way around this trap, as it were, was to actively make use of the secular dimension of the nation state; i.e. the realm of civil society. Thus it is not surprising that the *'ulama* would emphasize in the articles of the associations they created their apolitical nature and respect of political authority and existing laws (al-Humsi, 1991). Even those with the strongest political views were very clear about the fact that their objective was only to convince politicians that it was in their interest to adopt policies that were consistent with the religious sensibility of Syrian Muslims (al-Humsi, 1991).

The Kaftariyya and Qubaysiyyat adapt to the new political context

The traditional Damascene *'ulama* became uneasy when Kaftaru and his disciples began to adopt overtly political positions which were not consistent with their views. In 1957, during the parliamentary election of the Damascus District, Kaftaru publicly backed Riyad al-Maliki, the Ba'thist candidate, against Mustafa al-Siba'i from the Muslim Brotherhood (al-Humsi, 1991; Naddaf, 1998).

> Shaikh Ahmad was always searching for a strong man he could have an alliance with. He had the fortitude to realise that things were only going to get worse, that no matter how much the *mashaykh* [religious figures] screamed in their Friday sermons, they simply did not have enough popular support ... When he said we should support al-Maliki, we understood that he was trying to forge an alliance, and of course we all went along with his decision. (Imady, 2005)

Kaftaru's decision to support al-Maliki can be described as the first of a series of 'decision communications' that served to organizationally differentiate the nascent *Kaftariyya* movement. Those who identified themselves with this 'decision communication' and voted for al-Maliki were the first recognizable members of this movement. In 1964, one year after the Ba'th coup, elections of a new grand mufti took place. While, Hasan Habannaka received 17 votes, Kaftaru received 18. Undoubtedly, the alliance Kaftaru had forged in 1957 played an important role in the strong government support he received, which in turn must have translated into convincing at least some of the *'ulama* to support him (Böttcher, 2004).

Another important 'decision communication' which was initiated in the late 1950s was Kaftaru's decision to initiate into the Naqshbandi order al-Shaikha Munira al-Qubaysi, a woman who clearly intended to propagate a specific vision of Islam with Syrian Muslim women (Hamidi, 2006a; Nayyouf, 2007; Islam, 2012; Kalmbach, 2008; Khatib, 2011; Manea, 2011; Buergener, 2013). Her initiation into the order was a 'decision communication' that in essence endorsed the creation of an autonomous female branch of the Naqshbandi order. In the rich, and often fluid, history of Sufism, it isn't easy to find precedents for a Sufi order that is entirely female (Green, 2012).

> Al-Shaikha Shams [as al-Bani would refer to Munira al-Qubaysi for reasons he did not explain] would attend Shaikh Ahmad's lessons in Abu al-Nur [a mosque in Rukn Eddin] with her uncle ... Her brilliance lies in the fact that she did not make Shaikh Ahmad responsible for her actions. She took what she needed from him, and then moved on to create her own *jama'a* [group or movement]. Neither Shaikh Ahmad nor Shaikha Shams would speak about their relationship in public, but privately, Shaikh Ahmad would refer to her as *al-batala* [the heroine]. (al-Bani, 2005)

In 1958, during the unity with Egypt, government control over associations began to tighten with the decree of the current Law No. 93 on Associations. It was in essence a far more restrictive version of Law No. 47 of 1953, which had replaced the earlier Ottoman law (HRW, 2007). Since 1958 there have been many additions and modifications to this law, but in its essential components it remained largely the same (Abd Allah, 2011). The law placed the associations under the administrative authority of the Ministry of Social Affairs and Labour, and gave the minister the right to terminate any association by decree with no recourse to any appeal process. While the formal monitoring of associations was delegated to the Ministry of Social Affairs and Labour, the task of ensuring that these associations did not at any point constitute a political threat was of course the responsibility of the security apparatus, which had the right to terminate an association, suspend a specific activity or arrest members; and none of this had to be pre-approved by the Ministry (HRW, 2007). Nevertheless, associations continued to be active and even grew in number, reaching approximately 1,200 on the eve of the Syrian Uprising (SANA, 2010).

The decade of the 1960s was a transitional phase in the evolution of the *Kaftariyya* and *Qubaysiyyat* movements. The version of the Ba'th in power was a leftist, almost Marxist, version hostile to everything religious, regardless of how it was organizationally manifested (Khatib, 2011). When al-Asad overthrew this faction in 1970, and became Syria's president in March 1971, the patron that Kaftaru had long sought was finally found.

> It was clear to Shaikh Ahmad and to me that Asad [i.e. Hafez al-Asad] was on his way to becoming the president of Syria. Shaikh Ahmad would confide his opinion with other *'ulama* and he would say to them: '... we can either choose to surround him, and become his trusted advisors or we can lose him to those who are hostile to Islam. It doesn't matter what we choose to do, he is going to become the president no matter what.' (al-Bani, 2005)

Kaftaru's decision to support Syria's first Alawite president and to speak of him as a Muslim who should be respected as such constituted another major 'decision communication', which served to further identify his movement. Indeed, the movement would benefit from this for in the 1970s, both the *Kaftariyya* and the *Qubaysiyyat* would significantly expand organizationally. The Abu al-Nur complex, which was built on the spot of the old mosque of Abu al-Nur where Shaikh Amin would give his lessons, was initiated in 1971 and completed in 1974. It housed the headquarters of the Ansar Association, as well as a mosque comprising seven floors (6,000 square feet), which would eventually be utilized for several religious colleges (Böttcher, 2004). During the 1970s, the *Qubaysiyyat* were granted their first permission to establish an elementary/preschool in Damascus. Dar al-Farah constituted the first religious alternative to modern missionary schools such as the Franciscan and Freres schools (Hamidi, 2006a; Salam, 2015; Habash, 2014a).

Kaftaru's third 'decision communication' that was destined to define his movement, as no other decision prior or after it, was the position, which he proclaimed and publically repeated, regarding the insurgency of the Muslim Brotherhood (1979–1982) against the Asad regime (Böttcher, 2004).

> Many would say that Shaikh Ahmad had to support the government because of his position. The truth of the matter is that he would have made this decision even if he were not the Mufti. He regarded what the Ikhwan [the Muslim Brotherhood] was advocating as endangering everything that the

'*ulama* have been trying to achieve since independence. True, the Ikhwan was provoked, but we were all being provoked. Even Shaikh Ahmad was constantly provoked. The *mukhabarat* [security] even went as far as to kill his son Zaher [the official account that he was killed by peasants over a land dispute in 1979]. And when some of his followers attacked the government in front of him, he became very angry and said that this is a personal matter and no one is allowed to interfere in this. (al-Bani, 2005)

Kaftaru in essence was making it clear that when it comes to protecting the organizational setup of the movement, there are no limits for how tolerant the *'ulama* must be. Confrontation with the government would not only risk their associations, it would also mean that they would be barred in the future from engaging in civil society. Since their traditional organizations were already subject to government controls, to be barred from civil society was synonymous with the total marginalization of the *'ulama*, an outcome which Kaftaru was adamant at avoiding at all costs.

It was during the 1980s that the Abu al-Nur complex would begin to host its various educational components, all overseen by the Ansar Association. By the 1990s, the complex hosted a secondary shari'a school for both males and females; an institute to teach Arabic to foreigners; the College for Islamic Da'wah; the College of *usul al-din*; the College of Shari'a and Law; and the College of al-Imam al-Awza'i. Undergraduate and postgraduate degrees would eventually be granted. Concurrently, the *Qubaysiyyat* would establish elementary schools in Damascus and other major cities (Böttcher, 2004). In 1999, a large complex that included a school, an events hall and a catering service was completed in the neighbourhood of Kafr Susih (Hamidi, 2006a; Salam, 2015; Habash, 2014a). The first association established by students of al-Qubaysi, *jam'iyat al-nada al-tanmawiyyah* (the Nada Association for development), was formalized in 2005 (Azurni, 2015; Facebook, 2015). Students of al-Qubaysi succeeded in spreading her vision to Lebanon, Jordan, Kuwait and other countries (Hamidi, 2006a). The same organizational pattern of schools and associations and an events hall for women was replicated in various cities, and in recent years was also spread to some European countries and America (Abdullah, 2012; Grewal, 2013). During this period, sources estimated the number of those women who identified themselves as *Qubaysiyyat* to be over seventy thousand (Schleifer, 2014).

After the death of Hafez al-Asad in June 2000, the *Kaftariyya* and the *Qubaysiyyat* largely continued their activities in the same manner. What had been established and firmly planted was an organizational approach that was adopted by groups that were even hostile to Kaftaru. In a strictly organizational sense, they had all eventually identified with the 'decision communication' of Kaftaru regarding interacting with the Asad regime as a grand patron of their organizational activity. The very *'ulama* who had once regarded Kaftaru's decision to align himself with Hafez al-Asad as blasphemous, were now equally accommodating of his son and doing everything they could to protect their associations (Pierret and Selvik, 2009; Habash, 2013)

Organizational analysis

Prior to moving to the phase of the Syrian Uprising, we pause here to provide an organizational typology of the *Kaftariyya* and *Qubaysiyyat* movements. The typology touches upon the most important elements that should be kept in mind when analysing not only the *Kaftariyya* and *Qubaysiyyat*, but other Islamist movements as well.

At the core of the *Kaftariyya* and *Qubaysiyyat* is the Naqshbandi Sufi order (Stenberg, 1999; Ibrahim, 2012; Takao, 2010). Those who identify with these movements are invited to attend regular religious lessons and participate in 'worship events' that comprise prayer and *zikr* sessions – a meditative activity that is entirely silent. The gratification derived from such identification is purely expressive because these activities have no instrumental quality to them. They are no different from the gratification members of a book club obtain from reading assigned books and attending sessions to discuss them. This is the default organizational quality of both movements. In a hypothetical scenario when everything else is outlawed, such activities continue because, in the final analysis, they can be enacted by individuals in their own homes. During the 1980s, for example, when government tolerance was very low even of religious lessons that addressed individual morality, the *Kaftariyya* and the *Qubaysiyyat* would often resort to long *zikr* sessions; producing, in the process, humorous anecdotes about how members of the security who were attending these sessions felt after three hours of silence in a room with the lights off (al-Bani, 2005). This strong expressive quality explains, to a certain extent, why it is that for those who identify with these movements, what takes place in society (and what does not take place) is not the basis of their self-identification.

The schools, religious colleges and charity services, which these two movements embrace, operate within the framework of associations that may be described as both expressive and instrumental. They are expressive, because once again, those who are involved in these activities obtain gratification from benevolent work. Because these organizations have a specific societal objective, e.g. education, moral upbringing and charity, they may be also described as instrumental. When the instrumental quality is not actualized, however, e.g. a teacher fails to teach his student, a charity project fails to alleviate poverty, those who advanced these activities fall back on the expressive qualities of the organizations, i.e. the mere involvement in such benevolent work.

In terms of membership, organizations can be classified as formal or informal. Members of formal organizations (i) fill out applications to join, which may or may not be accepted; (ii) may be expected to perform certain duties or be required to pay regular contributions; and (iii) can, under certain conditions, be dismissed. Members of informal organizations, on the other hand, are more akin to 'supporters'. They neither formally join nor can they be dismissed, since there is no formal process for such a measure. Some formal organizations may have, in addition to their members, 'supporters' who are not formal members, but who nevertheless play an important role in advancing an organization's objectives.

In the context of Islamist organizations, the failure to capture this distinction often leads to erroneous evaluations. 'Supporters' of an informal organization, for example, may carry out activities that are not consistent with the organization's objective but are nevertheless used by some scholars to evaluate the organization as a whole. What is lost in translation, as it were, is in fact that there are no organizational mechanisms that are available to this informal movement that can either prevent 'supporters' from acting in a manner inconsistent with its objectives, nor are disciplinary or dismissal measures applicable since 'supporters' are not formal members to begin with. Followers 'chose' to identify with a 'decision communication' or not; and there are no organizational mechanisms to reward those who do or to discipline those who do not. In attacking the *Qubaysiyyat*, for example, opposition members often refer to the fact that women who identify themselves with this movement express positions that are in support of the Asad regime (Baladi, 2012). The implication here, though this is not actually stated, is that these women are formal members who are in effect articulating a proclamation on behalf of Munira al-Qubaysi. What is blurred here, again, is the distinction between a supporter and an actual member. Not only are statements by al-Qubaysi herself never used to back up this argument (since no such statements exist), but even statements in support of the regime by the very small group of teachers known to be part of her inner circle are not invoked, again because they do not exist. In addition, even statements by supporters may have, as some reports have suggested, been issued under duress. Nevertheless, the conditions under which statements are made are indeed far less important than the organizational context from which they emerge. This very error can even take place in reverse. After the Uprising, Facebook pages and YouTubes began to appear that spoke of young women 'defecting' from the *Qubaisiyyat* because the movement failed to take on a clear anti-regime position (Facebook, 2011). This is subsequently shared by scholars, without anyone stopping to examine the organizational implications of this event. How does one 'defect' from a movement that has no formal members? Defection implies a previous state of 'organizational' belonging, which simply does not apply here. These women, more accurately, decided to stop identifying with a movement they once supported. Many members of the Ba'th, on the other hand, did proclaim their 'defection' after March 2011 (Al-Jazeera, 2012), and here the term is organizationally sensible and applicable.

Neither the *Kaftarriyya* nor the *Qubaysiyyat* have what can be described as formal membership. The teachers at the Qubaysi schools dress in the style distinctive of the *Qubaysiyyat*, but are in the final analysis employees. Women who dress in this manner are found in many other institutions and a significant number are government bureaucrats. Indeed, this style of dress, with differences difficult to detect, was adopted by many religious women in Damascus who do not identify themselves as *Qubaysiyyat*, including female followers of the *Kaftarriyya* (Chagas, 2013). Likewise, teachers and students at the Kaftari schools and religious colleges may or may not be disciples of Kaftaru. In either case, the only individuals that can be termed formal members are those who held positions in either the Ansar Association or the much later Nada Association. Initiation into the Naqshbandi order by either

Kaftaru or al-Qubaysi transformed the individual into a 'disciple', but not into a 'formal member'. Hence, the vast majority of those who identified with either movement are more accurately described as supporters rather than members.

Leadership of an organization is grounded in either the charismatic nature of a specific leader or in the organizational authority embedded in a specific administrative position. Charismatic leadership appears far more capable of controlling the behaviour of 'supporters' (though clearly not all), whereas administrative leadership appears more likely to control formal members. Charismatic leadership generally produces a centralized, if informal, organizational structure while formal associations are associated with administrative leadership.

Islamist organizations often provide fascinating examples of the tension between these two forms of structure. Masters of Sufi orders, who became involved in political parties, had significant difficulty with the idea that they simply cannot expect members of a political party to act like obedient disciples of a Sufi order (Imady, 2005b). Both Kaftaru and al-Qubaysi, charismatic leaders in the purest sense, avoided this trap by distancing themselves from instrumental organizations. At most, they may choose to support a candidate to the parliament, or a specific official or even an administrator of a school, but these individuals, in the end, do not act on behalf of Kaftaru or al-Qubaysi, nor do they receive direct instructions from them. If they become influential, they can help advance the objectives of the movement, but if they fall, they fall alone.

Finally, organizations can be further classified on the basis of whether or not they operate within the formal legal structure of civil society. Secular organizations are (i) created in accordance with established laws, regardless of how restrictive they may be, and are thus formally registered; (ii) provide regular disclosures of finances; and (iii) pursue objectives which may seek to influence (but never to overtake or substitute for) the government (Sider and Unruh, 2004).

Islamist movements that fulfil these qualifications are found throughout the Muslim world (Schneier, 2015). The critical test lies in what happens when such organizations are faced with laws that effectively curb most, if not all of their activities. Are they willing to respect such laws, regardless of how unfair they seem? Do they wait for a time when such laws change, or perhaps find innovative ways to go around them? Or, do they, under such circumstances, choose to work outside the realm of what is legally permissible? These are the questions that differentiate between organizations that are genuinely secular and those that are willing, under certain circumstances, to operate in a manner that is contrary to these principles. Indeed, the *Kaftraiyya* and the *Qubaisiyyat* have unequivocally demonstrated that when it comes to their organizational nature, they are thoroughly secular.

Prelude to the Uprising: Attacking the organizational setup of the 'Ulama

Even before Kaftaru died in 2004, important events took place that started to undermine the intricate balance between state and religion in Syria. The US invasion of Iraq in 2003 was an event that not only had a catastrophic impact on Iraq, but it also had very serious consequences on the region as well. The *'ulama* of Damascus were not unaware of how easily this could jeopardize the balance they had strived so hard to reach. In the words of Bashir al-Bani:

> They [members of the Asad regime] were not this scared in a very long time. That wasn't good. They do not act rationally when they are scared. (al-Bani, 2005)

Rational or not, the Asad regime's response to the American invasion was to encourage and facilitate the creation of Islamist organizations in Iraq that opposed with violence everything the US was trying to achieve there. Suddenly, and in mosques across Syria, Imams delivered sermons that encouraged fighting the American invaders (Habash, 2014b). The very type of Islamist organizations that were crushed by the regime in the 1980s were now being encouraged by the regime to resurface to be utilized to deter the US from thinking about extending its intervention to Syria. So strong was the pressure on the *'ulama* to support the government's stand on events in Iraq that Kaftaru was made to issue a *fatwa* supporting suicide bombing in Iraq in 2003 (Terzieff, 2003). Privately, Bashir al-Bani would elaborate:

> They come to us with exactly what they want us to say written down. Sometimes it is even in poor Arabic. They do not even like it when we attempt to correct the style out of fear that we may be trying to water down the message they want us to convey. Shaikh Ahmad would never condone the idea of suicide bombings, even those that take place in Palestine, let alone those that take place in Iraq. And those who do not understand how political *fatwas* are issued in Syria should come here and visit and see for themselves. (al-Bani, 2003)

Though al-Bani's words were said in private, the supporters of the *Kaftariyya* fully understood that Kaftaru is not asking them to partake in such activity. Indeed, there is no documentation of supporters of the *Kaftariyya* participating in what was termed the *jihad* in Iraq. Years later, his son Salah would even vehemently deny that members of his father's movement were involved in what was taking place in Iraq (Mardini, 2009).

Concurrently, Bashar al-Asad made the decision to allow the rehabilitation of what is known as Jama'at Zayd, which was founded by Abd al-Karim al-Rifai (1901–1973) in the early twentieth century (Al-Khatib, 2014). In the 1980s, the Zayd movement did not identify with the 'decision communication' of Kaftaru to not join the Muslim Brotherhood insurgency, and in fact, many of its members fought with the Muslim Brotherhood. Osama al-Rifai, the eldest son of Abd Karim al-Rifai and his successor, left the country and settled in Saudi Arabia. He was allowed back in the mid-1990s, seemingly as a calculated move by Hafez al-Asad to harness popular support to the future presidency of his son (Al-Khatib, 2014). In 2002, Bashar al-Asad paid an unprecedented visit to Osama al-Rifai, which in turn reactivated the organizational activity of the movement in the realms of religious education, charity and social services (Al-Khatib, 2014). The irony here is that no such visit was paid to the Grand Mufti of Syria who had forged an alliance with the Asad regime since 1970. Clearly, Kaftaru was regarded in the same manner as many of the old pillars of the regime were regarded by the president, i.e. as officials who had fulfilled their functions, and whose loyalty could be assumed. They are tolerated out of respect for what they had undertaken in the past, but in so far as the Syria that the new president had in mind, they not only had no role to serve, they may even have proved to be an obstacle.

In September 2004, Kaftaru died and the two functions he once carried out pertaining to the *Kaftariyya* movement were now separated. The administration of the Abu al-Nur complex, which entails supervision over al-Ansar Association as well as all the other religious institutes hosted in the Abu al-Nur complex, was delegated to his son Salah Kaftaru (NoSawot, 2004). The successorship of the Sufi order, on the other hand, went to his right hand (and only surviving disciple of Amin Kaftaru) Bashir al-Bani (Imady, 2005a). Salah was infamous for his harsh temperament and for the use of inappropriate language during his fits of anger, a sensibility which alienated many of the *'ulama* who taught at the institutes of Abu al-Nur, as well as the administrators who worked with him (Elamata, 2006). At this time, Salah was fortunate because the Minister of Awqaf, Muhammad Ziyad al-Ayyubi, who regarded himself as a disciple of Ahmad Kaftaru, would do everything he could to maintain a cordial relationship with Salah. Indeed, al-Ayyubi was friendly to both the *Kaftariyya* and the *Qubaysiyyat* and is credited with convincing the authorities to allow the *Qubaysiyyat* to give their lessons in mosques rather than in homes (Hamidi, 2006a). Holding religious lessons at homes was in fact forbidden by the security; however, the Qubaysi teachers would disguise their events as celebrations of various types and social gatherings.

None of this, however – not the American invasion of Iraq and the Islamist instrumental organizations it unleashed, not the reactivation of the Zayd movement – were as significant for the future of state–religious relations as the government's decision to allow the Ministry of Awqaf to undermine an equation between the state and the *'ulama* that had been in place for nearly a century (since the 1909 Ottoman Law of Associations). The story begins with Law No. 32 of July 2002. All Syrian children must undergo a mandatory Basic Educational Cycle, which merges the primary and preparatory previous cycles into a unified nine-year cycle (al-Ayyubi, 2006; IISS, 2008; Mansur, 2012). Much of this can be seen as an attempt to rationalize the educational system. However, the direct implication of this law on religious education was that *shar'i* or religious schools were no longer permitted to accept pupils who had not completed this mandatory cycle. What this amounted to in the eyes of religious scholars was the systematic 'drying up' of potential new students that guaranteed the sustainability of these religious schools. Since most, if not all of these schools, were administered by associations in which the *'ulama* were active, this move was further seen as infringing on a realm of civil society that the state had so far respected. Though the law was issued in 2002, its actual implementation in a systematic manner did not begin until a few years later when, concurrently, the activity of many new *hawzat* or *shi'i* religious schools began to be noticed. This lethal combination, reducing the authority of *sunni* religious schools while allowing more authority to *shi'i* equivalents, was too much for the *'ulama* of Damascus to accept. On 30 June 2006, 39 religious scholars, including al-Buti, Osama al-Rifai, Salah Kaftaru, Mouaz al-Khatib and Hisham al-Burhani, signed a petition addressed to the president. The petition clearly articulated the sense of anger that the *'ulama* felt, not only because of the implications of this new law on their schools, but also because of the different treatment which the *shi'i hawzat* were receiving (Salem, 2006). The petition went on to propose a compromise solution of teaching religious subjects alongside the mandatory curriculum at the *shar'i* schools. Asad met with a delegation of the signatories and it was agreed to postpone the implementation of the decree (Al-Ayyubi, 2006). What was not addressed, however, during this meeting was the far more significant tampering with the autonomy of associations that the Ministry of Awqaf was undertaking. Less than a month later, the Minister of Awqaf dismissed Osama al-Khani, one of the signatories and the Director of the Department of Religious Education, from his position, and only five months later al-Ayyubi himself would be dismissed because of alleged embezzlement charges (IISS, 2008). His deputy, Muhammad Abd al-Sattar al-Sayyid, became the new Minister of Awqaf. Al-Sayyid was the son of a previous Minister of Awqaf who held his position in the 1970s and who was known for his antagonistic relationship with Ahmad Kaftaru. Al-Bani who was not one of the signatories to the petition, was very anxious about what all of this would entail. Only seven months before he died, he shared his private fears regarding the regime's reaction to the petition:

> None of this was wise. This regime cannot tolerate such a move. It is far too arrogant to accept to be challenged in this way. It may look like they [the *'ulama*] got what they wanted, but in fact what they have done is unleash something much worse. This new minister [al-Sayyid] comes with a mandate of revenge. (al-Bani, 2008)

In October 2008, the heads of several associations were summoned to the Ministry of Social Affairs and Labour to be notified of a decision that had to be implemented immediately (al-Najjar, 2008). In essence, all religious figures had to resign from the administrative boards of associations. The very associations which were created by religious figures in the late twentieth century now had to be 'cleansed' from even those who simply had a degree in religious sciences. The event used to justify this move, a car bombing in Damascus, allegedly carried out by a group that included a graduate from one of the religious colleges in Damascus, al-Fath (Thawara, 2008), was clearly nothing more than an excuse since the government was well aware that none of these religious figures were in any way involved in this act. Nor was this related to the organizations that the government had encouraged to fight in Iraq and subsequently turned against, since the activities of these benevolent associations was, again, entirely unrelated. From the administrative board of the Ansar Association the following were ousted: Salah Kaftaru, Bassam Ajak, Abd al-Salam Rajeh and Rajb Deeb (the current master of the order). Qubaiysi female teachers were summoned to the Ministry and were informed that they must all renew their security clearances to continue to give lessons (al-Najjar, 2008).

In June 2009, Salah Kaftaru was arrested on charges of embezzlement, and only two months earlier his brother, Mahmud, had been detained for 13 days (U.S. Department of State, 2010). Though he was replaced by a young disciple of Ahmad Kaftaru, Sharif al-Sawaf, and his removal was clearly a relief to the administrators who objected to his style of management, the void he left at the complex was instantly filled by the heavy handed control imposed by the Ministry of Awqaf. The culmination of these measures was no doubt Decree No. 48, issued only 19 days after the beginning of the Syrian Uprising, 4 April 2011 (Marasim wa-Qawanin, 2011). The Decree proclaimed the establishment of al-Sham Higher Institute for Religious Sciences (Ma'had al-Sham al-'Ali li-l-'Ulum al-Shar'iyya). The Decree effectively nationalized three religious colleges, once funded and administered by associations presided over by religious scholars. Ironically, news of this decree was first announced by al-Buti as though it were a significant achievement, even a compromise by the regime (Pierret, 2013).

In the Uprising

As the ruthless tactics of the regime in dealing with protestors became apparent, many notable religious scholars were quick to condemn the regime and, in time, eventually sided outright with the opposition. Those who did not follow this path chose to be silent even as the government demanded from them outright condemnation of the protests. Very few, notably, prominent Damascus Shaykh, Muhammed Said Ramadan al-Buti, were willing to adopt the government's line, and even as al-Buti condemned the protestors he repeatedly made reference to the errors of those in positions of authority, which had led the country to this tragic fate. Unlike Kaftaru, however, whose 'decision communication' in 1979 rallied thousands of his supporters to identify with his position, al-Buti had no *jama'a* or movement of his own, though of course he did have many who respected him as a scholarly authority. Once he sided with the government, however, many of those who looked up to him felt confused and alienated by his position. Perhaps al-Buti regarded himself as re-enacting what Kaftaru had done with the Muslim Brotherhood insurgency. But not only did he not have the popular organized support that Kaftaru had, but he was also dealing with a Damascus that was very different than that of 1979.

In a sense, the *'ulama* of Damascus were at their weakest point organizationally since the modern nation state had undermined their traditional organizations a century earlier. Not only did they lack a charismatic figure whom they regarded as their leader or even their representative, they were evicted from the administrative boards of their associations and informed that the religious schools and colleges that they had worked for decades to establish were now under the authority of their nemesis, the Ministry of Awqaf. With all his severe intolerance for political dissent, Hafez al-Asad had proved far more tolerant of the organizational activity of religious scholars than his son. His tolerance was not grounded in a genuine appreciation of civil society, but rather it was seen by him as a necessary compromise. To provide his regime with real support, religious scholars had to be organizationally empowered. Attacking their organizational setup is not only to make them deeply resentful and uncooperative, but more important, is to leave them unable to support the government even if they choose to do so since their primary medium of mobilization (their autonomous organizations) has been undermined.

Over the last four years, the influence and organizational activity of the *Kaftariyya* and *Qubaysiyyat* have receded to Damascus. Most of the schools that were founded by their members outside Damascus have either been closed down or destroyed. In Damascus, the complex of Abu al-Nur is now home to a branch of al-Sham Higher Institute, which is managed and supervised by the Ministry of Awqaf. The Sufi order component of the *Kaftariyya* is headed by Rajab Deeb, who is among those scholars who chose silence in regard to his position from the Syrian Uprising, as did many of the elder disciples of Kaftaru who are still alive. Though Deeb is at times presented as explicitly pro-regime, none of his public lessons, which are published on YouTube, make any statements in favour of the regime or condemn the Uprising (Deeb, 2012). Kafaru's son-in-law and prominent disciple, Muhammad Habash (Heck, 2004), who was a member of parliament when the Syrian Uprising began, tried in vain (along with vice president Farouk al-Shara') to mediate some type of national dialogue and to convince those officials he had contact with of the futility of the 'security option'. Convinced that the regime had no intention to change its course, Habash defected with his wife and resides now in the UAE (Owais, 2012).

The *Qubaysiyyat*, on the other hand, continue to manage their schools in Damascus, none of which are *shar'i* schools. They are simply schools in which women who identify themselves as followers of this movement serve as teachers. Nevertheless, control and supervision by the Ministry of Education on these schools is reported to be at its highest since they were established in the late 1970s. Like Rajab Deeb, al-Qubaysi opted for public silence; a path which all members of her inner circle adopted as well (Abu Rumman, 2013b). Government harassment, which the *Qubaysiyyat* have known since the 1970s, became far more intrusive and systematic. On a regular basis, and especially during the early phase of the Uprising, buses would arrive at the schools of the *Qubaysiyyat* with instructions for the teachers to be transported to various events in Damascus. Pictures of these events (showing the *Qubaysiyyat* in their distinctive style of dress) would be deliberately posted by media outlets loyal to the regime, and then, as though by mutual agreement, reposted by opposition outlets so as to attack the *Qubaysiyyat* for their alleged loyalist stand. In December 2012, one of these teachers described how she found herself suddenly in the presidential palace. The president arrived, gave the women a lecture in the presence of the Minister of Awqaf and then left. As usual, many pictures were taken and later posted of the event (Baladi, 2012).

In May 2013, one of the members of Qubaysi's inner circle of teachers, Fatima al-Khabaz, was shot dead at a government check point, allegedly because the car failed to stop fast enough (Swied, 2013). Another member of the inner circle, Amira Jibril, is often invoked by the opposition to make the point that the *Qubaysiyyat* are pro-regime because she is the sister of the Palestinian leader Ahmad Jibril who is closely aligned with the regime (Hamidi, 2006b; Zain, 2014). As noted earlier, however, neither Amira Jibril nor any other member of the inner circle had made any public (or private but documented) position that can be described in any manner as pro-regime, or pro-opposition for that matter. In March 2014, Salma Ayyash, a woman who dresses in the style of the *Qubaysiyyat*, was appointed as a Deputy Minister of Awqaf, a move which supporters and opposition alike used as evidence to the fact that the *Qubaysiyyat* are with the regime. Ayyash was neither a member of Qubaysi's inner circle or even a minor teacher in the movement. Like many other women who identify themselves with the movement, she happened to hold a position at the Ministry and was subsequently promoted. Doubtless, the regime did this deliberately as part of its adamant attempt to present itself as being supported by large segments of Damascene society; and, doubtless, al-Qubaysi fully understands this and deliberately chooses not to publicly contradict it. In many ways, all the basic elements, i.e. silence, excessive government control and the retreat to the Sufi order, characterize the *Qubaysiyyat* since 2011 as much as they characterize the *Kaftariyya*. In both cases, their followers are willing to cooperate with the government, as with the case of al-Sawaf at the Abu al-Nur complex, or Salma Ayyash at the Ministry of Awqaf.

The story of the *Kaftariyya* and the *Qubaysiyyat* is essentially the story of the rise and fall of an organizational setup in which the *'ulama* utilized the benevolent association to advance their objectives and to become organizationally empowered. By 2011, as the regime placed the final touches that were meant to undermine the existing setup of how the state interacted with the *'ulama*, the Syrian Uprising cascaded, and in a matter of four months became an event that would henceforth redefine everything Syrians had so far taken for granted. In these critical four months, from March until 31 July 2011, when the Syrian army marched into Hama, the event was still possibly reversible. The regime, however, opted for the now infamous 'security solution', not only because it felt that any other path would make it seem weak, and thus vulnerable, but also because there was no one within the realm of civil society, religious scholar or otherwise, who had the charismatic authority and a large popular movement that could effectively influence the thousands of young Syrians who flooded out of the mosques on Fridays to protest. After all, who was there to reach some sort of deal with the protestors? Ahmad Hassun, the Grand Mufti, was not only from Aleppo (the first non-Damascene to ever hold this office), but he had no popular following of any significance (Habash, 2013). Unlike his predecessors, he was appointed by decrees rather than by election by his peers, precisely because he had no chance of being elected (Pierret, 2013). Nor was the Zayd movement in which the regime had invested so much energy, of any help either. The instrumental aspect of this movement was far too strong to tolerate what the regime was doing, and once again, they chose exile rather than finding a way, however subdued, to tolerate the government's actions (Al-Khatib, 2014).

The regime turned to al-Buti, marginalized for years after Bashar al-Asad first took office (IISS, 2008), who was unable to even restrain the young men who attended his Friday sermon at the Omayyad mosque (Al-Buti, 2011). They not only interrupted him, but they stormed out of the mosque to protest. Furthermore, the most the regime could obtain from those with various levels of charismatic authority and popular movements, e.g. the *Kaftariyya* and the *Qubaysiyyat* was silence, and how different was the silence of Rajab Deeb and Munira al-Qubaysi from the 'decision communication' repeatedly proclaimed by Kaftaru during the Muslim Brotherhood insurgency. On this level, all of this can be explained by an exaggerated sense of self-confidence on the part of the regime. What Hafez al-Asad tolerated, even at times encouraged, his son would undermine and marginalize, until in 2010, even the Ramadan banquet Syrian presidents had held for the '*ulama* since independence was cancelled (Abu Zaid, 2010).

The significance of what remained in Damascus, the *Kaftariyya* and the *Qubaysiyyat*, in particular, lies not in what these movements are still capable of achieving, given the numerous restrictions they operate under, but rather in just how committed they have proven themselves to the expressive and in turn to the secular nature of their organizational activity. In a sense, the following principle summarizes their approach: what cannot be done legally will not be pursued; and when the government becomes overly repressive, we will withdraw into the realm of the Sufi order. In the rebuilding of Syria, which is bound to take place, the presence of Islamist movements that are this committed to what is termed here 'organizational secularism' will not only serve to balance those movements that are indifferent to this type of approach, but could also constitute the foundation on which a new civil society is established (Mamouri, 2015; Moubayed, 2015). Until some form of resolution of the conflict is reached, however, the primary challenge faced by both the *Kaftariyya* and the *Qubaysiyyat* is not to stay active, since this art has already been mastered, but rather to stay relevant.

Bibliography

Abd Allah, Abd al-Rahman (2011), Qanun al-Jam'iyyat (Law of Associations), *Muntada Muhami Suriyyah*. Available at: www.damascusbar.org/AlMuntada/showthread.php?t=20129 [Accessed 1 December 2016].

Abdullah, W.B. (2012), Saving Superwoman … and I'll add Superman, too. *The Sandal*. Available at: https://wbabdullah.wordpress.com/2012/07/21/saving-superwoman-and-ill-add-superman-too/ [Accessed 1 December 2016].

Abu Rumman, M.S. (2013a), *Islamists, Religion and the Revolution in Syria.* Amman: Friedrich-Ebert-Stiftung, FES Jordan & Iraq / FES Syria. Available at: http://library.fes.de/pdf-files/bueros/amman/10236.pdf [Accessed 2 November 2016].

Abu Rumman, Muhammad (2013b), Syrian Sufis Divided as Salafist Influence Grows, al-Monitor. Available at: www.al-monitor.com/pulse/originals/2013/10/syria-sufi-salafi-war-islam.html [Accessed 2 November 2015].

Abu Zaid, Nasir (2010), Limadha lam yad'u al-ra'is al-suri 'ulama' suriyyah lil-iftar al-revolution.mind11ramadani wa-khafaya ukhura (Why didn't the Syrian president invite the religious scholar of Syria to the Ramadan banquet and other secrets). *Thawrtalsoryienalahrar.* Available at: http://thawrtalsoryienalahrar.blogspot.co.uk/2010_09_12_archive.html [Accessed 1 December 2016].

Al-Ayyubi, Ahmad (2006), Ghazu Irani li-Surriyah yahmihi al-Asad (An Iranian Conquest of Syria protected by al-Asad). *Haqeeqa.* Available at: www.haqeeqa.net/Subject.aspx?id=104 [Accessed 1 December 2016].

Azurni, Qusay (2015), Shaqiqtan Fi-Suriyyah Tu'biran 'An "Irfanihma Li-Tafani Waldita-huma Fi-Taribiyatuhma (Two Sisters Express Their Gratitude for Their Mother's Selfless Upbringing). UNHCR. Available at: www.unhcr-arabic.org/557d554f6.html [Accessed 1 December 2016].

Badawi, Hayat Mutwali (2011), Ahlam wa-Ijtihadat Qada'iyyah Suriyyah. *Muhamat Net.* Available at: www.mohamah.net/answer/26357/أحكام-و-إجتهادات-قضائية-سورية [Accessed 1 December 2016].

Bechmann, G. and Stehr, N. (2002), The Legacy of Niklas Luhmann. *Society,* 39: 2, 67–75.

Berger, J. (2003), Religious Nongovernmental Organizations: An Exploratory Analysis. *Voluntas: International Journal of Voluntary and Nonprofit Organizations,* 14: 1, 15–39. Available at: www.global.ucsb.edu/orfaleacenter/luce/luce08/documents/Harvard%20Summary%20paper.pdf [Accessed 2 November 2015].

Böttcher, A. (2004), 'Official Islam, Transnational Islamic Networks, and Regional Politics: The Case of Syria'. In *The Middle East and Palestine: Global Politics and Regional Conflict,* edited by Dietrich Jung, 125–150. New York: Palgrave MacMillan.

Buergener, E. (2013), Becoming a true Muslim: Syrian women's journey to devoutness. PhD Thesis, University of Birmingham.

Al-Buti, Muhammad Ramadan (2011), Muzaharat Jami' al-Amwi (Demonstrations of the Ummayad Mosque). *muhammedsh 78.* Available at: https://www.youtube.com/watch?v=M-E7QnLRr_o [Accessed 1 December 2015].

Chagas, G.F. (2013), 'Female Sufis in Syria: Charismatic Authority and Bureaucratic Structure'. In *The Anthropology of Religious Charisma: Ecstasies and Institutions,* edited by C. Lindholm, 81–200, New York: Palgrave Macmillan.

Deeb, Sheikh Rajab (2012), Official Page of Sheikh Rajab Deeb. Available at: https://www.youtube.com/user/sheikhrajabdeeb [Accessed 2 November 2015].

Elamata (2006), Kaftaru yuhadid al-Jabban wa-Deeb al-ab wa-alibn wa-al-Sabbagh wa-al-Ayyubi (Kaftaru threatens al-Jabban and al-Deeb (father & son) and al-Sabbagh and al-Ayyubi), Elamata. Available at: http://elamata.blogspot.co.uk [Accessed 1 December 2016].

Enab Baladi (2012), Al-Qubaysiyyat: shukuk wa-rudud hawla al-'ilaqah ma' nizam al-asad (The Qubaisiyyat: Doubts & Reponses Concerning the Relationship of this Group with the Asad Regime), Al-Mundasah. Available at: http://the-syrian.com/archives/91963 [Accessed 1 December 2016].

Facebook (2011), Hara'ir al-thawara al-munshaqat 'an al-qubaisiyyat (The free women of the revolution who have defected from the Qubaisiyyat). Revolutionmind2011. Available at: https://ar-ar.facebook.com/women.splition.from.Qubaisiate/info/?tab=page_info [Accessed 1 December 2016].

Facebook (2015), Al Nada Charity. n.p., 2015. Web. 21 December 2015.
Gordon, C.W. and Babchuk, N. (1959), A Typology of Voluntary Associations. *American Sociological Review*, 22–29. [Online]. Available at: www.jstor.org/stable/2089579?seq=1#page_scan_tab_contents [Accessed 2 November 2015].
Green, N. (2012), *Sufism: A Global History*. New York: John Wiley & Sons.
Grewal, Z. (2013), *Islam is a Foreign Country: American Muslims and the Global Crisis of Authority*. New York: New York University Press.
Habash, Muhammad (2013), Sina'at al-fatwa li-maslahat hizb al-ba'th (The Manufacturing of Fatwas for the benefit of the Baath). Al-Muthaqaf al-Jadid. Available at: http://al-muthaqaf.net/index/news.php?action=show&id=268 [Accessed 2 November 2015].
Habash, Muhammad (2014a), Al-Qubayssiyyat – al-malf al-majuhul (The Qubaysiyyat – the Unknown File). All4Syria. Available at: http://all4syria.info/Archive/151719 [Accessed 2 November 2015].
Habash, Muhammad (2014b), Al-Tariq ila-da'ish (The Path to Daish). All4Syria. Available at: http://all4syria.info/Archive/171912 [Accessed 2 November 2015].
Hamidi, Ibrahim (2006a), Yalbisna al-hijab al-kuhli wa-yamlikna shabakat tadris wa-nufudh wasi'ah (They wear navy blue headscarves, and possess a wide network of education and influence). *Al-Hayat*. Available at: http://daharchives.alhayat.com/issue_archive/Hayat%20INT/2006/50/3 -يرتدين-الحجاب-الكحلي-ويملكن-شبكة-تدريس-ونفوذ-واسعة-آنسات-القبيسيات-يباشرن في-سورية-انخراط-النساء-في-الدعوة.html [Accessed 1 December 2016].
Hamidi, Ibrahim (2006b), Shaqiqat Ahmad Jibril fi-halaqat al-anisah Munira al-Qubaysi (The Sister of Ahmad Jibril attends the lessons of Munira al-Qubaysi). *Al-Hayat*. Available at: http://daharchives.alhayat.com/issue_archive/Hayat%20INT/2006/50/3 شقيقة-أحمد-جبريل-في-حلقات-الآنسة-منيرة-القبيسي-دمشق-تسمح-لـ-القبيسيات-بنشاط-علني.html [Accessed 1 December 2016].
Heck, Paul L. (2004), Religious Renewal in Syria: The Case of Muhammad al-Habash. *Islam and Christian–Muslim Relations*, 15: 2, 185–207. Available at: www.tandfonline.com/doi/abs/10.1080/0959641042000192792?journalCode=cicm20 [Accessed 2 November 2015].
Hopkins, J. (2015), *Knowledge, Networks and Policy: Regional Studies in Postwar Britain and Beyond*. London: Routledge.
Human Rights Watch (HRW) (2007), No Room to Breathe: State Repression of Human Rights Activism in Syria. *Syria*, 19 (6E). Available at: https://www.hrw.org/reports/2007/syria1007/syria1007web.pdf [Accessed 1 December 2016].
al-Humsi, Muhammad Hasan (1991), *Al-Du–at wa-l-Da–wa al-Islamiyya al-Mu–asira al-Muntaliqa min Masajid Dimashq* (Preachers and Contemporary Islamic Call Stemming from Damascus's Mosques), 2 vols. Damascus: Dar al-Rashid.
Ibrahim, Arwa (2012), Sufism and Modernity: A Comparative Study of Contemporary Social Movements, Turkey, Syria and Egypt. Available at: www.thedeeninstitute.com/mulitimedia/articles/85-sufism-and-modernity-a-comparative-study-of-contemporary-social-movements-in-turkey-syria-and-egypt.html [Accessed 2 November 2015].
IISS (2008), *Al-Ba'th al-shi'i* (The Shi'i Ba'th). (No place of publication): Al-Ma'had al-Dawli Lil-Dirasat al-Suriyyah.
Imady, Omar (2003), Muhammad Bashir al-Bani – Private Comments. 2003. In person.
Imady, Omar (2005), Muhammad Bashir al-Bani – Biographical Interview for the Introduction of Rasa'il al-Bashir, in person.
Imady, Omar (2005a), Rasail al-Bashir (Letter of al-Bashir). Damascus: Dar Tlas.
Imady, Omar (2005b), *The Rise and Fall of Muslim Civil Society*. Salinas, CA: MSI Press.
Imady, Omar (2008), Muhammad Bashir al-Bani – Private Comments. In person.
Islam, Sarah (2012), 'The Qubaysiyyat: The Growth of an International Muslim Women's Revivalist Movement from Syria (1960–2008)'. In *Women, Leadership, and Mosques:*

Changes in Contemporary Islamic Authority, edited by M. Bano and H. Kalmbach, 161–183. Leiden: Brill.

Ismail, Salam (2015), Jama'at al-Akhawat al-Qubaysiyyat (A Study on the Qubaysi Sisters). Barq. Available at: www.all4syria.info/wp-content/uploads/2015/08/جماعة-الاخوات-القبيسيات.pdf [Accessed 1 December 2016].

Al-Jazeera (2012), Khitab lil-Asad wa-al-mu'aradah tad'u lil-tadwil (Al-Asad delivers a speech and the opposition calls for the internationalization of the crisis). Jazeera.net. Available at: www.aljazeera.net/home/print/f6451603-4dff-4ca1-9c10-122741d17432/a520aa42-1ef8-453c-836e-32b12b3f67ac [Accessed 1 December 2016].

Kalmbach, H. (2008), Social and Religious Change in Damascus: One Case of Female Islamic Religious Authority. *British Journal of Middle Eastern Studies*, 35: 1, 37–57. [Online]. Available at: http://hilarykalmbach.com/Files/Kalmbach-SocialandReligiousChangeinDamascus-AuthorPost-Print.pdf [Accessed 2 November 2015].

Khatib, L. (2011), *Islamic Revivalism in Syria: The Rise and Fall of Ba'thist Secularism*. London: Routledge.

Lu, W. (2008), Exploring instrumental and expressive dimensions: Adapted origin of nonprofit and voluntary organizations. PhD Thesis, Florida State University, Tallahassee. Available at: http://diginole.lib.fsu.edu/etd/1021/ [Accessed 2 November 2015].

Makdisi, G. (1981), *The Rise of Colleges: Institutions of Learning in Islam and the West*. New York: Columbia University Press.

Mamouri, A. (2015), How Sufism could Balance Salafism. *Al-Monitor: the Pulse of the Middle East*, 16 January. Available at: www.al-monitor.com/pulse/originals/2015/01/islam-sufism-salafism-ties-extremism-reform.html# [Accessed 2 November 2015].

Manea, E. (2011), *The Arab State and Women's Rights: The Trap of Authoritarian Governance*. London: Routledge.

Mansur, Muhammad (2012), Al-Madaris al-dinyyah: Mirjal al-thawarah al-ladhi kana yaghli (Religious Schools – the jar of the revolution which was boiling). Orient Net. Available at: www.orient-news.net/ar/news_show/594 [Accessed 2 November 2015].

Marasim wa-Qawanin (2011), al-Marsum al-Tashri'I Raqm 48 (Legislative Decress Number 48). PNF. Available at: http://pnf.org.sy/?page=show_det&category_id=287&id=513&lang=ar&lang=ar [Accessed 2 November 2015].

Mardini, Bahiyyah (2009), Kaftaru li–ilaf – alsufiyyun lam wa-lan-yadhahbu lil-jihad fi-al-iraq (Kaftaru to Ilaf: The Sufis have not and will not go to Jihad in Iraq). Ilaf. Available at: http://elaph.com/Web/AkhbarKhasa/2009/6/453308.htm [Accessed 1 December 2016].

Moubayed, Sami (2015), Damascene Sufism: The Antidote to ISIS. *Huffington Post*. Available at: www.huffingtonpost.com/sami-moubayed/damascene-sufism-the-anti_b_8641630.html [Accessed 2 December 2015].

Mu'taz Al-Khatib (2014), Al-Tanafus 'ala-din wa-al-siyassah fi-suriyyah (Competing over Religion and Politics in Syria). All4Syria. Available at: www.all4syria.info/Archive/146118 [Accessed 2 November 2015].

Mykkänen, M. and Tampere, K. (2014), Organizational Decision Making: The Luhmannian Decision Communication Perspective. *Journal of Business Studies Quarterly*, 5: 4, 131–146.

Naddaf, Imad (1998), Al-Shuyu'I wa-al-shaikh-fi-Suriyyah: Sadaqah min-naw' khas (The Communist and the Shaikh in Syria: A Special Type of Frienship). *Al-Hayat*. Available at: http://daharchives.alhayat.com/issue_archive/Hayat%20INT/1998/2/5/-الشيوعي-والشيخ-في-سورية-صداقة-من-نوع-خاص.html [Accessed 1 December 2016].

al-Najjar, Ghassan (2008), Tahdhir min tadakhul al-dawlah (A warning from Government intervention), Rabitat Udaba' al-Sham. Available at: www.odabasham.net/ساحة-حرة/تحذير-من-تدخّل-الدولة-74341 [Accessed 1 December 2016].

Nayyouf, Hayyan (2007), Al-Shaikh Kaftaru yathadath 'an khafayah 'alam al-Qubaisiyyat fi-Suriyyah (Shaikh Kafatru speaks on the hidden world of the Qubaisiyyat in Syria). *Al-Arabiyyah*. Available at: www.alarabiya.net/articles/2007/05/10/34306.html [Accessed 1 December 2016].

NoSawot (2004), Wasiyyat al-rahil al-kabir al-shaikh Ahmad Kaftaru, rahimahu Allahu ta'ala (The will of the grand deceased al shaikh Ahmad Kaftaru, may God have mercy on him). Sawot. Available at: www.saowt.com/forum/showthread.php?t=7406&p=33147&view full=1#post33147 [Accessed 1 December 2016].

Owais, Ghada (2012), Muhammad Habash al-Azmah al-Suriyyah (Muhammad Habash, the Syrian Crisis). Aljazeera. Available at: www.aljazeera.net/programs/today-interview/ 2012/7/21/محمد-حبش-الأزمة-السورية [Accessed 1 December 2016].

Pierret, Thomas (2013), *Religion and State in Syria: The Sunni Ulama from Coup to Revolution*. Cambridge: Cambridge University Press.

Pierret, T. and Selvik, K. (2009), Limits of 'Authoritarian Upgrading' in Syria: Private Welfare, Islamic Charities, and the Rise of the Zayd Movement. *International Journal of Middle East Studies*, 41: 4, 595–614.

Qahf, Munzer (2006), *al-Waqf al-Islami, Tatawurhu, Idaratuhu, Tanmiyatuhu* (Islamic Charitable Trust – Evolution, Management, Development). Damascus: Dar al-Fikr. Available at: http://ia600400.us.archive.org/11/items/alwaqf_644/alwaqf.pdf [Accessed 2 November 2016].

Robinson, M. and White, G. (1997), The Role of Civic Organizations in the Provision of Social Services. *Research for Action*, 37.

Salem, Zuhair (2006), Bayan (Proclamation). The Arab Orient Centre. Available at: www.asharqalarabi.org.uk/m-w/b-mawaqif-43.htm [Accessed 1 December 2016].

Sahgal, Gita (2013), Secular space: bridging the religious-secular divide? Open Democracy. Available at: https://www.opendemocracy.net/5050/gita-sahgal/secular-space-bridging-religious-secular-divide [Accessed 1 December 2016].

Salvatore, A. (2005), The Euro-Islamic Roots of Secularity: A Difficult Equation. *Asian Journal of Social Science*, 33: 3, 412–437.

SANA (2010), Al-Jam'iyyat al-Ahlaiyyah al-Murkhasah fi-Suriyyah (Registered Benevolent Associations in Syria Exceed 1200). *De Press*.

Schleifer, A. ed. (2014), The Muslim 500: The World's 500 Most Influential Muslims, 2014/15. Available at: www.shianeali.com/books/english/personalities/The%20500% 20Muslims%20-%202014.pdf.

Schneier, E. (2015), *Muslim Democracy: Politics, Religion and Society in Indonesia, Turkey and the Islamic World*. London: Routledge.

Seidl, D. and Becker, K.H. (2006), Organizations as Distinction Generating and Processing Systems: Niklas Luhmann's Contribution to Organization Studies. *Organization*, 13: 1, 9–35.

Sider, R.J. and Unruh, H.R. (2004), Typology of Religious Characteristics of Social Service and Educational Organizations and Programs. *Nonprofit and Voluntary Sector Quarterly*, 33: 1, 109–134.

Skovgaard-Petersen, J. (2004), 'A Typology of State Muftis'. In *Islamic Law and the Challenges of Modernity*, edited by Y. Yazbeck Haddad and B. Freyer Stowasser, 81–97, Walnut Creek, CA: Altamira Press.

Stenberg, L. (1999), 'Naqshbandiyya in Damascus: Strategies to Establish and Strengthen the Order in a Changing Society'. In *Naqshbandis in Western and Central Asia: Change and Continuity*, edited by E. Ozdalga. London: Curzon Press.

Swied, Anas (2013), Istishhad al-Da'iyah Fatimah al-Khabbaz (The Martyrdom of the Propagator of Islam Fatimah al-Khabbaz). osama2012ify. Available at: https://www.youtube.com/watch?v=C6kpJB6pfMA [Accessed 1 December 2016].

Takao, K., タカオケンイチロウ and 高尾賢一郎 (2010), Sufi Genealogy of Shaykh Ahmad Kuftaru: Damascene Networking of Naqshbandi Sufi Order in 19–20th Centuries. 一神教世界, 1, 110–119.

Terzieff, Juliette (2003), Syrians Told to Prepare for Fight with U.S. / Iraq War is just the Beginning, Leaders Say. SFGATE. Available at: www.sfgate.com/news/article/Syrians-told-to-prepare-for-fight-with-U-S-2625143.php [Accessed 1 December 2016].

Al-Thawrah (2008), Munafidhu al-a'mal al-irhabiyyah ya'tarifun (Those who undertook terrorist acts confess). Thawra.sy. Available at: http://thawra.sy/_print_veiw.asp?FileName=31283024420081107020927 [Accessed 1 December 2016].

U.S. Department of State (2010), Syria. [online] Available at: www.state.gov/j/drl/rls/hrrpt/2009/nea/136080.htm [Accessed 11 March 2017].

Weismann, I. (2003), The Forgotten Shaykh: 'Īsā al-Kurdī and the Transformation of the Naqshbandī-Khālidī Brotherhood in Twentieth-Century Syria. *Die Welt des Islams*, 43: 3, 373–393 [Online]. Available at: www.jstor.org/stable/20140681?origin=JSTOR-pdf&seq=1#page_scan_tab_contents [Accessed 2 November 2016].

Zain, Nasir (2014), Al-Qubaisiyyat wa-Itharat al-Jadal (The Qubaisiyyat and the Triggering of Argumentation). *Zaman al-Wasl*. Available at: https://zamanalwsl.net/news/49879.html [Accessed 1 December 2016].

9

BASHAR'S FATEFUL DECISION

David W. Lesch

Syrian President Bashar al-Asad's speech to the nation on March 30, 2011, his first to address the protests in Syria that intensified following the debacle in Deraa in mid-March, was a seminal moment in modern Syrian history. The whole country, it seemed, supporters and opposition, waited with bated breath to hear what he had to say, after hearing barely a peep from him in the two weeks since the incidents at Deraa. His speech, given in front of a crowd of adulating supporters in the National Assembly, is now famous for having offered very few concessions to meet the protestors' demands; on the contrary, it was a defiant speech, blaming the Uprising on the insidious actions of terrorists and armed groups supported by Syria's external enemies in the region and internationally. Asad was taken to task in the international media for what was viewed as a blatant attempt to divert attention from the real socio-economic and political factors that laid the foundation for the unrest … either this or he and his inner circle were blind to the real causes of the protests. Certainly, the protestors were immensely disappointed, but so were many of Asad's supporters in and outside of the Syrian government.[1]

Interviews conducted with a number of former Syrian officials who were close to or in the decision-making apparatus behind Asad's policies reveal that the Syrian president definitely had a choice as to what direction to take in his March 30th speech.[2] There were apparently different factions within the regime who advocated a variety of responses, from one group wanting to make what they felt were the necessary concessions to dampen the rising tide of protests to another group that obviously influenced the president to make the speech he did in fact give, one that laid the groundwork for the regime's crackdown on protestors in the days and weeks to come. Some of these officials went to the National Assembly or watched the speech on television expecting the more lenient draft they had figured (or been told) Asad would give, only to be surprised with what actually happened. It is clear there was a tussle back and forth within the opaque Syrian decision-making apparatus surrounding Asad, with the decision by the Syrian president on what course to take, in effect which version of the speech to give, having taken place only a short time before delivering it.[3]

Why did Asad choose to deliver the more defiant and harsh version rather than the more conciliatory one? To answer this question is, in essence, to answer why the Syrian regime chose to brutally put down the Uprising, setting in motion a chain of events that has led to many years of devastating conflict. Was it an individual decision on the part of Bashar al-Asad and perhaps a few of his closest advisors, or was it something more systemic, i.e. the way in which the Syrian regime, or at least enough of the officials therein, uniquely viewed the nature of threat based upon its own conceptual paradigm?

Ultimately we may never know for sure, but I think there is enough circumstantial evidence and knowledge of recent Syrian history to suggest some answers. Whatever the case, that March 30th speech may be the single most important decision in modern Syrian history, one that sent Syria in a trajectory toward a catastrophic war that has forever changed the country; indeed, it has changed the heartland of the Middle East itself, the repercussions of which are still being felt.

Caught unawares?

In late 2010 and early 2011, Syria seemed to be a fairly stable place, especially when compared to Tunisia, Egypt, and Yemen, where events of the so-called Arab spring were beginning to percolate. Bashar al-Asad had improved his own and his country's image. Earlier in the decade, and particularly in the aftermath of the 2005 assassination of former Lebanese prime minister Rafiq Hariri, which was widely blamed on Damascus, that image had been severely tarnished. However, in Paris in December 2010, the Syrian president and his wife, Asma al-Asad, were described as cosmopolitan visitors and were widely photographed in their haute couture clothes, visiting museums and being hosted (if not feted) by the French elite.

In retrospect, Bashar's apparent complacency, denial of the facts, and/or ignorance amid the turmoil of the Arab spring was vividly on display in an interview he gave to journalists from the *Wall Street Journal* in late January 2011.[4] Asad stated in the interview that the protests in Tunisia, Egypt and Yemen signaled a "new era" in the Middle East where rulers would need to meet the rising political and economic demands of the people: "If you didn't see the need of reform before what happened in Egypt and Tunisia, it's too late to do any reform." He went on to say that, "Syria is stable. Why? Because you have to be very closely linked to the beliefs of the people. This is the core issue. When there is divergence…you will have this vacuum that creates disturbances."

This was actually a reference to Syria's position on the Israeli–Palestinian issue as well as to Bashar's perceived triumphal resistance to the "American project" in the region. The Syrian president also seemed confident in the level of reform he had implemented in Syria over the years. He admitted that he wished there had been more, but commented that his country needed more time to build up institutions and improve education in order to absorb such levels of reform. In this vein, he asked, "Is it going to be a new era toward more chaos or more institutionalization? That is the question."

In two essays in its February 2011 issue, *Forward Magazine*, a pro-government English-language monthly published in Damascus, dovetailed with Bashar's *Wall Street Journal* interview.[5] One essay was by the periodical's editor-in-chief and one of the leading Syrian commentators, Sami Moubayed, who was well-connected to the upper echelons of the Syrian regime, and the other was by Bouthaina Shaaban, one of the president's closest and most influential advisors. Political essays in this periodical are heavily vetted, and at this important juncture, were no doubt purposely placed in the publication, thus reflecting regime sentiments.

In Moubayed's essay, he repeatedly hammers home the point that the dictators in the Arab world who had either fallen by then (President Ben Ali in Tunisia) or were on their way out (President Husni Mubarak in Egypt and President Abdullah Saleh in Yemen) primarily because over the years they had been lackeys of the West, and particularly of the United States.

In her essay Shaaban, like Moubayed, castigates the West for being at the root of the unrest in the Arab world. Interestingly, she seems to recognize the pervasive socio-economic problems in the region, and by implication also in Syria, that in part gave rise to the unrest. However, she also identifies what in her (and Bashar's?) mind were the real reasons for the upheavals: Arab neglect of and complicity in the Palestinian problem, Israeli brutality and related US policies. In other words, if an Arab leader, such as Bashar al-Asad, has been on the correct side of history by opposing such policies and supporting the Palestinians and other Arabs suffering under stagnant, obsequious autocracies and foreign imperialism, he should be safe, because he is on the side of the people. She ended her article by saying, "If anger is directed today against governments and aims are to change rulers and their methods, there is no doubt that the position of these rulers over the question of the liberation of Palestine from Israeli occupation will be a major factor in what happens over the comings weeks and months." It was the correct identification of symptoms, but it was also the wrong diagnosis.

In addition, there were comments by Syrian officials that painted Bashar as someone who was relatively young, technologically savvy and thus in tune with the people, especially the younger generations at the epicenter of protests elsewhere. He was not the septuagenarian or octogenarian, entrenched autocrat who was totally out of touch with the people, such as Mubarak in Egypt. He was popular because he had opposed the West, Israel and their lackeys in the region. Surely Bashar was immune to the popular unrest he was witnessing around him in neighboring Arab states.

Indeed, Bashar al-Asad was, prior to the Uprising, generally well-liked in the country—or at least not generally reviled. He tended to live modestly and had a popular wife, both of whom were much better at domestic public diplomacy than his father had ever been. The image cultivated was that he and his family were normal—not distanced from the masses but rather aware of and concerned about their problems. Indeed, Bashar's supporters would often talk about him in reverential terms, almost like a prophet delivered to Syria to bring the country forward. Of course, this sort of sycophancy only fed Bashar's delusion that emerged over the years that the well-being of the country was synonymous with his well-being. Bashar had also gained a good bit of credit in the eyes of many Syrians for giving up his passion, ophthalmology, to serve the country when it needed him following his brother's death in 1994 and his father's passing in 2000. Of course, this was promoted as regime propaganda, and it may have bought Bashar a longer learning curve and more public patience with his incremental reform efforts, simply because the image was that he was not groomed to be president. Quite to the contrary, Bashar was portrayed as having kept the country together despite the regional and international pressures applied against Syria during the previous decade (the 2000s), and in so doing deserved the gratitude of the Syrian people. In addition, there was some economic growth, albeit very uneven, as well as fiscal, administrative, and education reform that perhaps has been too easily dismissed in the wake of the civil war.

Initially, calls by anti-Asad elements inside and outside the country for similar protests to be held in Syrian cities in January and February 2011 failed to elicit much of a response, as only a few dozen showed up, rather than the hoped-for thousands that had showed up in Tunisian and Egyptian cities. These protests usually fizzled out rapidly or were easily dispersed by security forces. There just did not seem to be the same energy for opposition in Syria as in other countries, and this only made the regime feel that much more secure. It is almost certain that Bashar al-Asad was absolutely shocked when the so-called Arab spring uprisings seeped into his country in force in March 2011. I believe he truly thought he was safe and secure and popular beyond condemnation. He probably believed so much in his own popularity in Syria that any protests must have been foreign-inspired.

There were other more tangible factors that led Bashar and his supporters—as well as many external experts and observers—to believe that the regime could weather the storm rising in the Arab world, or at least deflect and contain it if it did enter Syrian space: because of Syria's turbulent political development following independence in 1946, Syrians had generally disdained engagement in actions that could produce instability. In the decade prior to the Arab spring they only had to look across their borders, on either side, toward Lebanon and Iraq—two countries that, like Syria, are ethnically and religiously diverse—to see how political disorder can violently rip apart the fabric of society. Of course, this trepidation was constantly stoked by the regime to reinforce the necessity of maintaining stability at all costs. It frequently portrayed itself as the only thing standing between stability and chaos. So long as Asad remained the only viable alternative in the minds of many Syrians, they were not going to participate in an opposition movement that could destabilize the country over the long term. And with the brutality of the Syrian government crackdown in Hama in 1982 within the consciousness of most Syrians, the repressive apparatus of the state—military, *mukhabarat*, paramilitary groups—was daunting to anyone contemplating taking it on.

The fate of the Syrian military and security services is also closely tied to that of the regime. In contrast to Egypt, these institutions have not been as separate from the political leadership. They have aggressively led the violent crackdown on the protestors since the beginning of the Uprising. And over his decade-long tenure in power, by 2011 Bashar had successfully manipulated the ruling apparatus, both military and civilian, to put in place an extremely loyal and tight leadership at the top. There have really been remarkably few high-placed defections from the Syrian government when compared to other Arab states convulsed by uprisings, and by now their fates are tied together more than ever.

The minority-ruled Syrian regime, infused as it is with Alawites in important positions, had always represented itself as the protector of all minorities in a country that is about 65 percent Sunni Arab. In addition to the 10–11 percent Alawite population, there are various Christian sects comprising about 10 percent of the population, plus Druze (3 percent), and a smattering of smaller Shiite sects. The Sunni Kurdish population in Syria (another 10 percent) have often been a restless and repressed minority in Syria under the Asads; however, the Syrian government made a number of concessions to the Kurds, mostly in the area of political autonomy, in the early part of the Uprising in order to at the very least keep most of them neutral in the conflict. The Asads skillfully played the minority card over the years, practically guaranteeing for themselves at least a 20–30 percent support base in the country by playing on fears of the potential for repressive, even fanatical, Sunni Muslim rule and/or instability, in which minorities typically pay a high price. Then there are loyal Sunnis from the business class who had long been co-opted into supporting the Asads as well as numerous Sufi Muslim orders in Syria who were actively cultivated and supported by the Asads, especially by Bashar. When all these elements are added together, they probably account for about half of the Syrian population. For an authoritarian regime, this is not such a bad percentage: employing coercion, a pervasive spy apparatus, carefully constructed tribal and family alliances, co-optation and the tactics of divide and rule, maintaining control over the remaining half of the population is not as difficult for a minority-led regime as it would, on the surface, seem to be.

Finally, Syria's internal and external opposition prior to the Uprising was often uncoordinated and divided, with no generally recognized leadership, which carried over into the civil war itself. The Syrian regime had done a good job over the years of ensuring this. There was little if any experience with politics in a populace where there existed a very restricted political space. As such, there was no real alternative to Asad, especially after the regime survived—and indeed consolidated power—following the existential threat in the wake of the assassination of former Lebanese prime minister Rafiq Hariri in 2005.

Thus, for many reasons Asad thought his position was different from that of his peers in the other Arab republics, but as it turned out, Syria had been suffering from many of the same underlying socio-economic woes that existed in the non-oil producing Arab countries and that created a well of disenfranchisement and disempowerment, especially among an energized and increasingly frustrated youth. The perfect storm in the Arab world of higher commodity prices (which made basic items more expensive) and a youth bulge that created an irreparable gap between social mobilization and assimilation via employment into the system, threw into sharp relief the widespread socio-economic problems (especially gross unequal income distribution and growing poverty), corruption, and restricted political space marked by *mukhabarat* enforced political repression. In this, Syria was no different. And after the popular uprisings in Tunisia and Egypt led to the removal of the *ancien regimes* in each country, the barrier of fear of the repressive apparatus was broken.

To speech or not to speech

In response to the growing protests, the Syrian government announced a series of reforms on 24 March 2011. This seemed to repeat the pattern established by fallen regimes in Tunis and Cairo as well as other governments in the Arab world experiencing problems at the time. Regime insiders told this researcher that Bashar went back and forth in his mind between making concessions (and announcing them in a conciliatory speech) and cracking down hard on the protestors. The March 24 announcement included the formation of a committee to investigate and bring to justice anyone who had committed unlawful acts, including government soldiers and personnel. Bouthaina Shaaban, the political and media advisor to the president who had now assumed the role as a government spokesperson, stipulated that the wages of government workers would be raised by 20–30 percent (thus keeping an important support base mollified), and there would be income tax cuts and pension increases. She then spoke in general terms about new health reforms, judicial reform, the relaxation of media restrictions, the establishment of a new mechanism to fight corruption, and allowing more political parties to compete in elections. She also announced that a committee would be formed to examine the need to lift the state of emergency law that had been in place since the Ba'thist coup in 1963 (Decree No. 51).

Of course, Syrians had heard these promises before with little to no implementation. The real question people were asking amid the rising protests was "Where is Bashar?" He had not been heard from since the protest movement began in earnest in Deraa in mid-March, and he seemingly had retreated into seclusion. There are some possible reasons why Bashar was not personally responding to the growing crisis. I firmly believe he—and the Syrian leadership as a whole—was caught off-guard by the ferocity of the protests and how they spread from Deraa to other cities and towns. It is not as though the regime did not consider and take measures in the wake of what happened elsewhere in the Arab world. Before Deraa had erupted, Bashar had apparently ordered three separate security studies to examine the likelihood of the Arab spring spreading into Syria. The quality and methodology of the studies (and which branch or branches of the government carried out the studies) can, perhaps, be questioned, but all three concluded that Syria was safe and secure.[6] In addition, in Damascus police authorities were given orders to be more lenient in terms of traffic violations and other unlawful activities in order to minimize any potential incidents that could incite the public.[7] And there was certainly a mobilization of military and security forces just in case something happened, mostly in and around Damascus. Bashar probably still believed he had a target on his back dating from the days of the Hariri assassination. The security chiefs never believed that they were not under siege, or so the mentality went. Some certainly felt that after Egypt, Syria had to be on the lookout.[8] So, it was not as though the regime was totally complacent; but it obviously was focusing on Damascus (and perhaps Aleppo) too much, as the protests in other Arab countries, particularly in Egypt, tended to focus on and have the most significant impact in their respective capital cities, whereas the Syrian Uprising began and continued for some time as a mostly rural phenomenon outside of Damascus.

Regardless, the regime seemed to be rocked back on its heels by the events at Deraa. There were apparently pronounced differences in the inner circle surrounding the president over how to react.[9] Should the protests be repressed ruthlessly, as had been the Syrian way in the past? Or should Asad announce—and implement—meaningful reforms? There appeared to be a great deal of confusion within the inner circle, with varying responses to these questions, and comments and actions by the regime in these crucial two weeks made it seem as though it was talking out of both sides of its mouth, saying one thing while regime forces were doing quite the opposite on the ground. Interviews with both regime and opposition figures reveal a wide variety of stories/recollections on exactly what happened in Deraa in those crucial days of March 2011. Some of these may be filtered through agenda-ridden or traumatized lenses, but enough ambiguity exists that an accurate history of what actually went down in Deraa remains to be written. One top regime insider told me that Asad had intended to go down to Deraa and be apologetic, conciliatory, and possibly even get rid of his cousin, the governor, Atif Najib, who many held responsible for the civilian deaths.[10] This would have met many of the local demands and possibly would have taken the air out of the expanding protests. However, according to this official, there was a massacre (unreported in the media) of about a dozen policemen in Deraa in late-March by local elements bent on revenge, and after this occurred, Asad had no choice but to give the orders to respond more forcefully. Regardless of these different narratives of the events in Deraa, Asad was publicly nowhere to be found, so it appeared that the president was not taking charge.

Bashar al-Asad is also someone who does not typically act or decide on important issues in an expeditious fashion. It is difficult to discern exactly what was going on in those first few days and weeks, as the Syrian decision-making apparatus is fairly opaque. It is also hampered by deep bureaucratic inertia that makes quick decisions on policy exceedingly difficult. Decision-making at the top appears to be quite compartmentalized. There are small groups of advisors close to the president who advise him on different issues. Some officials serve on more than one of these ad-hoc committees, and often competing viewpoints are deliberately placed in the same group so that the president can hear different opinions. Asad tends to be very deliberate in his decision-making, often mulling things over for quite some time before making a final decision. This is not a system that is built for quick, efficient responses and reactions.

One high-ranking Syrian official informed me in December 2011 in a meeting in Europe that one of the driving forces behind the regime's response in the initial stages of the unrest had been to *not* do what the Tunisian and Egyptian presidents had done. The logic was inescapable: Ben Ali and Mubarak were removed from office in short order after making some concessions and not ordering widespread crackdowns; therefore, Bashar should pretty much do the opposite of what they did. These other leaders gave in too easily and appeared weak. I asked this Syrian official why Asad did not go in front of the cameras on live television, instead of giving televised, orchestrated speeches. The official told me that a number of people had tried to get him to do this in order to connect with a people with whom he had forged a bond over the years and while he still had some credibility. But there were other, obviously more influential, members of the inner circle, who strongly cautioned against doing this because it was what other—by then former—Arab leaders had done.

Maybe some of the more hardline elements in the regime thought it would be a sign of weakness for the president to admit any mistakes. Maybe they thought Bashar might be able to dissociate himself from the crackdown by connecting at a more personal level with the Syrian people, thus making their own positions more vulnerable. Indeed, several former high-level Syrian officials indicated that talk of internal coups was in the air. One recommended to Bashar that the president himself could carry out a coup against some of these hardline elements. The president's response, according to this official, was simply, "you are naive."[11] Another very well-placed former Syrian official, who had direct access to Bashar and was one of the more influential officials in Damascus, blatantly accused certain Ba'th Party officials in cahoots with the security establishment of using the crisis as an opportunity to force out the more reformist elements in the regime, of which he was one. Clearly there was confusion and intrigue at the top during this crisis period, and Bashar had to navigate his position—his response—very carefully.

Perhaps, as well, Bashar's decision to make a televised speech reflected his unswerving commitment to what is often the fiction of institutions; therefore, he spoke first at the People's Assembly on March 30th, speaking to his newly sworn in Cabinet in April, and to address a cast of supporters in an auditorium at Damascus University in June. It could be that Bashar, who is not the greatest orator and does not have a commanding presence, felt (or his advisors did) that he needed to be surrounded by supporters as a kind of prop, to create the spectacle and theater of drama he was seeking, with almost scripted applause and adulation that are so familiar to anyone who has heard speeches by him or his father in such venues.

A speech not worth waiting for

There was a great deal of anticipation regarding Bashar's March 30th speech. Many were hoping that the Syrian president would be magnanimous and humble, announcing serious political reforms. This was the moment when Bashar would finally come through, would finally live up to the high expectations raised when he first came to power over a decade earlier. They were to be disappointed. Many Syrians in the opposition later identified Bashar's speech as a turning point, i.e. their disappointment in the speech made them realize that Bashar, in the end, wasn't any different from his father, and it galvanized the protests.[12] In addition, the fact that Bashar did not punish his cousin, the governor of the province of Deraa, at least as a symbolic gesture in reaction to the civilian deaths in the city of Deraa, reinforced the view that any real concessions by the government would be few and far between. A number of Syrian opposition elements from inside the country, both civilian and armed activists, concede that if he had done one or both of these things, the Uprising may never have occurred. As one pro-government Hizbullah figure explained:

> Bashar had real popularity in Syria. It was not 90 percent, it was not total or unconditional support, but he had—I think that we had a clear majority who was hoping that Bashar was going to transform the system, little by little. Perhaps some of them were becoming less patient, but when the contestation movement began, if he had taken some measures to directly sanction the guy who tortured the kids in Deraa, if he had taken some anticorruption measures, even if it was symbolic, it would have made things better. He had to take the decision to confront some clans inside the leadership and the Syrian apparatus and administration and I think that he could have—this kind of measure would have divided the ranks of the contestation, and he would have had a larger popular base.[13]

One Syrian opposition activist frankly stated that Bashar could have remained in power "if he stayed with the Syrian people."[14]

A former high-level Syrian government official who was a part of the decision-making apparatus at the time said that Bashar made a

> terrible strategic mistake that week [the week after the March 15 Deraa incident] by not deciding what's the nature of this conflict. And I tried to say this is not a singular crisis, this is a multi-dimensional crisis, economic and political. Have a package, and a package that's clear in one particular direction. Don't give signals in two hundred directions … Let me put it simply: first, sack the governor. Then sack all the heads of security so his cousin doesn't stand out. That is what we used to do whenever there was trouble in any governorate.[15]

He went on to say that he (and others) advised Bashar to rain some largesse on Deraa, new roads, schools, etc., then send ministers, or even the president himself, down to Deraa to meet with city elders and tribal leaders to pacify the situation.[16]

These hypotheticals are difficult to prove in hindsight, but it is likely that at least some of the energy to the growing unrest would have been dampened had Bashar initiated such bold moves. This, is, indeed, one of the great tragedies of the conflict: unlike a Mubarak, Qadhdhafi, or even a Ben Ali, Bashar al-Asad still enjoyed a level of genuine popularity in his country, and he could have possibly rallied the population, if not all of the security forces or Ba'th Party leadership, behind him to compel the country in a more ameliorative direction rather than one of confrontation. It's easy for armchair historians to speculate about this. We are not the ones putting our lives on the line, and surely there would have been hard line elements in Damascus who would vigorously oppose any moves by the Syrian president to enact reforms that could undercut the power base of important factions in the government; however, it is times like these that separate the great leaders from the also-rans and conformists, who might save a country rather than plunging it into the depths and despair of many years of civil war.

Despite some references to the socio-economic causes of the unrest in Syria, Bashar's speech was clearly dominated by the attempt to place the blame on external forces and on the seditious activities of their domestic co-conspirators; indeed, the word "sedition" was used repeatedly during the speech. Toward the end of his speech, in a clear—and chilling—warning to opposition elements, Bashar said: "The Holy Quran says, 'sedition is worse than killing.' So all those involved intentionally or unintentionally in it contribute to destroying their country. So there is no compromise or middle way on this. What is at stake is the homeland and there is a huge conspiracy."

It seems that ultimately Bashar and a critical mass of the Syrian leadership concluded that the battle was on and that the protests had to be eliminated. The regime had to reassert control and stability through force and would play on the penchant of the Syrian population to believe conspiracy theories. He ended his speech by stating: "I shall remain the faithful brother and comrade who will walk with his people and lead them to build the Syria we love, the Syria we are proud of, the Syria which is invincible to its enemies." That he ended his speech with the word "enemies" revealed the direction the regime was taking in terms of its public evaluation of the main source of the crisis, as well as the nature of its response.

It was no surprise that in his speech Bashar blamed the protests largely on conspirators inside and (especially) outside the country. Anyone who has spent time in Syria can recognize this national paranoia. This conspiratorial mindset is commonplace even among the educated elite, many of whom attended university in the West. The problem is that there have been just enough actual foreign conspiracies in Syria over the decades to lend credence to such claims. And the regimes of both Hafiz and Bashar al-Asad have nurtured this paranoia through propaganda and censorship, in part to justify the necessity of the security state. So, the president probably figured he was preaching to the converted, certainly within the parliamentary chamber in which he was speaking. And a good many Syrians outside the chamber probably believed it as well; but in the new information age, a growing number of people could no longer be cowed or brainwashed as they had in the past. The Arab spring had changed the perspectives and the level of demands of ordinary citizens. By blaming unseen forces of conspiracy, the government denied responsibility for (and recognition of) the very real socio-economic and political problems, and for the growing clamor of Syrians expressing frustration with the government for lack of accountability, corruption, political repression, and rising poverty. Asad did not adequately address these issues, which had become much more important to ordinary citizens because they saw in other Arab countries a way to finally combat them.

No going back

Beyond his closest supporters, the reactions to Bashar's speech were almost universally negative. In the wake of the speech, protests broke out across the country (with the exceptions of Aleppo and Damascus for the most part) and were followed by violent crackdowns by government forces. The regime was probably taken aback that the speech was apparently not the panacea they perhaps thought it would be. Bashar subsequently replaced the Cabinet as well as announced a number of other measures, such as the termination of the 1963 Emergency Law; however, other announcements and provisions—and above all, actions—effectively made null and void any apparent concessions made by the regime. The Syrian population was used to announcements of reforms followed by very little substance, much less implementation. To them, this was no different. Bashar would probably have insisted that he had made serious concessions and that they were not appreciated in the West nor by duplicitous, naive elements of the growing opposition movement. And rather than lying through his teeth, he might actually have truly believed he was going far more than halfway to meet various demands. But this is what neither side particularly understood very well of the other. The Arab spring has raised the bar, and expectations were greater than what a *mukhabarat* state regime could possibly meet.

In the end, Bashar fell back into the default position, convinced by certain elements in his inner circle and security apparatus to do so, that the Uprising could be taken care of in a matter of weeks. As one former high-ranking Syrian military figure who was close to the inner circle stated, "He [Bashar] was tilting on both sides. At some point they [security chiefs] must have told him, move aside, relax, and we'll deal with it."[17] Perhaps this is just the typical response under the Asads. When a domestic threat appears, there is a push-button response of quick and ruthless repression. Survival instincts. No one really questions it. The *mukhabarat* and the elite units of the military swing into action. Maybe the real story in all of this would have been if Bashar did not press that button. He probably did not fret over it too much once the initial shock of the protests wore off. This is just how things are done. It was business as usual in the *mukhabarat* state, and Bashar had been convinced—or he had convinced himself—that he was actually saving the country from the enemies of the state.

During the first month or two of the Uprising, while the regime continued to make some concessions and announce reform measures and present an image of calm and cool control,[18] the military and security forces intensified their crackdown in cities across Syria. To the outside observer, this approach may seem contradictory and indicative of fissures within the ruling elite on how to respond to the crisis. On the other hand, from the perspective of Bashar and his inner circle, it could be seen as two sides of the same coin. In a way that came to be expected of the Asad regimes—old and new—it was something of an axiom of power politics that one offers concessions only from a position of strength, never from a position of weakness. Therefore, while there was a practical side to the Asad approach, in terms of quelling the unrest, it also clearly indicated that the regime wanted to portray itself as only making concessions and offering reforms (actually only re-stating measures previously made so as not to seem as if it was caving in to pressure) from a position of strength. Perhaps the reforms announced could separate the wheat from the chaff of the opposition, thus enabling the regime to land a knockout punch in relatively short order. But, of course, that never happened.

Ultimately, Bashar al-Asad had little faith that anything other than his continuance in power could lead the way forward. Bashar's strategic vision (dream even) for an internationally respected and integrated Syria became consumed by a paradigm of political survival. He was either unwilling or unable to stop what in Syria is a reflexive response to a perceived threat. He retrenched and retreated into a typically Syrian authoritarian mode of survival, an Alawite fortress to protect the sect's chokehold on power. In the end, when the pressure was greatest, Asad was not the enlightened, Western-educated ophthalmologist. He was—as he always really has been—a child of the Arab–Israeli conflict, the superpower cold war, and, most importantly, Hafiz al-Asad.

Yes, Bashar had a choice in the hours before giving his speech on March 30, 2011. But considering the parameters under which he was ruling, the conceptual paradigm of his perception of the nature of threat, a world-view that had been shaped by modern Syrian history, maybe in the end there was really only one option.

Notes

1 Excerpts from this piece appear in David W. Lesch, *Syria: The Fall of the House of Assad* (London: Yale University Press, 2013).
2 Unless otherwise noted, information gleaned from interviews were generated as part of the Harvard-NUPI Trinity Syria Research Project (hereinafter, HNT). This was a project that I developed and organized in late 2012, sponsored by the Harvard Negotiation Project, the Norwegian Institute for International Affairs (NUPI), and Trinity University in San Antonio, Texas. The project was funded by the Swiss and Norwegian governments and was focused on meeting with top officials in most of the stakeholder countries/entities involved in the Syrian conflict, including members of the Syrian government and elements of the Syrian opposition both in and outside of Syria. A Final Report was produced in the fall of 2013, the full version only available to certain parties in a confidential manner. An abridged version of the Final Report was more widely circulated and can be found at the following website: http://www.nupi.no/en/Publications/CRIStin-Pub/Obstacles-to-a-Resolution-of-the-Syrian-Conflict-Harvard-NUPI-Trinity-Syria-Research-Project-Primary-Author-David-W.-Lesch-Contributing-Autho. Some of the

endnotes include the date and location of the interview; others do not because it could reveal the identification of the interviewee.

3 I have yet to find this so-called more lenient version of the speech, if it even exists anymore, and I have not found any details on exactly what concessions Asad might have offered in this version. A *New York Times* article stated that, "according to [Syrian] officials, the speech...will offer significant political concessions, including the lifting of laws that restrict civil and political freedoms." Michael Slackman, "Syria's Cabinet Resigns: Concessions Expected," *The New York Times*, March 29, 2011. http://www.nytimes.com/2011/03/30/world/middleeast/30syria.html.

4 Jay Soloman and Bill Spindle, "Syria strongman: time for reform," *Wall Street Journal*, January 31, 2011.

5 Sami Moubayed, "Lesson from Egypt: West is not best," p. 4; and Bouthaina Shaaban, "The real evils plaguing the region," p. 16, *Forward Magazine*, 48, February 2011.

6 Interview with former high-level Syrian government official who received the results of the studies and discussed them with Bashar. HNT.

7 Interview with European diplomat present in Damascus in early stage of Uprising. HNT.

8 As one activist who knew Bashar al-Asad well before joining the opposition said, "Bashar and his guys prepared for this fight before and they choose for this fight. Everyone repositioned after Egypt. The cards were already shuffled; everyone wants to make the game for their side. Everyone prepared for the fight before it started. They are too smart to hesitate." Interview with opposition activist, Gaziantep, Turkey, December 2012. HNT.

9 Interviews with several former high-level Syrian government officials intimately engaged in the decision-making at the time. HNT.

10 Interview in Beirut, Lebanon, January 2015.

11 Interview with former high-level Syrian official. HNT.

12 Opposition elements were not the only ones disappointed in the speech, as there were a number of regime officials who were unhappy with it or at least surprised by it. One top former Syrian official close to Bashar said the following, "Normally, when he [Bashar] makes a speech he calls people back to listen to the vibes, and normally after tens of people would come and tell him 'wow', but no one called this time." Interview with former Syrian government official, February 2013, HNT.

13 Interview with Hizbullah figure, Beirut, August 2013, HNT.

14 Interview with Syrian opposition activist, Gaziantep, Turkey, December 2012, HNT.

15 Interview with former high-level Syrian government official, HNT.

16 Ibid.

17 Interview with former high-level Syrian military figure, HNT.

18 For instance, on March 25, 2011, the Syrian Minister of Information, Muhsin Bilal, said that "the situation is completely calm in all parts of the country." Alarabiya.net, "Deaths Reported as Protests Erupt across Syria," March 25, 2011, http://www.alarabiya.net/articles/2011/03/25/142927.html. A month later, a Syrian official was quoted as saying, "We will have a few months of difficult times, but I don't think it will go further … it will be a period of unrest and not an overthrow of the regime. That is highly improbable." Ian Black, "Six Syrians Who Helped Bashar al-Assad Keep Iron Grip after Father's Death," *The Guardian*, April 28, 2011, http://www.theguardian.com/world/2011/apr/28/syria-bashar-assad-regime-members. And, "the state-run Syrian Arab News Agency reported that normal life had returned to all Syrian provinces," Neil Macfarquhar and Liam Stack, "Syrian Protesters Clash with Security Forces," *The New York Times*, April 1, 2011, http://www.nytimes.com/2011/04/02/world/middleeast/02syria.html.

10

SYRIA'S ALAWIS

Structure, perception and agency in the Syrian security dilemma

Leon Goldsmith

Introduction

Since the start of the Syrian Uprising in March 2011, communal insecurities have been a major factor in the escalation of conflict, which has increasingly divided Syria's diverse society along identity lines. Syrian minorities have experienced a security dilemma due to uncertainty around the political and military intentions of the country's 65 per cent Sunni Arab majority, which causes most to cling to the embattled regime of Syria's Alawite president, Bashar al-Asad. Growing sectarianism in Syria has provided a dying regime with critical life support from the minorities and shifted the dominant narrative of events from 'popular street uprising' towards 'zero-sum' sectarian civil war; this effectively undermined Syria's revolutionary social movement and led the country to disintegration and external interventions. This chapter examines the role and predicament of the Alawite minority in this process, and explains how they found themselves trapped within a deadly predicament between the Asad regime, the moderate opposition, jihadist extremists and their respective external backers.

Three interconnected dimensions of the security dilemma need to be examined in order to understand Alawite and minority political behaviour and to assess whether the descent into conflict since 2011 was inevitable as the Syrian Ba'thist state deteriorated in power. First, structural factors such as historical legacies, internal and external geopolitics, and demographic realities have all undoubtedly played a part in shaping the political behaviour of the Syrian Alawites. Equally important are intangible factors such as perceptions (or misperceptions), which produce irrational or emotional assessments about the intentions and threat of the 'other' within the context of identity politics. The final factor, however, that is lacking attention in the security dilemma discourse is the question of agency. How do political actors affect the dynamics of the security dilemma through deliberate, politically strategic actions or policies? It should also be kept in mind, however, that political actors are also susceptible to the security dilemma in terms of it influencing their decisions and actions. The central argument presented here is that without the interventions of political actors – regardless of their mindset or rationale – in sparking and exploiting sectarian insecurity, the structural and intangible drivers of the security dilemma would not necessarily lead to conflict, or could be more effectively mitigated. This is a counterfactual inference as far as the Syrian conflict goes; however, addressing the question of agency in the security dilemma is of great importance for better understanding the drivers of ethno-religious conflict, finding solutions for resolving such conflicts, and for establishing processes of justice and accountability in the aftermath of conflicts with ethnic-religious dimensions.

Since the mid-2000s, conflict in the Middle East or the developing world more broadly, has come to be seen through an identity politics lens with common explanations for identity conflicts focusing on structural factors such as political geography, economic underdevelopment and colonial legacies. Syria seemed no exception as ethnic-sectarian dynamics quickly emerged as a critical factor in the slide to civil war. When we look to examples of mass violence in the twentieth century, however, explanations often centred on the culpability of regimes and more precisely the agency of executive leaders. During the first four years of the Syrian conflict industrial-scale state violence was waged against large parts of Syria's population in response to mass protests against the rule of Bashar al-Asad. Even with modern communications, a true record of the human and material destruction will only begin to be known by historians after the war's end. Meanwhile, the burden of political scientists is to try to explain mankind's recurrent capacity for 'beastliness' by applying different political theories to the problem of genocidal violence. In the Syrian case, scholars have often chosen security dilemma theory as an appropriate analytical device to explain the political behaviour of minority groups, the decision by most of them to remain loyal to the Ba'thist regime, and how this affected the onset and evolution of conflict (Goldsmith, 2015). However, there is also a case to be made to examine the conflict in Syria through a lens of executive agency, not only as an example of brutal repression of political dissent, but also for the way that minority insecurity has been manipulated by the Syrian regime to bring forth a security dilemma in the country that increased its chances for political survival.

Parsing the ethnic-religious security dilemma

Originally developed as a theory in international relations, the security dilemma was adapted by Barry Posen (1993) as a way to explain the violent ethnic-religious fragmentation of the Balkans in the 1990s. It provided a largely structural explanation based around a set of circumstances that can bring about ethnic conflict. To summarise his argument briefly, when overarching powers, multi-national states or empires, lose authority and/or legitimacy, a security vacuum occurs in which different groups face a dilemma regarding possible threats from other groups seeking security and control of territory or resources. Moreover, different ethnic groups may retain collective memories of historic persecutions or conflicts with other groups. Consequently, groups build up their defensive military resources, which in turn exacerbates the level of threat felt between groups; therefore 'what one does to enhance one's own security causes reactions that in the end, can make one less secure' (Posen, 1993: 28). This dilemma is very relevant to the predicament of the Alawite sect in Syria; the steps that they have taken to preserve their security during the Uprising (clinging to the regime) have paralleled and contributed to the expansion of grave threats to the group in the form of Sunni opposition groups who view the sect as complicit with the regime and its atrocities. More threatening still for Alawites, has been the entry into the chaotic environment of transnational extremist groups who view the Alawites as irredeemable infidels who must be purged from a future 'Islamic state'.

Also significant in Posen's theory are the relative levels of group solidarity based on shared history, geography, culture, beliefs or other commonly held identity symbols. This has an effect on the security dilemma, whereby groups that are more cohesive seem to pose a greater military threat than more divided groups (Posen, 1993: 30). In this sense, Ibn Khaldun has provided us with theoretical tools to measure the solidarity of groups and the consequent effect on the emergence and decline of political regimes or dynasties (Khaldun, trans. Rosenthal, 1967). One area that he did not examine, however, was insecurity, and more specifically sectarian insecurity and its effect on group solidarity. The Alawites of Syria have largely remained cohesive due to a type of Khaldunian *'asabiyya* reinforced by high levels of sectarian insecurity as a historically persecuted sub-sect of Shi'a Islam (Goldsmith 2013; 2015). Given such structural features of a group's situation and history, the security dilemma theory anticipates that a group will shape their behaviour according to 'worst case scenarios' based on assumptions that other groups harbour malevolent intentions towards them (Roe, 2000). In the case of the Alawites, there was a perception that a revanchist Sunni majority sought to reverse the period of Alawite integration in Syria from the mid-twentieth century, reduce Alawites to second-class citizens, or worse, violently persecute the sect as had occurred periodically in the past.

In this sense security dilemma theory has been critiqued for its lack of attention to more intangible factors, in particular misperception (Roe, 2000). According to some scholars, misperception plays a key role in bringing about a security dilemma. In this view, the misperceptions of parties regarding the intentions of other parties create unnecessary and therefore tragic conflicts based on mutually mistaken threat perceptions. Most relevant to the case of the Alawites is the potential for an imagined worst case scenario – i.e. xenophobic religious extremism – to become a reality; in other words 'fear of what initially may have never existed may subsequently bring about what is feared the most' (Herz, 1966, cit. in Roe, 2000: 377). In this interpretation of the security dilemma two parties may in fact be in pursuit of similar goals security but through misperception of the others' intentions instead arrive at a situation of hostility or even genocidal conflict.

The Alawites struggled throughout the late nineteenth and twentieth centuries to achieve social and political integration in the Levant and hoped for security and equal citizenship in pluralist systems (Goldsmith, 2013). In 2011, hundreds of thousands of protesters, including many Alawites, flooded the streets of Syrian cities demanding justice, dignity and freedom. Yet, by 2012 these seemingly shared goals had disaggregated into identity conflicts involving a deep polarisation between pro-regime minorities and largely Sunni Muslim opposition movements. An activating factor was that opposing sides largely adopted strategies and policies based on worst case scenarios. For instance, fearing Sunni Muslim revanchism or majoritarian intolerance, Alawites and other minorities predominantly clung to the regime and the political status quo. On the other side, Sunnis in the opposition were prone to generalise that Alawites collectively supported the regime and were enemies of the revolution; hence Alawites who joined the opposition were often treated with suspicion and contempt (anon. interviews).

Even with the presence of these types of structural and perceptional activators of the security dilemma, a descent into ethnic-religious conflict is not necessarily inevitable. However, when leaders or influential actors in one or more of the groups involved in the security dilemma has an interest in exploiting the insecurity of his/her group for political reasons, then the potential for conflict is increased dramatically. For instance, if leading political figures on either side of the conflict manipulated or scare mongered their groups to pique their insecurity and imbue a sense of mistrust along identity lines, it would upgrade the likelihood of a violent security dilemma occurring. In this sense it has been claimed by many Syrians and external observers that the regime actually sought to provoke sectarianism as a way to activate the security dilemma of minorities and keep them onside with the regime (Goldsmith, 2015: 197–198). Conversely, the state sponsors of many rebel groups, such as Saudi Arabia, Qatar and Turkey, have contributed to a 'Sunnification' of the opposition in line with their own religious identities and interests. The following sections explain the structural, intangible and agency factors related to the Alawite security dilemma in Syria.

The structure of Alawite insecurity

From the outset, Alawite (sometimes referred to as *Nusayri*) history contained episodes of persecution by political and religious authorities that shaped the community's identity of particularism, mistrust and insecurity. While there were long periods when the sect enjoyed relative security and interaction with wider society, these periods often gave way to renewed conflict and hostility. This regular return to conflict can be viewed as a result of structural insecurities between both hegemonic powers and the Alawites. The Mamluks and the Ottomans, especially, were highly suspicious of Alawite loyalty to their empires and, equally, the Alawites never felt secure enough to seek genuine integration or to reveal their real beliefs and identity. Nonetheless, the diverse ethnic-religious fabric of Levantine society remained cohesive during the greater part of the region's history. Most frequently it was during periods of state breakdown, decline, or external intervention that violent episodes of communal violence broke out. This general pattern follows the first premise of the security dilemma, that structural changes or the collapse of political systems in diverse states are a key factor in sparking conflict between different identity groups. History does indeed indicate that Alawites faced greater threats to their security during transition phases, and power struggles such as we are seeing today in Syria, generally impacted negatively on the security of the Alawites.

During the early period of the Alawite/Nusayri sect's history in ninth-century Iraq, the political environment was chaotic. The Abbasids were struggling to maintain their authority, Islam was fragmenting into distinct sects with political overtones and the caliphate was under pressure from a resurgent Byzantium in the north (Goldsmith, 2015: 14; Waines, 1977). In this environment, the nascent Alawite sect found itself targeted by the political authorities and the community's leader, Hamdan al-Khasībī, was imprisoned between 926 and 945 CE (Friedman, 2010: 22–23). Later, following the movement of the sect's centre of gravity to the coastal Levant, the crusaders lumped the Alawites together with other Muslims and many were massacred (Moosa, 1988: 269). Likewise in the early fourteenth century the Mamluk Empire – under pressure from Mongol conquests to the East and the Armenian kingdom to the north – cracked down on the suspect Alawites, prohibiting them from practising their religion. When 3000 Alawites rebelled in 1318 the sultan in Cairo ordered the extermination of the entire sect (Tsugitaka, 1997). Again, following the Mamluk collapse in 1516, the new Ottoman power again sought to eradicate the heretical Alawites, mainly because they were suspected of collusion with their arch enemies, the Shi'a Safavids of Iran. In this instance, it was possibly the rugged terrain of the coastal mountains that saved the Alawites from destruction and subsequently Alawites relied on a policy of *taqiyya* (dissimulation) in order maintain their security under Ottoman rule (Maundrell, 1963: 16–17).

Another salient example of Alawite insecurity during political shifts came in the late 1850s. When the powerful and ruthless Alawite chief Ismail Khayr Bey took advantage of declining Ottoman power in the Levant, imperial troops threatened to scourge the entire Alawite territory. With the community faced with catastrophe, Ismail was killed and beheaded by his own uncle who appeased the Ottomans by presenting them with the grisly trophy (Jessup, 1910: 152; Talhamy, 2008: 904). After 1936, with the French mandate winding down, the Alawites made the necessary compromises to survive in another potentially hostile environment. When an eccentric but influential figure named Suleiman al-Murshid (d. 1946) and later his son Mujib (d. 1952) tried to assert Alawite autonomy and raise rebellions, other Alawite tribes declined to assist and both father and son perished at the hands of the new Syrian government (Yaffe and Dann, 1993).

The capture of power by Alawite officer Hafiz al-Asad in 1970 represented a different kind of change whereby Alawites became directly – or indirectly – connected to the hegemonic power structure in Syria. This represented either a potential windfall for Alawite security or a dangerous overextension for the sect. Alawites therefore perceived grave threat in the Uprising against Asad by the Syrian Muslim

Brotherhood in 1976–1982. Asad, an astute political tactician, had, however, built a broad coalition including rural Sunnis, merchants in Damascus and Aleppo and, though generous donations and endowments, many Sunni clerics (Ziadeh, 2011: 139–40). The key cities of Damascus and Aleppo therefore remained quiet while the regime pulverised the rebels at the city of Hama in 1982. So rather than endangering the sect, Hafiz al-Asad was seen by Alawites as successfully protecting them from the 'extremism' of the Muslim Brothers. Overall, the effect of heightened insecurity during times of political transition and upheaval has been to increase the solidarity ('asabiyya) of religious minorities, especially during those periods of political flux (Hinnebusch in Kerr and Larkin, 2015: 107–108). The Alawites are no exception to this pattern.

Alawite insecurity has largely been a result of their religious divergences from 'orthodox' Islam. The Alawites are often considered an extremist (*ghulat*) break-away group from Shi'a Islam (Moosa, 1988); however, they consider themselves a legitimate school within Twelver Shi'a Islam (anon. interviews, 2011). Their principal point of difference from the Twelver Shi'a is their elevation of the fourth caliph, 'Ali ibn Abi Talib, and his descendants, the Imams of *Ahl al-Bayt* (People of the House of the Prophet), to near divine status (Friedman, 2010: 72–3). This aspect of Alawite religion is the main reason they have been accused of heresy by orthodox Sunnis and extremism (*ghulaw*) by orthodox Twelver Shi'a Muslims (Bar-Asher and Kofsky, 2002). In general, Alawite religious beliefs are highly syncretistic, containing elements from Christianity and paganism along with a belief in metempsychosis (transmigration of the soul after death). Alawite difference is palpable in contemporary Syrian society as they are relatively liberal in interpreting the role of religion in their daily lives. Alcohol is permitted, Alawite women are not required to wear headscarves and can associate freely in public, and fasting during Ramadan is not strictly observed. Alawites have traditionally not been required to pray in mosques, believing that expression of faith is a personal act. Instead, shrines of Alawite 'saints' and holy men act as focal points for Alawite religious devotion (see Prochazka and Prozchazka, 2010).

The divergence of Alawite religious practice from Islamic orthodoxy has made them targets of intolerance by political powers and religious establishments. The Mamluk era Sunni jurist, Taqil-din Ahmad Ibn Taymiyya (d.1328), was the most famous proponent of intolerance for Alawite heterodoxy (Friedman, 2005: 350). Ibn Taymiyya, had a profound impact on the future of the Alawites with his three religious rulings or fatwas, delivered between 1305 and 1318, which adjudged the Alawites as non-Muslims and worse heretics than Christians and Jews. This played a major part in the Alawites' continuous structural marginalisation under the Mamluk and Ottoman states (Talhamy, 2010; Winter, 2010; Tsugitaka, 1997). Subsequent Sunni based religious and political rulings in 1516 and in the 1820s continued and reinforced Alawite structural insecurity (Talhamy, 2010). In May 2013, the influential Sunni scholar Sheikh Yusuf al-Qaradawi gave a sermon in Doha, Qatar, in which he raised the spectre of the 700-year-old fatwas of Ibn Taymiyya as he judged Alawites collectively complicit in the state violence of the

Asad regime: 'the Nusayris [Alawites] are more disbelieving than the Jews and the Christians ... we see them today killing people like mice and cats by the thousands and tens of thousands' (*Al-Hadath al-'Arabī*, May 2013). The effect of religious difference, set against intolerance in some quarters of the Sunni establishment, clearly remains a major source of structural insecurity for Alawites that drives the security dilemma.

Alawites are also differentiated along class lines. Historically members of the sect were among the lowest socio-economic strata in Syrian society who remained impoverished rural peasants with extremely limited opportunities for upward mobility in Syria (Weulersse, 1940). This perception of Alawite inferiority has persisted even into the modern period, especially among the urban bourgeoisie in Damascus, even as many Syrians came to resent the extreme wealth of those few well-connected Alawite individuals close to the regime, such as the president's cousin Rami Makhlouf (Salamandra, 2000). Alawites are therefore sensitive to the possibility of losing their legal and social equality in Syria and many ordinary Alawites were reportedly outraged to hear the protest chant in Latakia in 2011 suggesting that Bashar al-Asad should 'should return to the farm' (Rosen, 2011). The structural features of the security dilemma in Syria include additional socio-economic factors. The Uprising largely began in rural Sunni majority areas like Dera'a that had suffered severe hardship in the period leading up to the Uprising. Drought and government neglect of rural Syria since the mid-2000s meant that masses of unemployed rural Sunnis became easy targets for jihadist recruiters from 2012 as the regime escalated its brutal repression and the Uprising turned towards armed resistance. Conversely, the regime sought to recruit loyalist militias that came to be known as 'Shabiha' from among the ranks of young working-class men from the minorities, especially poor Alawites (Lund, in Kerr and Larkin, 2015: 212).

The breakdown of the Syrian state's authority over the country's territory and inaction by the international community, fed into the security dilemma. The increasingly anarchic environment compelled Alawites to activate age-old self-defence strategies and villages and towns began arming themselves. Significantly, the vast majority of weapons were supplied to Alawite village militias by the Syrian regime (ibid.: 212), which added impetus to the structural conditions necessary for sparking an escalating ethnic-religious security dilemma. The fact that international actors either could not agree on measures to intervene, or were not prepared to take steps to provide any security for Syria's population, added to the spiralling situation. For the Alawites, caught between a regime that saw the Uprising in 'zero-sum terms' and an opposition that could not contemplate a reversion to the status quo, there was essentially no way out (Kerr and Larkin, 2015). Western hesitation to intervene inside Syria – even beyond firmly declared 'red lines' regarding the use of chemical weapons – meant that Syrian opposition movements had little choice but to rely on financial and military support from regional Sunni states. In mid-2012 Syrian rebels of the secular Free Syrian Army (FSA), which contained many defected soldiers, complained that they were unable to obtain sufficient ammunition and supplies in contrast to newly established Islamist groups who were generously supported by Turkey, Qatar and Saudi Arabia (Yazbek, 2015: 22). This added fuel to the sectarianisation of the conflict ensuring that Alawites felt they had no option but to cling to the Asad regime as a last line of defence against their perceived annihilation at the hands of a vengeful Sunni Muslim majority.

Intangible Alawite insecurities

Sensing or perceiving threats, which are not empirically obvious, is a common component of human nature. It is not always possible to explain why we feel fear other than a gut instinct or a sense of uncertainty. For Alawites, insecurity appears deeply ingrained in their collective consciousness. They have long undergone internal struggles, as a community and as individuals, to overcome their insecurity regarding coexistence with Syria's Sunni majority. In 1936 Alawite elites grappled with this dilemma as the majority Alawite coastal region looked set to be reattached to the Sunni dominated Syrian interior when France came under pressure to terminate its mandate. In that case Alawites, facing few alternatives and pressed into accepting the unionist option by the pure pragmatism of their religious leaders and influential political leaders like the famous shaykh Saleh al-Ali, overcame their fear and ultimately embraced their inclusion in the Syrian state (Yaffe-Schatzmann, 1995).

Throughout Syria's post-independence period Alawite uncertainty regarding a revival of collective Sunni Muslim identity or *'asabiyya* remained, and a level of mistrust existed between the communities, even during the height of the secular Ba'th regime in the 1980s and 1990s. The sectarian distribution of commands in the Syrian army and intelligence services in the Ba'thist period indicates a sustained level of mistrust of even loyal Sunnis by the regime. Alawites were generally privileged in the most sensitive security posts in a 'sectarian network of control'. Related to this mistrust, according to Hinnebusch, there has been little evidence of significant levels of intermarriage between Alawites and Sunnis, except at the level of political elites. This could be due to differences of belief, class or mutual chauvinism (Hinnebusch in Kerr and Larkin, 2015: 114–16). Mistrust and rising resentment among communities was made worse in the 2000s as socio-economic opportunities decreased for most, while a narrow clique of regime-connected Alawite elites became extremely wealthy – the common example is the first cousin of Syrian president, Rami Makhlouf (Goldsmith, 2015: 193).

Long-standing intangible insecurity among Alawites is also shown by a collective sense of uneasiness about their place in the Sunni dominated interior of Syria. Alawite migration into the Syrian interior from the mid-twentieth century was 'cautious', meaning many remained uncertain of their security and permanent acceptance in the urbanised interior (Batatu, 1981: 344). This uneasiness explains why much of Alawite migration to the interior has been 'circular' whereby most families retain very strong links to their traditional villages. For example, many Alawite residents of Hama, Homs or Damascus maintained dual lifestyles between the city and their villages of origin in the different parts of the Coastal Mountains (Jabal Sahiliyah) (Goldsmith in Kerr and Larkin, 2015: 153; Nakkash, 2013: 13).

The need to keep a refuge open in the Sahel and mountain villages is linked to perceptions of 'danger' that could arise in the event of political upheaval in the interior. In 1976–82, for example, Alawite security and military personnel responded to the Muslim Brotherhood revolt by sending their families back to the coastal region (*New York Times*, 28 Oct. 1979). Later, in 2005, the Syrian regime was implicated by international investigators in the murder of former Lebanese prime minister, Rafiq al-Hariri. While no explicit threat existed for Alawite security, the potential for a political crisis caused Alawites to consider the option of retreating to their territorial heartland, as one Alawite man explained, if there are problems 'the people in Damascus will return to the village and they'll find protection with their people' (Shadid, 2005). This impulse to retreat primarily shows a (mis)perception of threat from the Syrian majority population. In 2011–15 this impulse to retreat was again on display from mid-2012 with Alawites streaming into the coastal region from Damascus and Aleppo and other cities of the interior (Hendawi, 2012).

Ironically, the political upheavals of the 2005 Cedar Revolution in Lebanon, which followed the murder of Hariri, and the 2011 Syrian Uprising involved popular expressions of political pluralism and demands for political reform that could have been advantageous to Alawite long-term security and acceptance in Levantine society. The intangible insecurities of Alawites and other minorities, like the Druze, Christians and Ismailis, possibly obstructed a historic opportunity to achieve progress towards those pluralist aspirations along the lines of the original 2011 protest movement in Syria.

A comparable inner struggle to the one posed by the 1936 unification question faced Alawites in 2011 as the anti-government Uprising gathered momentum and challenged the foundations of the Asad regime (Hinnebusch in Kerr and Larkin, 2015: 109). Similar to the community's approach in 1936 many young Alawites joined anti-regime protests in early 2011, pragmatically recognising an inevitable and potentially beneficial political shift, and that the best option was to side with the Uprising and hope for a genuine pluralist change in Syria (Goldsmith, 2015: 196). Many others were afflicted by latent and intangible insecurity (Nakkash, 2013). The observable reaction of most Alawites witnessing the first protests in Latakia in March 2011 was terror based on perceptions of extreme danger from what were clearly peaceful protests (author's observation, March 2011).

Intangible sources of insecurity drove the security dilemma of Alawites from the early stages of the Uprising. When the regime mobilised gangs or militias of ruthless loyalists that came to be known as '*Shabiha*', mutual insecurities between sects were greatly exacerbated. The Shabiha perpetrated brutal atrocities against civilians including what some charge was a regime-sanctioned massacre of civilians in the village of Houla near Homs in May 2012 (Harris, 2015b: 179–80). As the crisis deepened and regime brutality increased, the term Shabiha was increasingly applied collectively to all regime loyalists and assumed a great deal of 'sectarian baggage ... as a synonym for pro-regime Alawis', which led to deepening sectarian mistrust and division (Lefevre in Kerr and Larkin, 2015: 213–14). On the other hand, the armed opposition's requirement for allies against the superior military capability of regime forces meant that they were compelled to cooperate with, or at least tolerate, radical jihadist groups who perpetrated similar atrocities against Alawites. In one example, Alawite civilians were massacred in the central Syria village of Adra by al-Qaeda-linked rebels in December 2013 (Reuters, 12 Dec. 2013). The overall effect of these types of incidents and the opposition's toleration of extremists was to breed fear and mistrust among Alawites about the ideology and intentions of the entire armed opposition (Lefevre in Kerr and Larkin, 2015: 129).

It is important to consider how the peaceful revolutionary protest movements in Syria tried to arrest the structural and intangible drivers of the security dilemma. Local coordinating committees, media centres, and determinedly peaceful activists like, for example, the well-known activist Raed Fares from Kafranbel (famous for its satirical political banners), were aware of the danger from communal insecurity, and attempted to confront the structural and intangible forces of the security dilemma. In the first half of 2011 sectarianism and violence was persistently rejected by protesters who tried to assuage the fears of Alawites and other minorities about the threat to their security in a new post-Asad pluralist Syria. One common protest chant went, 'not Alawi or Sunni, we want freedom … Syria in all its shades and sects' (Wieland in Kerr and Larkin, 2015: 231).

Conversely, the presence of Alawites in the early protests surprised many Sunni activists and challenged misperceptions about universal Alawite support to the political status quo. The efforts of the famous Alawite actress Fadwa Suleiman to support protesters in Homs carried vital symbolic value in countering mutual misperceptions between Sunni and Alawite communities. She addressed the peaceful rally in Clock Square with the chant, 'one, one, one, the Syrian people are one' (YouTube, 7 Dec. 2011). Other Alawites organised themselves into different opposition formations, including the Alawite League of Coordinating Committees, the Party for Modernity and Democracy, and when the struggle turned to armed resistance, the National Unity Battalions sought to fight alongside the opposition (Goldsmith, 2015: 196; Wieland in Kerr and Larkin, 2015: 231–39). Later in 2013, Alawite intellectuals arranged a conference in Cairo and attempted to rally Alawites to the opposition to stem the tide of the rising security dilemma. One of the delegates, Bassem Yousef, reached out to the different Syrian opposition groups to resist the agency of the regime in shaping events: 'we are inviting all of the opposition to confront the sectarian problem being ignited by the regime' (Wieland in Kerr and Larkin, 2015: 241). In a different act of extreme courage, the Alawite writer Samar Yazbek travelled throughout rebel-controlled northern Syria in 2012 and 2013 to foster civil-society among Syrian women, but also, by her presence, challenged rising preconceptions and hatreds towards Alawites by Sunnis (Yazbek, 2015).

The regime undertook rapid and ruthless steps to maintain Alawite solidarity and silence moderate Alawite voices that contradicted its narrative of an 'extremist and intolerant' Sunni opposition movement that offered no future for Alawites. Fadwa Suleiman was vigorously hunted in Homs and was forced to flee the country, the mixed protests in Homs Clock Square were dispersed with live fire on 18 April, 2011 with dozens killed (Wieland in Kerr and Larkin, 2015: 234). Likewise, the shifting nature of the opposition towards extremism fed into a deepening polarisation along identity lines. Samar Yazbek, due to her Alawite identity, was forced to depart from northern Syria as extremist groups began to overpower or absorb the moderate fighters and revolutionaries (Yazbek, 2015). Overall, Alawite revolutionaries quickly found their situation impossible, rejected by their families, co-sectarians and the opposition as the security dilemma of fear and mistrust set in.

As the Uprising expanded and the regime responded with increasing levels of force, Alawites talked of feeling hated; one Alawi resident of Aleppo explained '… since 2011 we have felt the hatred directed against us' (Balanche in Kerr and Larkin, 2015: 104). Cognisant of this Alawite insecurity regarding the Sunni majority, opposition groups have occasionally tried to reassure Alawites. On several occasions the Syrian Muslim Brotherhood have voiced their goal of 'a civil-state that protects the rights of minorities' (Lefevre in Kerr and Larkin, 2015: 126). To Alawite perception this type of discourse does not necessarily penetrate their feelings of insecurity, however, and at best may conjure feelings of a return to second-class or *dhimmi* status under Sunni Muslim 'protection'. Among the more extremist armed groups that have risen to prominence since 2013, including Ahrar al Sham, Jabhat al Nusra and Islamic State, there exists no thought of compromise with Alawites at all, with a common narrative – in private conversations – being that there is no place for Alawites in any future Syrian state (Yazbek, 2015: 234).

It should also be acknowledged that the regime itself is also susceptible to misperception. Whether due to a deficit of popular legitimacy, the Alawite identity of Bashar al-Asad, or a sense of siege by external enemies, the Syrian regime displays a paranoid and conspiratorial mindset. Bashar al-Asad has of course been socialised within his environment. Scholars with intimate knowledge of him have described Bashar as a 'child of the Arab-Israeli war' who believes in the cause of the 'resistance' (Lesch, 2011). It should also be recalled that Bashar was not supposed to be president and has had to struggle to prove himself; his older brother Basil was the heir apparent until his death in a road accident in 1994. Many external pundits predicted the 'weaker' sibling's early demise when he assumed the presidency in mid-2000 (Zisser, 2001: 115). His subsequent survival within the 'Machiavellian' Syrian political arena was testament to his durability and political guile. Moreover, his personal belief about his popularity among the Syrian people became entrenched after his first re-election by referendum in 2007 (Lesch in *Ha'aretz*, 21 June 2009). This belief in his domestic popularity may have been hard for him to let go of, even as the Uprising against his rule surged in 2011. In addition, the fact that Asad became highly popular in the wider Arab world between 2006 and 2009 for his strong support to Hezbollah and Hamas in their respective conflicts with the Israeli Defense Forces, perhaps fed a (mis)perception by Bashar al-Asad that the Uprising must have been, at least partly, a result of conspiracy by both external and internal enemies (Goldsmith, 2015: 156; 176–77).

The basic insecurity of the Syrian regime is encased by its ideological exterior. In Syria, the state continues to dutifully perform the moribund symbols and rhetoric of secular Ba'thism and resistance, which creates a type of mental prison that does not permit any alternative ideas to penetrate. Bashar al-Asad personifies this ideologically rigid mindset. In justifying the brutal repression of opponents in order to preserve Ba'thist Syria, he has compared himself to a heroic surgeon doing the necessary bloody operation to save a patient (*Al-Safir*, 4 June 2012, cit. in Harris, 2015a), or as he explained to the Russian foreign minister, 'I am Syrian, I was born here, I am protecting my people and I will die in Syria' (Kerr and Larkin, 2015: 21). This fixed ideology and belief by Bashar al-Asad that he is somehow personally vital to preserving Syria has created a readiness to undertake utterly ruthless measures in order to achieve his objectives, in a similar way that Stalin and his lieutenants were compelled by their fixed ideology to carry out mass exterminations in the 1930s (Arch and Naumov, 1999: 22). An important part of Asad's policy has been to take measures to ensure that the Alawite community remains inseparably bound to his regime (Kerr and Larkin, 2015: 18).

Agents of Alawite insecurity

A key concern for the Asad regime since the 1970s has been to preserve the idea that strong authoritarian rule is necessary to contain deep-rooted religious, ethnic or sectarian hatreds. So while Syrians have been fully aware of their lack of rights and the absence of political pluralism, many felt the alternative would be chaos. A Damascus merchant commented in June 2005, 'of course we all want change, but when you ask at what cost we all shut up' (Goldsmith, 2015). The Muslim Brotherhood perhaps assisted the regime in this regard in the 1970s and 1980s. At that time the Brotherhood attempted to play the sectarian card to inflame sectarian animosities and arouse the Sunni majority against the 'Godless' Ba'thist regime (Hinnebusch in Kerr and Larkin, 2015: 118). Subsequently the regime promoted itself as the sole guardian of secularism and social equality, which helped to consolidate its power. There remained a contradiction between the regime's championing of Syrian and Arab nationalism at the same time as it relied heavily on maintaining Alawite 'asabiyya as a means to hold power. This dichotomy of a secular regime actively exploiting sectarian identity for political advantage is not lost on many Syrians, for example, Syrian novelist Fadi Azzam critiqued regime strategy as 'sectarian scare mongering dressed up as Marxist critique' (ibid.: 61).

To uphold Alawite 'asabiyya, the regime followed a policy of continually 'stoking fears' of religious intolerance, subjecting the Alawites to a kind of 'Ibn Taymiyya syndrome', which traps the sect in a defensive, insecure mindset regarding the Sunni majority (Winter in Kerr and Larkin, 2015: 49–50). For example, when a bomb exploded in the Sayeda Zeinab neighbourhood of Damascus, killing seventeen people, including a high-ranking officer on 27 September 2008, Sunni Islamic extremists were immediately blamed in state media (SANA, 29 Sep. 2008). However, alternative explanations for the bombing suggested it was possibly a result of internal regime struggles, which provided an additional effect of piquing minority insecurities (Goldsmith, 2015: 175). The latter theory is given additional credence by the testimony of defected regime personnel, who claimed to have been ordered to park explosive laden vehicles in central Damascus in the early stages of the Uprising (Yazbek, 2015).

The Syrian regime under the leadership of Bashar al-Asad has shown itself to be highly durable in its response to the challenges it faced from revolutionary opposition forces since 2011 (Leenders in Kerr and Larkin, 2015: 244). Resorting to violent repression of peaceful protests had a sound logic in terms of authoritarian counter revolutionary measures. First of all, the fall of the regimes in Tunisia and Egypt in early 2011 after the respective security services refused to crush protests, convinced the Syrian regime that it should not make a similar mistake (Abbas, 2011). Verbal appeasements by Egyptian president Hosni Mubarak had done little to quell the surge of protests. Likewise, the dropping of the Syrian Emergency Laws by Bashar al-Asad in April 2011 had no effect on reducing the numbers of Syrians going into the streets. Therefore, the tactics of the Syrian regime understandably reverted to the military-security option that had worked for it in the past, including the destruction of the Muslim Brotherhood revolt at Hama in 1982. According to some scholars and many Syrian activists, 'a civil war scenario actually provided the Syrian regime with a better chance of survival' (Leenders in Kerr and Larkin, 2015: 272). In counterfactual terms, violently supressing a sustained peaceful Uprising, may have eventually forced the international community to take action under Chapter VII of the UN charter to preserve international security or under the 'responsibility to protect' principle. Russia and China would have found it increasingly difficult to justify vetoing UN Security Council resolutions regarding Syria under those conditions.

Whereas, security dilemma theory dictates that state breakdown and resulting power vacuums are key components for activating ethnic-religious conflict, in the Syrian case *the state itself became a prime agent of instability and insecurity*. To ensure the continued support of minorities, the Syrian regime had strong incentives to encourage continuation and intensification of sectarian divisions. Active promotion of a security dilemma between communities in Syria would allow the regime to retain durable support among its key communal social base, the Alawites. In addition, it would have the effect of altering the overall narrative of events from violent state repression of a popular Uprising into a life and death struggle between the 'secular' state and foreign backed 'Sunni terrorism'. This shift of narrative, especially after the rise of the Islamic State in 2013 (al-Tamimi, 2014), was effective among international actors also, who proved increasingly reluctant to support opposition groups who might have links to Islamic State, Jabhat al Nusra or other extremist labelled groups.

Consistent with the regime's long-time strategy of sectarian 'scare mongering', the regime responded immediately to the anti-regime protests in 2011 by proclaiming the Muslim Brotherhood was a driving force behind the protests (Lefevre in Kerr and Larkin, 2015: 126). This was highly unlikely to be the case as the Muslim Brotherhood had retained no organisational presence inside the country. Membership of the Brotherhood had remained a capital offence in Syria since 1980 and, moreover, in 2009 the Islamist group had entered a kind of truce with the regime following the Gaza war with Israel (Goldsmith, 2015: 101, 177). Nonetheless, ever since the destruction of the Brotherhood's revolt in February 1982 in Hama, Alawites had feared a possible reckoning for the massacre that killed around 20,000 people in the space of two weeks. This partly explains the intangible terror shown by Alawite citizens who witnessed protests in Latakia and elsewhere across the country. In order to give substance to Alawites fears the regime looked to inject an Islamist presence in the opposition by strategically releasing radical Islamists from its prisons in early 2011 (Harris, 2015a: 180; Wieland in Kerr and Larkin, 2015: 226). These figures included individuals who would go on to play leading roles in the rise of extremist groups including Jabhat al Nusra and the Islamic State (Yazbek, 2015; *The National*, 21 Jan. 2014).

The solidification of sectarian divisions was deepened by the recruitment of pro-regime militias along communal lines. The regime tapped into perceptions of threat among young poor Alawites regarding the protests to rapidly organise them into local gangs tasked with countering the early stages of the Uprising. This process was clearly on display in central Latakia in March 2011. Rather than attempting to cordon off and contain protests, security personnel actively directed these Alawite 'gangs' towards the scene of protests. In addition, to add to the terror and confusion, random gunmen aimed shots into the demonstrating crowds from rooftop positions (author's observation, 25 March, 2011). Alawites resident in the Syrian interior were less susceptible to recruitment into these militias at first – many in fact joined protests in Homs and Damascus. But after the regime used lethal force to disperse peaceful protesters in Homs' Clock Square in 18–19 April 2011 Alawite insecurities were activated by rising mutual sectarian mistrust; for example, Alawite youths began to question their situation relative to the Uprising after angry calls to jihad were broadcast from the minarets of Sunni mosques after the massacre of unarmed protesters by regime security forces (Nakkash, 2013). Thereafter, regime intelligence officers worked to recruit young Alawite men into the pro-regime militias with monthly salaries paid for by regime-connected businessmen, such as the Al Bustan fund (Lund in Kerr and Larkin, 2015: 219).

These initial gangs, which came to be known as Shabiha numbered around 5,000–10,000 in late March 2011, but would grow to form the nucleus of increasingly sectarian defined military formations separating Alawites off from the wider opposition movement in real terms. The establishment from late 2012 of the National Defence Forces (NDF), which comprised mostly Alawite recruits subjected to Iranian training and indoctrination – similar to the sectarian mobilisation of Lebanese Shi'ites by Iran in the 1980s – further entrenched the sectarianisation of the conflict in Syria (Nassief, 2014: 13; Spyer, 2013: 11; Lund in Kerr and Larkin, 2015: 219).

Against the backdrop of growing sectarianisation of the conflict, the International Red Cross officially declared the Syrian situation as a 'non-international armed conflict' (civil war) in early June 2012 (Reuters, 12 June 2012). This completed an important element of the regime's struggle for survival. A 'civil war' scenario freed the regime to deploy greater military force against the expanding pockets of territory that had been liberated from regime control without significant risk of international intervention. Beginning with the mass bombardment of the rebel held Homs suburb of Baba Amru in February 2012, the regime increasingly deployed its superior military power against the lightly armed rebels. Over the following three years heavy artillery, helicopter gun-ships, fighter jets, ballistic missiles, chemical weapons and barrel bombs were increasingly deployed against urban areas containing concentrated – mainly Sunni – civilian populations. The involvement of Arab Gulf states and Turkey to support Sunni rebels with weapons and funding was countered by the direct intervention of Shi'a Hizballah ground forces inside Syria from May 2013, escalating the sectarian and regional character of the conflict (Harris, 2015b: 181).

Overall, the Asad regime's gambit to spark sectarianism in Syria to preserve its rule has been successful in downgrading the threat posed by any viable secular and nationalist alternatives to the regime (Wieland in Kerr and Larkin, 2015: 226), but has come at massive cost. An estimated 260,000 people have been killed and the Syrian state's territory and society has been irreparably torn apart along ethnic-sectarian lines (Syrian Observatory for Human Rights, n.d.). Moreover, the direct entrance of Russian and Iranian air and ground forces into the Syrian theatre in September–October 2015 presented grave risks for regional stability as increasingly assertive Gulf Arab states vowed to counter what they view as a war against Syria's Sunni population (Pierret, 2015). At the street level, the Asad regime's use of mass violence against its population and the degradation of moderate rebels groups have provided fertile ground for the Islamic State and other jihadist groups to expand recruitment among young Sunni males. Within this polarising situation, Alawites find themselves caught in a perilous position between extreme forces; a regime that is not prepared to countenance any concession to any opposition forces which it views in blanket terms as terrorists, and a radicalised opposition that sees Alawites as religious deviants and complicit in an attempt to exterminate Syria's Sunni population.

Conclusion

The most tragic part about the course of events in Syria since 2011 is that it was not necessarily inevitable that the structural and intangible factors of the security dilemma at the outset of the Uprising would lead the country and the Alawites into the nightmarish abyss that existed with the post-2012 militarisation of the conflict. There is reason to believe that the Syrian regime through its agency and deliberative steps to preserve its rule carries much of the responsibility for the humanitarian crisis caused by the destruction of the country and the wave of desperate Syrian refugees who are landing on the shores of surrounding states and Europe. Saudi Arabia, Qatar and Turkey also bear some responsibility for pushing opposition forces into a Sunni framework, which stripped the revolution of its initial pluralist character.

The structural factors of a long history of Alawite marginalisation and religious and social difference undoubtedly played a part in sparking the security dilemma inside Syria. Moreover, in a fluid and volatile period of change across the region, it was natural for uncertainty around the intentions of the 'other' to emerge among minorities and other groups. Syrians from all backgrounds were, however, struggling to overcome those threats. In the face of political actors that were prepared to spark and exploit sectarian conflict, and an international community that was not prepared or able to provide any security for Syrians, the resistance of Syrians to the forces of the security dilemma would eventually break. The role of authoritarian regimes bent on preserving key allies or reducing foes, and Western democracies' lacking any coherent policy regarding the Syrian crisis has played a key role in the course of events in Syria; however, the initial conditions that laid the foundations for the sectarianisation of the conflict and opened the door to external intervention and state break up were created by the Syrian regime under the leadership of Bashar al-Asad.

Bibliography

Abbas, Hassan (2011), 'The Dynamics of the Syrian Uprising', *Arab Reform Initiative Brief*, 51, (October), www.arab-reform.net/sites/default/files/ARB_51_Syria_Oct_2011_H-Abbas_En.pdf.

Arch, Getty J., and Naumov, Oleg V. (1999), *The Road to Terror: Stalin and the Self-Destruction of the Bolsheviks, 1932–1939*, trans. Benjamin Sher, New Haven: Yale University Press.

al-Tamimi, Aymenn (2014), 'The Dawn of the Islamic State of Iraq and ash-Sham', *Current Trends in Islamist Ideology*, 16: 27 (Janurary).

Bar-Asher, Meir M. and Kofsky, Aryeh (2002), *The Nusayri-'Alawī Religion: An Enquiry into its Theology and Liturgy*, Leiden: Brill.

Batatu, Hanna (1981), 'Some Observations on the Social Roots of Syria's Ruling Military Group and the Causes for its Dominance', *Middle East Journal*, 35: 3 (Summer), 331–344.

Bengio, O. and Ben-Dor, G. (eds) (1999), *Minorities and the State in the Arab World*, Boulder: Lynne Rienner.

Butterfield, Herbert (1951), *History and Human Relations*, London: Collins.

Charbonneau, Louis (2012), 'Syria Conflict Now a Civil War, U.N. Peacekeeping Chief Says', *Reuters*, 12 June. http://uk.mobile.reuters.com/article/topNews/idUKBRE85B1FM20120612 (accessed 2 Aug. 2015).

Friedman, Yaron (2005), 'Ibn Taymiyya's Fatwa against the Nusayri-Alawi Sect', *Der Islam*, 82: 2.

Friedman, Yaron (2010), *The Nusayrī -'Alawīs: An Introduction to the Religion, History and Identity of the Leading Minority in Syria*, Leiden: Brill.

Goldsmith, L. (2011), 'Syria's Alawites and the Politics of Sectarian Insecurity: A Khaldunian Perspective', *Ortadoğu Etüdleri*, 3: 1, 33–60.

Goldsmith, Leon (2012), 'Alawites for Asad: Why the Syrian Sect Backs the Regime', *Foreign Affairs*, 16 April.

Goldsmith, L. (2013), 'God Wanted Diversity': Alawite Pluralist Ideals and their Integration in Syrian Society 1832–1973', *British Journal of Middle Eastern Studies*, 40: 4, 392–409.

Goldsmith, Leon (2015), *Cycle of Fear: Syria's Alawites in War and Peace*, London: Hurst.

Ha'aretz, Israel (2009), 'Assad No Longer Stands in his Father's Shadow', 21 June.

Harris, William (2015a), 'Syria's Firestorm: Where From? Where to?' *Ortadoğu Etütleri*, 6: 2 (January), 8–26.
Harris, William (2015b), *The Levant: A Fractured Mosaic*, 4th Edition, Princeton: Markus-Wiener.
Hendawi, Hamza (2012), 'Syria Sectarian Divide Turns to Fear and Flight', The Associated Press, 27 August.
Hertz, John (1966), *International Politics in the Atomic Age*, New York: Columbia University Press.
Jessup, Henry H. (1910), *Fifty Three Years in Syria*, London: Fleming H. Revell.
Kalin, Stephen (2013), 'Islamists kill 15 Alawite and Druze civilians in Syria – activists', Reuters, December, 12, www.reuters.com/article/us-syria-crisis-adra/islamists-kill-15-alawite-and-druze-civilians-in-syria-activists-idUSBRE9BB0PM20131212.
Kerr, M. and Larkin, C. (eds) (2015), *The Alawis of Syria: War, Faith and Politcs in the Levant*, New York: Oxford University Press.
Khaldun, Ibn (1967), *The Muqaddimah: An Introduction to History*, trans. F. Rosenthal, abr. N. J. Dawood, London: Routledge & Kegan Paul.
Lesch, David (2011), 'The Syrian President I know', *New York Times*, 29 March, 2011, www.nytimes.com/2011/03/30/opinion/30lesch.html?_r=0.
Maundrell, Henry (1963), *A Journey from Aleppo to Jerusalem in 1697*, Beirut: Kyats.
Moosa, Matti (1988), *Extremist Shiites: The Ghulat Sects*, New York: Syracuse University Press.
Nakkash, Aziz (2013), 'The Alawite Dilemma in Homs: Survival, Solidarity and the Making of a Community', Freidrich Ebert Stiftung, March.
Nassief, Isabel (2014), 'The Campaign for Homs and Aleppo', Middle East Security Report, Institute for the Study of War, No. 17.
Pierret, Thomas (2015), 'We Break it You Own It: Russia's Logic in Syria', *Global Observatory*, 20 Oct., http://theglobalobservatory.org/2015/10/russia-syria-putin-assad-nato-isis/ (accessed 23 Oct. 2015).
Posen, Barry R. (1993), 'The Security Dilemma and Ethnic Conflict', *Survival*, 35: 1, Spring, 27–47.
Prochazka-Eisl, G. and S. Prozchazka (2010), *The Plain of Saints and Prophets: The Nusayri-Alawi Community of Cilicia (Southern Turkey) and its Sacred Places*, Wiesbaden: Harrassowitz Verlag.
Roe, Paul (2000), 'Former Yugoslavia: The Security Dilemma That Never Was', *European Journal of International Relations*, 6: 3, 373–393.
Rosen, Nir (2011), 'Assad's Alawites: The Guardians of the throne', *Al Jazeera*, 10 October.
Salamandra, Christa (2000), 'Consuming Damascus: Public Culture and the Construction of Social Identity', in *Mass Mediations, New Approaches to Popular Culture in the Middle East and Beyond*, edited by W. Armbrust, 182–202, Berkeley: University of California Press.
Shadid, Anthony (2005), 'Death of Syrian Minister Leaves a Sect Adrift in a Time of Strife', *Washington Post*, 31 October.
Spyer, Jonathan (2013), 'Fragmented Syria', *Middle East Review of International Affairs*, 17: 3 (Fall).
Syrian Observatory for Human Rights (n.d.), website: www.syriahr.com/ (accessed 1 Oct. 2015).
Talhamy, Yvette (2008), 'The Nusayri Leader Isma'il Khayr Bey and the Ottomans (1854–1858)', *Middle Eastern Studies*, 44: 6 (Nov), 895–908.
Talhamy, Yvette (2010), 'The Fatwas and the Nusayri/Alawis of Syria', *Middle Eastern Studies*, 46: 2, 175–194.
The National, Abu Dhabi (2014), 'Assad regime set free extremists from prison to fire up trouble during peaceful uprising', 21 Jan., www.thenational.ae/world/syria/assad-regime-set-

free-extremists-from-prison-to-fire-up-trouble-during-peaceful-uprising (accessed 23 Oct. 2015).
Tsugitaka, Sato (1997), *State & Rural Society in Medieval Islam*, Leiden: Brill.
VOA, United States (2009), 'Syria Profits from Regional Diplomatic Upheaval after Gaza Conflict', 2 Feb., www.voanews.com/english/2009-02-02-voa39.cfm.
Waines, David (1977), 'The Third Century Internal Crisis of the Abbasids', *Journal of the Economic and Social History of the Orient*, 20: 3 (October), 282–306.
Weulersse, Jacque (1940), *Le pays des Alaouites* Tours: Arrault & Cie, Maitres imprimeurs.
Winter, Stefan (2010), *The Shiites of Lebanon under Ottoman Rule, 1516–1788*, Cambridge: Cambridge University Press.
Yaffe, Gitta and Uriel Dann (1993), 'Suleiman al-Murshid: Beginnings of an Alawi Leader', *Middle Eastern Studies*, 29: 4 (October), 624–640.
Yaffe-Schatzmann, Gitta (1995), 'Alawi Separatists and Unionists: The Events of 25 February 1936', *Middle Eastern Studies*, 31: 1 (January), 28–38.
Yazbek, Samar (2015), *The Crossing: My Journey to the Shattered Heart of Syria*, trans. Nashwa Gowanlock and Ruth Kemp, London: Rider Books.
YouTube website, 'Al-Khaldiyah, Homs: Actress Fadwa Sulaiman & Goalkeeper Al-Saroot Lead Protest', uploaded 7 Dec. 2011, https://www.youtube.com/watch?v=RjEwoZ6rZlY.
Ziadeh, Radwan (2011), *Power and Policy in Syria*, New York: I.B.Tauris.
Zisser, Eyal (2001), 'The Syrian Army: Between the Domestic and the External Fronts', *MERIA Journal*, 5: 1 (March).

11

EMERGENCE OF THE POLITICAL VOICE OF SYRIA'S CIVIL SOCIETY

The non-violent movements of the Syrian Uprising

Tamara Al-Om

Introduction

This chapter proposes that a political dimension of Syrian civil society emerged from amongst the non-violent movements of the Syrian Uprising. It seeks to show this by highlighting the changing nature of Syria's civil society and its various manifestations, particularly between the years of 2000 and 2015. After a conceptual introduction, the state of Syria's civil society pre-Uprising, under Bashar al-Asad's rule, is surveyed. Then, the chapter shows how Syria's non-violent movements acquired a space in civil society during the post-2011 Uprising. The chapter expands the wider debate on civil society by incorporating resistance as a central theme.

Civil society is commonly perceived to be 'outside of the State and marketplace' and 'the opposite of family' (Van Rooy 1998; Zinecker 2011), autonomous of both but interacting with, rather than subordinate to the state. For state and civil society to interact, the relationship would probably have to be built on the foundations of democracy and where government is non-democratic and restricts civil society, its role can evolve into non-violent resistance. Non-violent resistance (NVR) is a strategy to achieve political and social change using active 'non-violent methods, by withdrawing consent through non-cooperation or civil disobedience of unjust laws, so that governments can no longer operate' (Chenoweth and Cunningham 2013). Civil society's *political voice* is vital to its role as resistance, a voice which was long denied in Syria, but which began to develop in the early years of the Uprising.

The case of Syrian civil society

Syrian civil society prior to the Uprising in early 2011 was largely subdued, having to act within the constraints of a regime with a very limited conception of civil society. Many, if not all, of the arenas that would fall under the realm of civil society were controlled by the state. While there were certain elements of Syrian civil society that had some degree of presence and even autonomy, the existence of a political voice was limited in every respect (Sawah 2012). A corporatist form of associational life was established by the Ba'th Party itself that pre-empted space for alternative autonomous associations. In addition, there was also a more primordial civil society, groups one would be part of by virtue of birth and not choice per se – such as kinship, the tribe or religious affiliation. There was also a significant number of religious charities, both Islamic and Christian, that had a prominent role in society. However, all were required to undertake their activities under the conditions controlled by the regime. Civil society was harnessed to government ends, enabling the outsourcing of state welfare functions to charity organisations that supported the poor, elderly, disabled, the young and women. While certain areas of civil society of a certain limited kind did exist within Syria (Khalaf et al. 2014; Yassin-Kassab and Al-Shami 2016), it had little *political voice*. As Yassin Al Haj Saleh (2014) put it, there was:

> no space for internal political life, no space for public conversation or for any type of independent political organisation. Indeed, it was impossible for groups of Syrians to gather even in private homes to discuss public matters. The Syrian people lived in absolute political poverty, forbidden for more than forty years the right to assembly and the right to speech.

While under Hafez al-Asad's presidency, any independent political activities by civil society were suppressed, the coming to power of his son Bashar in 2000 saw the potentiality for change and many saw the new president as promising much needed economic and political liberalisation and modernisation. Accountability, transparency, development and reform were key words in his early speeches, particularly when it came to the realms of education and culture. Bashar stated, 'our educational, cultural and media institutions must be reformed and modernised in a manner that ... renounces the mentality of introversion and negativity' (George 2003: 129). Although some were sceptical of any real change occurring, many remained hopeful.

It was during the early phase of Bashar's presidency that the Damascus Spring became visible with the emergence of the phenomena of the 'salons', the civil society meetings and discussion groups which, although concentrated in Damascus, spread across Syria. Some of the most famous of these salons included Riad Seif's National Dialogue Forum, the Jamal Al Atassi Forum and Al Kawakibi Forum. These meetings revolved around issues of political reform. While consisting largely of a certain strata of Syrian society, its writers, poets and intellectuals, the meetings and events grew in popularity and gained attendees from more varied sections of Syrian society. Alan George (2003: 35) stipulates that it was the aim of these associations to 'revive the institutions of civil society and achieve balance between their role and that of the state'. Michel Kilo highlighted the aim of the movement as a revival of civil society based on an attempt to bring the people of Syria into the fold, in order for the movement to cease to be an elitist group that was not in touch with Syrian reality. He states (George 2003: 33–34),

> either we could work as an elite and found a new political party. Or we could work in a different way, offering knowledge, ideas, experiences, reflections and emotions [to that part of society] which is now outside of politics: to help society restore itself politically through a cultural project that we offered.

Numerous high-profile attempts to press the government for reform included the Statement of the 99, and the subsequent Statement of the 1,000 and the Damascus Declaration much later in 2005. All of these initiatives were essentially demanding an end to the state of emergency, an amnesty for all political prisoners and a return of those in exile, the establishment of a state of law which would include secularism and pluralism, freedom of the press, expression and assembly and the liberation of public life. At no point did these initiatives call for an outright change of regime and sought rather to work with the government to bring about reform *over time*. While initially these gatherings were tolerated, the government soon changed its position and arrests and detainment followed. According to Robert Rabil (2003) this was sending a 'clear message to the public that it would not tolerate any reform it could not control'. The beginnings of an independent civil society were seen as a threat to the stability and security of the state and as such were suppressed. The hard line of Hafez al-Asad would be upheld by his son (and the 'old guard'). Moreover, according to Wael Sawah (2009), even within the ruling Ba'th Party, 'activists have been unable to meet and discuss party policy, which has remained in the hands of small circles of leaders, and have been without the means to engage in healthy political life inside the party or in society, which [has] affect[ed] the performance of the civil society itself'. As a result, the majority of activities occurred in secret, between close knit circles of those deemed trustworthy. This forced many to cease their attendance, and crippled the movement. Despite attempts to involve a broader spectrum of people, the relentless government pressures and restrictions faced by these movements meant they were unable to penetrate mainstream society and remained without the support of the masses, and hence powerless to achieve the change for which they strove (Pace 2005).

In the years following the Damascus Spring, the regime attempted to create its own version of civil society, particularly following the establishment of the Syria Trust for Development in 2007 patronised by Asma al-Asad, the president's wife. The issue of civil society was put on the agendas of both the 10th (2006–2010) and 11th (2011–2015) Five Year Plans, which were interested in creating workshops and initiatives to further involve civil society in Syria's development, albeit under government leadership. These initiatives included such things as encouraging entrepreneurship among the younger population, the development of locally based and EU–Syrian partnership projects for rural development, and associations promoting rights of women, higher education standards, and culture as a means of increasing the role of civil society. One of the most significant initiatives was the introduction of laws granting a modern legal framework to civil society and its non-governmental organisations (NGOs) (Star, 2010). The problem with this, however, was the government's continued right to approve or reject formation of NGOs and its continued power over their activities. While certain initiatives addressed some important issues, including women's rights and poverty, a great deal of the reforms advocated were never realised in practice. For example, the work undertaken by NGOs on women's rights, who were fighting for 'the right of a Syrian woman to pass their nationality to their children' and for laws against honour killings and marital rape never came to fruition (Al-Om 2015). As a result, these GONGOS (Government non-governmental organisations) did little for social freedom and nothing for political freedom, which was overwhelmingly neglected. For Joshua Landis (2011), these initial efforts could be a government attempt to 'open up more space for civil society to grow, breathe and develop'. However, as Yahya al-Aous (2013) argues, it was purely within the confines of what the state deems acceptable. Religious institutions found themselves tightly controlled by the regime and its appointed officials, professional institutions were limited to Ba'thist organisations as were most of the educational institutions. Cultural institutions, which the regime advertised as 'humanity's highest need' remained firmly in the hands of the regime, which saw the need, in Miriam Cooke's words, for 'absolute control over the production of culture' (Cooke 2007). The permitted (and controlled) activities of NGOs largely remained in the realm of economics, providing more freedom and flexibility exclusively to business and enterprise which, had it deepened, might have resulted in the construction of 'a business-centred civil society' (Hinnebusch 1993) by a growing new bourgeoisie which could potentially have led to demands for a greater rule of law and a limiting of state power. However, the interests of the business elite rarely converged with the interests of the intellectuals within the civil society movement[1] and certainly did not with average Syrians.[2] The one-dimensional conception of civil society that the regime espoused, which attempted to *appear* to represent the needs of the people, was insufficient to drive social and political reform. Indeed as the Syrian thinker Burhan Ghalyun (Browers 2006) put it years earlier,

> the socially alienated state fears its own society and views every move or whisper coming from civil society as political opposition, a rejection of the state authority and a direct threat to the existence of the community, the nation and the revolution. As a result, the state has turned inward, toward its own coercive forces, which are developed at great expense, not to provide for the needs of society, but to better crush it.

Syria's civil society post-Uprising

It would be overly simplistic to assume that the lack of autonomy and freedom granted to Syrian civil society was the cause of the Uprising in 2011. However it was the lack of a political voice within civil society over an extended period of time that prevented people from having their needs heard and met that led to the emergence of the peaceful protests and also to the suppression of them.

When the uprisings began in Tunisia, shortly followed by Bahrain, Egypt, Libya and a number of other Arab countries, the situation in Syria remained relatively calm. President Bashar al-Asad stated, in an interview with the *Wall Street Journal* on 31 January 2011, that an Uprising in Syria was unlikely to transpire in the same way, while also articulating a reformist agenda and presenting an awareness of the need for immediate political and social reform. This apparent calm was explained by many experts and analysts as a combination of Bashar's nationalist foreign policy, certain reforms which opened up the country to a number of services that had previously been inaccessible, most notably the Internet; and the acceptance of many Syrians that change takes time and that Bashar should be given a chance. Another explanation for the initial absence of widespread protests was the fear of possible sectarian conflict: 'many Syrians believe[d] that the ruling Ba'th Party's emphasis on secularism [was] the best option (*Syria: Kingdom of Silence* 2011)'. According to Joshua Landis, society was vulnerable to fragmentation along sectarian lines and hence would not easily come together against the regime as had happened in the Egyptian and Tunisian Revolutions. Finally, according to Gerges, '… the army would fight to protect not only the institution of the army but the regime itself, because the army and the regime is one and the same' (Syria: Kingdom of Silence 2011).

The numerous Facebook calls mounted by expatriate (or exiled) Syrians for a 'Day of Rage' across Syrian cities in early February were initially met with deafening silence on the streets, apart from the presence of the undercover security forces, the *mukhabarat*, since public displays of discontent carried too high a risk. However, social media sites provided a public sphere enabling some freedom to activists to express themselves and disseminate information. Later it became a means for the organisation and mobilisation of people. As such, it didn't take long for the 'wall of fear to fall' and it quickly became clear that the dissatisfaction of the Syrian people was greater than perceived and for infectious feelings and desires for freedom, dignity and justice to spread. Unfortunately, the government responded to small peaceful protests with violent repression, which, in turn ignited larger peaceful protests that began to appear across Syria.

These movements began with acts of solidarity with the Tunisian and Egyptian people. A number of candlelight vigils were held in Bab Touma, Damascus, were quickly dispersed, with many demonstrators being monitored or detained by security forces. Concurrently, a number of school children were detained and tortured in Dera'a for scrawling slogans in public places: 'The people want the fall of the regime' and 'It's your turn next doctor'. Another impetus was provided by the torture, mutilation and murder of Hamza Al Khateeb, a thirteen-year-old boy, after being picked up by regime forces during a demonstration. Rima Dali, an attorney and prominent dissident, led the 'Brides of Damascus' group who dressed in traditional white wedding gowns in the streets of Souq Hamadiya of Old

Damascus, handed out roses and held bright red signs stating 'Stop the killing: We want to build a Syria for all Syrians, Stop all military operations in Syria, 100% Syrian'. These protests soon grew in size and spread in number, particularly with the increasing brutality of the regime, 'the wave of killings and arrests, torture and humiliation targeting people who were not even involved in the demonstrations drove many who steered clear of politics to join the protest movement' (Sinjab 2013).

The next few months saw hundreds of thousands of Syrians take to the streets across the country. And while many protests were organised online and via mobile phones, those attending were not only the youth of Syria but a multitude of people from various backgrounds. The sentiments of the protests were visible in the activities, slogans and songs that were adopted including: 'The Syrians won't be humiliated'. Trying to head off attempts to divide the public on sectarian lines, the protestors chanted, 'One, one, one, the Syrian people are one' and the handing out of roses and water bottles to soldiers, underlined the peaceful character of the protest (Sinjab 2013). As the violence increased, calls for the fall of the regime increased, with the introduction of songs such as 'It's time to leave, Bashar'[3] and 'The hearts of the army are dead' in an attempt to encourage soldiers to defect. Regardless of the peaceful nature of the protests or the sentiments espoused, protestors were soon met with tanks and bullets and Internet and mobile services were interrupted.

As the protests grew, so did government violence towards them. It was the city of Hama, the scene of the massacre of 1982 that witnessed the largest peaceful protests of over 400,000 people in July 2011 and, as a result, was faced with a violent siege. This was a scene that was replicated across Syrian towns and cities. The regime aim was to put a stop to the protests by any means necessary, with the use of tanks, snipers, checkpoints, and militia (*Shabiha*) who would attack, rape and murder people in their own homes. This strategy was partly successful because it became impossible for people to gather without severe consequence but the relentless targeting of peaceful protestors inevitably led to the emergence of an armed resistance. In this way, the initial calls for economic, social and political reform, with a desire to work with the government towards the establishment of 'a new social contract' (Abbas 2014) quickly turned to calls for regime change. The militarisation of the conflict followed which made it easier for foreign extremist groups to enter Syria and hijack the Uprising. Regrettably, the dominant narrative of the mainstream media has focused on the violence, ignoring the enduring impact of the work undertaken by Syria's non-violent movement (Al-Om 2014). Despite the fact that the movement was not allowed to move beyond demonstrations into a fully engaged civil resistance, its work persisted in the face of hostility, kidnappings, arrest and death perpetuated by both the regime and extremist groups active on the ground.

Syria's NVM is by no means homogeneous and was, rather made up of hundreds of quite varied groups. Activist Omar Aseel and members of the Syrian Non-violence Movement created a comprehensive mapping of these groups, the numbers and nature of which have changed significantly over the duration of the Uprising.[4] Another recent study, *Activism in Difficult Times: Civil Society Groups in Syria 2011–2014*, examines a multitude of these groups across various areas of Syria and explores their varying identities, activities and struggles (Khalaf 2014). Their differences in ideology, activity, organisation, interaction with external forces, etc., are dependent on numerous factors including their location, the presence of extremist groups, their ability to cross borders and their access to funds. There is also significant diversity among the members of these groups, Syrian citizens who come from all classes, sects and religions, many of whom had no previous experience of activism. As Al-Achi put it, 'in the past, most Syrians shunned civil society initiatives because these were the very activities stopped by the Ba'th Party. The revolution forced Syrians to reconnect with each other and to begin working together effectively' (quoted in Halasa 2014b).

While a great deal of these groups initially came together to organise and attend peaceful demonstrations and then later to provide humanitarian relief to the besieged areas once the violence erupted, their roles developed far beyond this. The establishment of civilian-led Local Co-ordination Committees (LCC) and Local Councils in many of the non-government controlled areas were, according to Al-Achi, 'among the earliest political networks to form cells across Syria. Their template for collective action helped spread the tactic of non-violent civil disobedience during the first year of the uprising' (Halasa 2014b). Some of the key areas of their work can be seen to fall into several categories.

Media

The LCC's created media centres that became key in the dissemination of information both within Syria between different groups, towns and cities and internationally. Furthermore, the emergence of the citizen-journalist, following the expelling of foreign correspondents and news agencies from the country, enabled an unrivalled access to and dissemination of photographic images and video footage of the events taking place on the ground. Omar Alassad (Halasa et al. 2014: 113) sees the establishment of informal news agencies as breaking the 'long history of censorship and disinformation'. A number of opposition media outlets opened, including numerous newspapers and radio stations, predominantly functioning online; examples include Radio SouriaLi established in October 2012 'in an attempt to bypass censorship and reach out to the largest number of Syrians, both within and outside the country …'[5] and the publication of a local newspaper in January 2012, *The Grapes of my Country*, by a women's group in Darayya, Damascus, who worked towards promoting 'the principles of the civil state and civil society'.[6] Most importantly, the use of new media in the virtual realm enabled NVMs to continue to work, as one research paper stipulates, 'clandestinely, even in areas under control of extremist armed groups' in order to ensure their interaction could continue 'with the Syrian diaspora and the international community' (Khalaf 2014). Even when the regime attempted to put restrictions on their ability to communicate by cutting off mobile phones and the Internet, they were still able to communicate, using satellite phones, more freely than they ever had been before the Uprising began.

Art and culture[7]

Graffiti, from which the Uprising began, became, 'despite extreme danger, little by little, wall by wall' one of the most 'powerful forms of resistance' (Halasa et al. 2014: 285). An example of the use of graffiti is the works of the *Lovers' Notebooks* on the walls of Saraqeb, Idlib. Upon the liberation of the city from regime forces in late 2012 many began to 'celebrate their new-found freedom by painting the walls of their city,'[8] depicting the experiences of their lives and using quotes from famous Arab poets. However, with the increased presence and dominance of extremist groups, many of the works were painted over and the activists' ability to continue their work was made impossible, with many having to flee the country. Some of them, however, continued their work in exile, recently releasing a film on the subject of the *Lovers' Notebooks*.

The creative and artistic expression of those within the NVMs extends beyond graffiti and has involved the production of art in its numerous forms, including film, music, comedy, comics, cartoons, poetry and literature. The publication and distribution of pamphlets and underground intellectual literature, the making and production of posters and magazines and the organising symbolic public acts were part of an explosion in long suppressed free expression. One of the most internationally visible acts of expression were the satirical banners, often in English, from the town of Kafranbel. The messages on the banners not only reflect the struggle of the people of Kafranbel and the rest of Syria but also highlight the hypocrisies of the international community, feature international current events and use international cultural symbols and icons in an attempt to universalise and humanise their struggle. Another example is the Damascus street campaign carried out by *Save the Rest*, which attempts to highlight the plight of the prisoners of conscience held by the Syrian regime. They distributed pamphlets across the city that were disguised as folded 500 Syrian pound notes with information about the suffering; some with messages from the prisoners themselves.[9]

Rebuilding of institutions

A large proportion of the work undertaken by the NVM was concerned with rebuilding, in non-regime controlled areas, the economic, legal, civic, social, cultural and moral foundations for a functioning civil society with a political voice. Part of this process was about developing strategies for rebuilding democratic communities by liberating minds, encouraging intellectual and creative thought and action, promoting reconciliation and attempting to counter pressure from extremist groups. Many of these NVM groups have also, according to Khalaf et al. (2014), 'contributed to containing the process of fragmentation along ethnic, sectarian, political and ideological lines, and continue to do so today despite the prevailing climate of violence'. Khalaf et al. also found that these groups and the local councils they set up introduced various public services including the distribution of aid, medical services and education, maintenance of the judiciary system and management of waste collection in areas that had previously been under regime control. Courts and security services were set up in many areas (until the spread of extremist groups took over many of them) and 'free' trade unions and students groups were also established to counter the decades-long restrictions of these groups under the Ba'thist umbrella. Other forms of organisation included youth networks, development associations and rights-based organisations (Khalaf et al. 2014).

The conducting of educational workshops has also been a priority for the NVMs, including running workshops on media and communication skills, humanitarian and medical assistance, legal awareness and many others. For example, the organisation 'Building the Syrian State' runs leadership and democracy building workshops[10] with the aim of arming the people with the ability to rebuild the country and not leave it in the hands of the government or foreign forces. Interestingly, some of the most popular workshops were based on Gene Sharp's teachings on civil disobedience and resistance (Halasa 2014b).

Inevitably, the need for legal assistance also emerged and as a result an organisation which began as a Facebook group soon developed into the Free Syrian Lawyers Association. According to members of the group who work between Turkey and Syria, they attempt not only to represent the Syrian people in need of legal assistance, but also to 'hold the revolution to higher standards' by supervising 'FSA interrogations of captured army soldiers, monitor[ing] rebel 'courts' and provide[ing] representation to defendants accused of supporting the government'. According to one of the founding members of the organisation, 'the ultimate aim is to set up temporary criminal courts in all liberated areas' (Syria's Legal Fight 2013).

The Syrian Civil Defence group known as the White Helmets have become a symbol of the Syrian struggle against violent and indiscriminate oppression. They are a group of 2,900 volunteer search and rescue workers from local communities who risked their lives – with 167 having been killed as of October 2016 – to save others following attacks and bombings. According to their website, they 'save people on all sides of the conflict ... deliver public services to nearly 7 million people, including reconnecting electrical cables, providing safety information to children and securing buildings'. They also state that they are 'the largest civil society organisation operating in areas outside of government control' which pledges 'commitment to the principles of 'Humanity, Solidarity, Impartiality" (White Helmets Website). They were nominated for the 2016 Nobel Peace Prize and in September 2016 Netflix released a film documenting their activities, with their motto 'To save a life is to save all of humanity'.

The imagery and image of the non-violent movements

As touched upon previously, many of the activities of these groups were an attempt to remind people of the original aims and values of the Uprising. A spokesperson from Kartoneh, an anonymous collective of artists and activists who produce banners in Deir Al Zour, highlighted this sentiment: regardless of the struggles activists faced 'we did not carry weapons, despite the siege ... we still insist on expressing ourselves in the same simple way in which we started' (Halasa 2014: 62). An interesting feature of a great deal of the activities of the NVM is the juxtaposition of the imagery and symbolism adopted by the various groups to the cult of personality and symbolism of the regime. They have purposely, as Charlotte Bank highlights, steered 'clear of creating new icons' (Halasa et al. 2014: 75) and leadership figures and instead have adopted images of the children and youth of Syria, symbols of the breaking away from the fear, paralysis and silence that their society was riddled with for so long and instead focusing on 'ideas based on choice, not force' as Zaher Omareen stated (Halasa et al. 2014: 102).

The NVM had to adapt and reinvent themselves with the evolution of events. One of the findings of Khalaf et al. in terms of the identity of the NVM groups was that, while a number of them could not be seen as 'progressive' as such, many still tended to be secular, socially responsible (calling for an inclusive, pro-poor economic system that provides opportunities for all), pluralistic (demanding democracy, justice, equality and respect for all segments of society), and interested in cooperating against oppressors with a strong, unified voice. However, increasingly they faced extremist groups selling their own ideas as a preferable alternative. Many activists became aware that they were unable to stop the armed and increasingly extremist turn of the conflict, with numerous of their own members having joined the armed struggle. With the increase in violence against and threat to those within the NVM by the regime and by the extremist groups, many were forced to leave Syria. In spite of this, they continue their work in their newly established places of residence.

Conclusion: The emergence of the political voice of Syria's civil society

The Syrian Uprising did not begin with demands for regime change – that was a subsequent demand in the face of indiscriminate and sustained violent repression by the government. However, the Syrian people did not have pre-existing autonomous civil society that could effectively aid them in their emancipation from the oppressive regime. Indeed, it could be argued that it was the very absence of a *free* civil society that resulted in the chaotic situation in which Syria finds itself. By no means is this to deprecate the work, dedication and sacrifices made by pre-Uprising pioneers, such as the intellectuals involved in the Damascus Spring, which in many ways laid the groundwork for those who participated in the Uprising. This, plus the weakening of the traditionally dominant autocratic Syrian state during the Uprising, opened new opportunities for civil society. Indeed, the Uprising was able to overcome the weakness of the earlier movements that were disconnected from much of the Syrian populace, as seen in the post-Uprising mobilisation of the masses (Pace 2005). Even amongst the total devastation of areas and the chaos that has taken place, people came together to act within a space of civil society that did not exist before, a realm of civil society as a means of expression, development, co-ordination, and community but mostly as *resistance*. Syrian civil society is transforming itself from one living under constraints to one that is able to create its own identity – an identity of resistance, against the once hegemonic state and also now against the tyrannical Daesh (IS) and other extremist and armed groups fighting for control and power.

A significant proportion of the activities undertaken within the NVMs of the Syrian Uprising are indicative of a critical and dynamic consciousness in the 'mentalités' of the Syrians who are now, as Zaher Omareen puts it, 'armed with their own instruments, which can contribute to undermining *all* authority that is not based on genuine democracy' (Halasa et al. 2014: 101). The movement has enabled many Syrian people to 'demonstrate that they are in possession of the very attributes that the regime denies them – agency, identity, diversity, intelligence, beauty and humour … [the movement] challenges and undermines narratives of power, no matter where they originate' (Halasa et al. 2014: 232). Moreover, the sharing of ideas, dialogue, debate, contestation and decision-making occur within a collective space described by Mezar Matar, as a 'committee of citizens' (Halasa et al. 2014: 102). In fact, it is only as citizens and through true citizenship that a diverse society such as Syria can be held together. While a positive relationship between the potential citizen and the state under the current circumstances in Syria is not possible, the political voice of civil society has been growing with the emergence of the expressions of the social freedoms fundamental for a practising 'active citizen' (Halasa et al. 2014: 56). The hope is that the public space that is emerging within Syria and also for Syrians outside it, will create the foundations on which a democratic polity can be enacted, for as McGee (2012) states 'civil society institutions are not simply an indicator of the flourishing of liberal democracy, but rather they are also instrumental in realising the transition towards such a system'. Thus, it is amongst the NVMs that an alternative lies to the dominant and often violent players that dominate the narratives of the Syrian conflict.

Notes

1 There are exceptions to this, including the role of Riad Seif who is a prominent oppositional figure, held post within parliament and was also a prominent businessman who inevitably benefited from the opening up of Syria's economic realm.
2 In fact, a number of those within this business-centred civil society have remained supporters of Asad throughout the Uprising.
3 This song emerged from the amateur poet and singer Ibrahim Qashoush who changed the lyrics of traditional songs to criticise Asad. He was later found with his throat cut and his vocal cords removed. There were other targeted attacks on key figures of the Uprising, including Ali Ferzat, a famous cartoonist whose fingers and hands were broken in an attempt to stop him drawing.
4 This mapping can be viewed at http://www.alharak.org/nonviolence_map/en/.
5 Syrian Creativity: Radio SouriaLi Broadcasts over the Internet (7 June 2013). Syria Untold.

6 The Grapes of My Country: Syrian Journalism Baptized in Blood (6 November 2013). Syria Untold.
7 The Creative Memory of the Syrian Revolution provides an exhaustive selection of examples of the creative expressions of those within the Syrian Uprising accessible at: http://www.creativememory.org/?lang=en.
8 Walls of Saraqeb: The Vitality of Colors in War-weary Syria (28 February 2015). Syria Untold.
9 Save the Rest: Campaigning Inside Assad's Stronghold (5 February 2015). Syria Untold.
10 Nonviolence in Syria (October 2013). Peace News.

Bibliography

Abbas, H. (2014), 'Between the Cultures of Sectarianism and Citizenship'. *Syria Speaks: Art & Culture from the Frontline*. Edited by M. Halasa *et al*. London: Saqi Books.

Al-Aous, Y. (2013), 'Feminist Websites and Civil Society Experience'. In *Syrian Voices from Pre-Revolution Syria: Civil Society against All Odds*. Edited by Kawakibi, S. The Hague, Netherlands: Knowledge Programme Civil society in West Asia, Hivos.

Alassad, O. (2014), 'Popular Collision'. In Halasa, M. *et al.*, *Syria Speaks: Art & Culture from the Frontline*. London: Saqi Books.

Al-Om, T. (2015), 'Syria's Arab Spring: Women and the Struggle to Live in Truth'. In *Routledge Handbook on the Arab Spring*. Edited by L. Sadiki. London: Routledge.

Browers, M.L. (2006), *Democracy and Civil Society in Arab Political Thought: Transcultural Possibilities*. Syracuse: Syracuse University Press.

Chenoweth, E. & Gallagher Cunningham, K. (2013), 'Understanding Nonviolent Resistance: An Introduction', *Journal of Peace Research*, 50: 3, 271–276.

Cooke. M. (2007), *Dissident Syria: Making Oppositional Arts Official*. Durham, NC: Duke University Press.

George, A. (2003), *Syria: Neither Bread nor Freedom*. London: Zed Books.

Gorman, D. (2014), 'From the Outside Looking In'. In *Syria Speaks: Art & Culture from the Frontline*. Edited by M. Halasa *et al*. London: Saqi Books.

Gramsci, A. (2005). *Selections from the Prison Notebooks*. London: Lawrence & Wishart.

Halasa, M. *et al.* (2014), *Syria Speaks: Art & Culture from the Frontline*. London: Saqi Books.

Halasa, M. (2014b), 'Mystery Shopper: Interview with Assaad Al-Achi'. In *Syria Speaks: Art & Culture from the Frontline*. Edited by M. Halasa *et al*. London: Saqi Books.

Hinnebusch, R. (1993), 'State and Civil Society in Syria', *Middle East Journal*, 47: 2 (Spring), 243–257.

Kaldor, M. (2003), *Global Civil Society: An Answer to War*. Cambridge: Polity Press.

Khalaf, R. *et al.* (2014), *Activism in Difficult Times: Civil Society Groups in Syria 2011–2014*. Badael Project / Friedrich-Ebert-Stiftung. Beirut: Lebanon.

Khalaf, R. (2015), 'Governance without Government in Syria: Civil Society and State Building during Conflict', *Syria Studies*, 7: 3.

Matar, M. (2014), 'Cartoons by Kafranbel'. In *Syria Speaks: Art & Culture from the Frontline*. Edited by M. Halasa *et al*. London: Saqi Books.

McGee, T. (June 2012), 'Syria: Promoting Civil Society in the Face of Civil War'. Fikra Forum, Washington Institute for Near East Policy. Available at: http://fikraforum.org/?p=2327#.V-0-GPl97IU.

Nasser, R. *et al.* (2013). 'Socio-Economic Roots and Causes of the Syrian Uprising', *Syrian Centre for Policy Research*. Available at: www.scribd.com/document/340805411/Socio economic-Roots-and-Impact-of-the-Syrian-Crisis.

Omareen, Z. (2014), 'The Symbol and Counter-Symbol in Syria'. In *Syria Speaks: Art & Culture from the Frontline*. Edited by M. Halasa *et al*. London: Saqi Books.
Putnam, R.D. (1993), *Making Democracy Work*. Princeton, NJ: Princeton University Press.
Rabil, R. (October 2003), 'Reform in Syria? Prospects and Assessments', *The National Interest*, October 23. Available at: www.licus.org/liclib/oped/Rabil10-22-03.pdf.
Roberts, A. (2010), *Civil Resistance and Power Politics*. Oxford: Oxford University Press.
Sadowski, Y. (1997), 'The New Orientalism and the Democracy Debate'. In *Political Islam: Essays from Middle East Report*. Edited by Beinin, J. & Stork, J. London: I.B.Tauris.
Sawah, W. (2009), 'The Dialectic Relationship between the Political and the Civil in Syrian Civil Society Movement', *Arab Reform Initiative*, issue 34, December. Available at: www.arab-reform.net/en/node/402 [Accessed on 17/9/2017].
Sawah, W. (2012), *Syrian Civil Society Scene Prior to the Syrian Revolution*. Knowledge Programme Civil Society in West Asia. Hivos: The Hague, Netherlands.
Star, S. (2010), 'Syrian Civil Society Empowerment 2010: New Directions for Syrian Society', *Syria Forward Magazine*, 37, 3 March.
Van Rooy, A. (1998), *Civil Society and the Aid Industry*. London: Earthscan.
Yassin-Kassab, R. (2014), 'Literature of the Syrian Uprising'. In *Syria Speaks: Art & Culture from the Frontline*. Edited by M. Halasa *et al*. London: Saqi Books.
Yassin-Kassab, R. & Al-Shami, L. (2016), *Burning Country: Syrians in Revolution and War*. London: Pluto Press.
Zinecker, H. (2011), Civil Society in Developing Countries – Conceptual Considerations. *Journal of Conflictology*, 2: 1.

Websites

Al Haj Saleh, Y. (16 November 2014). Forty-four Months and Forty-four Years/ 1- Two Blindfolds. Available at: www.internationaleonline.org/ [Accessed on 1.6.15]
Al Haj Saleh, Y. (January 2016), Syria is a Unique Symbol of Injustice, Apathy and Amnesia. Interview with Bostjan Videmsek. *The Chronikler*. Available at: http://chronikler.com/middle-east/iraq-and-the-levant/yassin-al-haj-saleh/ [Accessed on 21.4.16].
Al-Om, T. (7 June 2014), Don't Ignore Syria's Non-Violent Movements. *The Guardian Online*. Available at: www.theguardian.com/commentisfree/2014/jun/07/syria-nonviolent-movement-freedom-justice [Accessed on 21.4.16].
Creative Memory of the Syrian Revolution. Available at: www.creativememory.org/?lang=en [Accessed on 21.4.16].
Dudouet, V. Nonviolent Resistance in Power Asymmetries. Available at: www.berghof-foundation.org/fileadmin/redaktion/Publications/Handbook/Articles/dudouet_handbookII.pdf [Accessed on 15.11.15].
Human Rights Watch (3 February 2011) Syria: Gang Attacks Peaceful Demonstrators; Police Look On. Available at: www.refworld.org/docid/4d51019526.html [Accessed on 10.10.16].
Khalek, R. (9 September 2013), Syria's Nonviolent Resistance is Dying to be Heard. Al Jazeera America. Available at: http://america.aljazeera.com/articles/2013/9/9/syrias-nonviolentresistanceisdyingtobeheard.html [Accessed on 21.4.16].
Landis, J. Quoted in Wikstrom, C. (9 February 2011), Syria: A Kingdom of Silence. Al Jazeera English Online. Available at: www.aljazeera.com/indepth/features/2011/02/201129103121562395.html [Accessed on 1.6.15].
Mapping of the NVM. Available at: www.alharak.org/nonviolence_map/en/ [Accessed on 2.6.15].

Nonviolence in Syria (October 2013). Peace News. Available at: http://peacenews.info/node/7373/nonviolence-syria [Accessed on 29.5.15].

Pace, J. (2 September 2005), interview with Kamal al-Labwani, posted on *Syria Comment* blog by Joshua Landis. Available at: www.joshualandis.com/blog/ [Accessed on 21.12.13].

Qayyum, M. (24 March 2014), Syrian Non-Violent Movements Do Exist. *Huff Post Politics*. Available at: www.huffingtonpost.com/mehrunisa-qayyum/syrian-nonviolent-movemen_b_5007325.html [Accessed on 21.4.16].

Save the Rest: Campaigning Inside Assad's Stronghold (5 February 2015). Syria Untold. Available at: www.syriauntold.com/en/event/save-rest-campaigning-inside-assads-stronghold/ [Accessed on 1. 5. 15].

Sinjab, L. (15 March 2013), Syria Conflict: From Peaceful Protest to Civil War. BBC Online. Available at: www.bbc.co.uk/news/world-middle-east-21797661 [Accessed on 10.10.16].

Syria: A Kingdom of Silence (9 February 2011). Al Jazeera English Online. Available at: www.aljazeera.com/indepth/features/2011/02/201129103121562395.html [Accessed on 1.6.15].

Syrian Creativity: Radio SouriaLi Broadcasts Over the Internet (7 June 2013). Syria Untold. Available at: www.syriauntold.com/en/2013/06/syrian-creativity-radio-souriali-broadcasts-over-the-Internet/ [Accessed on 4.6.15].

Syria's Legal Fight amid the Gunfire (3 March 2013). Garden Court. Available at: https://gclaw.wordpress.com/2013/03/04/syrias-legal-fight-amid-the-gunfire/ [Accessed on 2.6.15].

The Grapes of My Country: Syrian Journalism Baptized in Blood (6 November 2013). Syrian Untold. Available at: www.syriauntold.com/en/2013/11/the-grapes-of-my-country-syrian-journalism-baptized-in-blood/ [Accessed on 4.6.15].

Walls of Saraqeb: The Vitality of Colors in War-weary Syria (28 February 2015). Syria Untold. Available at: www.syriauntold.com/en/creative/walls-saraqeb-vitality-colors-war-weary-syria/ [Accessed on 5.6.15].

Wall Street Journal interview with Bashar Al Assad (31 January 2011). *WSJ Online*. Available at: www.wsj.com/articles/SB10001424052748703833204576114712441122894 [Accessed on 10.10.2016].

White Helmets, Syrian Civil Defence. Twitter Page. Available at: https://twitter.com/syriacivildef [Accessed on 6.6.15].

White Helmets Website. Available at: https://www.whitehelmets.org/ [Accessed on 6.6.15].

12
DEMANDS FOR DIGNITY AND THE SYRIAN UPRISING[1]

Juliette Harkin

> 'When a man loses his country, he loses his dignity and life.'
> —*a Syrian citizen, Jarablus*[2]

Introduction

Invocations of dignity in the Arab, and Syrian, context stretch far and wide in time, place, and thus in meaning. The idea was, for example, manifested in struggles against colonial rule: on the airwaves of Arab nationalist radio, *Sawt al-Arab* (Voice of the Arabs) during the Abdel Nasser era, and in the liberation struggle for Palestine (Gerges, 2013; Chomsky, 2013; Rogan, 2009, 305; Wynn, 1959). Once again, and in new and interesting ways, dignity has emerged as an important idea in the latest Arab revolutions, from Tunisia to Egypt, Yemen and Syria (Saleh, 2011; Tripp, 2013; Pearlman, 2013; Schielke, 2015; Willis, 2016). In this chapter I argue that this latest assertion of the idea of dignity speaks to the political aspirations of the Syrian people and goes beyond the enforced binary confines of secularism versus Islamism or assumed inevitable sectarian divides (Phillips, 2015). The demonstrator, artist, media activist and the armed fighter in the Syrian revolutionary moment all reveal to us, with varying means, a common striving to assert their dignity in the face of imposed indignities and injustice. If we follow the uses and meanings of dignity in the Syrian revolution, we can more closely explicate the thinking and practices of the revolutionaries (and their ideas) as expressed 'from below'. With this approach we can start to discover the way that dignity might be discussed and acted on alongside ideas of freedom and social justice.

It is useful to place the notion of dignity in a historical setting reminding us of its origins as a reaction to the humiliation of colonial rule (AbuKhalil, 1992; Fanon, 1961/1963, 34; Chomsky, 2013). The Arab spring marked the beginning of what Ilan Pappé described as a new phase in 'the assertion of self-dignity' (2011;

Traboulsi, 2012). This new phase in asserting dignity is, in its current manifestations, part of the struggle against the domestic tyranny of authoritarian regimes (Hinnebusch, 2014; Heydemann & Leenders, 2013; Tripp, 2013, 2). These new assertions of dignity directly challenge long-assumed legitimacy claims of the Syrian state to be a leader in the 'resistance' against the injustice of foreign occupation and imperialism. Dignity's emergence draws out the ways in which Syrians have not gained their full citizenhood; how the social contract between the Arab state and its peoples has not provided for life's basic needs and how the people are living on the margins and at the extreme edges. This in turn alerts us to the necessity of considering the invocation of dignity in its raw political context, that is, as a *political* act of 'resistance' (Tripp, 2013, 2). As the Syrian Uprising was increasingly met with repression, it was dignity at the extremes; the kind of existence and struggle for survival which Tzevetan Todorov captures in his writings on the everyday gestures and examples of dignity in the Nazi concentration camps (1991/2000, 59–70).

Whilst there is an established and expansive literature on the concept of dignity, this has mostly been considered within a particular (neo)-liberal/Western setting and confined to a normative and/or legalistic human rights discourse (Kateb, 2011; Waldron, 2012; Rosen, 2012). There is also some interesting work being done on harnessing dignity for conflict resolution (Hicks, 2011; Lesch, 2015). Yet, I offer an alternative reading and approach. The very idea of dignity goes beyond valid concerns about the legal place and protection of human dignity (for the dignity we see in the revolutions cannot be *conferred* on people by states by recourse to abstract laws), and instead here I concentrate on the intricacies of its actual political uses, as *asserted* by the actors in the revolution. This chapter aims to shed light on the dynamic, diverse and contingent nature of actions in that revolutionary moment, but also can enable us to trace the conceptual history of the idea in the Arab and Syrian context, thus enabling a useful intersection of both the diachronic and synchronic levels to my investigation (Freeden, 1996).

As well as seeking to move beyond human rights treatments of the concept of dignity, another challenge is that such a ubiquitous concept (we refer to dignity in dying, in labour, in resigning, and so on), has tended to be regarded as too vague, contested, or abstract for any meaningful analysis and thus been discounted from serious scholarly attention. I partly avoid this concern by focusing on the use of dignity in a particular context: the Arab revolutions and Syria's Uprising. Although the possible meanings in the use of the concept of 'dignity' in the Syrian revolution[3] might indeed be variegated and contingent, my approach steers away from any reductionist and positivist assumptions. Instead, I draw on theoretical work to suggest an 'interpretative' approach to the concept of dignity; one which enables an investigation into the concrete political 'thought-practices' of Syria's divergent revolutionary actors and activists through a consideration of their ideas and of concepts brought to bear in discourse and in action (Freeden, 1996, 2008, 2013; Connolly, 1974/1993).

I acknowledge that the idea of dignity is put to use by different actors in the Syrian conflict: consider Syrian president Bashar al-Asad's speeches to the parliament (Wieland, 2012); and the Islamic State's leader al-Baghdadi who claimed he was giving Syrians back their dignity (in his announcement of the Caliphate). *The very fact that all sides in the conflict feel the need to invoke dignity itself attests to the power of the concept*, especially as unleashed in the latest Arab revolutions. However, and in any case, the focus of this study is on revolutionary practices and political language, not that of the state or of counterrevolutionary currents.

In this chapter I first discuss specific meanings and uses of dignity in the contemporary Syrian context. In the second part of the chapter I argue for a *political* interpretation of the idea of dignity in Syria's revolution. I introduce some instances of the utterances and use of dignity in the beginning of Syria's 2011 Uprising and the subsequent (but arguably not inevitable) arming of the revolution. I have limited my citations of the 'raw material'; much of it is embedded in pdf files and reams of newsfeeds on social networking sites (SNS) and content sharing sites such as Facebook, Twitter, YouTube, Vimeo and on various blogging platforms. Since such links cannot be accessed in print (and where they are not clearly searchable), I list the names of the SNS, the 'group' name, and the title in the bibliography (most groups are 'public' and anyone can 'like' or subscribe to access the material). This recourse to mediated content available on social networking sites and content sharing 'archives' poses a number of challenges and limitations, which I have discussed elsewhere (Harkin, 2013), and it requires careful attention in the era of social media if we wish to consider and theorise about contemporary revolutionary practices using such 'archives' (Hazareesingh & Nabulsi, 2008, 150–170). While recognising these limits, we can explore some of the uses and meanings of dignity, as mediated through SNS and websites, with a focus on the beginnings of Syria's revolution in 2011 and its revolutionary moment. First we turn to a brief linguistic context for the concept of dignity in the Arabic language.

Linguistic notes on *karama* (dignity)[4]

Looking at dictionary definitions of dignity does not help us to understand why a Syrian student wrote about dignity or scrawled the idea onto a banner. Also, it does not help us to explore the possible political implications of his action. However, here I set out some of the established definitions of dignity.

In modern standard Arabic (MSA) usage, dignity is commonly denoted by the noun *karamah*.[5] The dictionary explanations of this concept elaborate on the nobleness and on the standing and prestige such a term evokes. The idea of dignity, along with associated ideas of honour and pride, is pervasive in the Arab language and culture and can be found in Arabic music and poetry as with *Umm Kulthoum's* song, *asaun karamiti* 'Preserve My Dignity'[6] and in the poetry and customs of Syrian tribes (Stewart, 1994; Dukhan, 2012; Chatty, 2010)[7] and might appear in family, kinship, socioeconomic and community contexts. As well as *karama*, the Arabic noun *'ird* is used to denote honour or as an indicator of good repute (Stewart, 1994, 143–144; Abu-Lughod, 1986). A key point to bear in mind is that use, and therefore meaning, can change and vary in location, across social cleavages and so on; some of these considerations are examined in an anthropological study of the Bedouin and their usages of ʻird (Stewart, 1994). For example, the shift from traditional uses of honour relating to one's status and standing in society and to particular customs, to modern usages of dignity focused on individual human rights, can be noted both in the 'western' and the 'Arab' contexts (cf. Taylor, 1992, 27; Bayefsky, 2013; Stewart, 1994).[8] This idea of honour might be employed to emphasise the protection of Arab and Islamic land and sacred sites, or one's status garnered on a number of (patriarchal) levels – i.e. a respected family name and heritage, respected occupations and social standing and a level of (political/religious) influence and social status, including but not exclusively in tribal compositions (Thompson, 1999; Stewart, 1994).

An associated noun ʻizz (this is sometimes pronounced and transliterated as ʻizzah in colloquial Syrian Arabic) can connote honour and strength, as well as dignity, and is suggestive of how one is regarded in society. Also, in the Syrian context, the noun nakhwah can be used to express a sense of honour and pride, but it can also be a marker of the idea of dignity.[9] Important in the traditional framing of honour has been the social imperative to protect and provide for women, in the family context and in the wider community (Thompson, 1999; Schielke, 2015). As I argue in this chapter, it seems that dignity has been used in the revolutionary moment in Syria in a way that is neither merely traditional nor liberal, in a narrow sense of the Western neoliberal regimes dominant today, but offers an alternative. Importantly, what this dynamic, shifting 'family' or cluster of concepts suggests is that the idea of *karama* as used in the context of the Arab revolutions cannot be considered in isolation. Dignity is a signifier of (political) practices in a particular time and place. Among actors in the Syrian revolution there is a common thread of political action pursued in different ways (protest, civil disobedience, armed resistance) and that *karama* is one way to follow and unpick these differing practices, which are at times intertwined or overlap. My focus is thus on the active sense of the idea of dignity which does not necessarily place it in the stable of individuated rights which are protected, given or bestowed upon individuals, in a legal, state, or institutional-centric analysis.[10] Rather, we need to pay more attention to the idea of dignity in its *collective* sense, in the myriad, and sometimes contested and contrasting ways it is harnessed and claimed by Syrians through their actions (Ismail, 2011).[11] I do not mean to completely discount other readings, and indeed a human rights and humanitarian focus in the Syrian revolution has been necessary. But as will be shown briefly below, I focus on the idea of dignity in Syria as it has been asserted in the revolutionary testimony and literature and on alternative media platforms, the activist campaigns, and in the ways in which Syrians participate in the revolution – i.e. their day-to-day work in human rights and in the alternative revolutionary media outlets. The next section is an initial investigation into the uses of dignity by Syrian revolutionary actors.

Beginnings: dignity in resistance

Syria's Uprising was, in important ways, spurred on by wider regional revolutionary ferment and the fall of Tunisia's Ben Ali and Egypt's Mubarak in which we also saw the idea of dignity emerge. In the case of Syria, sites of protest simultaneously emerged in Damascus and Darʻa, then Banyas and other towns during February and March, 2011, respectively. Initially these were not connected but reflected local grievances, and were in some cases acts of solidarity in response to developments in Libya and other revolutions (Ismail, 2011; International Crisis Group, 2011; Yazbek, 2012). In the case of Darʻa, initial protests in March 2011 were in response to the local security agency detaining some children, the oldest aged 15, who had scrawled graffiti on the school walls saying 'the people want the downfall of the regime'. The children were held by the local authorities without any information or access to them. The anger about the detaining and torture of children is captured in the folk song called *Ya Hayf* (Oh Shame!) by a well-known Syrian singer, Samih Shouqair (2011).[12] Tribal leaders and family relatives in Darʻa responded to the arrest of the children by sending a delegation to meet with the local authorities to obtain their release (ICG, 2011; Macleod, 2011). An enduring narrative of this period recalls how the family representatives, wearing traditional Arab head dress (the *keffiyyah* and ‾*aqal*), following local custom removed their head bands or the black *aqal* and rested them on the table to be taken back after resolving the situation. The Syrian official is said to have responded by throwing the traditional head bands into the rubbish bin.[13] The insulting behaviour and responses of the Syrian officials were met with a collective assertion of dignity. So, in response, in the first weeks of the Uprising the idea of dignity was invoked, with the naming of the square outside the Omari mosque in Darʻa as 'dignity square' on the significant day of Friday 18 March 2011. On this day, public protests had come under fire and the first martyrs fell. Over time, Syrians posted the pictures of martyrs on the buildings around the square, as the numbers of dead grew at the hands of the security forces and army. In subsequent funerals (another rare form of being able to legally gather in public) and demonstrations Syrians were shot at, beaten or arrested by security forces.

By the autumn of 2011 there was a major campaign which indicates the growing uses of dignity – as a mobilisation tool, as a cause and value to fight for and hold to, and as a plea against on-going repression. The beginnings of the revolution were 'mediated' by local activists, citizen journalists and the demonstrators who uploaded content, or the raw material, from the protests (Harkin et al., 2012). This is well-captured in a documentary produced with support from the various local *tansiqiyyat* (local coordinating committees and groups), unions, media networks, and journalists operating in the Hawran region. The narrator of the documentary tells us that 'the beginning was 18 March and [this] first Friday was called the Friday of Dignity', with gatherings in the square in the southern city of Darʻa after Friday prayers. Utilising one of the few sites of legal gathering allowed in Syria, the mosques, Syrians could gather to demonstrate straight after the midday prayers (Pierret, 2012). In this documentary we also hear the voice of an old Syrian man explaining what happened: '… we called for dignity and freedom, no one said anything about toppling the regime until they started shooting at us' (FreeSyrianTranslator, 2012).

Syria's dignity strikes

The mobilisation of dignity strikes throughout the autumn 2011 and into 2012 was promoted by prominent Syrian activists such as Ayman al-Aswad and Fadwa Suleiman (2011) and by the local networks of *tansiqiyyat*. These strikes were in no way comparable in scale with the organised-labour strikes and protests that were well-established by the time of Egypt's 2011 revolution (Beinin & Vairel, 2011). In Syria, a number of small-scale initiatives calling for general strikes eventuated in a campaign for *idrab al-karamah* (the strike of dignity) and also *idrab al-īzz* (strike of pride). The dignity strike campaign was launched by Syrian activist groups and resulted in general and targeted strikes in Syrian towns and cities and rural areas throughout December 2011, and into 2012, in Homs, Damascus, Deir Az-Zour, Aleppo, Hama, Daraya, Idlib (including those 'liberated' and those still under Syrian government control). Whilst small-in-scale the breadth of and collective nature of these actions can be seen from material published and uploaded on YouTube and on Facebook and Twitter feeds; for example the Syrian group *Ayaam al-Hurriyah* (freedom days) and the *Idrab al-karama* (dignity strikes) Facebook page and Twitter account. They consisted of a series of strikes focused on different sectors: education, commercial traders and so on. In the activist material, available in online archives, we can find early examples of revolutionary communications. On 7 December 2011 activists posted a flyer that included the following information:

> Dignity Strike: begins at dawn, Sunday, 11 December (2011):
> Until the withdrawal of the army from the cities
> And until the release of the prisoners ...
> Look, you are important ... support your homeland and your strike

The idea of Syrians being 'important' and active is a theme which can be found in the flyers and can be read as an argument for the agency of the citizen against that of the state and its apparatus of control. The flyers appeal to Syrians in the colloquial language too, seeking to mobilise citizens and to persuade them that they are not alone and should not be afraid. On the first day of the dignity strike, Sunday 11 December 2011, there were over 40 video clips from around Syria uploaded by Syrian activists and the *tansiqiyyat*. In these social media 'archives', video messages and promotions are available alongside raw activist footage from strikes around the country. It is hard to find video footage, and perhaps none exists, that lasts longer than 30–40 seconds. This is because it was very difficult to openly 'film' events in public with the heavy presence of the security forces and with the culture of informants that remained pervasive in Syrian society. At the time activists posted user-generated content which showed shops with their shutters down and of short and sometimes shaky footage (because it was taken covertly to avoid arrest) of Syrian security officials forcibly opening the shutters. These actions and the campaign for the dignity strikes were covered by al-Jazeera Arabic online and on air, utilising material provided by Syrian activists and were much discussed in al-Jazeera Arabic's

Beyond the News programme (2011). Having set out an example of dignity in action in the beginnings of the Uprising in Syria, I want to move on to look at the ways in which the concept was developed: in the first year a defining and important shift was undoubtedly the move towards militarisation of the revolution. We can explore the ways here in which dignity manifested among the fighters and armed rebels.

Arming the revolution

My contention in this section is that an open exploration into the idea of dignity can lead us to consider not only the liberal or secular (as perceived by both Syrian actors in the revolution and by outsiders) nonviolent activists, but also those Syrians who took up arms to resist government repression and to fight the state more actively. Indeed, a central aim of this chapter is to interrupt these fixed divides and to argue that there was a commonality which can be seen among the nonviolent activists and the fighters: they were all struggling and demanding dignity in their different ways. The fully armed revolutionary response encompasses the battalions of the 'Syrian Free Army', as well as the emerging (and, ideologically, sometimes overlapping) multitude of 'Islamist' battalions.

Throughout the summer of 2011, in response to heavy state security and army repression there arose, locally and through the formal representation of the 'opposition', internal debate and disagreement among Syrians about whether or not to take up arms. Some elements of the Syrian opposition had formed the then Syrian National Council (SNC) and an associated military command that mainly operated from Istanbul in Turkey (Tripp, 2013, 57). While many media and nonviolent activists carried out overt and covert acts of disobedience, such as demonstrations, sit-ins, producing and delivering revolutionary newspapers, releasing large balloons into the sky above Damascus with revolutionary messages and acted as citizen journalists documenting the human rights abuses, there were others who felt that they needed to take up arms in order to defend their revolution. This turn to arming the revolution is illustrated by the early formation of the Free Syrian Army (FSA). Syrians who had either defected from the army ranks or taken up arms as citizens had initially the sole purpose of protecting the demonstrations – a very novel hybrid form of chiefly nonviolent struggle protected by local armed groups that developed before the full militarisation of the conflict. What Syrians did was to privilege the right to protest in public and then made arguments, not always reaching consensus, about ways in which to protect this sacred and newly found freedom. From the summer of 2011, armed groups worked to protect their local area (so, were initially defensive) and hold off government forces, thus creating small liberated areas in places in Homs, Idlib and elsewhere in Syria. It would be a mistake to assume that there was a seamless connection between local grassroots strikes, calls for civil disobedience, and the moves towards armed resistance. It can be gleaned from the raw video material that elements from the armed revolutionaries did take part in the dignity strikes and in some areas the strike campaign was coordinated by armed rebel groups with activists and citizen journalists who recorded the strike actions. It is illuminating to find that there was an early general modus operandi in which media and nonviolent activists operated alongside and in cooperation with the armed rebel groups (although this became more difficult and dangerous with time).

For the purposes of looking at dignity in use and meaning and in searching for some common ground across the Syrian revolutionary landscape, I want to contrast civil disobedience with other forms of resistance, as exemplified in the thought and practices of a prominent figure, Abdel Qader Saleh (also referred to as Abu Maria) of the Islamist brigade, *Liwa al-Tawhid* and the Syrian Islamist fighters who were also making claims to fight for 'freedom' and 'dignity'. It is not the aim here to attempt an analysis of the myriad Syrian brigades and rebel groups, which have been tracked and analysed in detail elsewhere (Lund, 2013; Tamimi, 2013), but rather to trace the ideas and thinking of a particular actor whose thought and practices exemplified a particular element of the rebel fighters. In the case of Saleh, religious rhetoric was used to motivate and to discipline the fighters in the brigade. This ability stemmed from Saleh's preaching past, as a committed and pious Muslim, and so reflected the everyday, lived religion and pious nature of many Syrian fighters and much of the population. Saleh was a young businessman and grain trader from the town of Mari' who joined the initial call for peaceful protests against the injustice of the Syrian government. Like other Syrians he spent some time participating in the demonstrations before he and others felt compelled to take up arms. Saleh was not involved in politics before the revolution and was not active within political Islam currents but became part of the nonviolent protest movement which grew from events in Der'a in March 2011.[14] His brigade was important regionally for some of its key battles, especially in Aleppo, and Saleh was well-respected, enabling him to garner support from Gulf funders.

More than two years after the start of Syria's Uprising, he discusses his motivations and feelings in a special Ramadan interview for the pro-revolution channel Orient TV (in 2013). He explains that Syrians were living in an unjust situation of oppression and that they wanted a return to a life of dignity.[15] He stated that Syrians do not want to be slaves to Bashar al-Asad and his system. Saleh added that Syrians would like a return to religion (Islam). He recounts the ways in which:

> [the] good days under Bashar al-Asad were still a humiliation, like being in prison but with access to luxuries ... whereas now we break our fast on onion and bread (on the frontlines in Aleppo) and we are happy and fighting for what we believe in.[16]

The 33-year-old Saleh was injured in Syrian government shelling in November, 2013, and transferred to Turkey for medical treatment. His death was announced via social media and on major Arab news channels from 17 November 2013 and he was buried in his hometown of Mari'.[17] He became a revolutionary icon of the Syrian fight against the government and it is significant that Syrian activists across all sects and ideological trends mourned his passing with a spectacular array of commemoration videos, *nasheed* (songs), interviews and commentary. Arab news channels sympathetic to the revolution covered the news in detail and provided extended analysis. In particular, the Facebook newsfeeds of Syrian activists and Syria commentators were flooded with (as well as smiling pictures of Saleh from the battlefields) a particular video clip of Saleh. The video footage was said to be his last appearance before he succumbed to the aerial bombing that was likely targeting him and other key rebels (Saleh, 2011). In this video of him with his brigade, he draws on verses in the Quran and from the *Hadith* of the Prophet Mohammed in mobilising and motivating his troops – invoking the battles of Badr and Hunain.

In this section I have set out an approach for considering the turn to arms in the beginning of Syria's Uprising. I have introduced the political thought and ideas of a prominent, perhaps exceptional, Syrian battalion fighter, and indicated the ways I think that he exemplifies the ideas of the revolution. From the political discourse used by actors like Saleh, I have indicated the ways in which the idea of dignity is present and active in the political language of the fighters in similar ways to which we have seen its appearance among the activists who spear-headed campaigns of civil disobedience and many of whom did not see armed revolution as an effective response. This helps us to see beyond differences in strategy to remind ourselves of the underlying and unifying elements of the Syrian revolution. It seems that the ideals of the revolution as attested by the use of the idea of dignity remain something Syrians feel worth striving for.

Conclusion

My aim has been to tentatively explore possible approaches towards the study of Syria's revolutionary moment by looking at and contrasting the common threads in thinking politically, specifically in regard to the overlap in the use of the idea of dignity by the nonviolent activists and the armed fighters who came to be dominated by Jihadists. I draw out the commonalities between different strands in the revolution by looking at the political practice and discourse of actors in the Syrian revolution. I briefly consider ideas from two different trends within the revolution through a consideration of the activities of the self-declared nonviolent and civil disobedience groups in organising the dignity strikes and of an armed 'Islamist' brigade exemplified through the political thought of one of its more prominent brigade members. I am suggesting that we start to question an assumed distinction and separation of these two ideational currents, as they played out in the revolutionary moment. Indeed, the claimed separation of the nonviolent strand from the armed wings of the revolution is not a reflection of actual political practices. Leading on from this, a central claim in this chapter is that, through an investigation of the uses of ideas like dignity, we can see that there is a certain commonality cutting across sect, religion and ideology, in that all these Syrians were demanding dignity. I therefore make two broader points about the conceptual framing of the idea of dignity by Syrian actors in the revolution.

Firstly, that the assertion of dignity was a specific and political response to the violent repression of the Syrian demonstrations from February and March of 2011: it was a refusal to be dehumanised or to be discounted and the chants of the demonstrators that 'the Syrians will not be humiliated' was one manifestation of 'dignity'. I suggest that this dignity-humiliation tension both underpins the socioeconomic problems that backgrounded the revolution, and, that it is a deeply political rejection of the actions of the state as represented in the streets during the protests by its government officials, army, and security apparatus. Therefore, I suggest that Syrian revolutionary invocations of dignity should be considered outside the mere legal framing of human rights, even though many of the civil society activists were to become deeply involved in gathering information on human rights abuses.

Secondly, and following some of the arguments made by Michelle Browers in her examination of Egypt (2009), in taking an interpretive approach to the idea of dignity in revolution we can start to see the ways in which ideas might cut across assumed fixed ideological divides. In following the idea of dignity wherever we find it, we can see the ways in which the nonviolent activists were working with the armed fighters as one small example of common cause and as a possible indication of the potential for unifying ideas like dignity. Overall I am suggesting that dignity became a constitutive part of the revolutionary culture and practice of the Syrian revolutionaries, activists and fighters. Dignity, understood in a particular context in Syria, cuts across and holds sway against sectarian and other divisive and fragmenting understandings of the revolutionary moment.

This consideration of the political sense and force of concepts such as dignity invites us to consider the wider ideational framework and the ways in which concepts act as building blocks for the ideological patterns which shape and change in our social and political world (Freeden). The concept of dignity in the Arab and Syrian context holds promise for a rethink about Arab ideologies and the way that political concepts and virtues are formed, change, and are contested. Dignity did this work in entering into the political discourse of those who are countering the dominant power and ideology of the Syrian state. An investigation into the idea of dignity interrupts fixed and assumed traditions and invites us to look more deeply at political ideologies and the ways in which ideas might shift and be prioritised in chaotic revolutionary settings. Some of the issues in the Arab context and some thoughts on the revolutions and implications for ideologies and for political thinking have been tackled already (Haugbolle, 2012; Browers, 2016). The aim of this chapter is to suggest that by pursuing the idea of dignity we open up onto a wider sub-field of theory and thinking which might further aid an understanding of what happens to our ideas and our ideological beliefs in a time of flux and revolution.

Notes

1 I thank Samantha Earle, Rupert Read and Muzna al-Naib, University of East Anglia, for discussions and suggestions as I grappled with the ideas for this chapter, and also Peter

Hill, University of Oxford, for comments on a draft. I also thank the co-editors for very valuable comments and suggestions, though, of course, any and all shortcomings remain my own.
2 Taken from a citizen documentary short produced by The Street Collective, supported by the Kayani organisation: 'Jarablus: Horizons of Freedom', available on YouTube via the Kayani channel, 2012 (not my translation).
3 I intentionally use 'revolution' and my wider research problematises political science approaches to revolution, which seek to generalise with universal models, tend to be state-centric and overly focus on defining and fixing causes instead of looking at revolutionary processes and practices.
4 Throughout this chapter I use a simplified version of the IJMES transliteration system for written Arabic and indicate the diacritical marks for the letters hamza (') and ayn (') only. In transliterating the Syrian dialect I try to simply capture the actual pronunciation of the words rather than the spelling, given that it is an aural language.
5 The noun is derived from the Arabic root letters k, r, m, and the perfect verb form of *karamah* means to honour and to be noble; derived verb forms also denote meanings implying honour and being noble, generous and liberal. Modern Standard Arabic (MSA) is the language of contemporary Arabic broadcast and print media, modern literature, and political discourse and is used in distinction to a richer and classical Arabic language reserved for more formal occasions, for classical poetry and literature, and for religious sermons.
6 This song featured in a 1947 Egyptian film called *Fatima*, directed by Ahmed Badrakhan. The song was written by Ahmed Rami and the music score was by Riyadh al-Sonbati. Fatima refuses her marriage suitor, who is of a higher social class than she is. I am grateful to Ahmed Abdelaziz for our discussions of this song and the film, which points to issues around social inequality. I am grateful to Rupert Read and Samantha Earle, University of East Anglia, for helping me to think about the important relational nature between the two opposing concepts of dignity and humiliation.
7 I am grateful to Haian Dukhan for our discussion, at the 2013 St Andrews conference on Syria, on dignity in the tribal context and for referring me to poetry and meetings in which the idea is used. See *sawt al-ramtha* (Ramtha Voice) which can be accessed online at www.ramthavoice.net.
8 The Arab trajectory on notions of dignity and honour and the shifting uses of the concepts echoes patterns of modernity elsewhere. As shown in the work of Kant, notions of honour were associated with tradition and social hierarchies, whereas dignity signifies the levelling effect of equality, heralding the liberal human rights (and human responsibilities) approach for individuals to act with dignity and to be allowed to live in dignity. See Taylor, *Politics of Recognition*, 1992, 27; For a treatment of Kantian conceptions of honour and dignity see R. Bayefsky, 'Dignity, Honour, and Human Rights, Kant's perspective', *Political Theory*, 4 (6), 809–837, Dec. 2013.
9 It is pronounced *nekhwey* in the Syrian dialect and can be heard voiced by a Syrian activist from the Hawran region of Syria, interviewed in a Syrian documentary which was mainly filmed by the prominent Syrian activist Basel Shehadeh, killed by Syrian government airstrikes in Homs. The documentary was uploaded with English subtitles and it should be noted that the choice of translation into English of 'dignity' offered by the translators raises questions regarding the layers of mediation of events and actions from within Syria. The sentence it is used in runs as follows in the spoken word in the documentary: *lissa fee amal wa lissa fee al-alaam nekhwey wa lissa fee dumeir* (there is still hope and there is still in the world a sense of pride and there is still consciousness; *my translation of Syrian dialect*).
10 Such as the United Nations Declaration on Human Rights and the Arab League Declaration on Human Rights.
11 More investigation is required, and is pursued elsewhere in my research, in consideration of the *collective* sense as opposed to a solely individualist trajectory that has flourished since Immanuel Kant's canonical work and his conception of *würde*.

12 Shouqair is an exiled Syrian Druze from the Golan. The song is dedicated to the children of Darʻa and asks: who kills their children with live bullets? The song has over 1.5 million views on YouTube (see bibliography for information). It is discussed in the michcafe blog available at michcafe.blogspot.co.uk, entitled 'Syria protest ode on YouTube'. I am grateful to Muzna al-Naib, University of East Anglia, for introducing me to this singer.
13 This is one of the narratives that emerged from the beginning of the revolution, Syrians sympathetic to the revolution will give similar accounts of this chain of events but it is difficult to find any hard evidence which has been published. Still, it is set out here in summary as a useful insight into the political emotions from this period and some of the ideas around dignity and honour.
14 Indeed investigations with Syrian contacts suggest that Saleh was in fact active in an apolitical religious group called the *Jamaʻat al-Daʻwah wa-al-Tabligh* (Society of Spreading Faith), which emerged from India and has a presence in Pakistan with adherents across East Asia and among Muslim populations worldwide. It is founded as a pious group which emphasises the non-material life and religious preaching. My source must remain anonymous. That is not to say that its individual members might not be swayed, especially if they undergo religious instruction in the same cities which also host training by more extremist and politicised elements.
15 He uses both *karama* and *ʻizz*.
16 This is a summary of his answer to a question from the interviewer about whether he misses the Ramadan holidays of years gone by. I am thankful to Muzna for translating and discussing the Arab source material with me.
17 Saleh's background and analysis of the brigade are documented in detail on this blog post: Aron Lund (2013) 'The death of Abdelqader Saleh', Sunday 17 November, available at http://www.joshualandis.com/blog/death-abdelqader-saleh/, accessed September 2015. The brigade is mapped out here: http://web.stanford.edu/group/mappingmilitants/cgi-bin/groups/view/527, accessed September, 2015.

Bibliography

AbuKhalil, Asad (1992), 'A new Arab Ideology? The Rejuvenation of Arab Nationalism', *The Middle East Journal*, Spring, 46: 1.

Abu-Lughod, Lila (1986), *Veiled Sentiments: Honour and Poetry in a Bedouin Society*. Berkeley: University of California Press.

Achcar, Gilbert (2013), *The People Want: A Radical Exploration of the Arab Uprising*, London: Saqi Books

Aya, Roderic (1979), 'Theories of Revolution Reconsidered: Contrasting Models of Collective Violence', *Theory and Society*, 8:1, 39–99.

Bayefsky, Rachel (2013), 'Dignity, Honour, and Human Rights: Kant's Perspective', *Political Theory*, 4:6, 809–837.

Beinin, Joel & Vairel, Frederic (2011), *Social Movements, Mobilization, and Contestation in the Middle East and North Africa*, California: Stanford University Press.

Browers, Michaelle (2009), *Political Ideology in the Arab World: Accommodation and Transformation*. Cambridge: Cambridge University Press.

Browers, Michelle (2016), 'Arab Political Thought after 2011 (Lines of Inquiry for a Research Agenda)', 24 January, published online at www.thedisorderofthings.com.

Chatty, Dawn (2010), 'The Bedouin in Contemporary Syria: The Persistence of Tribal Authority and Control', *The Middle East Journal*, 64:1, 29–49.

Chomsky, Noam (2013), 'Violence and Dignity: Reflections on the Middle East', The Edward W. Said Lecture, Friends House, London, 18 March.

Connolly, E. William (1974/1993), *The Terms of Political Discourse*, 3rd edn. Oxford: Blackwell Publishers.

Dukhan, Haian (2012), 'Tribes and Tribalism in the Syrian Revolution', opendemocracy, 19 December.
Fanon, Franz (1961/1963), *The Wretched of the Earth*. Harmondsworth: Penguin Books.
Freeden, Michael (1996), *Ideologies and Political Theory: A Conceptual Approach*. Oxford: Oxford University Press.
Freeden, Michael (2003), *Ideology: A Very Short Introduction*. Oxford: Oxford University Press.
Freeden, Michael (2008), 'Thinking Politically and Thinking about Politics: language, interpretation, and ideology', in *Political Theory: Methods and Approaches*, edited by Leopold, D. & Stears, M., 196–215. Oxford: Oxford University Press.
Freeden, Michael (2013), *The Political Theory of Political Thinking: The Anatomy of a Practice*. Oxford: Oxford University Press
Gerges, Fawaz (2013), Interview for: 'The Making of the Modern Arab World', Episode 2, BBC Radio 4 documentary series, presented by Tarek Osman and first broadcast in December, 2013.
Hanieh, Adam (2013), *Lineages of Revolt: Issues of Contemporary Capitalism in the Middle East*. Chicago: Haymarket Books.
Harkin, Juliette et al. (2012), 'Deciphering User-Generated Content in Transitional Societies: A Syria Coverage Case Study', commissioned by Center for Global Communication Studies, Annenberg School for Communication, Pennsylvania University, Washington DC: Internews Center for Innovation and Learning.
Harkin, Juliette (2013), 'Is it possible to understand the Syrian revolution through the prism of social media?', *Westminster Papers in Communication and Culture*, 9:2, April. London: University of Westminster.
Haugbolle, Sune (2012), 'Reflections on Ideology after the Arab Uprising', published online at Jadaliyya eZine, 21 March 2011, accessed September 2011.
Hazeeresingh, Sudhir & Nabulsi, Karma (2008), 'Using Archival Sources to Theorize about Politics', in *Political Theory: Methods and Approaches*, edited by Leopold, D. & Stears, M. Oxford: Oxford University Press
Heydermann, Steven & Leenders, Reinould (2013), *Middle East Authoritarianisms: Governance, Contestation, and Regime Resilience in Syria and Iran*. Stanford: Stanford University Press.
Hicks, Donna (2011), *Dignity: The Essential Role It Plays in Resolving Conflict*. New Haven: Yale University Press.
Hinnebusch, Raymond (2014), 'A Historical Sociology Approach to Resilient Authoritarianism in post-Arab Uprising MENA', published online by the Project on the Middle East Political Science (POMODS), 14 December, accessed September 2015.
International Crisis Group (2011), 'Popular Protest in North Africa and the Middle East (V1): The Syrian Regime's Slow-motion Suicide', *Middle East/North Africa Report*, International Crisis Group, 108, 6 July.
Ismail, Salwa (2011), 'The Syrian Uprising: Imagining and Performing the Nation', in *Studies in Ethnicity and Nationalism*, 11:3.
Kateb, George (2011), *Human Dignity*. Cambridge, MA: Harvard University Press.
Lesch, David (2015), Lecture: 'The Slow Fix: The CDI-Trinity Syria Initiative', 3rd Biannual Conference of the Centre for Syrian Studies, University of St. Andrews, 1–3 July 2015.
Lund, Aron (2013), 'Islamist Groups Declare Opposition to National Coalition and US Strategy', published on syriaComment, 24 September. Available at: http://www.joshualandis.com/blog/major-rebel-factions-drop-exiles-go-full-islamist/, accessed September 2015.
Macleod, Hugh (2011), 'Inside Deraa', published online, 19 April, on www.aljazeera.com/indepth, accessed February 2016.

Pappé, Ilan (2011), 'Reframing the Israel/Palestine Conflict', Interview by Frank Barat, 6 March 2011, uploaded on YouTube on 4 August.

Pearlman, Wendy (2013), 'Emotions and the Microfoundations of the Arab Revolutions', *Perspectives on Politics*, 11:2, 387–409.

Phillips, Christopher (2015), 'Sectarianism and Conflict in Syria', *Third World Quarterly*, 36:2, 357–376.

Pierret, Thomas (2012), 'The Role of the Mosque in the Syrian Revolution', *Near East Quarterly*, 20 March.

Rogan, Eugene (2009), *The Arabs: A History*, London: Penguin Books.

Rosen, Michael (2012), *Dignity: Its History and Meaning*, Massachusetts: Harvard University Press.

Saleh, Yassin al-Haj (2011), 'Thawrat al-karama', al-hiwar mutamadden', available online at www.ahewar.org.

Schielke, Samuli (2015), *Egypt in the Future Tense: Hope, Frustration, and Ambivalence before and after 2011*. Bloomington: Indiana University Press.

Shehabi, Omar (2014), 'Bahrain's Fate', Jacobin magazine online, January 2014, available at https://www.jacobinmag.com/2014/01/bahrains-fate/, accessed January 2014.

Stewart, Frank H. (1994), *Honor*. Chicago: University of Chicago Press.

Tamimi, A. J. (2013), 'Jihad in Syria', published on his personal blog, March, 2013, available at: http://www.aymennjawad.org/13097/jihad-in-syria, accessed September, 2015.

Taylor, Charles (1992), *Multiculturalism and 'The Politics of Recognition'*. New Jersey: Princeton University Press.

Thompson, Elizabeth (1999), *Colonial Citizens: Republican Rights, Paternal Privilege, and Gender in French Syria and Lebanon*. New York: Columbia University Press.

Todorov, Tzvetan (1991/2000), *Facing the Extreme: Moral Life in the Concentration Camps*. London: Phoenix.

Traboulsi, Fawwaz (2012), 'Syrian Revolutionaries Owe No One an Apology'. Interview by Mohammed al-Attar, available online at www.boell.de., accessed September, 2015.

Tripp, Charles (2013), *The Power and the People: Paths of Resistance in the Middle East*. Cambridge: Cambridge University Press.

Waldron, Jeremy (2012), *Dignity, Rank & Rights*, edited by Meir Dan-Cohen. The Berkeley Tanner Lectures. Oxford: Oxford University Press.

Wieland, Carsten (2012), *A Decade of Lost Chances: Repression and Revolution from Damascus Spring to Arab Spring*. Seattle: Cune Press.

Willis, Michael J. (2016), 'Revolt for Dignity: Tunisia's Revolution and Civil Resistance'. In *Civil Resistance in the Arab Spring: Triumphs and Disasters*, edited by Roberts, A., Willis, M., McCarthy, R. & Garten Ash, T. Oxford: Oxford University Press.

Wynn, Wilton (1959), *Nasser of Egypt: The Search for Dignity*. Cambridge, MA: Arlington Books.

Yazbek, Samer (2012), *A Woman in the Crossfire: Diaries of the Syrian Revolution*. London: Haus Publishing Limited.

Selected online sources and links

Aswad, A. (2011), Activist Aymen Aswad calls for Dignity Strike, uploaded on Facebook group 'idrab al-karama', 13 December, accessed September 2015. Available at: https://www.facebook.com/karamah.Dignity.Strike/videos/vb.169643846466525/10151044477855203/?type=2&theater.

Forfreedom (2011), idrab al-karama, published online at YouTube channel 'forfreedom', 6 December 2011, accessed September 2015. Available at: https://www.youtube.com/watch?v=ovrl5J_Kkqg.

FreeSyrianTranslator (2012), Dignity Revolution, English subtitles provided at YouTube channel 'freeSyrianTranslator', published 16 June 2012, accessed September 2015. Available at: https://www.youtube.com/watch?v=qQ_CkQ0HlRk&index=50&list=PL4-an89sTcZ 6DzKzdfKmCjRvd-Dtd-xSs.

al-Jazeera Arabic (2011), 'Beyond the News: idrab al-karama', uploaded 11 December, YouTube channel 'al-Jazeera Arabic', accessed September 2015. Available at: https://www.youtube.com/watch?v=rHniTzgkzwE.

al-Jazeera Net (2011), 'Electronic Demonstrations and the Dignity Strikes in Syria', published online 11 December, accessed September 2015. Available at: www.aljazeera.net/home/print/f6451603-4dff-4ca1-9c10-122741d17432/7b3acfad-ebd0-42bf-bd33-85d2b d2f95f8.

Saleh, A. (2013), 'Exclusive interview with Abdel Qader Saleh talking about his personal life', broadcast by Orient TV and published online on the YouTube channel 'Orient TV', 15 July 2013, accessed February 2016. No longer available on the channel.

Saleh, A. (2013), 'The last appearance of Abd al-Saleh al-Qadir al-Saleh (haji Marea) in the 80 Brigade Front', published on YouTube channel 'Thaer Al-Shamali', uploaded 17 December 2013, accessed September 2015. Available at: https://www.youtube.com/watch?v=Spsl09fQr-0&index=45&list=PL4-an89sTcZ6DzKzdfKmCjRvd-Dtd-xSs.

Shehadeh, Basel (2013), 'Streets of Freedom', produced by *The Street* collective and supported by Kayani, published online, April 2013. See YouTube channel at *'Kayani Web TV'*, accessed September 2015. Available at: https://www.youtube.com/watch?v=7v5Rj3AwWy0.

Shouqair, Samih (2011), *YaHayf* (oh Shame!), revolutionary song, available via the YouTube channel for the 'local coordinating group for the town of Yabrud', published 29 March 2011, accessed September 2015. Available at: http://michcafe.blogspot.co.uk/2011/03/syria-protest-ode-on-you-tube.html.

Soliman, Fadwa (2011), 'A call to strike', uploaded online 11 December 2011, YouTube channel '*FadwaSoliman*', accessed September 2015. Available at: https://www.youtube.com/watch?v=gvdfV8jL5_k#t=105.

Street Media and Development, The (2013), 'Jarablus Horizons' of Freedom (*ifaq al-hurriya*)', documentary short, published online March 2013; on their YouTube channel: muwassasat al-shara'a al-'ilaam (The Street Media, Incorporated), accessed September 2015. Available at: https://www.youtube.com/watch?v=118mfokZncw&list=PL4-an89sTcZ7 Tz8sXeLKUJcHuY1OsoPto&index=96.

13

MEDIATING THE SYRIAN REVOLT

How new media technologies change the development of social movements and conflicts[1]

Billie Jeanne Brownlee

> "Enemies are many ... the revolution is one ... and it will continue"
> Banner in the city of Kafranbel, Syria (3 January 2014)[2]

Introduction

The Syrian Uprising broke out at the time of what many defined as the "Arab Spring", a period of revolutionary ferment, popular mobilisation and protest against authoritarian and corrupt regimes in the Arab world (Anderson, 2011).[3] However, the peaceful protests of the early months later turned into an armed conflict that made Syria a fertile ground for Islamic fundamentalist groups, often with conspicuous participation of foreign fighters, waging a *jihad* aimed at establishing a reactionary interpretation of *sharia* law. Regional powers, like the Gulf Cooperation Council, Turkey, Hezbollah and Iran's Revolutionary Guards Corps (IRGC) have contributed to the conflict with military support and fighters, and international super powers, though not initially taking an active part in conflict, financed the opposing sides.[4] These external powers have engaged in a multisided proxy war, in which media wars have played a salient part.[5]

The unwrapping of Syria's chapter of the Arab Spring has been influenced by an unprecedented and overwhelming role that the new media technologies have played since the early days of the Uprising and to a large extent in the years that predated its outbreak.[6] The predominant role that the new media played at the time of the Uprising was not the effect of a *deus ex-machina* but the result of years of experimentation and maturation, wherein Syrians were actively employing digital tools to access information, to network and to disseminate campaigns on social and political issues. As the World Bank data shows, between 2002 and 2012 Syrian cell-phone usage rates increased by 2,347 per cent, compared to the 83 per cent in the US during the same time period (Kilcullen, 2013). Moreover, Syria's Internet penetration increased by 883 per cent, a greater increase than in Egypt,

Libya and Tunisia. The third-generation media, that is to say, satellite channels and social media networks like Facebook, Twitter and YouTube proved particularly influential in promoting social mobilisation. These tools deeply affected the spark and development of the revolt, its narrative, the making of news and the management of the conflict. The extensive use of the new technologies at the time of the Uprising is the expression of a global rise over the last decade in social mobilisation and protest movements, all heavily influenced in their tactics and strategies by the employment of the new media (Shirky, 2011). Movements like Occupy Wall Street, the Indignados of Puerta del Sol and those of Syntagma Square or of Brazil's 10-cent movement have been framed as mobilisations against austerity measures caused by the economic crisis, while those in the Arab world as mobilisations against authoritarian regimes (Brownlee and Ghiabi, 2016) and yet both demonstrate how the new media is offering citizens more opportunities to contest political authority and economic inequalities worldwide (Meyer and Tarrow, 1998).

This chapter examines the significant and multi-faceted role that the new media technologies played during the Syrian revolt, with the aim of reflecting on how the new information technologies have changed people's power, journalism and conflicts in many and diversified ways. In Syria, the new media technologies have been a game changer from many points of view: they have been used by citizens to vent their frustrations and sense of oppression; they have been employed to organise protest movements, to attack the regime's propaganda and to reach international audiences. On the other hand, the regime has also used the new media to launch a counter-offensive, countering anti-regime propaganda, strengthening the sentiment of its loyalists and deploying a digital army charged with spying on people's activities online, identifying and arresting them. Indeed, the confrontation between the regime and the rebels has not occurred in streets and battlefields only but in the virtual space as well. The extremist Islamic groups operating in Syria have also resorted to the new media to elicit fear, demand ransoms for hostages and recruit new followers.

The analysis of Syria's media field is here presented as a three-phase development which follows the evolution of the revolt: the initial period of protests and demonstrations; the country's entry into a state of armed conflict; and the subsequent draining stalemate of civil war. Understanding the changing role of the new media in the development of the Syrian revolution will allow a more thorough understanding of the events in Syria and expose the enormous potential that the new media technologies are offering people in closed regimes around the globe, as well as the harm that these same tools produce when handled by authoritarian governments, terrorist organisations and not least, international media outlets, often more concerned with sensationalist reporting rather than fundamental ethical principles.

Phase 1. The spark of the Uprising and the "syndrome of Hama": the Facebook and YouTube effects

Unlike Egypt that had enjoyed a high and unfettered rate of network connectivity before 2011, Syria's web surfers had faced sophisticated technical infrastructures of censorship and wiretapping that applied to the online space as much as to the offline one (Kilcullen, 2013). However, after the regime's decision to lift the ban on the use of Facebook and YouTube in February 2011, a move aiming both to appease the new generations and allow the regime to monitor anti-regime activists (Baiazy, 2012), both social networks were flooded by users and viewers. On 15 March 2011, a number of social rallies gathered in the main streets and squares of several Syrian cities in response to the call for mobilisation of a Facebook page "The Syrian revolution 2011".[7] A few days later, the page counted more than 41,000 fans (Baiazy, 2012).

Since that date, the Syrian Revolution Facebook page became the revolution's main manifesto and coordination network. Each Friday, the first day of the weekend in Syria, the page called for people to rally in defence of fundamental rights and values and to comfort the relatives of those who had lost a family member during the unrest (Fares, 2015). The Facebook page, imitating the Egyptian call for a Day of Rage, became instrumental to allow activists to communicate with citizens, motivate people to take part in the protests and create a sort of social glue through which people could find support in each other and acquire a sense of common destiny. The great success of the page, symbolised by growing numbers of followers, led to the opening of many other pages created in support to the Syrian revolt, like "the Syria Free Press" on 20 February 2011, "the Sham News Network" on 18 March 2011 and "the Ugarit Network" on 2 April 2011 (Fares, 2015). One year later the number of online pages had reached the thousands. Facebook was the springboard for the spark of the Syrian Uprising. Facebook pages were used as news-bulletins, building bridges with other activists in Arab countries and abroad, as well as simply for sharing opinions. Facebook pages were also popular among pro-regime supporters, sharing videos on the violence perpetuated by the rebels and uploading videos about the regime's military prowess and patriotic sacrifice. Activists also turned to other social media tools like YouTube, Skype and Twitter.

In this phase, from March to July of 2011, the role performed by social media was inspired by a collective memory of the 1982 mass killing of civilians (between 10,000 and 30,000 deaths) in Hama, which had received inadequate media coverage.[8] Determined to prevent a recurrence of this episode, Syrians held on to their smartphones and cameras and kept filming every protest and peaceful march and their brutal repression by the regime. The act of uploading photos or videos onto YouTube documenting the regime's brutality paradoxically encouraged more people to join civil resistance despite the high degree of risk and uncertainty. Doug McAdam defines this process as "cognitive liberation", an evolution that individuals experienced when exposed to the regime's wrong doings, which broke the barrier of apathy and drove them to reject perceived injustice collectively (McAdam, 1982). Events like the regime's harsh punishment of the children of Dera'a and the torture of the 13-year-old Hamza al Khateb, acted as "catalytic events" that lit the revolt (Ayoub, 2012).[9] These events exposed the regime's viciousness on a national level via alternative news outlets that the regime was unable to block and which had developed over the years prior to the Uprising. What marked the difference between the events in Hama of 1982 and those of 2011 was the public condemnation the latter provoked through the online media.

In a year's time YouTube surpassed Facebook's popularity, which actually relied on YouTube's videos posting on its pages. These networks are closely interconnected, as videos are usually uploaded on YouTube, shared on Facebook and then referred to on Twitter. The number of YouTube videos uploaded on the Syrian revolution, approximately 2 million in the first two years of the revolt, has led some to refer to the Syrian revolt as the "YouTube revolution", as opposed to the Egyptian "Facebook revolution" or the Iranian Green Movement "Twitter's revolution" (Khatib, 2014). The nature of the page drove its success, as everyone with a phone or any rudimentary technology was able to post and share his/her own experience of the revolution. As a result, Fares Abed held that the "Syrian revolution is the most documented revolution in history" (Baiazy, 2012). However, given the still limited number of Internet surfers in Syria, their relevance grew when the information and footage uploaded on these social media was portrayed on satellite TV channels, the mass communication medium *par excellence*. Hence, it is when these two media, social media and satellite TV interacted that the Syrian news coverage reached the highest audience rates (Baiazy, 2012). This made the work of Syrian activists vital for international media reporting, but it also helped the aim of the revolution, giving it an international echo.

The nature of video-documentation on the Syrian revolt is wide and diversified. Some testify to the creativity and humour of the Syrian people even in dark times, like *Top Goon: Diaries of the Little Dictator*, a web-based series puppet show that went on air in 2011 mocking President Bashar al-Asad and his violent repression of protestors.[10] A wide number of videos testify to the resilience of the Syrian people, like the women of Salamiyah, who organised sit-ins at home, where women in disguise and holding banners with political slogans were filmed and later posted on the web.[11] In this way women supported the cause of the revolution yet avoided the risk of being arrested. Other videos recorded the courageous demonstrations that ignited the Uprising, the conflict between regime and rebels, the hard days of people under siege.

In Syria, online media represented inexpensive means to communicate, fast ways to coordinate action and the only space where Syrians could express their dissent. In other Arab countries, citizens relied on social media to coordinate action, but expressed their dissatisfaction through massive gatherings in public spaces like Habib Bourghiba Street in Tunis, Tahrir Square in Cairo, Sittin Square in Sanaa and Pearl roundabout in Manama. In Syria, instead, the lack of large protest spaces, combined with the repressive security apparatus, pushed the concentration of protests to the peripheries (e.g. Dera'a, Banias) while Damascus and Aleppo, the two main urban agglomerations, were largely free of political rallies, at least in the initial stages of the revolt. For this reason, the new media were used to bridge these gaps and create a unifying force that, albeit online, was capable of keeping the revolution alive.

The extent to which the new media dominated the development of the Syrian conflict is indicated by the establishment of the regime's "Syrian Electronic Army" (SEA), a group of IT specialists specifically recruited to fight against the anti-regime online mobilisation. The group, which defines itself as "enthusiastic Syrian youth who could not stay passive towards the massive distortion of facts about the recent Uprising in Syria", was launched in 2011 to operate digital spamming campaigns and attacks on individuals, groups and organisations undermining the legitimacy of the Syrian government (Fowler, 2013). The regime had always kept a close eye on the Internet, being the last Arab country to allow public access and even then, being very cautious at permitting unlimited access to all its variations. However, at the onset of the Uprising in Syria, it became clear that new media were driving the social mobilisation and that to combat anti-regime sentiment it was not sufficient to crush it in the streets and squares but it was also necessary to wear it out online. The group operated on different fronts: hacking and shutting down Syrian opposition websites, spamming popular Syrian opposition websites with pro-regime comments; uploading fabricated videos on YouTube to discredit protestors (Khamis et al. 2012). When activists were identified and arrested, security forces extracted information with the use of force, obtaining usernames and passwords of activists' social media accounts, which would be passed to the Syrian Electronic Army to post pro-regime slogans on their pages and go after the user's "friends" (Baiazy, 2012). The regime's IT army worked in close collaboration with the Syrian Security Communication branch, codenamed 225, the hub for all telecommunication security in Syria, intensifying the electronic surveillance system by controlling text-messaging, e-mails and Internet use, and blocking messages that might contain terms such as "revolution", "meeting" or "demonstration" (Zaluski, 2015). Thus on the ground clashes in Syria were paralleled by clashes in the virtual world, through spy warfare and cyber espionage, an aspect of the conflict often neglected.

Social media not only provided space for news coverage of the Syrian revolt, they also opened venues of artistic expressions of resistance. While violence seems to dominate most of the cyberspace coverage of the Syrian conflict, local artists have transformed the Internet into a virtual gallery to exhibit their works of art. The Syrian net-art is an innovative phenomenon of cultural production that encompasses visual art, mash-ups, cartoons, jokes, songs and web-series. One example is represented by the "Raised Hands Campaign", a reaction to a campaign by the regime to gain popular support which entailed the putting up of billboards showing a colourful hand and the slogan "young or old, I'm with the law" (*ṣaghir aw kabir, ana ma' a al-qanuun*), ""whether a boy or a girl, I'm with the law" (*ṣabiy aw fatà, ana ma'a al qanuun*). Syrians reacted to this Orwellian atmosphere by reusing the same slogans and images and by posting them across the different social media with new slogans that said: "I'm free" (*ana hurr*), "I lost my shoe" ("*faqadhtu hidha'i*" – suggesting it had been thrown at the dictator). The popularity of the digital version of the "Raised Hands Campaign", as opposed to the offline one, obliged the regime to react to this manipulation and replace the old banners with new ones that displayed rhetorically more neutral mottos like "I'm with Syria. My demands are your demands" ("*Ana ma'a suriya. Maṭlabi huwwa maṭlabik*"). Once more, social media were filled up with the new version of the slogan, which read: "I'm with Syria, My demands are freedom").

As the scholar Donatella Della Ratta observes, this campaign, like many others, shows how Syrians did not accept the official rhetoric of the regime any longer, but rather challenged it, regaining control over the world of public symbols (Della Ratta, 2012). The art of resistance also emerged in the powerful canvases of Monif Ajaj and Yasser Abu Hamad and the banners of Kafranbel, a stronghold of resistance in the centre of Syria; likewise, it can be identified in the Facebook page "Meals under Siege", created by the people of Homs to share improvised and creative recipes with the scarce ingredients at their disposal. Hence, social media allowed Syrians to rediscover their creativity, once censored or excluded from the elite-driven cultural production. By posting the arts and crafts online, with no regime-interference and no censorship, this user-generated art, established a new relationship *vis à vis* state power and a new connection between ordinary citizens and artists (Della Ratta, 2012).

Phase 2. From Uprising to armed conflict, from citizen journalism to a revival of traditional media

When it became clear that popular demonstrations were not ending and that the regime was holding on to power, a military confrontation between rebels and regime began. Protestors started arming themselves, guerrilla groups emerged and the regime progressively lost control of numerous towns and cities. With the formation of the Free Syrian Army by defected Syrian officers, the Syrian Uprising progressively moved from popular protests to a militarised civil conflict. This change had an impact on the media scene. Activists across Syria organised in Local Coordination Committees, with media centres providing local news coverage and sharing information. This phase extends from the fall 2011 to the beginning of 2013 and ISIS's expansion within Syrian borders.

New media, in this context, progressively acquired a new status, one which was not linked exclusively to informing and documenting events, but that also had a positive impact on the organisation and management of communities. In this second phase, Syrians joined the revolt by fighting and by "doing journalism", signalling a transition from Facebook/YouTube "media activism", to "citizen journalism", a form of participation that supported social development, and focused on the needs of the domestic audience, rather than the international one. This new type of journalism, also known as "public", "participatory", "democratic", or "street" journalism, assigns the role of collecting, reporting, analysing and disseminating news and information to citizens. Citizens take up this role to compensate for the poor performance of official news outlets and to dispel the distorted propaganda offered by the regime's own journalists.

The profession of citizen journalist has been the object of extensive, though not exhaustive, debates: some consider it to be a contribution from an "insider" to the making of news or a courageous effort by the people, yet one lacking professionalism, owing to its strong political value content and militant language. News, as a result, became more visual and emphatic, including images of death and destruction, engaging the audience even more than traditional media. In this respect, the media became tools to protect the cause of the revolution. A media activist interviewed in Gaziantep during a media training session argued: "My aim is to use the media to help my people topple Bashar. Why shouldn't I serve the interests of my people and of myself? I have been silenced for my whole life by the regime, now I need to have my say".[12] As such, journalism in Syria was no longer exclusively reserved for accredited journalists or established media outlets as in the past; rather potentially every man or woman with a cell-phone camera in his/her hand could contribute to and even question news coverage.

However over time because of the durability of the conflict and because of technical and financial support received by media activists from foreign powers, journalism became more professionalised. Foreign powers supported media training for activists in Syria, with the alleged objective of securing professional media coverage of the conflict, as well as teaching a new profession to the new generations; however, in reality, the practice of media assistance projects, funded by international actors like the EC and USAID turned into the strategy by these powers to intervene indirectly in the conflict via a form of soft power, which supports civil society while pushing for regime change.

If in the initial stage of the Uprising the renaissance of the media landscape apparently developed through digital platforms, with the passing of time it moved towards the revaluation of traditional forms. As the conflict limited people's access to the Internet, traditional media like newspaper, radio and TV channels regained popularity.

Newspapers

Underground newspapers first appeared in Syria towards the end of 2011, marking an important change in the panorama of the Syrian revolution.[13] The publication and distribution of periodicals marked a symbolic rupture with the monopoly of information that the regime had imposed up to then. The production of newspapers as well as radio channels represented that necessary step that bridged the pre-revolutionary phase in which alternative news circulated only online and were thereby limited to those accessing the web, to a post-Uprising phase in which the non-regime news horizon expands to the offline production and is accessible to the wider public.

Between 2011 and 2012, a dozen independent grassroots newspapers, often with their online version, were printed in Syria, like *Suryitna* (Our Syria), *Hurriyat* (Freedoms), *Enab Baladi* (Local Grapes), only to mention a few.[14] The production and distribution of these periodicals jeopardised the lives of those involved, especially those working in the distribution of copies within pro-governmental areas.[15] Today the number of oppositional papers has grown enormously, with a production that operates both in government-held areas as well as in regions under the control of armed groups, sometimes produced in Turkey. Higher quality publications have appeared, thanks to the financial and technical support of international media organisations. Many of these papers are published in local dialects or languages (e.g. Kurdish and Arabic) and target audiences such as women, children, and religious minorities (De Angelis et al., 2014).

Among the numerous printed papers that have emerged, *Sayedat Souria* (The Lady of Syria) constitutes a meaningful voice. This magazine puts forward a vision outside the box of the revolution. The magazine is an advocacy paper in circulation since the beginning of 2014, which has been supported financially and technically by the French media organisations SMART and ASML. Printed in Gaziantep on the Turkish border with Syria – with a working plan to open branches also in the liberated areas – the paper has a distribution of 5,000 copies in the liberated territories and 2,000 copies in Syrian refugee camps. The magazine is also published online through *Issuu*, a digital publishing platform, along with Facebook and Twitter. With no political or religious orientation, *Sayedat Souria* aims at raising women's awareness about politics, society and justice by having women themselves address and write about other women. Yasmine Merei, editor in-chief of the magazine, affirms that before the revolt began people spoke only of one Syrian woman, Asma al-Asad, the president's wife, the female icon of Syrian society.[16] Now, with the revolution, the magazine portrays all Syrian women, regardless of whether they are for or against the regime. The aim of the magazine is not to put forward a certain reading of the conflict or push people to take sides, but to focus on the pressing issues that Syrian women face today, whether they are living in refugee camps, rebel-held areas or regime-controlled neighbourhoods. The paper touches upon pressing issues for the female community, victims of a civil war and faced with problems like forced marriage of minors, childcare, environmental and food constraints. It also pushed for increased female representation in the Syrian National Coalition, which was limited to only 5 per cent. With violence perpetuated by the regime and by Islamist groupings alike, *Sayedat Souria* attempted to provide a perspective that differed from the monolithic narratives of the contending sides, with a glance at what could be a future Syria.

Radio

After a first period of digital explosion, radio re-emerged as probably the most efficient way to reach local audiences inside Syria. Requiring only a cheap receiver and a small battery, radios could easily be used across the country and radio broadcasts could reach communities otherwise marginalised geographically. Radio waves have the advantage of not having to pass checkpoints and frontiers to reach areas under attack, offering the only possibility for isolated areas to receive news coverage. Numerous radio stations have been established with foreign support in Turkey (both Istanbul and Gaziantep) or have their offices further abroad, like *Rozana* whose main office is in Paris. A number of transmission options are available: some radios are only available online, while others broadcast both on short waves and online. In some cases, like *Radio Fresh*, a local radio station broadcasting from Kafranbel in Idlib province, they are available only to their local broadcast audience.

In May 2015, at least 17 Syrian radio stations were broadcasting, as indicated in Table 13.1.[17]

These radios stations are the by-product of the current civil war, therefore designed to support those Syrians afflicted by the conflict and suffering from economic restrictions, as well as the numerous refugees, scattered across the country. They presented programmes concerning daily life whether in regime or opposition-held areas such as how to deal with power-cuts, lack of water and gas, and how to cook amidst food shortages (De Angelis et al., 2015). They also presented cultural programmes based on the revival of Syrian history, culture, music, dialect and food.

TABLE 13.1 Opposition Radio Stations in Syria

Radio	Website	Main Office
AL-KUL	http://radioalkul.com	Istanbul, Turkey
ALWAN	http://radioalkul.com	Gaziantep, Turkey
ANA	www.ana.fm/ar/	Gaziantep, Turkey
ARTA	https://www.facebook.com/artradio?fref=ts www.arta.fm	Gaziantep, Turkey
FRESH	https://www.facebook.com7Radio.Frsh.90.00FM?fref=ts	Kafranbel, Syria
HARA FM	https://www.facebook.com/radioharafm?fref=ts	Gaziantep, Turkey
HAWA SMART	https://facebook.com/hawasmartradio	Gaziantep, Turkey
NASAEM SYRIA	https://www.facebook.com/radio.nasaem.syria/timeline	Gaziantep, Turkey
Roo7	https://www.facebok.com/RadioRoo7?fref=ts	Gaziantep, Turkey
ROZANA	http://rozana.fm	Paris, France
WATAN	https://www.facebook.com/alwan6070?fref=ts www.alwan.fm	Gaziantep, Turkey
YARMOUK 63	http://yarmouk63radio.weebly.com	No main office (team located in Syria, Lebanon and Turkey)

Adapted from Marrouch (2014).

A very good example was by *Radio SouriaLi*, an Internet-based radio broadcasting from October 2012, born from a project of a group of Syrians with different ethnic, religious and intellectual backgrounds, based inside and outside Syria. Caroline Ayoub, an activist who had been detained by the regime and one of the main contributors of the radio show, explains how the name "SouriaLi" sums up the current situation in her country. It is a play on words, which combines "sourialia", meaning surrealism, with "souria li", meaning "Syria for me", in order to refer to the surrealistic condition that Syria is experiencing and the need for all Syrians to come together to build a new Syria.[18] Ayoub affirms that the radio is trying to sew up the wounds of the war and reunite Syrians in the name of their rich cultural heritage. This is done through a number of programmes, like *"Ayam el Lulu"* (Good Old Days) in which well-known episodes of Syrian history are celebrated; *"Fattoush"* (a traditional Syrian salad dish), which airs a 15-minute cooking show on traditional food recipes; or *"Hakawati Souria"*, a 20-minute programme on traditional storytelling,[19] aiming to show how life in Syria endures and preserves the great culture of its people. *Radio SouriaLi* is the most successful Syrian media project, with 500,000 returning visitors to the website each month, 200,000 playbacks on their sound cloud account and 4 million online listeners (Marrouch, 2014). The radio broadcasts for three hours a day in Syria, using equipment and broadcasting capacity provided by *Hawa Smart* in Hama, Homs, Damascus, Latakia, and Aleppo.

Another example of a successful radio station is *Radio Fresh*, though very different with regards to its reach and quality. Founded in 2013, *Radio Fresh* was established by a group of media activists in Kafranbel, Idlib province, as a community-radio, which could cover local issues that were relevant for its local audience. As Rima Marrouch reports through the words of a Syrian researcher living in Gaziantep, "the success of Radio Fresh is that they really speak about issues that touch Kafranbel's residents. For example, fixing the local power plant or distribution of humanitarian aid in town. They don't speak about the Iranian nuclear programme or international affairs, stories that people can follow in mainstream Arabic-language media outlets". These radio stations are funded by a mix of donor contributions and self-generated funding (Marrouch, 2014).

The panorama of Syrian radios would not be complete without mentioning those radios that chiefly serve partisan ends, telling stories of mothers sending their children to take up arms to fight the regime, or chanting songs encouraging young people to join the battle or simply merging news coverage with propaganda and sensationalism. Particularly, with the emergence of the Islamic State within Syrian borders, radio became a means of jihadi propaganda. This is the case of radio *Al-Bayan*, established by the Islamic State after the seize of the city of Raqqa in January 2014 (Marrouch, 2014). This radio station broadcast daily news about the advancement of the Islamic State, read out political statements and described the benefits of living under Islamic law. Thus, the enthusiasm and creativity that characterised the beginning of the Uprising has given way to a more complex reality, where media can contribute to the escalation of violence and enmity.

Satellite TV

Two satellite channels, Orient TV and Barada TV, created before the Uprising and based abroad, assumed an explicit anti-regime position, adopting the discourse of the revolution. This was followed by the creation of up to nine opposition broadcasting channels, among which are Souria Al-Shaab (Syrian People), Souria Al-Ghad (Syria Tomorrow), 18th of March Channel and Aleppo Today. Despite the controversies regarding the financial support it received, Barada TV played a fundamental role in the years leading up to the revolt and in those that followed it (Witlock, 2011). This London-based TV channel, funded in 2008 by a group of Syrian expatriates with a low-budget production, covered topics that were taboo within Syria, often with explicit anti-regime stances and political debates usually left out of Syria's national channels. As soon as the first protests and manifestations started, the channel gave wide coverage to the events. It started streaming YouTube videos that protestors had posted online, inaugurating a technique that characterised the news coverage on Syria of most of the established international news networks. Beside the use of exclusive footages, the channel also relied on open debates, where people were able to call in and express their opinions, opening a venue for critical thinking and civic engagement.

However, the most significant development in the Syrian media war between opposition and regime came when the government of Saudi Arabia and Qatar decided to use their media assets, respectively al-Arabiya and al-Jazeera, to hasten Asad's demise (Al-Abdeh, 2012). Although this happened after protestors had already taken to the streets in massive numbers, it revolutionised the media landscape on the Syrian conflict, in terms of information available and owing to the strong influence the two channels had over public opinion (Abu Khalil, 2011). The two channels, founded by members of the Qatari and Saudi royal families, respectively, had won the hearts of the Arab audience by introducing a new type of journalism inspired by Western values of professionalism, accountability, precision and independent thinking. When the Uprising in Tunisia broke out, these channels played a fundamental role in representing local protest as the expression of a broader Arab popular Uprising that facilitated the spread of the protests from one country to another, as part of a common framework, something that would have hardly been possible without the unifying media narrative. Unfortunately, their professionalism was strongly undermined in the coverage of the Syrian conflict, which served the interests of their patrons and local proxies. As for the coverage of Syrian state television, it resisted reforms and became a weapon in the hands of the security apparatus and the old regime (Lynch, 2015). Unfortunately, as pointed out by Marc Lynch (2015), much TV coverage of the Uprising adopted a partisan tone.

Phase 3. Media professionalisation amidst war stagnation

The revolution had by 2013 entered a new phase, with new participants joining the conflict and an intractable civil war raging. With the fall of the regime not expected to happen any time soon, and with the radical Islamist guerrillas in control of large swaths of the country, the media sector also moved into a new phase. Despite the war, media centres and media professionals were working with higher standards of professionalism, inspired by Western models and supported by foreign media support programmes. This type of support to local journalists and media activists was conceived as necessary to keep news from Syria flowing, as international reporters had been barred from or had restricted access to the country, leaving local journalists as the only newsgatherers for Syria's war. Media development, intended to provide material support, technical assistance, training and financial support to media centres and activists, grew enormously, to an extent that it resembled an industry (Stanley, 2007). A variety of actors were involved in the media assistance, from governments, to multilateral organisations and a large number of national and international non-governmental organisations (NGOs). The US government and EU were two of the main donors, entrusting projects to a vast number of implementers like BBC Media Action, Internews Europe, the National Democratic Institute, HIVOS, Free Press Unlimited, Canal France International, l'Association du Soutien aux Médias Libres (ASML), and AVAAZ. These projects were usually based in Syria's neighbouring countries, with Turkey being the main host. Gaziantep, a city on the Turkish-Syrian border, became the hub for media organisations that operated training for Syrian media activists. Here they learned the basics of journalism and video shooting and were provided with broadcast equipment. Some returned to Syria to teach others media skills and provide them with the necessary equipment, in some cases establishing media centres in the different governorates. The protracted conflict and deteriorating situation inside Syria forced media support projects to return to working on traditional media, principally radio and newspapers, which could reach areas under siege. These programmes were specifically designed to respond to the needs produced by a crisis that has left people without houses, reduced many to being refugees across the country and in the region, and confined others in refugee camps, while sectarian strife and the terror caused by the prospect of an Islamist takeover spread across the country.

One of the main initiatives of this phase was the formation of platforms mediating between the online production of news and the public: checking the contents, contextualising the events and verifying their authenticity. One example was the Damascus Bureau, a news platform where independent journalists and inexperienced media activists publicised their articles, had them translated, and received comments from experts and the public.[20]

Other types of initiatives gathered news and videos provided by activists in the field, verifying, and contextualising raw material into useable footage, which was then distributed to the international media; for example, the citizen press group, ANA News Media Association, a Cairo-based network of journalists co-funded by the British-Syrian journalist Rami Jarrah, that provided training and equipment, often smuggled across the Lebanese border, to media activists working in Syria, with support from private donors and EU funding.[21] The organisation has grown substantially, reaching a network of 350 Syrians who file news from across the country.[22]

Of a different nature is the platform Syrian Media, funded by the media activist Monis Bokhari, which constituted a database of the different stories that had appeared since the outbreak of the revolution and also funded[23] the online radio Baladna (our country); it aimed to create a common language for Syrian journalism based on enhanced professionalism and collaboration among journalists (De Angelis, 2014). The emergence of these organisations guaranteed higher reliability of the news, as opposed to what was previously a chaotic, if not piecemeal, uploading of news by activists on social media.

Despite these initiatives, a large section of news outlets continued to lack professional rigour and ethical responsibility, adopting highly partisan narratives, which served specific state authorities/factions or political aims. This picture refers to both national and international media outlets, which, driven by political agendas, have contributed to the marketisation of fear, the sectarianisation of the conflict and the demonisation of specific minorities. As Lynch (2015) pointed out, if the media played a prominent role in enabling the outbreak of the Uprising, the fragmentation in the media coverage that followed also transformed it into a vehicle for proxy warfare by regional powers and encouraged the logic of violence. For instance, the emphasis put on the sectarian nature of the Syrian civil war, whether by the regime, some opposition groups or regional state actors, was employed and manipulated by the different parties operating on the ground to serve their political aims. The Syrian regime inevitably stressed the sectarian nature of the conflict to justify its repression of rebel forces and its call for national unity against the *takfiri* Islamist threat. Regional actors, such as Saudi Arabia and Iran, embarked on a proxy war through competing media channels and networks.

ISIS and the cyber Caliphate

The analysis of the Syrian media-scape would not be complete without mentioning the hi-tech jihadi war directed by the so-called Islamic State in the third phase of the Syrian conflict. Despite the retrograde aim of restoring an Islamic caliphate over the territories of Iraq and Syria, the new Islamic State is anything but retrograde in terms of the sophisticated media campaign it launches.[24] ISIS has invested enormously in its marketing strategy, which has improved greatly since the "fuzzy, monotonous camcorder sermons" of Osama bin Laden (Rose, 2014). The ISIS global media operation makes use of YouTube, Twitter, Instagram, Tumblr and other social media to instil fear, discredit and stir hatred against its enemies (i.e. Iran and Shi'i groups), provoke the US and its allies and recruit from outside the Middle East. The group also founded al-Hayat Media Centre, a broadcaster aimed at non-Arabic speakers, with programmes shaped on the model of Western TV channels, streaming in several languages, with the intent of showing the perfect life that exists for those living within the confines of the Islamic Caliphate.

Different from the dreadful video footages showing the brutality of the group when killing Western hostages or different ethnic and religious groups caught up in their military advance, are other videos circulating on the *mujdatweets*, few-minutes videos under the shape of a jihadi travel show, showing colourful scenes of street life, children at play or eating an ice cream, with people joyfully coming up to the camera to express the security and peace that the "land of the Khalifah" offers, saying "We don't need any democracy, we don't need any communism or anything like that, all we need is shari'a" (Rose, 2014). The Western origin of many of its fighters is revealed by the professional audio and visual techniques being used as well as by the expressions of pride in the fashion of shooting selfies by Islamic fighters (Diab, 2015). Sadly, these "poster boys", posing in Rambo-like selfies and circulating through ISIS followers' social networks (regardless of the religious "legality" [*haram* vs. *halal*] of these photos) proved effective in recruiting followers.

The emergence of ISIS further complicated the conflict in Syria, presenting a third contending party in the already fragmented conflict and deepening the crisis. However, beside the actual brutality of the group, experienced by all those falling under its authority, the group is also waging a war that transcends the borders of the presumed Islamic caliphate, reaching Western countries through cyberspace and raising fundamental questions about the idea of territorial sovereignty. ISIS' "electronic war", waged against Europe and the US, threatened Western computing systems, hacked business and government websites and provoked serious economic and national challenges. For examples in April 2015 ISIS hacked the French Television network TV5 Monde, preventing it from broadcasting for three hours and controlling its social media accounts on Twitter and Facebook.

Thus, the expansion of the Islamic State did not just occur in Syrian and Iraqi territories but also through the virtual world. It is in the cyberspace that the power of the caliphate was rooted. Here, digital platforms became the main tool for attracting recruits who discovered not only ISIS, but as Adam Shatz argues on the *London Review of Books*, Islam itself (Shatz, 2015). Indeed, digital media paradoxically bridged the gap between two crises of citizenship: the exclusion of young Muslims in Europe and the exclusion of Sunnis in Syria and Iraq (Shatz, 2015).

This confirms that the media are ductile tools that can serve popular democratic movements, authoritarian governments and terrorist organisations alike as they can equally bridge gaps between atomised citizens, drive regime changes and gather disfranchised people inebriated by fanaticism and violence.

Conclusion

The role and development of the new media in Syria has been a revolution within a revolution. Social networking sites, web-aggregators, TV channels, satellite stations, radios, magazines, online and printed newspapers, have emerged in the midst of the revolt, eager to replace what had been the official and meagre news diet that the Syrian regime had offered thus far. It was the combination of old and new media, online and offline protests, that marked the success of the media campaign. Activists opened new webpages and uploaded videos reporting on the brutality of the regime; underground newspapers were distributed in rebel-held areas, radio stations operating from neighbouring countries reached the Syrian airwave space and satellite TV channels spread the news of Syrian social networks to an international audience. All of this amplified the capacity of the opposition movement and the reach of its message across the population.

The events, *à la* Alain Badiou, unfolding in Syria have been influenced by the media in all its phases and aspects, to the extent that it would be very difficult to think of the Syrian Uprising separately from the media. Based on these assumptions, this chapter analysed the diversified role that the new media technologies have played during the course of the Syrian Uprising – from its early days to the current civil war – identifying the actors employing them, the strategies used and the impact they produced on the development of the conflict. Specifically, the chapter argues that the Syrian media scene experienced three major phases in its development: the emergence of alternative sources of information through the digital space that acted as catalysts, mobilisers and organisers of the popular movement; the evolution from media activism to citizen journalism and finally, the professionalisation and diversification of the media sphere amidst an intractable conflict.

Analysing the role of the media in the Syrian conflict is important for several different reasons. The most evident one is that with the spark of the Syrian revolt, the monopoly of information held by the Syrian regime crumbled before citizens' access and employment of the new media technologies. These tools did not simply offer a new and diversified news panorama, but they set up platforms where interaction and coordination occur, where collective action is organised and where everyone, government included, are asked to be accountable for their actions. The new information technologies damaged the regime's stability by putting an end to its control over the flow of information and people's interaction. Moreover, the Syrian conflict became the expression of another important phenomenon, namely that the new media have not simply increased the opportunities for social movements to emerge, but they have changed the way conflicts are fought, becoming at the same time tools to inform and weapons to attack. Today the media are not just tools to spread information, but to "perform" in the conflict (Zelizer, 2007). Nowadays conflicts are not simply fought on the ground with heavy artillery but online, with real electronic armies fighting over the control of space, power and language. And yet the role of the new media in the Syrian conflict has not simply empowered citizens against authoritarian ruling and duplicated the conflict in a real and virtual dimension but it has also produced a new type of journalism, less professional but more vivid and crude. If the Vietnam War was the first televised war and the Gulf War the first 24/7 cable war, the Syrian conflict is the first social media war. Lynch defines it as the "most socially mediated civil conflict in history", with a range of videos, information and discourses flowing from Syria that is unprecedented and at times, ungovernable (Lynch et al., 2014).

Images and live footages have dominated the news coverage of the Syrian revolt since its onset and have profoundly affected its development. Some images are now glued in our collective memory, like the massacre of Izra', near Dera'a on 22 April of 2011 and the picture of an anguished father carrying the dead body of his son, who had been shot in the head (Al-Abdeh, 2012). The videos of the singer

Ibrahim Qashush who gathered thousands in the streets of Hama by tuning the song "Come on, Bashar, leave!" (*yallah, irhal ya Bashar!*) and who was found dead in a river with his throat cut, is another symbolic icon (Shadid, 2011); and even more, the rows of dead children heaped up after the chemical attack in East Ghouta province in August 2013 (Mahmoud and Chulov, 2013). Daunting videos and images like these have encouraged Syrians to participate and have shaped the world's understanding of the violent repression of peaceful protestors by the Syrian regime. Equally shocking videos like the one of the rebel commander eating the heart of a fallen enemy, have proved how the enduring state of war and devastating humanitarian catastrophe is dis-humanising, on whichever side they occur.[25]

The rise of citizen journalists and their performance with new media is progressively changing the nature and the limits of journalism, extending "journalists authority in questionable ways" (Zelizer, 2007). If on the one hand the media coverage offered by citizen journalists can be criticised for being imbued with political value and militant language, on the other hand one should also question the agenda of international media outlets that collect the material uploaded by citizens journalists to build a narrative serving the interests of their patrons, local proxies or simply to sell papers – focusing their coverage on sensationalism, inciting hatred against political adversaries and deepening ethnic and religious divisions. This suggests that the media are powerful tools, which can be equally effective to encourage collective action and drive popular mobilisations as they can produce fear, resentment and divisions (Lynch, 2015).

The recent catastrophe of Syrian refugees fleeing their country and embarking on an unknown journey is assigning the media the decisive role of documenting the crisis and calling for the international community to act promptly. When the image of a dead Syrian boy, Aylan Kurdi, in September of 2015, washed ashore the coastal city of Bodrum in Turkey, appeared on social media and on international newspapers, it reminded the international community that the Syrian crisis has not ended, thus is widening and coming closer to Europe with the calamity of its refugees fleeing the war. The image has provoked an unprecedented involvement of civil society actors around European countries, rallying in the streets and pushing their governments to provide temporary asylum to the many Syrian refugees, a fact that, per se, shows the unprecedented potentialities that the new media have in changing society and politics. And yet the role of the media does not terminate here. Once the conflict is over, the new media will have to take part in a much harder task: sewing the wounds that the violence caused by sectarian, religious and political divides has provoked during these years of civil war.

Notes

1 For transliteration, I have modified the system developed by the *International Journal of Middle East Studies*, dispensing with diacritical marks, and, where possible, adopting the spelling used in the mainstream media.

2 Slogan written on a banner by the city of Kafranbel, known for its courageous spirit and carrying out distinctive acts of civil activism in the midst of a civil war. See Daher (2014).
3 As terminology is a locus of lasting influence, this chapter attempts to avoid the unfinished debate about the definitions of the Arab uprisings favouring terms like "uprising", "upheaval" or "revolts" and "revolution".
4 The Asad regime has received backing from Russia, Iran and Lebanon, while the rebel groups have been fattened by Turkey, the conservative Arab states, specifically Qatar and Saudi Arabia, the EU member states and the US, with financial revenues by Gulf countries fuelling the Islamic groups.
5 This covert intervention has been justified on two grounds, that the Syrian regime is authoritarian (despite many authoritarian nations have been also allied with the West) and because the Syrian government has been charged with using illegal chemical weapons.
6 The development of Syria's media landscape in the years that predated the Uprising of 2011 is the issue of enquiry of my PhD thesis. University of Exeter.
7 The page was created on 18 January 2011. See Landis (2011).
8 "Emergence: Inform to Protect", *ASML*, http://medialibre.fr/en/evolution-of-media-in-syria/emergence-inform-to-protect/, accessed 28 April 2015.
9 See also, Hugh Macleod, Annasofie Flamand, "Tortured and Killed: Hamza al-Khateeb, Age 13", *al-Jazeera*, 31 May 2011, http://www.aljazeera.com/indepth/features/2011/05/201153185927813389.html,accessed 28 April 2015.
10 The series was created by 10 artists from inside Syria and is made of two seasons. It received an incredible success with more of 40,000 viewers. See, "Little Dictator", *al-Jazeera*, 21 August 2015, http://www.aljazeera.com/programmes/witness/2012/08/2012820111648774405.html, accessed 27 April 2015.
11 "Salamiyah Coordination Committee", *Syria Untold*, 8 May 2014. http://www.syriauntold.com/en/work_group/salamiyah-women-coordination-committee/, accessed 27 April 2015.
12 Interview with Syrian activists in Gaziantep, on the Turkish border with Syria, 8 August 2013.
13 Syria has a long history of underground papers. See James A. Paul, *Human Rights in Syria* (New York: Human Rights Watch, 1990).
14 'Revolutionary Press Blooms Underground in Syria', *al-Arabiya*, 27 September 2012, http://english.alarabiya.net/articles/2012/09/27/240428.html, accessed 24 April 2015.
15 "Activists Take Big Risks to Deliver Underground Newspapers in Syria", *France 24*, 11 November 2011, http://observers.france24.com/content/20111121-syria-syrian-activists-take-risks-distribute-underground-newspaper-hurriyat-damascus-homs-appelo-opposition, accessed 24 April 2015.
16 Interview with the editor in-chief of Sayedat Souria, Yasmine Merei, via Skype, 4 March 2014.
17 Table adapted from Rima Morrouch's report, "Syria's Post-Uprising Media Outlets: Challenges and Opportunities in Syrian Radio Startups", *Reuters Institute*, 2014, http://reutersinstitute.politics.ox.ac.uk/publication/syria%E2%80%99s-post-uprising-media-outlets-challenges-and-opportunities-syria, accessed 16 December 2015.
18 Interview with one of the main contributors of Radio SouriaLi, Caroline Ayoub, via Skype, 3 March 2014.
19 Interview with Caroline Ayoub, via Skype, 3 March 2014.
20 The Damascus Bureau's website: https://damascusbureau.org/en/, accessed 7 May 2015.
21 Brendan McGeagh, Amy Johnson, "Citizen Journalism in Syria: Rami Jarrah", *Canadian Journalists for Free Expression*, 27 November 2012, https://cjfe.org/resources/features/citizen-journalism-syria-rami-jarrah, accessed 7 May 2015.
22 "Syria: A War Reported by Citizen-Journalists, Social Media", *Radio Free Europe*, 7 April 2015, http://www.rferl.org/content/syria-war-reported-by-citizen-journalists-social-media/24630841.html, accessed 6 May 2015.
23 Syrian Media's website (in Arabic): http://www.syrianmedia.com/, accessed 5 May 2015.

24 Jean Pierre Filu, *From Deep State to Islamic State* (London: C. Hurst & Co., 2015).
25 Paul Wood, "Face-to-Face with Abu Sakkar Syria's 'Heart-Eating Cannibal'", *BBC News*, 5 July 2013, http://www.bbc.com/news/magazine-23190533, accessed 6 May 2015.

Bibliography

Abu Khalil, Asad (2011), "Syrian Protests and the Media: Al-Jazeera and Al-Arabiya", *Al-Akhbar*, 29 September, available at http://english.al-akhbar.com/node/752, accessed 27 December 2015.

Al-Abdeh, Malik (2012), "Syria, the Activists Grow Up", *Open Democracy*, 14 November, available at https://www.opendemocracy.net/malik-al-abdeh/syria-activists-grow-up, accessed 20 January 2016.

Al-Abdeh, Malik (2012), "The Media War in Syria", The Majalla, 4 October, available at http://eng.majalla.com/2012/10/article55234370/the-media-war-in-syria, accessed 6 January 2016.

Anderson, Lisa (2011), "Demystifying the Arab Spring", *Foreign Affairs*, May/June.

Ayoub, Ayman (2012), "Syria's Revolution a Year On", Open Democracy, 22 March, www.opendemocracy.net/ayman-ayoub/syrias-revolution-year-on, accessed 28 April 2015.

Baiazy, Amjad (2012), "Syria's Cyberwars: Using Social Media against Dissent", Media Policy, available at www.academia.edu/3555530/Syria_Cyber_Wars, accessed 27 December 2015.

Brownlee, Billie Jeanne (2016), New Media and Revolution: Syria's Silent Movement towards the 2011 Uprising, PhD, *Exeter University*.

Brownlee, Billie Jeanne and Maziyar, Ghiabi (2016), "Passive, Silent and Revolutionary: The 'Arab Spring' Revisited", *Middle East Critique* 25: 3.

Daher, Joseph (2014), "The Roots and Grassroots of the Syrian Revolution (Part 4 of 4)", Open Democracy, 5 April 2014, https://www.opendemocracy.net/joseph-daher/roots-and-grassroots-of-syrian-revolution-part-4-of-4-3, accessed 27 April 2015.

De Angelis, Enrico (2014), "Tre Anni Dopo lo Scoppio della Rivoluzione: la Sfera Virtuale Siriana si Trasforma", Arab Media & Report, 12 May, available at http://arabmediareport.it/tre-anni-dopo-lo-scoppio-della-rivoluzione-la-sfera-virtuale-siriana-si-trasforma/, accessed 2 February 2016.

De Angelis, Enrico, Della Ratta, Donatella, and Badran, Yazan (2014), "Against the Odds: Syria's Flourishing Mediascape", Al-Jazeera, 30 August, available at www.aljazeera.com/indepth/opinion/2014/08/against-odds-syria-flourishing-201483094530782525.html, accessed 27 December 2015.

Della Ratta, Donatella (2012), "Towrds Active Citizenship in Syria", Mediaoriente Blog, 12 June, available at www.sidint.net/content/towards-active-citizenship-syria-donatella-della-ratta, accessed 20 December 2015.

Diab, Khaled (2015), "The Jihadist Selfie is Changing the Image of the Holy War", Al-Jazeera, 11 March, www.aljazeera.com/indepth/opinion/2015/02/jihadist-selfie-changing-image-holywar-150224053159076.html, accessed 5 January 2016.

Fares, Obaida (2015), "Pro-regime Versus Opposition Media: During the Revolution, 2011–2013", in *Routledge Handbook of the Arab Spring*, edited by Sadiki, Larbi, 187–196, Abingdon: Routledge.

Fowler, Sarah (2013), "Who is the Syrian Electronic Army?", BBC News, 25 April, available at www.bbc.co.uk/news/world-middle-east-22287326, accessed 5 January 2016.

Khamis, Sahar et al. (2012), "Beyond Egypt's 'Facebook Revolution and Syria's You Tube Uprising:' Comparing Political Contexts, Actors and communication strategies", *Arab Media & Society*, Spring, available at www.arabmediasociety.com/articles/downloads/20120407120519_Khamis_Gold_Vaughn.pdf, accessed 27 December 2015.

Khatib, Lina (2014), "Transforming the Media: From Tool of Rulers to Tool of Empowerment", in ed. *Arab Human Development in the Twenty-First Century: The Primacy of Empowerment*, New York: The American University in Cairo Press.

Kilcullen, Davis (2013), *Out of the Mountains: The Coming Age of Urban Guerrilla*, London: C. Hurst & Co Publishers.

Landis, Joshua (2011), "The Man behind 'Syria Revolution 2011': Facebook Page Speaks Out", SyriaComment Blog, 24 April, www.joshualandis.com/blog/the-man-behind-syria-revolution-2011-facebook-page-speaks-out/, accessed 16 April 2015.

Lynch, Marc (2015), "After the Arab Spring: How the Media trashed the Transitions", *Journal of Democracy* 26: 4.

Lynch, Marc, Freelon, Deen and Aday, Sean (2014), "Syria's Socially Mediated Civil War", US Institute of Peace, 13 January.

McAdam, Doug (1982), *Political Process and the Development of Black Insurgency 1930–1970*, Chicago: University of Chicago Press.

Mahmoud, Mona and Chulov, Martin (2013), "Syrian Eyewitness Accounts of Alleged Chemical Weapons Attacks in Damascus", *The Guardian*, 22 August, available at https://www.theguardian.com/world/2013/aug/22/syria-chemical-weapons-eyewitness, accessed 5 January 2016.

Marrouch, Rima (2014), "Syria's Post-Uprising Media Outlets: Challenges and Opportunities in Syria", Reuters Institute, University of Oxford. Available at http://reutersinstitute.politics.ox.ac.uk/publication/syria%E2%80%99s-post-uprising-media-outlets-challenges-and-opportunities-syria, accessed 5 January 2015.

Meyer, Davis and Sidney Tarrow (1998), *The Social Movement Society*, Lanham: Rowman & Littlefield Publishers.

Rose, Steve (2014), "The ISIS Propaganda War: a Hi-Tech Media Jihad", *The Guardian*, 7 October, available at https://www.theguardian.com/world/2014/oct/07/isis-media-machine-propaganda-war, accessed 2 February 2016.

Shadid, Anthony (2011), "Lyrical Message for Syrian Leader: 'Come on Bashar, Leave' 'Come on Bashar, Leave'", *New York Times*, available at www.nytimes.com/2011/07/22/world/middleeast/22poet.html, accessed 5 January 2016.

Shatz, Adam (2015), "Magical Thinking about ISIS", *London Review of Books* 37: 23, available at www.lrb.co.uk/v37/n23/adam-shatz/magical-thinking-about-isis, accessed 5 January 2016.

Shirky, Clay (2011), "The Political Power of Social Media", *Foreign Affairs*, January/February.

Stanley, Bruce (2007), "Crafting the Arab Media for Peace-Building: Donors, Dialogue and Disasters", in *Arab Media and Political Renewal*, edited by Naomi Sakr, London: I.B.Tauris.

Whitlock, Craig (2011), "US Secretly Backed Syrian Opposition Groups, Cables Released by Wikileaks Show", *The Washington Post*, 17 April, available at https://www.washingtonpost.com/world/us-secretly backed-syrian-opposition-groups-cables-released-by-wikileaks-show/2011/04/14/AF1p9hwD_story.html, accessed 5 January 2016.

Zaluski, Richard (2015), "Syria's Cyberwar Branch 225 at Work", Centre for Strategic Cyberspace + Security Science, http://cscss.org/cscssdev1/?p=3668, accessed 5 May.

Zelizer, Barbie (2007), "On 'Having Been There': 'Eye Witnessing' as a Journalistic Key Word", *Critical Studies in Media Communication* 24: 5, 408–428.

14

UNBLURRING AMBIGUITIES

Assessing the impact of the Syrian Muslim Brotherhood in the Syrian revolution

Naomí Ramírez Díaz

In March 2011, when the Syrian revolution against the four-decade long rule of the Asad family officially started, the Syrian Muslim Brotherhood (SMB), with a long history of opposition to the Asad regime, did not hesitate to engage in the revolution at various levels. It is the aim of this chapter to study the participation of the SMB in the revolutionary movement of the country, its ups and downs and its future prospects but with a particular focus on the early stages of its involvement when its role was more pivotal. In addition, it will contribute to the debate on how the SMB's policies have affected their internal dynamics, especially regarding the regional divisions that the organization has suffered from for decades, and the role of the younger generations and their commitment towards the traditional top-to-bottom structure of the group.

Contradicting narratives on SMB early activities

From the day they were expelled from Syria after the 1982 Hama massacre, following on a decree issued two years previously that punished an individual's membership in the organization with death or exile, the SMB's activities and prominence in Syria had been very much reduced. The organization had also been handicapped by a history of factionalism. In founding the Brothers, Mustapha Sibai had unified various regional religious groups with different perspectives and views, under the same banner and inevitably, those differences would haunt the group after his early death in 1964. The most notorious division, which is still relevant in the group's activity, was the one that took place in 1986 when the election of a new leader, meant to unify the rival factions, actually provoked a schism between two rival leaderships in the organization: the Hama and Aleppo wings. After a temporary leadership, the Aleppo branch took control and kept it until 2010, when the last Aleppine leader, Ali Sadr al-Din al-Bayanouni, lost power to Muhammad Riad

Shaqfa from Hama. This division has continued to affect the revolutionary activities of the SMB.

In 2009, for reasons that exceed the scope and goals of this chapter, the SMB decided to put their opposition activities on hold. At the time, Ali al-Bayanouni was still the leader of the organization, a position he had held since 1996. When the popular mobilizations began in Syria in 2011, the organization did not officially change its stance until 1 May 2011, when it announced the resumption of opposition to the regime. At this point, though, the SMB limited their activity to issuing some supportive statements.[1]

When the mobilizations began in Egypt in January 2011, those who hoped for a similar situation to take place in Syria opened a Facebook page called "the Syrian Day of Rage" on 15 February 2011 calling for mass mobilizations in the Syrian capital, Damascus, which, however, failed. But, indicative of the mood among many Syrians, a few days later, on 17 February 2011, a spontaneous episode took place in the Damascene Hariqa souk, where hundreds of people shouted at a law enforcement agent who had mistreated one of the merchants in the area. The slogans they repeated were: "the Syrian people will not be humiliated" and "death before humiliation".[2]

Another Facebook page was created on 18 January 2011, under the name "The Revolution against Bashar al-Asad".[3] Media outlets close to the Syrian regime claimed that the SMB were behind this move and pointed at Fidaa al-Sayyid as its manager.[4] Although this eventually proved to be true, as will be noted below, people responded to the regime's claims by emphasizing the fact that they had taken to the streets for a very simple reason: "Neither SMB, nor Salafis, we want freedom."

Finally, two years after the beginning of the mobilizations, the SMB publicly explained to the Syrian people the steps they had taken to prepare themselves for a potential Uprising. Molhem al-Droubi (2013), one of the most prominent figures of the SMB, explained this in the organization's 2013-born *Al-Ahd* newspaper. According to him:

> The SMB have participated in the Syrian revolution from the very beginning ... In January 2011, its leadership met to study the revolutions in Tunisia and Egypt and I was put in charge of the elaboration of a plan on what could happen in our country. And that is what I did ... I presented a plan called "Leave, Bashar" (*Erhal Bashar*), where I summarised what I believed we should do in case of a revolutionary outbreak ... One of the most important points that we agreed upon was that we would make no individual or specific demand, and that we would simply support the population's demands. On the other hand, we decided that our priorities would be the preservation of the peaceful nature of the revolution and its national character, the preservation of Syria's territorial unity and the rejection of all forms of foreign military intervention [an intervention carried out by non-Arab and non-Muslim countries].

In the next issue of *Al-Ahd*, Hamza al-Abdallah and Fidaa al-Sayyid (2013) explained how they had set the above-mentioned Facebook page in motion:

> The Syrian street had reached a boiling point and it was about to explode ... it just needed someone to shout or to knock at the door first ... The 'Syrian Revolution Against Bashar al-Asad' page did exactly that, and thank God, it sparked a revolution in the whole country.

Hamza al-Abdallah, in turn, added the following:

> It is important to note that the "Syrian Revolution Against Bashar al-Asad" page was not the first to appear in this context, but many others paved the way. Through them, *we called* for demonstrations on February 4 and 5, 2011, but they were not successful. Because of that, *we set* a new date for mid-March. Among those pages, we can highlight "Towards a popular movement for a Syrian Day of Rage" and "The Syrian Day of Rage".[5] [emphasis added]

Their accounts take credit for the first "official" calls for an Uprising. In a press statement published by Reuters, the SMB said the following: "Unite your voices and shout for freedom and dignity. God created you as free men, so do not let tyrants or the powerful elites turn you into slaves. God is great."

Into the political sphere: ideology, organization, alliances

From the beginning, the Syrian revolution suffered from an acute scarcity of leaders, due to its popular and spontaneous nature, but also due to the fact that many of the initial young organizers were jailed, tortured, or killed, prompting many others to flee the country. Therefore, the revolution needed the establishment of some form of leadership and political representation. In order to achieve this, and very probably following the Libyan National Transition Council's success in achieving international recognition as opposition and government in exile, the SMB promoted the organization of a conference to found a similar body in Antalya (Turkey) in early June 2011.

Among the different issues raised, the thorniest one was the nature of the future Syrian state in the event of a regime collapse. While some political forces supported the establishment of a secular system, the SMB refused to accept such an idea, since "separating the State from religion means depriving the State from its morals" (Salim 2011). For the SMB, Syria must become a civil state with an Islamic framework or reference, a loose concept which is still being defined. The question that still needs to be answered is what the SMB and other groups understand by the civil state and by the Islamic framework. Most members of the SMB interviewed by the author agree that "'civil' means it is neither religious, nor military".[6] However, the concept has no agreed upon definition and its meaning depends on the intention of the speaker. To make matters worse, it is a neologism, usually articulated in "negative terms" – stating what it is not, but omitting what it actually is (Kantz Feder 2014). Therefore, some argue that it is a "local and not a political or a judicial concept, [and] does not belong to the sphere of political science or of political philosophy" (Katbeh 2012).

Rafik Habib, of the Egyptian Muslim Brotherhood, defines it in opposition to the authoritarian state:

> The civil state is the antithesis of the authoritarian state where it is primarily under military authority regardless of its reference and essentials. The secular authoritarian state is similar to the religious, communist or capitalist authoritarian state since they are all forms of the military idea, which is the opposite of the civil … [The Muslim Brotherhood] agrees that the general Islamic authority can't be primarily maintained unless we accomplish the mandate of the nation and its full right to choose its own rulers and representatives. Only when the nation is represented by the honorable will it be possible to hold the rulers accountable and ousted for their errors. Therefore, the civil state in this sense is the essence of the Islamic reform project. (Habib 2009)

Following this logic, the Islamic State and the civil state would be two terms for the same concept, as different documents have affirmed, because in both the same rights and obligations would be guaranteed.[7]

As opposed to this, the Egyptian writer Alaa al-Aswani claims that:

> The civil State is neither lay nor irreligious: it simply remains at the same distance from all religions and respects citizens equally; however, the Brotherhood have come up with a new slogan: a civil State with an Islamic framework. This is strange because there's no civil State with a religious framework … If what they mean is the Islamic principles of justice, freedom and equality, those are already the bases on which the civil State is based, so there is no need for any additional reference.[8] If what they mean is the imposition of indisputable sacred legislation in the name of religion, we would then be facing a purely religious State, even if the term changes. (Al-Aswani 2011)

Therefore, the problem is neither the concept of the civil state, nor the presence of religion in the social sphere, but the addition of an "Islamic reference", which mixes religious and civil terminology, and, therefore, gives the political sphere prerogatives over people's private lives. Trying to understand what this reference stands for remains a difficult task. For example, Ali al-Bayanouni claimed that, since the "identity of the Syrian nation" is inspired by Islamic values, the government must also be inspired by those values.[9] Following this argument, Omar Mushaweh, current editor in-chief of *Al-Ahd* newspaper and unofficial spokesman of the SMB, claimed that "Islam or the Islamic reference recognizes the existence of an elected ruler, a parliament, the principle of separation of powers, the rule of law, and the fact that all citizens are equal before the law; however, within a framework which does not contradict sharia".[10] Nevertheless, Faruq Tayfur, ex deputy leader of the SMB, explained that they supported the loosest and most tolerant understanding of this reference, in order to adapt it to the modern state and accommodate differences "just like it was the case with the Pact of Hudaybiyya signed by the Prophet with different tribes in the early days of Islam".[11] What is clear is that laws and the government must not contradict *sharia*.

Due to the minimal success of the Antalya meeting, the SMB took part on 16 July that same year in the National Salvation Conference, ironically organized by Imad al-Din al-Rashid, former vice-dean of the Faculty of *Sharia* in Damascus, who Thomas Pierret defined in 2013 as the "main Islamist rival of the SMB in forming the Syrian National Movement" (Pierret 2013). According to Ali Sadr al-Din al-Bayanouni, the conference would be the starting point for the transition to a civil participative and democratic system: "This is a revolution to establish equality."

However, the most controversial subject he raised during his speech was the emphasis on the Arab-Islamic identity of Syria, which sparked certain tensions with both religious and ethnic minorities. Months later, in a conciliatory tone, Muhammad Riad Shaqfa, then leader of the SMB, presented his condolences on the death of the Kurdish leader Mishal Tammo,[12] insisting on the fact that the SMB would continue their efforts to build a nation for everyone "without exclusion or marginalisation". Nevertheless, tensions between the Kurdish parties and other opposition groups remained uneasy, as the events on the battlefield suggest, regardless of the situation in the political front and the attempts at reconciliation.

Eventually, in October 2011, the Syrian National Council (SNC) was founded. According to Riad Shaqfa, SMB leader from 2010 to 2014, "had we not pushed towards the formation of the SNC, it would never have taken shape, for there were no other parties" (Riad Shaqfa 2013). What he meant was that they were the eldest established group in the opposition with a defined worldview and a political programme for Syria,[13] even if there were other political trends or coalitions. Unlikely as it may seem that all the parties agreed upon something, there was a common attitude: the refusal to negotiate with the regime.

This explains why many members of this opposition body rejected the creation of the National Coalition for Syrian Revolutionary and Opposition Forces (NCSROF) in November 2012 as a substitute for the SNC, fearing that they would be forced to negotiate with the regime. Among those who most fiercely opposed this new body were the SMB.[14] Despite their rejection, they had to surrender to the *fait accompli*. As a sign of protest, for instance, Ali Sadr al-Din al-Bayanouni became a member of the General Assembly of the NCSROF as a "patriotic personality" (*shakhsiyya wataniyya*) and not as a member of the SMB or the SNC. Regardless of the tension, the SMB were able to gain a certain hegemony (by means of the establishment of alliances with other Islamist forces and personalities of patriotic background, like communist George Sabra or secular academic Burhan Ghalioun) in the NCSROF, and so, keep a high profile.

This establishment of alliances had already been explained by the now ex leader of the SMB, Muhammad Riad Shaqfa, in October 2011:

> We are currently working on two different levels: one with the opposition, which includes all groups who work against the regime, which is embodied in the SNC (the NCSROF had not been created yet), and we also work with a view to uniting the Islamic opposition. In order to achieve that, we are in contact with different Islamic groups, because we are members of the SMB. We have met the Salafis, the Sufis, etc., in an attempt to unify our stances and create a common project for the day after the fall of the regime.[15]

However, such a project implied dealing with Salafi Islamist forces whose origin was more military that political, and who insisted on their will to turn Syria into an Islamic state; thus contravening the SMB concept of "civil state" or "civil state with an Islamic reference".

On 25 March 2012, the SMB issued what they called the National Document-Pact, where references to Islam were almost non-existent and where they asked for the establishment of a civil, democratic and plural state, with alternation in power and led by a "republican representative" government. Far from establishing an official religion, the document supported equality, regardless of religion, ethnicity or sect. Despite the advanced and progressive nature of this document, Muhammad Sarmini, member of the younger generations, who eventually left the Brotherhood in 2015, believed it necessary to be more consistent in their statements. In his article "The Syria of the future ... The one we want", he stated that: "It is necessary to elaborate a clear plan that erases the fear and doubts that the components of Syrian society might have regarding the SMB ... and afterwards, a clear plan that guarantees the minimum necessary services for the Syrian people to have a dignified life" (Sarmini 2013).

However, before Sarmini's contribution, on 27 September 2012, the SMB re-published a much more conservative text and with a very similar title: "The Syria that we want" which originally accompanied the SMB's political programme of 2004. As opposed to the total omission of religion in the Document-Pact, this text supported the creation of a state with an Arab and Islamic identity where all citizens would have the rights and duties established by God's law. This apparent contradiction might have been related to the need to keep some proximity to Salafi elements, who rejected the elimination of references to religion or the support of concepts like democracy, citizenship and pluralism.

In 2012, Muhammad Riad Shaqfa announced the SMB's will to create a political party. "The political party that we intend to create will be neither an alternative to the organisation, nor its political arm ... Instead, it will be a national party with an Islamic reference founded by upright men from all religious and ethnic backgrounds that accept such reference."[16] Five years before, Ali Sadr al-Din al-Bayanouni had said something very similar in an interview conducted by Yaqub Haddad, member of the Syrian Socialist National Movement. "The SMB ... originated as an Islamic association devoted to preaching ... so it is only natural that its members are Muslims who believe in its principles." However, "when the situation allows the formation of a political party in Syria ... this party will be in charge of the political activities and it will be open to all citizens who share our project". In June 2013, the SMB founded the National Party for Justice and the Constitution, *Al-Wa'd* ("the promise") in its Arabic acronym. At least two Christians, Nabil Qasis (vice president and leader of the political bureau) and Raymun Ma'jun (chief of the trade unions and civil society organizations' office), became active members of the party. However, somewhere between late 2015 and early 2016, the party's records simply disappeared from the net.

> First, there was a polarisation between those who supported Nabil Qasis and those who supported Jihad Al-Atasi, who was at the time the secretary of the party. This polarisation blocked the party's functioning. The SMB organised a meeting, but only those who were members of the SMB itself attended it. They formed a new leadership but to no avail, and the other members of the party did not even take a stance on the matter. We can say that the party reached a dead-end at that moment. It was originally created to fail.[17]

In spite of this failure, the founding document of the party is still worth studying. According to it, the party wanted to become representative "of all sectors of society that for thousands of years have lived in the same territory in peace, friendship and brotherhood and share the same destiny".[18] The party claimed its desire to work in order to "offer radical and enduring solutions to the problems of the nation and the citizen ... without contravening our traditions, customs and heritage". This heritage and traditions can be summed up in the fact that the party's programme was framed, according to its founding documents, in the Islamic reference and a moderate (*wasati*) understanding of Islam. They explicitly stated that they would not accept anything forbidden by *sharia*, confirming that the Islamic reference is a synonym for respecting the limits established by *sharia*.

Despite this failed attempt at separating their religious and social activities from the political sphere, for one SMB ex-activist, the organization needed a whole internal revolution that would incorporate the thinking of the younger generations whose know-how on politics was much more developed than that of the elders, who had been in charge for decades and had even closed the doors to new members for fear that it might precipitate a reaction within Syria by the security forces:

> It is not only a party that the SMB need as an alternative, they need to re-found the whole organisation and its mindset from the start, and put an end to the era of the holistic organisation. Of course, Islam is holistic, but the different activities must be independent from each other ... If they understood that, changed the situation, started working with a new mentality, and dealt with public affairs in a different way, I would not hesitate to return to the organisation.[19]

This is reflective of a serious generational cleavage that the SMB faced in its engagement with the revolution, even if some of those young members have been incorporated into the leadership, such as the above-mentioned Omar Mushaweh, and Hussam al-Gadban, leader of the Young Member's office, both in their forties.

Humanitarian campaigns

One of the strongest aspects of the SMB's activity from March 2011 was the delivery of humanitarian aid, both inside and outside Syria. Knowing that the political sphere was very much dependent on international trends and that military activity was difficult to control, although they have played a role in it, the SMB concluded that the best way to gain supporters was by means of the provision of humanitarian aid and, later on, schooling and housing for refugees. Therefore, their activities in this sphere became wide-ranging albeit mostly focused on education and medical assistance, especially in Turkey, where they established their headquarters in 2013.

From the early days, the SMB leaders agreed upon a decentralization policy, mostly resulting from their own regional splits and networks. Therefore, in the field of humanitarian aid, the Hamawis, led by the Brotherhood leader, Riad Shaqfa, led the way from the beginning, reactivating their latent connections on the ground with a view to keeping their hegemony. It is not surprising, in this sense, that Faruq Tayfur was the president of the Syrian Association for Humanitarian Aid and Development founded in Istanbul in 2012 and the only one recognized by the SNC at that time (Tayfur 2012).

This, however, was detrimental to cities like Raqqa, Latakia, Daraa or Deir Ezzor, that had fewer members (Lefèvre 2013).

> When the initial protests became a real revolution, the SMB began to increase their scope of influence in Syria by means of humanitarian aid campaigns [they established a specific organisation for that, which began working immediately] ... [Nevertheless] it soon became obvious that the division between Hama and Aleppo still had its impact in the work of the SMB: Aleppo and the Eastern areas of Syria received less logistical support than Hama and Idlib ... [This paved the way for] the formation of a new organisation formed by the Aleppine members [second generation, born in the eighties] with the support of the spiritual fathers [Bayanouni and Zuhair Salim[20]], the so-called National Action Group (NAF) led by Ahmad Ramadan. (Al-Haj 2012)

Such attempt at separation became symptomatic of the need to give a larger role to new generations, and mostly those who disagreed with the Hamawi leadership, many of whom eventually left the Brotherhood in 2015. Among them, many, like Ramadan himself, as well as Obeida Nahas, former prominent member of the SMB, became full members of the NAF after cutting the organizational ties with the SMB.

Another open front: the militarization of the revolution

Until mid-2013, the SMB held a prominent position in the opposition's political organs, not only because they had maintained their networks (Abu Ruman 2013), but also because the revolution had remained mostly peaceful. The SMB were very enthusiastic in their support for this discourse as a counter to the regime's narrative about them. In fact, they never made a formal decision to arm the revolution, which resulted in a reduction of their weight in comparison to the jihadist movements that became dominant in the country. Their first formal call for jihad was not announced until October 2015, and it was declared against the official Russian military campaign in the country. "The SMB, in the light of this clear occupation of our country by the forces of evil, declare that defensive jihad has become today an individual duty for everyone capable of carrying weapons" (Syrian Muslim Brotherhood 2015).

This late endorsement of the armed struggle as a means of self-defence resulted initially in the Brotherhood's marginalization within the armed struggle, despite the continuous references to the SMB owning several brigades and battalions.

> The SMB do not have their own brigades. This, however, does not exclude the fact that some Islamist brigades have contacted us for coordination purposes before their formal announcement. In this sense, we talk to everyone. (Riad Shaqfa 2012a)

Despite this, "in August 2012, the SMB, through Molhem al-Droubi, acknowledged that three months before they had created a series of armed brigades in the interior of Syria, for purposes of self-defence and the protection of the oppressed" (Dibo 2013). Long before, some accounts claim that in December 2011, a dozen brigades had been financed by the SMB under the umbrella of the Body for the Protection of Civilians – theoretically focused on humanitarian tasks – which later became the main component of the Sham Legion (*Faylaq al-Sham*) formed in March 2014. Eventually, Muhammad Riad Shaqfa stated the obvious.

> With a view to uniting the moderate brigades and divisions who trust the SMB, we invited them to Istanbul [in December 2011], and there we created *Duru' al-thawra* [Revolution Shields] as an independent organisation with an Islamic tendency, but close to us. (Riad Shaqfa 2012a)

The close links between the Revolution Shields, which in March 2014 became integrated into the Sham Legion, and the SMB were explained by Hassan al-Hashimi, from the political bureau, who is also considered as part of the younger generation:

> The Shields are the closest brigades to our way of thinking, and we have designed a plan to communicate between the political bureau and the interior,

in order to establish a connection between the political sphere and the activities on the ground, which facilitate our contacts with the Shields.[21]

On his part, Muhammad Adel Fares, member of the SMB who had been a rival of Bayanouni for the leadership of the organization, explained that "we support them all without any particular interest, and when we see that one of them has an extremist behaviour, we simply stop supporting it".[22] With this, he might have been referring to a detailed list of groups by means of which the SMB had tried to influence the armed opposition, very probably with a view to avoiding radicalization more than in order to Islamize the revolt itself (Hassan 2014).

In such a context, it is interesting to highlight the reaction of the SMB to the inclusion of Jabhat al-Nusra (now Jabhat Fath al-Sham, after allegedly severing ties with Al-Qaeda) in the EU list of terrorist groups in December 2012, a fact that the NCSROF through its president at the time, Moaz al-Khatib, condemned.[23] The SMB issued the following statement:

> The SMB consider that labelling certain revolutionary forces on the ground as terrorists by some parties is a mistaken, hasty and reprehensible measure [which goes against] the aim that unites all Syrians [which] is establishing a State of justice, equality and brotherhood.[24]

Furthermore, Muhammad Riad Shaqfa, when asked if they were ready to dialogue with Al-Nusra, stated: "They are our brothers in faith ... We will not ignore anyone for Syria's sake, but that does not mean we share the same ideas" (Riad Shaqfa 2012b). In fact, in January 2015, Muhammad Hikmat Walid, leader of the SMB after Shaqfa, insisted that the organization would side with any bullet directed against the regime (Al-Omar 2015).

The question remains what the SMB's take was on the suppression of protesters in Ma'rrat al-Nu'man by Al-Nusra in March 2016, when, during the partial 'cessation of hostilities', the people took back to the streets feeling safe from air raids. Ibrahim al-Olabi, ex prominent member of the young generations, who left the SMB in late 2015, stated his disapproval in Facebook. "If you [al-Nusra] are 'Islamic' as you pretend, and think that you are in contradiction with people's natural instinct and movements, in which they do not raise your slogans, please note that you are like a plague for Islam and Muslims even if you believe you are being loyal (to them)."[25] No official statement had been made by the SMB or any of its most prominent figures on the subject in March 2016. In fact, the only mention of the subject appeared in the SMB's newspaper *Al-Ahd*, in an interview with Labib Nahhas, member of Ahrar al-Sham, who said that Al-Nusra's behaviour had "become worrying for everyone in the past months", but that his organization was still collaborating with them on the battlefield, even if "our project and vision for the future Syria is totally different from theirs" (Nahas 2016). In an informal conversation with a prominent member of the SMB the day before the Nusra Front's disengagement from Al-Qaeda, he stated that: "The best for the revolution would be both an organizational and ideological withdrawal. If someone wants to work for the Syrian revolution, all his ideas and relationships must be Syrian, so as to avoid pushing us into a global war with which we or the revolution bear no relationship."[26] Labib Nahas, from Ahrar al-Sham, made a very similar statement in Al-Hayat newspaper. Although he welcomed al-Nusra's withdrawal from al-Qaida, he insisted that it had to "certify that the severing of ties had not only taken place at the organizational level" (Al-Hayat 2016).

The only formal (and utterly brief) statement by the SMB on the subject, on 29 July 2016, explained that the SMB will always welcome any step which brings a group closer to the people's will and the revolution's goal of liberation from oppression. In this sense, Al-Nusra decision is a "first step" in this direction, but it "needs a deeper integration into the popular base", by means of returning them their rights and compensating them for the injustices they have suffered. As such, "everyone must carry out a complete revision whose outcome is useful and helpful for our people and their revolution".

Indeed, the most interesting relationship is the one the SMB established with Ahrar al-Sham (Abboud 2013), the main component of the Islamic Front founded in late 2014, with which they co-signed an important document known as the Revolutionary Honour Pact. Ahrar's leader at the time, Hassan Abboud, claimed that he did not accept the idea of democracy and that he wanted to establish an Islamic State (Abboud 2013). However, after the attack on the group's command on 10 September 2014, as a result of which, Abboud and other prominent figures were killed, the SMB's newspaper published very positive opinions on him. In the words of Abdallah Zayzan, from the political bureau of the Shields of the Revolution, Ahrar's leader was "moderate, conscious and realistic, and had understood the time he was living in, without renouncing Islamic values" (Zayran 2014). According to the same author, Abboud had explained that: "There is no difference at all between the SMB and me, except for one aspect, which is democracy, but we are ready to revise our stance on the subject and change it if a legal Islamic study is carried out." This could have been the motivating factor for the SMB's establishment of the *Hay'at ta'sil al-shar'iyya* (Legal Founding Organism), focused on the study of different concepts like the civil state, in order to establish whether or not it is a model of state legally sanctioned by *sharia*.

Whatever the reasons behind those declarations, there were and still are several trends within Ahrar al-Sham besides a significant division between the political and the military sectors, with the latter holding more extremist views. In any case, the SMB's priority has never been the leadership of military campaigns, but the establishment of contacts with brigades once they had been created, with the aim of attracting – and diluting – radical discourses towards their moderate way of thinking. As a result of this process, the Revolutionary Honour Pact was issued.

This was the first document signed by groups close to the SMB (Faylaq al-Sham) and the Salafis, as a step towards a rapprochement. According to Omar Mushaweh, head of the media office of the SMB, the above-mentioned National Document-Pact and this Revolutionary Honour Pact had a high degree of confluence. On 18 May 2014, he wrote in his personal *Facebook* wall the following statement:

> The Revolutionary Honor Pact is the jihadi version of the National Document-Pact that the SMB issued two years ago. There are many similarities between them, and the main difference is that the first focuses on the jihadi and current revolutionary context, whereas the second one focuses on the civil context and provides a view for the future. That is the reason why there are some issues mentioned in the first one that do not appear in the second, and vice versa: it is just the consequence of the differences of context between them. Regardless of that, they share the same spirit, soul and way of thinking. In fact, some excommunicated the SMB and now they do the same with the Jihadi factions that have signed the Revolutionary Honour Pact.

Instead of focusing on *sharia*, which is not even mentioned, the Revolutionary Honour Pact claims that the principles that guide the actions of the forces of the revolution are those of "our true religion (*dinuna al-hanif*[27])", without relating it to any specific laws, but to doctrines of behaviour and ethics.

Another aspect that sets this document closer to the one issued by the SMB is the fact that it commits to the safeguarding of Syria's territorial unity. Limiting the combat field to Syria implies the recognition of the country's borders, without including it in the framework of the international jihad, as it is the case of Al-Qaeda or Daesh. That is, their jihadi struggle is limited to the national context, even if it is shaped in more religious than nationalistic terms. Moreover, the document does not speak of "jihadi action", but of "military action", and the fighters are referred to as "combatants" (*muqatilun*), and not as "mujahidin". Therefore, it is interesting that Mushaweh mentioned the jihadi context, which no one else, not even the document, had mentioned.

In the end, the document expresses its support for the creation of a "State of justice, law and freedom" as the aim of the Syrian revolution. With such blurry expressions, each signing faction might have referred to a different thing, specially bearing in mind that Faylaq al-Sham has close links with the SMB (which means that they would prefer a civil state with an Islamic reference). Abboud denied any support to the idea of a civil state and claimed that what the pact had achieved was finding some common ground for the different factions (Abboud 2014). The document was an attempt to avoid intra-Islamic competition, and unify action around minimum revolutionary parameters.

Consequently, although both documents bear many similarities, the fact remains that the scarce references to the nature of the state, the political future of the country and the ambiguity of some stances in the case of the Revolutionary Honour Pact put the intentions of the movements that signed it in question. Furthermore, the assassination of the Ahrar al-Sham command put the application of the document in abeyance. Other powerful groups, such as Jaysh al-Islam, never signed it and the death of its leader, Zahran Alloush, in December 2015 further left the issue of the Pact unresolved.

Conclusion

Through the examination of the role of the SMB in the Syrian revolution, it has become apparent that they have tried to touch upon all the different spheres of action. More prominent in the early stages were the political activities they carried out; however, as time went by, they realized that the military struggle had taken over the political and social in many areas, due to the escalation of state violence against the population. All this, combined with their role in providing basic services to the displaced exposed the weaknesses of the organization. This was due to the many years in which new memberships were very limited because of its absence from Syria, to the resurgence of old regional cleavages and to more recent generational ones inside the movement.

Despite these difficulties, the discourse of the SMB has not changed regarding the national character of their project, far from all forms of exclusion. To illustrate this, no example is more significant than the National Document-Pact of March 2012, where the SMB supported a republican and democratic system based on citizenship, although the publication a few months later of a 2004 document, where the religious references absent in the former came back to the fore, placed a question mark on the degree of the SMB's commitment to a system based on religious equality.

In this sense, it is necessary to understand that, for the time being, facing the difficulty of controlling armed groups, and the sponsorship of rival militant Islamist groups by outside patrons, the SMB chose to direct their efforts towards the moderation of these groups' discourse. The fact that some jihadi brigades signed the Revolutionary Honour Pact, where the ideas of Islamic state and jihad in its bellicose meaning are omitted, is the result of those efforts; however, its ambiguity and the fact that it does not mention democracy or citizenship, are additional factors adding to the doubts about the SMB's discourse. This ambiguity arguably must be seen as essential if the SMB is to be able to play the role of shield against radicalization and against the advance of violent Salafism in the country: to carry out that role, it is evident that the religious and the political must remain intertwined. Yet, the extent of the Brotherhood's success in bridging radical and moderate currents is still difficult to assess for both secularist and Salafi currents remain suspicious of it. The reason behind that might be the lack of definition in many aspects, which is disliked by both more rigorous Islamists and the rest of the opposition, in addition to the mental image most Syrians have of the SMB as a violent and sectarian organization. Making their stances clearer might be the key to the SMB's success in being the hinge between apparently irreconcilable forces. Much depends on whether the Syrian conflict is resolved in a way compatible with the Brotherhood's stance in favour of pluralism; in that case, the way forward might have been prefigured by the creation of the – no longer functional – *Al-Wa'd* party as a national project of which the Brothers were just members, but not the dominant block, and wherein they worked with partners of other confessions and currents.

Notes

1 Ramírez (2011).
2 The demonstration can be retrieved from: http://www.youtube.com/watch?v=Yb5l L5YdCOs [Date consulted: 03/03/2016].
3 It eventually changed its name to "Shabakat al-thawra al-suriya" (The Syrian revolution network): https://www.facebook.com/Syrian.Revolution/info [Date consulted: 03/03/2016].
4 https://www.facebook.com/note.php?note_id=209661022394433 [Date consulted: 03/03/2016].
5 Ibid.
6 According to Ali Al-Bayanouni, leader of the SMB from 1996 to 2010, the Islamic State has a civil nature because "we do not want anyone to govern it as if he were the Prophet". Nevertheless, it should be a State "inspired by Islamic values, which conforms to society's identity" (interview in Istanbul, August 2014).
7 Hay'at al-ta'sil al-shar'i (2014). "Al-dawla al-madaniyya wa-l-dawla al-diniyya" (The civil state and the religious state). In *Al-Ahd*, n. 32, 1 July: 8.
8 Some elder members of the SMB insist that this reference is not necessary precisely because a civil State implies all those principles (interviews in Istanbul, August 2014).
9 Interview in Istanbul (13/08/2014).
10 Interview in Istanbul (13/08/2014).
11 Interview in Istanbul (14/08/2014).
12 Retrieved from: http://www.youtube.com/watch?v=B46s812K1ol&feature=plcp [Date consulted: 03/03/2016].
13 Published in 2004, the document is compiled in a more than a hundred-page long booklet entitled *Political Program for the Future Syria*.
14 Interview with Asaad al-Aachi, representtive of the civil movement in Syria, in Beirut (04/04/2013).
15 Originally published in the YouTube channel *Ikhwantube*, the video was eliminated.
16 Interview originally published in the SMB's old webpage whose link is no longer available (20/11/2012).
17 On-line interview with an ex-member of the SMB (18/03/2016).
18 Due to the disappearance of the party, the link to the document is no longer available.
19 On-line interview with an ex-member of the SMB (18/03/2016).
20 Both eventually resigned from their positions in the leadership in 2013–2014.
21 Interview in Istanbul (16/08/2014).
22 Interview published by the old SMB's webpage and whose link is no longer available (20/11/2012).
23 Statement by Moaz al-Khatib in the meeting of the Friends of Syria in Marrakech, on 12 December 2012. Retrieved from: https://www.youtube.com/watch?feature=player_embedded&v=oSQh3qA_y0o [Date consulted: 18/05/2014].
24 Statement of rejection of the designation of Al-Nusra as a terrorist organization under the title "Al-irhab suluk wa laysa hawiyya wa Bashar al-Asad huwa al-irhabi al-waheed 'ala ard suriya" (Terrorism is a way of behaving and not an identity, and Bashar al-Asad is the only terrorist in Syria), 12 December 2012. Retrieved from: http://www.elaph.com/Web/news/2012/12/779536.html?entry=arab [Date consulted: 03/03/2016].
25 Al-Olabi, I. (2016). Facebook status, 4 March. No link available.
26 On-line conversation (27/07/2016).
27 This concept is usually applied to Islam, but includes the other two monotheistic religions, drawing from the fact that Abraham was the first prophet in charge of sending the message.

Bibliography

Abboud, H. (2013), Interview by Tayseer Alony in *Al-Jazeera*, 9 June. Retrieved from: www.youtube.com/watch?v=GRPb4nFU2UA [Date consulted: 03/03/2016].

Abboud, H. (2014), Intervention in Orient TV regarding the Revolutionary Honour Pact, 19 May. Retrieved from: www.youtube.com/watch?v=QIOjIIfCSBU&feature=youtu.be [Date consulted: 03/03/2016].

Abu Ruman, M. (2013), *Al-Islamiyyun, wa-l-din wa-l-thawra fi Suriya* (Islamists, religion, and revolution in Syria), Beirut: Friedrich Ebert Stiftung.

Al-Abdallah, M. and Al-Sayyid, F. (2013), "Qari'u abwab al-hurriyya: mu'assisu safhat al-thawra al-suriyya 'ala safahat Al-Ahd" (Those who knocked at the doors of freedom: the founders of the Syrian Revolution page in Al-Ahd). Interview in *Al-Ahd*, n. 2, 5 March, 12.

Al-Aswani, A. (2011), "Hal tasmah al-dawla al-madaniyya bi-tatbiq al-sharía?" [Does a civil state allow the establishment of the sharia?], *Al-masry al-yaum*, 14 June.

Al-Droubi, M. (2013), "Al-qiyadi al-ikhwani Molhem al-Droubi yaftah awraqahu al-khassa li-sahifat Al-Ahd" *(The SMB leader Molhem al-Droubi shows his cards in Al-Ahd newspaper)*, n.1, 1 March, 8.

Al-Haj, A. (2012), Al-islam al-siyasi wa-l-thawra al-suriyya (Political Islam and the Syrian revolution), Marzak al-Jazeera li-l dirasat. Retrieved from: http://studies.aljazeera.net/reports/2012/05/2012521101415565424.htm [Date consulted: 03/03/2016].

Al-Hayat (2016), Qiyadi fi Harakat Ahrar al-Sham yurahhib bi-qarar al-Nusra (One of Ahrar al-Sham's leaders welcomes Al-Nusra's decision), 10 August.

Al-Omar, S. (2015), "Al-Muraqib al-'am al-jadid l-ikhwan Suriya: li-l-Quds al-arabi: Natafahham masaliha Rusia lakinna didda baqa' Al-Asad wa-al-alawiyyun irtakabu khat'an kabiran bi-ta'yiidihim li-l-nizam" (The new SMB leader to Al-Quds al-Arabi: We understand Russia's interests, but we refuse to accept Assad's stay in power, and the Alawites have committed a terrible error by supportng the regime), 21 January. Retrieved from: www.alquds.co.uk/?p=283462 [Date consulted: 03/03/2016].

Dibo, M. (2013), "Ikhwan Suriya: hikayat fashl tawil" (The SMB: A Long Story of Failure), Maaber, May. Retrieved from: www.maaber.org/issue_may13/lookout3.htm [Date consulted: 03/03/2016].

Habib, R. (2009), "Understanding the Riddle of the Modern Civil State," Ikhwanweb, 11 September. Available at: www.ikhwanweb.com/article.php?id=20968.

Hassan, Hassan (2014), "In Syria, the Brotherhood's Influence is on the Decline," *The National*, 1 April. Retrieved from: www.thenational.ae/thenationalconversation/comment/in-syria-the-brotherhoods-influence-is-on-the-decline [Date consulted: 01/03/2016].

Kantz Feder, R. (2014), "The 'Civil State' in Political Discourse after the Arab Spring". In Tel Aviv Notes, 2. Available at: www.dayan.org/sites/default/files/Rachel_Kantz_Feder_TA_NOTES_Civil_State_Discourse_26052014.pdf.

Katbeh, A. (2012), "The Civil State - The New Political Term of the Arab World", 1 June. Available at: www.internationalpeaceandconflict.org/profiles/blogs/the-civil-state-the-new-political-term-of-the-arab-world?xg_source=activity.

Lefèvre, Rafael (2013), "The Brotherhood Starts Anew in Syria," *al-Majalla*, 19 August. Retrieved from: www.majalla.com/eng/2013/08/article55244734 [Date consulted: 03/03/2016].

Nahas, L. (2016), "Hiwar khass: mas'ul al-'alaqat al-siyasiyya al-kharijiyya fi harakat Ahrar al-Sham al-islamiyya" (Special interview: the man responsible for the foreign political relations of Ahrar al-Sham). Interview by Arwa Abd al-Aziz in *Al-Ahd*, n. 58, pp. 4–5.

Pierret, Thomas (2013), "Les oulémas: une hégémonie religieuse ébranlée par la révolution." In *Pas de Printemps pour la Syrie: Les clés pour comprendre les acteurs et les défis de la crise (2011–2013)*, edited by Burgat, F. and B. Paoli, Paris: La Découverte.

Ramírez, Naomí (2011), "Los Hermanos Musulmanes apoyan las manifestaciones del día de la ira contra el régimen en Siria". In *Los Hermanos Musulmanes: un observatorio de la organización islámica*, April 29. Retrieved from: http://hermanosmusulmanes.wordpress.com/2011/04/29/los-hermanos-musulmanes-apoyan-las-movilizaciones-del-dia-de-la-ira-contra-el-regimen-en-siria/ [Date consulted: 01/03/2016].

Riad Shaqfa, M. (2012a), "Taraddud al-garb faqama al-tatarruf" (Western Doubts have triggered extremism). Interview by Abd Allah al-Gadui in *Okaz*, January 12. Retrieved from: www.okaz.com.sa/new/issues/20130112/Con20130112563741.htm [Date consulted: 01/03/2016].

Riad Shaqfa, M. (2012b), "Lan nantaqim, wa sanuhawir Al-Nusra, wa Tlass istayaba li-nasihatina" (We will not take revenge, we will dialogue with Al-Nusra and Tlass has taken our advice). Interview by Abd Allah Raja in *Zaman al-Wasl*, 3 December. Retrieved from: http://zaman-alwsl.net/readNews.php?id=33598 [Date consulted: 03/03/2016].

Riad Shaqfa, M. (2013), "Exiled Muslim Brotherhood Plans to Return to Syria". Interview by Rula Khalaf and Abigail Fielding-Smith in *Financial Times*, 25 April. Retrieved from: www.ft.com/intl/cms/s/0/00a7865a-ad86-11e2-a2c7-00144feabdc0.html#axzz3GcIacnYW [Date consulted: 01/03/2016].

Salim, Z. (2011), Interview in Al-Mustaqilla Channel, 2 June. Retrieved from: http://asharqalarabi.org.uk/ruiah/b-sharq-262.htm [Date consulted: 03/03/2016].

Sarmini, M. (2013), Suriyat al-mustaqbal … allati nuriduha (The Syria of the future … The Syria that we want). In *Al-Ahd*, n. 15, 1 October, 10.

Syrian Muslim Brotherhood (2015), Al ihtilal al-rusi sawfa yadfa'uhu al-sha'b al-suri bi-l-jihad (The Syrian people will expell the Russian intervention by means of jihad), 4 October. Retrieved from: http://goo.gl/OTRCLC [Date consulted: 03/03/2016].

Tayfur, F. (2012), "Suqut nizam al-Asad qabla bidayat al-'am al-muqbil … wa ma yahduh fi Suriya laysa hadathan mahaliyyan" (The Assad regime will be toppled before next year, and what is happening in Syria is not a local issue). Declarations to *Ikhwan* Suriya, 13 October. Retrieved from: http://goo.gl/hOs6Rl [Date consulted: 03/03/2016].

Zayran, A. (2014), "Ightiyal qadati ahrar al-sham: tasa'ulat wa shukuk" (The assassination of Ahrar al-Sham's leader: questions and doubts). In *Al-Ahd*, n. 36, 15 September, 6.

15

SECTARIANISM AND THE BATTLE OF NARRATIVES IN THE CONTEXT OF THE SYRIAN UPRISING

Enrico Bartolomei

This chapter examines the formulation and projection of competing narratives on sectarianism in the context of the Syrian Uprising. Sectarian framings have been employed by rival forces to mobilize populations or specific groups according to their perceived or real national, ethnic, cultural, or religious differences. The focus will be on three relevant narratives on sectarianism that have emerged from the beginning of the civil Uprising until the June 2013 battle for al-Qusayr, which marked a major turning point for the "sectarianization" of discourses and practices in Syria: the Syrian regime's manipulation of sectarianism as a mechanism of power and strategy for survival; the anti-sectarian narrative of grassroots activists and organizations, which promoted cross-sectarian solidarity, mobilization and political identities; and the sectarian discourse and practice introduced by Salafi-jihadists, which turned a sectarian understanding of religion into one of the most effective mobilization tools, identity markers and ideological common denominator of the armed opposition. The primary argument is that the sectarianization of politics was the result of the deliberate manipulation of ethnic and religious identities by "entrepreneurs of cynical sectarianism" (Lynch 2013) for political and economic purposes. The emergence of a sectarian master narrative as the dominant framework for understanding the conflict in Syria also led to the empowerment of sect-centric political actors, pulling communities into the cycle of violence and reprisals while driving a wedge between various components of Syrian society along perceived ethnic, religious and sectarian lines.

Sectarianism as a discourse of power

In the context of conflicts, frames are the lenses through which disputants interpret what the conflict is about, their place in it and how they should act and behave. The conceptual framing of a conflict determines whether protagonists perceive it in terms of material interests, specific cultural values, universal principles of human rights, class struggle or primordial ethnic, religious, and sectarian loyalties (Kaufman et al. 2003). As state and non-state actors are fighting for legitimacy as much as they are fighting on the battlefield, framing can be critically evaluated as a discourse of power used by multiple actors in a conflict with the aims of influencing political decision making of state actors and international organizations and of mobilizing internal support (Nissen 2013).

Therefore, discourses on sectarianism are a manifestation of the larger "battle of narratives" in which competing actors invest considerable efforts to frame the Syrian civil war to foster support for their political objectives. Even the categorization of the conflict in Syria as a "civil war" became part of the battle over shaping the narrative. For instance, both the Syrian regime and opposition activists have disputed the claim that the Syrian conflict has descended into a civil war, as asserted by a senior UN official in June 2012. As Shehadi (2013) points out, "the importance of narrative goes beyond mere semantics" as each component of a narrative has underlying policy implications. In fact, if events in Syria are framed as nationwide "revolution" against an oppressive regime, then the implication is that "the people need protection" from state violence; whereas if it is characterized as "a sectarian civil war" then the implication is that "all sides have to stop the violence and sit around the table". While grassroots activists and organizations have argued that the term civil war suggests an equivalence between the two sides, ignoring the history of the peaceful protest against the al-Asad regime and, rather, defined the struggle as a national popular Uprising against an authoritarian, corrupt and repressive regime. Bashar al-Asad has characterized the confrontation as a foreign-backed terrorist plot to overthrow his legitimate rule and divide Syria. Salafi-jihadist groups within the armed opposition led to the emergence of a third narrative, which describes the conflict as a jihad against the heretic Alawite rule and its Shi'a allies.[1]

This chapter relies on instrumentalist and constructivist approaches to the study of ethnicity and sectarianism, rejecting the notion that they are rooted in some cultural or primordial essence. It follows Makdisi's understanding of sectarianism as a process through which a religious identity is politicized as part of a struggle for power (2008, p. 559). The main assumption is that ethnicity and sect are social constructions, ways to perceive events and represent the social world and not inherent objective, or immutable traits. Therefore, throughout history, entrepreneurs of cynical sectarianism such as authoritarian regimes or competing groups strategically manipulated sectarian divisions to mobilize popular support or build their own power base. In response to the wave of popular protests sweeping the Arab world, authoritarian regimes have exacerbated sectarian divisions among Sunni and Shi'a communities in order to fracture and prevent the creation of a cross-sectarian opposition front (Matthiesen 2013). As the Syrian civil Uprising escalated into a full-fledged civil war, there has been an increasing tendency to explain the dynamics and drivers of the conflict through the lenses of sectarianism, pointing at the historical schism and at the doctrinal differences between Sunnis and Shi'a as the driving factor behind present-day conflicts in the Middle East.

The Syrian regime's sectarian strategy

Over the decades the Syrian regime manipulated ethnic and sectarian cleavages in order to preserve and perpetuate its rule, for example by according positions within the army and security forces to a core of Alawites loyal to al-Asad family. At the same time, although discussions of sectarianism were totally banned from public debate, accusations of instigating sectarian tensions were part of a political discourse adopted by the regime to criminalize dissent and as part of its claim that only an authoritarian regime was capable of preserving the complex mosaic of Syrian society from sedition and sectarian chaos (Dibo 2014).

Bashar al-Asad's role in actually fomenting sectarianism in the early period of the Uprising was part of what Frederic C. Hof (2013) called the regime's "sectarian survival strategy". It aimed to undermine the legitimacy of the popular Uprising by portraying the demonstrators as foreign-backed takfiris[2] and terrorists and to raise the spectre of sectarian strife in order to present itself as the sole guarantor of Syria's national unity and social fabric.

Indeed, the articulation of the regime discourse passed through a number of distinct phases (Spyer 2012). During the first weeks of the civil Uprising, when protests demanding political reforms rather than the fall of the regime were largely confined to the southern province of Deraa and Syria's coastal cities, the Syrian regime did not yet aggressively deploy the sectarian argument. At this early stage its purpose was preventing conservative Muslims from joining the protest movement while presenting itself as the legitimate representative of a moderate and tolerant form of Islam against violent religious extremism imported from abroad. Still, long before Syria's first homegrown Salafi-jihadist groups appeared, government spokeswoman and long-term adviser Buthaina Shaaban blamed foreign elements for causing sectarian strife in the country, saying that "it is obvious Syria is the target of a project to sow sectarian strife to compromise Syria and the unique co-existence model that distinguishes it".[3] On 30 March 2011, President Bashar al-Asad made his first public appearance since anti-government protests began, addressing the country in a speech before Parliament (President Bashar Al-Asad's Speech at the National Assembly, 2011). He claimed that the protests had been instigated by a foreign conspiracy, denying that the country was witnessing a wave of popular protests demanding political reforms. Even if he did concede that not all the demonstrators could be conspirators, Bashar al-Asad referred to the Uprising as a "conspiracy", warning that "a few people who wanted to stir chaos and destroy the national fabric" managed to "mislead many people who demonstrated with good intensions". In his view, the conspiracy started with "incitement" weeks before the beginning of the unrest, using satellite TV stations and the Internet, then conspirators moved to "sedition", producing fake information to be circulated on the Internet, and finally "they started to use the sectarian element" with the purpose of setting one sect against the other.

The second speech, delivered by Bashar al-Asad on 16 April 2011, followed a few concessions aimed at appeasing specific group such as Syria's Kurds and conservative Muslims (President Al-Asad's Speech to the New Government 2011). This time the tone was more conciliatory, focusing on a narrative of reform distinguished from "sabotage": "there are clear differences between the demands for reform and the intentions of creating chaos and sabotage", he said to the newly appointed Cabinet. The Syrian president acknowledged that Syrians had legitimate grievances and outlined a series of proposed reforms that in his view would have removed any legitimate grounds for future protests.

Nevertheless, as local demonstrations turned into a widespread call for the end of the regime, reaching the central provinces of Homs and Hama as well as the suburbs of Damascus, Bashar al-Asad's propaganda strategy once again shifted. The third speech (President al-Asad Damascus University Speech 2011) marked a turning point inasmuch as he abandoned any attempt at denying or minimizing the presence of large proportion of Syrians revolting against his rule and openly accused demonstrators of fomenting sectarian divisions. Although at this stage protests had still mostly stuck to nationalist slogans with little signs of protesters or defectors taking up arms in self-defence or in retaliation for regime brutality, Bashar al-Asad reiterated the narrative of Syria being the target of a foreign-inspired conspiracy. During the third speech, he distinguished between one component of demonstrators, whose demands were raised "underneath the national umbrella", a second component consisting of "outlaws and [those] wanted for various criminal cases", and a third "more dangerous component", despite its small size, formed by those holding "extremist and takfiri ideology". These people "invoked detestable sectarian discourse" and used peaceful demonstrations with legitimate demands for reform as a pretext to move into armed confrontation with the regime. Since then, subsequent public addresses by Bashar al-Asad together with private and public pro-government media reiterated the themes of the first speeches, portraying Syria as the victim of an international conspiracy to overthrow a defiant Arab nationalist and resistance state and depicting opponents as terrorists from al-Qaeda and its offshoots who were being used by foreign states to incite sectarian sedition and tear the Syrian national fabric apart.

The survival of the al-Asad regime largely depended on the credibility of its sectarian argument. The creation of a shared threat perception arising from a sectarian civil war was meant to bolster support for the existing power structure within core military and security forces as well as among minorities communities, which consider themselves a potential target of Salafi-jihadists. In his statements, interviews and speeches, the Syrian president constantly referred to the rebels as "terrorists", "takfiris", or "al-Qaida members". State propaganda such as Syrian state TV, the private TV al-Duniya, state controlled Sana news agency and official newspapers incessantly replicated the regime's rhetoric of being the target of a sectarian foreign plot. Internally, the sectarian strife argument was employed by al-Asad to tarnish the image of the civil Uprising with the aim of persuading both internal and external audiences that he was fighting a terrorist-led and al-Qaida-inspired insurgency devoid of any social and political content, which could only be resolved militarily. The claim that takfiris constituted a significant part of the protest movement was generalized to cover all the opposition to the regime, which during the civil Uprising phase was mostly peaceful and cross-sectarian. Thus, on 10 January 2012, two weeks before al-Nusra Front released its first video statement, Syria's president (President al-Asad's Damascus University Speech 2012) declared he was fighting "terrorists taking cover under Islam". During this speech words like "terrorism" or "terrorists" appeared over 30 times while in the June 2012 speech at the People's Assembly more than 40 times (Speech Delivered by H.E. President Bashar al-Asad 2012). This passage from Asad's Opera House speech (2013) held on 6 January 2013, provides a sample of regime discourse:

> Takfiris, terrorists, al-Qaeda members calling themselves Jihadis streamed from everywhere to command the combat operations on the ground.... We are fighting those, most of whom are non-Syrians, who came for twisted concepts and fake terms they call Jihad, but nothing can be farther from Jihad and Islam. Most of them are terrorists instilled with al-Qaeda thought.

Besides Syrians, the other target audience of the regime's propaganda campaign was the international community, particularly the West. The sectarian strife argument allowed the regime to present itself as "the last stronghold of secularism, stability and coexistence in the region"[4] leading the battle against al-Qaida affiliated groups and their sectarian ideology, as Syrian President Bashar al-Asad said in an interview with Russia TV on 9 November 2012. The regime's communication strategy, especially when addressing foreign audiences, was to claim that its presence was indispensable for regional stability, warning that a foreign intervention in Syria "will have a domino effect that will affect the world from the Atlantic to the Pacific".

Furthermore, part of the regime's strategy of turning the popular Uprising into a sectarian civil war was a depopulation campaign that aimed at forcing Sunni civilians out of insurgent-held areas using artillery shelling, air strikes, and massacres of Sunni villages and neighbourhoods. This policy of population displacement "hardened sectarian lines as communities grouped together out of fear and the need for self-protection" (Holliday 2013, p. 19). The fact that largely Alawite-heavy military units, *shabiha* militias – armed loyalists of mostly Alawite origin – and foreign Shi'i militias were indiscriminately attacking predominantly Sunni populations, and that Iran and Hizbullah were among the main supporters of the regime, substantiated the sectarian storyline of a Sunni fight against perceived Alawite rule and a Shi'i-dominated regional order. This largely accounted for the sharp increase in anti-Alawite and anti-Shi'i rhetoric among larger sections of the anti-government forces, which started to perceive the conflict as a sectarian confrontation against the Sunnis as a religious group. The regime's atrocities had also the effect of implicating the entire Alawite community in its crimes in the eyes of the anti-government forces while also strengthening the sectarian narrative held by Salafi-jihadist groups operating in Syria.

The anti-sectarian discourse of the opposition

The civil Uprising phase against the regime of Bashar al-Asad, ranging from March 2011 until the militarization of the opposition following the creation of the Free Syrian Army (FSA) on 29 July 2011, was characterized by genuinely spontaneous, geographically widespread and community-based protests. Youth activists and grassroots organizations emphasized the cross-sectarian and peaceful nature of the Uprising, while developing a strong nationalist and anti-sectarian discourse which framed events in Syria as a popular national Uprising against an oppressive regime under which all components of Syrian society had equally suffered.

Through the use of social media and the organization of civil disobedience campaigns and countless other cross-sectarian peaceful activities, activists invested considerable efforts in highlighting the involvement of Alawis, Druze, Kurds, and Christians in the protest movement. In their public statements and founding documents they began to forge a new political language that prioritized national affiliation over ethnic, religious or sectarian identities while affirming a commitment to a civil democratic state based on equal citizenship for all components of Syrian society. The "Syrian Revolution 2011" Facebook page can be considered as one of the most influential social networking tools in the early mobilization of protesters. As early as March 2011, it issued (Syrian Revolution 2011) a *Code of ethics against sectarianism in Syria*, warning against sectarian thinking and behaviour, which were considered a threat to the Syrian national fabric. The Code stated that sectarianism as well as any form of discrimination between Syrians would be rejected in the context of a democratic civil state that would regard all its inhabitants as equal citizens. The "Syrian Revolution 2011" also provided an effective platform for translating social media campaigns into street politics. Every week the administrators of the page posted a poll calling on sympathizers to choose the names of the upcoming Fridays' mass protests. Especially during the early months of the popular Uprising these names tended to be representative of all components of the opposition, reflecting the need for reassuring minorities that they will be participants in the new Syria and their rights respected once Asad's rule ends. For instance, Friday June 17, 2011, was named the "Friday of Honorable Sheikh Saleh al-Ali", an Alawite who commanded the Syrian revolt of 1919 against French colonialism and who became one of the symbols of Syria's unity and independence (Atassi & Wikstrom 2012; Badran 2012).

Banners, graffiti campaigns and protest chants videotaped and uploaded on social networking websites also indicated that during the civil Uprising phase, mobilization did not occur on religious, ethnic or sectarian basis; on the contrary, demonstrators showcased the role of minority activists and shouted anti-sectarian slogans such as "Muslims, Christians, Alawis are all one". Chants often during funerals, solidarity rallies and weekly mosque prayers included: "Neither Salifist nor Ikhwan", "Sunnis and Alawites ... peaceful, peaceful"; "Sunnis and Alawites, we all want freedom"; "One, one, one, the Syrian people are one" (Kahf 2013).

By the summer of 2011 a number of coalitions began to coordinate the networks of local activists and committees that sprouted during the first weeks of the

Uprising. They were involved in multiple activities, such as reporting on violations committed by the Syrian government, organizing social media campaigns and street protests, and providing aid to areas under bombardment or siege (Al Shami 2013). The Local Coordination Committees (LCCs) were committed to nonviolent struggle and civil disobedience acts, such as staging protests, sit-ins, and media campaigns, while consistently developing a counter-discourse against sectarianism and religious fanaticism and for building a democratic, pluralistic, and civil state based on freedom and equality for all Syrian citizens (Abu Hamed 2014).

On 22 April 2011, the LCCs (2011) issued a statement of principles in which they stated that the peaceful demonstrations aimed at reclaiming freedom, dignity and equal citizenship through a series of "constitutional amendments that will allow for a democratic transition of Syria to become a respected, multi-national, multi-ethnic, and religiously tolerant society". The LCCs laid blame on the Syrian regime for "gambling with our national unity by playing sectarian, ethnic, and religious divisions against each other" in order to divert the revolution from its initial objectives of democracy, freedom, and dignity. A statement (2011b) issued on 15 May 2011, three months after the beginning of the Uprising clearly warned that the "systematic media disinformation campaigns" of the Syrian regime aimed at "ignit[ing] sectarian tension and break[ing] apart the social and national Syrian unity" while also "weakening the civil peaceful movement and disrupting it". In the June 2011 "Vision for the Political Future of Syria," the LCCs openly denounced the sectarian strategy of the regime, which is trying "to harm the unity of Syrians by all possible and dirty means and to create fear among their groups, cause concerns for the ethnic minorities, and build up the sectarian speech addressed by the official and semi-official media", while stating that the aim of the revolution is the creation of a "civil state" based on the idea that the Syrian people are "equal free citizens", regardless of their ethnic or religious backgrounds. On Friday 8 June 2012, under the banner "Freedom is my sect" (2012a) the LCCs organized a campaign called "My sign expresses me" in which they raised signs and carried placards bearing symbols of all Syrian sects. They also reaffirmed that the motto of the revolution was "one against injustice and sectarianism" and for the establishment of a nation "for all Syrians, of all different religions, sects, and beliefs".

Other grassroots opposition networks were also pivotal in portraying the Uprising as inherently non-sectarian. They all shared the belief that a vision of citizenship based on equality of rights and responsibilities under a democratic and plural political system would serve as the principal remedy against all sorts of sectarian or ethnic divisions. For instance, in its August 2011 founding document, the Syrian Revolution General Commission, a coalition of more than 40 opposition groups inside and outside of Syria actively supporting armed rebels, confirmed (2011) its commitment towards "toppling the oppressive and abusive regime and then building Syria as a democratic and civil State" based on equality and respect of human rights for all citizens. In an April 2011 statement the Supreme Council of the Syrian Revolution (2011), another grassroots opposition network inside the country, also clarified that Syria is "the homeland of all Syrians of all religious affiliations, ethnic, national, cultural, intellectual, and political without discrimination or exception or exclusion" and asserted that it was a lie to depict the revolution as one of any "party, or denomination, or sect, or organization from within or outside Syria".

Although the significance of civilian grassroots opposition was drastically reduced as a consequence of the militarization of the Uprising, they still continued to exert some influence on the ground throughout the first half of 2012, particularly in ensuring that the ethical principles of freedom, citizenship, and dignity were still part of the narrative of the armed and political opposition. A striking example is the role played by the LCCs in drafting a "Code of ethical conduct" that established the moral and political principles for the military action of the Free Syrian Army, at the time the largest umbrella armed group composed of Syrian military defectors and civilians who took up arms. The document served to state to world public opinion that any practice contradicting the basic principles of the revolution, namely "freedom, dignity, and justice", will not be considered in line with the moral and national foundations of the revolution. The Code of conduct was initially published (2012b) by the LCCs on 8 August 2012 and committed the FSA to respecting human rights and international humanitarian law. The leading ethical role that the LCC still retained within the opposition was confirmed by the fact that nearly 30 commanders and battalions signed the pledge. Article IX explicitly addresses the sectarian issue:

> I pledge not to exercise reprisals on the basis of ethnicity, sect, religion, or any other basis, and to refrain from any abusive practices, in word or in deed, against any component of the Syrian people.

Signed a week after reports of armed anti-government forces executing suspected pro-Asad militiamen in Aleppo, the Code was a response to widespread concern over human rights violations and abuses by the armed opposition, as documented in a number of human rights groups' reports (Human Rights Watch 2012; Amnesty International 2012). A few days after the publication of the Code, the Commission of Inquiry on Syria (2012) concluded in a report that opposition forces had actually committed war crimes in a number of incidents.

With the creation of the FSA, the Uprising entered a new phase. As the civil resistance movement turned into armed insurgency, activist networks were being sidelined by armed groups while the discourse on Syria came to be dominated by issues of militarization, external intervention and sectarianism. However, the vision of the first armed militants was still dominated by the anti-sectarian framing of the grassroots protest movement. Early FSA units publicly embraced principles of non-sectarianism, framing their armed confrontation as a national liberation struggle against an oppressive dictatorship. Their rhetoric employed secular themes such as self-defence, national unity and the creation of a pluralistic civil state, also with the purpose of reassuring minority communities that they will not be subjected to acts of vengeance after the fall of the regime. For instance, on 10 June 2011, Syrian Army Lieutenant Colonel Hussein Harmoush publicly announced (Holliday 2012, p. 14) his defection in a video statement that would serve as a model for other defecting officers. He declared that his mission was "the protection of the protestors", assuring the "great people of Syria and all its diverse sects and groups" that his objectives were "freedom and democracy".

The Syrian National Coalition (SNC), the largest coalition of Syrian opposition leaders and political groups formed abroad on 2 October 2011, also understood the importance of presenting itself as the legitimate representative of all sections of the Syrian people while at the same time reaffirming the anti-sectarian nature of the Uprising. This has been done in a number of public statements and official documents, and bolstered by appointing as heads of the exiled opposition groups figures such as the long-time Christian-Marxist dissident George Sabra and Ahmed Moaz al-Khatib, the widely respected preacher of the historic Ummayad Mosque in Damascus who from the very beginning of the Uprising repeatedly called for unity among Syria's religious groups and for freedom "for every Sunni, Alawite, Ismaili and Christian, whether Arab or a member of the great Kurdish nation".[5] In late February 2012, the SNC (2012) released a statement stating that the members of the Alawite sect are "an essential element of Syria's cultural and ethnic fabric" and that they will continue to "enjoy the same rights as other citizens as we build one nation of Christians, Muslims, and other sects". It charged the government with trying to "fragment Syrian society and drive a wedge within mixed communities by dividing cities along military and security lines". The Muslim Brotherhood, the most influential Islamic group within the SNC, promoted a moderate Islamist approach with the aim of distancing itself from the sectarian rhetoric of militant Salafi-jihadist groups while reassuring secular opposition forces, foreign governments, and Syria's religious minorities (Lund 2013b). The Brotherhood's rejection of sectarianism was reiterated in a number of interviews and statements released by high-ranking member of the organization in an attempt to dispel suspicions that its anti-sectarian stance arose out of pragmatism rather than genuine political commitment. In March 2012, the organization (2012) issued a political programme framing the conflict as a national revolution encompassing all sectors of the Syrian nation. It also announced its support for religious equality, standing in favour of the creation of "a state [based on] citizenship and equality, in which all citizens are equal regardless of their ethnicity, faith, school of thought, or [political] orientation".

In April 2013, the National Coalition for Syrian Revolutionary and Opposition Forces (2013), a newly formed and more inclusive coalition of opposition groups, released a statement of principles[6] reaffirming its commitment to "a democratic, pluralistic Syria" where "all Syrians will be equal regardless of their ethnic, religious and sectarian background" and with "no room for sectarianism or discrimination on ethnic, religious, linguistic or any other grounds".

A stance against sectarianism was also adopted by other components of the opposition to the regime of Bashar al-Asad, like the National Coordinating Committee for Democratic Change (NCC), a Syria-based coalition of nationalist and leftist political parties and figures. The NCC, which sought to portray itself as representing the internal opposition in contrast to the foreign-backed exile coalitions, initially favoured a negotiated settlement with the regime and committed to three basic principles: "No" to foreign military intervention, "No" to religious and sectarian instigation, and "No" to violence and the militarization of the revolution. On 23 September 2012, the NCC (2012a) held the "Syria Salvation Conference" in Damascus, where it reaffirmed its "rejection of sectarianism and everything else that contributes to dividing Syrian society on a pre-civic basis". It also outlined an overview of the new Syria (NCC 2012b) that was to be built on the basis of "absolute equality of men and women, and the prohibition of any form of discrimination on the basis of race, family, gender, sect, political opinion, language, ethnicity or religion".

Being very sensitive to the regime's charges that the Uprising was driven by takfiris and terrorist groups, the main components of the non-Salafi-jihadi Syrian opposition, comprising exiled dissidents, grassroots activists and FSA armed militants, tended to downplay the radical Islamist dynamic emerging within the armed insurgency and minimized the growth of anti-Alawite sentiment in anti-government protests. Wishing to present itself as the legitimate representative of all segments of the Syrian people, the SNC strove to reassure both the West – from whom they hoped for political support and military assistance – and minority communities that the fight is for the overthrow of the Asad regime and not against any particular sect. However, while being quick to condemn the sectarian massacres committed by the Syrian regime, the SNC was reluctant to condemn war crimes and attacks targeting Shi'i and Alawite civilians and religious shrines perpetuated by the FSA or affiliates, particularly during the early August offensive in the countryside of Lattakia.

Yet, notwithstanding the regime's propaganda campaign to portray its opponents as sectarian religious extremists and foreign terrorists and despite its indiscriminate and deliberate attacks against Sunni civilian populations, the main components of the Syrian opposition largely refrained from retaliating against minority communities. According to an investigation by the Syrian Network for Human Rights (2016), from March 2011 until June 2013, the vast majority of massacres involving a pattern of sectarian killing were carried out by government forces or their local and foreign militia allies. As the armed insurgency transitioned to a civil war during the summer of 2012, international human rights organizations and institutions increasingly reported a growing number of war crimes and other violations of international human rights law committed by government forces and its affiliated militias and also by opposition armed groups. In a report covering the five-month period before the battle for al-Qusayr, UN human rights investigators (Commission of Inquiry on Syria 2013b, p. 1) concluded that "violations and abuses committed by anti-government armed groups did not reach the intensity and scale of those committed by government forces and affiliated militia".

In the end, however, neither the opposition's strong nationalist and anti-sectarian discourse, rhetorical commitments to a "democratic, pluralistic, and civil state" and appointment of members from minority communities to a number of positions inside the SNC proved sufficient to alleviate minorities' fears of sectarian retribution if Syria's radical Sunni militants were to come to power. And while the FSA also initially attempted to marginalize hardline jihadist groups in order to reassure minorities and the international community, it did not succeed in asserting control over independently operating brigades and battalions nor was it able to produce a coherent narrative on sectarianism that may have challenged the rising ideological influence of Salafi-jihadist groups, which also exerted growing influence on the ground.

The sectarian narrative of the Salafi-Jihadist groups

As the regime's brutal crackdown on protesters intensified, the armed opposition's original emphasis on national unity and self-defence was gradually challenged by a more explicitly Islamist discourse. Indeed, the first half of 2012 witnessed the appearance of a strong Salafi-jihadist current within the Syrian armed opposition that described the struggle against the Asad regime as being essentially sectarian in nature and that eventually proved decisive in reshaping the terms of debate within Syria (International Crisis Groups 2012, p. 10). Sunni Islamists, particularly Salafis, often resorted to what Zelin & Smyth (2014) has called "the vocabulary of sectarianism" to describe their Shi'i Islamist foes – those that support or are fighting with the Asad regime. They have routinely used the derogatory term *Rawafid*, literally rejectionists, plural of *Rafida*, in reference to Twelver Shi'a, or the word *Nusayri* to emphasize that Alawites worship their founder Abu Shuayb Muhammad Ibn Nusayr and as such are outside Islam, rather than employing the term Alawite which refers to Ali Ibn Abi Talib, considered by Sunnis to be the fourth Caliph.

In the discourse of the most radical Salafi-jihadists the dichotomy "revolutionaries vs. al-Asad regime" presented by the mainstream opposition was replaced with a narrative of "jihadists or believers vs. infidels or heretics". This sectarian narrative aimed at fuelling perceptions of community divisions along sectarian lines in order to gain the support of Syria's predominantly Sunni population while allowing Salafi-jihadists to be presented as the defenders of Sunnis against the "heretical" religious group of the Alawites.

Al-Qaeda-affiliated al-Nusra Front announced its creation in late January 2012. It identified the struggle in explicitly sectarian terms, calling on Sunni Muslims to wage war against the "Alawite regime" and its "Shi'ite agents". However, while rejecting the vision of a civil democratic state in Syria where all groups enjoy equal rights, it has been careful to minimize indiscriminate civilian casualties and sectarian massacres that could result in the loss of support from the Syrian population (Benotman & Blake 2013). Nonetheless, the group openly affirms that its battle is not only with the "infidel" Asad regime, that represents the sect of the Alawites, *al-Nusayrin*, but also with the other minority sects and religions, considered "infidels" or "apostates", and its regional "Shiites proxies".

The removal of the regime of Bashar al-Asad is presented as the short-term goal of the fight, while the end-goal is to establish a "Caliphate" in *Bilad al-Sham*

(Greater Syria), which will be ruled by a strict interpretation of Islamic law. Its statements openly embrace sectarian rhetoric: Shi'a are derogatorily referred to as *Rawafid* while Alawites as *Nusayris* (International Crisis Group 2012a). On January 24, 2012, al-Nusra leader Muhammad al-Julani announced the establishment of the organization:

> any sane people can feel the Iranian efforts in the previous years, side by side with this [Asad] regime, to spread the Safavid ideology in this blessed land in order to restore the Persian Empire. The Levant is the lungs of this Iranian project.[7]

Al-Nusra Front justifies its military actions as retaliations for the massacres committed against the Sunnis by the Alawites, which are identified with the regime of al-Asad. In a video (Jabhat al-Nusra Claims Credit for Twin Bombings 2012) posted online[8] claiming responsibility for two suicide bombings attack in Damascus on May 10, 2012, the sectarian nature of its mission is all too evident: "Stop your massacres against the Sunni people, otherwise you hold the sins of the Nysayris (the Alawites) and what's coming thereafter is worse and more bitter Allah-willing." On 20 May 2012, al-Nusra released a statement claiming responsibility for a bomb attack on a Syrian state security compound in Deir al-Zor, explaining that "the blessed operations will continue until the land of Syria is purified from the filth of the Nusayris and the Sunnis are relieved from their oppression".[9]

Various Salafi armed groups represent a middle ground between al-Qaeda affiliates and FSA factions. Unlike al-Nusra Front, they have downplayed the rhetoric of global jihad and the use of indiscriminate violence, while in contrast with secular nationalist FSA brigades, they often refer to their enemy in overtly sectarian terms and justify their resort to violence exclusively within an Islamist frame of reference. Ahrar al-Sham Brigade soon emerged as one of the most prominent Salafist groups in Syria. It was the principal organization operating under the umbrella of the Syrian Islamic Front (SIF).[10] In April 2012 Ahrar al-Sham (International Crisis Group 2012, p. 15) released its first video in which it clearly declared that its objective is to replace al-Asad's regime with an Islamic state. It also framed the Uprising as "a jihad against a Safawi [Iranian Shi'a] plot to spread Shi'ism and establish a Shi'ite state from Iran through Iraq and Syria to Lebanon and Palestine". Should the plot succeed, the statement continues, it would benefit the Zionists "because it's well known that al-Rafidha don't fight the enemy; they only turn their swords against Sunnis". In a June 2013 interview for *Al Jazeera Arabic*, Hassan Abboud (Zelin & Smyth 2014), leader of Ahrar al-Sham, was quoted as saying that Syria "has been ruled by a Nusayri idea, a Shi'a group that came to power and started discriminating against the Sunni people". The leadership of SIF also embarked on a propaganda campaign with a view to strengthening the Islamist character of the conflict. This also meant that the organization frequently resorted to sectarian rhetoric in its public statements, labelling Alawites and Shi'a as *Nusayris* and *Rawafid* (Lund 2013a). However, although SIF leaders are likely to share the view of Alawites as apostates, the group has developed a less inflammatory discourse than al-Nusra Front in which it has somewhat reassured non-Sunnis who are not fighting for al-Asad. On 21 January 2013, SIF released its official charter in which it clearly states that the goal of the Front is "to build an Islamic, civilized society in Syria ruled by the law of God" (Carnegie Endowment for International Peace 2013). In the fourth section of the Charter, the Front (Islamic Forces in Syria Announce Establishment of Joint Front 2012) outlines its vision for the religious minorities in the future society.[11] Despite calling for "coexistence between the sons of one nation" and for the "rejection of any plan to divide it [Syria] on an ethnic or sectarian basis", its views on minority rights are clearly based on its interpretation of *shari'a*: "all Syrians enjoy the rights required for them by law"–that is, Islamic *shari'a*. Therefore, while "non-Muslims" will be treated with "justice and fairness", suggesting a second-class citizenship, the status of Shi'a and Alawites remains unclear.[12]

The emergence of a sectarian master narrative

The increasingly polarized discourses on sectarianism in Syria reflected a larger struggle of narratives over the nature and the objectives of the Uprising. As the protest movement escalated into an armed confrontation, the main actors created and projected competing narratives of the conflict with the aims of mobilizing specific constituencies to either support them or fight against the enemy and of fostering international support for their policies. Youth activists and grassroots organizations engaged in delivering consistent anti-sectarian messages in accordance with their framing of the Uprising as a popular and cross-sectarian national revolution against an autocratic regime. The regime's sectarian argument was meant to bring the international community to perceive the conflict as a confrontation of a legitimate government with criminal gangs or foreign-supported jihadists, while internally to convince local constituencies that it is either the government of President Bashar al-Asad or al-Qaida affiliated groups that will rule the country once the civil war ends. As for the Salafi-jihadist sectarian narrative, by describing the conflict as one pitting a minority Alawite rule and its Shi'a allies against the Sunni Muslim majority, Syrian jihadist groups represented themselves as the most effective defender of the Sunni community. The convergence between the regime's policy of manipulating sectarian cleavages as a survival strategy and the virulently sectarian rhetoric propagated by Salafi-jihadist groups led to the emergence of a sectarian master narrative that portrays the Uprising as part of the broader Sunni struggle against the threat of Shi'i domination in the region.

A major turning point in the emergence of this master narrative was the June 2013 battle of al-Qusayr, after which the Salafi-jihadist sectarian rhetoric seriously challenged the uprising's original non-sectarian narrative. Indeed, this event deepened sectarian polarization and exacerbated the role of identity politics in the region as a whole. The fierce fighting that ended with the regime's forces, backed by Hizbollah, wresting the strategic border town from rebels' control represented "a significant inflection point in the intensity of sectarian rhetoric from outside Syria" (Reese 2003, pp. 14–15). Furthermore, as acknowledged by the International Commission of Inquiry on Syria (2013), the fact that some attacks were launched by Hizbullah and that many of the government's artillery positions were located within Shi'i villages led to a strong undercurrent of sectarianism in the interpretation of events by those who lived through them.

On the one hand, the public emergence of Lebanese Hizbullah and Shi'i militias operating with Syrian government forces stirred up sectarian tensions between Shi'a and Sunnis. In his May 25, 2013, televised speech, Hizbullah Secretary-General Hassan Nasrallah (2013) vowed to stand by the Syrian regime in the fight against "takfiri groups and mentality".[13] As Usmaa Butt (2014) points out, both Hizbullah and Shi'i militias developed a political discourse entrenched in radical political Shi'ism. The religious narrative of the Battle of Karbala and the Martyrdom of Hussein together with the rhetoric of defending Shi'i religious shrines functioned as formidable political tools to mobilize support and justify intervention (Anzalone 2013; Smyth 2013).

On the other hand, prominent Sunni clerics throughout the Arab world increasingly recurred to sectarian language and rhetoric against Hizbullah and the Shi'a, issuing calls for jihad against the *Rawafid* (Varulkar et al. 2013). In a sermon delivered in Qatar on 31 May 2013, influential Qatar-based Egyptian cleric Yusuf al-Qaradawi (2013) used an inflammatory sectarian rhetoric, condemning Hizbullah, which he called "the party of Satan", and Iran, for helping Syria's "Alawite regime" in its war against the Sunnis. He referred to the *Nusayris* as being "greater infidels than the Jews and the Christians". This inciting sectarian language was widely amplified by other contemporary Salafi religious figures such as Sheikh Adnan Arour and Abul-Mondher al-Chinguetti, who issued fatwas demonizing Alawites and calling for "jihad against Nuseris" (Lund 2013a, p. 22; International Crisis Group 2012a, pp. 30–33). Their virulent anti-Shi'i rhetoric, characterizing the Syrian Uprising as a Sunni jihad against a polytheistic Alawite regime and its Shi'i allies, validated the regime's sectarian strife argument while also rejecting the grassroots activists' framing of the Uprising as a popular national cross-sectarian revolution. Concepts of "equal citizenship" and "democratic, pluralistic, and civil state" were replaced by "protection of minorities" and "state based on sharia law".

The open involvement of transnational actors overtly embracing sectarian rhetoric for justifying their intervention and for the mobilization of constituencies represented a major step towards the "sectarianization" of discourses and practices in Syria. With Salafi-jihadist groups taking a prominent role in the fight against the regime of Bashar al-Asad, sectarian language became more acceptable even among non-jihadist sections of the armed opposition, obscuring as a result the anti-sectarian counter narrative produced by grassroots activists and organizations. The regime, on its part, have been successful in producing "a self-fulfilling prophecy" (Frederic C. Hof & Alex Simon 2012, pp. 19–21) where the manipulation of sectarian identities also encouraged the emergence of sectarian feelings and hatred among opposition groups, lending credence to its narrative of an opposition made up of religious extremists that would not hesitate to wreak sectarian violence against Syria's minorities regardless of whether they supported or opposed the regime.

The rising ideological influence of the sectarian discourse not only contributed to the escalation of anti-Alawite and anti-Shiite rhetoric, but also provided legitimization for perpetrators of sectarian and communal violence, as increasingly reported by human rights organizations and institutions (Human Rights Watch 2013; Commission of Inquiry on Syria 2013a). Over time a dynamic of polarization emerged, in which religious identity groups increasingly held one another collectively responsible for violations, real and perceived (Hof 2013). With communities trapped in a sectarian security dilemma, believing that they are facing an existential threat, religious groups increasingly aligned themselves with the competing political camps in order to ensure their own security, in turn deepening sectarian divides and reinforcing perceptions that the main drivers of the conflict are the age-old divides between Sunnis and Shi'a.

Conclusion

During the civil Uprising phase, when the opposition strategy to overthrow the regime remained largely focused on street protests and grassroots mobilization, the prevailing discourse of the Uprising remained largely anti-sectarian, emphasizing cross-national unity, a shared Syrian identity, and equal citizenship in a future civil and pluralistic Syria. The struggle against sectarianism was perceived by youth activists and grassroots organizations as an integral part of the struggle to overthrow the Asad regime. The anti-sectarian framing of the Uprising helped the crossing of boundaries between ethnicities and sects, with prominent intellectuals and activists from across the various minority groups – Alawites, Christians, Druze, Ismailis and Kurds – joining the campaign to topple the regime.

However the Uprising began to assume a growing sectarian dimension as a result of certain internal and regional developments that took place in the early stages of the Uprising (Shadid 2011; Rosen 2012; International Crisis Group 2012b). The disillusionment of many protesters with peaceful means of struggle together with the failure of the international community to stop indiscriminate attacks by Syrian government forces and militias on civilians accounted for the rising ideological influence of Salafi-jihadists within anti-government forces, in addition to pushing large parts of the protest movement to call for foreign intervention. The original focus on national unity, cross-sectarian solidarity, and the calls for a civil, pluralistic, democratic state were progressively challenged by a more radical Islamist discourse reframing the conflict from a "cross-confessional popular Uprising against an authoritarian regime" to a "jihad against the heretic Alawite rule". The trajectory towards further sectarianism was highlighted in a report by the Independent International Commission of Inquiry on Syria, covering the period September–December 2012, warning that the conflict was "overtly sectarian in nature", with government forces and supporting militias attacking Sunni civilians, and reports of anti-government armed groups attacking Alawites and other minority communities perceived to support the regime of Bashar al-Asad (Commission of Inquiry on Syria 2013a). Although the conflict in Syria should not be regarded as inherently sectarian, it cannot be denied that the increasing use of sectarian cleavages for political mobilization represented one of the key factors behind the polarization of Syrian society along sectarian lines. Nevertheless, the sectarian paradigm fails to highlight the decisive role played by entrepreneurs of cynical sectarianism in turning the popular Uprising into a civil war with increasingly sectarian overtones. Sectarian narratives reframed and depoliticized the Syrian Uprising, identifying ethnic or religious differences as the main source of violence while ignoring more fundamental economic and political factors that were the driving forces behind the outbreak of protests against the regime of Bashar al-Asad.

Notes

1 This article does not strictly follow a formal method of transliteration. Diacritical marks have not been used, except for the mark 'to indicate the 'ayn in certain instances, for example, "Shi'a" and "shari'a" but not "'Alawites". Arabic names of cities or prominent political and cultural figures are spelled according to the accepted English spellings.
2 The word "takfiri" usually refers to a Muslim who accuses other Muslims of apostasy.
3 "Asad adviser warns of sectarian strife in Syria" 2011, *Reuters*, 26 March.
4 "Assad to RT: 'I'm not Western puppet – I have to live and die in Syria'" 2012, *RT*, 8 November, https://www.rt.com/news/assad-exclusive-interview-syria-240/.
5 "Damascus suburb is new centre of defiance" (2011), *Gulf News*, 10 April.
6 National Coalition of Syrian Revolution and Opposition Forces (2013), "Declaration", http://en.etilaf.org/coalition-documents/declaration-by-the-national-coalition-for-syrian-revolutionary-and-opposition-forces.html.
7 "Announcement of the Al Nusrah Front" (2012), *Ansar al-Mujahidin Forum*, 24 January, in B. Fishman (2012), "The Evidence Of Jihadist Activity in Syria", *CTC Sentinel*, 22 May, Vol. 5, no. 5, p. 4.
8 "Jabhat al-Nusra Claims Credit for Twin Bombings in Damascus" 2012, 20 March, *Flashpoint Partners*, http://azelin.files.wordpress.com/2012/03/jabhat-al-nue1b9a3rah-22operation-against-the-directorate-of-air-security-and-the-department-of-criminal-security-in-damascus22-en.pdf.
9 "Militant group claims suicide bombing in Syria", *Reuters*, 21 May 2012.
10 The Syrian Islamic Front (SIF), created on 21 December 2012, was a Salafist umbrella organization that brought together eleven Islamist groups. In November 2013, the SIF joined with the Syrian Islamic Liberation Front, and the Kurdish Islamic Front to create the Islamic Front.
11 "Islamic Forces in Syria Announce Establishment of Joint Front Aimed at Toppling Assad, Founding Islamic State", *The Middle East Media Research Institute*, Special Dispatch No. 5107, 26 December 2012.
12 For the contemporary Salafi movement, which often refers to a series of *fatwas* by the medieval scholar Taqieddin ibn Taimiya (1223–1328), the position of Christians is less problematic than that of the Alawite, the Druze or the Twelver Shia, clearly referred to as "rejectionists" or follower of a "polytheist sect".
13 "Hezbollah Leader Hassan Nasrallah's Speech on Syria", *Voltaire Network*, 25 May, 2013, http://www.voltairenet.org/article178691.html.

Bibliography

Abu Hamed, A. (2014), Syria's Local Coordination Committees: the Dynamo of a Hijacked Revolution, Knowledge Programme Civil Society in West Asia, Amsterdam.

Al Shami, L. (2013), "Syria: The Struggle Continues: Syria's Grass-roots Civil Opposition", *Tahrir-ICN*, 16 September, https://tahriricn.wordpress.com/2013/09/16/syria-the-struggle-continues-syrias-grass-roots-civil-opposition/.

Amnesty International (2012), "Syria: Disturbing Reports of Summary Killings by Government and Opposition Forces", 25 July, https://www.amnesty.org/en/press-releases/2012/07/syria-disturbing-reports-summary-killings-government-and-opposition-forces/.

Anzalone, C. (2013), "Zaynab's Guardians: The Emergence of Shi'a Militias in Syria", CTC Sentinel, July.

Atassi, B. & Wikstrom, C. (2012), "The battle to name Syria's Friday Protests", Al Jazeera, 14 April, www.aljazeera.com/indepth/features/2012/04/201241314026709762.html;

Badran, Y. (2012), "Naming Friday: Debating Syria's Day of Revolt", *al Akhbar* English, 29 January, http://english.al-akhbar.com/node/3743.

Benotman, N. & Blake, R. (2013), Jabhat al-Nusra: A Strategic Briefing, Quilliam Foundation, 8 January.

Butt, Usama (2014), "Hezbollah: Syria and the Manipulation of Narrative", *Future Foreign Policy*, 14 January, www.futureforeignpolicy.com/hezbollah-syria-and-the-manipulation-of-narrative/.

"Charter of the Syrian Islamic Front" (2013), Carnegie Endowment for International Peace 4 February. Arabic version available at: https://docs.google.com/document/d/1fACS9tltlmZDmomlB1ZtiJLZaAckWOT0yhtRwoskgIE/edit?pli=1.

Dibo, M. (2014), "Asad's Secular Sectarianism", Open Democracy, 27 November, https://www.opendemocracy.net/arab-awakening/mohammad-dibo/Asad"s-secular-sectarianism.

Hof, Fred (2013), "Syria 2013: Will the Poison Pill of Sectarianism Work?", Atlantic Council, 3 January.

Hof, F. & Simon, A. (2012), Sectarian Violence in Syria's Civil War: Causes, Consequences, and Recommendations for Mitigation, *Paper Commissioned by The Center for the Prevention of Genocide, United States Holocaust Memorial Museum*, pp. 19–21.

Holliday, J. (2012), "Syria's Armed Opposition", *Middle East Security Report 3, Institute for the Study of War*, p. 14.

Holliday, J. (2013), "The Asad Regime: From Counterinsurgency to Civil War", Middle East Security Report 8, Institute for the Study of War, March.

Human Rights Council (2012), "Report of the Independent International Commission of Inquiry on the Syrian Arab Republic", Office of the United Nations High Commissioner for Human Rights, A/HRC/21/50, 15 August, www.ohchr.org/EN/HRBodies/HRC/IICISyria/Pages/Documentation.aspx.

Human Rights Council (2013a), "Report of the Independent International Commission of Inquiry on the Syrian Arab Republic", Office of the United Nations High Commissioner for Human Rights, A/HRC/24/46, 5 February, www.ohchr.org/EN/HRBodies/HRC/IICISyria/Pages/Documentation.aspx.

Human Rights Council (2013b), "Report of the Independent International Commission of Inquiry on the Syrian Arab Republic", Office of the United Nations High Commissioner for Human Rights, A/HRC/24/46, 11 September, www.ohchr.org/EN/HRBodies/HRC/IICISyria/Pages/Documentation.aspx.

Human Rights Watch (2012), "Open Letter to the Leaders of the Syrian Opposition", 20 March, https://www.hrw.org/news/2012/03/20/open-letter-leaders-syrian-opposition.

Human Rights Watch (2013), You Can Still See Their Blood, October, https://www.hrw.org/sites/default/files/reports/syria1013_ForUpload.pdf.

International Crisis Group (2012a), "Tentative Jihad", Middle East Report no. 131, 12 October.

International Crisis Group (2012b), Syria's Mutating Conflict, Middle East Report No.128, 1 August.

Kahf, M. (2013), Then and Now: The Syrian Revolution to Date, Friends for a Nonviolent World, St. Paul, MN.
Kaufman, S., Elliott, M. & Shmueli, D. (2003), "Frames, Framing and Reframing", in *Beyond Intractability*, edited by G. Burgess & H. Burgess, The Conflict Information Consortium, University of Colorado, www.beyondintractability.org/essay/framing.
Local Coordinating Committees (2011), LCC Statements, 22 April, www.lccsyria.org/1103. For a more accurate translation see the Arabic version www.lccsyria.org/1234-2.
Lund, Aron (2013a), "Syria's Salafi Insurgents: the Rise of the Syrian Islamic Front", Swedish Institute for International Affairs, 19 March.
Lund, Aron (2013b), "Struggling to Adapt: The Muslim Brotherhood in a New Syria", Carnegie Endowment for International Peace, 7 May.
Lynch, Marc (2013), "The Entrepreneurs of Cynical Sectarianism", *Foreign Policy*, 13 November.
Makdisi, U. (2008), "Pensee 4: Moving Beyond Orientalist Fantasy, Sectarian Polemic, and Nationalist Denial", *International Journal of Middle East Studies*, 40: 4.
Matthiesen, Toby (2013), *Sectarian Gulf: Bahrain, Saudi Arabia, and the Arab Spring That Wasn't*, Stanford: Stanford University Press.
National Coalition of Syrian Revolution and Opposition Forces (2013), "Declaration", http://en.etilaf.org/coalition-documents/declaration-by-the-national-coalition-for-syria nrevolutionary-and-opposition-forces.html.
NCC, National Coordinating Committee for Democratic Change (2012a), "Syria Salvation Conference: Our Main Principles", National Conference for Syria Salvation, Preparatory Committee National Conference for Syria Salvation, 22/9/2012: http://syrianncb.org/2012/09/23/syria-salvation-conference-our-main-principles/.
NCC, National Coordinating Committee for Democratic Change (2012b), "Syria Salvation Conference: An Overview of the New Syria", National Conference for Syria Salvation, Preparatory Committee National Conference for Syria Salvation, 22/9/2012: http://syria nncb.org/2012/09/24/syria-salvation-conference-an-overview-of-the-new-syria-2/.
Nissen, T.E. (2013), "The Ever Changing Narrative of Conflict", in C. Jensen (ed.), *Democracy Managers*, Copenhagen: Forsvarsakademiets Forlag, pp. 73–83.
"President al-Asad's 2012 Damascus University Speech" (2012), 10 January, www.presidenta ssad.net.
"President al-Assad 2011 Damascus University Speech" (2011), 20 June, www.presidentassa d.net.
"President Al-Assad's Speech to the New Government" (2011), 17 April, www.presidentassa d.net/.
"President Bashar Al-Asad's a Speech at the People's Assembly" (2011), 30 March, www.presidentassad.net/.
"President Bashar Al-Assad's January 6th, 2013 Speech" (2013), 6 January, www.presidenta ssad.net/.
Reese, A. (2013), "Sectarian and Regional Conflict in the Middle East", Middle East Security Report, Institute for the Study of War, Washington, DC.
Rosen, Nir (2012), "Q&A: Nir Rosen on Syrian sectarianism", Al Jazeera English, 18 February, www.aljazeera.com/indepth/features/2012/02/2012218165546393720.html.
Shadid, Anthony (2011), "Syrian Unrest Stirs New Fear of Deeper Sectarian Divide", *New York Times*, 13 June.
Shehadi, Nadim (2011), "Syria: Violence as a Communications Strategy", European Union Institute for Security Studies (EUISS), 16 August, www.iss.europa.eu/fr/publications/deta il-page/article/syria-violence-as-a-communications-strategy/.
Shehadi, Nadim (2013), "Revolution or Civil War. The Battle of Narratives in Syria", OpenDemocracy, 29 March.

Smyth, P. (2013), "Hizballah Cavalcade: What is the Liwa'a Abu Fadl al-Abbas (LAFA)?: Assessing Syria's Shia 'International Brigade' Through Their Social Media Presence", Jihadology, May, http://jihadology.net/2013/05/15/hizballah-cavalcade-what-is-the-liwaa-abu-fadl-al-abbas-lafa-assessing-syrias-shia-international-brigade-through-their-social-media-presence/.

"Speech Delivered by H.E. President Bashar al-Asad at the People's Assembly" 2012, 4 June, www.presidentassad.net/.

Spyer, J. (2012), "Syrian Regime Strategy and the Syrian Civil War", *Middle East Review of International Affairs*, 16:3, Fall, 43–50.

Syrian Muslim Brotherhood (2012) "We Will Establish a Democratic, Civil, Egalitarian State once Assad Is Ousted", MEMRI Report, Special Dispatch No. 4631, April 5, http://www.memri.org/report/en/print6250.htm

Syrian National Council (2012), "SNC Extends Hand to Alawite Community in Syria", *Naharnet Newsdesk* 26 February, www.naharnet.com/stories/en/31370.

Syrian Network For Human Rights (2016), "Most Notable Sectarian and Ethnic Cleansing Massacre", 16 June, http://sn4hr.org/blog/2015/06/16/8049/.

Syrian Revolution General Commission (2011), "Press Release", Arab Digest, 19 August.

The Syrian Local Coordinating Committees (2011c), LCC Statements, 16 June, http://www.lccsyria.org/923.

The Syrian Local Coordination Committees (2012b), "New Battalions Sign the Code of Conduct", Facebook update (Arabic page), 8 August,: www.facebook.com/note.php?note_id=508232342537240.

"The Syrian Revolution" (2011), Code of Ethics against Sectarianism in Syria, 24 March, https://www.facebook.com/syrian

The Supreme Council of the Syrian Revolution (2011), "Statement", 24 April, Facebook update (Arabic page), 22 May, https://www.facebook.com/pages/%D8%A7%D9%84%D9%85%D8%AC%D9%84%D8%B3-%D8%A7%D9%84%D8%A3%D8%B9%D9%84%D9%89-%D9%84%D9%84%D8%AB%D9%88%D8%B1%D8%A9-%D8%A7%D9%84%D8%B3%D9%88%D8%B1%D9%8A%D8%A9-Supreme-Council-of-Syrian-Revolution/116159318470147.

UN Independent International Commission of Inquiry on Syria (2012), "Syrian Government and opposition forces responsible for war crimes – UN panel", United Nations News Center, 15 August, www.un.org/apps/news/story.asp?NewsID=42687#.VrtxehjhDwd.

Varulkar, H., Barkan, L. & Green, R. (2013), "Following Nasrallah's Statements On Syria Fighting, Calls Emerge For Sunnis To Wage Jihad Against Hizbullah, Shiites", MEMRI Report, 6 June.

"Yusuf al-Qaradawi Calls on Muslims to Support the Rebels in Syria" (2013), The Meir Amit Intelligence and Terrorism Information Center, 16 June, www.crethiplethi.com/yusuf-al-qaradawi-calls-on-muslims-to-support-the-rebels-in-syria/global-islam/2013/.

Zelin, A. Y. & Smyth, P. (2014), "The Vocabulary of Sectarianism", *Foreign Policy*, 29 January.

16
SUNNI/ALAWI IDENTITY CLASHES DURING THE SYRIAN UPRISING
A continuous reproduction?

Ola Rifai

The Syrian Uprising created conditions for an ongoing fight for hegemony between a regime instrumentalizing Alawi identity and opposition groups instrumentalizing Sunni identity. The former co-existence between these identity groups was destroyed, with each party attempting to maximize its gains over the other. This chapter addresses the interaction between several elements that account for this conflict. The chapter is divided into three main sections: the first section provides a short historical background to the Sunni/Alawi identity clashes in modern Syria. The second section examines the orchestration of Sunni and Alawi identity clashes from above, focusing on the roles of the Syrian regime, the Sunni political entrepreneurs and the external state and non-state actors. The third section analyses the roles of symbolic features (such like flags and myths) in inciting identity clashes from below. Based on a qualitative research method, this chapter employs a discourse analysis technique. The chapter is based on fieldwork carried out by the author in Syria during the first two years of the Uprising. It should be noted that the chapter does not aim to limit the Syrian conflict to identity clashes, nor to disregard the fact that many Syrian Sunnis and Alawis adhere to a secular civil identity.

The identity puzzle in Syria (1946–2011)[1]

The Alawi/Sunni identity clashes that exploded during the Uprising seem to be rooted in Syria's modern history. Although Syria enjoyed relative sectarian stability during the Asads' tenure, the Uprising indicates that the problem of identity was buried away rather than addressed. Present-day Syria came into existence as a result of the political game of the Western great powers that imposed arbitrary borders after WWI on a heterogeneous community. Therefore, neither a solid national identity nor a sense of nationhood underpinned the creation of the Syrian state.

Instead, sectarian cleavages persisted and were thereafter aggravated by political conflicts (Kessler 1987).

Alawites are followers of the Alawite sect, an offshoot of Shiite Islam, comprising an estimated 12% of Syria's total population, inhabiting the coastal areas in the interior lowlands east of the Alawite Mountains, the mountains themselves and the rural areas around cities of Homs and Hama. In recent decades tens of thousands migrated to Damascus. Throughout its history, the Alawi community has been persecuted politically, socially and economically, and was dominated by a hostile Sunni community that disparaged the Alawi religious beliefs. After the Ba'th Party, dominated by Alawi officers, took power in 1963, parts of the Sunni majority (making up an estimated 69% of the population), perceived the Alawis as an non-Islamic group that sought hegemony over them (Faksh 1984).

In this context, Syria's late president Hafiz Asad (1971–2000), a master in the art of *realpolitik*, attempted to build his regime on a cross-sectarian coalition and to construct a balance between the Alawi and Sunni identity groups, yet he took a contradictory approach. Since Asad belonged to the Alawi minority, he adopted a Khaldounian/neo-patrimonial strategy to build his regime. This strategy relied on Alawi *assabiyya* 'group feeling' (Tibi 1997)[2] to forge a coherent elite, commanding high-ranking positions in political and military institutions. Indeed, Alawi *assabiyya* signifies the backbone of the Asad regime and, notwithstanding that Asad never engaged in direct sectarian rhetoric, he covertly exploited the Alawi identity and encouraged Alawis to view the regime as 'theirs' without ever admitting this publicly (Hinnebusch 2012) which provoked Sunnis and Alawis to perceive each other as rivals. Yet, at the same time, Asad sought to contain the risk the Sunni majority might pose to his rule and he shrewdly constructed a social contract with the Sunni peasantry in the rural areas and also crafted an alliance with urban Sunnis (ibid). Indeed, Asad employed carrot-and-stick tactics, carrots vis-à-vis most Sunnis, while wielding the stick against his most powerful Sunni adversary of that time, the Muslim Brotherhood. In February 1982, Asad suppressed a Sunni rebellion in Hama that was seeking to overthrow his regime on the grounds that it was Alawi. Nevertheless, soon afterward, he aimed to 'accommodate and empower the apolitical Islamic organizations' (Khatib 2012, 29). By doing so, Asad sought to establish a modus vivendi with the Sunni majority and to foster a state-controlled Islam.

Bashar Asad inherited the presidency in June 2000 but failed to protect the fragile balance his father had constructed. As Carsten Wieland argues, during Bashar's tenure 'the regime had become more Alawite compared to Hafez's time' (Wieland 2012, 74). A good indicator is his removal of some of the Sunni old guard of Hafiz's regime such as the former vice president, Abdul al-halim Khaddam, and the former Chief of staff Hikmat Shihabi. Moreover, Bashar advanced an economic liberalization project that unintentionally damaged the delicate balance between the identity groups. Its effect was to empower the elite, whether Sunni or Alawite, and was mainly directed towards the benefit of the big cities, like Damascus and Aleppo whilst neglecting the socio-economic conditions of other cities and towns, such like Dar'a (southern Syria) and Banias (western Syria). This, subsequently, widened the socio-economic gaps and demolished the social contract that Hafez Asad strove to establish with Sunni workers, peasants and members of the rural class (Hinnebusch 2012). In fact, Bashar's policies enriched a loyal group of crony capitalists, such as Bashar's first cousin, Rami Makhlouf, who played a vital role in triggering Sunni resentment against the Alawis since he enjoyed a monopoly over key economic sectors (Bloomfield 2011). Although the crony capitalists included some Sunni businessmen, like Ratib al-Shalah and Mohamed Hmashu, other urban Sunnis were excluded. Hereafter, in the eyes of many Sunnis, Bashar's economic project was limited to the regime-connected cronies who were drawn from his clan and the Sunni bourgeoisie. This fostered what became reinforcing class/communal cleavages. Not surprisingly, offices belonging to Makhlouf were among the buildings targeted by Sunni protesters in Dar'a during the early days of the 2011 Uprising. Yet, it has to be noted that many Sunnis who benefited from the regime policy stood with the Asad regime against the Uprising.

Indeed, in parallel with the fostering of cross-sectarian crony capitalism, Bashar sought to co-opt the Islamic movements and to advance the arrangements that his father crafted with Sunni factions (Khatib 2012). Thus, he gave a free hand to Sufism, a largely non-political tradition of Sunnism. Nevertheless, his tactical alliance with Sufis in Damascus did not mend fences with all Sunnis of Syria, particularly with those of the remote areas who were deprived as a result of the regime's neo-liberal approaches. Furthermore, in addition to his manipulation of the Sufi identity, Bashar instrumentalized the Salafis for *realpolitik* gains. During the early years of the 2000s, Bashar allowed some Syrian Salafis to infiltrate Iraq to counter the US, unwittingly bolstering a Salafi sentiment that was at odds with his supporters among the Sufis, the Alawis and the secularists. In short, Bashar Asad's policy contained myriad flaws that contributed to inflaming identity conflicts.

This is not to say that policies of the Asad dynasty are solely responsible for the eruption of identity clashes during the Uprising. Rather, as has been argued above, in the establishment of the current Syrian state, a concrete national identity was not achieved and each sectarian group was seeking empowerment within the state. Nevertheless, the Asads' instrumentalization of sectarianism to bolster their regime caused more fragmentation in an already fractured national identity and played the identity game in a way that eventually backfired on the dynasty and on the country.

Orchestrating Sunni and Alawite identity clashes from above

The Syrian regime rhetoric vis-à-vis the Uprising: playing with sectarian fire?

From its very beginnings, the Syrian regime saw the Uprising as endangering its very existence. Its strategy was to crush the Uprising and only once this was accomplished to institute some reforms to contain future rebellion. However, this approach only served to exacerbate the 'crisis'. Observers agree that the regime played the sectarian card since the outbreak of the Uprising by inciting the Alawi religious minority to fight against a Sunni-dominated opposition, and by continuously accusing Sunni fundamentalists of *tatiyyf* ('sectarianization') of the 'crisis'. In parallel, the regime strove to promote itself as the only entity capable of preventing civil war and of maintaining sectarian stability (International Crisis Group (ICG) 2012).

Within its broader strategy two phases can be identified in its approach to the Uprising, both of which have had significant repercussions on the ongoing construction of Alawi and Sunni identities. These strategies have been labelled as *al-hal al-'amny* (security solution) and *al-hal al-'askary* (military solution). The security solution was activated in April 2011, and denotes the deployment of the security services and *Shabiha*. *Shabiha* refers to the pro-Asad militias that consist mainly of Alawis, and which played a vital role in attempting to suppress the Uprising. According to an Alawi resident of Homs, with relatives working with a *Shabiyha* network in Damascus, a *Shabiyh* (singular of *Shabiha*) earns around $300 per month and works an eight-hour day.[3] In Arabic, *Shabiha* derives from the word *Shabah*, meaning 'ghost'. Originally, it referred to the Alawi mafia that operated during the 1970s under Rifat al-Asad (uncle of Bashar Asad), and which 'smuggled contraband, all the while earning a reputation for unrelenting violence' (*Middle East Online*). Unlike the security services, who are official employers at governmental institutions, *Shabiha* networks were not formally registered as government forces, despite having been funded and armed by the regime and some of its patrons. The Syrian intelligence services and the *Shabiha* consisted mainly of Alawi conscripts, whose main mission was to punish anti-Asad activists, the majority of whom were Sunnis.

With the eruption of the Uprising, these loyalist forces frequently besieged and attacked mosques in rebel areas that were the primary sites for anti-Asad protests, and which were mainly to be found in Sunni districts. A case in point is Jdiyydyt 'Artuz in northern Damascus. In this neighborhood *Shabiha* resided in *Masaken al-Hars* ('Guards' Houses'), established in 1998, a type of residential compound located north of Jdiyydyt 'Artuz where Alawi officers and soldiers reside with their families. During the Uprising, these informal Alawi forces besieged the central mosque in Jdiyydyt 'Artuz and attacked protesters.[4] This situation also applied to Homs, where *Shabiha* of the muhajreen quarter (a lower-class district at the edges of eastern Homs predominated by Alawis), cracked down on protesters in the nearby Dyr-B'lba area, which is inhabited mainly by Sunnis. According to an Alawi resident of Homs, *Shabiha* of muhajreen played an essential role in protecting Alawi neighbourhoods: 'Muhajreen's *Shabiha* protected our areas. Without them, the Sunnis would have smashed us'.[5]

Notably, forces loyal to the regime often displayed identifiers of their communal belongings, such as the Zulfiqar sword, a sword with two blades that the Prophet Mohamed gave to his cousin, Ali bin abi Talib – an icon for the Alawis as he represents the first Shi'i Imam (Muhaiyaddeen 2002). Many members of the Shabiha revealed tattoos that depicted their religious identity. For instance, one member's tattoo was a piece of Arabic script, which read *ya Ali* ('Oh Ali') referring to Ali bin abi Taleb. Moreover, members of the security forces and *Shabiha* spoke with strong Alawi accents while undertaking their missions.[6] Additionally, *Shabiha* and soldiers allowed themselves to be filmed as they tortured Sunni protesters while speaking in tough Alawi accents. Such videos were widely circulated among Syrians on social media and on other online mainstream networks, and they elicited a collective radicalization of Sunni identity. Whether these were authentic or not and if authentic, whether or not it was intended, what such videos did was to further catalyse the reinforcement of sectarian identities amongst the various identity groups.

The regime loyalist forces' looting of houses in opposition zones (and the selling of these looted items in public markets established mostly in Alawi districts) further heightened sectarian animosities. These markets were dubbed as *souq al-sunnih li al-masrwqat* ('the Sunni market for looted items'). One popular market was located nearby Masaken Al-hars in the mu'damiyaa area, northern Damascus. Here, furniture and electronic devices like LCD televisions and iPads were displayed under huge portraits of Asad, and in which the salesmen were members of the Alawi identity group.[7] Certainly, looting is a natural consequence of civil war, but the deliberate and targeted exploitation in this case, constitutes an act of sectarian aggression and violation of the Other's identity. Consequently, the looting helped to inflame Sunni-Alawi communal identity polarization.

The regime's security solution actually exacerbated the 'crisis' as the violence used against protesters turned more and more Syrians against the regime. Most importantly, the Alawis' involvement in combating the rebels resulted in a Sunni counter-mobilization. When, in consequence, protesters in huge numbers marched in central squares of cities like Hama and Homs while chanting anti-Asad slogans, this scared the regime as it mimicked scenes from the uprisings in Egypt and Libya. Therefore, in February 2012, the regime's 'security solution' was upgraded to a 'military solution', which involved the nationwide deployment of the Syrian army and heavy shelling of rebel regions. Homs, in western Syria, was the first zone to be subjected to this military solution, with bombardments targeting Sunni areas such as Bab-'Amur. The fact that the Alawi quarter in the very same district remained unharmed by the shelling helped to fuel sectarian clashes. Furthermore, these areas were not subjected to the same humanitarian crisis resulting from fuel and food shortages as the Sunni districts were subjected to. An Alawi resident of al-nizha gave an eyewitness account of the situation at the time: 'Life looks very normal here. Most shops are open, flour and fuel are available. You can see people smoking shisha at the coffee shops. We hear the shelling next door, we try to act normally, but all of us are afraid. None of us dares to leave *hartu* ('his alley')'.[8]

In essence, by deploying Alawi-dominated forces, the Syrian regime projected the Uprising as an anti-Alawi movement, and as a result, Alawis were made to feel that they were fighting for their communal survival. Certainly, the attitudes of many anti-Asad Sunnis have verified the claims of the regime and hence, many Alawis could not perceive any alternative way of surviving, other than fighting for the regime. In this light, the *security dilemma* played on Alawi fears, constructing an

Alawi identity at odds with that of the Sunnis. A 28-year-old Alawi of Latakia expressed fears for the Alawis fate in post-Asad era:

> Although Latakia is relatively calm, we are extremely afraid. They [anti-Asad Sunnis] claim that they will forgive those Alawis who do not have blood on their hands. But how they would be able to identify every single Alawi who has blood on his hands? And what would happen to us if the regime failed? I keep asking myself.[9]

It is worth noting here that this chapter does not suggest that all Alawis are united in their stances vis-à-vis the Uprising. Rather, it argues that the Syrian regime instrumentalized Alawis for *realpolitik* ends. More importantly, the *security dilemma* interacts with the regime policies and triggered the majority of Alawis to support Asad for their own survival. Indeed, the insecurity crisis has provoked Alawis who reside in ethnically mixed areas to flee to the villages that they originally came from. Manar, a 26-year-old Sunni of Jdiyydyt 'Artuz explains that, with the escalation of violence, Alawi men of Masaken el-Haras evacuated their families for fear that they would be executed. This, in his eyes, is a likely prospect in a post-Asad era. Manar blames not only the regime for initiating the clashes between Alawis and Sunnis, but also those Alawis who, according to him, have allowed themselves to be manipulated by the regime. In his words:

> Prior to the Uprising, Alawis of Masaken al-Haras seemed to integrate fairly well with the Sunnis of 'Artuz town. They used to send their children to schools in Jdiyydyt 'Artuz and do their shopping there. Everything looked normal at that time, but after the Uprising I do not think that these Alawis would be able to live peacefully with us again. I do not know what would happen, but what I'm sure about is that in a post-Asad era, Masaken al-Haras would not stand there anymore. Not a single Alawite would be allowed to stay there. Too much blood has been shed by them.[10]

As the conflict continued to escalate, several incidents of mass killing were reported, particularly in areas that are divided across ethnic lines and in which each identity group tended to blame the other for perpetrating such killings. A case in point was the massacre in al-Houla, a tiny town northwest of Homs that is dominated by Sunnis. The massacre took place on the evening of 25 May 2012 when armed men killed 92 Sunni civilians, including 32 children. The Syrian regime accused 'terrorist gangs', while Sunni rebels claimed that the perpetrators were Alawis from the bordering town of al-Qabu, which is mostly populated by Shiite and Alawis (CNN 2013). A second case in point took place in Jdiyydyt 'Artuz on the 1 August 2012 in which, Sunni residents of 'Artuz interviewed by the author, claimed that Alawis of Masaken al-Haras executed some 35 anti-Asad Sunnis. However, only one week before the massacre, Sunni rebels of Jdiyydyt 'Artuz kidnapped three Alawi men from Masaken al-Haras (*Huffington Post* 2012). Graphic videos of the brutal killings that showed how some of the dead had been killed with knives or blunt objects spread like wildfire. In March 2013, a United Nations Human Rights report affirmed that Asad's forces had 'commit[ed] mass killings which are at times sectarian in nature' (cited in *Huffington Post* 2013).

Yet, the report stresses that both sides were guilty of carrying out violations against civilians during the conflict, and that Sunni militants executed Alawi militiamen and established detention centres in Homs and Aleppo. This is corroborated by the enormous number of video clips uploaded to the Internet that showed Sunni militants torturing Alawites. Some Sunnis applauded these videos, while others strongly denounced the brutal sectarian violence.[11] Despite the fact that the authenticity of these videos and the accuracy of the reports of mass killings cannot be guaranteed, their existence gives a broad indication of the nature of the insecurity crisis that each identity group was confronting. This situation served to intensify the identity clashes.

The Syrian regime's security and military solutions vis-à-vis the Uprising ultimately failed to quell it. At the heart of these policies rested a reversion to communal solidarities – *assabiyya* based on sectarian, familial or tribal ties. The Asad regime was able to exploit *assabiyya* to mobilize Alawis from different socio-economic backgrounds, from lower-class neighbourhoods like Muhajreen in Homs to the ranks of the elite, of which Asad's cousin and business magnate Rami Makhlouf was a member. Together, these socially disparate Alawis would combine against the Uprising and link their survival explicitly to that of Asad. By inciting Alawis to engage in warfare with the Sunnis, the regime ignited strife between the Alawis and the Sunnis that had not been seen in centuries and destroyed the 30-year alliance that Asad senior had established with the Sunni community.

Shaping Sunni identity; Sufism, Salafism and Salafi-Jihadism

For many Sunni clerics and activists, the Syrian Uprising offered a unique opportunity to recast Syrian Sunni identity. Multiple Sunni actors used the Uprising to establish a Sunni orthodoxy and to mobilize the majority community in attempts to influence or take power. The following section examines the reproduction of three key trends in Syrian Sunni identity: Sufism, Salafism and Salafi-Jihadi.

The Sufi identity

Sufi identity is considered to be apolitical, as it does not seek the establishment of an Islamic state. Rather, it focuses on promoting Islamic principles among individuals to advance the self-regulation of society. Some of the Sufi ulama (such as Ramadan al Buti) opted to support Asad – fearing a Salafi take over – while others decided to support the Uprising. Sheikhs Usama Rifai and Kraiyym Rajih, represent powerful Sufi players who, prior to the Uprising, enjoyed great influence over Damascene Sunni religious society. The grassroots support for these clerics stemmed from the Damascene upper and middle classes, and had a strong influence over the

Kafrsuseh, Midan, and Malki quarters of Damascus, upper- and middle-class areas, inhabited mostly by Sunni Damascenes. In the early months of the Uprising, protests exploded from the mosques where Rifai and Rajih gave their Friday sermons. Both Sheihks aimed to reinforce a Sufi identity that is based on *al-Islam al-mu'tadel*, a moderate version of Islam. They backed the Uprising but sought to promote a particularly Sufi interpretation of Sunni identity. Unlike fundamentalists, Rifai and Rajih represented the Syrian Uprising as a popular movement to oust an authoritarian regime and not as a religious struggle against the Alawi faith. Neither of them promoted the creation of a theocracy. Instead, they advocated democracy and tolerance whilst emphasizing the significance of these norms in Islamic doctrines. For instance, in a broadcast interview, Rifai stressed the importance of pluralism and democracy in post-Asad Syria, claiming that: 'The Syrian revolution is for all shades of Syrian society ... after the fall of the regime, God willing, sectarianism will be erased from our history'.[12] In another interview, however, Rifai emphasized that Islamists should occupy supreme roles in Syrian politics after the Uprising: 'Islamists should be represented because they sacrificed their blood for the revolution while others were just watching'.[13] Unlike fundamentalists, Sufis did not use anti-Alawi discourse, nor did they promote a bellicose rhetoric in relation to secular ideologies. Also, unlike Salafis and Jihadis, these clerics were not funded by state or non-state actors. Rather, they relied on the Damascene elite, their longstanding social foundation, to fund their charitable networks that functioned mostly in Damascus.

The Salafi identity

One crucial consequence of the Syrian Uprising is the rise of Salafism as a potent movement that proved capable of crafting a power triangle consisting of arms, money and public support. Salafism is a strict form of Sunni Islam that seeks to revive *al-salaf al-salih*, a pure and authentic form of Islam. It aims to restructure the state and society in line with Quranic and Sharia law. Salafism is hostile 'towards other Islamic teachings like Sufism and Shia Islam' (Lund 2013, 5). Amidst the three-year-old conflict in Syria, Salafi groups struggled to reshape a Salafi identity for Sunni Syrians, an identity that excluded Syrians who adopted different religious ideas.

Among Salafi Sheikhs and activists, the most noticeable in the Damascus suburbs were Sheikh Zahran 'Alloush and Sheikh 'Adnan 'Ar'our. 'Adnan 'Ar'our (b. 1948) fled his hometown of Hama to Saudi Arabia in 1982, owing to the regime's oppression of Hama's Islamist rebellion. During the 2011 Uprising, 'Ar'our emerged as a symbolic figure, and styled himself as its godfather. His discourse portrayed the Uprising as a Sunni movement that sought to achieve religious aims. He regularly appeared on the Salafi Satellite TV channels *wisal* and *shada al-hurriya* making anti-Alawi speeches in which he cited Salafi theorists and made rhetorical use of symbols from the Salafi tradition, particularly the Salafi flag. In a live-aired programme on *wisal*, 'Ar'our explicitly threatened to execute each Alawi who supported Asad, saying: 'I swear to God that we would grind the flesh of pro-regime Alawis and feed it to the dogs'.[14] Footage of 'Ar'our shaking a warning finger at the camera while vowing to kill pro-regime Alawis spread throughout the online community. Unsurprisingly, this fuelled the fire of sectarianism.

Another powerful Salafi actor was Sheikh Zahran 'Alloush, the leader of *Liwa' al-Islam* ('the Islam Brigade') which consisted of some 25,000 fighters. 'Alloush is a former Islamist prisoner, whom the Syrian regime set free in the early months of the Uprising. Thereafter, he established a base in his hometown of Duma, northern Damascus (Hamidi 2013). 'Alloush used hostile rhetoric towards Alawis, describing them as *kuffar* (atheists) and portraying the Uprising as a holy war against the Alawis. For example, during a graduation ceremony for Islam Brigade fighters, 'Alloush stressed that the motivations for the Uprising must be purely religious, stating that: '[We] are going to take up arms and to raise our flag [the Salafi flag] to fight for the sake of God and to destroy the *Kufr* '('atheism') and the *Kuffar* [referring to Alawis]'.[15] Moreover, in his official page on Twitter, 'Alloush accused Alawis of plotting to kill the Sunnis.

The Salafi-Jihadi identity

Among the many Salafist groups seeking to mobilize a transnational *jihad*, Nusra Front (NF) was the strongest. An al-Qaeda affiliated group formed in January 2012, it called for the establishment of an Islamic Caliphate and was distinguished from other Salafi groups in its adoption of an anti-Western agenda advocating global *jihad*. It won legitimacy as a result of its military prowess in the struggle with the regime. As a resident of Idlib puts it 'NF comprises the best fighters who are always on the frontline'.[16] Essentially, the NF portrays the Uprising as a religious struggle against Alawis and Shiites, while strongly denouncing any secular national affiliations. NF comprises both Syrian and foreign fighters – mainly Iraqis, Afghanis and Libyans – who flocked into Syria to participate in the *jihad*; on the other hand, NF's Syrian members are less captivated by the NF's Jihadi ideology than by the efficiency of its military operations. As one FSA soldier who was fighting with the NF stated: 'NF is an extremely professional paramilitary, it hits the regime in the eyes. I do not agree with their agenda or with their sectarian logic, but I want to get rid of Asad. Thus, I'm ready to collaborate with the devil to achieve this end.'[17]

★★★

Sunni political entrepreneurs vary from moderate to extreme but all of them employed a sectarian discourse that prioritized explicit adherence to Sunnism, thus helping to incite identity clashes with the Alawis. Each of these actors concocted strategies for mobilizing followers and for asserting power over the others. Sufism sought to assert a moderate Sunni identity that acknowledged the norms of democracy. However passively, it still embodied the predominance of Sunni identity and accentuated the line between Sunnis and Alawis. Sufis remained concentrated among the urban elite and middle classes, their longstanding constituencies. Their foothold was fragile in comparison with that of the Salafis, as they did not have a military presence; suffered from association with Asad prior to and during the Uprising; and from a lack of the external economic, political and military support that the Salafis secured. On the other hand, Salafis acted to reproduce a fundamentalist Sunni identity that rejected all secular ideologies like nationalism, and which directed a bellicose rhetoric towards the Alawites. They managed to obtain grassroots support, money and military leverage. Many rural, middle and lower-class Sunnis perceived Salafism as a legitimate presence that fights effectively on the battlefield and paves the way for rural Sunnis to enter Syria's political theatre, contesting the power of the urban Sunnis newly established as a result of Bashar al-Asad's neo-liberal policies. They were divided between those whose *jihad* was confined within the territorial state and those that advocated global *jihad*; the former succeeded in mobilizing the rural middle classes while the latter mobilized the rural lower classes in remote areas as well as many non-Syrians who travelled to Syria to fight the regime. Nevertheless, the global jihadists chances of achieving hegemony were limited, as most Syrian Sunnis tended to reject their extremist version of Islamic caliphate.

The Shiite axis vs. the Sunni bloc: reproducing Sunni and Alawi identities from beyond the Syrian borders

Given Syria's geostrategic position and her potential as a regional actor, it is unsurprising that the repercussions of the Uprising reached beyond its borders. A radical change in Damascus would catalyse a drastic shift in the balance of the regional system and the ongoing conflict in Syria jeopardized the stability of all contiguous actors. Therefore, since the onset of the Uprising regional actors have been striving to minimize the risks while seeking *realpolitik* gains. Both the Sunni and the Alawi identity were vital instruments in the hands of regional actors vying for power. Unquestionably, this helped to inflame identity clashes. The policies of the so-called 'Shiite axis' (comprising Iran, Iraq and Hezbollah) and those of the 'Sunni-bloc' (represented mainly by some Gulf States and Turkey) manipulated sectarian identities in order to advance their interests. Each player sought to empower an identity group over the others by providing it political, economic and military support. This gave a sectarian trajectory to the Syrian Uprising, and sharpened its representation as a Sunni versus Shiite holy struggle.

The intimate involvement of Iran and Hezbollah had been acknowledged since the very beginning of the Uprising, as both actors have openly and fervently backed the Syrian regime. Certainly, the Syrian regime's survival is critical to Iran's regional power and, moreover, to Hezbollah's de facto existence. This is owing to the fact that Syria has long been a potent ally for both actors, as well as a conduit for providing weapons to Hezbollah. Therefore, Iran and Hezbollah struggled to defend their embattled ally and supplied the Asad regime with comprehensive political and military support. Furthermore, Hezbollah and Iranian fighters were shadowing the regime's forces in some sectarian mixed areas, mainly in the suburbs of Homs, which fuelled the Sunni versus Alawi clashes (Wood 2012). This led to the Free Syrian Army's (a Sunni-dominated anti-Asad militant group) capture in August 2012 of 48 Iranians who, according to the Syrian opposition, were members of the

Iranian Revolutionary Guards while Iranian official sources claimed that these were pious Shiite pilgrims. This kidnapping incident heightened the sectarian tensions, as it positioned Shiite and Alawi identity at odds with Sunni identity. The views of anti-Asad Sunnis interviewed by the author were exemplified by those of Abdullah, a Sunni of Homs: 'These Iranians are Shiite fighters, they are representing a Shiite theocracy allied to an Alawi regime. They came to Syria in order to empower their Alawi allies and to weaken the Sunnis.'[18] In January 2013, the Iranian detainees were released under a Turkish-sponsored deal by which the Syrian regime freed some 2,000 anti-Asad protesters. The Syrian State TV broadcasted footage of Iranian officials in Damascus giving a heroic welcome to the released hostages.

In a similar vein, Mehdi Taeb, a senior Iranian cleric, inflamed sectarian resentment in February 2013 by declaring Syria as an essential province of Iran: 'Syria is the 35th province [of Iran] and a strategic province for us. If the enemy attacks us and wants to take either Syria or Khuzestan [in western Iran], the priority for us is to keep Syria. If we keep Syria, we can get Khuzestan back too; but if we lose Syria, we cannot keep Tehran' (cited in Yaliban 2013). Taeb's statement dominated the news bulletins and fuelled the sectarian polarization, since it was perceived by many Sunnis as a clear indicator of the Shiite-Alawi alliance against the Sunnis. For many Alawis, on the other hand, this statement strengthened their stance in relation to the Sunnis. According to Aseel, a 26-year-old Alawi of Damascus: 'Taeb's declaration assures that they will defend us against them until the end'.[19]

Paralleling Iran's rhetoric is the official discourse by Hezbollah leader, Hasan Nassrallah, who, since the beginning of the Uprising, expressed a steadfast commitment to the Syrian regime and portrayed the popular movement as a conspiracy against the so-called 'resistance axis'. Although Nasrallah denied any physical presence of his party in Syria during the first two years of the Uprising, he did admit that Syrian Shiites in villages on the border with Lebanon 'took up arms to protect themselves from the armed-gangs there [in reference to the Sunni militias]' (Nasrallah 2013).

Hezbollah's solidarity with the Syrian regime was interpreted as backing for Shiite identity in its struggle against the Sunni identity, hence accelerating the sectarian narrative. As a result, Nasrallah's approach towards the Uprising resulted in a radical decline in his popularity among most Syrians, who for two decades had regarded him as a national hero: the cross-sectarian legitimacy that Nasrallah once used to enjoy was destroyed, and his status as a hero turned to that of a Shiite enemy (Barnard 2012). As a Sunni resident of Damascus expressed it: 'Nasrallah is backing Asad because a Shiite would support an Alawi and not a Sunni. Resistance is only a cover for Hezbollah sectarian ends'.[20]

In this context, the discourse of the former Iraqi Prime Minister, Noury Maliki, seems to overlap with Iran and Hezbollah's approaches towards the Uprising. With the eruption of the Uprising, Maliki expressed his vocal support for the Syrian regime. As he is the Shiite leader of a government that is considered to be part of the Shiite axis, Maliki's stances were framed in a Shiite and Alawi versus Sunni perspective. Moreover, in a controversial statement, Maliki emphasized the sectarian nature of the Uprising that, in his words, forced the Alawites in Syria to fight 'bravely by their men and by their women in order to survive' (Al-Arabiya 2013). Certainly, such a commentary indicated the sectarian grounding of Maliki's attitudes towards the Uprising, and heightened the tension between Alawis and Sunnis by portraying the Alawi identity as an endangered species fighting for its survival. Notably, sectarian tension extended to Iraq in late 2012, when Iraq's Shiite-led government faced several protests from Sunnis angered by perceived discrimination. The protests erupted from the Sunni stronghold of Falluja and rapidly spread to other Sunni Arab areas of Iraq. Some Syrian Sunni rebels praised these 'anti-Shiite' demonstrations in Iraq and linked them to the Syrian Uprising. For instance, anti-Asad activists proposed *Souriyya wa al-Iraq: thawra tutfi' nar al-majows* ('Syria and Iraq: a revolution that will quench the fire of the Magi' [in reference to the Shiites and to the Alawites]) as the title for the protest in Syria on 8 March.[21] Although Maliki opted not to intervene militarily in Syria, Iraqi forces at the border areas provided a defensive cover for the Syrian regime; for example, in the early months of 2013, sporadic clashes occurred between Syrian rebel forces and Iraqi troops safeguarding Asad's forces on the border (CBS news 2013). In June 2014 a jihadist group with links to fighters in Syria, which later turned into the Islamic state in Iraq and Syria (ISIS), seized several cities in northern Iraq and by late June, Iraq lost its control over the border with Syria and Jordon (BBC 2014). It vigorously promoted the struggle in both countries as a Sunni war against the Alawis and the Shiites.

On the other hand, political, economic and militarily support given to the Syrian Sunni rebels by Turkey and some of the Gulf States also heightened the sectarian narrative and seemed to instigate identity clashes, since their involvement was portrayed as part of a broader struggle against the Shiite axis in the region. In fact, each of these players exploited Sunni identity by empowering Sunni-dominated factions of the opposition against pro-Asad forces dominated by Alawis and supported by the Shiite axis. This is the message of the media coverage of the Gulf States, such as *Al-Jazeera* Satellite TV network in Qatar and the *Al-Arabiya* Satellite TV network in Saudi Arabia. These networks broadcast sectarian logic and played integral roles in reproducing sectarian identities (Kessler 2012). In parallel, non-Syrian Salafi Sheikhs who were supported by some Gulf States played crucial roles in triggering identity clashes, since they characterized the Uprising as an anti-Alawi/anti-Shiite movement. Some examples of these Sheikhs are Ahmed Asyr of Lebanon and Nabil al-'Audy of Kuwait who endorsed anti-Shiite and anti-Alawi logic and described the Uprising as a fight for existence between the Shiites and the Sunnis in the region. For instance, in one of his speeches, Asyr declared: 'Hezbollah is sending his soldiers to kill our [Sunnis] siblings and to rape our women' (Asyr 2013). Asyr was funded by Salafi networks based in Lebanon and in Saudi Arabia. He also ran a charity network that supplied humanitarian aid to Syrian refuges in Lebanon, and light weaponry to militants in the suburbs of Homs.[22] Moreover, both of these Sheikhs often cited Ibn Taimiyya, a medieval scholar (d. 1328) who issued the controversial declaration that Alawis are *murtadon* 'apostates' (Kazimi

2010). They sought to project the Syrian Uprising as a holy war against the 'Shiite threat'. For example, in a televised speech, Audi praised Syrian Sunni militants for confronting the Shiite agenda: 'Syrian Sunni rebels are facing the biggest and the most dangerous project for the Islamic Umma [which is] the Safavid project [in reference to Shiites]'.[23]

External actors played integral roles in constructing Sunni versus Alawite identity clashes, shaping sectarian discourse and feeding popular public imagination through new media sources. On the one hand, the vocal and visible support that the Shiite axis gave to the Syrian regime triggered a backlash from the Sunnis who perceived it as backing Alawis against Sunni rebels, since the fall of the Asad regime would fracture the Shiite axis and empower the Sunni bloc. On the other hand, the political, economic and military support that Sunni state and non-state actors gave to the Sunni rebels reinforced the Alawi identity. From an Alawi perspective, these actors threatened Alawi security and sought to make Sunni identity dominant in the region. Moreover, the anti-Alawi discourse used by non-Syrian Sunni political entrepreneurs helped to incite identity clashes, as each of them sought to reinforce the Sunni identity against the Alawi identity. This characterized the struggle as being crucial to the survival of each identity group. Therefore, despite being outsiders, external actors seem to be capable of redrawing the ethnic boundaries inside Syria. Their discourses played pivotal roles in prioritizing sectarian sentiment over national affiliation and henceforth producing transnational affiliation by which a Syrian Sunni might associate his or her identity with a Saudi Sunni fighting against a Syrian Alawite. Equally, a Syrian Alawite may feel an affinity with a Shiite Lebanese fighting against a Syrian Sunni.

Sunni identity vs. Alawi identity: the reproduction from below

Identity clashes are not simply manufactured from above. Symbols and myths also operated at the grassroots level, and their symbolic power was unleashed when the *security dilemma* reached a crisis, igniting identity clashes from below. Sectarian symbols, slogans, songs and jokes highlighted the boundaries between 'us' and 'them', reinforcing identities and inciting clashes between identity groups. Throughout the Uprising, several slogans chanted by Sunni rebels were explicitly inciting identity clashes, since they conveyed anti-Alawi sentiment. The most controversial example is the Sunni vow to cleanse Syria of Alawis: *al-alwiyyah la al-qubour w al-masiyhyyah la Beirut*, 'Alawis to graves and Christians to Beirut'. Another similar example is *bidna nbyd al-alwiyyah*, 'we want to massacre the Alawis'. These slogans were sung by some anti-Asad Sunnis and began to be expressed around the fifth month of the Uprising. Unsurprisingly, they elicited collective responses of anger and fear among the Alawis. An anti-Asad Alawi activist recounted this experience while she was taking part in a protest in the town of Yabroud, north of Damascus: 'We were chanting 'the people want to overthrow the regime', and then suddenly, couple of protesters yelled 'we want to massacre the Alawites'.

Rapidly, the rest of the protesters reiterated this slogan. I stood aside while watching the crowd. I felt afraid about my future and about Syria's future.'[24]

Likewise, slogans were repeated by Alawi forces loyal to the Asad regime such as: *Shabiyyha lil abad la'ajl 'ayunak ya Asad* '[we will remain] *Shabiyyha* forever, for your eyes oh Asad'. A similar one says: *ya Bashar la tihtam 'andak sh'ab byshrab dam* ('Oh Bashar, do not worry, you have people who drink blood').[25] These Pro-Asad Alawis also flaunted indicators of their communal belonging, such as the Zulfiqar sword and the Alawi accent.[26]

In parallel, flags waved in the conflict visibly advocated particular identities over others. For example, the black flag emblazoned with Arabic script that reads, 'there is no God but God', was flown by transnational jihadists while they chanted *al-sh'ab yuryd al-khilafa Islamiyya*, 'the people want the establishment of an Islamic Caliphate'. Similarly, the green or the white flag with the same writing is associated with the Salafis and was often flown by Sunni rebels chanting Islamic slogans, like *qa'idna li al-abad saydna Mohamed* ('Our leader forever is our prophet Mohamed'),[27] anti-Shiite slogans such as *la Iran w la Hezbollah, bidna Muslim ykhaf Allah*, 'neither Iran nor Hezbollah, we want a Muslim who fears God'. On the other hand, slogans against the Sunni bloc were commonly shouted during pro-Asad rallies. One popular anti-Qatari slogan runs: *il ma bysafi'. 'amu qatariyya*, 'you are a son of a Qatari if you do not applaud'. Another slogan says: *bi saraha w 'al makshouf 'ikhwanji ma bedna nshouf*, 'frankly and openly, we do not want to see any member of the Muslim brotherhood'.[28] Seen in this light, the regime's forces (particularly *Shabiyyha*) attached the Syrian flag to portraits of Asad while writing anti-Islamist and anti-Uprising graffiti, such as *la 'ilah ila Bashar* ('No God but Bashar'), *al Asad aw la ahad* ('either Asad or no one') and *al-Asad aw nahriq al-balad* ('either Asad or we will burn the country').[29] Such graffiti directly linked the fate of the Alawites to that of Bashar Asad and, henceforth, characterized Alawi identity as an endangered identity group, struggling for its survival against the Sunnis. Likewise, from the onset of the Uprising many Alawi singers produced pro-Asad songs that were commonly sung during pro-Asad demonstrations and car rallies. In these car rallies, Alawi youths drove their tinted-windowed Mercedes and Range Rovers displaying pictures of Asad and the Zulfiqar sword. Playing these songs at high volume, the youths cruised around the upmarket districts of Damascus, such as Malki and Abu-rummanah. It should be noted that Damascenes would have known that these were Alawi youths, as they largely came from Alawi elite in Damascus, such like those of the Ismail, Ibrahim and Suliman families. Hence, all of the components (the songs, singers, pictures and the people displaying them) were associated with Alawite identity and reinforced it. One example of these songs is the one by Ali al-Dyk, which says 'Oh Bashar [Asad] whatever happens … we shall remain your soldiers.' Interestingly, in the middle of this song, there is a soundbite of Hassan Nasrallah saying 'life for Syria's Asad'.[30] A second example is a song by Wafiq Habib that runs: 'Oh Bashar do not worry, Syria is with you.'[31] A final example is a song by Hussein al-Dyk, that says: 'Syria is fine and our leader is fine … Oh Bashar your army is protecting the house.'[32]

Equally important in inciting identity clashes was the sectarian language adopted by a number of anti-Asad Sunnis. Some examples of this language are the sectarian names referring to militias, commanders and military operations. These names evoke Sunni symbols, such as the Sunni Hawks Militia and the Ibn Taimiyya Battalions. In addition, many Sunni Internet activists refer to Alawites as *qurud al-jabal* ('monkeys of the mountain'), which recalls the Alawis' history as a persecuted group. This sectarian discourse served to spread anti-Alawi sentiment, and to depict the Alawis as outsiders. A popular jihadi songs first sung in Idlib named: *shurta nusayriyya* ('nussayri police') goes: 'Oh Alawis wait, we are going to slaughter you … They say that I am a terrorist; I'm honored, I replied …'[33] A second song expresses the Uprising as an anti-Alawi fight: 'Oh you listen Bashar [Asad], Sunni people revolted, opened fire on *Shabiyyha* and murdered them.'[34]

Many sectarian jokes were also circulated amongst Syrians, which bolstered communal affiliations at the grassroots level. The following are some examples:

> A Sunni tells an Alawi, I can assure you a hundred percent that all Alawis will be treated fairly after the Uprising. All of them will be sent back to mountains to collect olives.
>
> How beautiful is the religious coexistence that we have in Syria. We have a mosque for Muslims, next to a church for Christians and just next to them stands a security branch for the Alawis.

By using sarcasm and irony, theses jokes express anti-Alawi and anti-Sunni affiliations and reproduce the sectarian identity of each group. In summary, symbols, songs, slogans, graffiti and jokes that express support or enmity for the Sunni or Alawite identity groups played a crucial role in reproducing sectarian identities at the grassroots level.

Conclusion

Throughout the Uprising, Sunni/Alawite identity clashes were provoked by internal and external actors, and by material and symbolic factors. The interaction between sectarian discourses directed from above and from below established the necessary context for the outbreak of identity clashes. The Asad regime and Sunni oppositionists both instrumentalized sectarian identities in the power struggle – to create enemies and to mobilize followers.

The regime's security and military solutions, in pitting Alawite-dominated forces against Sunni rebels, reproduced the Alawite identity and provoked sectarian action by the Sunnis. This served to embody the Uprising as a sectarian fight per se and linked Asad's survival to that of the Alawites themselves. On the other hand, the geopolitical alliances that the regime and the rebels enjoyed, manipulated identities for *realpolitik* gains, and thus fuelled sectarianism from without. Paralleling these discourses manufactured from above, sectarian symbolism took root at the grassroots, such like Zulfiqar sword and the Salafi flags, signified how an individual is different from the 'other', and emphasizing the 'otherness' by visibly excluding or including members of a specific identity group. Thus, these elements played significant roles in reproducing identity. Moreover, the *security dilemma* that affected both Alawites and Sunnis led both parties to believe that they were fighting for their survival, empowering sectarian identities and accelerating the outbreak of identity clashes. Indeed, top-down and bottom up sectarianism, reinforced each other, including and excluding members of a group, and inciting clashes. Are any of these identity groups capable of single-handedly winning this war? Can the hardening of these sectarian identities ever be reversed or subsumed under a common civic national identity? Would a material balance of power and power sharing between groups pave the way for tolerance of identity diversity? Or will the current identity clashes be suppressed by one materially victorious actor? If none is able to prevail over the other, will the outcome be a reconfiguration of territorial borders to reflect mutually exclusive identity groups? These questions are yet to be answered.

Notes

1 Some material in this section was previously published.
2 The Tunisian sociologist Ibn Khaldoun (d. 1406) defines *assabiyya* as 'the ties that enable a group to form a solidarity vis-à-vis other groups'.
3 Author's interview with an anonymous Alawite, 8/9/2012 in Damascus.
4 Fieldwork, *Jdiyydyt 'Rtuz* on 24/7/2012.
5 Author's interview with an anonymous Alawite via Skype 13/3/2013.
6 Fieldwork in Damascus and its suburbs, February – October 2012. As a reaction, many Sunni activists replaced the letter *qaf* in Arabic (which is stressed in the Alawite accent) with the letter *hamza* while writing commentaries on social media, which sparked a wave of criticism among Syrians.
7 Field work in mu'damiyaa on 1/6/2012 where the author conducted myriad of interviews with residents. Cited in *Syrian Center for Political and Strategic Studies*, scpss.org/en/?p=205.
8 Author's interview with an anonymous Alawite, 20/2/2012 email.
9 Author's interview with an anonymous Alawite, 4/4/2013.
10 Author's interview with Manar, 5/8/2012 in *jdiyydyt 'rtuz*.
11 For samples of such videos see ''idam al-Shabiyyha al-alawiyyn b'd tahrir sraqeb' ('The execution of an Alawite Shabiha after the liberalization of Saraqeb'), YouTube, accessed on 3/5/2013 available, at https://www.youtube.com/watch?v=Gv7hAJ-1HAU. Also see ''urqusi ya 'aniaa: 'idam al qanasa al-alawiyyn al-arb' fi die al-zour', ('Dance you Anysa' the execution of four Alawite snipers in Deir al-Zour), YouTube, accessed on 5/5/2013, available at https://www.youtube.com/watch?v=jGYkxRxhgy4.
12 'mudakhalt al-shikh Usama Rifai 'ala qanat oreiyyant' ('Interview with Usama Rifai on Orient Satellite TV station'), YouTube, accessed on 28/3/2013, available at http://www.youtube.com/watch?v=BCkjdMz8lYk.
13 al-jazeera: muqabala m' al-shikh Usama Rifai (Interview with Sheikh Usama Rifai *on al-Jazeera*), 29/12/2012. Accessed on 4/5/2013, available at https://www.youtube.com/watch?v=v5ZU_IBvNn8.
14 al-'ar'our sayafrum al-alawiyyn bil mulinkis w yut'im lahmahum lil kelab' ('ar'our will grind the Alawites by mulliniks and will feed their meat to dogs'), YouTube, accessed on 3/5/2013, available at: https://www.youtube.com/watch?v=WbkDiWZh2fI. Also see 'The Charm of Telesalafism', The Economist Website, accessed on 3/5/2013, available at: http://www.economist.com/news/middle-east-and-africa/21564913-influential-rebel-preacher-who-needs-tone-things-down.

15 'tadrybat wa takhrij duf'ah men abtal liwa' al-islam' ('exercises and graduation of the heroes of al-Islam Brigade'), YouTube, accessed on 6/10/2013, http://www.youtube.com/watch?v=tPT0rx1CTwA.
16 Author's interview, 1/8/2012.
17 Author's interview via Skype with an anonymous FSA soldier, 1/2/2013.
18 Author's interview with Abdullah, 6/8/2012, Damascus.
19 Author's interview with Aseel, 20/2/2013, via Skype.
20 Authors' interview with Maram, in Damascus 10/3/2012.
21 This sparked a heated debate among secular activists who opposed the sectarian discourse endorsed by the Syrian Revolution Page on Facebook. In response, some secular activists created a page on Facebook to refute this proposed name for Friday's protest. See 'no for the name of Friday's protest', Facebook, accessed on 3/11/2013, available at https://www.facebook.com/naralmjoss. Eventually, the Friday was not given this name, but was named 'Syrian women' instead, as 8 March marks the international women's day.
22 Author's interview with an anonymous Sunni activist associated with Asyr on 9/1/2013, Lebanon.
23 'Sermon of Damascene heroes and the Safavid project', 24/3/2012. Accessed on 09–01–2017 available on http://www.youtube.com/watch?v=0EE3SCkO64U&feature=youtube_gdata_player. 'Safavid project' refers to shi'ism as the former is a 13th century dynasty that ruled the Persian Empire and established the Twelver Shia Islam as its official religion and attempted to advance Shi'ism by military means.
24 Author's interview with an anonymous Alawite, 3/1/2013 in Beirut, Lebanon.
25 Fieldwork, Syria on 27/3/2012, at a pro-Asad mass rally in Damascus.
26 Fieldwork, Syria on 15/3/2012, at a pro-Asad mass rally in the Umayyad Square in Damascus, and on 20/4/2012 at pro-Asad mass rally in the sabi'a bahrat square in Damascus.
27 Fieldwork, Syria 2012 during protests in Lawan area in the suburb of Damascus on 4/5/2012, 30/5/2012 and 9/7/2012. Also, during a funeral for anti-Asad activists in Kafrsuseh, Damascus on 30/4/2012 and on 5/5/2012.
28 Fieldwork, Damascus on 3/3/2012 during a pro-Asad rally in Sabi' bahrat.
29 Fieldwork in Lawan on 21/3/2012. Also in Mazih area in Damascus on 8/3/2012; in Jdiyydyt 'artuz on12/7/2012 , and in Sahnaya suburb of Damascus on 2/6/2012.
30 hiyyw souriyya' ('Salute Syria'), YouTube, accessed on 3/11/2013, available at http://www.youtube.com/watch?v=F9mMVLAWRRw.
31 hiyyw souriyya' ('Salute Syria'), YouTube, accessed on 3/11/2013, available at http://www.youtube.com/watch?v=F9mMVLAWRRw.
32 'Souriyya bi khyr' ('Syria is fine'), YouTube, accessed on 2013, available at https://www.youtube.com/watch?v=0cN4Zn-3RNg .
33 It was uploaded on YouTube 'nashid min tfl souriyy mujahed' ('Song by a Syrian Mujahed child'), YouTube, accessed on 6/10/2013, available at http://www.youtube.com/watch?v=B6RCaUQEU4c .
34 jabhit al-nusra tuhni' al-muslimiyyn bi eid al-'adha' ('Nusra Front greets Muslims for Adha Eid'), YouTube, accessed on 3/11/2013, available at http://www.youtube.com/watch?v=r_BXDMvacW427/10/2012.

Bibliography

Al-Arabiyya (2013), 'Al-maliki; al-alwiyyn fi souriyya yuqatiloun bi shaja'it al ya's' ('Maliki: Alawites in Syria are fighting with the courage of despair'), *Alarabiya* website, accessed on 29/3/2013, available at: www.alarabiya.net/articles/2013/02/09/265327.html.
Barnard, Anne (2012), 'Loyalty to Syrian President Could Isolate Hezbollah', *New York Times* (5/4/2012).

BBC (2014), 'Iraq Conflict: militants 'Seize' City of Tal Afar', BBC Website, accessed on 2/7/2014, available at: www.bbc.com/news/world-middle-east-27865759.

Bloomfield, Adrian (2011), 'Syria; The Hardliners Responsible for State Brutality', *Telegraph Newspaper* (27/04/2011).

CBS (2013), 'Officials: 42 Syrian Troops Ambushed in Iraq', CBS news website, accessed on 28/3/2013, available at: www.cbsnews.com/8301-202_162-57572365/officials-42-syrian- troops-ambushed-in-iraq/.

CNN (2013), 'Why the Syrian Regime is Killing Babies', CNN website, accessed on 3/5/2013, available at: http://edition.cnn.com/2012/05/31/opinion/ghitis-syria-killing-children.

Faksh, Mhamud (1984), 'The Alawi Community of Syria: A New Dominant Political Force', *Middle Eastern Studies*, 20: 2 (April), 133–153.

Figueira, Daurius (2011), *Salafi Jihadi Discourse of Sunni Islam*, Bloomington, IN: Universe.

Hamidi, Ibrahim (2013), 'kata'ib Islamiyya souriyya tatawahad bi da'm iqlimy istibaqan li hal syasy' ('Syrian Islamist militias unit in an anticipation of a political solution'), *Alhayat* (6/10).

Hinnebusch, Raymond (2012), 'Syria: From Authoritarian Upgrading to Revolution', *International Affairs*, 88: 1, 95–113.

Huffington Post (2012), 'Syria Video Purport to Show New Killing in Jadeite Artuz', *Hufflingtonpost* website, accessed on 8/5/2013, available at: www.huffingtonpost.com/2012/08/02/syria-video-massacre-jdeidet-artouz_n_1733591.html.

Huffington Post (2013), 'Syria Massacres: Government Reportedly Using Local Militias for Mass Killings', *Huffingtonpost* website, accessed on 3/5/2013, available at: www.huffing tonpost.com/2013/03/11/syria-massacres-government_n_2851665.html.

International Crisis Group (ICG), 'Syria's Mutating Conflict', N 128–121 (Brussels and Damascus, August 2012), pp. 5, 6.

Kazimi, Nibras (2010), *Syria: Through Jihadist Eyes: A Perfect Enemy*, Stanford, CA: Hoover Institution Press.

Kessler, Martha Neff (1987), *Syria: Fragile Mosaic of Power*, Washington, DC: NDU.

Kessler, Oren (2012), 'The Two Faces of Al-Jazeera', *Middle East Quarterly* (Winter), 47–56.

Khatib, Line (2012), 'Islamic Revival and promotion of moderate Islam from above', in *State and Islam in Baathist Syria: Confrontation or Co-operation?*, St Andrews: University of St Andrews.

Lund, Aron (2013), 'Syria's Salafi Insurgents: The Rise of The Syrian Islamic Front' (UI Occasional papers #17 March 2013. Published by the Swedish institute of International Affairs).

Middle East Online (2013), 'The Rise of Shabiha', *Middle East Online* Website, accessed on 22/3/2013, available at: www.middle-east-online.com/english/?id=53322.

Muhaiyaddeen, M. R. Bawa (2002), *Islam & World Peace: Explanations of a Sufi*, Philadelphia, PA: Fellowship Press.

Nasrallah, Hassan (2013), 'Statement of Hezbollah Chief, Sayyed Hassan Nasrallah', Lebanonfile website, accessed on 13/3/2013, available at: http://lebanonfiles.com/news/511529.

Tibi, Bassam (1997), *Arab Nationalism: Between Islam and Nation State*, London: Macmillan Press.

Wieland, Carsten (2012), *A Decade of Lost Chances: Repression and Revolution from Damascus Spring to Arab Spring*, Seattle: Cune Press.

Wood, Josh (2012), 'Hezbollah Offering Direct Help to Syrian Army, Rebels Say', *New York Times*, 17 October.

Yaliban (2013), 'Iranian Cleric: Losing Syria is Like Losing Tehran', website, accessed on 29/3/2013, available at: www.yalibnan.com/2013/02/16/iranian-cleric-losing-syria-is-like-lo sing-tehran/. See also Tareq al-Hashemi, 'if we lose Syria we lose Tehran', *asharq al-aawsat* (17/2/2013).

17

THE RISE OF SYRIAN SALAFISM

From denial to recognition[1]

Issam Eido

Introduction

This chapter examines the emergence of Salafism in the current Syrian context. Is Salafism one thing or does it have different discourses and presences and what are they? What is the reality of Salafi existence inside Syria before and after the Syrian revolution?

Defining Salafism and its various manifestations

Salafism etymologically is derived from the word "salaf"[2] which means a return to the beginning and an adopting of the practices of the early Muslim community as the most suitable ideal for understanding the "pious life." Most Salafists reject "later generations" conduct and more specifically the foreign elements that don't fit with the initial authentic Islam and accordingly are considered "*bid'a*" which means religiously deviant innovation.[3] That being said, this definition is debated even among various Salafi factions.[4]

Salafism has tended to appear during times of crisis in the Muslim community, whether political or religious.[5] In these crisis moments, Salafi discourse as the identity of the Muslim community intensifies because it is seen as unifying all Muslims on the religion's primary texts, namely the Qur'an and sound canonical Sunna, the original sources of their cohesion.

In recent history, Salafism has witnessed diverse manifestations that can be outlined as follows. First, *Reform Salafism* emerged in the late nineteenth century and beginning of the twentieth century led by a number of prominent scholars such as Jamal al-Deen al-Afghani, Muhammad Abduh and Rasheed Rida.[6] Although all of them have a common approach, which is the necessity of returning to primary texts and bypassing the later legal tradition, they differ on other issues such as their attitudes towards relations with the Western world. The Levant reform school that Jamal al-Deen al-Qasimi led can also be included in this group.[7] Second, *Traditional Salafism* is concerned with the principles of Salafi methodology.[8] Nasir al-Deen al-Albani's works are considered the most important in this category and they define the core of the "Traditional Salafi" approach. In these books, al-Albani discussed two key terms: *tasfiya* (purification) and *tarbiya* (individual upbringing). The former is concerned with returning to the authentic primary texts of the Qur'an and the Sunnah (statements of the Prophet Muhammad) via the two sciences of *'ilm usul al Hadith*[9] and *'ilm al Takhreej*,[10] which seek to classify authentic and inauthentic hadith, with the former surpassing the authority of the jurists (*fuqaha'*). The latter, *tarbiya*, focuses on the importance of individual's following authentic prophetic and religious teachings in their private religious affairs. An individual's self-reformation is seen as having public consequences, as exemplified in the statement of al-Hudaiby, "if you apply the state of Islam in your hearts, then this state will be reality in your land" (Abdul Mun'im Salim 2008: 20). Traditional Salafi discourse is concerned in particular with individual reformation through returning to the authentic primary texts and rejects the idea that political issues are a primary goal of human beings. According to Traditional Salafi, the goal of human beings is to worship God and follow His commandments. On this point, their discourse is similar to Sufi teachings, with a focus on the piety of a Muslim and self-reformation; indeed, al-Albani's definitions of these terms (*tasfiya* and *tarbiya*) share the same linguistic meaning that Sufism ascribes to them (Abdul Mun'im Salim 2008: 21–22). Third, *Jihadi Salafism* is a branch of the Salafi discourse that is consistent with the other two approaches in that the main idea is returning to authentic primary texts and bypassing the legal schools, but differs with these others by containing a violent political dimension. This political and violent dimension can be either local, focusing on oppressive and infidel regimes, or global, focusing on infidel global regimes that are considered enemies of Islam and Muslims (International Crisis Group 2012).

Syrian Salafism before the revolution

The Ba'th regime has striven since 1970 to bring all Islamic communities and discourses under its control in two parallel ways. On the one hand, the regime sought to eliminate all types of opposition Islamic thought by banning or repressing it;[11] Salafism and the Muslim Brotherhood were two of the many opposition groups which the Ba'th regime strived to exclude from Syria in the aftermath of the Islamist Uprising of 1978–82. Hafiz al-Asad, in his speech on June 30, 1979 said: "they [the Muslim Brotherhood] have exploited the atmosphere of freedom in order to tempt some young people into committing crimes and to cause [them] to become enemies of Islam. We cannot be lenient with this group, which has committed various acts of murder and one of the most odious massacres ever known in the history of Islam" (Van Dam 1996: 95). Most Syrian Salafis fled the country, were arrested, or killed.[12] From the 1980s, the Salafis, in particular jihadi Salafism, and the Muslim

Brotherhood disappeared in Syria and no longer had a noticeable influence on the masses. This was assisted by the fact that traditionally the Syrian people embrace moderate interpretations of Islam that refuse political violence.[13]

The Ba'th regime also worked at co-opting religious discourse in order to make it politically passive and focused on the private religious reform of individuals. This resulted in most *'ulama* and their students vilifying and distorting the Salafi discourse and there was no critical work that criticized this discourse seriously even from within local academia.[14] Throughout the Ba'th period many official and semi-official religious institutes were founded that remained apolitical, which were directly or indirectly associated to the regime (Pierret 2011: 64–100) and promoted a discourse mostly conforming with the regime's version of reality.[15] While the regime gave its blessing to these new faces in Damascus, only in the late 2000s were some new religious institutes established in other Syrian cities, such as the Shari'a faculty (*kulliyyat ash-shari'a*) in Aleppo, founded 2006–2007.

Thus, there were only a few Salafi scholars in Syria before the revolution, such as Shaykh Abd al-Qader al-Arnaout, who can be classified as Traditional Salafists. Al-Arnaout remained in Syria limiting himself to working on editing manuscripts of various works of hadith for publication (Pierret 2011; Al-Kayyal 2012). Syria also witnessed other Salafi faces such as the pro-regime supporter Abu al-Qaqaa (Mahmoud Qul Aghasi)[16] who was active in Aleppo before and after the Iraq occupation and was known to encourage his followers to go to Iraq and fight American forces.

As for Syrian Salafis residing outside of Syria, the most famous was Shaykh Nasir al-Deen al-Albani who left Syria early and Shaykh Adnan al-Arour who resided in Saudi Arabia after he left Syria in the 1980s.[17] Al-Arour became a famous religious personality owing to his public TV program on the Safa Channel where he focused on criticizing Shiite thought. The program was watched only by those limited number of Syrians who were concerned about sectarian conspiracies against Sunnis. However, since the beginning of the Syrian revolution and in particular after the growth of armed resistance to the regime, Arour's popularity has significantly increased and he is considered one of the most motivating and inspiring people for many Syrian rebels. Some of them wrote his name on the slogans that they were carrying in the demonstrations in Homs and Idlib (Pierret 2011: 236–238).

The Syrian revolution and factors leading to the spread of Salafism

From the beginning of Syrian revolution in March of 2011 up until December of 2011, the Syrian people had hopes of a peaceful change of the regime that would result in the establishment of a civil state based on democracy and citizenship. Therefore, all political slogans which people were raising in their demonstrations focused on the unity of the people such as "wahed, wahed, wahed, al-shaab alsouri wahed" ("one, one, one, the Syrian people is one").[18] The Syrian regime depicted rebels as Islamist "radicals" aiming to spread chaos in the country[19] but while the majority of Syria's rebels were Sunni, there were, in fact, many Christians, Druze,

Alawites and Ismailis — individuals and groups — participating in the protests[20] and there were Sunni individuals and groups that supported the regime. This suggests that the large proportion of Sunni rebels only reflects the predominant proportion (75–80%) of Sunnis in the Syrian population,[21] rather than evidence of a "Sunni revolution."[22] Thus, according to one source, the Syrian opposition was initially a democratic-leaning movement in which "the Islamist quotient among the opposition is very low" (Weiss et al. 2011).

While the presence of Salafis during the first year of the revolution was at a low level, the violence of the regime served as a source of radicalization that activated the jihadists inside the country (al-Shishani 2011) so that, in the following year, the landscape of the revolution begun to change gradually. With the increase of regime brutality against all peaceful resistance,[23] the Syrian people begun to discuss the idea of the armed resistance to defend people and their properties, led by soldiers who defected from the regime army but many activists were unwilling to change the peaceful nature of the revolution (International Crisis Group 2012). This created a situation congenial to the spread of jihadist versions of Salafism (ICG 2012). First, as the Uprising turned into armed conflict, liberal, secular, and moderate Syrians could not offer the rebels as valid and convincing a motive as that provided by religion for risking their lives in fighting a regime which violated everything they held to be of value (Swehat 2013; Sa'eed 2012). A year into the conflict, the rebels no longer had a way to survive and resist the regime except by appealing to strong religious motivations which promised martyrs a great reward in the afterlife. Additionally, the government media gave credibility to the violent jihadi Salafists by justifying its oppression as a fight against such groups, despite the fact that most opposition forces had rejected these groups or ignored them (al-Haj Salah 2012, 2013; Sa'eed 2012; ICG 2012). Finally, funding from private and non-official Gulf sources backed the Salafist groups among the rebels (ICG 2012; Kouja 2013).

Certain features of Salafism made it an attractive ideology of resistance against the regime. Since Salafism entails a return to the earliest period of Islam and rejects the official legal schools as a valid source of religious authority, it is congruent with challenges to established authority. Salafism focused on the authentic primary texts as the foundation of the Shari'ah, while the Islam represented by the four legal schools (*madhahib*), often allied itself with the political powers of the time (International Crisis Group 2012; Haykel 2009: 35–50).[24] Salafism also appeals to the masses who are most concerned with following righteous pure Islam rather than that of the jurists, while, in parallel, Traditional Salafists believed that the masses had the capacity to understand the texts directly and as a result, generally refused the idea of juristic authority, points clear in the writings of al-Albani.[25] Reflecting the popular feeling against inflexible official religious authorities, which neglected the values of justice and dignity, Salafism became an interpretation of Islam congenial to a period of mass popular mobilization unleashed by the Arab Uprisings. Leadership in these revolutions fell to political activists, not trained jurists.[26] In addition, the traditional *'ulama* entered the debate on the Uprising reluctantly and their role was very unclear to Syrians.[27] Accordingly, a new group of young Syrians formed to take a lead role to improve the direction of religious thought, differing from the semi-official and official religious thought and growing closer to the Salafi vision that fed the crucial needs of the rebels; these people found the primary texts of the Quran and Sunnah to be important resources to constitute a popular version of pure and revolutionary Islam.

The reality of Syrian Salafism through the revolution

Although most Syrian Salafi groups share the above features since early 2012, they differ from each other in certain ways. There are debates over whether the Sharia includes the life and conduct of the pious ancestors (hadith) or is only the Quran and Sunna texts. The most debatable topics among these groups is the nature of jihad.[28] From the earliest date of the revolution, Salafism was associated with the idea of local jihad against the regime which it began to describe as an occupying force (Swehat 2013; ICG 2012) but later, because of the ambiguous role and perceived complicity of international society in regime repression, there was a shift from the idea of local jihad to global one and therefore the idea of fighting for a trans-national Islamic umma and of the restoration of the caliphate. As a result, the belief became that the Uprising in Syria was a step to establishing the Islamic state and liberating Palestine.

As for the ruler and the shape of the state, they agree on the Islamic identity of the state and on rejecting the citizenship concept (ICG 2012). But some of them go to the extreme of refusing democracy as a Western concept. Broadly speaking, Salafism opposes the notion of democracy since it opens the door for establishing disputing parties and divergent voices represented in parliaments; this model of political life is seen as "usurping God's role as lawmaker and party politics as violating the Qur'anic command not to split into factions (McCants 2012).[29] The last idea is a part of Traditional Salafi thought, but it appears strange when we see it in the context of a popular revolution. The writings of Abu Basir al-Tartusi – a Syrian scholar described as one of the "primary Salafi opinion-makers guiding the jihadi movement" (Heffelfinger 2006) – could be a good example on how Salafists see democracy. In his treatise "the Islam's perspective on Democracy" "*Hukm al-Islam fi ad-Dimoqratiyya*", al-Tartusi (n.d) argues that Islam is in a battle with democracy since "the major crusader states work hard – in all ways – to spread and pose the religion of democracy – (*deen ad-dimoqratiyya*) over the oppressed people."

Thus, Syrian Salafism is a heterogeneous mix of intellectual ideas. The most important commonality of all these groups and all of their supporters is the desire to see the fall of the regime.[30]

The proliferation of Salafist groups in Syria

Syrian Salafism's turn to violence should be linked to the extreme and unstable political circumstances in which it emerged. Initially, in the many discussions among rebels and activists on websites, the idea that the revolution would be religious in nature was rejected[31] in favor of the national dimension. The first military emergence of Syrian Salafism appears around January 2012, ten months after the beginning of the revolution (ICG 2012). Many discussions had occurred on Facebook pages and in various discussion forums about the possibility of announcing *al jihad* against the regime[32] and at this point the first jihadist organization, *Jabhat al-Nusra li Ahli al-Sham* (Nusra Front) declared itself.[33] Since that time, Syrian Salafism began to crystallize, became attractive to individuals and groups and also began to form into a military entity that paralleled the Free Syrian Army yet differed from it in terms of structure and resources.

The following are the most important Salafist groups that emerged in 2012 and the beginning of 2013 in Syria:

Jabhatu al-Nusra li Ahli al-Sham: Since its emergence, and up until now, many discussions among rebels and activists are taking place about this organization's controversial goals and leaders.[34] Many were suspicious of the fact that it announced its responsibility for the first bombing (al-Qazzaz) which most Syrians had previously attributed to the regime.[35] Moreover, the head of Jabhat, Abu Muhammad al-Julani, was seen as an ambiguous personality.[36] However, the most important attacks against the regime were made by Jabhat al-Nusra, a fact that led many rebels to support it, and led the Syrian National Coalition to oppose, putting it on the American terrorism list.[37] Jabhat al-Nusra, which is distinguished by an obvious Salafist discourse, is affiliated with al-Qaeda which presents its messages on its website "Shumoukh al-Islam"[38] and, in line with al-Qaida's thinking, Jabhat al-Nusra held that the conflict with al-Asad was the first half of the battle, and the second half would be to establish an Islamic state with a Salafist vision (ICG 2012). Jabhat al-Nusra was most active in the north of Syria especially in Aleppo and the countryside, and the east, especially in Dair al-Zour, but it sometimes claimed responsibility for operations in Damascus.[39]

Ahrar al-Sham[40] emerged in the first month of 2012 (ICG 2012). This group believes in an Islamic state, aims at waging a jihad against the regime and the "Nusairi Devil (al-taghut)" and establishing an Islamic society that follows Shari'ah.[41] It was also focused on waging jihad against Shiite Iranian missionaries in the east.[42] It also considered itself, in spite of its cooperation with the Free Syrian Army, an alternative Salafist army. Although its activities are primarily located in the north-west of Syria, it claims that it spread throughout the country (ICG 2012).

Jabhat Tahreer Souria al-Islamiya was the first attempt to unite the disparate Islamist-influenced, formerly FSA-linked, armed groups. In its first statement on September 12, 2012, it declared itself a group which unified the majority of the influential military groups in Syria that sought the fall of the Asad regime. It declared a mission to protect all Syrians regardless of their different beliefs, ethnicities, and sects, and to defend Syrian sovereignty, unity and independence. This group included around 22 military groups, foremost amongst which are the following (ICG 2012; JTSI 2012). *Suqour al-Sham Brigade*, which is considered one of the earliest military groups, was formed at the end of 2011 and is led by Ahmad Isa Ahmad al-Shaykh. It was active in Idlib and was known to have a strong Salafi orientation. It unequivocally aimed at establishing an Islamic state. Its stand on minorities was contradictory, with some statements at times rejecting unity between Sunnis, Alawites, and Christian as forbidden in the Sharia, and other statements seemingly in favor of guaranteeing minority rights. *Liwaa al-Umma*, founded in November of 2012 in the north of Syria, aimed to conduct a violent jihad until Syria was liberated, eliminating the Devil, the Asad regime (al-Taghout), establishing an Islamic state, and following the fighting rules in Shari'a which orders Muslims to fight only the enemy (ICG 2012; https://www.youtube.com/watch?v=gUg_2A82QBw). The *Farouq Brigade* is famous for leading the seizure of east Aleppo from the regime. Other groups under the Muslim Brotherhood umbrella included *Liwa' al-Islam* (Damascus); *Tawhid Birgade* (Aleppo); *the Deir ez-Zor Revolutionary Council* (Deir ex-Zor).; *Liwaa Amr Ibn al-Aas* (Aleppo); *Suqur al-Kurd Brigade* (al-Qameshli); *Liwa''Ibad al-Rahman* (Idlib), *Liwa' al-Fath* (Aleppo), *Tajmu' Ansaar al-Islam* (Damascus), and *Liwaa al-Iman* (Hama).

Al-Jabha al-Islamiya al-Souriya (JIS) was founded in December 2012 by Ahrar ash-Sham, bringing together more radical Salafist groups that had not accepted the authority of the Muslim Brotherhood-influenced Islamic Liberation Front. Its goal was to gather all military groups that share the same Salafist vision. In its first public statement, it declared that it was an inclusive Islamic organization based on the path of Ahl al-Sunna wa al-Jamaa and the pious predecessors (salaf al-salih), and aiming to bring about the fall of the Asad regime and establish an Islamic society which follows Shari'a where Muslims and non-Muslims enjoy the justice of Islam.[43] To accomplish its aims, the JIS employed several different means: military, educational, relief work, public preaching, and efforts to bring about cooperation and unity with other Islamist groups. JIS included, in addition to Ahrar ash-Sham, the following local military groups (ICG 2012; ATS 2013): *Liwa' al-Haqq*, located in Homs which includes ten military groups (ICG 2012); *Harakat al-Fajr al-Islamiyyah*, located in Aleppo and its countryside; *Jama'at al-Tali'ah al-Islamiyyah*, located in the countryside of Idlib;[44] *Ansar al-Sham Brigades* (Lattakia); *Mus'ab bin Umair Brigades* (Rural Aleppo); *Al-Haqq Brigades* (Hama); *Al-Iman Fighting Brigades* (Damascus and its countryside);[45] *Al-Tawhid Army* (Deir ez-Zor);[46] *Al-Iman Fighting Brigades; Saraya al-Maham al-Khassah*; and *Hamza bin Abd al Mutalib Brigade* (all located in Damascus and its countryside).[47]

This is a general image of the Salafist political landscape in the early years of its emergence, although new permutations emerge regularly.

Conclusion: Syrian Salafism from denial to recognition

The regime wanted from the beginning of the revolution to convey to all observers an image that the opposition was made up of violent Salafist terrorist groups, a claim that a majority of Syrians and non-Syrians, external and internal observers, rebels and opponents denied, ignored, and mocked. But the regime worked on several fronts to develop this narrative and to achieve its goals of making it a self-fulfilling prophecy. This strategy was meant to strengthen the regime's position with the international society and justify its oppression of the Uprising. In time, jihadism became a reality, with military Salafist groups spread over the country. These Salafi groups had in common their Salifist identity and the goal of eliminating the so-called heretical Alawite-Nusairi regime. Moderate Syrians who believed in a democratic state rejected these groups and argued that they were fostered by the regime to serve its narrative. Yet, the reality on the ground forced most Syrians to recognize the importance of these groups, without whom the Syrian people would not have experienced the attacks of military aircraft and the shelling of their cities.

Notes

1 This chapter was presented as a lecture at the Center for Syria Studies (CSS) of the University of St Andrews, March 2013. Special thanks to Forum Regionale Studien in Berlin for hosting me during writing this paper, Michelle Burgis, Thomas Pierret and Raymond Hinnebusch for comments and rich discussions.
2 For more linguistic details, see the word سلف and its diversities in Lane's *Lexicon*, pp. 1407–1409.
3 For more details on the concept of innovation Bidʻa, see Kamrava (2011).
4 Salafism has different definitions, and "is notoriously difficult to define because its practitioners prefer to say what it is not rather than what it is." William McCants (2012); Duderija (2012) and International Crisis Group (2012).
5 This can be noticed in the time of Ibn Taymiyya and his students and more recently with the consequences of Ottoman empire's demise which witnessed what it is called "Reform Salafism" established by Jamāl ad-Dīn al-Afghānī and his student Muhammad ʻAbdū. After that, many varieties of Salafism emerged. See International Crisis Group (2012).
6 On the nature of Reform Salafism and its characteristics, see Aziz Ahmad (2012), and Khaled Ahmed, Book review: Rashid Rida's 'lighthouse' today, http://archives.dailytimes.com.pk/editorial/26-Apr-2009/book-review-rashid-rida-s-lighthouse-today-by-khaled-ahmed.
7 For more details on the history of Salafism in Damascus, see Pierret (2011: 102–03).
8 For an overview of the history and the evolution of Syrian Salafism, see Pierret (2011: 102–108): al-Kayyal (2012) and Crisis Group (2012).
9 This science explains the criterion that ʻulama relied on in order to verify the prophetic reports (*hadith*). For more details, see Dickinson (2012).
10 This science explains what are canonical, sound, weak or hadith, their resources and how we access them.
11 For more details on how Baʼth regime dealt with Islamists, see Pierret (2011: 64–100), and al-Kayyal (2012).
12 For more details on the relationship between the Baʼth regime and Salafi groups and individuals, see Muhammad Sami al-Kayyal, *On the Syrian Salafism*, http://faroukit.blogspot.com/2012/04/blog-post_9060.html.
13 On the nature of Syrian people and the relationship with Salafi and Sufi movements and individuals, see al-Kayyal (2012), Saʼeed (2012), and International Crisis Group (2012).
14 For an example of how traditionalist ʻulama addressed this issue, see Saeed Ramadaan al-Buti's book *"al-Salafiyya Marhala Zamaniyya Mubaraka laa Madhhad Islami"*. On the image the Salafism among Syrian people during the Baʼth reign, see Saʼeed (2012).

15 This elimination and persecution was noticed clearly during the brutal 1980s events. For more details, see Pierret (2011) and al-Kayyal (2012).
16 He founded an organization called "Ghurabaa' ash-Shaam", and he was assassinated in 2007. See al-Kayyal (2012).
17 For more details on al-Arour and his influence, see Pierret (2011), al-Kayyal (2012) and International Crisis Group (2012).
18 For the nature of Syrian revolution and the idea of united Syrian people, see al-Haj Saleh (2012, 2013) and Sa'eed (2012).
19 President Bashar al-Asad made it clear in his speech on June 20 that the country faced external forces, outlaws and radicals who are exploiting the "movement seeking legitimate reforms" (BBC Arabic, June 20, 2011).
20 For more details on the presence of these sectarian groups and the nature of the Syrian revolution, see al-Sa'eed (2012) and al-Haj Saleh (2012).
21 For more details on the proportions of the sects in Syria and the role of Sunni sect in the society, see al-Haj Saleh (2012).
22 On the reality of Sunni engagement in the revolution and why the Sunni sect as a majority aligned with the revolution, see Sa'eed' (2012) and al-Haj Saleh (2012).
23 June 2011 witnessed the first defection from the Syrian army by Lieutenant Colonel Hussein Harmoush who declared that the aim of this defection was to "protect the unarmed protesters who demand freedom and democracy," adding: "'No' to sectarianism, the Syrian people are one." See International Crisis Group (2012) and Holliday (2012). For the video of Harmoush's defection, see https://www.youtube.com/watch?v=2XeIFv1B7no.
24 For more details on the trajectory of Salafi adherence to *madhahib*, the genealogy of their thought and the relationship between Salafism and Wahhabi thought see Haykel (2009); McCants (2012).
25 For example see his detailed introduction to his book *sifat salat al-nabi*, al-Riyaad: Maktabat al-Ma'arif.
26 For more details on the perspectives of official and non-official *'ulama* towards the revolution, see Pierret (2011: 216–238; Eido 2014). On why Salafism is welcomed and accepted during the revolution, see al-Haj Saleh (2012) and International Crisis Group (2012).
27 For an overview on the *'ulama*'s perspectives, see Pierret (2011: pp. 216–238); Eido (2013) and International Crisis Group (2012).
28 This will be explained with details later in this paper.
29 The Qur'anic command is mentioned in this verse: "And be ye not as those who separated and disputed after the clear proofs had come unto them. For such there is an awful doom." Qur'an, 3:105 (Pickthall translation; http://tanzil.net).
30 See Crisis Group Middle East Report, N: 131 *Tentative Jihad: Syria's Fundamentalist Opposition*, October 12, 2012.
31 See International Crisis Group (2012). To understand the religious nature of the Syrian revolution and why the new Syrian generation rejected violence, see Sa'eed (2012).
32 See International Crisis Group (2012) and Wasim Umawi, "the next Friday is a Friday of the people, announces jihad" "الجمعة القادمة جمعة الشعب أعلن الجهاد": http://www.muslm.org/vb/showthread.php?468658-%D8.
33 See International Crisis Group (2012); also http://www.dailymotion.com/video/xnys9x_%D8%A5%D8%B9%D9%84%D8%A7.
34 On these discussions that reflect the secrets and puzzles of Jabhat al-Nusra, see Kouja (2013), and International Crisis Group (2012).
35 For more details on analyzing the two-side, opposition-regime, nature of Jabhat al-Nusra, see Mannaa (2012), Yassin al-Haj Saleh (2013), and International Crisis Group (2012): 33.
36 On al-Julani's character and other al-Nusra's fighters, see this interview with Abu Adnan, a leader in Jabhat al-Nusra: http://world.time.com/2012/12/25/interview-with-a-newly-designated-syrias-jabhat-al-nusra/. On the relationship between Nusra and Liwaa' al-Tawheed, see International Crisis 2012.

37 For the US move against al-Nusra and the Syrian opposition's opposition to that, see these links: http://www.cnn.com/2012/12/11/world/meast/syria-civil-war/, http://archive.arabic.cnn.com/2012/middle_east/12/27/Syrian-Jabhat-alNusra/; see also al-Haj Salah (2013).
38 For more details on Shumoukh al-Islam and other media resources, see the interview with Abu Adnan, a leader at Jabhat al-Nusra http://world.time.com/2012/12/25/interview-with-a-newly-designated-syrias-jabhat-al-nusra/ and International Crisis Group 2012. On the relationship between al-Nusra and al-Qaida, see Kouja (2013) and International Crisis Group (2012).
39 On the presence of al-Nusra in Deir al-Zour, see http://foreignpolicy.com/2012/12/20/all-syrian-politics-is-local/.
40 "Estimating the number of fighters within any given group is particularly difficult. Most factions call themselves katiba (battalion), kataa'ib (battalions) or liwaa' (brigade). While this provides some indication of size – kata'ib implies that the group is more than a single unit, while liwa suggests several 'battalions' within the command structure of a larger 'brigade' – in practice these words are used very loosely, and the number of fighters within a battalion or brigade can vary widely." See International Crisis Group (2012).
41 http://ahraralsham.net/?p=4640.
42 Ibid. Also see http://archive.aawsat.com/details.asp?section=4&article=690359&issueno=12310#.Vp_SHPkrLIU.
43 The following link includes the JIS's public statement and all Islamic factions that are fighting under JIS's umbrella: https://docs.google.com/document/d/1fACS9tltlmZDmomlB1ZtiJLZaAckWOT0yhtRwoskgIE/edit?pref=2&pli=1.
44 https://docs.google.com/document/d/1fACS9tltlmZDmomlB1ZtiJLZaAckWOT0yhtRwoskgIE/edit?pref=2&pli=1.
45 https://docs.google.com/document/d/1fACS9tltlmZDmomlB1ZtiJLZaAckWOT0yhtRwoskgIE/edit?pref=2&pli=1.
46 https://docs.google.com/document/d/1fACS9tltlmZDmomlB1ZtiJLZaAckWOT0yhtRwoskgIE/edit?pref=2&pli=1.
47 Ibid.

Bibliography

Abdul Mun'im Salim, Amr (2008), al-Fataawaa al-Manhajiyya (al-Qahira, Dar al-Diaa'), http://dar.bibalex.org/webpages/mainpage.jsf?PID=DAF-Job:86182.
Ahmad, Aziz (2012), "Iṣlāh," *Encyclopedia of Islam*, Second Edition, Brill Online 20.
ATS (2013), *Ahdath al-Thawrah al-Suriyyah*, http://rewayat2.com.
Dickinson, E. (2012), Uṣūl al-Hadīth, *Encyclopedia of Islam*, Second Edition, Brill Online.
Duderija, Adis (2012), *What is Salafism?*, www.newageislam.com/the-war-within-islam/what-is-Salafism?/d/6624.
Eido, Issam (2014), *Religious Groups and Scholars of Islam in the Syrian Revolution*, www.joshualandis.com/blog/religious-groups-scholars-islam-syrian-revolution-isam-eido/.
al-Haj Saleh, Yassin (2012), *The Group of "What's Remained": The Syrian Sunni and Policy*, http://aljumhuriya.net/237.
al-Haj Saleh, Yassin (2013), *What is our Problem with Jabhatu al-Nusra*, http://aljumhuriya.net/581.
Haj Saleh, Yassin (2013), *The Most Dangerous Phase of the Syrian Revolution*, www.alhayat.com/Details/476394.
Haykel, Bernard (2009), "On the Nature of Salafi Thought and Action." In *Global Salafism: Islam's New Religious Movement*, 33–57, edited by Roel Meijer, New York: Columbia University Press.
Heffelfinger, Chris (2006), "The Ideological Voices of the Jihadi Movement," *Terrorism Monitor*, 4: 24.

Holliday, Joseph (2012), *Syria's Armed Opposition*, Institute for the Study of War, March.
International Crisis Group (ICG) (2012), N: 131, Tentative Jihad: Syria's Fundamentalist Opposition, *Middle East Report*, October 12.
Jabhat Tahrir Suriyyah al-Islamiyyah (JTSI) (2012), Official Website, http://archive.li/LyFov.
Kamrava, Mehran (2011), "Contextualizing Innovation in Islam." In *Innovation in Islam: Traditions and Contributions*, 1–20, edited by M. Kamrava, Berkeley: University of California Press.
al-Kayyal, Muhammad Sami (2012), *On the Syrian Salafism*, http://faroukit.blogspot.com/2012/04/blog-post_9060.html.
Kouja, Kinan (2013), *The Puzzles of Jabhat al-Nusra*, http://aljumhuriya.net/549.
Mannaa, Haytham (2012), www.alalam.ir/news/1431669.
McCants, William (2012), The Lesser of Two Evils: The Salafi Turn to Party Politics in Egypt, *Middle East Memo*, Brookings, Number 23, May, www.brookings.edu/research/papers/2012/05/01-Salafi-egypt-mccants.
Pierret, Thomas (2011), *Religion and State in Syria: The Sunni Ulama from Coup to Revolution*. Cambridge: Cambridge University Press.
Sa'eed, Yaser Nadeem (2012), *On the Possibilities of Success of a Political Sunni Sect in Syria*, http://aljumhuriya.net/140.
al-Shishani, Murad Batal (2011), "Jihadists in Syria: Myth of Reality," *Terrorism Monitor*, 9: 34.
Swehat, Yasin (2013), *Thoughts on Jabhatu al-Nusra*, http://aljumhuriya.net/546.
al-Tartusi, Abu Basir (n.d), *Hukm al-Islam fi ad-Dimoqratiiya wa at-ta'addudiyya al-hizbiyya*, pp. 4, www.abubaseer.bizland.com/books/read/b11.pdf.
Van Dam, Nikolaos (1996), *The Struggle for Power in Syria: Politics and Society under Asad and the Ba'th Party*. London: I.B.Tauris.
Weiss, Michael, Hannah Stuart and Samuel Hunter (2011), *The Syrian Opposition: Political Analysis with Original Testimony from Key Figures*. London: Henry Jackson Society.

18

FROM A WINDOW IN JARAMANA

Imperial sectarianism and the impact of war on a Druze neighbourhood in Syria

Maria Kastrinou

Introduction

By providing a window into Jaramana from 2011 until today, this chapter pieces together the local micro-history of events and the shifting socio-political dynamics in a Druze neighbourhood at a time of war in Syria. Starting with a dramatic and violent event that shocked and inevitably changed the neighbourhood of Jaramana, it seeks to understand two broad concerns regarding the Syrian war (1) how sectarian violence emerged; and (2) why minorities in Syria, the Druze, in particular, did not join the anti-regime opposition. In order to address these concerns, the chapter firstly delineates how sectarian violence has been theorised with reference to the anthropology of war, globalisation and the state. Secondly, ethnographically it explores ideologies of sectarianism, paying attention to the rhetoric of 'imperial sectarianism' employed by the Syrian state before the war as a way of understanding the dialectics between state and sects; and, lastly, it presents an empirical micro-history of war and sectarianism in Jaramana by analysing how both identities and political dynamics have changed on the ground over the past five years. More broadly, the site of Jaramana is a unique case-study of minority belonging and the evolution of sectarian ideology at a time of war, because it involves the study of the Druze community vis-à-vis its changing relations with the Syrian state, the internally displaced people who find refuge in Jaramana, and the territorial conflicts raging between different opposition fractions.

From a window in Jaramana

'Jaramana is the only place where religious freedom really exists in Syria', I remember Umm Nidal telling me while I was helping her clean the dishes. Her kitchen had a large window above the sink which looked down on *sharia al-'alam*,

Jaramana's high street whose Arabic name translates into 'Street of the World'. Umm Nidal explained to me that Jaramana welcomed Iraqi refugees fleeing their country, as it had welcomed Palestinians before them. Jaramana was multi-ethnic and multi-religious; Druze and Christians had for many years lived together here. More recently, people from all religious denominations, had started buying or renting property in Jaramana because it was cheaper than Damascus, but at only 4 kilometres away, still only a ten-minute *servis* (minibus) ride to Baramkeh station. For this reason, many students, emerging artists and celebrities had also started to move into Jaramana, and over the years many cafes, restaurants and nightclubs had emerged – something that gave a cosmopolitan pride to the younger group of my Druze friends.

Jaramana, despite its high population density (Fahmi and Jaeger 2009), and its reputation as a chaotic refugee city, was rapidly becoming trendy and gentrified (Kastrinou 2014). Yet, its geographical, social, and political centre of gravity had remained where it had always been: between *sahat-arrawda* and *sahat al-shioyf* (the Square of the Swords), around the discreet shrine of Al-Khoudr (Fahmi and Jaeger 2009). This was the old centre of what used to be an agricultural Druze village, which economically and socially was part of the surrounding fertile region of al-Ghouta (Batatu 1999). From the 1970s onwards the village, like those surrounding it, had become industrialised and part of the national economy (Hinnebusch 1990), while, with the decline of local industry and the coming of Iraqi refugees, it had become a hotbed of real estate development. However, the central geographical location described above was still inhabited by an overwhelming majority of Druze residents, especially local elites.

Known in 'traditional' Middle Eastern nomenclature by the name of a religious apostate, al-Darazi (Khuri 2004), the Druze are a distinct religious community whose contemporary members live in Lebanon, Syria, Palestine, and worldwide in diaspora communities such as in the United States, Venezuela and Australia. They are estimated to be one million worldwide, forming between 3 to 5 per cent of the population in Syria. In Syria, an estimated 500,000 live in Jabal al-Arab – the district of Suwayda, in Jaramana, and between Aleppo and Idlib in Jabal al-Samak. However, as statistical measurements of minorities often contradict nationalist ideology and hence fall outside the realm of civil censuses in the Middle Eastern countries inhabited by the Druze, estimates of their numbers are approximations at best.

With origins in the 11th-century-Fatimid Dynasty in Cairo, Druze religious doctrine, *tawhid*, is historically related to the Ismaili branch of Shia Islam, and was divinely revealed to the Fatimid ruler of Cairo al-Hakim bi-Amr Allah (996–1021) (Firro 1992). In 1017, al-Hakim publicly declared the advert of the final gnostic revelation of the divine truth: *tawhid*. Translated as unitarianism or monism, *tawhid* is the religious doctrine of its followers, the *muwahhidun* or *Banu Marouf* – the names that the Druze would prefer to be known by. Many theological, social and practical rituals bind the transnational Druze communities together, such as belief in reincarnation and the strict practice of endogamy.

However, religious doctrine and ritual practice do not override historical, social, political and economic differences across, but also within, Druze communities. Conformity to religious doctrine does not translate into transnational politics. Instead, the Druze are valorised as nationalists within their respective nation-states: for example, as leaders of the nationalist Syrian revolt against the French Mandate in 1925, as the only Arabs 'to be trusted' to serve in the Israeli army, and as the 'kingmakers' in the confessional politics of Lebanon. The Druze inhabit and partake in the political communities of diverse nation-states (Hazran 2014); at the same time, they often partake in political life and civil society through identifications other than sectarian and identities other than Druze. Political participation and activism, connection to the religious establishment, class and status – all these are significant factors that differentiate the Druze internally, upon lines of social, political and economic stratifications that cross-cut the Syrian polity before the war (Kastrinou 2014). This is not to say that religious identities were not important but rather to note that religious identities have a political economy that must be studied, not assumed (Kastrinou 2016). The designation 'the Druze' is deeply problematic as it overly generalises and homogenises a diverse group of people on the basis of often unfounded and ahistorical assumptions about the unchanging nature of both 'community' and 'sect'.[1] Indeed, members of the Druze intelligentsia, or university students like my friend Zahir, often ridiculed the religious shaykhs for lack of secular education, perceiving them as the left-over relics of a peasant and uncivilised past.

By the end of 2010 a new Druze shrine, much larger and more imposing than the tucked away Al-Khoudr, was being built near *sahat* Al-Khoudr. The imposing size and architecture were perhaps signs of the times: that the close-knit esoteric Druze were becoming more wealthy and confident in their public religious proclamations. Indeed, proclaiming one's religion, increasingly visible since the invasion of Iraq, had become a social practice in Damascus; a reaction to both foreign interventions as well as chronic political repression, religious politics were becoming popular.

When the so-called Arab Spring unrolled in Tunisia and Egypt, my friends and families all expressed their surprise and welcomed the hoped-for popular change. They speculated whether Jordan or Lebanon would be next. Some, a small minority already involved with leftist politics, hoped for creating a new space for internal debate and reform in Syria. Most did not believe that a popular Uprising would reach Syria. Following the bloodbath in Dara'a, there were demonstrations and tensions began to rise. Anna, a left-wing Alawi friend sent me this message on Skype:

'It is very easy to be dead now, without knowing why or how or who did that. And nobody knows the truth. Some say it is the security, some say outside forces. Some say they are the people in Syria. Some say that they want the freedom. Some say they want a war.' (Anna, Skype, 24/4/11)

Jaramana was, again, about to become a shelter for the newly internally displaced people of the Syrian war. Soon, Anna found refuge there with Druze friends when her home near Yarmouk camp was looted, almost a year later. This war claimed more than 250,000 lives between 2011 and 2016, displaced almost half of the entire Syrian population, and has contributed to what the UN calls the worse refugee crisis since WWII. Moreover, this is a war that has indiscriminately endangered large parts of the civilian population, both through disproportionate use of force by the Syrian state, as well as through terrorist attacks and the existential threat of extermination or enslavement of religious and ethnic minorities by the increasingly totalitarian oppositions posed by the Islamic State and Jubhat al-Nusra. Religious minorities, like the Druze, find themselves dangerously placed between an authoritarian regime that claims to protect them, and the increasing threat of sectarianism and extermination at the hands of the most fundamentalist of the 'revolutionaries'. The 'protection of minorities', moreover, features prominently in the ideological renditions justifying the international proxy war that is currently unfolding in Syria. Many a times in the Middle East over the past centuries, the alleged protection of minorities and human rights have paved the way for the colonial and imperialist intervention and invasion. In the remainder of this chapter, I outline the consolidation of sectarian politics as a *result* rather than a cause for the war in Syria by (a) contextualising state ideology prior to the war in order to show continuities and discontinuities in the national imaginary; and (b) providing a chronological account of the events that have shaped Jaramana's Druze political relationships internally in the neighbourhood, with the regime in Damascus, and with the oppositions in the neighbouring Damascus countryside.

Methodology

The war has meant that I have not been able to return to Syria since late 2010. The 'loss' of one's field-site is a very peculiar situation for an anthropologist, since our research is based on the empirical and iterative participant observation method. Indeed, anthropologists are known to be able to deal with events of trauma and war only 'after the fact' (Geertz 1995; Caton 2005; Nordstrom and Robben 1995). This chapter, however, is based on somewhat different, experimental, and for this reason incomplete, methods that I had to devise. Mediated communication, whether through telephone, Facebook, or Skype, has become the primary means of data collection. What my friends and families are able to say, or more often not to tell, comprise the main source for data and analysis. I owe much to the generosity of these interlocutors who not only accommodated and accepted me as their resident ethnographer, a 'catholic' Druze as they joked, in times of peace but also who continue to trust me with their stories in these new perilous times of war. Much of the empirical data in this chapter I owe to my research assistant, Tariq, who shared his dairies with me, although I bear all the responsibility for its presentation, analysis and interpretation.

This chapter, then, is an incomplete local history, and although not exclusively based on fieldwork, it offers a window to Jaramana from the particular vantage point of my interlocutors. I have tried to integrate their voices, dissonances, disagreements wherever this was possible, in order to emphasise how war, sectarianism, and politics are experienced by the people I have known who, as much as I can tell, are not significant activists and represent an 'average'. As detailed and embedded accounts of the political manoeuvres of religious and military landscapes amongst the Druze in Suwayda and beyond have emerged through the meticulous work of Ayman Jawad Al-Tamimi, I hope here to bring to the fore the microhistory of war from a very particular window in Jaramana: one of its everyday residents. In this way, I hope this research contributes to better understanding of the 'social condition of war' (Lubkemann 2008: 23).

A point of no-return: The event of sectarian violence in Jaramana

The Druze residents of Jaramana organised and mobilised in the early days of the war along pre-existing *political* rather than sectarian lines: the known regime supporters, the known members of the secular liberal and left political oppositions, the nationalists, the religious. Many times, my friend Zahra, one of my key informants and friends who has been a long-time member of the secular left opposition in Syria, provided me with potent examples of divisions along political and not sectarian lines. Internal political fragmentation combined with Jaramana's geographical position as a neutral ground between regime-held Damascus and opposition-supporting countryside, turns it into a kind of 'natural' buffer zone. The increasing numbers of internal refugees that were finding shelter in Jaramana further fostered its claim to political neutrality despite the engulfing violence. I will detail these processes in the course of this chapter. Yet, by contrast, I also describe a violent *event* that shocked and achieved a dramatic political change on the ground in Jaramana that ushered in new economic and policing regimes. Its effects included the silencing of internal political opposition while tending to 'sectarianize' and homogenise the Druze of Jaramana into a singular identity. I employ the term *event* analytically, following Caton (1999, 2005), in order to understand this incident that broke the normative structure of politics and everyday life in Jaramana, without either reducing it to causal structural explanations, nor relegating it as a completely exceptional, and hence tautological, occurrence.

In 2013, a young man from the bordering town of Saqba was publicly tortured, and killed, in the central Square of the Swords (*sahat al-sioyf*). This act had been perpetrated by the Druze popular committee (*al-lijan al-sha'biyah*) that was formed of young volunteers patrolling the neighbourhood's borders. Such committees had emerged out of what some saw as the increasing need to control borders as a means for the community's self-defence and self-preservation vis-à-vis its majority opposition neighbourhoods along its southeastern frontiers. After the public torture and execution, the corpse of the young man was put on the back of a truck and paraded throughout Jaramana.

The killing reportedly had happened in retaliation for the murder of a Druze man at a checkpoint. However, what is significant in this event is not the revenge killing – regrettable but not peculiar or unique. It is, rather, the *performance* of killing: the public torture, execution and parade. The ritual elaboration of the killing that turned what under other circumstances would be a personal or family vengeance story into collective murder.

This event shocked local society, but also marked a point of no-return: the Druze were no longer neutral but found themselves within the camp of regime supporters. Indeed, only the regime and its weapons could protect them now. Jaramana was no more part of the wider social geographic environ of al-Ghouta; its neighbours had now become its enemies. Internally, this show of force muted dissent and opposition and also signified that the role of religious authority began to wane. Jaramana, previously multi-ethnic and multi-religious, known for its hospitality as a place of refuge for the displaced, was changed. A new form of power – or violence – was consolidating.

How can we understand this event, and more broadly the emergence of sectarian violence? The first step is to point out cross-cultural examples of violence that locate ethnic and religious violence as the results of contemporary practices of war, and *not* as culturally specific. In a provocative cross-examination of contemporary violence between majorities and minorities, Appadurai (2006) suggests that both globalisation's large-scale extension of the possibilities for grand idioms of belonging, as well as the proliferation of the nation-state, are *structurally* responsible for these new forms of violence emerging. This is because, Appadurai argues, the modern nation-state is built upon the assumptions of an homogeneous 'ethnic genius', hence from their foundations, modern nations are constructed as both imagined homogeneous communities (Anderson 1991), but also through the making of internal others, such as ethnic, religious, or political minorities, that act as a foil to a presumed 'pure' nation. There was, in fact, nothing 'Druze' or 'traditional' to this execution: the perpetrators did not follow the traditionally prescribed honour code for blood money and revenge (Khalaf 1990; Khuri 2004). On the contrary, such public performances of killings are examples of late modernity's aesthetics of ethnic cleansing. 'Through violence', writes Malkki on the Rwandan genocide, 'bodies of individual persons become metamorphosed into *specimens* of the ethnic category for which they are supposed to stand' (Malkki 2004: 132, emphasis in the original). The public execution in the Square of the Swords aimed to ritually transform the man from Saqba into a specimen of the Other, the Enemy.

Second, rather than discussions on human nature, or assumptions about the essential existence of 'primary' identities, and the inevitability of civilisational clashes, anthropological studies situate sectarianism as a historically recent and politically contingent phenomenon. To do this, the thesis that religious communities represent 'compact minorities' (Rabinovich 1979) must be challenged on two fronts: firstly, on account of ethnographic works that demonstrate the internal heterogeneity that exists is such communities (Kastrinou 2016; Khuri 2004). Secondly, although both 'sectarianism' (*ta'ifiyyah*) and related notions such as 'tribalism' are increasingly questioned by historians (Neep 2012; White 2012) and anthropologists (Chatty 2013; Salamandra 2013), in understanding current political conflicts, they are still deployed in softer forms, as the 'natural and culturally specific bases of politics in the Middle East' (Van Dam 2011: 144). This position, however, tends to ignore the recent and important history of sectarianism as a modern form of political subjectivity and citizenship that emerged under a complex mixture of local and global forces in the weaning of the Ottoman empire in late 19th century (Makdisi 2000).

In this chapter, I follow Makdisi's definition of sectarianism as both a practice through which historically specific collective identities are formed, and as a discourse, an ideology that imagines difference and constitutes Others on the basis of eternal religious or ethnic differences. I contend, with Neep (2012), and White (2012), that sectarianism and minorities were further institutionalised through the colonial French Mandate. Ever since, the politics of minorities and majorities have precipitated and excused hard and soft forms of external interventions in Syria and throughout the Middle East (Mahmood 2012). Today's sectarian fragmentation in Syria is the newest chapter in this history of using religious identities as a means of global and local politics. Sectarian identities are not unchanging and exclusive of other identities but are, rather, constructed through practices and discourses which need to be analysed in context (cf. Phillips 2015). Let us now turn to understanding the latent conditions of sectarianism in pre-war Syria.

Imperial sectarianism: State ideology and sectarianism in pre-war Syria

For Gramsci, folklore was a gate to the life world of popular strata that could reveal their views and contestations of 'official' renditions of history and morality (Gramsci 1999: 360). But what happens when the state inserts itself into this intimate world, and funds it to come perform on stage?

The manipulation of minorities has been instrumental to the consolidation and maintenance of Ba'th rule in Syria – and this is not only because such loyalties were politically manipulated in the army and the security apparatuses. Coercion alone does not sustain a government, however brutal, for over 40 years: 'violence can always destroy power; out of the barrel of a gun grows the most effective command, resulting in the most instant and perfect obedience. What never can grow out of it is power' (Arendt 1970: 53). 'Power' here is understood as *voluntary compliance*, not coercion, to different forms of domination (see Lukes 2005).

The 'smart' use of sectarianism by the state lay in that, while public discourse spoke of secular Arab nationalism, populist cultural policy allowed for the controlled expression of religious and ethnic 'cultural' difference. In a sense, *'sectarianism' rather than an imposed rigid and homogeneous nationalism* was the 'dirty secret' of the state as well as the reason for its endurance. During fieldwork in Syria, I went to many folklore festivals, organised and sponsored by the Syrian state, through the Ministry of Tourism or the Directorate of Theatre and Music. In the contexts of authoritarian, one-party rule and in the absence of fair and free elections, these festivals provided opportunities as well as excuses for the interaction of the Syrian state with its subjects as means of renewing and consolidating legitimacy, consent and animated enforcement of state loyalties.[2] Folklore festivals offered a unique opportunity to investigate the mechanisms that the Syrian state used to present itself in pre-war Syria, since, following Abrams:

> the state ... is a bid to elicit support for or tolerance of the unsupportable and intolerable by presenting them as something other than themselves, namely, legitimate, disinterested domination ... the legitimating of the illegitimate. (Abrams 2006: 122)

State interest and investment in cultural affairs began during the age of Syria's union with Nasser's Egypt (UAR 1959–1963). Nasser's Egypt, the UAR and the subsequent Ba'thist Syrian Arab Republic were also influenced by Soviet policy – especially cultural state policy in the valorisation of national, working class values and practices (Wedeen 1999). Cultural policies and cultural politics are important arenas for 'forging the nation' (Seale 1989: 441–460), significant tropes of statecraft. As public performances and spectacles, the officially sanctioned narratives of history and culture were manifested, appropriated and performed in ways that went beyond verbal propaganda: as embodied practices, dances do not only relay the sanctioned story which substantiates government's power, but they embody state narrative, its contradictions and limitations.

Promoting an internal cosmopolitan policy of 'unity in diversity' the Syrian state not only allowed heterogeneity but also actively encouraged it through public spectacles such as folklore festivals. The cosmopolitanism of the Syrian state was based on the strategic use of diversity, heterogeneity and difference. However, this 'difference' was not any difference but state-defined, sanctioned and regulated. Let us call this state-managed-sectarianism 'imperial sectarianism' (Kastrinou 2016: 151–152). While nationalism imposes homogeneity (Anderson 1991; Scott 1998), imperial sectarianism constitutes, manages and is sustained by internal heterogeneity. Otherwise, why does a state that is renowned for being oppressive, authoritarian and inflexible spend so much time and effort on the maintenance, nurturing and reification of 'difference'? The theoretical point proposed here is that both nationalism and sectarianism are historically closely related identities by which state power may be legitimated. The Syrian state, through such policies simultaneously pursued both these two, apparently opposing, strategies of homogenisation *and* difference; homogeneity and heterogeneity, are the rhetorical devices that the state utilises in different ways with different audiences and contexts. Whereas nationalism aims to obliterate difference, imperial sectarianism aims to command difference, in the name of harmony or co-existence, and only under its patronage.

The Syrian choreographic politics of state-sponsored folklore festivals help forge an idea of the state as the precondition for 'cultural' harmony within a bounded polity and territory. In crises, however, cultural policies were replaced by threats as the regime asserted: 'it is us or it is (sectarian) chaos.' In this way, the sectarian violence of the public torture and killing in Jaramana that took place in 2013 (described above) did not emerge from nowhere. The cultural script for the construction and antagonism of sectarian-based identities had long been choreographed through the latent construction of sectarianism as part of the state's ideological justification – as the precondition of social and sectarian co-existence. The moment the state's monopoly of violence was challenged, the foundations of 'social harmony' also began to shake. The current phase of 'state deconstruction' (Hinnebusch 2014), therefore, is characterised by the manipulation of pre-existing – but latent – political discourses of sectarianism and nationalism. These now openly sectarian identities do not essentially challenge the binary foundations that modern states are built on (Appadurai 2006), but instead justify with new force their identitarian politics on the basis of demography, purity of identities, and claims for representation.

Jaramana and its Druze residents since 2011

Historically, Druze communities are fiercely attached to their land, which is viewed as a necessary prerequisite for the exercise of autonomy (Khuri 2004; Firro 1992). Ideologically, especially during times of conflict, the land constitutes perhaps the most evocative terrain upon which claims of autochthony are made, while both theological doctrine and historical memory are used (Kastrinou and Layton 2016). Theology and memory have found renewed political potency through the Druze self-preservation rhetoric that has emerged post-2011. This rhetoric, although internally contested, holds that the preservation of the community must happen at whatever cost. In the sections below, I analyse these developments and dynamics through five more or less distinct phases we can see in the evolution of the conflict on the ground

Revolutionary Jaramana or, 'al yasar shayal'

'*Al yasar shayal!*': 'the left has been turned on', as if the lights had suddenly been switched on, wrote Salih, a friend from Jaramana, in a message when the first demonstrations began in March 2011. Early calls for reform and social justice found support in Jaramana, especially from two distinct groups. Many political activists and intellectuals from Jaramana had significant links with existing secular political parties, movements, and civil society fora (for a summary of the political landscape in Syria after the Damascus Spring, see Pace and Landis 2009: 120–125), for example, local intellectuals associated with the Damascus Spring, members of different legal and illegal parties, the Qassioun movement, the communists, and Nasserists. The second group comprised a younger generation of youth and university students. There were important differences between the two groups: the first groups were older, reluctant to participate in spontaneous public protests, less radical but more ideologically cohesive around liberal or social democracy. The second group was more enthusiastic, public and vocal, and very diverse in terms of its political theory and practice. Moreover, this group of students was an important link between Jaramana, Damascus and the countryside as they interacted in the university with students from Duma, Ain Terma, and Dara'a who told them of police brutality.

Tariq, my research assistant, admitted to me in a slightly confessionary tone: 'I thought it was impossible, I did not want to believe it but it was true.' He was finishing his degree in architecture in 2011 at that time, and, coming from a religious Druze family in Jaramana, Tariq was politicised as a result of the protest movement at Damascus University (see Kastrinou 2014, for a lengthy description of Tariq's family). Before the war, Tariq was a largely apolitical, even naive, young man who little questioned official discourse. I remember that one time, talking with fellow students from the Golan Heights in 2009, he was so surprised to find out that the 1973 war between Syria and Israel was not the 'victory' that his schoolbooks had presented.

This was a time, however, that people in Jaramana, as in most of Syria, had hoped for political reforms. They were not anticipating an 'Arab Spring' as violent or as drastic as in other places but there were hopes for a second Damascus Spring that would bring multi-party politics, and much needed economic reforms to alleviate corruption, increasing poverty and rural–urban inequalities. But hopes were guarded as the use of disproportionate force from the regime vis-à-vis protests in the countryside escalated. The blood that shrouded the protests in Dara'a fed fears as well as hopes. 'The society was shocked by what happened in Dara'a,' Tariq told me. Demonstrations for political reform and for solidarity started happening in Jaramana. Yet for every '*mouthahara*' (demonstration), there was also a '*masira*' a pro-regime march, generally organised by local members of the Ba'th Party, and with alleged participation from civil servants and other white-collar state employees.

Finding shelter in Jaramana

By 2012, once again in its history, Jaramana was welcoming refugees, this time from the internally displaced Syrians fleeing violence in the surrounding Damascus countryside, from Dera'a and Homs. Jaramana was and is a good option for many internal refugees because it has more affordable rents relative to Damascus, but also because of its existing humanitarian infrastructure, which includes the UN and Red Crescent. Since the first internal refugees appeared in Jaramana, local residents, especially the young, mobilised to create ad-hoc associations for the help and relief of the newcomers. Tariq was a member of one of these associations, the *Jamaya shabab Jaramana*, the youth association of Jaramana, that collected food and clothing and distributed it to refugees. He describes his experience, which echoes descriptions from other young Druze friends in Jaramana:

'Jaramana was receiving hundreds of families a day, [I] do not forget the sight of displaced families who lined the sidewalks and squares … We collected food from homes of families and friends and acquaintances, and every day we were cooking a meal … And the feeling was wonderful, we do our duty to our people and our friends …' (Tariq, personal communication 2013)

However, as violence escalated and more refugees arrived in Jaramana, the tensions between residents and newcomers appeared. Below, I take two such examples from Tariq's notes, which he brought with him out of Syria, when he left in September 2013:

> The displaced families, most of whom are Sunni, see Jaramana as a place that is unethical because of the restaurants and nightclubs on the outskirts of the town ... One day a car full of women stops in front of Abu Ali's house and ask him for water. He asks them where are your men, they say '*bi jahido*' [which means that they fight a holy war]. From personal experience, I heard once a woman saying the following statement 'God curse him who made us break our feast among the infidels.' She meant spending the month of Ramadan here ... but this is an individual case, the vast of the displaced people were requesting a safe place to escape the killings. (Tariq, field notes, September 2013).

In the above quotation, Tariq carefully lays out the social architecture of the events that he describes, paying attention to context, situation and stereotypes. He points our attention to the necessity of survival, to 'escape the killings', and at the reproduction of the conflict through sectarian stereotyping from both sides: cursing the 'infidels' and offending the hospitality and generosity of hosts by fighting in a religious war, *jihad*, with the implication that they are fighting against infidels and perceived apostates, like the Druze. The need to survive, the right to life, is a unifying human condition that both hosts and internal refugees are well aware of. The divisive element is sectarianism: the perceived religious difference that might serve to reproduce tensions and violence, firstly by diminishing one of the most fundamental aspects of social behaviour: hospitality. Yet, sectarianism and war can be lucrative businesses:

> I was returning from work and there was a veiled woman. She was walking holding a carrier bag, mostly containing only clothes, fleeing the bombing, and was asking the [bus] driver: Do you have a room for rent? The driver began to haggle on price, he said: six thousand pounds for the two rooms and a bathroom. This was huge exploitation! She said to him: I am a refugee from the bombing and you tell me six thousand pounds ...

Although subjective, Tariq's observations, which were regularly recorded for the purposes of our research, provide a vantage point, a window, into seeing how perspectives and practices were changing in Jaramana as a result of the war. By the end of 2012, other factors were affecting the ways that the Druze residents of Jaramana reacted to the ongoing violence, such as the increasing demands made on them for conscription, which caused many young Druze men to emigrate. More importantly, however, as the revolution became increasingly weaponised and violent, the Free Syrian Army was formed and along with it other forces began to emerge. These new formations took hold in Damascus' countryside, especially in the areas surrounding Jaramana. With open confrontations between regime and oppositions, Jaramana became a frontier caught in the crossfire. Moreover, with the retreat of the state from the countryside smugglers and criminal gangs emerged.

Along with the first mortar shelling that claimed the lives of six people (on 2012/11/18), deadly car bombs in Jaramana in August, October and November were estimated to kill more than a hundred people (Sherlock 2012; Human Rights Watch 2015). A double car bomb on 28 November 2012 officially claimed some 50 lives – while locals put the number of casualties at 70 people. In December, reportedly 25 young men from Jaramana were kidnapped for ransom in the space of only two weeks. One of these was Tariq's younger brother, who was kidnapped for 52 days. As the Syrian war began to make an incision into the Druze neighbourhood, collective organisation increasingly became a necessity.

Neutrality and the politics of religion

From welcoming refugees at the start of the war, social attitudes begin to alter in Jaramana at the start of 2013. An internal Druze political struggle was taking place regarding the direction the neighbourhood should follow: should it join the revolution along with all their geographical neighbours or should they sit within the regime's encampment and within the protection of the status quo?

In this phase, there was an increasing political visibility of religious authority in Jaramana. This is significant because prior to the Syrian war religious leaders and elders were less prominent in political decision-making. Religious and elder authority, especially through the council (*majlis*) of the religious shaykhs emerged as the voice of reason and reconciliation between different political voices internal to the Druze community. The shaykhs took the position that the Druze had more to lose if they aligned to any other power and should strive to remain neutral: not to rebel against the state but also to help and welcome refugees and neighbours. They demanded the combining of autonomy with strong territorial self-defence. They mediated between quarrelling factions in Jaramana, but also they built formal local networks of communication and decision-making between other religious representatives, including Christians but also religious representatives from the newcomers. In this way, a substantial effort was initiated to build communication networks, and in a way to keep Jaramana out of the conflict. This attempt, as we shall see, was not totally successful.

War in Jaramana

Since 2013, the time when Tariq got out of Syria to escape army conscription, the conflict escalated into an all-out war. Foreign weapons and fighters provided a steady flow of fuel to the fire in Syria. In many ways, what happened on the ground in Syria is best described as a proxy war, better analysed through geopolitics, and less by anthropology. This feeling is strengthened, sadly, by reports from friends and families on the loss of hope on their part, on their feelings of desperation that even if at one point this conflict was about Syria, this is no longer the case. In many ways, the brutal event of the public torture and killing of the man from Saqba in the Square of the Swords in 2013, described at the start of the chapter, ushered Jaramana violently into war proper.

The event of the public torture, killing, and parade of the dead man's body contested visually but also materially the rhetoric of unity and non-interference propagated by the religious authorities in Jaramana. The event was a visual public declaration that political power and sectarian representation had shifted away from established political parties or religious authorities. The community's self-preservation and self-defence was now becoming incumbent upon the emerging military formations that took it upon themselves to police the borders of the neighbourhood (Cambanis 2015): the 'people's committees' (*al-lijan al-sha'biyah*). Allegedly, such committees started emerging, organically or not, already in 2012, in Damascus and among religious minorities (Lund 2013). These were, at first, loosely organised associations of neighbours, usually young men, that played diverse roles between neighbourhood watch and vigilantism (Reuters 2012). However, from late 2012 onwards these became increasingly absorbed within the umbrella pro-government National Defence Forces (*Quwat ad-Difāʿ al-Waṭanī*). The NDF was an attempt by the central government in Damascus to encompass and hence professionalise the volunteer forces in local militia groups and people's committees (Lund 2013). As Jaramana found itself increasingly under fire, it also found itself uncomfortably squeezed between a violent state (however, one that does not have the monopoly of violence anymore), and a fragmented opposition that was increasingly threatening to minorities. In Jaramana, like in the Druze governorate of Suwayda (Al-Tamimi 2015c; Fadel 2015), popular committees soon became the local NDF.

Indeed, staging the public execution of the man from Saqba at the Square of the Swords was a public show-off of the ability to inflict violence and death. To local residents, who were both shocked and afraid to react publicly, the event symbolically 'inaugurated' the Druze NDF militia that would now, with support from state military structures, take on the policing of the neighbourhood, its borders, and its people. By locating the torture and execution at the Square of Sword, which is an important local landmark commemorating Druze resistance to French colonialism, the militia evoked local sectarian identity, honour and bravery, as well as legitimate resistance. Through both violence and symbolism, the Jaramana NDF provocatively proclaimed to represent 'the Druze'. This declaration had two important effects: (1) with its monopoly over violence, it silenced internal opposition, and minimised the political authority of the religious shaykhs who has urged for neutrality; and (2) by using sectarian identities for legitimacy, it claimed to politically represent the Druze on the basis of sectarian identity. The significance of the violence in the Square of the Swords is that sectarianism was the *result*, not the cause of violence, the *result* of the formalisation and weaponisation of popular committees into NDF, and the *result* of policing contested borders.

However, contrary to expectations regarding the formation of completely sectarian political identities, in the context of increasing violence and militarisation in Jaramana's society, it seems that the ideology of social nationalism is also developing. Interestingly, media reports from SANA convey an increasing presence and influence of the pro-regime Syrian Social Nationalist Party (SSNP) in Jaramana as well as in Suwayda (Al-Tamimi 2015c). Although more research is necessary, this could nevertheless be another indication of the constitution of political identities in situations of war on the bases of exclusive ideologies rather than primordial identities.

Based on sources from a local journalist, since the war began Jaramana has had 8 car bombs, 12 explosive devices, about 4,000 shells, and civilians' deaths are estimated to be about 850. When Tariq left Syria, along with his notes and stories he brought photographs showing that, despite the ongoing destruction, a huge, mainly illegal, construction boom was occurring. A war economy was developing, and new political players were often part of this scene. Most people, however, more than ever before began to fear. The silences during the telephone conversations with Umm Nidal or Umm Samir became more telling than their answers to how is the situation there: '*na'sqour 'allah* … '*adi* …' (we thank God … normal …).

It is in these shifting contexts that we begin to locate and understand the significance of the public execution in 2013. The incident did not emerge from nowhere but through the intensification of the conflict, sustained because of external interventions on the regional and international levels. The conflict emerged out of economic, social and political conditions of pre-war Syria, such as the previous neo-liberalisation of the economy (Haddad 2012) – both of which contributed to increasing poverty, internal migration and population shifts. Jaramana found itself on this rural–urban split – and as it was becoming urbanised and its Druze residents benefited from real estate development – its difference with the poorer agricultural neighbours also became more evident. The study of internal dynamics, moreover, reveals an interesting finding: the effect that the war had on the Druze community in Jaramana was to mute internal politics and oppositions, and to build and maintain social and political boundaries on the basis of sect. The Druze now as a result of the conflict resemble a 'compact minority' more than ever before. Internal dynamics, therefore, helped to consolidate a *renewed politics of sectarianism*: the formation of political identities and political citizenship and belonging on the basis of an imagined homogeneous religious community under the threat of extinction and the urgent rhetoric of self-preservation.

Dignity: The straw that breaks the camel's back?

In five years of war, most Druze areas in Syria, largely in regime-held territories, have welcomed hundreds of displaced internal refugees, and attempted to maintain neutrality without challenging Damascus' claim over state sovereignty. From the relative security that proximity to the capital gives, the Druze in Jaramana have been watching with concern developments that happened in other Druze locations in Syria, specifically the Druze massacre in Qalb Lawza in June 2015 (Kastrinou 2014), and the twin bomb explosions in Suwayda in September of the same year.

Along with other Druze villages in March 2015, Qalb Lawza in northern Syria accepted a truce with the advancing al-Nusra Front (Al-Tamimi 2015a). The truce included an Islamisation programme that appears to reflect in practice the ideas of al-Jowlani, the leader of the Nusra Front, about religious minorities under an al-Nusra administration (Lund 2015). But, the massacre of more than 20 Druze men on 10 June, allegedly after a dispute with Nusra fighters over property, heightened fears of sectarian retribution in the context of increasing regime losses to both the Nusra coalition and the Islamic State.

Indicative of the wider geopolitical alliances, Walid Joumblatt, Druze Lebanese political leader opposing al-Asad, viewed the event as an 'isolated incident', calling his Druze brothers to accept the al-Nusra apology, and to side with the Turkish backed 'moderate' Islamic opposition. On the other side, the Syrian state, not affording to lose the support of the third largest minority, emphasised the existential threat posed by sectarian conflict and its international sponsors, blaming the attack on 'takfiri terrorists' from Jabhat al-Nusra and Islamic Ahrar al-Sham Movement 'affiliated to 'al-Saud and Erdogan regimes' (SANA 2015). Yet, the June offensive mounted by Islamic State and rebel forces on the fringes of the Druze province of Suwayda at army base 52 withered the Druze's trust in the continuing ability of the regime to protect them. In this context, Israel did not let the opportunity pass to openly contest Syrian sovereignty by proclaiming itself as a Druze protector; arguing that the 'memory of Holocaust requires action to avert "mass genocide"', Israel stepped up talk on a 'safe' or 'buffer' zone along its Syrian border (Reback 2015).

On 4 September, 2015, a twin bomb-attack in the centre of Suwayda claimed more that 25 lives. The first bomb killed one of the most prominent regime-sceptical Druze Shaykhs, Abu Fahad Waheed al-Bal'ous (see Al-Tamimi 2015b). The second bomb detonated near the hospital at the time that victims of the first attack were being transferred there. Syrian state media were quick to condemn the attack as terrorist. Shaykh Bal'ous was the leader of Rijal al-Karama (translated as Men of Dignity) and he advocated the self-defence and self-preservation of the Druze in Suwayda, but was more critical and independent from the regime, in comparison with other Druze militia leaders (Gillespie 2015).

In the days prior to the bombs, there had been large anti-corruption demonstrations in the city of Suwayda demanding, among others things, electricity and bread. One of the slogans shouted was the following: 'the people want the downfall of the governorate'. The governorate (*muhafez*) of Suwayda, largely Druze and not aligned with opposition forces, allegedly responded by shutting down the Internet. In the aftermath of the bombs, spontaneous demonstrations took place, and clashes between protestors and security resulted in the death of six security personnel. Fearful of the reaction of the central government in Damascus, Tariq noted: 'But you know what the protesters were shouting? It was not '*Syriah,* 'allah, Bashar wa bas' (Syria, God and Bashar only), but 'Syriah, 'allah, kareme wa bas' (Syria, 'allah, and dignity only). Sometimes it is just enough. We made a deal for the preservation of our community, but we have dignity!' Tariq then went on to quote an Arabic proverb: 'I really believe that this might be the straw that breaks the camel's back', he said, meaning the event that will turn Druze public support from the regime. 'But it is very difficult', he continued, 'there are no best options, who can we ally ourselves with? And they [the regime] are using emotions for propaganda.' The year 2016 witnessed further mobilisation of youth protest movements in Suwayda (Rollins 2016). Whether this will affect Jaramana, or 'break the camel's back' remain to be seen.

Conclusion: Minorities and sectarianism from a window in Jaramana

This chapter has offered an anthropologically based perspective of what has happened in the Druze neighbourhood of Jaramana since the start of the war in Syria. The resulting accounts that piece together a micro-history of Jaramana at a time of war differ from the fieldwork based research that anthropologists usually do. As visiting the 'field' would be too dangerous, I have relied on the stories that I could gather from the same reliable people that informed my anthropological research before the war.

The work presented here, moreover, attempts to address two concerns: (1) how can we understand sectarian violence and (2) why does the Syrian state still hold sway among minorities. To answer the first question, the chapter outlined the latent uses of sectarianism by the Syrian state prior to the war, in a way that made imperial sectarianism a basis for the political belonging to the state. Secondly, we must also understand sectarian violence as a consequence, rather than a motive, of the war and its emergent practices of border controlling. To this effect, this chapter provides evidence from both the wider literature as well from the micro-historical description of conflict dynamics specific to the Druze in Jaramana.

Putting recent developments in Suwayda in perspective, the second question should be perhaps rephrased into why minorities have not *yet* abandoned the regime. An obvious answer to this question comes from looking at the increasingly anti-secular and minority-threatening rise of totalitarian religious oppositions. While, the state has a long history of ideologically projecting itself in the national imagination as the protector of minorities, this rhetoric of non-secular but socially harmonious, has yet to be articulated fully by any of the oppositions.

Moreover, the rhetoric of communal self-preservation has played a significant ideological role in mobilising and re-organising the political basis of the Druze in Jaramana, specifically in the homogenisation process through the idea of self-preservation and autochthony. Therefore, this chapter has addressed the two questions posed through recourse to state ideology and policy prior to the war, Druze ideology generally, and the local dynamics within the Druze during the ongoing war. A window into Jaramana, perhaps, but I hope one that problematises views and perspectives on sectarianism, the state and minorities more broadly.

Notes

1 For a discussion on the history and anthropology of sect in Syria, see Kastrinou (2016).
2 For an in-depth analysis of the politics of folklore and sectarianism in pre-war Syria see Kastrinou (2016: 130–161).

Bibliography

Abrams, P. (2006), 'Notes on the Difficulty of Studying the State'. In *The Anthropology of the State: A Reader*, edited by A. Sharma and A. Gupta, 112–130, London: Blackwell.
Al-Tamimi, A. J. (2015a), 'Jabhat al-Nusra and the Druze of Idlib Province'. *Syria Comment* (24 Jan), URL: www.aymennjawad.org/15969/jabhat-al-nusra-and-the-druze-of-idlib-province, accessed: 8/2/2016.
Al-Tamimi, A. J. (2015b), 'The Assassination of Sheikh Abu Fahad al-Bal'ous: Context and Analysis'. *Syria Comment* (5 Sep), URL: www.aymennjawad.org/17811/the-assassination-of-sheikh-abu-fahad-al-balous, accessed: 8/2/2016.
Al-Tamimi, A. J. (2015c), 'The New Druze Militia Factions of Suwayda Province'. *Syria Comment* (8 Aug), URL: www.aymennjawad.org/17695/the-new-druze-militia-factions-of-suwayda-province, accessed: 8/2/2016.
Anderson, Benedict (1991), *Imagined Communities*. London: Verso.
Appadurai, A. (1998), 'Dead Certainty: Ethnic Violence in the Era of Globalization'. *Public Culture*, 10: 2, 225–247.
Appadurai, A. (2006), *Fear of Small Numbers: An Essay on the Geography of Anger*. Durham, NC: Duke University Press.
Arendt, Hannah (1970), *On Violence*. London: A Harvest Book, Harcourt.
Batatu, Hanna (1999), *Syria's Peasantry, the Descendants of its Lesser Rural Notables, and Their Policies*. Princeton, NJ: Princeton University Press.
Cambanis, T. (2015), 'Behind the Lines in Damascus, a War of Neighbors'. (16 Oct.), URL: http://thanassiscambanis.com/tag/jaramana/, accessed: 9/2/2016.
Caton, S. C. (1999), 'Anger be now thy song': The Anthropology of an Event. Unpublished, provided by The Occasional Papers of the School of Social Sciences, Institute for Advanced Study, Princeton. URL: www.sss.ias.edu/files/papers/paperfive.pdf accessed: 2011 May.
Caton, S. C. (2005), *Yemen Chronicle: An Anthropology of War and Mediation*. New York: Hill and Wang.
Chatty, Dawn. (2013), 'Syria's Bedouin Enter the Fray: How Tribes Could Keep Syria Together'. *Foreign Affairs*, 13 November.
Fadel, L. (2015), 'Sweida Residents Fight Back against ISIS: Terrorist Group Suffers Heavy Losses'. *Al-Masdar News*. URL: www.almasdarnews.com/article/sweida-residents-fight-back-against-isis-terrorist-group-suffers-heavy-losses/, accessed: 9/2/2016.
Fahmi, F. and Jaeger, P. (2009), 'Jaramana: Refugee city'. Zurich: ETH, Studio Basel, Contemporary City Institute. URL: www.studio-basel.com/Projects/Beirut-Damascus/Student-Work/Damascus-Jaramana.html accessed: 2010 May.
Firro, K. M. (1992), *A History of the Druzes*. Leiden: E. J. Brill.
Geertz, Clifford (1995), *After the fact: Two Countries, Four Decades, One Anthropologist*. Cambridge, MA: Harvard University Press.
Gillespie, K. (2015), 'As War Swirls around Suwayda, a Complex Picture Emerges of Druze Interests'. *Syria: Direct* (15 Mar), URL: http://syriadirect.org/news/as-war-swirls-around-suwayda-a-complex-picture-emerges-of-druze-interests/, accessed: 8/10/16.
Gramsci, Antonio (1999), *A Gramsci Reader: Selected Writings 1916–1935*, edited by D. Forgacs. London: Lawrence and Wishart.

Haddad, Bassam (2012), *Business Networks in Syria: The Political Economy of Authoritarian Resilience*. Stanford: Stanford University Press.

Hazran, Y. (2014), The *Druze Community and the Lebanese State: Between Confrontation and Reconciliation*. Abingdon: Routledge.

Hinnebusch, Raymond (1990), *Authoritarian Power and State Formation in Ba'thist Syria: Army, Party, and Peasant*. Oxford: Westview Press.

Hinnebusch, Raymond (2014), 'Syria-Iraq Relations: State Construction and Deconstruction and the MENA State System'. *LSE Middle East Centre paper*, 04. Middle East Centre, London.

Human Rights Watch (2015), '"He didn't have to die": Indiscriminate Attacks by Opposition Groups in Syria'. *Human Rights Watch Report* (March), URL:https://www.hrw.org/sites/default/files/reports/syria0315_ForUpload.pdf, accessed: 8/10/2016.

Kastrinou, Maria (2014), 'Sect and House in Syria: History, architecture and Bayt amongst the Druze in Jaramana'. *History and Anthropology*, 25: 3, 313–335.

Kastrinou, Maria (2016), *Power, Sect and State in Syria: The Politics of Marriage and Identity amongst the Druze*. London: I.B.Tauris.

Kastrinou, M. and R. H. Layton (2016), 'The Politics of Reincarnation, Time and Sovereignty: A Comparative Anthropological Exploration of the Syrian Druze and the Australian Anangu'. In *World Anthropologies in Practice: Situated Perspectives, Global Knowledge*, edited by J. Gledhill, ASA Monograph 52. London: Bloomsbury Academic.

Khalaf, Suleiman (1990), 'The Settlement of Violence in Bedouin Society'. *Ethnology*, 29: 3, 225–242.

Khuri, Fuad I. (2004), *Being a Druze*. London: Druze Heritage Foundation.

Lubkemann, S. C. (2008), *Culture in Chaos: An Anthropology of the Social Condition in War*. London: The University of Chicago Press.

Lukes, S. (2005), *Power: A Radical View*, Second Edition. New York: Palgrave Macmillan.

Lund, Aron (2013), 'The Non-State Militant Landscape in Syria'. *CTC Sentinel* (27 Aug), URL: https://www.ctc.usma.edu/posts/the-non-state-militant-landscape-in-syria, accessed: 9/2/2016.

Lund, Aron (2015), '"Abu Mohammed al-Golani's Aljazeera Interview" by Aron Lund'. *Syria Comment* (29 May), URL: www.joshualandis.com/blog/abu-mohammed-al-golanis-aljazeera-interview-by-aron-lund/, accessed: 8/2/2016.

Mahmood, S. (2012), 'Religious freedom, the minority question, and geopolitics in the Middle East'. *Comparative Studies in Society and History*, 54: 2, 418–446.

Makdisi, U. (1996), 'The Modernity of Sectarianism in Lebanon: Reconstructing the Nation-state'. *Middle East Report*, 200: 26. URL: www.merip.org/mer/mer200/modernity-sectarianism-lebanon, accessed: 4/9/2015.

Makdisi, U. (2000), *The Culture of Sectarianism: Community, History, and Violence in Nineteenth-Century Ottoman Lebanon*. London: University of California Press.

Malkki, L. H. (2004), 'From Purity and Exile: Violence, Memory, and National Cosmology among Hutu Refugees in Tanzania'. In *Violence in War and Peace: An Anthology*, edited by N. Scheper-Hughes and P. Bourgois, 129–135, Oxford: Blackwell Publishing.

Mitchell, T. (2006), 'Society, Economy, and the State Effect'. In *The Anthropology of the State: A Reader*, edited by A. Sharma and A. Gupta, 169–186, London: Blackwell.

Neep, Daniel (2012), *Occupying Syria under the French Mandate: Insurgency, Space, and State Formation*. Cambridge: Cambridge University Press.

Nordstrom, C. and A. C. G. M. Robben (eds) (1995), *Fieldwork under Fire: Contemporary Studies of Violence and Survival*. Berkeley: University of California Press.

Pace, Joe, and Joshua Landis (2009), 'The Syrian Opposition: The Struggle for Unity and Relevance, 2003–2008'. In *Demystifying Syria*, edited by Fred Lawson, 120–143, London: Saqi Press.

Phillips, C. (2015), 'Sectarianism and the Conflict in Syria'. *Third World Quarterly*, 36: 2, 357–376.
Rabinovich, I. (1979), 'The Compact Minorities and the Syrian State, 1918–1945'. *Journal of Contemporary History* 14: 4, 693–712.
Reback, G. (2015), 'Israel Weighs 'Safe Zone' for Syria's Embattled Druze'. *Times of Israel*, (14 Jun), URL: www.timesofisrael.com/israel-weighs-safe-zone-for-syrias-embattled-druze/, accessed: 8/2/2016.
Reuters (2012), 'Insight: Minority Militias Stir Fears of Sectarian War in Damascus'. Reuters, URL: www.reuters.com/article/us-syria-crisis-militias-idUSBRE88612V20120907, accessed 9/2/2016.
Rollins, T. (2016), 'Unrest Grows among Druze in Syria's Sweida'. *Middle East Eye*, URL: www.middleeasteye.net/news/syria-druze-sweida-1534888183, accessed: 7/9/2016.
Salamandra, C. (2013), 'Sectarianism in Syria: Anthropological Reflections'. *Middle East Critique* 22: 3, 303–306.
SANA (Syrian Arab News Agency) (2015), 'Al-Nusra terrorists perpetrate another massacre in Idleb countryside'. (11 Jun), URL: http://sana.sy/en/?p=44531, accessed: 8/2/2016.
Scott, J. C. (1998), *Seeing like a State: How Certain Schemes to Improve the Human Condition Have Failed*. London: Yale University Press.
Seale, Patrick (1989), *Assad of Syria: The Struggle for the Middle East*. Berkeley: University of California Press.
Sherlock, R. (2012), 'Syria: 50 Dead in Damascus Car Bomb Attacks'. *The Telegraph* (28 Nov), URL:www.telegraph.co.uk/news/worldnews/middleeast/syria/9709945/Syria-50-dead-in-Damascus-car-bomb-attacks.html, accessed: 8/2/2016.
Van Dam, N. (2011), *The Struggle for Power in Syria: Politics and Society under Asad and the Ba'th Party*. London: I.B.Tauris.
Wedeen, Lisa (1999), *Ambiguities of Domination: Politics, Rhetoric, and Symbols in Contemporary Syria*. Chicago: University of Chicago Press.
White, B. T. (2012), *The Emergence of Minorities in the Middle East: The Politics of Community in French Mandate Syria*. Edinburgh: Edinburgh University Press.

19

THE LEFT IN THE SYRIAN UPRISING

*Ferdinand Arslanian**

Introduction: The Left's predicament

Examining the social media and pundits on the Syrian Uprising, one can note a plenitude of assaults on the Syrian ideological Left with regards to its stance on the Uprising. What makes this confusing is that the Syrian conflict has continuously been viewed through the lens of sectarian or identity politics with no reference whatsoever to the Left. To add to the confusion, these assaults take place from both those who oppose the regime and from those who support it. Oppositionists depict the Left as being captivated by anti-imperialist rhetoric and failing to realise that an actual revolution is taking place, while regime supporters perceive the Left as naïve idealists failing to realise that what they are actually romanticising is global Jihad.

This reflects the predicament of a marginalised, fractured and outdated political movement in dealing with a complex situation in which an Uprising is taking place against a political regime that while internally highly repressive and based on crony capitalism shares the same ideological roots as the Left and shares an archetypal enemy, 'Western Imperialism.' The demonstrative case of the brutal civil war in neighbouring Iraq in the aftermath of the US invasion further intensified this predicament.

In dealing with the role of the Syrian Left in the Syrian Uprising, Massouh refers to 'the Balkanisation of the Syrian Communists' as a deliberate strategy of the Syrian regime in marginalising and undermining Syria's communist parties throughout the decades, which explains the unmet expectations of the young protesters that Syria's left-leaning intelligentsia would unequivocally support the Uprising (Massouh 2014: 58). However, his analysis is confined to the case of the official communist parties and fails to address the whole spectrum of the Syrian Left. Bunni fills this gap by addressing the plethora of left-wing political organisations existing in the Syrian political scene (Bunni 2014). Nevertheless, his analysis is restricted to merely mapping these organisations and outlining their political positions without providing any in-depth explanation of their positions or how they've developed throughout the conflict.

As such, the chapter will make several contributions. First, it will classify the Syrian Left in terms of its positions regarding the Uprising and discuss the development of each political bloc throughout the Syrian conflict. For the purpose of this study, the Left is defined as entailing both Arab nationalist parties and Marxist communist parties with all their ramifications including Ba'thist, Nasserite for the former and Stalinist, Trotskyite and Guevarists parties for the latter, but excluding groups that have shifted completely towards liberal democratic positions. This study will not discuss the case of the traditional Left within the Syrian-Kurdish political scene and will only refer to this brand within the context of the broad political blocs that the Kurdish Left participated in. In terms of their position regarding the Uprising, the Left can be divided into four main political blocs: the loyalists represented in the National Progressive Front dominated by the ruling Ba'th Party; the traditional Left opposition represented by the National Coordination Bureau for Democratic Change (sometimes referred to as the National Coordination Committee – NCC, but hereafter as NCB); the centrists represented by the Front for Change and Liberation; and the Left embedded in the grassroots protest movement. This chapter will discuss the first political bloc briefly and the last three more thoroughly. It will address the predicament of the Syrian Left through a trilemma of regime change, internationalisation and militarisation and explain how each political bloc resolved this trilemma. Finally, it will argue that the Uprising contributed to the transformation of these blocs to better fit the current political situation.

The loyalists: The Ba'th Party and the National Progressive Front

The Arab Socialist Ba'th Party has been the ruling party in Syria since 1963 and, up till February 2012, was designated in Article 8 of the Syrian constitution as 'the leader of state and society'. Ostensibly, the Ba'th Party rules within the framework of the National Progressive Front comprised of various communist and Arab nationalist parties. The NPF was formed by the former president, Hafiz al-Asad, in 1972 as a mechanism for co-opting the 'progressive opposition' (Hinnebusch 2002: 66). In reality, the other parties of the NPF are merely decorative while even the Ba'th Party itself has been marginalised within regime institutions in favour of the security services (Ziadeh 2012: 23).

One main impact of the Syrian Uprising was that the de facto marginalisation of the Ba'th Party within the ruling institutions of the regime was complemented by a *de jure* corrosion of its constitutional status with the abolishment of Article 8 in the new constitution of February 2012. Nevertheless, this didn't affect its standing in the subsequent parliamentary elections – given the staged nature of these elections – as its share of seats remained unchanged (134 out of 250 seats) and well above the 126 seats required for forming a majority in the parliament (*Carnegie Middle East*, 8 May 2014).

The Syrian Uprising barely affected the internal cohesion of the party. Nevertheless, some events are worth mentioning. To begin with, a wave of resignations occurred among its members in Daraa during April 2011 in protest of the crackdown taking place in the Governorate. More importantly, the party witnessed internal friction between Farouq al-Sharaa, the country's vice president, and party hardliners following Sharaa's 'democracy speech' at the national dialogue consultative meeting during July 2011 in which he argued that one party rule has become outdated. Subsequently, Sharaa underwent 'informal political retirement' with suspicions against him intensifying following the Arab League's January 2012 call for Asad to relinquish power to his deputy (*Carnegie Middle East*, 27 September 2012). The month of July 2012 witnessed a severe blow to the central committee of the party with several members being killed in the bombing of the regime 'crisis cell' while others defected (*Carnegie Middle East*, 17 November 2013). During the following July, a Ba'thist reshuffle took place with the meeting of the central committee in which all members of the political high command (Regional Command), including Sharaa, were ousted with the exception of Asad himself who retained his position as secretary-general of the party (*The Independent*, 12 July 2013). Another development, indicative of the adaptation of the party to Uprising was the emergence of, the Ba'th Brigades in Aleppo in mid-2012 following the advance of the armed opposition inside the city. The formation of the Ba'th Brigade emerged within the context of the increasing presence of militias fighting alongside the Syrian army; most notably the National Defense Forces (*Carnegie Middle East*, 13 January 2014). It consisted of volunteering party members estimated to number around 7,000; its task evolved from guarding party's building towards fighting side by side with the Syrian army (*Al-Akhbar*, 30 December 2013).

As for the other parties in the NDF, it was business as usual as they merely re-iterated the regime discourse of Syria facing an international conspiracy. Many members of these parties acted as regime apologists entering live debates with opposition figures on Satellite TV channels, most notably, Khaled al-Abboud from the Nasserite Socialist Unionist party. Furthermore, the Syrian Communist Party formed its own quasi-militia 'the Youth of Khaled Bakdash' inside public universities with the aim of monitoring and suppressing opposition activities among students (*The New Arab*, 21 March 2015).

The traditional Left opposition: The National Coordination Bureau for the Forces of Democratic Change (NCB)

Roots and formation

The roots of the NCB can be traced back to the National Democratic Gathering (NDG) formed in 1979 as an opposition coalition comprising Arab nationalist and Marxist splinter groups that had previously defected from the ruling parties of the NPF at different points in time. The NDG participated in the Damascus Spring of the early 2000s and took part in forming the Damascus Declaration (DD) in 2005

(Ziadeh 2012: 25). The DD represented the widest ever opposition bloc formed against the Syrian regime. Its creation was spearheaded by the liberal Syrian Democratic People's Party (SDPP), an ex-communist splinter group[1] and brought together NDG, the Muslim Brotherhood (MB) and various Kurdish and Assyrian parties in addition to other individual activists emerging from the Damascus Spring. However, the coalition did not last long. In 2006, the MB suspended their activities within the DD and allied with the, then, recently defected vice president Abdul Haleem Khaddam creating the National Salvation Front. Another schism occurred during the DD's leadership elections in December 2007, this time between the NDG and the Marxist Left Gathering (MLG),[2] from the one side, and the liberals (SDPP) from the other. The main point of difference was related to the strategy of relying on external powers to force change in domestic politics as inspired by the US invasion of Iraq; with the latter advocating and the former opposing. Consequently, the Left defected and the DD was confined to the SDPP and other minor like-minded parties. The defected Left attempted to create a third way between the regime and the DD with many meetings taking place between January 2008 and July 2010 among the NDG, the Marxist Left Gathering (MLG), and left-wing Kurdish parties along with other intellectuals and independent personalities in order to reach a common vision; however, these attempts resulted in failure (*Al-Hewar Al-Mutamaden*, 4 August 2011).

With the outbreak of the Uprising, attempts were made to create an opposition coalition consisting of the four main internal political opposition blocs: the DD, NDG, MLG and the National Kurdish Movement. Nevertheless, it became apparent during the month of June, 2011 that the differences among these blocs were too wide to bridge. The final outcome was a meeting that took place on 25 June consisting mainly of the NDG and MLG parties as well as half of the Kurdish parties, whereas none of the parties affiliated with the DD attended. The outcome of the meeting was the formation of the NCB (*Al-Hewar Al-Mutamaden*, 4 August 2011). In other words, the Uprising was successful in uniting the different left-wing groups after years of failed attempts.

The spokesperson of the NDG (and leader of the Democratic Arab Socialist Union faction), Hasan Abdul Azim, was appointed as the General Coordinator of the NCB with Hussein al-Oudat, an ex-Ba'thist journalist, and Burhan Ghalioun, a Sorbonne professor, as his deputies (*NCB*, 30 June 2011). The founding document identified the Bureau as comprising Arab nationalist, Marxist, Leftist and Kurdish parties open to the inclusion of all the other political forces, with the objective of achieving a democratic transition through dialogue with the regime. This dialogue was conditional upon the government creating a suitable environment by halting its security/military approach towards the Syrian Uprising (*NCB*, 30 June 2011). The NCB sought to move beyond its leftist core and to include figures from other social and political strata such as the Democratic Islamic Current and figures and groups from the grassroots protest movement. Table 19.1 depicts the heterogeneous factional composition of the NCB. Most of the groups included in it had, through decades of political repression, been reduced to small groups of intellectuals, even one-man parties or empty skeletons of once vibrant political parties.

TABLE 19.1 The Political Composition of the NCB

Political Blocs	Political Parties
National Democratic Gathering	Democratic Arab Socialist Union (DASU)
	Arab Socialist Movement (ASM)
	Democratic Ba'th Arab Socialist Party (DBASP)★
	Arab Revolutionary Workers' Party (ARWP)
Marxist Left Gathering	Communist Action Party (CAP)
	The Syrian Communist Party – The Political Bureau
	The Marxist Democratic Gathering
	The Association of Syrian Communists
	The Kurdish Left Party in Syria
Kurdish / Syriac Parties	Democratic Union Party (PYD)
	The Syrian-Kurdish Democratic Party
	The Kurdish Democratic Party in Syria
	The Kurdish Yekiti Party★★★★
	The Syriac Union ★★
Others (Grass Root/Independents)	Committees for the Revival of Civil Society
	17 April Youth Movement
	Ma'n movement★★★
	The Islamic Democratic Current

★Joined August ★★Joined October ★★★Joined September ★★★★ Left August

Source: Adapted from the Establishing Document (*NCB*, 30 June 2011).

The failed quests for opposition legitimacy and unity

The first test the NCB faced was the issue of its participating in the July 2011 dialogue consultation meeting initiated by the Syrian regime. The grassroots coordination committees expressed their rejection of dialogue through naming the Friday preceding the meeting as the Friday of 'No Dialogue' (*Al-Jazeera*, 7 July 2011). Similarly, both the DD and the MB rejected dialogue as a matter of principle (*Aksalser*, 11 July 2011). From its side, the NCB refused attending the meeting due to the absence of what they perceived as a 'suitable environment for dialogue' in the light of the continuation of the military/security approach in facing the protest movement. Therefore, the consensus in rejecting dialogue despite differing rationales delayed the rise of tension between the NCB and the other blocs of opposition. Nevertheless, divisions were slowly fermenting among the 'three rights' (Islamic, Liberal and Kurdish) as opposed to the NCB's 'three lefts' (Marxist, Arab nationalist and Kurdish) (*al-Hewar al-Mutamaden*, 4 August 2011), which would come also to be referred to as the external and internal oppositions respectively.

The month of August 2011 represented a turning point in relations within the opposition. The faltering of the Qaddafi regime in Libya led to a swing in the mood of the protest movement in support of international military intervention, especially within the external opposition. Within this context, a meeting in Istanbul was held on the 23 August with the aim of forming a council similar to the Libyan National Transitional Council (Lund 2012: 3). This took place in parallel to the NCB holding their exile branch meeting in Berlin. The surprise was that Burhan Ghalioun, the exile branch's deputy coordinator, rather than going to Berlin went to Istanbul with the plan for him to preside over what would become the Syrian National Council (SNC) (*Al-Akhbar*, 6 October 2011). The final attempt for unification took place at the Doha Consultative Meetings in September attended by the NCB, DD, MB as well as the 'Istanbul Group.' Contrasting narratives exist on what actually happened during that meeting, nevertheless, a week later, the Syrian National Council (SNC) was formally announced in Istanbul comprising the Istanbul Group, DD and MB without the NCB (*Al-Akhbar*, 6 October 2011) (Lund 2012: 46–47).

In response, the NCB held their own meeting in Damascus two days after the formal establishment of the SNC. In differentiating their stance from the newly formed SNC, the NCB announced its 'Three No's' slogan of 'No to international military intervention, No to sectarianism, No to militarisation', and thus setting out its conditions for any future unification with the SNC. It reaffirmed the cessation of the security solution as a condition for dialogue with the regime (*All4Syria*, 18 September 2011; *Day Press*, 18 September 2011). The 'Dignity and Rights Covenant' was presented as its political vision for the future of Syria. It addressed general principles of geographical integrity, equal citizenship and civil liberties, called for a democratic presidential system and an economic system that preserves private property while acknowledging the productive and distributive roles of the public sector (*NCB*, 17 September 2011). Overall, the NCB's vision was more in line with liberal democracy, with a slightly greater role for the government in the economy, than with espousing any radical political and economic outlooks.

With the crystallisation of opposition divisions, the battle for legitimacy among the wings of the protest movement emerged and resulted in the utter and immediate failure of the NCB. Throughout late September and early October, several grassroots opposition groups endorsed the newly formed SNC culminating in naming the Friday of the 7 October as 'the SNC represents me' Friday (*Al-Mundaseh*, 29 September 2011) (Lund 2012: 28). Relations further deteriorated with Haytham Mannaa, the new deputy general coordinator in exile, waging an attack on the SNC. Mannaa accused the Council of over-representing Islamists and being heavily financed by Western NGOs.[3] To make matters worse, the attack was carried out on the Iranian channel al-Alam, further raising suspicions about the political direction of the NCB within opposition circles (*Al-Mundaseh*, 10 November 2011).

In this environment of isolation, the NCB clutched at the Arab League initiative as the final bulwark against the internationalisation of the conflict (*Syria Steps*, 19

October 2011). The initiative called for the cessation of violence, the creation of a national unity government, with presidential elections to be held in 2014 in addition to sending a mission from the League to monitor the progress on the ground (*Al-Jazeera*, 6 September 2011). Tensions with the SNC – which perceived the initiative negatively – were further exacerbated when the Syrian regime accepted the initiative in early November. On its way to a meeting at Arab League headquarters in Cairo, the NCB's envoys were attacked by a mob of SNC supporters. The protestors scorned them as regime agents, threw eggs at them and physically assaulted them (*Al-Akhbar*, 11 November 2011). Resentment further reached the internal ranks of the NCB with some dissidents raising accusations against the leaders of abandoning the revolution and being regime agents, leading to the defection of the 'Freedom and Dignity Gathering' and the more symbolic defection of activist Marwa al-Ghamian, further severing the few remaining ties with the protest movement (*Global Arab Network*, 6 November 2011; *Ajel*, 10 November 2011). The resentment within the protest movement became so widespread that 'the NCB does not represent me' was actually one of the suggested names for Friday 11 November, while protestors in Homs raised slogans depicting the NCB as traitors.[4]

Despite all the dramatics, talks between the two pillars of the Syrian opposition resumed under the auspices of the Arab League and, by the end of the year 2011, the NCB announced reaching a draft agreement with the SNC (*NCB*, 31 December 2011). It represented a compromise between the two positions on the issue of foreign intervention, where it stated its rejection of foreign military intervention but asserted that 'Arab intervention does not represent foreign intervention'. However, this compromise did not prove satisfactory to the main body of the SNC and the draft agreement was rejected from their side (*Al-Majjala*, 4 January 2012).

The Arab League initiative proved to be short-lived and the Syrian case was transferred to the UNSC. With the ending of the Arab League mission, the NCB lost the straw that it had clutched and, with its emphasis on pacifism and rejection of internationalisation, it appeared irrelevant to a conflict growing in both militarisation and internationalisation. This situation stimulated a second wave of defections, more far-reaching than the first one, represented mainly by the breakaway group the Democratic Platform (DP) formed by the writer and opposition figure, Michel Kilo. Kilo lamented the absence of political representation of the protest movement due to the dismal performance of both blocs of the political opposition. The DP envisaged a coordinative role among the different opposition groups as a step towards creating a political representation of the Uprising (*Assafir*, 3 March 2012). This defection represented a severe blow to the NCB with the departure of many of its prominent independent figures, mostly related to the Damascus Spring era 'Committees for the Revival of the Civil Society', such as Fayez Sara and Samir Aita (*Al-Mundaseh*, 9 September 2012).

Other defections took place as well. The formation of the National Kurdish Council (NKC) in October 2011 resulted in having Kurdish parties as well as the independent Kurdish figures affiliated with both the NCB and the SNC freeze their membership within their affiliated political blocs in a tactic to coordinate with whichever of the two political blocs was more willing to accommodate Kurdish political demands for self-determination. Within this context, all NCB affiliated Kurdish parties, with the exception of the PYD, froze their membership in the NCB in January 2012 (*Elaph*, 17 January 2012). 'The Path for Peaceful Change' (PPC) was another breakaway group from the NCB, albeit taking a more critical stance towards the Uprising. The breakaway was led by Fateh Jamous, the historical leader of the Communist Action Party, within the Marxist Left Gathering, along with other 20 NCB members (*Syria Truth*, 24 February 2012). Jamous discarded the notion that Syria was witnessing a revolution but rather a three-sided conflict among loyalists, oppositionists and the in-between, a conflict prone to escalation given Syria's geopolitical significance and its fragile social fabric. Consequently, rather than overthrowing the regime the task foreseen was exiting the crisis with least possible losses which implied creating a political representation of the in-between 'the third popular block' as well as initiating unconditional dialogue among all sides of the conflict (*Syria Truth*, 24 February 2012; *Al-Nida'*, 14 April 2013).[5]

The quest for a political solution amid militarisation

With the official ending of the Arab mission in February 2012, both the internationalisation and the militarisation of the Syrian conflict had become facts that the NCB had to accommodate itself to. The referral of the Syrian case to the UNSC was met with a double Russian/Chinese veto and was followed by the joint UN/Arab League Kofi Annan plan (*Al-Jazeera*, 27 March 2012). Another facet of internationalisation was the initiation of the 'Friends of Syria' conferences. Within this new context, NCB's strategy was based on endorsing the Annan plan, rejecting the 'Friends of Syria' conferences and building closer ties with Russia and China.

The welcoming of the Annan plan was based on the view that it re-activated the Arab League initiative. The argument went that the consensual nature of the plan would alleviate many of its negativities emanating from its international nature and therefore neutralising the threat of its transformation into a platform for international intervention (*NCB*, 28 March 2012). Conversely, the 'Friends of Syria' was viewed as the exact opposite of the Annan plan. It represented a manifestation of a specific international axis – that of the Western/Turkish/Gulf countries – as well as a platform for both militarisation and imposing the SNC as the sole representative of the Syrian opposition (*NCB*, 28 February 2012). The third pillar of the NCB's new foreign policy was its tilt towards Russia and China. This represented a shift from the position adopted during the Arab initiative where – being part of the international community – they were viewed as part of the problem especially given their close links with the Syrian regime (*Al-Quds Al-arabi*, 2 February 2012). Nevertheless, the changing international context of the Syrian conflict compelled the NCB to change its attitude. From one side, the NCB realised that the Russians and Chinese, with their veto powers, were indispensable for any solution (*NCB*, 5

February 2012). From another side, a convergence of interests emerged between them as they both emphasised a non-military political resolution to the Syrian conflict (*Taht Al-Mijhar*, 17 February 2012). Again, the Annan plan proved to be incapable of dealing with the intensification of violence. After failing to achieve any negotiating progress, Annan manged to have the UNSC members agree on an action plan on Syria referred to as the Geneva Communiqué. The Communiqué referred to a transitional government with full executive powers but failed to specify the fate of Asad (*The Telegraph*, 30 June 2012).

Directly following the Geneva Communiqué, the different opposition factions held a conference in Cairo under the auspices of the Arab League. The conventional narrative was that this conference agreed on two documents, a Joint Political Plan for the Transitional Phase and the National Pact, while failing to agree on creating follow-up committees (*Carnegie Middle East*, 25 September 2013). The National Pact, envisaging Syria's future, drew heavily from the NCB's Dignity and Rights Pact. In the Joint Political Plan, the transitional phase surpassed the Geneva Communiqué in explicitly linking the initiation of the transition phase with Asad's relinquishing of power. It also witnessed the NCB's overt endorsement of the FSA (*Asharq al-Arabi*, 4 July 2012). Behind the scenes, the Cairo conference was an attempt to have the opposition and, in particular, the SNC endorse the Geneva Communiqué. Given that Geneva diluted the potential for military intervention and even failed to mention that Asad ought to step down, it was rejected by the SNC. 'We will take issues with our own hands' was Farouq al Taifour's response to Annan's deputy, Nasser Al Qudwa (*Al-Akhbar*, 14 November 2013). As such, Cairo, more than being a disagreement on follow-up committees, was an absolute failure. It launched a new era in the Syrian conflict in which opposition violence as a means for overthrowing the Syrian regime was applied to the fullest, leading to a complete divergence between the two main blocs of the political opposition (*Al-Akhbar*, 14 November 2013).

The Cairo conference was followed by the fiercest offensive launched by the Syrian armed opposition, with battles reaching the metropolises of Damascus and Aleppo forcing the regime to retreat from large swathes of rural areas especially in the north. Within this new reality, the NCB focused its international diplomacy on using the adverse impact of increasing militarisation to reignite the choice of a peaceful diplomatic solution through carrying out visits to numerous international and regional countries (*NCB*, 28 July 2012).[6] Another focus was the inauguration of a conference for the Syrian opposition inside Syria. The 'Conference for Salvation' convened in September 2012 after receiving guarantees from the regime's international allies. In the middle of Damascus and in the presence of the Russian, Chinese and Iranian ambassadors, it explicitly called for regime change (*Al-Jazeera*, 24 September 2012). Two days prior to the conference the NCB announced that one of its leaders, Abdul Aziz al-Khayer, had disappeared following his return from a visit to China along with two other members of the NCB; the NCB accused the Syrian intelligence of abducting them on their way from the airport to Damascus, while the Syrian government officially denied any role in their disappearance

(*NCB*, 21 September 2012). The conference did not impress the main body of the opposition with both the SNC and the FSA viewing it negatively (*Al-Jazeera*, 24 September 2012). Internally, the conference itself enticed a third wave of defections, albeit less significant than the previous one. Both the grassroots Ma'n and the Association of Syrian Communists Left the NCB as they considered the conference a retreat from the opposition consensus reached in Cairo (*All4Syria*, 14 September 2012; *Syria News*, 19 September 2012).

The subsequent events in late 2012 would re-inforce the NCB's convictions of the futility of a military solution to the Syrian crisis, because even though the Syrian regime had retreated significantly, it was nowhere near collapsing. Furthermore, the humanitarian cost of the conflict appeared appalling. The rise of Jihadist groups within the armed opposition further complicated issues especially with blowback effects of similar groups materialising in Libya and Mali (*al-Hewar al-Mutamaden*, 18 July 2013). Within this context, the already weak potential for direct military intervention was further dimmed while the US sought to increase its direct influence on Syrian affairs most notably through replacing the SNC with the more inclusive National Coalition of Syrian Revolutionary and Opposition Forces (NC) as the main representative of the opposition (*al-Hewar al-Mutamaden*, 18 July 2013). In reality, the NC was nothing other than the SNC extended to include more liberal figures and to be headed by Moaz al-Khatib, the former cleric of the Grand Mosque of Damascus, and seen as holding the middle ground between the secularists and the Islamists. The NCB received the creation of the NC with scepticism, fearing that it would, in line with its predecessor, attempt to monopolise the opposition scene (*NCB*, 12 November 2012).

The year 2013 commenced with Asad launching a dialogue initiative in early January. The initiative entailed establishing a conference for national dialogue leading to an inclusive new cabinet as well as parliamentary elections. Although both sides of the opposition rejected the initiative (*Day Press*, 7 January 2013), it instigated two counter dialogue initiatives: the first by the NCB itself, which emphasised Geneva 1 as the platform for dialogue (*NCB*, 8 January 2013). The second, more surprising, initiative was announced by al-Khatib himself, albeit as an individual initiative rather than that representing the NC (*Assafir*, 31 January 2013). The NCB welcomed the al-Khatib initiative realising that the NC was no longer acting as a unified bloc and saw an emerging Damascene faction within it that was more prone towards dialogue – due to fears the devastation in Aleppo would be repeated in Damascus – which they could coordinate with. At the end of the day, all initiatives were rendered obsolete.

Later in January, the NCB, via the Scandinavian Institute for Human Rights – headed by Manaa' himself – organised a 'For Democratic Syria and Civilian State' conference in Geneva. The conference comprised, in addition to the NCB, another internal opposition group called 'Building the State Current.' The main outcome was the adoption of the Geneva Communiqué as the platform for future political settlement of the Syrian crisis as well as calling for convening an international conference on Syria (*Day Press*, 30 January 2011). This conference was convened in parallel to another Syrian NC-led opposition meeting held in France. Rumours circulated that the French deliberately organised this meeting with the intention of undermining the NCB gathering in Geneva. Manaa' would go further, accusing France of pressuring the Swiss to reject visas for many invitees to his gathering (*Al-Akhbar*, 28 January 2013).

The quest for fair representation: Geneva II and beyond

With the 7 May 2013 visit of the US foreign minister, John Kerry, to Russia, the two international powers announced their willingness to solve the Syrian conflict through political means based on the Geneva Communiqué and agreed on arranging an international conference on Syria (BBC, 7 May 2013). The NCB welcomed the US–Russian initiative and announced their readiness to participate in the proposed Geneva 2 in contrast to the initial rejection from the Turkey-based National Coalition (*Taht al-Mijhar*, 12 May 2013; *al-Huraa*, 30 May 2013). By November 2013, the NC accepted to participate and discussions were initiated between the two sides to form a unified delegation for the opposition (*Al-Mayadeen*, 11 November 2013).[7] However, these discussions were cancelled altogether with the agreement between the two international powers on dividing the responsibilities of delegation formation under which Russia would be responsible for the government's delegation while the US would be responsible for the opposition.[8] The US maintained that the opposition delegation was to be carried out under the umbrella of the NC, which the NCB rejected.[9] The end result was that the NCB boycotted Geneva 2 while the NC attended it. The irony herewith was that the group that ardently advocated Geneva 2 boycotted it while the group that reluctantly accepted it was its sole opposition representative.

With the failure of Geneva 2, there was a halt in diplomatic initiatives from the two international powers, especially with the escalation of the Ukrainian Crisis. Henceforth, the NC would appear weak and impotent, especially given the internal divisions among its Saudi-, Turkish- and Qatari-linked factions. This situation coincided with a new foreign policy approach to Syria led by President al-Sisi's Egypt which found in the NCB a suitable local partner since it endorsed a political solution as well as countered the influence of the NC, in which the Muslim Brotherhood were heavily influential. As such, the Egyptian Foreign Ministry hosted an NCB-organised workshop in May 2014 which included 11 members of the Syrian opposition from different political factions; most notably, Moaz al-Khatib, the former head of the NC, along with Manna' and Arif Dalilah from the NCB (*Aksalser*, 21 May 2014). Nevertheless, rapprochement attempts between the NCB and NC remained stagnant until late 2014.

The month of November 2014 witnessed the revival of diplomatic initiatives with the UN envoy, Stephan De Mistura, announcing his Aleppo freeze plan while Russia announced its plans to host a meeting between the regime and the opposition in Moscow. Within this context, the NCB and the NC worked on creating a common vision prior to any potential dialogue with the Syrian regime

(*Al-Modon*, 12 December 2014). By the end of December, a draft memorandum of understanding was reached in Cairo in which the Geneva Communiqué was adopted as the basis for the negotiation process (*Al-Mayadeen*, 28 December 2014). The January 2015 Cairo conference would reflect what had been agreed upon in the draft memorandum of understanding. Nevertheless, attendance was restricted to the Saudi faction within the NC since MB-affiliated members had their visas rejected by the Egyptian authorities and thus the conference failed to act as a platform for uniting the opposition (*The New Arab*, 19 January 2015; *The New Arab*, 21 January 2015). The Cairo conference was followed by Moscow 1, which the NC boycotted while the NCB attended with a low profile representation, giving priority to Cairo (*The New Arab*, 26 January 2015).

This sudden prominence of the Egypt/NCB axis on the diplomatic scene was met with unease by both the French and the Turks and, in response, a meeting in Paris on 26 February was organised between a few members of the NCB and NC. The meeting led to an internal crisis within the NCB between the 'independent' faction led by Manna' and the 'parties' faction led by DASU and CAP, with the former opposing the meeting while the latter supported it. The independent faction viewed the Paris meeting as an attempt to abort the Cairo conference, and the end result was a wave of resignations taking place within the NCB, leading Manna' to declare the establishment of the Qamah movement (*Assafir*, 3 March 2015; *The New Arab*, 26 February 2015). The second round of the Cairo conference took place in June with the NC officially boycotting the conference while its Saudi faction attended on a personal basis (*DotMsr*, 8 June 2015). On the other hand, a follow-up from the Paris meeting between the NCB and the NC took place in Brussels in July 2015 which cemented the links between the two after the NCB had been emancipated from the pressure of its 'independent' faction (*Assafir*, 24 July 2015; *The New Arab*, 22 July 2015).

The centrists: The Front for Liberation and Change

Roots and formation

The National Committee for the Unity of the Syrian Communists (NCUSC) originates from debates and power struggles taking place in the early 2000s within the official Syrian Communist Party. Qadri Jamil led an initiative to rejuvenate and unite the party through fostering change from below against what was perceived as an ideologically ossified and fractured leadership. Ironically, the attempt to invigorate the party led to another split under the banner of the NCUSC (*Levant News*, 29 December 2010) related to the power struggle between Jamil and the ruling Bakdash family, where the former created his new faction after the latter ousted him from the leadership of the Syrian Communist Party (*Al-Arab*, 3 November 2013). Following the split, NCUSC distanced itself from the regime-dominated NPF, established its own media outlet, Kassioun, and participated in the 2003 parliamentary elections on its own (*Al-Hewar Al-Mutamaden*, 24 June 2005).

At the onset of the Uprising, Jamil supported the Uprising, perceiving it as a natural response to the social tensions emanating from the adoption of the neo-liberal economic policies in the years preceding the Uprising. Consequently, he called on the government to undertake comprehensive reform measures, politically, through the issuance of a new constitution and legislation related to political parties and the electoral system and, economically, through reversal of its neo-liberal policies.[10,11] Jamil was one of the very few opposition figures to participate in the July 2011 dialogue consultative meeting with the regime. He preceded the meeting by creating a coalition with a dissident faction from the Syrian Social Nationalist Party named Intifada headed by Ali Haidar, called the Popular Front for Change and Liberation (PFCL) in order to represent a distinct brand of 'patriotic' opposition (*Kassioun*, 9 July 2011). During the meeting, Jamil criticised both the Syrian regime for its use of violence against protestors and the Syrian opposition for boycotting the meeting, viewing the boycott as an implicit endorsement of violence.[12] Again, radical and comprehensive reforms were espoused as a means of fortifying the internal situation against its potential exploitation by foreign powers in response to regime claims of the existence of an international conspiracy against Syria.[13]

The patriotic opposition facing internationalisation

The growing internationalisation of the Syrian crisis set the PFCL a new test for an opposition that labelled itself patriotic and emphasised its rejection of international intervention. The PFCL appeared more radical than the Syrian regime in its animosity towards the American ambassador's direct involvement in Syrian politics and called for his expulsion (*Kassioun*, 10 July 2011). The same logic applied towards the Syrian external opposition with Jamil threatening to boycott dialogue with the regime if the later were to agree to dialogue with the DD. The first Russian/Chinese double veto on the Syrian case was hailed as protecting civilians in Syria through sparing the country a Libyan scenario as well as protecting the protest movement from being hijacked by external powers.[14]

However, it was the freezing of Syria's membership in the Arab League in November 2011 that acted as a turning point for the PFCL. Accusing the Arab League of being an Imperialist/Zionist tool, the PFCL called for creating a national unity government that would both initiate dialogue and implement reforms (*Kassioun*, 13 November 2011; *Kassioun*, 27 November 2011). Consequently, the NCUSC transformed itself into a political party (The Popular Will) and announced its participation in the May 2012 parliamentary elections (*Day Press*, 7 December 2011; *Kassioun*, 31 March 2011). It also formed a wider coalition 'the Coalition of Forces for Peaceful Change' (CFPC) envisaging itself as a third way combining the aforementioned NCB-breakaway group PPC along with other minor groups such as the Marxist Democratic Gathering; another NCB-defected group, the Third Current for Syria, as well as a few grassroots entities (*Bokra*, 3 May 2012).

The cabinet period: the attempt to reform from within

As mentioned above, the PFCL participated in the May 2012 elections, gained five seats out of 250, and subsequently joined the Syrian cabinet. With the absence of the NCB – viewed as the other half of the patriotic opposition – the PFCL viewed the cabinet as a quasi-unity government rather than a genuine one, its formation necessitated by the peculiar conditions of the country. The PFCL was granted two ministries in the cabinet. Ali Haidar was given the newly founded Ministry for National Reconciliation, while Jamil assumed both the position of the Deputy Prime Minister for Economic Affairs – previously held by Abdullah Dardari – as well as the Minister of Economy and Foreign Trade.[15] Later on, he would be assigned the position of the Director of the Syrian Investment Agency.[16] The assigned positions reflected the Front's vision of addressing the root political and economic causes of the Uprising, with Haidar tackling addressing the political aspect through national reconciliations while Jamil implementing the task of reversing the previously adopted neo-liberal economic policies.[17]

However, things did not materialise as planned, because after forming the cabinet, the country witnessed the grand opposition offensive of July 2012. The impact of the military situation on the economic front was obvious with the exchange rate deteriorating, material supply shortages and power outages. Given the pressure of the situation, the government was compelled to concentrate on contingency procedures rather than pursue long-term economic strategies.[18] With the commencement of the year 2013, the cabinet started to undertake drastic price liberalisation measures, raising the tension between Jamil and the rest of the cabinet. Further tension was raised when Kassioun published an article calling for the nationalisation of the Syrian mobile phone operators, an issue directly affecting the inner core of the Syrian regime because of the involvement of Rami Makhluf, the president's maternal cousin. Consequently, Jamil was dismissed from his position as the director of the Syrian Investment Agency (*Kassioun*, 2 February 2013; *Aksalser*, 16 February 2013).

The path to no man's land: Geneva II and beyond

Following the May 2013 US-Russian rapprochement and with preparations for Geneva 2, Jamil sought to be represented as an independent opposition faction and not part of the government delegation.[19] But rather than his previous stance of threatening to boycott a meeting that included the external opposition, his new argument was that Syria includes various oppositions rather than a single opposition and that this state represents a healthy phenomenon in line with Syria's democratic envisaged future.[20] Within this context, Jamil visited Moscow in October 2013 where the Russians arranged a meeting between him and Robert Ford. The Syrian government's response was to sack Jamil from his official positions, news he ironically received on air while conducting an interview with Russia Today channel (*Carnegie Middle East*, 1 November 2013).[21] At the end of the day and similar to the case of the NCB, the CFPC declined to participate in Geneva 2 after the Americans required all opposition participation to be carried out under the umbrella of the NC. Organisationally, the CFPC transformed into the Front for Liberation and Change (FLC) as a result of what was argued to be a 'merger' among the previous groups in the coalition (*Kassioun*, 18 March 2014).

The 2014 Syrian presidential elections resulted in a further divergence in the relations between the FLC and the Syrian regime as the FLC explicitly boycotted the elections claiming that they are neither comprehensive nor pluralistic (*RT*, 24 April 2014). As a result, the SSNP faction Left the FLC since they supported the elections and endorsed Asad as their candidate (*Dam Press*, 6 May 2014). The FLC emerged as the prominent participant at the Moscow Conferences given NC's boycott and NCB's low profile delegation. As the main output agreed upon was a 10-point consensual document proclaiming the Geneva Communiqué as the basis for future negotiations, Jamil considered this a major breakthrough since the Syrian government, for the first time, endorsed the Communiqué (*RT*, 10 April 2015). The final tie between Jamil and the Syrian state was severed on the 30 June 2015 with his expulsion from the Syrian parliament along nine other parliamentarians. Lund considered the decision to represent a pre-emptive measure from the Syrian regime to undermine Jamil and thwart his potential in playing a pivotal role in a future settlement in the light of Russia's increasing diplomatic activity (*Carnegie Middle East*, 4 August 2015).

The Left in the grassroots protest movement

The outbreak of the Syrian Uprising witnessed the explosion of a plethora of activists with many having links to the aforementioned traditional Left parties. Within the older generation, many former members of the Syrian Communist Party-Political Bureau (Riyad al-Turk faction) and Communist Action Party were heavily involved in the protest movement. Yassin el-Hajj Saleh, for example, is a former member of SCP-PB and widely regarded as the conscience of the revolution, while well-known activists such as Jalal Nawfal and Samirah al Khalil were former members of CAP. Among the younger generation, many party affiliates played a pivotal role in initiating the protest movement (*Syria Untold*, 27 June 2013). Barout mentions the case of the youth section within the Nasserite party DASU which, as mentioned, was to become part of the NCB. The youth section was able to reach an agreement with the leadership in DASU to act as a separate movement, giving it the opportunity to pursue its opposition political activity without embarrassing the party itself. As such, it became one of the main organisers of the pre-Uprising February 2011 protest in front of the Libyan embassy in Damascus (Barout 2012: 179, footnote 13). More importantly, it played a pivotal role in organising protests in the city of Douma and even organised the city's first popular committee which elected the Nasserite doctor Adnan Wahbe (Barout 2012: 210–11). With the formation of the NCB, the youth section of DASU would gradually become disillusioned with its policies and in April 2012, it announced that the leadership in

DASU and NCB no longer represented them (*Al-Fikr Al-Arabi*, 19 April 2012). Gradually, Douma would be dominated by Islamist armed groups, most notably, the Army of Islam, and Wahbe himself was assassinated in mid-2012, while it has been argued that the Nasserite youth movement fed into the Army of Islam (*Al-Hadath News*, 18 May 2014; *Syria Truth*, 15 November 2012).

By the fall of 2011 and parallel to the formation of the main political opposition blocs, several small left-wing groups – the Coalition of Syrian Left (CSL), the Coalition of the Revolutionary Left in Syria (CRLS) and the Coordination Committees of the Syrian Communists (CCSC) – rooted in the protest movement announced their formation and political agenda. The CSL identified itself as a coalition of left-wing groups and individuals participating in the Uprising led by the Palestinian Marxist intellectual Salameh Kileh (*Al-Hewar Al-Mutamaden*, 4 July 2011). The CCSC claimed to represent the disillusioned base of the official communist parties against their leadership's position on the Syrian Uprising while the CRLS is a Trotskyist group (*Shiou3e* (Facebook), 27 January 2012) (Bunni 2014: 22). Overall, these activists viewed the Uprising as a revolution of the impoverished classes and establishing a liberal democracy a transitional goal towards longer range more direct forms of democracy (*Al-Hewar Al-Mutamaden*, 4 July 2011; *Al-Khat Al-Amami*, 15 October 2011). These groups were at odds with both the NCB and the SNC in rejecting dialogue with the regime, from one side, as well as rejecting militarisation and international intervention from another side (*Al-Khat Al-Amami*, October 2011; *Shiou3e* (Facebook), 15 September 2011; *Al-Manshour*, 8 September 2011). Instead, they placed emphasis on the power of the masses and espoused non-violent measures such as strikes and civil disobedience as means for overthrowing the regime (*Al-Khat Al-Amami*, 5 February 2012; *Shiou3e* (Facebook), 24 October 2011).

Nevertheless, militarisation, increasingly prevalent during the first half of 2012, would eventually be taken for granted and even endorsed by them. As clashes reached Damascus and Aleppo, they depicted the situation as 'the beginning of the end' and mass defections from the military were anticipated leading to the collapse of the Syrian regime, a fact that did not materialise (*Al-Khat Al-Amami*, 22 July 2012; *Al-Hewar Al-Mutamaden*, 18 July 2012). The subsequent chaos and complexity of the Syrian crisis was initially perceived as a by-product of a revolutionary process and the CRLS used Lenin's quote 'Whoever expects a "pure" social revolution will never live to see it' to justify the situation (*Al-Khat al-Amami*, 18 August 2012). Eventually, new terminology for dealing with the situation was developed. The dysfunctional NC was said to represent the ambivalence of the bourgeoisie in leading the revolution (*Al-Khat Al-Amami*, 14 June 2013); the Jihadist involvement and its regional patrons were referred to as a 'counter revolution' (*Al-Khat al-Amami*, 19 July 2013; *Al-Manshour*, 25 February 2013) while Russia represented a new 'Eastern Imperialism' as opposed to the conventional 'Western Imperialism' (*Al-Jazeera*, 30 January 2014). Eventually, these groups would diverge in terms of their envisaged solution to the Syrian crisis. While CSL and CCSC would endorse the idea of a transitional government (*The New Arab*, 6 April 2015; *Shiou3e*

(Facebook), 24 May 2013), the CRLS called for reorganising the coordination committees, the FSA and the democratic and left-wing forces in a united revolutionary front (*Al-Khat Al-Amami*, 10 June 2015).

Another contribution of the Left to the grassroots protest movement was its role in the creation of local councils. The idea of these councils was derived from the anarchist Omar Aziz who Left his job in information technology in Saudi Arabia and returned to Damascus to join the Uprising (*Sham Journal*, 25 February 2013). In late 2011, he disseminated a discussion paper arguing the necessity of establishing self-governance structures in rebellious areas (Aziz 2013: 3). The paper identified an overlap between 'the time of revolution' and 'the time of authority' in the sense that daily affairs are implemented by the very authorities (the time of authority) that the masses are attempting to overthrow (the time of revolution). This overlap would always carry the potential risk of having the general populace become exhausted in running their daily affairs and becoming disillusioned with the revolution. Therefore, it was deemed imperative to separate the day-to-day activities from the dominion of state authorities through having the protest movement assume the latter role (Aziz 2013: 3). The first local council materialised in the town of Berzeh at the outskirts of Damascus in early 2012 and similar councils spread instantly all across Syria. Aziz was arrested in November 2012 by the Syrian authorities and died in prison in February 2013 due to heart failure (*Sham Journal*, 25 February 2013). The fate of the local councils became more tragic than the fate of Aziz himself, as they increasingly became subordinate to funders (NC, EU, MB) and armed groups (*Sham Journal*, 25 February 2013; *Suwar*, February 2014). As such, they appeared to belong to 'the time of a newly established authority' rather than 'the time of the revolution' (*Sham Journal*, 25 February 2013).

Conclusion

While, in most cases, liberal democrats are likely to advocate peaceful reform whereas the Left tends to be more revolutionary, in Syria this trend was reversed. The nationalist and leftist ideological roots of the Syrian regime, its confrontational stance towards the US and Israel and the experience of Iraq were all factors that led to the Left's adoption of a peaceful and gradualist approach towards regime change in contrast to Syria's resurgent liberal democrats who were more prone towards adopting violent measures for achieving regime change.

All the three variants of the Left opposition faced the trilemma of changing the regime while maintaining pacifism and rejecting international interference. This trilemma intensified with regime resilience and intransigence, from one side, and the increasing militarisation and internationalisation of the Uprising from the other. The centrist PFCL considered internationalisation to be the greatest threat and, consequently, lowered their already low criteria for regime change and attempted change from within through joining the cabinet. The NCB gradually endorsed non-military internationalisation as a means for pressuring the Syrian regime to democratise. The grassroots leftist parties relaxed the condition of pacifism and endorsed militarisation while rejecting any compromise on regime change and international involvement.

Despite their proclaimed rejection of internationalisation, both the NCB and PFCL were successful in exploiting the latest trends in the international system. Their better understanding of international dynamics – in the sense that they realised that the international balance of power would not allow for a military victory by either side in Syria – led them to challenge the military solution adopted by the mainstream opposition through creating ties with international and regional powers opposing this solution. With the US–Russian consensus on resolving the Syrian conflict in a political manner, the task was transformed towards challenging the monopoly of opposition representation. By then, they were totally absorbed within the international system as the conflict changed into an international proxy war. Qadri Jamil's FLC represented the Russian faction of Syrian politics and fell into a no man's land with the regime perceiving them as a threat and the opposition seeing them as regime agents. The intimacy between the NCB and the Russians faded with its failure to be represented in Geneva 2. Later on, the NCB with its Arab nationalist fervour found in Sisi's Egypt its perfect partner. Although the main intention might have been to challenge the existing hegemony of the opposition, their alliance acted as a platform for converging with the mainstream opposition after ensuring their fair representation in the latter – as the latter developments of the Riyadh conference indicate – albeit at the expense of its unity. The grassroots Left also witnessed similar transformations: the local councils rather than representing an anarchic manifestation of self-governance appear more as embryonic forms for municipalities in emerging Islamic statelets, while, similarly, in Douma, the Nasserite youth fed into the eastern Ghouta Islamist movement.

In brief, the Syrian Left, despite being a fractured and outdated political movement, had retained, throughout the decades of stagnation of the Syrian political scene, a margin of political activity enabling it to contribute to the outbreak of the Uprising and its politics. In turn, the Uprising itself stimulated the transformation of these factions towards better congruence with the current state of Syrian and international politics.

Notes

* The author wishes to acknowledge the support of The Calouste Gulbenkian Foundation for the research conducted for this chapter.
1 The SDPP emerged in 2005 as a liberal democratic party after its ideological transformation from the Syrian Communist Party – The Political Bureau (SCP-PB).
2 The Marxist Left Gathering was created in April 2007 as a coalition of Marxist groups headed by the Communist Action Party with the aim of creating a united Marxist party (*Al-Hewar Al-Mutamaden*, April 26, 2007).
3 https://www.youtube.com/watch?v=v9eDki3Z_WY.
4 https://www.youtube.com/watch?v=9WtxRH918c0.
5 https://www.youtube.com/watch?v=lOmkEx0g074.
6 https://www.youtube.com/watch?v=2fvFrrrlNtU.
7 https://www.youtube.com/watch?v=J63vbJeljz0.

8 https://www.youtube.com/watch?v=J63vbJeljz0.
9 Ibid.
10 https://www.youtube.com/watch?v=iZjYwBKxUo8.
11 https://www.youtube.com/watch?v=iouXMSBAG_Y.
12 https://www.youtube.com/watch?v=h6Y2p85dw1o.
13 Ibid.
14 https://www.youtube.com/watch?v=mAQPJZqINWw.
15 Ibid.
16 https://www.youtube.com/watch?v=bD1ANDQiOh8
17 https://www.youtube.com/watch?v=7LsPX0z5EcQ.
18 https://www.youtube.com/watch?v=Ig7wx3MP0WM.
19 https://www.youtube.com/watch?v=lC3mTYIeUVQ.
20 Ibid.
21 https://www.youtube.com/watch?v=f2bR6b6MGKQ.

Bibliography

Aziz, Omar (2013), *A Discussion Paper on Local Councils in Syria*, The Anarchist Library, https://tahriricn.wordpress.com/2013/09/22/syria-translateda-discussion-paper-on-local-councils-in-syria-by-the-martyr-and-anarchist-comrade-omar-aziz/.

Barout, Muhammad Jamal (2012), *Syria in the Last Decade: The Dialectic of Stagnation and Reform* [in Arabic] Arab Center for Research and Policy Studies.

Bunni, Akram (2014), An Analysis of the Realities of the Syrian Left, in *Mapping of the Arab Left*, edited by Jamil Hilal and Katja Hermann, 102–125. Ramallah: Rosa Luxemburg Stiftung.

Hinnebusch, Raymond (2002), *Syria: Revolution from Above*. London and New York: Routledge.

International Crisis Group (2013), Anything but Politics: The State of Syria's Political Opposition. Middle East Report, No. 146. https://www.files.ethz.ch/isn/171564/146-anything-but-politics-the-state-of-syrias-political-opposition.pdf.

Lund, Aron (2011), *The Ghosts of Hama*. Stockholm: Swedish International Liberal Centre.

Lund, Aron (2012), *Divided They Stand: An Overview of Syria's Political Opposition Factions*. Uppsala: Olof Palme International Center, Foundation for European Progressive Studies.

Massouh, Firas (2014), Left Out? The Syrian Revolution and the Crisis of the Left. www.academia.edu/3497857/Left_Out_The_Syrian_Revolution_and_the_Crisis_of_the_Left.

Ziadeh, Radwan (2012), *Power and Policy in Syria: Intelligence Services, Foreign Relations and Democracy in the Modern Middle East*. London: I.B.Tauris.

20

POLITICAL INCONGRUITY BETWEEN THE KURDS AND THE 'OPPOSITION' IN THE SYRIAN UPRISING

Deniz Çifçi

Introduction

This chapter will focus on the underlying motives for the political distance between the Syrian opposition – including the Syrian National Council (SNC) and the National Coordination Committee (NCC) – and the Kurdish opposition, which is represented by the Democratic Union Party (Partîya Yekîtiya Demokrat – PYD) and the Kurdish National Council (Encûmena Niştimani ya Kurdî li Sûriyê – KNC). The Syrian opposition group, the SNC, and its affiliated armed group, the Free Syrian Army (FSA), were especially powerful during the first two years of the Syrian Uprising, but were later weakened with the rise of jihadist groups such as Jabhat al-Nusra (Nusra Front) and Islamic State of Iraq and Sham (ISIS), which eclipsed the FSA on the ground. At the same time, a group known as the PYD and its military wing, the People's Defence Unit (Yekîneyèn Parastina Gel – YPG), gained power by militarily establishing territorial control of the Kurdish area in northern Syria since 2012. The other Kurdish opposition group, the KNC, does not have military power on the ground, but enjoys international recognition.

At the onset of the Uprising, most thought that either the Kurdish opposition would join the Syrian opposition or that both parties would at least cooperate since the Ba'th Party (Ba'thism as an ideology), had for decades persecuted the Kurds. However, the Syrian opposition, in particular the SNC/FSA, and the Kurdish opposition, the PYD/YPG and the KNC, instead of gathering together around a common political goal(s), pursued their own agendas. The indifference of the Syrian opposition and the majority of Syrian Arabs to the Kurds' political rights and suffering before the Uprising led the Kurds to become a lot more cautious in their approach to the opposition, even though they strongly supported stripping Bashar al-Asad of his power. Fragmentation within the Syrian opposition in general, and division between the two main dominant opposition groups, the Kurdish and the Syrian opposition, in particular, has played a significant role in the failure of the Syrian Uprising.

This chapter will analyse the incongruity between the political aims of the Syrian opposition and the Kurds, primarily by analysing data obtained from interviews conducted with the Syrian Kurdish party leaders in the UK, Turkey and Iraq. The chapter consists of two parts. The first discusses the marginalised place of the Kurds within a Syrian state that identified itself as Arab, tracing the Ba'th regime's policy towards the Kurds and the relationships that developed in the 2000s between the Syrian Arab and Kurdish oppositions to the regime. The second part examines the disagreements between the Syrian opposition and the Kurdish opposition that emerged after the Uprising started by examining the KNC's and the PYD's political stances over the course of the Uprising.

From Syria's formation to Ba'th Party rule: the exclusion of Kurdish identity

The Kurds, with a population of more than 40 million, are the largest stateless ethnic group in the Middle East. The Kurdish region in Syria, also known as West Kurdistan (in Kurdish literature) and now *Rojava* (the West in Kurdish language), consists of nearly 10% of the Syrian population (International Crisis Group 2013, 6; Phillips 2015, 357). Kurds, who held semi-autonomous status for almost three centuries during the Ottoman Empire, were left with no political status within the re-mapped Middle East following the empire's collapse. With the Sykes–Picot Agreement of 1916, which showed little concern for the ethnic and religious realities of the region, the Kurdish populated territories were divided among their neighbouring nations: Turkey, Iran, Iraq and Syria (see Yıldız 2005). Of these regions, the Syrian portion is the smallest both in population and territory.

During France's Syrian mandate (1920–1946) the Syrian Kurds were not granted territorial rights but, unlike the Kurds in other countries, benefited from cultural rights at an individual level (Tejel 2009, 27; Vanly 1992, 117). Kurds were allowed to use the Kurdish language and practise their ethno-cultural values in the public sphere. They were also free to form their own cultural and political organisations. For instance, the Kurdish nationalist organisation Xoybûn ('freedom') was founded in 1927 in Syria, which led to the Kurdish revolt (1927–1930) in Turkey (Alakom 1998). Nonetheless, things quickly began to change for the Kurds following Syria's independence in 1946. Syria followed a homogeneous national identity creation project. In parallel with the revival of Arab nationalism, Arab identity begun to gain in importance and become dominant in internal Syrian politics and the Kurds were not granted any (Kurdish) national rights in independent Syria (Savelsberg 2014, 90). Arab nationalism and identity was further consolidated and systematised by the formation of the United Arab Republic (uniting Syria and Egypt on 1 February 1958 – UAR) (McDowall 2004, 472). Under the heavy influence of the Egyptian President Gamal Abdel Nasser's nationalist Pan-Arab unity project, the

Syrian government strengthened its pressure on non-Arab ethnic identities, and the Kurds were the first of all the minority groups to be regarded as a threat to Arab identity in Syria (Zisser 2014, 199). This, in turn, pushed the Kurds to create the first Kurdish party – the Kurdistan Democrat Party of Syria (Partîya Demokrat a Kurdistanê li Sûriyê – PDKS) – in 1957. The party demanded equality, access to economic and political resources, an end to political oppression, and ethno-cultural rights for the Kurds (Bedreddin 2014, 36–37). Despite its moderate demands, the PDKS was prohibited from taking part in politics, and therefore had to remain an underground organisation and carry out its activities secretly. However, with many of its leadership cadres arrested in 1960 (Bedreddin 2003, 25), the party was weakened and factionalised along leftist, rightist and centrist lines (Bedreddin 2014). These groups then split still further; as a result, there were a total of 17 active Kurdish political parties in Syria when the Uprising commenced in 2011.

The situation for the Kurds worsened once the Ba'th Party was in power. Syria's harsh policies towards the Kurds increased and the Ba'th Party started to seek ways to eradicate Kurdish ethnic identity. In line with this aim, the Ba'th regime carried out a special census (under Decree No. 93) in the Al-Jazira region, which denationalised almost 120,000 Kurds, which they then referred to as *Ajanib* (foreigners), justifying their actions by stating that these Kurds were unable to prove their residence in Syria prior to 1945 (Tejel 2009, 51). At the same time, another 50,000 (whom they referred to as *Maktoum*, or non-registered, literally 'with no country') were deprived entirely of their political and civil rights; their situation was even worse than the *Ajanibs*' (Zisser 2014, 201). The Ba'th regime essentially attempted to eliminate Kurdish ethno-national consciousness. In line with this aim, the regime established the 'Arab Cordon Project' in 1973 that aimed to Arabise the Kurdish region (Vanly 1992, 123–124). The project forcefully either replaced Kurds with Arabs or settled Arabs among Kurdish enclaves – a well-planned attempt to destroy the Kurds' territorial concentration and cut their affiliations with the Kurds in Turkey and Iraq (Zisser 2014, 200). As indicated by the measures taken, the Ba'th regime was determined to assimilate the Kurdish ethno-national identity into a dominant Arab identity.

Relations between the Kurds and the Syrian state took another turn as Hafiz al-Asad hosted the Kurdistan Workers Party (PKK) leader in Turkey, Abdullah Ocalan (1978–1998) and provided the PKK with a (de facto) safe haven in Syria. For Hafiz al-Asad, the PKK was a valuable card to use in Syria's disputes with Turkey over the distribution of Euphrates river water and the Turkish annexation of Iskanderun, while the PKK in return gained logistics and, to some extent, political support and security for its leadership (Zisser 2014, 204–205). Through the PKK, Hafiz al-Asad also aimed to take control of Syria's Kurds. Based on its secular and nationalist campaign, particularly the fight for the creation of a united Kurdistan and its armed struggle (PKK Program ve Tüzüğü 1995), the PKK attracted a large number of Syrian Kurds. In fact, it is estimated that more than 20% of the organisation's military are Syrian Kurds (Landinfo 2011, 16; see also

Alkan 2012; Ozcan 2006). Pragmatic relations between Hafiz al-Asad and the PKK came to an end in 1998 as a result of Turkey's threat to go to war with Syria unless Abdullah Ocalan was banished. As a result, Abdullah Ocalan was expelled, and under the Adana Agreement with Turkey, Syria's support for the PKK diminished (McDowall 2004, 479–480). Following Hafiz al-Asad's death (10 June 2000) there was further rapprochement between both countries, and Syria's estrangement from the PKK and the Kurds therefore continued during the Bashar al-Asad period.

Bashar al-Asad seemingly created a positive climate for the reform and democratisation of the country during his initial years of power, especially between 2000 and 2001, the 'Damascus Spring' period. During this period, opponents from diverse backgrounds raised their voices and organised discussion forums in support of freedom, equality, an independent judiciary and democratic elections (Wikas 2007, 4–7). Kurds also took advantage of the Damascus Spring. For instance, the Kurdish politician Mashal Temo organised a Jaladat Bedirkhan discussion forum in Qamishlo at the same time (ibid, 6). The Damascus Spring marked the first notable step in the process of building relations between the opposition to the regime and the Kurds (Ziadeh 2009, 5–6), because, as Ibrahim Mustafa has highlighted, both sides, and particularly their affiliated organisations in Europe, believed that if they could cooperate this would bring pressure to bear on the Syrian regime to take more steps towards democratisation (Ibrahim Mustafa, interview by author, London, 25 March 2015). In line with this aim, the initial talks between Syrian oppositionists and the Kurds began in Europe and were then initiated in Syria. The Damascus Spring, however, did not last long. Bashar al-Asad's tolerance of the opposition, including the Kurds, and his promise of reforms switched to persecution (Zisser 2014, 206). Affiliations between the Syrian opposition and the Kurds were sharply reduced. Nonetheless, the Qamishli riot and the Damascus Declaration, which will be covered in the coming sections, initiated a new phase in Kurdish politics in Syria, particularly in the Kurds' relations with both the Ba'th regime and the Syrian opposition.

Turning points

The Qamishli riot

The B'ath regime ended its assistance to the PKK after the Adana Agreement and the PKK and affiliated organisations' activities were banned and many members and supporters of the PKK were either arrested or extradited to Turkey. The Qamishli riot of 2004 (*Serhildan* in Kurdish) resulted from this and was a turning point for Kurdish politics and the Kurds' relations with the regime and Arabs. The riot was sparked by a football match between a Kurdish and an Arab team in Qamishli. Tensions started at the stadium as the Arab fans expressed their support for Saddam Hussein and shouted slogans against the Iraqi–Kurdistan leaders, Masoud Barzani and Jalal Talabani, due to both leaders' cooperation with the US during the Iraq invasion in 2003. The Kurds began to chant in support of the US and Iraqi–Kurdistan leaders (Kurdwatch 2009, 4–5). The tension spilled out onto the streets of many of the Kurdish enclaves as thousands of Kurds joined in (Savelsberg 2014, 92). Syrian security forces entered the Kurdish enclaves in order to end the protests. They adopted drastic and harsh measures, resulting in at least 36 deaths, hundreds injured, over 2,000 individuals detained and countless human rights violations (Wikas 2007, 17; also see Amnesty International 2005). The security forces' severe measures increased the Kurds' anger and further encouraged their mobilisation. Protests continued for more than two weeks, until the military forces withdrew from the streets, leaving behind a significant residue of anger.

With the Qamishli riot, the Kurds had shown strong solidarity and the will for mass mobilisation in the Kurdish regions of Syria (Tejel 2014, 223). The protests attracted a diverse group of Kurds from various political parties and ideological backgrounds, and followed an ethno-national line which strikingly contributed to the development of Kurdish self-awareness, with some identifying the idea of 'Kurdishness', as noted in Gunter (Gunter 2014, 94). The Qamishli riot also indicated that the Syrian regime's plan to take its own Kurds under control by hosting the PKK leader Abdullah Ocalan had not been successful.

Following the suppression of the Qamishli riot, Bashar al-Asad promised to deal with the Kurdish issue. In a talk at Damascus University regarding the Kurdish issue, for instance, he stated, 'we started solving it in 2002 by studying the criteria put for solving the problem, i.e. granting nationality [but] political developments delayed this issue … We will solve this issue soon in an expression of the importance of national unity in Syria' (Speech of President Bashar Asad at Damascus University, 10 November 2005). Bashar al-Asad, however, did not keep his promise, but even further intensified pressure on Kurdish identity. All of the measures taken, however, could not stop the Kurdish masses from organising further and demanding their ethno-cultural rights and status as a separate nationality in Syria.

It was not long after the Qamishli riot that the Kurds' discontent with the Ba'th regime deepened and once again escalated into another mass demonstration, which erupted as a result of the kidnapping and killing of the Kurdish cleric Sheikh Mohammed Mashouq al-Khaznawi in 2005. Khaznawi was an influential religious figure among the Kurds, who, shortly before his kidnapping, had started to demand that Kurds be given political rights (Lowe 2006, 6). The Ba'th regime did not welcome Khaznawi's opinions on the Kurdish issue. Kurds therefore blamed the regime for his assassination, and thousands gathered at his funeral (Allsopp 2014, 106). Syrian security forces infiltrated the funeral, resulting in many wounded and arrested, including Khaznawi's son (Rubin 2007, 94; also see Human Rights Watch 2009, 18). Nevertheless, this did not hinder the Kurds from once again taking to the streets collectively. Both the Qamishli and Khaznawi cases illustrated that the Ba'th regime's continued ethnic discrimination policies contributed to the further politicisation of Kurdish identity (Lund 2012, 67). Kurdish politics gained a collective and nationalist narrative and thus took a new turn in Syria.

Damascus Declaration

The Kurds and the Syrian opposition shared some common concerns regarding the Ba'th regime; however, this was not sufficient to create a strong relationship between them. The Damascus Spring of 2000 established a foundation for relations to develop, but full cooperation was not achieved because of the considerable suspicion and distrust between the parties. Despite this, the Qamishli riot illustrated that the Kurds were well organised and had the ability to mobilise collectively. This capability opened up an opportunity for the opposition in its struggle against the regime, even though the Kurds' ethno-national claims provoked disquiet amongst them. A common ground between the parties did eventually develop after the opposition's challenge to Bashar al-Asad's policies over Lebanon, Iraq and Palestine following the murder of Lebanon's former Prime Minister Rafic Hariri (14 February 2005), which also ended Syria's military presence in Lebanon (Lund 2012, 13–14). To strengthen the opposition against Bashar al-Asad's policies, the Kurds and the Syrian opposition intensified their relations. Conciliation between the two parties was affirmed by the *Damascus Declaration for National Democratic Change* on 16 October 2005, which was signed by five political groups and nine recognised opposition figures (Wikas 2007, 7).

The Declaration was successful in uniting most of the Kurdish and Syrian Arab opponent groups inside and outside Syria around a joint programme. However, due to the ideological differences and political competition, most of the Kurdish parties signed the Declaration separately. On the Kurdish side, the Patriotic Party (Partîya Demokrat a Welatparèz), the Progressive Party (Partîya Pêşverû), the Democratic Yekîtî (Partîya Yakîtîya Demokrat), the Equality Party (Partîya Wekhevî), the Abdulhakim Bashar-led Kurdish Democratic Party in Syria (el-Partî), the Left Party (Partîya Çep a Kurdî), Nasruddin Ibrahim's Partîya Demokrat a Kurdî li Sûrîye (el-Partî) and the Kurdish Accord (Wifaq) Party (Rêkeftin) were among the signatories (Kurdwatch 2011d, 29–30). On the Syrian Arab side, many of the regime's opponents, pro-democracy protesters and human rights organisations were represented.

The Damascus Declaration emphasised the creation of a 'democratic national regime', 'recognition of others' and equality between all citizens. In this context, it proposed 'a democratic solution to the Kurdish issue in Syria, in a manner that guarantees the complete equality of Syrian Kurdish citizens with the other citizens, with regard to nationality rights, culture, learning the national language, and the other constitutional, political, social, and legal rights on the basis of the unity of the Syrian land and people' (Damascus Declaration 2005). The Damascus Declaration in that sense was a significant step in developing relations between the Syrian Arab and Kurdish oppositions, as well as in moving the Kurdish issue onto Syria's political agenda. As a result, Kurds were given the opportunity to voice their demands in their own words and on more influential platforms.

However, the Damascus Declaration did not convince all Kurds, since they had doubts about how policies would be implemented once the regime was reformed

(Allsopp 2014, 198), and because the Declaration neglected to highlight the Kurds' 'territorial' national identity and fundamental rights. These Kurds, Ibrahim Mustafa noted, wanted the Kurdish issue to be solved within the concept of a territorial decentralisation, particularly federalism. To Ibrahim Mustafa, sharing a separate ethnic identity and being located on a particular territory that had a historical continuance were deemed requisite conditions for Kurdish rights, which was not clearly expressed in the Damascus Declaration (Ibrahim Mustafa, interview by author, London, 25 March 2015). Based on this, the Kurdish groups, the Democratic Union (Yekîtî), the Kurdish Freedom Party (Azadî) and the Kurdish Future Movement (Şèpela Pèşeroje ya Kurdî li Sûrîye) refused to sign the Declaration (Allsopp 2014, 111). They challenged the idea of solving the Kurdish issue within a citizenship context and demanded that the notions the 'land' and 'people' also be considered (Wikas 2007, 18).

Despite the Declaration's significance, discussions of it, particularly between the Kurds and Arab nationalists, greatly intensified later on. But it was unable to advance cooperation on the ground. Increased Arab nationalism, and some signatories' tough stance on the Kurds' self-administration demands, forced most of the Kurdish parties to withdraw their signatures from the Declaration, and pushed them to establish a Kurdish Political Congress in 2009, known as the Kurdish National Council from 2011 (Wikas 2007, 18). Nevertheless, the Damascus Declaration did form a basis for the development of relations between Kurdish groups and the SNC when the protests erupted in mid-2011.

The Kurdish opposition in the Syrian Uprising

Syria was overwhelmed by peaceful demonstrations against Bashar al-Asad starting in March 2011. These continued for a number of months in the hope of toppling al-Asad and transitioning to a democratic political system. Public political mobilisation offered a sense of hope for the Kurds at the time, as was the case for many Arabs. At the peak of the demonstrations Kurdish politics was, however, rather fragmented, as 17 parties (see ORSAM 2012), along with a number of social, cultural and political youth organisations were active (Tejel 2014). Many of these parties were associated with two main bodies: the PYD (which is part of the PKK-led Union of Communities in Kurdistan or Koma Civakèn Kurdistan – KCK) and the KNC (which was founded by the Kurdistan Democratic Party or Partîya Demokrata Kurdistanè – PDK) (International Crisis Group 2013, 43–44).

The PKK and the PDK are the two main influential but rival Kurdish groups, and differ significantly in their ideology, organisational structure and, to some extent, the political models they demand on behalf of the Kurds (International Middle East Peace Research Centre 2014, 24). That being said, the underlying motives behind their rivalry and their contradictory policies on Syria (particularly their approach to the Syrian Uprising, the Syrian opposition and the Bashar al-Asad regime) derive from their power struggle, and most importantly their alliances with different regional powers. Although considered to be the two main Kurdish political groups in Syria, the policies of the KNC and the PYD are closely aligned with the PDK in Iraq and the Turkish-based PKK respectively. The KNC enjoys international recognition, while it is claimed that the PYD still maintains links with the PKK, which is on the terrorist lists of both the US and the EU. Although not internationally acknowledged for a long time, the PYD is better organised and has more power on the ground than the KNC. This power has been proved to the West during the YPG's successful struggle against ISIS, a struggle that provided the PYD with support and, most importantly, legitimacy in most countries, including the US (Stephens and Stein 2015).

Despite their different views on the Kurdish issue, the PYD and the KNC formed the Kurdish Supreme Council (Desteya Bilind a Kurd Sûrîyè, KSC) in order to develop a common Kurdish policy in Syria. This was confirmed through the Erbil I (Hewler) Agreement on 6 December 2012 under the guidance of the Kurdish Regional Government (KRG) President, Massoud Barzani. The Agreement was built on the idea of power-sharing between the two groups in the Syrian Kurdish region. Referring to the Uprising and Kurdish issue the Erbil I Agreement stated that: 'all components of the Syrian people should be involved in working towards the fall of the oppressive and despotic regime', and demanded a multi-cultural, democratic Syria as well as recognition of Kurds' ethno-national rights within the context of political decentralisation (Hewler Declaration 2012). The Erbil Agreement did not work in practice due to the power struggles between the two parties, their differing opinions on relations with Bashar al-Asad and the Syrian opposition, and, most importantly, their differing relationships with the regional powers, especially with Turkey and Iran. This pushed the parties to draft two new agreements: Erbil II in December 2013 (Çelebi 2015) and Duhok in October 2014, the latter based on the power-sharing between the two sides (the PYD and the KNC) following the former's failure (Rudaw 2014). Again, neither agreement was put into action. Each group has accordingly pursued a different strategy towards the Syrian Uprising. This illustrates that although they share some common demands regarding the Kurdish issue, different variables play a role in shaping their relations with the Syrian opposition, particularly the SNC. To explore this further, separate analyses of each group's approach to the Syrian Uprising and the opposition will be undertaken.

Disagreements between the KNC and the Syrian opposition

As a means of developing a collective Kurdish policy, a coalition of 11 Kurdish parties was founded on 26 October 2011, now known as the Kurdish National Council (KNC). As of March 2012, this rose to 15 parties (Hossino and Tanir 2012). Many of the KNC's component parties took part in the demonstrations on the Kurdish streets at the beginning of the Syrian Uprising. However, in order to avoid further aggression from the regime, to see how the demonstrations would evolve, and to learn the Syrian opposition's approach to the Kurds' demands, some of the Kurdish parties withheld their party names and attended demonstrations at an individual level (Selah Bedreddin, interview by author, Saladin, 26 February 2015). In contrast, the Freedom Party (Azadî), the Kurdish Union Party (Yekîtî Kurd), the Future Movement of Mashal Tammo, and the majority of Kurdish youth groups, actively and collectively took part in demonstrations under their party names (Tejel 2014, 228). Kurdish demonstrators highlighted the Kurdish issue through symbols and slogans, along with general messages which reflected the main goals of the Uprising: for instance, 'yes to a democratic state', 'yes to political and ethnic diversity', 'no to life without a native language' (Kurdwatch 2011b). Some even included a national(ist) narrative. This was also a clear indication of the "Kurdification' of the protest discourse' (Savelsberg 2014, 94), the Kurds' demand for their ethno-national identity to be acknowledged.

To prevent the Kurds from joining the demonstrations, and to halt any potential cooperation between the Kurdish and Syrian opposition, Bashar al-Asad took certain measures to appease the Kurds. He repealed Decree 49 'that was prejudicial to Kurdish economic rights in border areas' (Lowe 2014, 232), and granted some Kurds citizenship rights, which they had been stripped of in 1963 (Tejel 2014, 226). Yet in an interview, the Iraq representative of the Kurdish Union Party in Syria (Partîya Yekîtiya Kurdî li Sûrîyè), Newaf Hesen Reshid, claimed that only a small number were given citizenship rights (Newaf Hesen Reshid, interview by author, Arbil, 27 February 2015). To establish good terms with the Kurds, Bashar al-Asad also invited the Kurdish parties to Damascus for the first time; however, both the KNC and the PYD rejected the invitation (Kurdwatch 2011a). The KNC openly opposed any form of cooperation or even interaction with the regime because of its severe suppression of the Kurds in the past. It therefore called the Uprising a revolution and demanded the removal of Bashar al-Asad from power (Allsopp 2014, 201). The Kurds also did not trust Asad because they felt he was only buying time with his gestures until the threats to his regime were eradicated (Mahmoud Ahmad Arabo, interview by author, Arbil, 27 February 2015). Consequently, and following in the footsteps of the SNC, the KNC took a direct stance against Asad's Ba'th regime. This naturally raised expectations that the KNC would join the Syrian opposition. The KNC, however, acted very cautiously in its approach to the opposition, and in particular the SNC. Two fundamental factors lay behind the KNC's 'initial' distant attitude towards the SNC, as will be explained in the following in more detail: these were the Arabs' indifference to the Kurdish issue before the Uprising (Lund 2012, 67), for example in ignoring the Qamishli riot in 2004 (Savelsberg 2014, 94); and the Kurds' distrust of the SNC's Turkish links. Disagreements about the Kurds' political demands in a post-Asad era and the involvement of non-state extremist Sunni groups in the Uprising, particularly ISIS, Jabhat al-Nusra and the Islamic Front, further heightened the rift between the two parties. These extremist groups, although differing in their methodology, share almost the same political goal: the establishment of an Islamic emirate. Concerning the Kurdish issue, too, they have almost the same opinion and share Turkey's aims: refusal to agree to the Kurds' territorial demands and insistence on the removal of the Kurdish forces (YPG) (Salih 2015, 5–7).

The KNC, at its inauguration assembly on 26 October 2011, clarified its approach to the Syrian Uprising and its political demands for the Kurds in a post-Asad regime. The party emphasised its desire for a peaceful transition of power and the creation of a democratic Syria 'that secures national rights for the Kurdish people'. Within this context, the KNC called for all forms of discrimination to be eliminated and insisted on 'constitutional recognition of the Kurdish people as a key component of the country' (cited in the National Coalition of Syrian Revolution and Opposition Forces 2011). In an interview, the KNC chairman (at the time), Faisal Yusuf, summarised the party's demands as acceptance of the Kurds as a nation, constitutional recognition of the Kurdish identity, 15% representation in the SNC, support for all national armed groups, and the re-naming of the country as the Republic of Syria (Kurdwatch 2012). By publicly announcing these demands, without reference to territorial de-centralisation, the KNC aimed to remove the SNC's concerns over the division of Syria and started to explore ways in which it could act together with the opposition. However, as will be explained further on, political developments that took place during the Uprising, mostly from 2012, had by then substantially weakened the chances of forming a common ground between the two parties.

As the Syrian Uprising moved into a new phase of resistance to the regime, particularly after 2012, Islamist extremist groups both in and outside the SNC developed, and more states were getting involved. The once-peaceful demonstrations, by gaining a sectarian and ethnic nature, were turning into a 'civil war' (Kirtley and Curtis 2013). Furthermore, a 'de facto' Kurdish autonomous region (structured as three cantons: Efrîn, Kobanî and Qamishli) was established in 2012 but was attacked by extremist groups, Jabhat al-Nusra and ISIS, who both sought to create an Islamist state (Rawi and Jensen 2014). These extremist groups consider the Kurds to be 'ideological enemies as well as rivals for the control of territory and resources' (Lowe 2014, 231–232). ISIS's success in capturing almost one-third of Syrian land and escalating the Syrian Uprising into a 'civil war' greatly damaged the foundations that keep Syrians united. Bloodshed between Alawi and Sunni Arabs and Kurds and Salafi-Jihadist groups destroyed trust between Syrians. These developments, particularly the rise of ISIS, doubled the Kurds' and the KNC's concerns regarding Syria's future and the Kurds' status in a non-Asad Syria (Ali Semdin, interview by author, Sulaymaniyah, 28 February 2015). Due to the emerging conditions in Syria, the KNC recognised that it was becoming necessary for the Kurds to acquire an autonomous territorial status. Otherwise, they believed, Kurds would be defenceless, because none of the alternative powers, including the SNC, could guarantee that the Kurds would have security following Asad's ousting (Ibrahim Mustafa, interview by author, London, 25 March 2015). The KNC therefore demanded political decentralisation for the Kurds in a post-Asad Syria. In other words, the KNC argued that Kurds should be given the right to federalism (Seit Mirani, interview by author, London, 15 May 2015). The party based their federalism demand on notions of Kurdish national identity and territorial concentration, as well as concerns over security (Amine Brimo, interview by author, London, 15 May 2015).

The SNC, particularly its Muslim Brotherhood and Arab nationalists members, rejected the KNC's political demands. Newaf Hesen Reshid, who took an active role in talks between the two parties in Syria, stated that the KNC initially wanted to develop a dialogue with the SNC. However, the talks were unable to make progress because of the Muslim Brotherhood's strict stance against the Kurds' political claims (Newaf Hesen Reshid, interview by author, Arbil, 27 February 2015). A similar argument explaining their failure was also pointed out by Ibrahim Mustafa, a UK representative of the Kurdistan Union Party in Syria (Partîya Yekîtî ya Demokrat a Kurdî li Sûriyê – PYDKS). He stated that the PYDKS strived to develop relations and cooperation between the SNC and the KNC in the EU; however, due to the SNC's challenge to the Kurds' political claims, particularly federalism, the attempts at conciliation failed (Ibrahim Mustafa, interview by author, London, 25 March 2015).

Rejecting the demands of the KNC, the SNC formulated its Kurdish policy through the concept of democratic state 'citizenship' and the party noted in its political programme released on 20 November 2011: 'the Constitution guarantees national rights for the Kurdish people and a solution to the Kurdish question in a democratic and fair manner within the framework of the unity of Syrian territory and people, as well as the exercise of rights and responsibilities of equal citizenship among all citizens' (Political Programme for the Syrian National Council 2011). The SNC stressed the recognition of Kurds' national rights in a 'democratic manner', but avoided discussing the Kurds' demands for political decentralisation. The SNC's first chairman, Burhan Ghallion, who himself is of Kurdish origin, deemed the Kurds' demands for political decentralisation as a 'delusion' (Carnegie Endowment for International Peace 2012). Disparities between the KNC and the SNC regarding the political demands of the Kurds became more evident with the declaration of the National Charter at the 'Friends of Syria' meeting held in Tunisia on 31 March 2012. The Charter guarantees 'constitutional recognition of the Kurdish national identity' within Syria's territorial and national unity without alluding to the idea of political decentralisation (Syrian National Council 2012). To put it simply, the SNC rejected constitutional recognition of the Kurds' national identity in any territorial sense and denied their political decentralisation demands because it believed that this, as noted by Robert Lowe, would lead to the re-identification of the Syrian state, 'which remains the last outpost of Arab nationalism' (Lowe 2014, 235–236). Burhan Ghalliun revealed in an interview that the SNC respects the idea of protecting the Kurdish identity as well as granting Kurds their fundamental rights – including education in the Kurdish language and administrative decentralisation. However, he added that it would not accept Kurds' demands for federalism because to Ghalliun, although there are areas with a high Kurdish population, 'there is no such thing as Syrian Kurdistan' that can be established as a federal entity, as was the case with Iraq (cited in Kurdistan National Assembly Syria 2012). Robert Lowe underlines that the two leading motives behind the Syrian opposition refusing the Kurds' demand for political decentralisation – in other words, for an autonomous government – are Arab nationalism and their 'fears of Syria fracturing' (Lowe 2014, 232). The SNC's actions and its stance on this issue only strengthened the KNC's distrust of it. This led the KNC to believe that there was no difference between the SNC's and the regime's approach to the Kurds because, they believed, both groups challenged the Kurds' demands for political decentralisation and sought to establish Syria with an Arab-first identity (Ismail Hassaf, interview by author, Arbil, 27 March 2015). These are the two primary reasons why the KNC has been hesitant to join the internationally recognised Syrian opposition, the SNC, and why it has concerns regarding a post-Asad era.

The PYD: Its 'third way' policy and the Syrian opposition

The PYD was founded in 2003 and its ideology is almost identical to that of the PKK. The PYD's outlook derives from PKK leader Abdullah Ocalan's 'philosophy' and 'ideology' (Kurdwatch 2011c). Ocalan's challenge to territorial political models, particularly concepts of nation-state and federalism, as well as his demand for democratic autonomy for the Kurds (Ocalan 2009, 2010) has therefore been adopted by the PYD for the Kurds in Syria. The PYD does not include nation-state and federalism in its agenda. 'We believe the Nation-state is the main problem and the source behind the problem in the Middle East ... We want to get away from a nation-state position', said the party's current co-chairman Salih Muslim (Salih Muslim, talk at the House of Commons, UK, 25 March 2015). The PYD calls for a "democratic autonomy" model that would confer considerable power on the Kurdish autonomous regions (cantons), including the right to muster self-defence forces, granting of ethno-cultural rights, establishment of local parliament (s) and self-rule. The model is not based on a particular ethnicity and/or territory and calls for acknowledgement of identical rights for all ethnic and religious groups, without drawing territorial borders, which differs from federalism. It envisions developing relations between democratic autonomous regions in Kurdish areas (in Turkey, Iraq, Syria and Iran) without damaging the territorial integrity of existing states (Draft submission for a democratic autonomous Kurdistan 2011). This also distinguishes the PYD's stance from the KNC's Syria policy, as the latter propose the territorial political model, i.e. federalism.

Although there are certain common policies between the parties, the PYD has implemented a different strategy for the Syrian Uprising called the 'third way', which privileges neither the Syrian opposition nor the regime, and underlines that the Kurds will have their way without being attached to any side (Altuğ 2013, 128–129). When demonstrations erupted on the streets of Syria, hundreds of PYD members were either in Syrian prisons or, including Salih Muslim, based outside the country. The Uprising was, in fact, a noteworthy opportunity for the PYD on many levels. For many, it sparked expectations that the PYD would actively take part in the Syrian opposition and fight against the Asad regime. Yet, although the PYD's support for the Syrian Uprising was clear, the party distanced itself from the Syrian opposition from the outset. The PYD deemed the Kurds as a 'third party' and therefore primarily focused on the Kurdish region. Its priorities were focused on the autonomous organisation of the Kurds in the region, both in a political and military sense. The PYD, therefore, avoided conflict with the regime's security forces, which led Bashar al-Asad to redeploy his military forces in the south of the country, where the militarily threat was the highest. Bashar al-Asad thus refrained from opening up a new battlefront, and ceded his power over the Kurdish regions to the PYD (Hamid Hajj Darwish, interview by author, Sulaymaniyah, 28 February 2015). This led to de facto Kurdish autonomy in 2012 (Caves 2012). As a result, the PYD is now able to prevent extremist groups and the SNC affiliated military forces, particularly the Free Syrian Army, from entering Kurdish enclaves.

With the PYD gaining authority over Kurdish territories and the party's distance from the SNC, suspicions of a partnership between the PYD and the Asad regime were rife. Hamid Hajj Darwish, the leader of the Kurdish Progressive Party (Pêşverû movement), revealed that the PYD had, since the beginning of the Uprising, been affiliated with the regime in some way; this was one of the main reasons, he stated, why the PYD did not allow other Kurdish parties, who harshly challenge Bashar al-Asad, to carry out their political activities in Kurdish enclaves in Syria (Hamid Hajj Darwish, interview by author, Sulaymaniyah, 28 February 2015). Similar claims were also strongly highlighted in a report published by the UK government. The report linked the PYD to the Asad regime, with a particular focus on the party's lack of cooperation with the Syrian opposition (UK Government Report 2015). In response to these claims, the PYD's co-chairman, Salih Muslim, asserted that the party did not have any direct or indirect link with the Asad regime. He further asserted that it fought against the regime's security forces in some regions. In regards to the PYD's distance from the Syrian opposition, Salih Muslim stated that the party sought cooperation with moderate opposition groups; 'however' he claimed, 'the so-called "moderate Syrian opposition" is exclusionary and has ignored the demands and rights of minorities including the Kurds' (Pikcampaign 2015). In the light of the allegations made and the PYD's response, it is safe to say that both parties – Bashar al-Asad and the PYD – have pragmatic relations (Atassi 2014).

The rise in extremist Islamist groups, particularly ISIS, the Nusra Front and the Islamic Front, in Syria, and their onslaughts on the Kurds, further established grounds for both parties (the PYD and the Syrian regime) to act in parallel, albeit not as allies. Thus, 'Asad correctly estimated that the rebels' Islamism would prove not to be appealing to the secular-minded Kurds. As such, while Kurdish militia formed and filled the power vacuum following the regime's withdrawal, they have refused to align with any rebel groups' (Phillips 2013, 28). Salih Muslim's interview with Kurdwatch clearly reinforced this: 'we are profiting from the unrest. It is a historical chance for us. We have a right and are making use of it … We are preparing our people and ourselves for the period after the fall of the regime' (Kurdwatch 2011c).

As an external power, Turkey's anti-PKK and PYD policies, and, in relation to this, its influence on the Syrian opposition, is also a significant factor in the PYD's distance from the Syrian opposition. Due to its own Kurdish issue, Turkey has always been wary of any Kurdish activity and successes in its neighbouring countries. The country anticipates that Kurdish political achievements in other Kurdish regions could potentially strengthen the PKK, as well as influence and radicalise Kurds in Turkey (Gunes and Lowe 2015, 8). In that sense, fear of a Kurdish identity developing has become a key factor in determining Turkey's foreign policy (Karakoç 2012). As a result, Turkey became heavily involved in the Syrian Uprising by supporting the SNC, particularly the Muslim Brotherhood. Some factions of the Muslim Brotherhood, especially those with moderate Islamic views (also known as the Aleppo group), have close affiliations with Turkey, in particular with the Justice and Development Party (Adalet ve Kalkinma Partisi – AKP) (Lund 2012, 61). The Muslim Brotherhood, like many other Islamist groups, is opposed to the idea of a federal Kurdish entity in Syria (Carnegie Endowment for International Peace 2012). Addressing similar issues, Walid Saffour, who was appointed Ambassador to the UK for the Syrian National Coalition (2012–2013), stated that, under current conditions, it was not the right time to talk about the Kurds' federalism demands (Walid Saffour, interview by author, London, 12 August 2015). By using the influence it has on the Muslim Brotherhood and the SNC, Turkey has aimed to design the Syrian opposition's Kurdish policy (Altuğ 2013); based on this effort, Salih Muslim stated, 'the Muslim Brotherhood does not acknowledge the existence of the Kurds. They have signed an agreement with Turkey that they will deny the existence of the Kurds if they come to power in Syria' (Kurdwatch 2011c).

In another effort to destroy Kurdish autonomy, Turkey made attempts to create a no-fly zone in northern Syria comprising mostly Kurdish enclaves. Turkey rejected allegations that it intended to destroy Kurds' political accomplishments by building this no-fly zone. Ibrahim Kalin, spokesman and adviser to President Recep Tayyip Erdogan, stated that, 'our security measures are entirely aimed at preserving our border security' (*Daily News* 2015). However, arguably, the main motive behind Turkey's efforts is its desire to challenge the PYD and oppose the formation of Kurdish autonomy (Quilliam and Friedman 2015). Turkey considers the PYD and its affiliated armed unit, the YPG, as sister groups of the PKK. Both these groups and the formation of Kurdish autonomy across its Syrian border are regarded as threats to Turkey's national interests, as was openly highlighted by President Recep Tayyip Erdogan (*Today's Zaman* 15 June 2015). And, based on this policy decision to prevent the PYD/YPG from strengthening and Kurdish autonomy from forming, Turkey was also reluctant to act against ISIS and Jabhat al-Nusra's activities across its Syrian borders (Barkey 2014). Especially during ISIS's attacks on the Kurds in Kobanî canton, Turkey closed its borders to the transfer of logistical aid to the YPG for a long time, during which time it condoned ISIS's activities across its Syria border, as was witnessed by many of the Kurds who live on both sides of the Turkey-Syria border (Sidar, Demhat and Jiyan (fictitious names), interview by author, Diyarbakir, 25 February 2015).

Turkey's stance is welcomed and shared by the SNC. The head of the Syrian opposition interim government, Ahmed Toma, in an interview with the Turkish daily *Milliyet*, stated that the interim government supports a 'buffer zone' to be established in Syria by Turkey. Toma further added that they would not allow any Kurdish autonomy or federal formation in a post-Asad Syria. Furthermore, he explained that, to ensure this, they would fight with the PYD after the elimination of Bashar al-Asad and ISIS (Milliyet, 10 July 2015). Turkey and the SNC's stance on Kurdish autonomy have heightened the PYD's concerns regarding both the Uprising and the SNC. The PYD, as highlighted by Alan Semo, argues that neither the current regime nor the SNC recognises the Kurds' national demands. Consequently, the party underlines that the only way to protect Kurds' ethnic existence is to form a powerful democratic autonomy and implement a policy against both sides (Alan Semo, interview by author, 18 December 2014). In other words, the PYD wants to distance itself from the Syrian opposition and establish its own policy – the 'third way', which, as noted earlier, aligns neither with Bashar al-Asad nor to the Syrian opposition.

Despite the lack of cooperation between the PYD and the SNC, the PYD developed a relationship with another moderate Syrian opposition group, the National Coordination Committee or Bureau (NCC/NCB), announced on 30 June 2011. The NCC consists of 16 left-leaning parties: three Kurdish political parties and a certain number of independent parties and some youth groups. The NCC has harshly criticised the SNC for its close relationship with Turkey and the Gulf countries, and challenges proposals for a foreign-led military intervention in Syria (Lund 2012, 26). This approach is also supported by the PYD (Tejel 2014, 227).

Regarding the Kurdish issue, the NCC has distanced itself from granting political decentralisation (territorial autonomy) to the Kurds, which is one of the reasons behind the rising tensions between it and the KNC (National Coordination Body for Democratic Change 2013). The NCC calls for a 'democratic resolution of the "Kurdish National Case"' within Syria's social and territorial integrity (cited in Abbas 2013, 86). In support of this, the PYD's UK-based representative, Alan Semo, explained that within the context of democratic and peaceful change in Syria the NCC accepts constitutional recognition of Kurdish national identity. Semo highlighted that the NCC recognises the self-determination rights of the Syrian Kurdish people. However, this does not indicate separation, he said. In explaining their and NCC's distance from the SNC, Semo stated that the SNC acts in line with what Turkey, Saudi Arabia or Qatar says – it is not independent (Alan Semo, interview by author, 18 December 2014). The NCC, similar to the SNC, is weak on the ground, but maintains ties with the PYD.

Conclusion

A consensus among the opponents of Asad has yet to be reached more than five years after the Syrian Uprising. Contrary to what was expected at the outset of the demonstrations in mid-2011, the Kurds did not and have not joined the Syrian opposition, although this could potentially have put pressure on Bashar al-Asad. Both the Kurdish opposition and the SNC agree on the overthrow of al-Asad but they are not in agreement on the Kurds' political status in a post-Bashar al-Asad regime. One of the main factors explaining why the parties are not in consensus is the Kurds' desire for political decentralisation; in other words, their demand for federalism: the KNC persists in this goal, whereas the SNC challenges it. The SNC also rejects the PYD's model of local autonomy (democratic autonomy) – even refusing to communicate with the PYD. The SNC does offer administrative decentralisation, a system in which the Kurds will be granted democratic rights, so there was scope for the parties to reach a compromise on the Kurdish issue during the first months/year of the Uprising. However, militarisation and the evolution of the Uprising into a 'civil war' along sectarian and to some extent ethnic lines impeded this. Kurdish anxieties about a post-Asad era further intensified. For the KNC, federalism, and for the PYD, democratic autonomy, were not only the sole models that could provide constitutional recognition of the Kurdish identity; these were also the models that would allow Kurds to establish their security forces and provide a sense of security – as is the case in Iraq. Kurds' lack of trust in Bashar al-Asad and the Syrian opposition drives their desire to act and be considered as a third power in a post-Asad period.

Bibliography

Abbas, Hassan (2013), 'Perspectives from Syria: Collection of Essays Two Years into the War'. Istanbul: Menapolis. file:///Users/denizcifci/Desktop/cok%20guzel%20ozetlem%C4%B1s.pdf.
Alakom, Rohat (1998), *Hoybun Örgütü ve Agrı Ayaklanması* [Khoybun Movement and Agri Revolt]. Istanbul: Avesta.
Alkan, Necati (2012), *PKK'da Semboller, Aktörler Kadınlar* [Symbols, Actors and Women in PKK]. Istanbul: Karakutu.
Allsopp, Harriet (2014), *The Kurds of Syria: Political Parties and Identity in the Middle East*. London and New York: I.B.Tauris.
Altuğ, Seda (2013), 'The Syrian Uprising and Turkey's Ordeal with the Kurds'. *Dialectical Anthropology*, 37:1, 123–130.
Amnesty International (2005), 'Syria Kurds in the Syrian Arab Republic One Year after the March 2004 Events'. Index number: MDE 24/002/2005. London: Amnesty International.
Atassi, Nader (2014), 'Rojava and Kurdish Political Parties in Syria Quoted from Jadalliya'. *Jadalliya*, 3 March. www.jadaliyya.com/pages/index/16673/rojava-and-kurdish-political-parties-in-syria.
Barkey, Henri J. (2014), 'Turkey's Syria Predicament'. In *Middle Eastern Security, the US Pivot and the Rise of ISIS*, edited by Toby Dodge and Emile Hokayem. London: Routledge.
Bedreddin, Selah (2003), *The Kurdish National Movement in Syria: A Critical Approach from Inside (1)*. Translated by Klkc. First. Berlin and Beirut: Kurdish Kawa Cultural Society.
Bedreddin, Selah (2014), *Kürt Ulusal Özgürlük Mücadelesi-Suriye* [*Kurdish National Struggle in Syria*].Translated by Umid Demirhan. Istanbul: Hivda.
Carnegie Endowment for International Peace (2012), 'The Kurdish National Council in Syria'. 15 February. http://carnegieendowment.org/syriaincrisis/?fa=48502.
Caves, John (2012), 'Syrian Kurds and the Democratic Union Party (PYD)'. *Institute for the Study of War*, December. www.understandingwar.org/backgrounder/syrian-kurds-and-democratic-unionparty-pyd.

Çelebi, M. Ali (2015), 'On the Possibility of a "Rojava Agreement"'. *The Rojava Report*, 28 September. https://rojavareport.wordpress.com/2015/09/28/on-the-possibility-of-a-rojava-agreement/.
DailyNews (2015), 'ISIL Exists Because Al-Assad Exists: Erdoğan Aide'. *Daily News*, 30 June. www.hurriyetdailynews.com/isil-exists-because-al-assad-exists-erdogan-aide.aspx?PageID=238&NID=84758&NewsCatID=510.
Damascus Declaration (2005). http://faculty-staff.ou.edu/L/Joshua.M.Landis/1/syriablog/2005/11/damascus-declaration-in-english.htm.
Gunes, Cengiz, and Robert Lowe (2015), 'The Impact of the Syrian War on Kurdish Politics Across the Middle East'. Research Paper. London: Chatham House.
Gunter, Michael M. (2014), *Out of Nowhere: The Kurds of Syria in Peace and War*. London: Hurst Company.
Hewler Declaration (2012), 'Hewlêr Declaration of Both Councils (Kurdish National Council in Syria and People's Council of West Kurdistan) Salahuddin', 7/11/2012. www.kurdwatch.org/pdf/KurdWatch_D031_en_ar.pdf'. 11 July.
Hossino, Omar, and Ilhan Tanir (2012), 'The Decisive Minority: The Role of Syria's Kurds in Anti-Assad Revolution'. The Henry Jackson Society. http://henryjacksonsociety.org/wp-content/uploads/2012/03/The-Decisive-Minority.pdf.
Human Rights Watch (2009), 'Group Denial: Repression of Kurdish Political and Cultural Rights in Syria'. 1-56432-560-1. New York: Human Rights Watch. https://www.hrw.org/sites/default/files/reports/syria1109web_0.pdf.
International Crisis Group (2013), 'Syria's Kurds: A Struggle within a Struggle'. *Middle East Report* No.136. Brussels. file:///Users/denizcifci/Desktop/136-syrias-kurds-a-struggle-within-a-struggle.pdf.
International Middle East Peace Reserach Center (2014), 'Suriye Kürtlerinin Türkiye'deki Kürt Sorunu ve Çözümüne Yönelik Algısı [Syrian Kurds' Perception of Turkey's Kurdish Issue and Its Solution]'. Ankara.
Karakoç, Jülide (2012), 'The Impact of the Kurdish Identity on Turkey's Foreign Policy from the 1980s to 2008'. *Middle Eastern Studies* 46:6, 919–942.
Kirtley, William M., and William R. Curtis (2013), 'Syria: From Uprising to Civil War'. *National Social Science Proceedings* 53, 59–72.
Kurdistan National Assembly Syria (2012), 'Burhan Ghalioun: There Is No Such Thing as Syrian Kurdistan'. Quoted from Sirwan Heji Berko. 17 April. http://kurdnas.com/en/index.php?option=com_content&view=article&id=449:burhan-ghalioun-there-is-no-such-thing-as-syrian-kurdistan&catid=3:newsflash&Itemid=54.
Kurdwatch (2009). 'The "Al-Qamishli Uprising" The Beginning of a "new Era" for Syrian Kurds?' Report 4. Berlin: Kurdwatch. www.kurdwatch.org/pdf/kurdwatch_qamischli_en.pdf.
Kurdwatch (2011a), 'Al-Qamishli: Kurdish Parties Refuse Dialogue with Bashar Al-Assad'. www.kurdwatch.org/index?aid=1651.
Kurdwatch (2011b), 'Al-Qamishli: New Mass Demonstrations for Freedom and Democracy'. 1 May. www.kurdwatch.org/index.php?aid=1466&z=en&cure=232.
Kurdwatch (2011c), 'Salih Muslim Muhammad, Chairman of the PYD: Turkey's Henchmen in Syrian Kurdistan Are Responsible for the Unrest Here'. 20 October. www.kurdwatch.org/html/en/interview6.html.
Kurdwatch (2011d), 'Who is the Syrian-Kurdish Opposition? The Development of Kurdish Parties, 1956-2011'. 8. Berlin: Kurdwatch. http://kurdwatch.org/pdf/kurdwatch_parteien_en.pdf.
Kurdwatch (2012), 'Faysal Yusuf, Chairman of the Kurdish National Council: "Sometimes Things Are Demanded of the Council That Only a Government Could Accomplish"'. 7 December. www.kurdwatch.org/syria_article.php?aid=2721&z=en&cure=240.

Landinfo (2011), 'Kurds in Syria: Groups at Risk and Reactions against Political Activists'. Oslo: Landinfo-Country of Origin Information Centre. www.refworld.org/pdfid/519cab2c4.pdf.

Lowe, Robert (2006), 'The Syrian Kurds: A People Discovered'. MEP BP 06/01. London: Chatham House.

Lowe, Robert (2014), 'The Emergence of Western Kurdistan and the Future of Syria'. In *Conflict, Democratization, and the Kurds in the Middle East: Turkey, Iran. Iraq, and Syria*, edited by David Romano and Mehmet Gurses, 225–246. New York: Palgrave Macmillan.

Lund, Aron (2012), 'Divided They Stand: an Overview of Syria's Political Opposition Factions'. Uppsala: Foundation for European Progressive Studies.

McDowall, David (2004), *A Modern History of The Kurds*. Revised Edition. London and New York: I.B.Tauris.

Milliyet (2015), "Özgür Suriye Ordusu Gruplarının PYD'ye Katılımını Kınıyoruz' [We Condemn Free Syrian Army Groups Joining to PYD]. Quoted in Namik Durukan. *Milliyet*, 10 July. www.milliyet.com.tr/-ozgur-suriye-ordusu-gruplarinin/dunya/detay/2085766/default.htm.

National Coalition of Syrian Revolution and Opposition Forces (2011), 'Kurdish National Council'. http://en.etilaf.org/coalition-components/national-blocks/kurdish-national-council.html.

National Coordination Body for Democratic Change (2013), Carnegie Endowment for International Peace. http://carnegieendowment.org/syriaincrisis/?fa=48369.

Ocalan, Abdullah (2009), *Özgürlük Sosyolojisi* [Sociology of Freedom]. Neuss: Mezopotamya Yayınları.

Ocalan, Abdullah (2010), Demokratik Özerklik [Democratic Autonomy]. Komunar, no. 47 (Agustos-Eylül-Ekim).

ORSAM [Ortadoğu Stratejik Araştırmalar Merkezi] (2012), 'Kurdish Movement in Syria'. 120. Ankara. www.orsam.org.tr/files/Degerlendirmeler/48/48%20Eng.%20pdf.

Ozcan, Ali Kemal (2006), *Turkey's Kurds: A Theoretical Analysis of the PKK and Abdullah Ocalan*. New York: Routledge.

Phillips, Christopher (2013), *The Civil War in Syria: The Variety of Opposition to the Syrian Regime*. Barcelona: IEMed Mediterranean Yearbook.

Phillips, Christopher (2015), 'Sectarianism and Conflict in Syria'. *Third World Quarterly* 36: 2, 357–376.

Pikcampaign (2015), 'PYD Responds to Government Criticisms of the Party in Recent Report'. *Peace in Kurdistan*, 16 April. http://peaceinkurdistancampaign.com/2015/04/16/pyd-responds-to-government-criticisms-of-the-party-in-recent-report/.

PKK (Partiya Karkerên Kurdistan) (1995), Program ve Tüzüğü *[the PKK Party Regulation program]*, Cologne: Wesanen Serxwebûn 71.

Political Programme for the Syrian National Council (2011), 20 November. www.lccsyria.org/2630.

Quilliam, Neil, and Jonathan Friedman (2015), 'Syria Safe Zones Will Undermine US Fight Against ISIS'. Chatham House. www.chathamhouse.org//node/18254.

Rawi, Waleed Al, and Sterling Jensen (2014), 'Syria's Salafist Networks: More Local than You Think'. *Prism* 4, 43–57.

Rubin, Barry (2007), 'How the Arab Regimes Defeated the Liberalization Challenge'. *Middle East Review of International Affairs* 11:3, 89–109.

Rudaw (2014), 'Divided Syrian Kurds Reach Deal in Face of ISIS Threat'. *Rudaw*, 22 October. http://rudaw.net/english/kurdistan/221020141.

Salih, Cale (2015), 'Turkey, The Kurds, and the Fight Against Islamic State'. ECFR/141. European Council on Foreign Relations. www.ecfr.eu/page/-/EngagingWithIran-Final1.pdf.

Savelsberg, Eva (2014), 'The Syrian-Kurdish Movements: Obstacles Rather than Driving Forces for Democratization'. In *Conflict, Democratization, and the Kurds in the Middle East: Turkey, Iran, Iraq, and Syria*, edited by David Romano and Mehmet Gurses, 85–107. New York: Palgrave Macmillan.

Speech of President Bashar Assad at Damascus University, 10 November 2005. www.leba nonwire.com/1105/05111001ASAAD_SPEECH.asp.

Stephens, Michael, and Aaron Stein (2015), 'The YPG: America's New Best Friend?'. Quoted in *Aljazeera*, 28 June. www.aljazeera.com/indepth/opinion/2015/06/ypg-am erica-friend-isil-kurds-syria-150627073034776.html.

Submission for a democratic autonomous Kurdistan (2011), Democracy Society Congress (Handbook). http://demokratischeautonomie.blogsport.eu/files/2012/10/DTK.engl_.pdf.

Syrian National Council (2012), 'National Charter: The Kurdish Issue in Syria'. 31 March. http://kurdwatch.org/pdf/KurdWatch_D026_en_ar.pdf.

Tejel, Jordi (2009), *Syria's Kurds: History, Politics and Society*. Translated by Emily Welle and Jane Welle. London and New York: Routledge.

Tejel, Jordi (2014), 'Toward a Generational Rupture within the Kurdish Movement in Syria?' In *Kurdish Awakening: Nation Building in a Fragmented Homeland*, edited by Ofra Bengio, 215–229. Texas: University of Texas Press.

Today's Zaman (2015), 'Erdoğan Views PYD as Threat, Prefers ISIL Control in Northern Syria'. 15 June. www.todayszaman.com/anasayfa_erdogan-views-pyd-as-threat-prefers-i sil-control-in-northern-syria_387065.html.

UK Government (2015), 'Government Response to the House of Commons Foreign Affairs Committee Report: UK Government Policy on the Kurdistan Region of Iraq'. Cm 9029. London: Secretary of State for Foreign and Commonwealth Affairs. https://www. gov.uk/government/uploads/system/uploads/attachment_data/file/415796/48533_Cm_ 9029 Accessible.pdf.

Vanly, Ismet Cheriff (1992), 'The Kurds in Syria and Lebanon'. In *The Kurds: A Contemporary Overview*, edited by Philip G. Kreyenbroek and Stefan Sperl, 112–234. London and New York: Routledge.

Wikas, Seth (2007), 'Battling the Lion of Damascus: Syria's Domestic Opposition and the Asad Regime', 69. Washington: The Washington Institute. www.washingtoninstitute. org/policy-analysis/view/battling-the-lion-of-damascus-syrias-domestic-opposition-a nd-the-asad-regim.

Yıldız, Kerim (2005), *The Kurds in Syria: The Forgotten People*. London and Ann Arbor, MI: Pluto Press.

Ziadeh, Radwan (2009), 'The Kurds in Syria Fueling Separatist Movements in the Region?' 220. Washington: United States Institute of Peace.

Zisser, Eyal (2014), 'The Kurds in Syria: Caught between the Struggle for Civil Equality and the Search for National Identity'. In *Kurdish Awakening: Nation Building in a Fragmented Homeland*, edited by Ofra Bengio, 193–213. Texas: University of Texas Press.

Interviews

Arabo, Mahmoud Ahmad. Interview by author. Arbil, 27 February 2015.
Bedreddin, Selah. Interview by author. Saladin, 26 February 2015.
Brimo, Amine. Interview by author. London, 15 May 2015.
Darwish, Hamid Hajj. Interview by author. Sulaymaniyah, 28 February 2015.
Hassaf, Ismail. Interview by author. Arbil, 27 March 2015.
Mirani, Seit. Interview by author. London, 15 May 2015.

Mustafa, Ibrahim. Interview by author. London, 25 March 2015.
Reshid, Newaf Hesen. Interview by author. Arbil, 27 February 2015.
Saffour, Walid. Interview by author. London, 12 August 2015.
Sidar, Demhat and Jiyan (fictitious names). Interview by author, Diyarbakir, 25 February 2015.
Semo, Alan. Interview by author. London, 18 December 2014.
Semdin, Ali. Interview by author. Sulaymaniyah, 28 February 2015.

21

CONCLUSION

The early trajectory of the Syrian Uprising: From agency to structure

Omar Imady and Raymond Hinnebusch

This conclusion brings together the arguments and evidence of the book's chapters to explain key issues and questions about the early (2011–13) trajectory of the Uprising. While the introduction addressed structural roots of the Uprising, here we focus on how agency – the interests and actions of the actors in the Uprising – constructed a multitude of structures that, in turn, constrained their agency. Thus, once peaceful protests became a violent Uprising in which the territory of the country was divided between regime and opposition, two or more exclusivist governance structures came into competition to fill – or alter – the Syrian space, squeezing secular reformists between a sectarianized regime and a jihadist opposition. Once the conflict was sectarianized, new exclusivist identities were forged that would constrain possibilities for ending what became an intractable conflict.

Why did anti-regime mass mobilization lead to stalemate rather than revolution or regime collapse?

By 2012 many believed the regime was on the ropes, but this proved mistaken. Conditions that allowed revolution in Egypt and Tunisia were not realized in Syria, namely, what might be called "bandwagoning" mobilization – in which a big majority combine against a regime people believe is on the way out – did not constitute the cross-class coalition against the regime that would have been needed for revolution from below. To be sure, a coalition of youthful urban middle-class protestors and deprived youth from rural towns and suburbs did take form. However, cross-class mobilization was crosscut by communal and urban-rural cleavages, and hence diluted. This allowed a pro-regime counter-mobilization by those with a stake in the regime. The crony capitalists who had benefited from political connections to enrich themselves did not generally abandon the regime; indeed, some of them actually financed pro-regime militias. Said (this volume) stressed the interests that the military-mercantile complex had in regime survival. Lawson (this volume) observed that the impact of the global financial crisis (and the move to neo-liberalism) in Syria had a differential impact, with some suffering and others able to preserve the gains they had made in the boom period: those whose economic interests were served by the status quo – newly emergent businessmen and public sector workers – failed to join the protests. Goldsmith and Bartolomei showed how the regime exploited fears of the Alawis and other minorities of radical Islamists to rally them. Many others, who were put off by both regime and opposition, refrained from anti-regime mobilization. The secular urban upper-middle class who has benefited from the end of socialist austerity and feared plebeian insurgents remained inactive or exited as explained by Lawson. As Zintl (2012) showed elsewhere, many Western educated Syrians had been co-opted by the regime's ostensible modernization drive. As Imady shows, many Sufis, the dominant tendency among Syria's Sunni Muslims before the Uprising, also refrained from joining the anti-regime movement (but suffered as a result from opposition vituperation). Illustrative of those in the middle were the attitudes of the "Left", explained in Arslanian's contribution. The Left wanted a peaceful transition but opposed external intervention, militarization and sectarianization; as a result, it was denounced by both regime and opposition and lost much of its youthful following. Çifci (this volume) explains why the regime was able to exploit divisions between the main Kurdish movement, the PYD, and the Arab opposition. Bandwagoning mobilization requires a combination of high grievances and opportunity structure; in the Syrian case, there were enough grievances in part of society and enough opportunity structure for anti-regime mobilization to be sustained and massive but not enough to rapidly remove the regime. As such, the outcome was *protracted conflict*, with extended *stalemate* between regime and opposition.

Why did peaceful protest turn into armed civil war, framed in sectarian terms, that has proved intractable?

The main explanation for the turn from peaceful protest to armed civil war was the use of increased violence by the regime that stimulated counter arming of the opposition and militarization of the Uprising. Rifai (this volume) recounts how regime strategy escalated from a "security solution" – in which the police and pro-regime *shabihas* used violence against or detained protestors – to the "military solution" in which artillery and aerial bombardment was unleashed against whole cities – in part to prevent the creation of "liberated zones" that would facilitate a Libya-type Western intervention. At first, as Harkin showed, the non-violent movement armed defensively to protect the protestors against the security forces, a "hybrid" phenomenon, midway between non-violent protest and armed struggle. In time, enough defectors from the army fuelled the construction of the Free Syrian Army (FSA) engaged in an armed struggle against the regime; but not enough to precipitate the collapse of the regime's Syrian Arab Army or to allow the FSA to take over the country. Instead, each came to dominate certain areas.

Once violence descended into civil war, there was no way back for either regime or opposition since they could never trust the other: each believed it must prevail by further escalating violence. "Competitive interference" by external powers and trans-state movements ratcheted up the unwillingness to compromise on both sides. The external arming of and safe haven given the opposition by Sunni states such as Turkey, Saudi Arabia and Qatar, led to counter balancing by Iran and Russia, which, together, greatly increased the violence of the conflict and made it more intractable: despite the high costs inflicted on the country, neither side perceived itself in a hurting stalemate that could only be ended by a compromise settlement; on the contrary, each thought if only its external patrons provided more resources it could win a victory; however, external powers provided enough resources for their clients to keep fighting but not to prevail over the other.

In parallel, sectarianism gave the conflict a special intensity. As Khatib argued, the regime's flirtation with Islamism had facilitated its spread to rural areas before the Uprising. Anti-regime protestors had initially promoted a civic discourse, welcoming minorities to their ranks but this did not persist. The instrumentalization of sectarianism by the regime, and thereafter also the opposition, to mobilize their constituents is documented in the chapters of Goldsmith, Bartolmeni and Rifai. The regime's use of indiscriminate violence to de-populate Sunni areas; plus the Alawi dominance of the coercive forces and the later backing of Hizbollah and Iran for them allowed Sunni militants to frame the issue as a Shia war on Sunnis. From-mid 2012, the jihadist sectarian narrative began to predominate, with regime backers depicted as infidels, militant armed groups presenting themselves as defenders of the Sunni community and anti-Alawi animus exacerbated by preachers in the Gulf media. In reaction, the regime, Hizbollah and Iraqi Shia militias (who entered Syria ostensibly to defend Shia shrines but ended up fighting on the side of the regime), portrayed the Shia as facing an existential threat from Sunni "takfiris" who were denouncing them as infidels liable to be killed. Rifai shows how what began as the instrumentalization of sectarianism "from above" resulted in sectarian identities seeping down to the grassroots level, e.g. with people on both sides flaunting sectarian markers. Identity change – internalization of sectarianism by individuals – began as the Sunni underclass was mobilized, which as Eido shows, was particularly susceptible to the simplicities of Salafism. Amidst mounting violence, religion provided the motivation for fighting, with new "jihadist" identities constituted in the struggle. A similar sort of zealotry was displayed by Shia militias who celebrated the possibility of martyrdom in defence of Shia communities. The convergence of pro- and anti-regime narratives resulted in the dominance of the sectarian narrative.

Moderate Islam, whether that of Sufis, traditional *ulama* or even modernists of the Muslim Brotherhood variety, tended to be squeezed out by the rise of jihadist Salafism. A case in point was the Muslim Brotherhood, which made an effort to bridge the moderate and Salafist Islamist factions, as recounted by Ramirez (this volume). In its discourse regarding its vision of the post-Asad state, it wavered between civil and Islamic content. In terms of tactics, it was at first reluctant to enter the armed struggle and concentrated on using humanitarian aid to build a constituency in refugee camps of displaced Syrians in neighbouring countries; yet, eventually it threw its weight behind the decision to adopt armed struggle and it constituted affiliated armed groups without which it would have had no influence in Syria itself; indeed these led the assault that wrested a part of Aleppo from regime control.

External funding by Gulf states and Turkey who armed and gave safe haven to the most militant jihadis, partly because they were the most effective anti-Asad fighters, and the large-scale movement of foreign jihadists into Syria led to the further spread of jihadist identities, both exclusionary and intolerant. The extraordinary change in identities can be measured by Rifai's judgement that Syrian Sunnis and Shia were starting to identify more with their trans-national sectarian kin than with Syria's citizens of the other sect.

As, with state failure, order broke down, the security dilemma kicked in – as each communal group came to depend for security on their group's militia and sought to purify their neighbourhoods of the threatening "Other". The grassroots sectarianism initiated as an instrument of warring leaders now fed back from the grassroots to the leadership level, where Rifai shows, to get support competitors had to outbid each other in animosity to the "Other", hardening sectarian identities, exclusionary views of the other and in-group solidarity that put a compromise settlement off actors' agendas. The peaceful secular middle class, squeezed between regime and jihadists, and not willing to take up arms or adopt sectarian discourses, increasingly exited the country, contributing to further polarization into two sectarian-defined camps. Overlapping with this was the emerging territorial division of the country that allowed war economies to grow up on both sides, with gang-like racketeering, smuggling, and kidnapping giving warlords a stake in the conflict's continuance (see Valter, this volume).

Outcomes of competitive regime formation

Schmidt (this volume) argued that Syria's "Sultanist" heritage made it less likely the revolt could have led to democratization and more likely that it would end in a failed state; this seems to be borne out. Despite state failure there is governance in Syria, but it is divided and different from that before the Uprising. "Competitive regime formation" was undertaken by the Asad regime and the opposition/s, each seeking to fill vacuum left by state failure.

How did the Asad regime reconfigure itself for civil war?

The regime reconfigured itself to survive amidst sectarian civil war. At the national level, the narrowing of the elite core concentrated power more exclusively in the hands of the Asad family, the multiple security apparatuses and elite military units. All those uncommitted to the struggle for victory that had not defected were purged. Thus, in July 2013, the whole party Regional Command, with the exception of Asad, was dismissed, including Vice President al-Sharaa who had advocated a compromise political settlement. Any military officer that showed leniency was denounced, as Valter observed. A much more coercive and exclusivist form of neo-patrimonial regime emerged in which the security forces enjoyed impunity. As, however, bureaucratic institutions were debilitated by resource decline and loss of territorial penetration, and the army suffered from defections and demographic obstacles to recruitment, the regime assumed a more decentralized form, in which power was diffused to militias at the local level, to neighbourhoods, often communally cleansed and armed for self-defence; and also backed by Shia militias from Lebanon and Iraq.

What governance alternatives to the regime have emerged in opposition-controlled territories?

In the opposition-controlled areas, Salafist-jihadist counter-regime building took place around charismatic leaders with radical Islamist ideologies leading armed movements; these were combined with remnants of bureaucratic capabilities, (most notable with IS) often centred on sharia courts and other Islamized organs. They were highly intolerant of all those that did not hold to their fundamentalist puritanical version of Islam. Fragmented into multiple formations and alliances – but with a few dominant, notably IS, Jabhat al-Nusra and Ahrar ash-Sham – Eido notes that they agreed on the Islamic character of the state and in rejecting equal citizenship and democracy as a Western invention. The groups chiefly varied in the extent to which they sought a trans-state caliphate or Islamization of the Syrian state.

On a third tangent, were the areas where the armed Kurdish movement managed to wrest governing power from the regime and defend it against jihadists. Its Leninist-inspired governance techniques ostensibly accorded equal rights to non-Kurds in its domain while centralizing actual power in Kurdish hands; its tendency toward expansionism, accompanied by a certain ethnic cleansing suggests it is little less exclusivist that the regime and the jihadists (see Çifçi, this volume).

In the interstices between regime and Islamist control, the remnants of the Local Coordinating Council activists persisted for a period, grouped with armed elements of the FSA and traditional notables, and often governing through elected councils. They defended, with limited success, the initial ideology of the Uprising, the ideal of an inclusive civic state, with equal citizenship for all. However, in many areas, criminal-like warlords fragmented and anarchized governance, while surviving areas of opposition civil governance were targeted by regime bombing and or food sieges meant to extinguish any effective alternative to the regime and extremist Islamists.

Neglected nuances and the horizons for future scholarship

Nearly six years have passed since the inception of the Syrian Uprising, and yet this phenomenon remains difficult to fully grasp, both in terms of underlying forces and long-term implications. Part of the difficulty lies in the fact that this particular story continues to unfold, and has not reached its conclusion and it may look very different after a decade. Nevertheless, our thirst to understand is not a patient one and this volume constitutes an attempt to understand not only why the Syrian Uprising began, but also why it evolved into something very different from what most analysts anticipated. The chapters that we have included provide significant insights into the various dynamics of the Syrian Uprising, but they also inadvertently shed light on just how elusive this phenomenon remains. Thus, many of the articles provide alternative explanations for the same events, which at this point, cannot necessarily be reconciled or their differences fully resolved. Moreover, while various such arguments may be compatible they are often located at different levels of analysis – e.g. structure or agency – requiring that we establish links between them.

Take, for example, Lesch's chapter "Bashar's Fatal Decision". This argument, paralleled by others before him and most likely to be repeated by others in the future, explains the event as a function of how Asad decided to respond to the initial protests and privileges agency. The implication is that so much would have been different today had Asad decided to respond differently. The problem here lies in whether or not anyone, including Asad, was in a position to respond differently in March 2011 since certain kinds of authoritarian systems appear incapable of a smooth transition to democracy: as Schmidt and Valter suggest, the regime was structured so as to make repression its only imaginable response. Moreover, it is far from certain that any concessions Asad could have offered would have appeased his opponents, as the ineffectiveness of conciliatory speeches by Ben Ali and Mubarak demonstrated.

Economic explanations for the Uprising encounter the same difficulty. Lawson, for example, emphasizes global economic dynamics that intertwined with more local factors such as the drought and Bashar's liberal economic policies. This argument is repeated in various ways by different authors, each emphasizing in essence that the Uprising was essentially rooted in economic grievances. Here the problem lies in the fact that it is very difficult to establish a cause and effect relationship between the Uprising and the state of Syria's economy in late 2010 and as Lawson, indeed, acknowledged many of the important indicators, including GDP per capita, hard currency reserves and foreign debt were more positive than during other periods in Syria's recent past, especially the 1980s. Though it is clear that poverty, rural poverty in particular, existed, many Syrians had experienced no sharp downturn running up to 2011: as such, the classic revolutionary scenario, boom followed by a sharp downturn cannot really be identified in Syria.

Other authors emphasize an explanation focusing on the impact of social institutions on the Uprising. Imady, for example, explores the relationship between the systematic institutional disempowerment of religious scholars in the years prior to the Uprising and their subsequent unwillingness to cooperate with Asad after the Uprising unfolded. What is still needed, though, is process tracing that can identify how the grievances of the religious class added agency to the Uprising; although mosques did indeed host protests, the young protestors appeared to be self-mobilized, with, indeed, the uprisings apparently leaderless and prepared to acknowledge no established leadership, whether urging rebellion or calm. At the same time, it remains a complex academic challenge to explain how a country known for a moderate, overwhelmingly Sufi, brand of Islam would so quickly become known for some the most Jihadist Salafi versions of Islam produced since at least the fall of the Ottoman Empire. Khatib shows how the regime's flirtation with Islamism provided the initial structural context and Eido shows how the structural conditions of civil war further enabled a radicalization via the agency of Salafist and jihadist movements. But how could the identities of lifetimes appear to be so quickly transformed? Equally challenging is understanding how the Syrian regime, long regarded as lacking popularity even amidst the Alawite community, managed to turn a popular Uprising into a sectarian civil war in which not only minorities find it natural to identify with this regime but also, as Said illustrates, vested interests, including those generated by an economy of war, perpetuate the regime's narrative.

All of this highlights the need for new, and innovative, scholarly approaches to the Syrian Uprising. The Arab Spring caught us at a time when existing literature was well established in understanding how states survive. Authoritarian upgrading and other similar theories shed light on the creative ways by which authoritarian regimes, in particular in the Middle East, managed to continue despite significant odds. We were not adequately prepared, however, on the level of understanding the dynamics and typography of social protest, especially in the age of social media. Brownlee and others emphasize some of the new issues at work that we must take stock of as we attempt to understand this new phenomenon; and Imady, in employing contributions from communication theory and sociology highlights, the need for an interdisciplinary approach in understanding some of the more subtle aspects of popular protest.

The Syrian Uprising has significantly challenged some of our most basic assumptions about states and society in the Middle East. In the long run, understanding the full implications of this phenomenon will require innovative and interdisciplinary approaches that seek to capture the full complexity of the phenomenon. If this volume succeeds in providing the spadework for such an approach, it would have fulfilled its objective.

References

Zintl, Tina (2012), "Modernization Theory II: Western-Educated Syrians and the Upgrading of Civil Society", *Syria Studies*, 4:2, 33–71.

INDEX

Abboud, Samer 87
accountability 23–4, 138, 142, 160
activists 38, 67, 77, 86, 93–5, 100, 103–04, 161–8, 177–81, 193, 228, 254, 333; corporation with rebels 179–80, 230; media 173, 194, 197, 199–200; violence against 168, 192
Adesnik, Ariel 78–9
Aflaq, Michel 19
agency 1–2, 33, 141–4, 169, 178, 329
agriculture 4, 82, 86
Ahrar al Sham 216–18, 234, 265, 330
aid 3, 61, 214, 253
al Arabiya 198, 253
al Asad, Asma 52, 100–01, 129, 161
al Asad, Bashar: presidency 1–2, 4–6, 34–5, 44–54, 56, 64–5, 83–4, 97, 151–2, 160, 243, 312–13, 321–24; engagement with religious organisations 116–17, 120, 244; response to protests 9, 33, 101, 128, 133–8, 317, 334; speeches 12, 101, 128–139, 160, 225–7; promises of reform 26–7, 51, 160, 226; succession 26, 34, 37; image of 130–1; supporters of 131, 290; popularity of 136–7, 151
al Asad, Basil 45
al Asad, Hafiz 3, 18–28, 44–9, 56–7, 69, 93–7, 160, 243, 291, 311–12; assassination attempt 24; enemies of 25–6; death of 26, 312
al Asad, Jamil 22
al Asad, Maher 36, 48
al Asad, Rifat 22–6, 45, 63, 245

al Ayyubi, Mohammad Ziyad 117–18
al Azm, Sadiq 60, 86
al Baghdadi, Khalid 108
al Bani, Muhammad Bashir 106, 108, 116–18
al Bayanouni, Ali Sadr al Din 207–09, 211–12
al Buti, Muhammed Said Ramadan 119, 122
al Fadil, Nibras 51
al Haj Saleh, Yassin 160, 304
al Jabha al Islamiya al Souriya 266
Al Jazeera 100, 178, 234, 253
al Kawakibi Forum 160
al Khatib, Mo'az 103, 231, 299–300
al Khaznawi, Mohammed Mashouq 313
al Kurdi, Isa 108
al Midani, Abu Khair 108
al Nasser, Jamal Abd 18
al Nihlawi, Abd al Karim 18
al Nusra Front 233–4
al Qubaysi, Shaikha Munira 110, 112, 114, 122
al Qusayr 235–6
al Rifai, Abd al Karim 116
al Sharaa, Farouq 9, 292, 332–3
al Turk, Riyad 95–6, 304
Alawite: dissent 51; history 144–48, 243; insecurity 141–156; presence in protests 150; revolutionaries 150–1
Alawites 5, 8–9, 45–6; gangs 47, 50; *see also militia*; in positions of power 20–2, 132; in the military 3, 34, 49, 57, 60

Aleppo 84, 146, 178, 191, 243, 292, 298, 305, 332
alienation 4, 21, 117, 162
Alloush, Zahran 102, 219, 249–50
Annan, Kofi 297–8
Ansar association 108, 111–12, 114, 117, 119
anti-imperialist 3, 290
Arab League 68, 292, 295–8, 302
Arab nationalism 13, 152–3, 277–8, 310, 315, 319
Arab nationalist 15, 18–22, 226, 291
Arab Spring 6, 30, 56, 129–33, 138, 173, 188, 273
Arab unity 12, 15, 19
army: control over 49–51, 54; *see also* military
Ar'our, Adnan 249–50
art: oppositional 166, 192–3
assabiyya 243, 248
associations 110–13, 118–19, 160–1; laws on 110–11, 115, 117–18
Assyrian parties 293–4
Atassi, Nur al Din 20–1
authoritarian: regime 12, 21, 21, 25–7, 64, 78, 132, 156, 174, 188–9, 224–5, 274; rule 22, 25, 152, 202, 277; system 30–2, 39–40, 210; upgrading 1–6, 26, 92
authoritarianism 2, 92–104
autonomy 40, 53, 95, 160, 162, 279; of the military 34, 48; of the state 23, 33

banks 4, 62, 80–3
Ba'th: brigades 292; ideology 12, 18–27, 34–5, 64, 309, 311; party 10, 60, 83, 96–7, 160–5, 291;
populism 3; rise to power 12, 16, 31, 243, 311; rule 3–4, 87, 148, 152, 261–2, 310–; state building 3, 12–28
Ba'thism: founding of 19; under Asad 21, 34, 37, 94; weakening of 23, 141, 291
Ben Ali 8, 130, 135
Bitar, Salah al Din 19
bourgeoisie 3, 21, 60, 82, 86–7, 244,
bribery 64–7
British rule 13, 17–8
Bunni, Akram 290–1
businessmen 38–9, 60–1, 63, 77, 82, 86–7, 244, 330

caliphate 13, 233–4, 250, 264, 333; cyber 200–201
capitalism 2–3, 39–40, 281; crony 4–5, 8–10, 27, 38–39, 54, 61, 65, 244, 329

change: political 15, 20, 68, 275; social 12, 15, 19–20, 159
China 297–8, 305
citizen: active 169, 178; journalist 165, 177–9, 190, 193–4, 203; role of 38, 169
citizenship 169, 229, 314–15, 317
civil disobedience 167, 179–81, 191, 228–9, 305
civil society 6–7, 9, 30, 94, 96, 107, 109, 112, 115, 159–69; conception of 159–60, 162; and democracy 159, 169; government control over 161–2; government sponsored 100, 161–2; Islamic 98; movements 160–2, 168; organisations 5; post-uprising 162–9; pre-uprising 159–60; primordial 160; as resistance 169; and state 159
civil state: 165, 229–30, 262; of the Muslim Brotherhood 209, 212, 217–18
civil war 1–2, 30, 153–5, 224, 318, 324, 330; impact of 2, 30, 155, 274; sectarian 30, 141, 224–7; 1979–82 25–6
clan: Of Asad 51, 61, 64–5, 244
classes: capitalist 4; elite 243–4; merchant urban 21, 83, 86; middle 4–6, 332; peasant 37, 243–4; rural 16, 38, 243–4; state employed 3, 16; support for the uprising 32; widening gap between 97–8, 133, 244
clientism 36, 60, 63, 67, 82
coalition 21–4, 31, 98–99, 146, 231–2, 243, 329
Coalition of Syrian Left 305–06
Coalition of the Revolutionary Left in Syria 305–06
coercion 21–2, 48, 132
collective action 6–7, 86, 165, 202–03
colonial: legacies 142; post- 14–16, 31; powers 13–4, 274; rule 15, 31, 173–4, 228, 310
Committee for the Revival of Civil Society in Syria 99, 296
communist parties 15, 290–2, 301–05
communities: religious 38, 94–5, 272
concessions 9, 50, 128, 132–9, 155, 225
conflict: ethno-religious 144; identity 144, 311; structure of 1–2
conscription 34, 52, 281
conspiracy 137–8, 225–6
constituency 3–4, 38, 66
constitution 37, 59, 291
control: education 23, 117–18; knowledge production 23; media 23; in state building 14–5; over the population 37,

47–9, 132; over the economy 82; political 15, 20; in state building 14–5
co-optation 21–3, 37, 51, 94, 96, 98, 132, 244, 262, 330
Coordination Committees of the Syrian Communists 305–06
Corrective Revolution 21
corruption 23–4, 46–54, 60–1, 63–4
Council of Ministers 85
cult of Asad 23, 35–6, 53, 163
Cultural Forum for Human Rights 99
culture: oppositional 166; production of 162, 278–9

Damascene Islamist Movement 106–122; as education providers 112, 117–18; interaction with the state 106, 109–12, 115–19; leaders of 115; members of 113–14; as political 109–12; position on the uprising 106, 114, 119–22, 249; as secular 108–9, 115
Damascus 5, 134, 146–9, 163, 191, 208, 298, 305–06
Damascus Declaration 99–100, 161, 292–5, 312, 314–15
Damascus Spring 26, 32, 99, 160, 168, 292–3, 312
Damascus-Beirut Declaration 100
Dardari, Abdullah 64–5, 84
debt 81, 334
decision communication 107, 110–12, 119
Declaration of the 99 99, 161
Deeb, Rajab 120–22
defections 8, 34, 49, 56, 67, 69–71, 132, 193
Defence Companies 24–5
Defence Units 22
democracy: conditions for 30–1, 40; facades of 36; pro- 93, 95
Democratic Arab Socliast Union 294, 304–5
Democratic National Bloc 95
Democratic Platform 296
democratic transition: 1–2, 8–10, 30–3, 40, 211; role of the military in 31, 40
Democratic Union Party (PYD) 309–10, 315–17, 320–24
democratization 1, 8–10, 15, 40, 92, 332
demonstrations *see protests*
demonstrators *see protestors*
Deraa 27, 48, 128, 133–4, 136, 163, 177, 273, 280
dialogue consultative committee 292, 302
dignity 6–7, 163, 173–182; in the Arabic language 175–6; as political and revolutionary 174–5; strikes 178–9; in the uprising 176–82
discontent 78, 86, 163
displaced: internally 273–4, 280–2, 284
displacement: as strategy 227
dissident 53, 92–3, 100–01, 232, 302
divisions 15, 18–20; identity 23–5, 141, 311; ideological 18; sectarian 23, 154, 173
documentary 177
Doha Consultative Meeting 295
domination 14–15; struggle for 12
drought 4, 38, 86, 147
drug trade 63–4
Druze 18–9, 271–87; background of 272–3; response to uprising 273–4, 279–286
dynamic: identity 271; political 271; sectarian 51, 142; secular-religious 92–104; socio- economic 271; socio-political 271
dynasticism 35–6

economic: crisis 61, 63; opening (infitah) 61; restrictions 59, 61, 63–4
economic global crisis 77–9, 330; impact on MENA 79–80; impact on Syrian economy 80–88
economy 6, 13–5, 38; and the army 56–71; domestic 77–88; national 51; political 3–4; socialist 38, 59–60,
education 4–5, 16, 48
Egypt 6–8, 30–1, 56, 68, 153, 300–01; relations with 22–3, 26; union with 18, 310
Eid, Abdularazak 100
elections 9–10, 30, 36, 291, 303–04
eleventh five-year plan 84, 161
elite: control 12; cross-sectarian 3; economic 63, 65, 67, 82, 84, 86–7, 98, 162, 244; military 60–1, 72; military forces 8–9, 12, 34; political 8; religious 98
EU 4, 64, 68, 103
Executions 275–6, 283–4
exile 9, 96, 99–100, 163, 332; forced 150–1, 168
export 13–14, 61, 80–1, 85
Export Development and Promotion Agency 85
external forces: blame on 130–1, 137, 225
external players: in the conflict 188, 331
external: pressure 25–7, 99–100

Fares, Raed 150
Farouq Brigade 266
fear 200, 203, 280, 284; loss of 7, 133, 163, 190; of sectarian conflict 102, 132, 150, 154, 163, 233, 246–8, 285

Ferzat Ali 96, 101
fitna (discord) 9, 101
folklore 277–9
foreign intervention 8, 23, 25, 83, 86, 147, 296
foreign trade 63–5
Forum for National Dialogue 99, 160
Fourth Armoured Division 57
fragmentation of social order 21, 27
Free Syrian Army 147, 179, 193, 230, 234, 281, 306, 309, 330, 333
Free Syrian Lawyers Association 167
free trade agreements 64, 84
freedom outside regime control 163, 166, 169, 179
Freedom and Dignity Gathering 296
freedom of expression 23, 37–8, 96; illusion of 53
French rule 13–7
French relations 51
Friends of Syria 297, 319
Front for Liberation and Change 301–03
funding: external 194, 263, 332; war effort 51–2

Geneva 2 300, 303
Geneva Communique 298–301, 304
gentrification 5, 272
geopolitical: location 17; threats 23
George, Alan 160–1
Ghalyun, Burhan 162, 293, 295, 319
Golan Heights 4, 22
graffiti 166, 177, 228, 255–6
Gramsci, Antonio 277
Grand Mufti 109–10, 117, 121
grassroot 101, 194, 223–4, 228–30; opposition groups 294–5; protest movement 291, 293, 296, 304–07
grievances 6–7, 15, 27, 86, 138, 177, 226, 330, 334
Gulf States 3, 22–3, 83, 253; role in uprising 147, 155

Haddad, Bassam 87
Hafiz, Amin 19–20
Hama: during uprising 164; massacre 24–5, 131, 164, 190, 295; uprising 6, 94, 243
Hamas: alliance with 27, 151
Hariri, Rafic: assassination of 27, 100, 129, 132, 148
Hawrani, Akram 95
Hizbullah: alliance with 26–7, 151; support from 71–2, 155, 235–6, 251–2
Homs 148–50, 178–9, 226, 245–6, 251–3; Clock Square 150, 154

human rights violations 95, 179, 182, 230, 248
humanitarian crisis 155, 299

Ibn Khaldun 143
identity 13, 19, 144, 329, 332, 335; Alawite 242–9, 251–7; clashes 242–57, 331; ethnic 13, 311; Kurdish 311, 313, 315, 318–19, 322–4; national 17; networks 17; politics 142; religious 13, 24, 144, 223–4, 273, 277; Salafi 249–57; Salafi-jihadi 223–7, 250–1, 305, 331; sectarian 10, 24, 223, 332; Sufi 244, 248–50; Sunni 242–57; Sunni Islamist 32; symbolism 254–6; Syrian 211
ideology 14, 19; Arab nationalism 13, 22; Islamism 13; of the military 58; regime 27
imports 50, 59–64, 81, 84
independence: call for 13, 16; political 15, 19; Syrian 15
insecurity: minority 141–3, 153, 330; sectarian 143, 223, 246–7
instability 21, 131–2, 153
institutionalization of political life 33–5
intellectuals 93–6, 99, 160, 168, 279, 293
intelligence agencies 22
international community 147, 153, 156, 166, 203, 227, 235–7, 297, 300, 307
International Red Cross 154
Internationalisation of the conflict 295–7, 302–3, 307
Internet see media
investment: foreign 2–4, 60, 64, 80; private 2, 60, 64, 86
Iran 3, 16–8; against Iraq 26; alliance with 26; support from 70–2, 154–5, 251–2
Iranian Revolutionary Guards 252
Iraq 253; invasion of 4, 26, 116, 290, 293
ISIS 200–201, 309, 333
Islam: moderate 5–6, 262, 331, 335; political 1, 98; promotion of 98–9; radical 5, 199; Salafi 10, 98, 102, 212, 219, 233, 335; Sufi 108, 113, 244, 331
Islamic: leaders 95, 98; militants 93, 98; piety 95; rebellion 94–5; sector 98
Islamist: attraction to 38, 263; insurgency 34; rise of 103, 153–4, 233; threat 102
Ismail, Ammar 49–50
Isolation 21, 26–7
Israel 3–4, 20, 273, 285
Issa, Mahmoud 100

Jabhat al Nusra 216–18, 250, 265, 285, 309, 330
Jabhat Tahreer Souria al Islamiya 265

Jadid, Salah 19–24
Jaish al Islam 102
Jama'at Zayd 116, 122
Jamal al Atasi Forum 99, 160
Jamil, Qadri 301–03
Jamous, Fateh 297
Jaramana 271–87
jihad 154, 188, 215, 218, 237, 250–1, 224, 236, 251, 264, 290
jihadist: groups 150, 155, 218–19, 233, 309, 317–18; radio 197; videos 200–201, 234
jihadists 98, 141, 147, 155, 181, 251, 299, 331–2

Kafranbel 150, 166
Kaftariyya 106–122
Kaftaru, Ahmad 106, 108–12, 115–17
kidnap 47, 52, 252, 282,
Kilo, Michel 96, 99–100, 160–1, 296
Kurdish: autonomy 310, 318–24; decentralisation 315–16, 318–20, 323; federalism 315, 318–320, 323–4; issue 313–17, 321–23; political rights 309, 312–13, 315–18, 321–22; region 310, 318, 320–2; and Syrian relations 311–12, 317
Kurdish Democratic Party of Syria 311
Kurdish National Council (KNC) 315–320
Kurdish National Party 309–10
Kurdish opposition in the uprising 315–24; see also opposition
Kurdistan 310–11, 319
Kurdistan Democratic Party (PDK) 315–16
Kurdistan Workers Party (PKK) 311–12, 315–16
Kurds 132, 310; marginalization of 310–13; Syrian 311–12

Latakia 47
leadership: neo-patrimonial 44–45
Lebanon: intervention in 26, 60–1, 63–4, 100; withdrawal from 27
legitimacy 92, 174; see also regime legitimacy
liberalization: economic 4, 9–10, 21, 60–1, 63–5, 82, 97, 243; political 9–10, 99–100
Liwaa al Umma 266
Local Coordination Committees 102, 150, 165, 177–8, 193, 229–30, 333
Local Councils 165–7, 306
loyalists: Asadist 5, 28, 70, 147, 149, 189, 227, 245, 291–2
loyalty 51, 56, 61, 63, 67–70, 87
Luhmann, Niklas 106–07

Makhlouf, Rami 36, 39, 51, 65, 148, 244, 303
Maliki, Nouri 252–3
Manna, Haitham 295, 300–01
Marxist Left Gathering 293–4
media Syrian 52–3, 226, 252, 263,
media 7, 181; internet 7, 9, 53, 188; mainstream 164, 200; new 7, 165, 188–203; oppositional 165–6, 179–80, 193; as partisan 198, 200; satellite TV 7, 53, 189, 191, 198, 249–50; social; *see social media*; support programmes 194, 199; traditional 199; videos 191–2, 202–03, 247–8,
militarization of the conflict 2, 32, 70, 164, 179–81, 193, 215, 281, 295–7, 305, 324, 330
military: control 8, 15–6, 20; coups 16–21, 57, 69; economic activity of 56–67; as fragmented 71–3; housing 68–9; ideology 58; industrial complex 8; national 34; recruits 16; regime control over 34, 132; relationship to regime 33–4, 56, 68; role of in suppression of protests 67–8, 70–2, 132, 139; socio-economic background of 57–8; solution 245–8, 299–300
Military Housing Institution 62, 65–66
Militia: opposition 38, 332; pro-regime 71, 154, 332; pro-regime (shabiha) 7, 51, 70–1, 148, 154, 164, 227, 245, 330
Ministry of Culture 96
Ministry of Defence 58
Ministry of Industry 83–5
Ministry of Information 53
Ministry of Religious Endowments 98, 109, 117–21
Ministry of Social Affairs and Labour 109–11, 118
minorities 16, 132, 141–2, 271–86; influence 20; insecurity 141–3, 153, 330; manipulation of 277; in military 19; protection of 93, 101, 132, 274; representation of 16; support of uprising 32, 271; threat to 274, 283; in uprising 228, 262–3
mobilization: anti-regime 6–8, 20, 329; cross-class 329; political 23–4; popular 24, 27, 30, 168; pro-regime 329; social 24, 133, 189
modernization 6, 64
monopoly 14–6, 19; of the military 61–65; of power 44–45
Moubayed, Sami 130
Mubarak, Hosni 8, 67–8, 130, 135, 153,
Mujahedeen 24

Mukhabarat 69, 72, 131, 138, 163,
Muslim Brotherhood 9, 15, 24–6, 30, 45, 111–12, 116, 152–4, 243, 262, 293–5, 300, 319, 322, 331; and armed struggle in the uprising 215–18; civil state 209, 212; Egyptian 209; humanitarian campaigns 214; internal dynamics 207–08, 211–19; and minority relations 211; political party 212–13; in the uprising 207–19, 231

Naqshbandi 108, 110, 113
narratives 150–1, 153; on MB 207–09; media 164, 169, 195, 198, 200, 203; sectarian 223–38, 266–7
Nasrallah, Hasan 236, 252–3
Nasserites 19
National Assembly 128
National Coalition for Syrian Revolutionary and Opposition Forces 103, 211, 231, 299–301, 305
National Committee for the Unity of the Syrian Communists 301
National Coordination Committee for Democratic Change vision for a future Syria 295, 309–10, 323
National Coordination Committee for Democratic Change 102, 231–2, 291–301, 304–05
National Defence Forces 71, 154, 283, 292
National Democratic Gathering 292–4
National Institute for Security 47
National Kurdish Council 296–7
National Kurdish Movement 293
National Party for Justice and the Constitution 213
National Progressive Front 21–2, 96, 291
National Salvation Front 293
National Welfare Fund 85
neo-liberal 2–3, 8, 10, 38, 56, 65, 174, 244, 251, 302
non-government organisations 7, 96, 162, 295
non-violent: imagery 167–8; movements 159, 164–9, 330; protest 30–3, 40, 67, 163–4, 228, 330; resistance 8–9, 159, 229, 305

oil 3–4, 54, 85
opposition 2, 8, 24–5, 32, 40, 136; as anti-sectarian 228–33; armed 52, 71, 149–50, 193, 298; calls for reform 161; detainment of 94–6, 100; divisions within 295; external 102, 132, 294; forces 78; as fragmented 102–4, 132, 283, 290–307, 309–10; groups 102; internal 102, 132, 294; Islamist 24–5, 34, 84, 93; Kurdish 211, 293–4, 309–24, 330, 333; marginalization of 103; moderate 32; political 23, 290–307, 309–; relations between different groups 290–307, 309, 312, 314–24; secular 5, 92–6, 99; Sunni 144; suppression of 32, 93–6, 99–100, 161
oppositional: art 166, 192–3; culture 166; newspapers 165, 179, 194–5; radio 165, 195–7; satellite TV 198
Ottoman rule 13, 15

Palestine: liberation of 15, 130, 264; support for 130, 151
Palestinian Liberation Organisation 26
paramilitary 57, 69, 131
parliament 36–7
Path for Peaceful Change 297
patronage 5, 17, 19, 22–24, 27, 31–6, 69–70, 72
Pei, Minxin 8–9
People's Assembly 21–2, 85
People's Committees 283
People's Defence Unit (YPG) 309, 315–17
pluralism 28, 271–2
policies: agricultural 21; defence 21; economic 61, 77; foreign 3–4, 21–3, 163; socio-economic 21
political: action 22, 25 176; aspirations of the Syrian people 173; boundaries 13; contestation 96; exclusion 12, 23; fate 28; influence 37; problems 138; repression 20, 23–5, 94–100, 142, 261, 293; solution 297–300; stability 21; struggle 19; survival 139, 142
political parties 17, 20–1, 36–7, 290–307
Political Security Agency 53
political space 102, 132, 169; limited 37
populace: depoliticised 38
Popular Front for Change and Liberation 291, 302–03
popular revolt 77, 86
popular unrest: immunity to 130
populist 2, 34; post 2–3, 5
Posen, Barry 142–3
poverty 4, 97, 138, 280, 334
power centralization of 37–8; consolidation of 22–3, 92; constraints on 34–5; international 2; ministerial 33; monopolizing 20; regional 23; regional Sunni 2; rentier 92; shift in 17–8, of the state 93; struggle for 16–21, 27
presidential monarchy 3, 5, 26
pressure: external 25–7, 99–100,

price: of food 79–82, 86; of oil 86
prisoners 23–4, 48–9, 52
prisons 23–4, 45, 49, 52
private sector 3–4, 56, 61, 63, 84–5
privatization 66
problems: socio-economic 132–3, 138, 243
propaganda: regime 131, 137, 193, 226–7, 232
protest movement 56, 70, 150
protestors: demands of 9, 32, 46, 77, 101, 163–4, 168, 225–6, 262, 280, 329,
protests 2, 6, 30, 48, 67, 86–88, 101, 316–17; mosques during 7, 334; role of expatriates during 7–8, 163; spread of 133–4, 163–4, 177–8, 226; suppression of 56, 70, 163
public: discipline of 23; sector 3, 59, 61, 84–5; sphere 23
public-private partnerships 83–4

Qaddafi, Muamar 9, 295
Qamishli riot 312–13
Qatar 144, 148, 155, 198, 300
Qubaysiyyat 106, 110, 112, 114, 117, 119–22

Radio Fresh 197
Radio SouriaLi 165, 197
ransom 47, 52
rape: as weapon of war 53
rebels 27; anti-regime 38, 155, 263; armed 52, 179–81, 332; cooperation with non-violent activists 179–80, 230
reform 2, 133, 138–9; agenda 163; economic 4–5, 27, 32, 64–6; land 3, 13, 21, 59; political 32, 271, 280; socio-economic 15
refugees 272; Syrian 155, 203
regime: adaptation of 2; change 9; collapse 329; decision makers 134–6; erosion of 12, 23–4, 27; hard-liners 8–9, 135; legitimacy of 3–4, 25, 93–4; moderates 8–9; new guard 65; old guard 5, 15, 27, 45, 65; power of 44; protection of 34; resistance to 24; response to uprising 129, 133–9, 153, 190, and society relations 22–3; soft-liners 8–9; structure of 1–2; survival of 2, 25, 226, 330, 332–3; support of 2–4, 25; vulnerability of 2–5, 12, 23–6, 151–2; weakening of 8
regional actors 200, 251
Regional Congress 34
relations: state-religious 106, 109–12, 115–22, 261–2

repercussions beyond borders 251–4
Republican Guard 45, 50, 57
resistance 14–5, 164, 169, 174, 192–3; armed 147, 150, 164, 263,
revolt: popular 77–8
Rifai, Usama 248–9
rural areas: in protests 134, 178, 331
Russia 78, 297–8, 300, 303–04; support from 70–3, 155

Sadat, Anwar 26
Salafi-jihadi: groups 227, 230–5, 333
Salafism: before uprising 261–2; definition of 260; divisions within 264–6; emergence of 260–1; rise of during revolution 262–7, 273, 283
Salafist: groups 264–6
salaries 52, 60, 67–9, 85–6, 133
Saleh, Abdel Qader 180–81
Saleh, Abdullah 130
sanctions 4, 68, 102
Saudi Arabia 144, 148, 155, 198, 200, 232, 300, 331
Sayadet Souria 195
Seale, Patrick 44, 62
Sectarian: identities 10, 46, 223, 335; massacres 71, 145, 149–50, 227, 232–4, 247–8; narratives 223–38; solidarity 7, 49; uprising as anti- 223, 228–233
solidarity 7, 49
sectarianism 2, 6, 8, 17–20, 45–6, 54, 141, 223–38, 271, 274–7, 331–2; as a discourse of power 223–4; ideology of 271–2, 277; imperial 277–9; as a regime tool 69, 101, 131–2, 151–6, 223, 225–38, 244–57, 266–7, 277–86, 331; as jihadis/ Salafis tool 223, 233–5; of transnational actors 236, 251–4
sectarianization of the conflict 148, 154–6, 200, 223–238, 281, 318, 324, 329, 331
secular: ideology 19–21, 231, 249–51; model 16; state 19, 153, 209–11
secularism 92–104
security: dilemma 141–56, 246–7, 254, 257, 332; forces 9, 32–4, 139; services 45–9, 52–4; solution 245–6, 330
Seif, Riad 160
separatism 16–7
Shaaban, Bouthaina 130, 133, 225
Shabiha see militia
Shaqfa, Riad 211–12, 214–15
Shawkat, Asif 48
Shi'a: alliance 27; axis 251–3, 331–2
smuggling 47, 60, 63, 332; see also trafficking
social contract 3–4, 174, 243–4

social media 163, 175, 178, 189–203, 228; Facebook 7, 50, 114, 163, 175, 178, 181, 190, 208, 228; as a tool for extremist groups 189, 200–201; as a tool for mobilization 163, 189–203; Twitter 175, 178; YouTube 7, 120, 175, 178, 191
social mobility 5, 8, 22
social movement theory 1, 6
social movements: organization of 106–15
social networks 23, 175, 201–02
social structure of accumulation 77–8, 82
social welfare 83, 97
socialism 19, 27, 59–60
solidarity: with uprisings 101, 163, 167, 177, 280, 313
Soviet Union 3, 17–8, 23
Special Forces 57
stalemate 329, 331
state: administrative apparatus 51, 82; building 12–28; de-formation 23, 27–8; disintegration 12, failed 2, 32; as guardian 93, 274; institutions 33; relationship to market 39–40
state formation: external forces in 17
state of emergency 37, 133, 161
Statement of the 1, 000 99, 161
Suleiman, Fadwa 150, 178
sultanism 1, 8, 30–40, 332; removal of the sultan 40; semi-sultanistic system 32–5
Sunni 3, 5–6, 16, 19–20; bloc 251–4, 331–2; clerics 236, 248–9; in government 16, 22; majority 141, 243, 248; peasantry 3, 243; officers 16, 18, 49, 67; rebellion 243; supporters of the regime 132; uprising 24–5; urban 21; versus Shi'a 251–4
Suqour al Sham Brigade 266
surveillance 47, 99, 192
Suwayda 283–6
Sykes Picot agreement 13
Syria Trust for Development 161
Syrian Democratic People's Party 293
Syrian Electronic Army 192
Syrian Islamic Front 234–5
Syrian Left 290–307
Syrian National Council 102–3, 179, 211, 231–2, 295–6, 309–10, 317–20, 322–4
Syrian Socialist Nationalist Party 15–18, 284, 304
Syria's Writers' Union 96

takfiri 200, 225–7, 232, 236, 285, 331
tansiqiyyat see Local Coordination Committees

technocrats 5, 33
territories: loss of 70–1; opposition controlled 2, 166–7, 333
Tlas, Firas 49–50
Tlas, Manaf (General) 9, 50
Tlas, Mustafa 20–1, 49
torture 49–50, 100, 136, 163–4, 177, 190, 209, 246, 275, 283
trafficking: of antiquities 52, 63
trajectory of the conflict 1–2
transition: pacted 8–9
tribes 8, 13, 16, 38, 175–6
Tunisia 6–9, 30–1, 56, 153
Turkey 4, 300, 312, 317, 322–3; role in uprising 155, 253; trade with 65, 84

ulama 9, 109–12, 115–19, 122, 262
Umran, Mohammad 19–20
UN 297–8, 300
unemployment 4, 79–80, 86, 88
unions 5, 9, 21, 83, 96–7
United States 17–8, 300
uprising: aims/ideals/values of 167–8, 181, 229–31, 290, 333; economic factors 77–88; as non-sectarian 101, 150, 223, 228–33; scholarship 77, 335; as secular 101; seeds of 1, 4–5, 23–5, 77, 86–88, 128, 132, 271, 284; support for 32, 38, 77–8, 86–7, 330

violence 16, 19, 21; against activists 168, 192; against civilians 2, 6, 8–9, 177, 190; against protestors 32–3, 48–50, 142, 153, 163–4, 177, 190–1; against regime 9, 24–5; as a regime tool 24–8, 48–51, 54, 142, 155, 164, 245–7, 330; sectarian 271–86, 331
voices: Alawite 150; non-Ba'thist 22; political 6, 159–60, 163, 169, 282

Wall Street Journal 129–30, 163
war crimes 230, 232
war economy 69, 71, 284, 332
Weber, Max 31
White Helmets 167
women: Islamic order 110, 112, 114, 117, 119–21; in the uprising 101, 150, 165, 178, 181, 190–1, 195
workers: public sector 77, 85–6, 133, 330
World Trade Organisation 64

Yazbek, Samar 150–1
Yemen 25, 129–30, 173
youth in the uprising 164, 192, 228, 235, 279–80, 286, 329, 334

Taylor & Francis eBooks

Helping you to choose the right eBooks for your Library

Add Routledge titles to your library's digital collection today. Taylor and Francis ebooks contains over 50,000 titles in the Humanities, Social Sciences, Behavioural Sciences, Built Environment and Law.

Choose from a range of subject packages or create your own!

Benefits for you
- Free MARC records
- COUNTER-compliant usage statistics
- Flexible purchase and pricing options
- All titles DRM-free.

Benefits for your user
- Off-site, anytime access via Athens or referring URL
- Print or copy pages or chapters
- Full content search
- Bookmark, highlight and annotate text
- Access to thousands of pages of quality research at the click of a button.

REQUEST YOUR FREE INSTITUTIONAL TRIAL TODAY
Free Trials Available
We offer free trials to qualifying academic, corporate and government customers.

eCollections – Choose from over 30 subject eCollections, including:

Archaeology	Language Learning
Architecture	Law
Asian Studies	Literature
Business & Management	Media & Communication
Classical Studies	Middle East Studies
Construction	Music
Creative & Media Arts	Philosophy
Criminology & Criminal Justice	Planning
Economics	Politics
Education	Psychology & Mental Health
Energy	Religion
Engineering	Security
English Language & Linguistics	Social Work
Environment & Sustainability	Sociology
Geography	Sport
Health Studies	Theatre & Performance
History	Tourism, Hospitality & Events

For more information, pricing enquiries or to order a free trial, please contact your local sales team:
www.tandfebooks.com/page/sales

Routledge
Taylor & Francis Group

The home of
Routledge books

www.tandfebooks.com